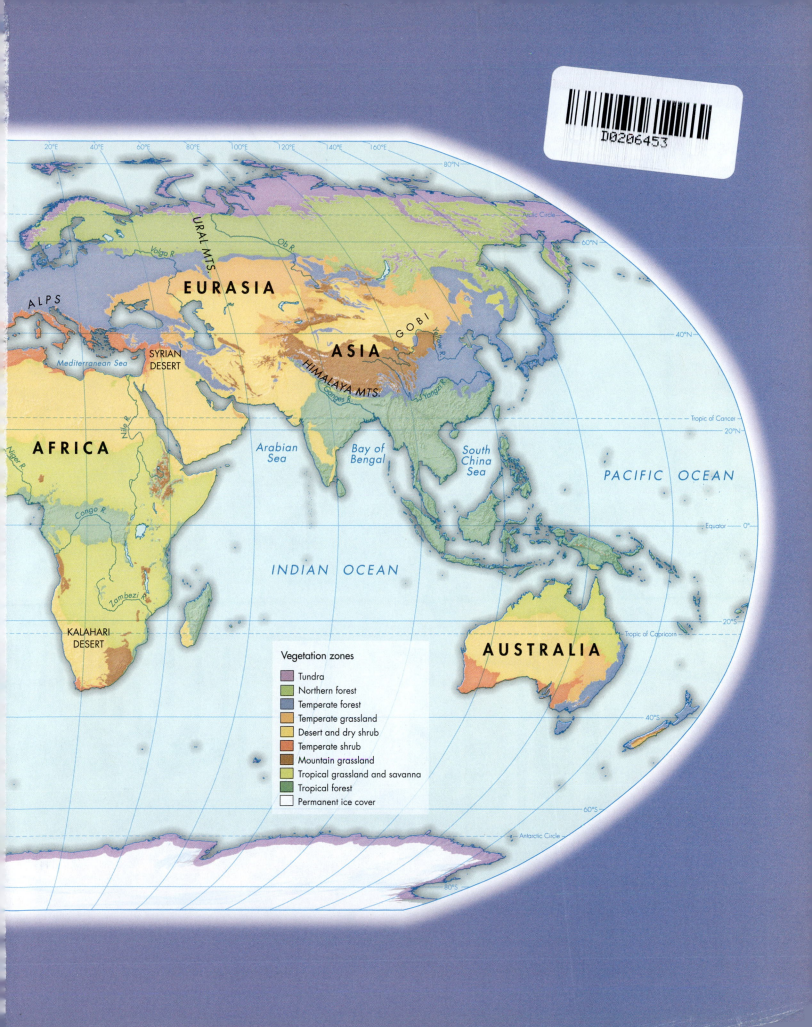

VOLUME B 500–1750

Crossroads and Cultures

A History of the World's Peoples

Bonnie G. Smith
Rutgers University

Marc Van De Mieroop
Columbia University

Richard von Glahn
University of California, Los Angeles

Kris Lane
Tulane University

Bedford/St. Martin's

Boston ■ New York

FOR BEDFORD/ST. MARTIN'S

Publisher for History: Mary Dougherty
Executive Editor for History: Elizabeth M. Welch
Director of Development for History: Jane Knetzger
Senior Developmental Editor: Heidi Hood
Senior Production Editor: Anne Noonan
Senior Production Supervisor: Andrew Ensor
Executive Marketing Manager: Jenna Bookin Barry
Associate Editor: Jennifer Jovin
Assistant Production Editor: Laura Deily
Editorial Assistant: Emily DiPietro
Production Assistant: Elise Keller
Copy Editor: Dan Otis
Map Editor: Charlotte Miller
Indexer: Leoni Z. McVey
Cartography: Mapping Specialists, Ltd.
Photo Researcher: Rose Corbett Gordon
Permissions Manager: Kalina K. Ingham
Senior Art Director: Anna Palchik
Text Designer: Jerilyn Bockorick
Cover Designer: Billy Boardman
Cover Art: Grand Canal and Santa Maria della Salute church
© Atlantide Phototravel/CORBIS
Composition: Cenveo Publisher Services
Printing and Binding: RR Donnelley and Sons

President: Joan E. Feinberg
Editorial Director: Denise B. Wydra
Director of Marketing: Karen R. Soeltz
Director of Production: Susan W. Brown
Associate Director, Editorial Production: Elise S. Kaiser
Managing Editor: Elizabeth M. Schaaf

Library of Congress Control Number: 2011943843

Manufactured in the United States of America.

7 6 5 4 3 2
f e d c b a

For information, write: Bedford/St. Martin's, 75 Arlington Street, Boston, MA 02116   (617-399-4000)

ISBN: 978-0-312-41017-9 (Combined edition)
ISBN: 978-0-312-57158-0 (Loose leaf)
ISBN: 978-0-312-44213-2 (Volume 1)
ISBN: 978-0-312-57159-7 (Loose leaf)
ISBN: 978-0-312-44214-9 (Volume 2)
ISBN: 978-0-312-57160-3 (Loose leaf)
ISBN: 978-0-312-57161-0 (Volume A)
ISBN: 978-0-312-57167-2 (Volume B)
ISBN: 978-0-312-57168-9 (Volume C)

A CONVERSATION WITH THE AUTHORS

The Story Behind *Crossroads and Cultures*

Bonnie G. Smith
Rutgers University

Marc Van De Mieroop
Columbia University

Richard von Glahn
University of California,
Los Angeles

Kris Lane
Tulane University

Bedford/St. Martin's is proud to publish *Crossroads and Cultures: A History of the World's Peoples,* which incorporates the best current cultural history into a fresh and original narrative that connects global patterns of development with life on the ground. This new synthesis highlights the places and times where people interacted and exchanged goods and ideas and in doing so joined their lives to the broad sweep of global history. Below the authors discuss their goals and approach.

Q. How does the title *Crossroads and Cultures: A History of the World's Peoples* tell the story of your book?

Crossroads

Bonnie: From the beginning we knew that we would be stressing interactions and engagements among the world's peoples. We looked for the places where they would meet—the **crossroads**—whether those were actual places or the intersections reflected in the practices of everyday life. We want students to see how crossroads, interactions, and connections among the world's peoples have changed over time and continue to shape their own lives.

Richard: This focus is a result of our recognition that world history is not simply a matter of covering more areas of the world; it requires rethinking what matters in world history. World history must center on cross-cultural interactions and the ways in which peoples and cultures are influenced and are sometimes transformed by political engagement, cultural contact, economic exchange, and social encounters with other societies.

Cultures

Bonnie: The second half of our title reflects our heartfelt judgment that the past is shaped by **cultures**. Beliefs, ways of living, artistic forms, technology, and intellectual accomplishments are fundamental to historical development and are a part of the foundation of politics and economies. Cultures also produce structures such as caste, class, ethnicity, race, religion, gender, and sexuality—all of which are important themes in our book.

> **"We looked for the places where the world's peoples would meet—the crossroads—whether those were actual places or the intersections reflected in the practices of everyday life."**

A History of the World's Peoples

Marc: The book's subtitle, *A History of the World's Peoples*, is crucial. History often focuses on kings and states, but in the end the peoples of the past are the most interesting to study, however difficult that may be considering the nature of the sources for world history. People interact with their immediate and more distant neighbors, and these interactions are, indeed, often a cause of historical change.

Bonnie: *Crossroads and Cultures* focuses on people—individual and collective historical actors—who have lived the history of the world and produced global events. We want to capture their thoughts and deeds, their everyday experiences, their work lives, and their courageous actions—all of which have helped to create the crossroads we travel today.

Q. To follow up on the idea of "crossroads," what are some of the places and interactions that you emphasize in the book, and why?

Marc: In the ancient world, the period that I cover in the book (Part 1, from human origins to 500 C.E.), two regions figured prominently by virtue of their location—the Middle East and Central Asia. From earliest times, the Middle East formed a nexus of interactions among the African, European, and Asian continents, which I try to convey when I discuss the first human migrations out of Africa and when I show how the Roman and Persian empires met—and yes, battled! But I emphasize as well that vast open areas also served as crossroads in antiquity. Indeed, Central Asia, an enormous region, acted as a highway for contacts between the cultures at its fringes: China, South Asia, the Middle East, and Europe. Seas also can play this role, and I include the gigantic Pacific Ocean, which, although a formidable barrier, functioned as a road for migration for centuries.

Richard: Since I also deal with a period remote from the present (Part 2, 500–1450 C.E.), I try to balance my coverage between familiar and recognizable places that remain crossroads today—Rome and Jerusalem, Baghdad and Istanbul, Beijing and Delhi, the Nile Delta and the Valley of Mexico—and places that have faded from view, such as the trading cities of the West African savanna; Melaka, the greatest port of Asia in the fifteenth century; Samarkand, which had a long history as the linchpin of the Central Asian Silk Road; and the Champagne fairs in France, which operated as a "free trade" zone and became the incubator of new business practices that enabled Europeans to surpass the older economic centers of the Mediterranean world.

Kris: Since my section of the book (Part 3, 1450–1750) treats the early modern period, when the entire globe was interconnected for the first time in recorded history, I have almost too many crossroads to choose from. In this period, Seville and Lisbon emerged as hugely rich and important ports and sites of redistribution, but so also did Manila, Nagasaki, and Macao. Most of the obvious crossroads of this seafaring era were ports, but great mining centers like Potosí, deep in the highlands of present-day Bolivia, also became world-class cosmopolitan centers. In other books many of these sites have been treated simply as nodes in an expanding European world, but I try to show how local people and other non-European residents made Manila and Potosí quite different from what the king of Spain might have had in mind. Indeed, I emphasize crossroads as places of personal opportunity rather than imperial hegemony.

Bonnie: The crossroads that we describe are often the obvious ones of war, empire building, and old and new forms of trade, but we also enthusiastically feature the more ordinary paths that people traveled. For example, in my own section of the book (Part 4, 1750 to the present), I trace the route of the young Simon Bolivar, whose travels in Spain, France, and the new United States helped to inspire his own liberation struggles. I also follow the rough road from factory to factory along which a seven-year-old English orphan, Robert Blincoe, traveled. His life occurred at the crossroads of industrial development, where he suffered deliberate torture as the world began industrializing. For me, these personal journeys—filled with interactions—are at the heart of our endeavor to make history vivid and meaningful for students.

> "The crossroads that we describe are often the obvious ones of war, empire building, and old and new forms of trade, but we also enthusiastically feature the more ordinary paths that people traveled."

Q. Author teams of world history textbooks typically divide the work based on geographic specialty. Why did you decide to take responsibility for eras instead of regions?

Bonnie: Our goal is to show the interactions of the world's peoples over time and space. Had we divided history by region, our purpose would have been confounded from the start. Many books still take a "civilizational" approach, shifting from one region or nation to another and dividing each author's coverage according to national specialization. We aimed for a more interconnected result by each taking responsibility for narrating developments across the globe during a particular period of time.

Marc: When we look at any period globally, we can see certain parallels between the various parts of the world. There is a huge benefit to weighing what happened in different places at the same time.

Richard: Right. World history fundamentally is about making comparisons and connections. Defining our subject matter by time period rather than by geographic region enabled us to see the connections or parallel developments that make societies part of world history—as well as the distinctive features that make them unique. Our format has the virtue of bringing a coherent perspective to the many stories that each part of the book tells.

Kris: In my chapters, certain themes, such as slavery and the spread of silver money, took on new meaning as I traced them across cultures in ways that regional specialists had not considered. Writing the book this way entailed a huge amount of reading, writing, and reconsideration, but I feel it was a great decision. It allowed each of us to explore a bit before coming back together to hash out differences.

Q. The table of contents for *Crossroads and Cultures* blends both thematic and regional chapters. Why did you organize the book this way?

Bonnie: There is no orthodoxy in today's teaching of world history. Although textbooks often follow either a

> **"Defining our subject matter by time period rather than by geographic region enabled us to see the connections or parallel developments that make societies part of world history—as well as the distinctive features that make them unique."**

regional or a thematic structure, we felt that neither of these told the story that a blended approach could tell.

Richard: I particularly relished the opportunity to develop thematic chapters—for example, on cross-cultural trade and business practices, or on educational institutions and the transmission of knowledge—that illustrate both convergence and diversity in history. The thematic chapters were especially suitable for introducing individuals from diverse levels of society, to help students appreciate personal experiences as well as overarching historical trends.

Kris: In my period, the rapid integration of the world due to expanding maritime networks had to be balanced against the persistence of land-based cultures that both borrowed from new technologies and ideas and maintained a regional coherence. The Aztecs, the Incas, the Mughals, and the Ming were all land-based, tributary empires headed by divine kings, but whereas the first two collapsed as a result of European invasion, the latter two were reinforced by contact with Europeans, who introduced powerful new weapons. I felt it was necessary to treat these empires in macroregional terms before grappling with more sweeping themes. I found that in the classroom my students made better connections themselves after having time to get a firm handle on some of these broad regional developments.

Q. Each chapter includes a Counterpoint section as substantial as the main sections of the narrative itself. What purposes do the Counterpoints serve?

Kris: The **Counterpoint** feature helps students and teachers remember that alternative histories—or paths—are not only possible but that they exist alongside "master narratives." In each chapter we have selected a people, a place, or a movement that functions as a Counterpoint to the major global development traced in that chapter. Some Counterpoints highlight different responses to similar circumstances—the successful resistance of the Mapuche of Chile against the European conquistadors, for example, in a chapter that tells the story of the collapse of the Aztec and Incan empires. Other Counterpoints show cultures adapting to a particular environment that either enables persistence or requires adaptation—such as the Aborigines of Australia, gatherer-hunters by choice, in a chapter that treats the rise of agriculture and spread of settled farming. Counterpoint is about human difference and ingenuity.

Richard: The Counterpoint feature is fundamental to our approach. It reminds us that there is much diversity in world history and helps us to think about the causes underlying divergence as well as convergence.

Marc: Right. It helps counter the idea that everyone goes through the same stages of evolution and makes the same choices. There is no uniform history of the world, as nineteenth-century scholars used to think.

Bonnie: One of my favorite Counterpoints centers on the importance of nonindustrialized African women farmers to the world economy during the Industrial Revolution. From a pedagogical standpoint, Counterpoints not only expose basic questions that historians grapple with but also offer material within a single chapter for compare-and-contrast exercises.

Q. Each chapter also offers a special feature devoted to the way that people made their living at different times and at different crossroads in the past. Would you explain how this Lives and Livelihoods feature works?

Richard: The **Lives and Livelihoods** feature helps us provide more in-depth study of one of our key themes, namely how people's lives intersect with larger cross-cultural interactions and global change.

Bonnie: We often spotlight new means of making a living that arose as the result of cross-cultural exchange or that contributed to major global developments. For example, the Lives and Livelihoods feature in Chapter 6 shows students how papermaking originated as a carefully guarded invention in classical China and became a worldwide technology that spawned numerous livelihoods. Similarly, the feature in Chapter 24 on workers on the trans-Siberian railroad exemplifies influence in both directions: the workers built a transportation network that advanced interconnections and fostered global change—change that they and their families experienced in turn.

Q. *Crossroads and Cultures* has a rich art and map program, and it also includes plentiful primary-source excerpts and clear reading aids. Can you talk about how you had students in mind as you developed these features of the book?

Kris: Throughout the book we chose **images** to match as closely as we could the themes we wanted to stress. We did not conceive of the images as mere illustrations but rather as documents worthy of close historical analysis in their own right, products of the same places and times we try to evoke in the text.

Richard: And our carefully developed **map program** provides sure-footed guidance to where our historical journey is taking us—a crucial necessity, since we travel to so many places not on the usual Grand Tour! Our **Seeing the Past** and **Reading the Past** features, which provide excerpts from visual and written primary sources, give students direct exposure to the ideas and voices of the people we are studying. These features also help students build their analytical skills by modeling how historians interpret visual and written evidence.

Bonnie: Among the many reading aids, one of my favorites is the chapter-opening **Backstory**, which provides a concise overview of previously presented material to situate the current chapter for the student. It is at once a review and an immediate preparation for the chapter to come.

Richard: And we use every opportunity—at the start of chapters and sections, in the features, and at the end of each chapter—to pose **study questions** to help students think about what they are reading and make connections across time and space.

Kris: We wanted to hit as many bases as possible in order to make our book accessible for different kinds of learners. I imagine I'm like most teachers in that I never teach a course in exactly the same way each year. I like to use or emphasize different aspects of a textbook each time I assign it, sometimes hammering on chronology or working through study questions and sometimes paying closer attention to maps, works of art, or material culture. It all needs to be there; I like a complete toolbox.

> **"The Lives and Livelihoods feature supports one of our key themes: how people's lives intersect with larger cross-cultural interactions and global change."**

Q. You have written many well-received and influential works. What response to *Crossroads and Cultures: A History of the World's Peoples* would please you most?

Bonnie: Our hope is that our approach to world history will engage students and help them master material that can otherwise seem so remote, wide-ranging, and seemingly disconnected from people's lives.

Richard: I would like from students who read this book what I want from my own students: a recognition and appreciation of the diversity of human experience that fosters understanding not only of the past and where we have come from but also of our fellow world citizens and the future that we are making together.

Kris: The practical side of me wants simply to hear, "At last, a world history textbook that works." The idealistic side wants to hear, "Wow, a world history textbook that makes both me and my students think differently about the world and about history."

Marc: And I hope that students start to realize not only that the pursuit of answers to such questions is absorbing and satisfying but also that the study of history is fun!

Crossroads and Cultures: A History of the World's Peoples makes its new synthesis accessible and memorable for students through a strong pedagogical design, abundant maps and images, and special features that heighten the narrative's attention to the lives and voices of the world's peoples. To learn more about how the book's features keep the essentials of world history in focus for students, see the "How to Use This Book" introduction on the following pages.

HOW TO USE THIS BOOK

STEP 1

Use the part opener's features to understand the place, time, and topic of the era.

PLACE
Ask yourself what regions are covered.

TIME
Ask yourself what era is under investigation.

TOPIC
Ask yourself what topics or themes are emphasized.

PART **2**

TOPIC and TIME

The Formation of Regional Societies

500–1450 C.E.

CH 9

ALTHOUGH NO SINGLE LABEL adequately reflects the history of the world in the period 500–1450, its most distinctive feature was the formation of regional societies based on common forms of livelihoods, cultural values, and social and political institutions. The new age in world history that began in around 500 c.e. marked a decisive break from the "classical" era of antiquity. The passing of classical civilizations in the Mediterranean, China, and India shared a number of causes, but the most notable were invasions by nomads from the Central Asian steppes. Beset by internal unrest and foreign pressures, the empires of Rome, Han China, and Gupta India crumbled. As these once-mighty empires fragmented into a multitude of competing states, cultural revolutions followed. Confidence in the values and institutions of the classical era was shattered, opening the way for fresh ideas. Christianity, Buddhism, Hinduism, and the new creed of Islam spread far beyond their original circles of believers. By 1450 these four religious traditions had supplanted or transformed local religions in virtually all of Eurasia and much of Africa.

The spread of foreign religions and the lifestyles and livelihoods they promoted produced distinctive regional societies. By 1000, Europe had taken shape as a coherent society and culture even as it came to be divided between the Roman and Byzantine Christian churches. The shared cultural values of modern East Asia—rooted in the literary and philosophical traditions of China but also assuming distinctive national forms—also emerged during the first millennium c.e. During this era, too, Indian civilization expanded into Southeast Asia and acquired a new unity expressed through the common language of Sanskrit. The rapid expansion of Islam across Asia, Africa, and

266

TOPIC
Read the part overview to learn how the chapters that follow fit into the larger story.

CH 10

TOPIC, TIME, and PLACE

CH 11

even parts of Europe demonstrated the power of a shared reli-

500–1450 C.E.

CH 13

faiths grew ever wider. The rise of steppe empires—above all, the explosive expansion of the Mongol empires—likewise transformed the political and cultural landscape of Asia. Historians today recognize the ways in which the Mongol conquests facilitated the movement of people, goods, and ideas across Eurasia. But contemporaries could see no farther than the ruin sowed by the Mongols wherever they went, toppling cities and laying waste to once-fertile farmlands.

After 1300 the momentum of world history changed. Economic growth slowed, strained by the pressure of rising populations on productive resources and the effects of a cooling climate, and then it stopped altogether. In the late 1340s the Black Death pandemic devastated the central Islamic lands and Europe. It would take centuries before the populations in these parts of the world returned to their pre-1340 levels.

By 1400, however, other signs of recovery were evident. Powerful national states emerged in Europe and China, restoring some measure of stability. Strong Islamic states held sway in Egypt, Anatolia (modern Turkey), Iran, and India. The European Renaissance—the intense outburst of intellectual and artistic creativity envisioned as a "rebirth" of the classical civilization of Greece and Rome—flickered to life, sparked by the economic vigor of the Italian city-states. Similarly, Neo-Confucianism—a "renaissance" of China's classical learning—whetted the intellectual and cultural aspirations of ed... Ma... Bla...

Eurasia's major land-based economies struggled to regain their earlier prosperity.

In 1453 Muslim Ottoman armies seized Constantinople and deposed the Byzantine Christian emperor, cutting the last thread of connection to the ancient world. The fall of Constantinople symbolized the end of the era discussed in Part 2. Denied direct access to the rich trade with Asia, European monarchs and merchants began to shift their attention to the Atlantic world. Yet just as Columbus's discovery of the "New World" (in fact, a very ancient one) came as a surprise, the idea of a new world order centered on Europe—the modern world order—was still unimaginable.

CH 15

TIME and PLACE
Scan the timeline to see how events and developments in different regions of the world fit together.

Americas
- 500 First permanent settlements in Chaco Canyon
- 500–1000 Andean state of Tiwanaku
- 550–650 Collapse of Teotihuacán
- 700–900 Heyday of Andean state of Wari
- 800–900 Collapse of the Maya city-states
- Rise of Chimú state 900
- 950–1150 Height of Toltec culture
- 1050 Consolidation of Cahokia's dominance
- 1200 Incas move into Cuzco region
- 1150 Abandonment of pueblos in Chaco Canyon
- 1250–1300 Collapse of Cahokia
- 1325 Aztecs found Tenochtitlán
- Columbus reaches the Americas 1492 •
- 1430–1532 Inca Empire

Europe
- 507 Clovis defeats Visigoths and converts to Christianity
- 590–604 Papacy of Gregory I
- Charles Martel halts Muslim advance into Europe 732 •
- Charlemagne crowned emperor 800 •
- 793 Earliest record of Viking raids on Britain
- 988 Rus prince Vladimir converts to Christianity
- 1066 Norman conquest of England
- 1150 Founding of first university at Paris
- 1150–1300 Heyday of the Champagne fairs
- Mongol conquest of Kiev 1240 •
- 1270–1300 Introduction of overseas navigational aids
- 1337–1350 Outbreak of Black Death
- 1337–1453 Hundred Years' War
- 1400–1550 Italian Renaissance
- Reconquista completed 1492 •

Middle East
- 527–565 Reign of Byzantine emperor Justinian I
- 570–632 Life of Muhammad
- 661–743 Umayyad caliphate
- 680 Permanent split between Shi'a and Sunni Islam
- 750–850 Abbasid caliphate at its height
- First Crusade ends with Christian capture of Jerusalem 1099 •
- Saladin recaptures Jerusalem 1187 •
- 1120 Founding of order of Knights of the Temple
- 1258 Mongols sack Baghdad
- 1291 Mamluks recapture Acre, last Christian stronghold in Palestine
- 1347–1350 Outbreak of Black Death
- 1453 Fall of Constantinople to the Ottomans

Africa
- 500 Spread of camel use; emergence of trans-Saharan trade routes
- 750 Islam starts to spread via trans-Saharan trade routes
- 969 Fatimids capture Egypt
- Fall of kingdom of Ghana 1076 •
- Mali Empire 1230–1255
- Reign of Sunjata, founder of Mali Empire 1230–1255
- 1250 Kingdom of Benin founded
- 1100–1500 Extended dry period in West Africa prompts migrations
- 1250–1517 Mamluk dynasty

Asia and Oceania
- 581–618 Sui Empire
- 618–907 Tang Empire
- 600–1000 Polynesian settlement of Pacific islands
- 668 Unification of Korea under Silla rule
- 755–763 An Lushan rebellion
- 850–1267 Chola kingdom
- 939 Vietnam achieves independence from China
- 960–1279 Song Empire
- 1100–1500 Easter Island's stone monuments
- Formation of first Hawaiian chiefdoms 1200–1400
- 1206–1526 Delhi Sultanate
- 1271–1368 Yuan Empire
- 1336–1573 Ashikaga Shogunate
- 1368–1644 Ming Empire
- 1392–1910 Korean Yi dynasty

Use the chapter's introductory features to understand the place, time, and topic of this chapter.

15

AT A CROSSROADS ▶

The fall of Constantinople to the Ottoman Turks in 1453 marked the end of the Byzantine Empire and heralded the coming age of gunpowder weapons. The Ottoman forces under Sultan Mehmed II breached the massive walls of Constantinople using massive cannons known as *bombards*. The Turkish cannons appear in the center of this book illustration of the siege of Constantinople, published in France in 1455. (The Art Archive/Bibliothèque Nationale Paris.)

PLACE and TOPIC
An important crossroads opens every chapter.

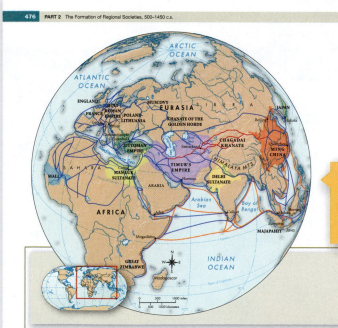

enough cannons to match the heavily armed Ottoman army and navy, which expelled the Venetians from the Black Sea in 1475. Although Venetian merchants still flocked to Constantinople, which Mehmed renamed Istanbul, to obtain spices, silks, and other Asian goods, the Ottomans held the upper hand and could dictate the terms of trade.

The fall of Constantinople to the Ottomans marks a turning point in world history. After perpetuating ancient Rome's heritage and glory for a thousand years, the Byzantine Empire came to an end. Islam continued to advance; in the fourteenth and fifteenth centuries, it expanded most dramatically in Africa and Asia. Italian merchants and bankers lost their dominance in the eastern Mediterranean and turned westward toward the Atlantic Ocean in search of new commercial opportunities. And this shift in commercial power and focus was not the only profound change that followed the Ottoman capture of Constantinople. The bombards cast by the Hungarian engineer for the Ottoman sultan heralded a military revolution that would decisively alter the balance of power among states and transform the nature of the state itself.

The new global patterns that emerged after Constantinople changed hands had their roots in calamities of the fourteenth century. The Ottoman triumph came just as Europe was beginning to recover from the previous century's catastrophic outbreak of plague known as the Black Death. The demographic and psychological shocks of epidemic disease had se-

PLACE and TOPIC
The Mapping the World feature gives a geographical overview of the chapter and highlights important routes and crossroads.

MAPPING THE WORLD
Afro-Eurasia in the Early Fifteenth Century

After the Mongol Empire disintegrated, trans-Eurasian trade shifted from the overland Silk Road to the maritime routes stretching from China to the Mediterranean. Muslim merchants crossed the Sahara Desert and the Indian Ocean in pursuit of African gold, Chinese porcelain, and Asian spices. Although Chinese fleets led by Admiral Zheng He journeyed as far as the coasts of Arabia and Africa, the Ming rulers prohibited private overseas trade.

ROUTES ▼
— Major trade route
— Silk Road
— Voyages of Zheng He

1315–1317 Great Famine in northern Europe
1325–1354 Travels of Ibn Battuta in Asia and Africa
1336–1573 Ashikaga shogunate in Japan
1337–1453 Hundred Years' War between England and France
• 1378 Ciompi uprising in Florence
• 1381 Peasant Revolt in England
1392–1910 Yi dynasty in Korea
• 1405 Death of Timur; breakup of his empire into regional states in Iran and Central Asia
• 1453 Ottoman conquest of Constantinople marks fall of the Byzantine Empire

| 1300 | 1325 | 1350 | 1375 | 1400 | 1425 | 1450 |

1347–1350 Outbreak of the Black Death in Europe and the Islamic Mediterranean
c. 1351–1782 Ayudhya kingdom in Thailand
1368–1644 Ming dynasty in China
1405–1433 Chinese admiral Zheng He's expeditions in Southeast Asia and the Indian Ocean
• 1421 Relocation of Ming capital from Nanjing to Beijing
1428–1788 Le dynasty in Vietnam

TIME and TOPIC
The timeline previews key events and developments discussed in the chapter.

Collapse and Revival in Afro-Eurasia

1300–1450

In the spring of 1453, as the armies of the Ottoman sultan Mehmed II encircled Constantinople, the Byzantine emperor Constantine XI received a visit from a fellow Christian, a Hungarian engineer named Urban. Urban had applied metallurgical skills acquired at Hungary's rich iron and copper mines to the manufacture of large cannons known as *bombards*. He came to the Byzantine capital to offer his services to repel the Ottoman assault. But although Urban was a Christian, he was a businessman, too. When Constantine could not meet his price, Urban quickly left for the sultan's camp. Facing the famed triple walls of Constantinople, Mehmed promised to quadruple the salary Urban requested and to provide any materials and manpower the engineer needed.

Seven months later, in April 1453, Ottoman soldiers moved Urban's huge bronze bombards—with barrels twenty-six feet long, capable of throwing eight-hundred-pound shot—into place beneath the walls of Constantinople. Although these cumbersome cannons could fire only seven rounds a day, they battered the walls of Constantinople, which had long been considered impenetrable. After six weeks of siege the Turks breached the walls and swarmed into the city. The vastly outnumbered defenders, Emperor Constantine among them, fought to the death.

Urban's willingness to put business before religious loyalty helped tip the balance of power in the Mediterranean. During the siege, the Genoese merchant community at Constantinople—along with their archrivals, the Venetians—maintained strict neutrality. Although the Italian merchants, like Urban, were prepared to do business with Mehmed II, within a decade the Venetians and Ottomans were at war. Venice could not produce

Fourteenth-Century Crisis and Renewal in Eurasia

FOCUS How did the Black Death affect society, the economy, and culture in Latin Christendom and the Islamic world?

Islam's New Frontiers

FOCUS Why did Islam expand dramatically in the fourteenth and fifteenth centuries, and how did new Islamic societies differ from established ones?

The Global Bazaar

FOCUS How did the pattern of international trade change during the fourteenth and fifteenth centuries, and how did these changes affect consumption and fashion tastes?

COUNTERPOINT Age of the Samurai in Japan, 1185–1450

FOCUS How and why did the historical development of Japan in the fourteenth and fifteenth centuries differ from that of mainland Eurasia?

BACKSTORY

In the fourteenth century, a number of developments threatened the connections among the societies of the Afro-Eurasian world. The collapse of the Mongol empires in China and Iran in the mid-1300s disrupted caravan traffic across Central Asia, diverting the flow of trade and travel to maritime routes across the Indian Ocean. Although the two centuries of religious wars known as the Crusades ended in 1291, they had hardened hostility between Christians and Muslims. As the power of the Christian Byzantine Empire contracted, Muslim Turkish sultanates—the Mamluk regime in Egypt and the rising Ottoman dynasty in Anatolia (modern Turkey)—gained control of the eastern Mediterranean region. Yet the Crusades and direct contact with the Mongols had also whetted European appetites for luxury and exotic goods from the Islamic world and Asia. Thus, despite challenges and obstacles, the Mediterranean remained a lively crossroads of commerce and cross-cultural exchange.

bazaar, and this isolation contributed to the birth of Japan's distinctive national culture. For most Afro-Eurasian societies, however, the maritime world increasingly became the principal crossroads of economic and cultural exchange.

OVERVIEW QUESTIONS

The major global development in this chapter: Crisis and recovery in fourteenth- and fifteenth-century Afro-Eurasia.

As you read, consider:

1. In the century after the devastating outbreak of plague known as the Black Death, how and why did Europe's economic growth begin to surpass that of the Islamic world?

2. Did the economic revival across Eurasia after 1350 benefit the peasant populations of Europe, the Islamic world, and East Asia?

3. How did the process of conversion to Islam differ in Iran, the Ottoman Empire, West Africa, and Southeast Asia during this period?

4. What political and economic changes contributed to the rise of maritime commerce in Asia during the fourteenth and fifteenth centuries?

Use the chapter tools to understand what is important.

Islam's New Frontiers

FOCUS

Why did Islam expand dramatically in the fourteenth and fifteenth centuries, and how did new Islamic societies differ from established ones?

Focus questions, which also appear at the start and end of the chapter, tell you what you need to learn from each major section.

In the fourteenth and fifteenth centuries, Islam continued to spread to new areas, including central and maritime Asia, sub-Saharan Africa, and southeastern Europe. In the past, Muslim rule had often preceded the popular adoption of Islamic religion and culture. Yet the advance of Islam in Africa and Asia came about not through conquest, but through slow diffusion via merchants and missionaries. The universalism and egalitarianism of Islam appealed to rising merchant classes in both West Africa and maritime Asia.

During this period, Islam expanded by adapting to older ruling cultures rather than seeking to eradicate them. Timur, the last of the great nomad conquerors, and his descendants ruled not as Mongol khans but as Islamic sultans. The culture of the Central Asian states, however, remained an eclectic mix of Mongol, Turkish, and Persian traditions, in contrast to the strict adherence to Muslim law and doctrine practiced under the Arab regimes of the Middle East and North Africa. This pattern of cultural adaptation and assimilation was even more evident in West Africa and Southeast Asia.

Islamic Spiritual Ferment in Central Asia 1350–1500

The spread of Sufism in Central Asia between 1350 and 1500 played a significant role in the process of cultural assimilation. **Sufism**—a mystical tradition that stressed self-mastery, practical virtues, and spiritual growth through personal experience of the divine—had already emerged by 1200 as a major expression of Islamic values and social identity. Sufism appeared in many variations and readily assimilated local cultures to its beliefs and practices. Sufi mystics acquired institutional strength through the communal solidarity of their brotherhoods spread across the whole realm of Islam. In contrast to the orthodox scholars and teachers known as *ulama*, who made little effort to convert nonbelievers, Sufi preachers were inspired by missionary zeal and welcomed non-Muslims to their lodges and sermons. This made them ideal instruments for the spread of Islam to new territories.

Topical headings in the margin focus on important topics and are useful for reviewing the chapter.

Timur

One of Sufism's most important royal patrons was Timur (1336–1405), the last of the Mongol emperors. Born near the city of Samarkand (SAM-ar-kand) when the Mongol Ilkhanate in Iran was on the verge of collapse, Timur—himself a Turk—grew up among Mongols who practiced Islam. He rose to power in the 1370s by reuniting quarreling Mongol tribes in common pursuit of conquest. Although Timur lacked the dynastic pedigree enjoyed by Chinggis Khan's descendants, like Chinggis he held his empire together by the force of his personal charisma.

From the early 1380s, Timur's armies relentlessly pursued campaigns of conquest, sweeping westward across Iran into Mesopotamia and Russia and eastward into India. In 1400–1401 Timur seized and razed Aleppo and Damascus, the principal Mamluk cities in Syria. In 1402 he captured the Ottoman sultan in battle. Rather than trying to consolidate his rule in Syria and Anatolia (modern Turkey), however, Timur turned his attention eastward. He was preparing to march on China when he fell ill and died early in 1405. Although Timur's empire quickly fragmented, his triumphs would serve as an inspiration to later empire builders, such as the Mughals in India and the Manchus in China. Moreover, his support of Sufism would have a lasting impact, helping lay the foundation for a number of important Islamic religious movements in Central Asia.

Marginal glossary definitions provide further explanation of key terms boldfaced in the narrative.

The institutions of Timur's empire were largely modeled on the Ilkhan synthesis of Persian civil administration and Turkish-Mongol military organization. Like the Ilkhans and the Ottomans, Timur's policies favored settled farmers and urban populations over pastoral nomads, who were often displaced from their homelands. While Timur allowed local princes a degree of autonomy, he was determined to make Samarkand a grand imperial capital.

Sufism A tradition within Islam that emphasizes mystical knowledge and personal experience of the divine.

Again, as with Islam in West Africa, the intellectual ferment of the Renaissance was nurtured in an urban environment. Humanist scholars shunned the warrior culture of the old nobility while celebrating the civic roles and duties of townsmen, merchants, and clerics. Despite their admiration of classical civilization, the humanists did not reject Christianity. Rather, they sought to reconcile Christian faith and doctrines with classical learning. By making knowledge of Latin and Greek, history, poetry, and philosophy the mark of an educated person, the humanists transformed education and established models of schooling that would endure down to modern times.

Nowhere was the revolutionary impact of the Renaissance felt more deeply than in visual arts such as painting, sculpture, and architecture. Artists of the Renaissance exuded supreme confidence in the ability of human ingenuity to equal or even surpass the works of nature. The new outlook was exemplified by the development of the techniques of perspective, which artists used to convey a realistic, three-dimensional quality to physical forms, most notably the human body. Human invention also was capable of improving on nature by creating order and harmony through architecture and urban planning. Alberti advocated replacing the winding narrow streets and haphazard construction of medieval towns with planned cities organized around straight boulevards, open squares, and monumental buildings whose balanced proportions corresponded to a geometrically unified design.

Above all, the Renaissance transformed the idea of the artist. No longer mere manual tradesmen, artists now were seen as possessing a special kind of genius that enabled them to express a higher understanding of beauty. In the eyes of contemporaries, no one exemplified this quality of genius more than Leonardo da Vinci (1452–1519), who won renown as a painter, architect, sculptor, engineer, mathematician, and inventor. Leonardo's father, a Florentine lawyer, apprenticed him to a local painter at age eighteen. Leonardo spent much of his career as a civil and military engineer in the employ of the Duke of Milan, and developed ideas for flying machines, tanks, robots, and solar power that far exceeded the engineering capabilities of his time. Leonardo sought to apply his knowledge of natural science to painting, which he regarded as the most sublime art (see Seeing the Past: Leonardo da Vinci's *Virgin of the Rocks*).

The flowering of artistic creativity in the Renaissance was rooted in the rich soil of Italy's comm[...] [...]from the Islamic world and Asia. Intern[...] [...]roduction across maritime Asia and gave[...] [...]nd consumption. In Japan, however, grow[...] [...]fostered the emergence of a national cultu[...] [...]ted the rest of East Asia.

> The final Counterpoint section offers an important exception to the Major Global Development discussed in the chapter.

Cultural Innovations

COUNTERPOINT
Age of the Samurai in Japan 1185–1450

In Japan as in Europe, the term *Middle Ages* brings to mind an age of warriors, a stratified society governed by bonds of loyalty between lords and vassals. In Japan, however, the militarization of the ruling class intensified during the fourteenth and fifteenth centuries, a time when the warrior nobility of Europe was crumbling. Paradoxically, the rise of the **samurai** (sah-moo-rye) ("those who serve") warriors as masters of their own estates was accompanied by the increasing independence of peasant communities.

from[...] [...]apter, Japan became more isolated [...]ural exchanges with China reached a pea[...] [...]invasion of Japan in 1281, ties with conti[...] [...]apanese see this era as the period in which Japan's unique national identity—expressed most distinctly in the ethic of *bushidō* (boo-shee-doe), the "Way of the Warrior"—took its definitive form. Samurai warriors became the

> Phonetic spellings follow many potentially unfamiliar terms.

FOCUS

How and why did the historical development of Japan in the fourteenth and fifteenth centuries differ from that of mainland Eurasia?

samurai Literally, "those who serve"; the hereditary warriors who dominated Japanese society and culture from the twelfth to the nineteenth centuries.

STEP 4
Do historical analysis.

Lives and Livelihoods features underscore the connections between daily life and global developments.

LIVES AND LIVELIHOODS

Urban Weavers in India

Industry and commerce in India, especially in textiles, grew rapidly beginning in the fourteenth century. Specialized craftsmen in towns and regional groups of merchants formed guilds that became the nuclei of new occupational castes, *jati* (JAH-tee). Ultimately these new occupational castes would join with other forces in Indian society to challenge the social inequality rooted in orthodox Hindu religion.

It was growth in market demand and technological innovations such as block printing that drove the rapid expansion of India's textile industries. Luxury fabrics such as fine silks and velvet remained largely the province of royal workshops or private patronage. Mass production of textiles, on the other hand, was oriented toward the manufacture of cheaper cotton fabrics, especially colorful chintz garments. A weaver could make a woman's cotton *sari* in six or seven days, whereas a luxury garment took a month or more. Domestic demand for ordinary cloth grew steadily, and production for export accelerated even more briskly. At the beginning of the sixteenth century, the Portuguese traveler Tomé Pires, impressed by the craftsmanship of Indian muslins and calicoes (named after the port of Calicut), observed that "they make enough of these to furnish the world."[1]

Weaving became an urban industry. It was village women who cleaned most of the cotton and spun it into yarn; they could easily combine this simple if laborious work with other domestic chores. But peasants did not weave the yarn into cloth, except for their own use. Instead, weaving, bleaching, a[...] professional [...] living in sepa[...]

Like oth[...] pation that c[...] Families of w[...] guilds with b[...] within their g[...] not have ex[...] could include[...] could becom[...]

Indian Block-Printed Textile, c. 1500
Block-printed textiles with elaborate designs were in great demand both in India and throughout Southeast Asia, Africa, and the Islamic world. Craftsmen carved intricate designs on wooden blocks (a separate block for each color), which were then dipped in dye and repeatedly stamped on bleached fabric until the entire cloth was covered. This cotton fabric with geese, lotus flower, and rosette designs was manufactured in Gujarat in western India. (Ashmolean Museum, University of Oxford/[...])

[...]ning prosperity of weavers whetted their aspirations for social recognition. Amid the whirl and congestion of city life, it was far more difficult than in villages to enforce the laws governing caste purity and segregation. As a fourteenth-century poet wrote about the crowded streets of his hometown of Jaunpur in the Ganges Valley, in the city "one person's caste-mark gets stamped on another's forehead, and a brahman's holy thread will be found hanging around an untouchable's neck."[2] Brahmans objected to this erosion of caste boundaries, to little avail. Weaver guilds became influential patrons of temples and often served as trustees and accountants in charge of managing temple endowments and revenues.

In a few cases the growing economic independence of weavers and like-minded artisans prompted complete rejection of the caste hierarchy. Sufi preachers and *bhakti* (BAHK-tee)—devotional movements devoted to patron gods and goddesses—encouraged the disregard of caste distinctions in favor of a universal brotherhood of devout believers. The fifteenth-century bhakti preacher Kabir, who was strongly influenced by Sufi teachings, epitomized the new social radicalism coursing through the urban artisan classes. A weaver himself, Kabir joined the dignity of manual labor to the purity of spiritual devotion, spurning the social pretension and superficial piety of the brahmans ("pandits") and Muslim clerics ("mullahs"):

a trinity of labor, charity, and spiritual devotion. The Sikhs, who gained a following principally among traders and artisans in the northwestern Punjab region, drew an even more explicit connection between commerce and piety. In the words of a hymn included in a sixteenth-century anthology of Sikh sacred writings:

> The true Guru [teacher] is the merchant;
>
> The devotees are his peddlers.
>
> The capital stock is the Lord's Name, and
>
> To enshrine the truth is to keep His account.[4]

Sikh communities spurned the distinction between pure and impure occupations. In their eyes, holiness was to be found in honest toil and personal piety, not ascetic practices, book learning, or religious rituals.

1. Tomé Pires, *The Suma Oriental of Tomé Pires*, ed. and trans. Armando Cortes (London: Hakluyt Society, 1944), 1:53.
2. Vidyapati Thakur, *Kirtilata*, quoted in Eugenia Vanina, *Urban Crafts and Craftsmen in Medieval India (Thirteenth–Eighteenth Centuries)* (New Delhi: Munshiram Manoharlal, 2004), 443.
3. Quoted in Vanina, *Urban Crafts and Craftsmen*, 149.
4. *Sri Guru Granth Sahib*, trans. Gophal Singh (Delhi: Gur Das Kapur & Sons, 1960), 2:427.

QUESTIONS TO CONSIDER

1. In what ways did the organization of textile production reinforce or challenge the prevailing social norms of Hindu society?
2. In what ways did religious ideas and movements reflect the new sense of dignity among prosperous Indian merchants and craftsmen?

Reading the Past and Seeing the Past features provide direct exposure to important voices and ideas of the past through written and visual primary sources.

[...]at ease [...] mullahs, [...]come [...]toil, [...]asure. [...]liesced [...]red on

[...]*n India.* Delhi: Oxford University Press, 1985.
[...]*India (Thirteenth–Eighteenth Centuries).* New Delhi: Munshiram Manoharlal, 2004.

SEEING THE PAST

Leonardo da Vinci's *Virgin of the Rocks*

Virgin of the Rocks, c. 1483–1486
(Erich Lessing/Art Resource.)

Leonardo's Botanical Studies with Star-of-Bethlehem, Grasses, Crowfoot, Wood Anemone, and Another Genus, c. 1500–1506 (The Royal Collection © 2011 Her Majesty Queen Elizabeth II/Bridgeman Art Library.)

the menacing [...] the cavern; de[...] there was any [...] thing within."[1]

Fantastic as the sce[...] might seem, Leonardo's [...] meticulous rendering of [...] rocks and p[...] based on cl[...] of nature. Th[...] lehem flowe[...] left of the pa[...] izing purity a[...] also appear[...] contempora[...] cal drawing [...] Geologists h[...] Leonardo's [...] sandstone n[...] and his prec[...] of plants wh[...] most likely t[...]

Master[...] the *Virgin o[...]* display Leonardo's careful study of human a[...] landscapes, and botany. Although he admire[...] tion of nature, Leonardo also celebrated the h[...] rational and aesthetic capacities, declaring th[...] arts may be called the grandsons of God."[2]

1. Arundel ms. (British Library), p. 115 recto, cited i[...] *Leonardo da Vinci: The Marvelous Works of Natu[...]* (Oxford: Oxford University Press, 2006), 78.
2. John Paul Richter, ed., *The Notebooks of Leonar[...]* of 1883 ed.; New York: Dover, 1970), Book IX, 32[...]

While living in Milan in the early 1480s, Leonardo accepted a commission to paint an altarpiece for the chapel of Milan's Confraternity of the Immaculate Conception, a branch of the Franciscan order. Leonardo's relationship with the friars proved to be stormy. His first version of the painting (now in the Louvre), reproduced here, apparently displeased his patrons and was sold to another party. Only after a fifteen-year-long dispute over the price did Leonardo finally deliver a modified version in 1508.

In portraying the legendary encounter between the child Jesus and the equally young John the Baptist during the flight to Egypt, Leonardo replaced the traditional desert setting with a landscape filled with rocks, plants, and water. Leonardo's dark grotto creates an aura of mystery and foreboding, from which the figures of Mary, Jesus, John, and the angel Uriel emerge as if in a vision. A few years before, Leonardo had written about "coming to the entrance of a great cavern, in front of which I stood for some time, stupefied and uncomprehending. . . . Suddenly two things arose in me, fear and desire: fear of

EXAMINING THE EVIDENCE

1. How does Leonardo express the conne[...] between John (at left) and Jesus throug[...] gesture, and their relationships with the[...] Mary and the angel Uriel?
2. The friars who commissioned the painting sought to celebrate the sanctity and purity of their patron, the Virgin Mary. Does this painting achieve that effect?

Thus, China influenced patterns of international trade not only as a producer, as with

READING THE PAST

A Spanish Ambassador's Description of Samarkand

In September 1403, an embassy dispatched by King Henry III of Castile arrived at Samarkand in hopes of enlisting the support of Timur for a combined military campaign against the Ottomans. Seventy years old and in failing health, Timur lavishly entertained his visitors, but made no response to Henry's overtures. The leader of the Spanish delegation, Ruy Gonzalez de Clavijo, left Samarkand disappointed, but his report preserves our fullest account of Timur's capital in its heyday.

> The city is rather larger than Seville, but lying outside Samarkand are great numbers of houses that form extensive suburbs. These lay spread on all hands, for indeed the township is surrounded by orchards and vineyards. . . . In between these orchards pass streets with open squares; these are all densely populated, and here all kinds of goods are on sale with breadstuffs and meat. . . .
>
> Samarkand is rich not only in foodstuffs but also in manufactures, such as factories of silk. . . . Thus trade has always been fostered by Timur with the view of making his capital the noblest of cities; and during all his conquests . . . he carried off the best men to people Samarkand, bringing thither the master-craftsmen of all nations. Thus from Damascus he carried away with him all the weavers of that city, those who worked at the silk looms; further the bow-makers who produce those cross-bows which are so famous; likewise armorers; also the craftsmen in glass and porcelain, who are known to be the best in all the world. From Turkey he

had brought their gunsmiths who make the arquebus. . . . So great therefore was the population now of all nationalities gathered together in Samarkand that of men with their families the number they said must amount to 150,000 souls . . . [including] Turks, Arabs, and Moors of diverse sects, with Greek, Armenian, Roman, Jacobite [Syrian], and Nestorian Christians, besides those folk who baptize with fire in the forehead [i.e., Hindus]. . . .

> The markets of Samarkand further are amply stored with merchandise imported from distant and foreign countries. . . . The goods that are imported to Samarkand from Cathay indeed are of the richest and most precious of all those brought thither from foreign parts, for the craftsmen of Cathay are reputed to be the most skillful by far beyond those of any other nation.

Source: Ruy Gonzalez de Clavijo, Embassy to Tamerlane, 1403–1406, trans. Guy Le Strange (London: Routledge, 1928), 285–289.

EXAMINING THE EVIDENCE

1. What features of Timur's capital most impressed Gonzalez de Clavijo?
2. How does this account of Samarkand at its height compare with the chapter's description of Renaissance Florence?

South[...] and Rai[...]

496

502

STEP 5

Review what you have learned.

> **Remember to visit the Online Study Guide for more review help.**

REVIEW

Online Study Guide
bedfordstmartins.com/smith

The major global development in this chapter ▶ Crisis and recovery
in fourteenth- and fifteenth-century Afro-Eurasia.

> **Review the Major Global Development discussed in the chapter.**

> **Review the Important Events from the chapter.**

IMPORTANT EVENTS

1315–1317	Great Famine in northern Europe
1325–1354	Travels of Ibn Battuta in Asia and Africa
1336–1573	Ashikaga shogunate in Japan
1337–1453	Hundred Years' War between England and France
1347–1350	Outbreak of the Black Death in Europe and the Islamic Mediterranean
c. 1351–1782	Ayudhya kingdom in Thailand
1368–1644	Ming dynasty in China
1378	Ciompi uprising in Florence
1381	Peasant Revolt in England
1392–1910	Yi dynasty in Korea
1405	Death of Timur; breakup of his empire into regional states in Iran and Central Asia
1405–1433	Chinese admiral Zheng He's expeditions in Southeast Asia and the Indian Ocean
1421	Relocation of Ming capital from Nanjing to Beijing
1428–1788	Le dynasty in Vietnam
1453	Ottoman conquest of Constantinople marks fall of the Byzantine Empire

> **Review the Key Terms.**

KEY TERMS

Black Death (p. 478)
humanism (p. 498)
janissary corps (p. 489)
Little Ice Age (p. 479)
Neo-Confucianism (p. 486)
oligarchy (p. 483)

pandemic (p. 478)
Renaissance (p. 498)
samurai (p. 501)
shogun (p. 503)
Sufism (p. 488)
theocracy (p. 489)
trade diaspora (p. 492)

CHAPTER OVERVIEW QUESTIONS

1. How and why did Europe's economic growth begin to surpass that of the Islamic world in the [...] after the Black Death?

2. Did the economic revival across Eurasia a[...] benefit the peasant populations of Europe [...] Islamic world, and East Asia?

3. How did the process of conversion to Islam differ in Iran, the Ottoman Empire, West Africa, and Southeast Asia during this period?

4. What political and economic changes contributed to the rise of maritime commerce in Asia during the fourteenth and fifteenth centuries?

> **Answer these big-picture questions posed at the start of the chapter.**

SECTION FOCUS QUESTIONS

1. How did the Black Death affect society, the [...] omy, and culture in Latin Christendom and [...] Islamic world?

2. Why did Islam expand dramatically in the fourteenth and fifteenth centuries, and how did new Islamic societies differ from established ones?

3. What were the principal sources of growth in international trade during the fourteenth and fifteenth centuries, and how did this trade affect patterns of consumption and fashion tastes?

4. How and why did the historical development of Japan in the fourteenth and fifteenth centuries differ from that of mainland Eurasia?

> **Explain the main point of each major section of the chapter.**

MAKING CONNECTIONS

1. What social, economic, and technological c[...] strengthened the power of European mona[...] during the century after the Black Death?

2. How and why did the major routes and con[...] ties of trans-Eurasian trade change after the collapse of the Mongol empires in Central Asia?

3. In what ways did the motives for conversion to Islam differ in Central Asia, sub-Saharan Africa, and the Indian Ocean during this era?

4. In this period, why did the power and status of the samurai warriors in Japan rise while those of the warrior nobility in Europe declined?

> **Connect ideas and practice your skills of comparison and analysis.**

507

VERSIONS AND SUPPLEMENTS

Adopters of *Crossroads and Cultures: A History of the World's Peoples* and their students have access to abundant extra resources, including documents, presentation and testing materials, the acclaimed Bedford Series in History and Culture volumes, and much, much more. See below for more information, visit the book's catalog site at bedfordstmartins.com/smith/catalog, or contact your local Bedford/St. Martin's sales representative.

Get the Right Version for Your Class

To accommodate different course lengths and course budgets, *Crossroads and Cultures: A History of the World's Peoples* is available in several different formats, including three-hole punched loose-leaf Budget Books versions and e-books, which are available at a substantial discount.

- Combined edition (Chapters 1–31)—available in hardcover, loose-leaf, and e-book formats
- Volume 1: To 1450 (Chapters 1–16)—available in paperback, loose-leaf, and e-book formats
- Volume 2: Since 1300 (Chapters 15–31)—available in paperback, loose-leaf, and e-book formats
- Volume A: To 1300 (Chapters 1–14)—available in paperback
- Volume B: 500–1750 (Chapters 9–22)—available in paperback
- Volume C: Since 1750 (Chapters 23–31)—available in paperback

Your students can purchase *Crossroads and Cultures: A History of the World's Peoples* in popular e-book formats for computers, tablets, and e-readers by visiting bedfordstmartins.com/ebooks. The e-book is available at a discount.

Online Extras for Students

The book's companion site at bedfordstmartins.com/smith gives students a way to read, write, and study by providing plentiful quizzes and activities, study aids, and history research and writing help.

FREE Online Study Guide. Available at the companion site, this popular resource provides students with quizzes and activities for each chapter, including multiple-choice self-tests that focus on important concepts; flashcards that test students' knowledge of key terms; timeline activities that emphasize causal relationships; and map quizzes intended to strengthen students' geography skills. Instructors can monitor students' progress through an online Quiz Gradebook or receive e-mail updates.

FREE Research, Writing, and Anti-plagiarism Advice. Available at the companion site, Bedford's **History Research and Writing Help** includes **History Research and Reference Sources**, with links to history-related databases, indexes, and journals; **More Sources and How to Format a History Paper**, with clear advice on how to integrate primary and secondary sources into research papers and how to cite and format sources correctly; **Build a Bibliography**, a simple Web-based tool known as the Bedford Bibliographer that generates bibliographies in four commonly used documentation styles; and **Tips on Avoiding Plagiarism**, an online tutorial that reviews the consequences of plagiarism and features exercises to help students practice integrating sources and recognize acceptable summaries.

Resources for Instructors

Bedford/St. Martin's has developed a rich array of teaching resources for this book and for this course. They range from lecture and presentation materials and assessment tools to course management options. Most can be downloaded or ordered at bedfordstmartins.com/smith/catalog.

HistoryClass for Crossroads and Cultures. *HistoryClass*, a Bedford/St. Martin's Online Course Space, puts the online resources available with this textbook in one convenient and completely customizable course space. There you and your students can access an interactive e-book and primary source reader; maps, images, documents, and links; chapter review quizzes; interactive multimedia exercises; and research and writing help. In *HistoryClass* you can get all our premium content and tools and assign, rearrange, and mix them with your own resources. For more information, visit yourhistoryclass.com.

Bedford Coursepack for Blackboard, WebCT, Desire2Learn, Angel, Sakai, or Moodle. We have free content to help you integrate our rich materials into your course management system. Registered instructors can download coursepacks easily and with no strings attached. The coursepack for *Crossroads and Cultures: A History of the World's Peoples* includes book-specific content as well as our most popular free resources. Visit bedfordstmartins.com/coursepacks to see a demo, find your version, or download your coursepack.

Instructor's Resource Manual. Written by Rick Warner, an experienced teacher of the world-history survey course, the instructor's manual offers both experienced and first-time instructors tools for preparing lectures and running discussions. It includes chapter review material, teaching strategies, and a guide to chapter-specific supplements available for the text.

Computerized Test Bank. The test bank includes a mix of fresh, carefully crafted multiple-choice, matching, short-answer, and essay questions for each chapter. It also contains the Overview, Focus, Making Connections, Lives and Livelihoods, Reading the Past, and Seeing the Past questions from the textbook and model answers for each. The questions appear in Microsoft Word format and in easy-to-use test bank software that allows instructors to easily add, edit, resequence, and print questions and answers. Instructors can also export questions into a variety of formats, including WebCT and Blackboard.

The Bedford Lecture Kit: Maps, Images, Lecture Outlines, and i>clicker Content. Look good and save time with *The Bedford Lecture Kit*. These presentation materials are downloadable individually from the Instructor Resources tab at bedfordstmartins.com/smith/catalog and are available on *The Bedford Lecture Kit* Instructor's Resource CD-ROM. They provide ready-made and fully customizable PowerPoint multimedia presentations that include lecture outlines with embedded maps, figures, and selected images from the textbook and extra background for instructors. Also available are maps and selected images in JPEG and PowerPoint formats; content for i>clicker, a classroom response system, in Microsoft Word and PowerPoint formats; the Instructor's Resource Manual in Microsoft Word format; and outline maps in PDF format for quizzing or handing out. All files are suitable for copying onto transparency acetates.

Make History—Free Documents, Maps, Images, and Web Sites. *Make History* combines the best Web resources with hundreds of maps and images, to make it simple to find the source material you need. Browse the collection of thousands of resources by course or by topic, date, and type. Each item has been carefully chosen and helpfully annotated to make it easy to find exactly what you need. Available at bedfordstmartins.com/makehistory.

Videos and Multimedia. A wide assortment of videos and multimedia CD-ROMs on various topics in world history is available to qualified adopters through your Bedford/St. Martin's sales representative.

Package and Save Your Students Money

For information on free packages and discounts up to 50%, visit bedfordstmartins.com/smith/catalog, or contact your local Bedford/St. Martin's sales representative.

Sources of Crossroads and Cultures. The authors of *Crossroads and Cultures* have carefully developed this two-volume primary source reader themselves to reflect the textbook's geographic and thematic breadth and the key social, cultural, and political developments discussed in each chapter. *Sources of Crossroads and Cultures* extends the textbook's emphasis on the human dimension of global history through the voices of both notable figures and everyday individuals. With a blend of major works and fresh perspectives, each chapter contains approximately six sources, an introduction, document headnotes, and questions for discussion. Available free when packaged with the print text.

Sources of Crossroads and Cultures e-Book. The reader is also available as an e-book for purchase at a discount.

The Bedford Series in History and Culture. More than one hundred titles in this highly praised series combine first-rate scholarship, historical narrative, and important primary documents for undergraduate courses. Each book is brief, inexpensive, and focused on a specific topic or period. For a complete list of titles, visit bedfordstmartins.com/history/series. Package discounts are available.

Rand McNally Historical Atlas of the World. This collection of almost seventy full-color maps illustrates the eras and civilizations in world history from the emergence of human societies to the present. Available for $3.00 when packaged with the print text.

The Bedford Glossary for World History. This handy supplement for the survey course gives students historically contextualized definitions for hundreds of terms—from *abolitionism* to *Zoroastrianism*—that they will encounter in lectures, reading, and exams. Available free when packaged with the print text.

World History Matters: A Student Guide to World History Online. Based on the popular "World History Matters" Web site produced by the Center for History and New Media, this unique resource, edited by Kristin Lehner (The Johns Hopkins University), Kelly Schrum (George Mason University), and T. Mills Kelly (George Mason University), combines reviews of 150 of the most useful and reliable world history Web sites with an introduction that guides students in locating, evaluating, and correctly citing online sources. Available free when packaged with the print text.

Trade Books. Titles published by sister companies Hill and Wang; Farrar, Straus and Giroux; Henry Holt and Company; St. Martin's Press; Picador; and Palgrave Macmillan are available at a 50% discount when packaged with

Bedford/St. Martin's textbooks. For more information, visit bedfordstmartins.com/tradeup.

A Pocket Guide to Writing in History. This portable and affordable reference tool by Mary Lynn Rampolla provides reading, writing, and research advice useful to students in all history courses. Concise yet comprehensive advice on approaching typical history assignments, developing critical reading skills, writing effective history papers, conducting research, using and documenting sources, and avoiding plagiarism—enhanced with practical tips and examples throughout—have made this slim reference a best-seller. Package discounts are available.

A Student's Guide to History. This complete guide to success in any history course provides the practical help students need to be effective. In addition to introducing students to the nature of the discipline, author Jules Benjamin teaches a wide range of skills from preparing for exams to approaching common writing assignments, and he explains the research and documentation process with plentiful examples. Package discounts are available.

Worlds of History: A Comparative Reader. Compiled by Kevin Reilly, a widely respected world historian and community college teacher, *Worlds of History* fosters historical thinking through thematic comparisons of primary and secondary sources from around the world. Each chapter takes up a major theme—such as patriarchy, love and marriage, or globalization—as experienced by two or more cultures. "Thinking Historically" exercises build students' capacity to analyze and interpret sources one skill at a time. This flexible framework accommodates a variety of approaches to teaching world history. Package discounts are available.

NOTE ON DATES AND USAGE

Where necessary for clarity, we qualify dates as B.C.E. ("Before the Common Era") or C.E. ("Common Era"). The abbreviation B.C.E. refers to the same era as B.C. ("Before Christ"), just as C.E is equivalent to A.D. (*anno Domini,* Latin for "in the year of the Lord"). In keeping with our aim to approach world history from a global, multicultural perspective, we chose these neutral abbreviations as appropriate to our enterprise. Because most readers will be more familiar with English than with metric measures, however, units of measure are given in the English system in the narrative, with metric and English measures provided on the maps.

We translate Chinese names and terms into English according to the *pinyin* system, while noting in parentheses proper names well established in English (e.g., Canton, Chiang Kai-shek). Transliteration of names and terms from the many other languages traced in our book follow the same contemporary scholarly conventions.

BRIEF CONTENTS

CONTENTS

PART 2 — The Formation of Regional Societies, 500–1450 C.E.

9

The Worlds of
Christianity and Islam,
400–1000 *270*

Major Global Development ▶ The spread of Christianity and Islam and the profound impact of these world religions on the societies of western Eurasia and North Africa.

10

Religion and Cross-
Cultural Exchange in
Asia, 400–1000 *304*

Major Global Development ▶ The cultural and commercial exchanges during the heyday of the Silk Road that transformed Asian peoples, cultures, and states.

17

The Fall of Native American Empires and the Rise of an Atlantic World, 1450–1600 *546*

Major Global Development ▶ European expansion across the Atlantic and its profound consequences for societies and cultures worldwide.

18

Western Africa in the Era of the Atlantic Slave Trade, 1450–1800 *580*

Major Global Development ▶ The rise of the Atlantic slave trade and its impact on early modern African peoples and cultures.

MAPS

SPECIAL FEATURES

ACKNOWLEDGMENTS

Writing *Crossroads and Cultures* has made real to us the theme of this book, which is connections among many far-flung people of diverse livelihoods and talents. From the first draft to the last, the authors have benefited from repeated critical readings by many talented scholars and teachers who represent an array of schools and historical interests. Our sincere thanks go to the following instructors, who helped us keep true to our vision of showing connections among the world's people and whose comments often challenged us to rethink or justify our interpretations. Crucial to the integrity of the book, they always provided a check on accuracy down to the smallest detail.

Alemseged Abbay, *Frostburg State University*

Heather J. Abdelnur, *Augusta State University*

Wayne Ackerson, *Salisbury University*

Kathleen Addison, *California State University, Northridge*

Jeffrey W. Alexander, *University of Wisconsin–Parkside*

Omar H. Ali, *The University of North Carolina at Greensboro*

Monty Armstrong, *Cerritos High School*

Pierre Asselin, *Hawai'i Pacific University*

Eva Baham, *Southern University at Baton Rouge*

William Bakken, *Rochester Community and Technical College*

Thomas William Barker, *The University of Kansas*

Thomas William Barton, *University of San Diego*

Robert Blackey, *California State University, San Bernardino*

Chuck Bolton, *The University of North Carolina at Greensboro*

Robert Bond, *San Diego Mesa College*

James W. Brodman, *University of Central Arkansas*

Gayle K. Brunelle, *California State University, Fullerton*

Samuel Brunk, *The University of Texas at El Paso*

Jurgen Buchenau, *The University of North Carolina at Charlotte*

Clea Bunch, *University of Arkansas at Little Rock*

Kathy Callahan, *Murray State University*

John M. Carroll, *The University of Hong Kong*

Giancarlo Casale, *University of Minnesota*

Mark Chavalas, *University of Wisconsin–La Crosse*

Yinghong Cheng, *Delaware State University*

Mark Choate, *Brigham Young University*

Sharon Cohen, *Springbrook High School*

Christine Colin, *Mercyhurst College*

Eleanor Congdon, *Youngstown State University*

Dale Crandall-Bear, *Solano Community College*

John Curry, *University of Nevada, Las Vegas*

Michelle Danberg-Marshman, *Green River Community College*

Francis Danquah, *Southern University at Baton Rouge*

Sherrie Dux-Ideus, *Central Community College*

Peter Dykema, *Arkansas Tech University*

Tom Ewing, *Virginia Polytechnic Institute and State University*

Angela Feres, *Grossmont College*

Michael Fischbach, *Randolph-Macon College*

Nancy Fitch, *California State University, Fullerton*

Terence Anthony Fleming, *Northern Kentucky University*

Richard Fogarty, *University at Albany, The State University of New York*

Nicola Foote, *Florida Gulf Coast University*

Deanna Forsman, *North Hennepin Community College*

John D. Garrigus, *The University of Texas at Arlington*

Trevor Getz, *San Francisco State University*

David Goldfrank, *Georgetown University*

Charles Didier Gondola, *Indiana University–Purdue University Indianapolis*

Sue Gronewold, *Kean University*

Christopher Guthrie, *Tarleton State University*

Anne Hardgrove, *The University of Texas at San Antonio*

Donald J. Harreld, *Brigham Young University*

Todd Hartch, *Eastern Kentucky University*

Janine Hartman, *University of Cincinnati*

Daniel Heimmermann, *The University of Texas at Brownsville*

Cecily M. Heisser, *University of San Diego*

Timothy Henderson, *Auburn University at Montgomery*

Ted Henken, *Baruch College, The State University of New York*

Marilynn J. Hitchens, *University of Colorado Denver*

Roy W. Hopper, *University of Memphis*

Timothy Howe, *St. Olaf College*

Delridge Hunter, *Medgar Evers College, The City University of New York*

Bruce Ingram, *Itawamba Community College*

Erik N. Jensen, *Miami University*

Steven Sandor John, *Hunter College, The City University of New York*

Deborah Johnston, *Lakeside School*

David M. Kalivas, *Middlesex Community College*

Carol Keller, *San Antonio College*

Ian Stuart Kelly, *Palomar College*

Linda Kerr, *University of Alberta*

Charles King, *University of Nebraska at Omaha*

Melinda Cole Klein, *Saddleback College*

Ane Lintvedt-Dulac, *McDonogh School*

Ann Livschiz, *Indiana University–Purdue University Fort Wayne*

George E. Longenecker, *Vermont Technical College*

Edward Lykens, *Middle Tennessee State University*

Susan Maneck, *Jackson State University*

Chandra Manning, *Georgetown University*

Michael Marino, *The College of New Jersey*

Thomas Massey, *Cape Fear Community College*
Mary Jane Maxwell, *Green Mountain College*
Christine McCann, *Norwich University*
Patrick McDevitt, *University at Buffalo, The State University of New York*
Ian F. McNeely, *University of Oregon*
M. E. Menninger, *Texas State University–San Marcos*
Kathryn E. Meyer, *Washington State University*
Elizabeth Mizrahi, *Santa Barbara City College*
Max Okenfuss, *Washington University in St. Louis*
Kenneth Orosz, *Buffalo State College, The State University of New York*
Annette Palmer, *Morgan State University*
David Perry, *Dominican University*
Jared Poley, *Georgia State University*
Elizabeth Ann Pollard, *San Diego State University*
Dana Rabin, *University of Illinois at Urbana-Champaign*
Norman G. Raiford, *Greenville Technical College*
Stephen Rapp, *Universität Bern*
Michele Reid, *Georgia State University*
Chad Ross, *East Carolina University*
Morris Rossabi, *Queens College, The City University of New York*
Steven C. Rubert, *Oregon State University*
Eli Rubin, *Western Michigan University*
Anthony Santoro, *Christopher Newport University*
Linda B. Scherr, *Mercer County Community College*
Hollie Schillig, *California State University, Long Beach*
Michael Seth, *James Madison University*
Jessica Sheetz-Nguyen, *University of Central Oklahoma*
Rose Mary Sheldon, *Virginia Military Institute*
David R. Smith, *California State Polytechnic University, Pomona*
Ramya Sreenivasan, *University at Buffalo, The State University of New York*
John Stavens, *Bristol Eastern High School*
Catherine Howey Stearn, *Eastern Kentucky University*
Richard Steigmann-Gall, *Kent State University*
Anthony J. Steinhoff, *The University of Tennessee at Chattanooga*
Stephen J. Stillwell, *The University of Arizona*
Heather Streets, *Washington State University*
Jean Stuntz, *West Texas A&M University*
Guy Thompson, *University of Alberta*
Hunt Tooley, *Austin College*
Wendy Turner, *Augusta State University*
Rick Warner, *Wabash College*
Michael Weber, *Gettysburg College*
Theodore Weeks, *Southern Illinois University*
Guy Wells, *Lorain County Community College*
Sherri West, *Brookdale Community College*
Kenneth Wilburn, *East Carolina University*
Pingchao Zhu, *University of Idaho*
Alexander Zukas, *National University*

Many colleagues, friends, and family members have helped us develop this work as well. Bonnie Smith wishes to thank in particular Michal Shapira and Molly Giblin for their research assistance and Patrick Smith, who gave helpful information on contemporary world religions. Her colleagues at Rutgers, many of them pioneers in world history, were especially helpful. Among these, expert historian Donald R. Kelley shaped certain features of the last section of the book and always cheered the author on. Marc Van De Mieroop thanks the friends and colleagues who often unknowingly provided insights and information used in this book, especially Irene Bloom, William Harris, Feng Li, Indira Peterson, Michael Sommer, and Romila Thapar. Richard von Glahn thanks his many colleagues at UCLA who have shaped his thinking about world history, especially Ghislaine Lydon, Jose Moya, Ron Mellor, Sanjay Subrahmanyam, and Bin Wong. He is also grateful for the exposure to pathbreaking scholarship on world history afforded by the University of California's Multi-Campus Research Unit in World History. Kris Lane thanks the many wonderful William & Mary students of History 192, "The World Since 1450," as well as colleagues Abdul-Karim Rafeq, Scott Nelson, Chitralekha Zutshi, Hiroshi Kitamura, Philip Daileader, Chandos Brown, and Ron Schechter. All offered valuable advice on framing the early modern period. He also owes a huge debt to the University of Minnesota for graduate training and teaching assistant experience in this field.

We also wish to acknowledge and thank the publishing team at Bedford/St. Martin's, who are among the most talented people in publishing that we as a group have ever worked with and who did so much to bring this book into being. Among them, our special thanks go to former publisher for history Patricia A. Rossi, who inspired the conceptual design of the book and helped bring us together. The current publisher for history, Mary Dougherty, then picked up the reins from Tisha and advanced the project, using her special combination of professional expertise and personal warmth. It is hard to convey sufficiently our heartfelt appreciation to president Joan E. Feinberg and editorial director Denise Wydra. They always kept us alert to Bedford's special legacy of high-quality textbooks, a legacy based on the benefits a book must have for students and teachers alike. We aimed to be part of that legacy while writing *Crossroads and Cultures*.

President emeritus and founder Charles Christensen was also present at the beginning of this project, and he always cheerfully lent his extraordinary knowledge of publishing to the making and actual production of this book. We know that it would have been less than it is without his wisdom. Alongside all these others, director of development for history Jane Knetzger patiently and skillfully guided the development process, during which each chapter (and sentence) was poked and prodded. We thank Jane for being such a quiet force behind the progress of *Crossroads and*

Cultures. Special thanks go to senior editor and expert facilitator Heidi Hood and the editorial assistants who joined Heidi in providing invaluable help on many essential tasks: Lynn Sternberger, Jennifer Jovin, and Emily DiPietro. All of them moved the project along in myriad ways that we hardly know. We also appreciate the countless schedules, tasks, and layouts juggled so efficiently and well by senior production editor Anne Noonan. On the editorial team were John Reisbord and Daniel Otis, who helped edit and polish our final draft. All along the way Rose Corbett Gordon and Charlotte Miller, our superb photo researcher and talented map editor, respectively, provided us with striking and thought-provoking images and up-to-date, richly informative, and gorgeous maps. No author team could ask for more than to have the book's content laid out in such a clear and attractive design as that provided by Jerilyn Bockorick, with assistance from senior art director Anna Palchik. Jerilyn's special attention to the overall look of our work makes us feel that we and our readers are especially lucky. Senior designer Billy Boardman created our six beautiful covers with help from senior art director Donna Dennison. We are grateful for their craft in building the book's appeal.

Crossroads and Cultures has a wealth of materials for students and teachers to help support the text. Editor Annette Fantasia has guided our creation of the sourcebook that accompanies the main book, and we could hardly have achieved this task without her help; she also edited the instructor's resource manual. The work of associate editor Jack Cashman, who supervised the development of the other elements in our impressive array of supplements, will be appreciated by all teachers and students who use these materials. Jenna Bookin Barry, senior executive marketing manager; Sally Constable, senior market development manager; and Katherine Bates, market development manager, have worked tirelessly at our side to ensure that the book is in the best shape to meet the needs of students and teachers. We are deeply grateful for all the work they have done in the past and all that they will do in so sincerely advocating for the success of *Crossroads and Cultures* in today's classrooms.

Among the authors' greatest *Crossroads* experiences has been our relationship with brilliant executive editor Elizabeth M. Welch and her support team of ace development editors Sylvia Mallory, Margaret Manos, and Jim Strandberg. Beth has guided many a successful book from inception to completion—all to the benefit of tens of thousands of students and their instructors. We thank her for bringing us her historical, conceptual, visual, and publishing talent, all of which she has offered with such generosity of spirit, good humor, and grace. It has been a privilege for all of us to work with Beth and to have spent these *Crossroads* years with the entire Bedford team.

Finally, our students' questions and concerns have shaped much of this work, and we welcome all our readers' suggestions, queries, and criticisms. We know that readers, like our own students, excel in spotting unintended glitches and also in providing much excellent food for thought. Please contact us with your comments at our respective institutions.

Bonnie G. Smith
Marc Van De Mieroop
Richard von Glahn
Kris Lane

The Formation of Regional Societies

500–1450 C.E.

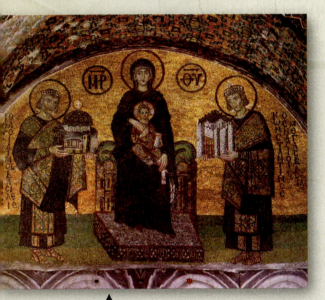

CH 9

ALTHOUGH NO SINGLE LABEL adequately reflects the history of the world in the period 500–1450, its most distinctive feature was the formation of regional societies based on common forms of livelihoods, cultural values, and social and political institutions. The new age in world history that began in around 500 C.E. marked a decisive break from the "classical" era of antiquity. The passing of classical civilizations in the Mediterranean, China, and India shared a number of causes, but the most notable were invasions by nomads from the Central Asian steppes. Beset by internal unrest and foreign pressures, the empires of Rome, Han China, and Gupta India crumbled. As these once-mighty empires fragmented into a multitude of competing states, cultural revolutions followed. Confidence in the values and institutions of the classical era was shattered, opening the way for fresh ideas. Christianity, Buddhism, Hinduism, and the new creed of Islam spread far beyond their original circles of believers. By 1450 these four religious traditions had supplanted or transformed local religions in virtually all of Eurasia and much of Africa.

The spread of foreign religions and the lifestyles and livelihoods they promoted produced distinctive regional societies. By 1000, Europe had taken shape as a coherent society and culture even as it came to be divided between the Roman and Byzantine Christian churches. The shared cultural values of modern East Asia—rooted in the literary and philosophical traditions of China but also assuming distinctive national forms—also emerged during the first millennium C.E. During this era, too, Indian civilization expanded into Southeast Asia and acquired a new unity expressed through the common language of Sanskrit. The rapid expansion of Islam across Asia, Africa, and

CH 10

CH 11

even parts of Europe demonstrated the power of a shared religious identity to transcend political and cultural boundaries. But the pan-Islamic empire, which reached its height in the eighth century, proved unsustainable. After the authority of the Abbasid caliphs ebbed in the ninth century, the Islamic world split into distinctive regional societies in the Middle East, North Africa, Central and South Asia, and Southeast Asia.

We also see the formation of regional societies in other parts of the world. Migrations, the development of states, and commercial exchanges with the Islamic world transformed African societies and brought them into more consistent contact with one another. The concentration of political power in the hands of the ruling elites in Mesoamerica and the Andean region led to the founding of mighty city-states. Even in North America and the Pacific Ocean—worlds without states—migration and economic exchange fostered common social practices and livelihoods.

Nomad invasions and political disintegration disrupted economic life in the old imperial heartlands, but long-distance trade flourished as never before. The consolidation of nomad empires and merchant networks stretching across Central Asia culminated in the heyday of the overland "Silk Road" linking China to the Mediterranean world. The Indian Ocean, too, emerged as a crossroads of trade and cultural diffusion. After 1000, most of Eurasia and Africa enjoyed several centuries of steady economic improvement. Rising agricultural productivity fed population expansion, and cities and urban culture thrived with the growth of trade and industry.

Economic prosperity and urban vitality also stimulated intellectual change. Much of the new wealth was channeled into the building of religious monuments and institutions. New institutions of learning and scholarship—such as Christian Europe's universities, the madrasas of the Islamic world, and civil service examinations and government schooling in China—spawned both conformity and dissent.

Cross-cultural interaction also brought conflict, war, and schism. Tensions between Christians and Muslims erupted into the violent clashes known as the Crusades beginning in the late eleventh century. The boundaries between Christendom and the House of Islam shifted over time, but the rift between the two

CH 12

CH 13

faiths grew ever wider. The rise of steppe empires—above all, the explosive expansion of the Mongol empires—likewise transformed the political and cultural landscape of Asia. Historians today recognize the ways in which the Mongol conquests facilitated the movement of people, goods, and ideas across Eurasia. But contemporaries could see no farther than the ruin sowed by the Mongols wherever they went, toppling cities and laying waste to once-fertile farmlands.

After 1300 the momentum of world history changed. Economic growth slowed, strained by the pressure of rising populations on productive resources and the effects of a cooling climate, and then it stopped altogether. In the late 1340s the Black Death pandemic devastated the central Islamic lands and Europe. It would take centuries before the populations in these parts of the world returned to their pre-1340 levels.

By 1400, however, other signs of recovery were evident. Powerful national states emerged in Europe and China, restoring some measure of stability. Strong Islamic states held sway in Egypt, Anatolia (modern Turkey), Iran, and India. The European Renaissance—the intense outburst of intellectual and artistic creativity envisioned as a "rebirth" of the classical civilization of Greece and Rome—flickered to life, sparked by the economic vigor of the Italian city-states. Similarly, Neo-Confucianism—a "renaissance" of China's classical learning—whetted the intellectual and cultural aspirations of educated elites throughout East Asia. Maritime Asia, spared the ravages of the Black Death, continued to flourish while

CH 14

	500		750	
Americas	**500** First permanent settlements in Chaco Canyon **500–1000** Andean state of Tiwanaku **550–650** Collapse of Teotihuacán		**800–900** Collapse of the Maya city-states Rise of Chimu state **900** **700–900** Heyday of Andean state of Wari	
Europe	▪ **507** Clovis defeats Visigoths and converts to Christianity **590–604** Papacy of Gregory I	Charles Martel halts Muslim advance into Europe **732** ▪ Charlemagne crowned emperor **800** ▪	▪ **793** Earliest record of Viking raids on Britain	
Middle East	**527–565** Reign of Byzantine emperor Justinian I **570–632** Life of Muhammad	▪ **680** Permanent split between Shi'a and Sunni Islam **750–850** Abbasid caliphate at its height **661–743** Umayyad caliphate		
Africa	▪ **500** Spread of camel use; emergence of trans-Saharan trade routes		▪ **750** Islam starts to spread via trans-Saharan trade routes	
Asia and Oceania	**581–618** Sui Empire **618–907** Tang Empire **600–1000** Polynesian settlement of Pacific Islands	▪ **668** Unification of Korea under Silla rule	**755–763** An Lushan rebellion	

Eurasia's major land-based economies struggled to regain their earlier prosperity.

In 1453 Muslim Ottoman armies seized Constantinople and deposed the Byzantine Christian emperor, cutting the last thread of connection to the ancient world. The fall of Constantinople symbolized the end of the era discussed in Part 2. Denied direct access to the rich trade with Asia, European monarchs and merchants began to shift their attention to the Atlantic world. Yet just as Columbus's discovery of the "New World" (in fact, a very ancient one) came as a surprise, the idea of a new world order centered on Europe—the modern world order—was still unimaginable.

CH 15

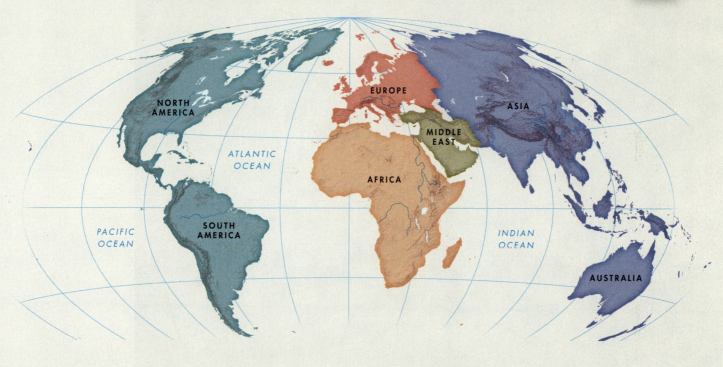

1000	1250	1500

950–1150 Height of Toltec culture   • **1200** Incas move into Cuzco region   Columbus reaches the Americas **1492** •

• **1050** Consolidation of Cahokia's dominance   • **1150** Abandonment of pueblos in Chaco Canyon   • **1325** Aztecs found Tenochtitlán   **1430–1532** Inca Empire

1250–1300 Collapse of Cahokia

988 Rus prince Vladimir converts to Christianity   • **1066** Norman conquest of England   • **1150** Founding of first university at Paris   **1347–1350** Outbreak of Black Death   **1400–1550** Italian Renaissance

1150–1300 Heyday of the Champagne fairs   **1337–1453** Hundred Years' War   Reconquista

Mongol conquest of Kiev **1240** •   **1270–1300** Introduction of overseas navigational aids   completed **1492** •

First Crusade ends with Christian capture of Jerusalem **1099** •   • **1120** Founding of order of Knights of the Temple   • **1291** Mamluks recapture Acre, last Christian stronghold in Palestine

• **1258** Mongols sack Baghdad   **1347–1350** Outbreak of Black Death   • **1453** Fall of Constantinople to the Ottomans

Saladin recaptures Jerusalem **1187** •

969 Fatimids capture Egypt   Reign of Sunjata, founder of **1250–1517** Mamluk dynasty

Fall of kingdom of Ghana **1076** •   Mali Empire **1230–1255**   • **1250** Kingdom of Benin founded

1100–1500 Extended dry period in West Africa prompts migrations

850–1267 Chola kingdom   **1100–1500** Easter Island's stone monuments   **1336–1573** Ashikaga Shogunate

939 Vietnam achieves independence from China   Formation of first Hawaiian   **1206–1526** Delhi Sultanate   **1368–1644** Ming Empire

960–1279 Song Empire   chiefdoms **1200–1400**   **1271–1368** Yuan Empire   **1392–1910** Korean Yi dynasty

AT A CROSSROADS ▲

The emperors of Constantinople had grand ambitions to rebuild the Roman Empire on new foundations of Christian faith. They displayed special devotion to the Virgin Mary, the patron saint of their capital. This mosaic in the Hagia Sophia, Constantinople's greatest Christian church, shows Emperor Constantine (right) offering a model of the city to Mary and the infant Jesus. Emperor Justinian I (left) presents a model of the Hagia Sophia, which he rebuilt in 562. (Erich Lessing/Art Resource, NY.)

The Worlds of Christianity and Islam

400–1000

In 550, Médard, the bishop of Noyon, northeast of Paris, faced a dilemma. Radegund, the pious wife of the Germanic king Clothar, had come to him seeking to become a nun. But Médard was reluctant to offend Clothar, his patron and benefactor, and the king's men had threatened to drag him from his church should he attempt to place a nun's veil on their queen. According to her biographers, Radegund, sizing up the situation, entered the sacristy, put on a monastic garb, and proceeded straight to the altar, saying, 'If you shrink from consecrating me, and fear man more than God, pastor, He will require His sheep's [Radegund's] soul from your hand.'" Chastened, Médard laid his hands upon Radegund and ordained her as a deaconess.

Radegund (520–587) was the daughter of a rival German king who was a bitter enemy of Clothar's tribe, the Franks. When Radegund was eleven, the Franks slaughtered her family and took her prisoner. Later she was forced to marry Clothar and became, in her words, "a captive maid given to a hostile lord." Raised a Christian, Radegund took refuge in religion. Even before renouncing secular life, "she was more Christ's partner than her husband's companion."[1] Her biographers describe in great detail the physical torments she inflicted on herself, her ministrations to the poor and the sick, the miracles she performed, and the rich gifts she bestowed on the church and the needy. After Clothar's death, Radegund founded a convent at Poitiers and took up a life of full seclusion. But she continued to play the role of Christian queen, maintaining a vigorous correspondence with the leading clergy of the day and trying to act as peacemaker between feuding Frankish kings.

BACKSTORY

As we saw in Chapter 7, the Roman Empire enjoyed a period of renewal in the early fourth century under Constantine, who reinvigorated imperial rule and adopted Christianity as an official religion. But the western part of the empire, wracked by internal conflicts and Germanic invasions, crumbled in the fifth century. By contrast, the emperors at Constantinople, buoyed by the diverse and resilient economy of the eastern Mediterranean, continued to preside over a strong state, which historians call the Byzantine Empire. The resurgent Persian Empire of the Sasanid dynasty struggled with the Romans for control of Syria, Mesopotamia, and Armenia. The rise of Islam in the seventh century would transform political, religious, and economic life from the Mediterranean to Persia.

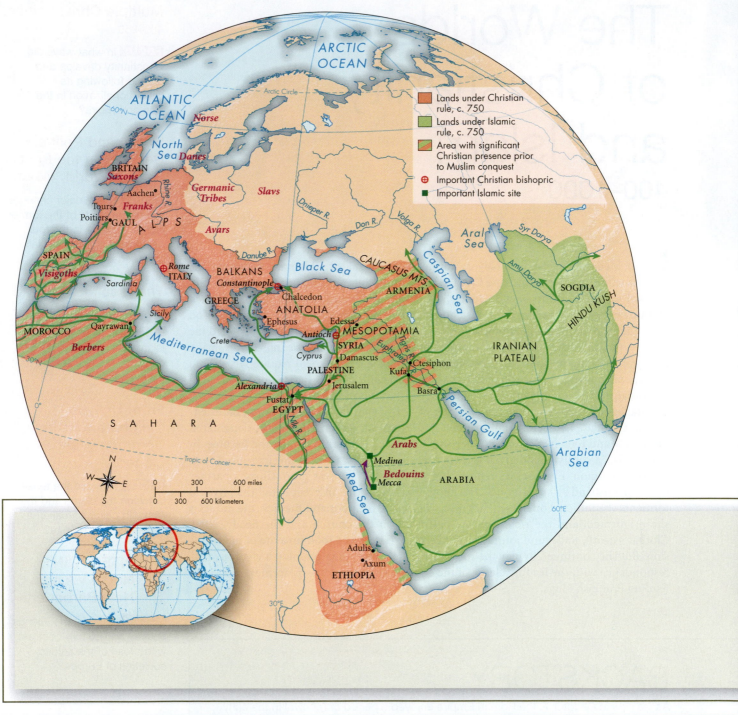

Legend:
- Lands under Christian rule, c. 750
- Lands under Islamic rule, c. 750
- Area with significant Christian presence prior to Muslim conquest
- ⊕ Important Christian bishopric
- ■ Important Islamic site

ARCTIC OCEAN

ATLANTIC OCEAN
Arctic Circle
60°N

Norse

North Sea
Danes
Germanic Tribes
Slavs
BRITAIN
Saxons
Aachen
Tours
Franks
Poitiers
GAUL
A L P S
Avars
Rhine R.
Dnieper R.
Don R.
Volga R.
Aral Sea
Syr Darya
Amu Darya
SOGDIA
HINDU KUSH
CAUCASUS MTS.
Caspian Sea
ARMENIA
SPAIN
Visigoths
Sardinia
⊕ Rome
ITALY
BALKANS
Constantinople
GREECE
Chalcedon
ANATOLIA
Ephesus
Edessa
Black Sea
Danube R.
IRANIAN PLATEAU
MOROCCO
Qayrawan
Sicily
Crete
Antioch ⊕
MESOPOTAMIA
SYRIA
Damascus
Ctesiphon
Kufa
Euphrates R.
Tigris R.
Berbers
Mediterranean Sea
Cyprus
PALESTINE
Jerusalem
Basra
Persian Gulf
Alexandria ⊕
Fustat
EGYPT
Nile R.
S A H A R A
Tropic of Cancer
Red Sea
■ Medina
Arabs
Bedouins
■ Mecca
ARABIA
Arabian Sea
60°E
Aral Sea
0°
30°E
30°N

N W E S
0   300   600 miles
0   300   600 kilometers

Adulis
Axum
ETHIOPIA

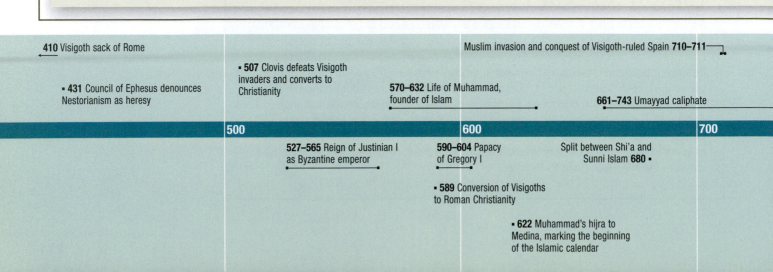

410 Visigoth sack of Rome

Muslim invasion and conquest of Visigoth-ruled Spain **710–711**

■ **507** Clovis defeats Visigoth invaders and converts to Christianity

■ **431** Council of Ephesus denounces Nestorianism as heresy

570–632 Life of Muhammad, founder of Islam

661–743 Umayyad caliphate

500

527–565 Reign of Justinian I as Byzantine emperor

590–604 Papacy of Gregory I

Split between Shi'a and Sunni Islam **680** ■

600

700

■ **589** Conversion of Visigoths to Roman Christianity

■ **622** Muhammad's hijra to Medina, marking the beginning of the Islamic calendar

By Radegund's day, Christianity had become deeply entrenched in all of the Roman Empire's former territories and had spread beyond to Iran, Armenia, and Ethiopia. Pagan societies on the fringes of the old empire, such as the roving Germanic tribes and the Slavic peoples of Eastern Europe, gradually adopted the Christian religion as well. Even the Norse Vikings, at first reviled as the mortal enemies of Christianity, remade themselves into models of Christian piety.

Unity proved elusive in Christendom (the realm of Christianity), however. Radegund's contemporary Justinian I (r. 527–565), the emperor at Constantinople, tried to reunify the old Roman Empire through military conquest. But Justinian's triumphs barely outlasted his death in 565. New adversaries in the east—above all, the rising religion of Islam—drew the emperors' attention away from the western provinces of the old empire. The rulers of Constantinople began to identify themselves exclusively with their capital's Greek heritage, spurning Roman traditions and replacing Latin with Greek as the official language of the empire. By 600 the religious and cultural gulf between the Latin west and the Greek east had so widened that historians speak of the latter as the Byzantine Empire (from *Byzantium*, the Greek name for Constantinople).

At the same time that the Latin west and the Greek east took increasingly divergent paths, a new and powerful culture arose that would challenge both. The emergence and spread of Islam in the 600s occurred with astonishing speed and success. The Muslim conquests sowed the seeds of Islamic faith and Arab social institutions in diverse societies in Africa, Europe, and Asia. The pace of conversion to Islam varied greatly, however. Islam quickly made deep inroads among urban merchants and among pastoral nomads such as the Berbers of North Africa. In agrarian societies such as Syria, Mesopotamia, and Spain, the Arabs long remained a tiny elite ruling over Christian majorities, who only gradually accepted Islam. In regions hemmed in by the expansion of Islam, such as Armenia and Ethiopia, the Christian faith became the hallmark of political independence. Thus Islamic expansion did not impose a uniform culture over a vast empire. Local conditions in each

MAPPING THE WORLD

Christian and Islamic Lands, c. 750

By 750, the old Roman Empire had been partitioned between two faiths, Christianity and Islam. Christendom itself was increasingly becoming a house divided between two rival churches centered at Constantinople and Rome. The Abbasid caliphate had deposed the Umayyad dynasty of caliphs, based at Damascus, in 747. The new Abbasid capital at Baghdad soon eclipsed Damascus and the holy cities of Mecca and Medina as the political and religious center of the Islamic world.

ROUTES ▼

→ Major campaign of Islamic forces, 625–732

→ Muhammad's hijra, 622

868–883 Zanj revolt against the Abbasid regime

793 Earliest record of Viking raids on Britain

988 Vladimir, the Rus prince of Kiev, converts to Christianity

870–930 Vikings colonize Iceland

| 800 | 900 | 1000 |

747–1258 Abbasid caliphate

800 Coronation of Charlemagne as emperor by Pope Leo III

909 Fatimid dynasty founded

732 Charles Martel halts Muslim advance into Europe

Muslim territory shaped the terms and consequences of cultural exchange among Muslim conquerors, subject peoples, and neighboring states.

However, like Christianity, Islam claimed to be a universal religion. Both religions offered a vision of common brotherhood that brought a new religious sensibility to daily life and integrated disparate peoples into a community of faith. Although Christianity and Islam spread along different paths, both were beset by an abiding tension between sacred and secular authority. The Christian church preserved its autonomy amid political disorder in the Latin west, whereas the Byzantine emperors yoked imperial power and clerical leadership tightly together. The vision of a universal Islamic empire combining spiritual faith with political and military strength was crucial to the initial expansion of Islam. In the ninth and tenth centuries, however, the Islamic empire fragmented into numerous regional states divided by doctrine, culture, and way of life. Nonetheless, the economic vibrancy and religious ferment of the far-flung Islamic world created a vast territory through which Muslim merchants, missionaries, and pilgrims moved freely, drawing together the separate worlds of Asia, Africa, and Europe. Islamic cities and ports became global crossroads, centers for the exchange of goods and ideas that helped create new cultural connections stretching from the Iberian peninsula to China.

OVERVIEW
QUESTIONS

The major global development in this chapter: The spread of Christianity and Islam and the profound impact of these world religions on the societies of western Eurasia and North Africa.

As you read, consider:

1. How and why did the development of the Christian church differ in the Byzantine Empire and Latin Christendom?

2. In what ways did the rise of Christianity and Islam challenge the power of the state?

3. Conversely, in what ways did the spread of these faiths reinforce state power?

4. Why did Christianity and Islam achieve their initial success in towns and cities rather than in the rural countryside?

Multiple Christianities 400–850

FOCUS

In what ways did Christianity develop and spread following its institutionalization in the Roman Empire?

In the century following the Roman emperor Constantine's momentous conversion to Christianity in 312, Christian leaders were confident that their faith would displace the classical Mediterranean religions (see Chapter 7). Yet the rapid spread of the Christian religion throughout Roman territories also splintered the Christian movement. Their fierce independence honed by hostility and persecution, Christian communities did not readily yield to any universal authority in matters of doctrine and faith. Efforts by the Byzantine emperors to impose their will on the Christian leadership met strong resistance. The progress of conversion throughout the territories of the old Roman Empire came at the cost of increasing divisions within the church itself.

The Christian Church in Byzantium

In the eastern Mediterranean, where imperial rule remained strong, the state treated the Christian church and clergy as a branch of imperial administration. Although the Christian communities of the eastern Mediterranean welcomed imperial support, they also sought to preserve their independence from the emperors' direct control. For example, bishops elected by their local followers exercised sovereign rule over religious affairs within their jurisdictions. In the late fourth century a council of bishops acknowledged the special status of the bishop of Constantinople by designating him as patriarch, the supreme leader of the church. But the bishops of Alexandria in Egypt and Antioch in Anatolia (modern Turkey) retained authority and influence nearly equal to that of Constantinople's patriarch (see Map 9.1). Thus, although Byzantine emperors sought to use the Christian church as a vehicle to expand and reinforce their power, church leaders contested this agenda throughout the empire.

Tensions between secular and religious officials were not the only source of division in eastern Christianity. The urban elite of imperial officials and wealthy merchants adopted the new religion, but alongside such new Christian practices as prayer, repentance, and almsgiving they often continued to uphold the old forms of Greek religion. Their vision of Christianity reflected the strong influence Greek culture continued to exert on Byzantine city life. These were urban people, and their religious beliefs and practices grew out of a cosmopolitan urban context.

In Syria and Egypt, however, rural inhabitants embraced a more austere form of Christian piety. Some of the most impassioned Christians, deploring the persistence of profane Greco-Roman culture in the cities, sought spiritual refuge in the sparsely inhabited deserts, where they devoted themselves to an ascetic life of rigorous physical discipline and contemplation of the divine. Perhaps the most famous of these ascetics was Symeon the Stylite, who for many years lived and preached atop a sixty-foot pillar. After his death in 459, thousands of pilgrims flocked each year to Symeon's shrine in northern Syria.

The Ascetic Movement

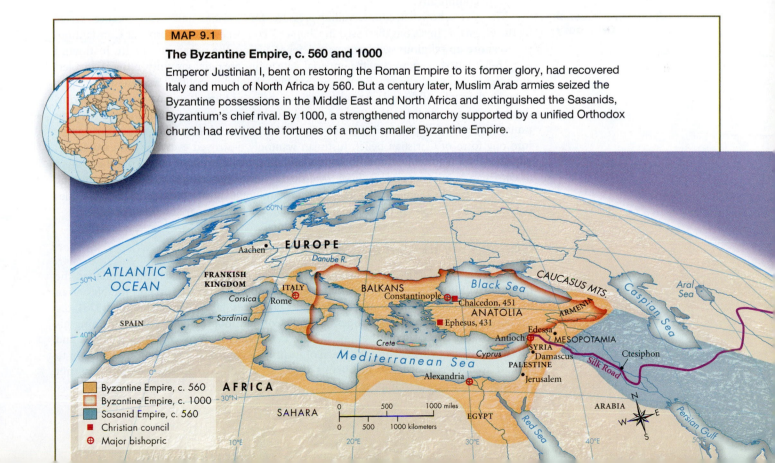

MAP 9.1

The Byzantine Empire, c. 560 and 1000

Emperor Justinian I, bent on restoring the Roman Empire to its former glory, had recovered Italy and much of North Africa by 560. But a century later, Muslim Arab armies seized the Byzantine possessions in the Middle East and North Africa and extinguished the Sasanids, Byzantium's chief rival. By 1000, a strengthened monarchy supported by a unified Orthodox church had revived the fortunes of a much smaller Byzantine Empire.

Byzantine Empire, c. 560
Byzantine Empire, c. 1000
Sasanid Empire, c. 560
Christian council
Major bishopric

Rise of Christian Monasteries

While also serving as spiritual guides for the Christian population at large, other ascetics founded monasteries that attracted like-minded followers. The monastic movement began sporadically in Egypt and Syria in the late third century and surged in the fourth and fifth centuries. The austerity of monastic life endowed monks with an aura of holiness and sacred power that outshone the pomp and finery of church leaders in the cities. Whether hidden away in the monasteries or preaching their convictions among the people, these holy men became alternative sources of sacred authority independent of the official church hierarchy.

Disputes over Doctrine

The divisions within eastern Christianity went beyond differences in style and presentation to disagreements over basic Christian beliefs. Straying from orthodoxy—established church doctrines—became common among recluses, itinerant preachers, and even those in the church's highest ranks. Already in the time of Constantine, the bishops had been locked in debate over the divinity of Jesus (see Chapter 7). Nestorius (neh-STORE-ee-us), elected patriarch of Constantinople in 428, renewed this controversy by proclaiming that Jesus had two natures, one human and one divine. Nestorius especially objected to the idea that a human woman, Mary, could give birth to the son of God. But Nestorius's views outraged Cyril, the bishop of Alexandria, who insisted that Jesus had a single, fully divine nature, a principle that became known as the Monophysite ("single nature") doctrine. Councils of bishops held at Ephesus (431) and Chalcedon (KAL-suh-dahn) (451) denounced Nestorius's views as heresy (see again Map 9.1). To counter the claims of Nestorius, the Ephesus council formally declared Mary "mother of God" (see Seeing the Past: Mary as Mother of God). The Chalcedon council, in an effort to heal the split among the clergy, adopted a compromise position, that Jesus was both "fully divine and fully human." But the bishops of Alexandria remained committed to their Monophysite views, whereas the Nestorian doctrine gained a considerable following among local clergy in Syria and Mesopotamia. This debate may seem esoteric to modern observers, but it is important to remember that, from the point of view of the participants, the stakes could not have been higher. At issue was the very nature of Jesus and, thus, the essential nature of Christianity. It is, therefore, not surprising that this debate led to long-lasting divisions within the Christian community.

Justinian's Imperial Orthodoxy

There were, however, countervailing pressures for Christian unity. The pressure exerted by the Germanic invasions discussed in Chapter 7 compelled the emperors at Constantinople to shore up religious solidarity as a defense against the pagan onslaught. Justinian I (r. 527–565) used the powers of the imperial state to impose religious unity, refusing to tolerate heretics and nonbelievers. Born a peasant but schooled in political intrigue while rising through the ranks of the palace guard, Justinian believed himself to have been divinely ordained to restore order to the Roman world. He began his campaign to impose religious uniformity on his empire soon after his coronation. "His ambition being to force everyone into one form of Christian belief, Justinian wantonly destroyed everyone who would not conform," wrote Procopius, the great historian of Justinian's reign.[2] He also put the content of Christianity in service of his drive toward religious orthodoxy as a means of promoting political unity. The theology elaborated at Constantinople during the next several centuries reiterated the principles of order and hierarchy on which the imperial state was built.

Christianity in Asia and Africa

Far from restoring unity, though, Justinian's often strong-arm tactics only widened the fractures within the church. Alexandria resisted imperial domination, and the Nestorian heresy became entrenched in the easternmost provinces. Jacob Baradaeus (died 578), the Monophysite bishop of Edessa, openly defied Constantinople's authority by forming his own separatist church (what became known as the Jacobite movement) in Anatolia and Syria. Christians living beyond the reach of Justinian's control were even more reluctant to submit to imperial dictates. Justinian's vision of a unified Christian empire was not matched by the power to impose his will.

Mary as Mother of God

***The Virgin of Vladimir* (artist unknown):** This icon, sent to the Rus prince of Kiev from Constantinople in 1131, became renowned for its miracle-working powers. (Scala/Art Resource, NY.)

over the question of Jesus's divinity that reached a climax at the 431 Council of Ephesus elevated Mary to a position in Christian devotion second only to Jesus himself.

Devotion to Mary intensified through a proliferation of festival days, liturgies, miracle stories, and visual images. When Constantinople's patriarch renovated the city's principal Christian church, Hagia Sophia, after the defeat of the iconoclasm movement in the mid-ninth century (see page 281), the mosaic shown at the start of this chapter of an enthroned Mary and the child Jesus flanked by two haloed Byzantine emperors was placed prominently over an entrance to the church's nave.

Icons intended for personal, private devotion depicted the Virgin and Child in a very different manner. The example reproduced here, known as the Virgin of Vladimir (the Kievan prince who commissioned it), portrays the Virgin and Child locked together in a tender maternal embrace, faces touching. The tiny head and hands of Jesus accentuate his infantlike helplessness. In contrast to her public portrayal as the enthroned Mary, in this personal icon Mary's gaze is fixed on the viewer, with her left hand upraised in a gesture of prayer that likewise beckons toward the viewer. Many icons of this type also were brought to Italy and had a strong influence on the religious art of the early Renaissance, a European cultural movement that we will discuss in Chapter 15.

Source: Maria Vassilaki, ed., *Mother of God: Representations of the Virgin in Byzantine Art* (Milan: Skira editore, 2000), plates 61, 24.

There is little scriptural authority for the central place that Mary, mother of Jesus, eventually came to occupy in Christian beliefs and rituals. The few references to Mary in the Gospels make no mention, for example, of her lifelong virginity or her ascent to heaven. Nonetheless, early Christian writings singled Mary out as a role model for women, stressing her obedience and virginity in contrast to the biblical Eve. The virginity of Mary also provided inspiration for the ascetic and monastic movements that began to flourish in the third and fourth centuries. Ultimately, the theological controversy

EXAMINING THE EVIDENCE

1. How does the "At a Crossroads" mosaic from Hagia Sophia (see page 270) and the icon shown here differ in their depiction of Mary as a maternal figure? What do these contrasts tell us about the differences between public and private devotion to Mary?

2. How does the Byzantine conception of imperial authority expressed in the mosaic from Hagia Sophia compare with the Roman conception as evidenced in the image of Augustus on page 217?

Armenia, at the frontier between the Roman Empire and the Persian Sasanid Empire, nurtured its own distinctive Christian tradition. Christianity had advanced slowly in Armenia following the conversion of its king in the early fourth century. But after Armenia was partitioned and occupied by Roman and Sasanid armies in 387, resistance to foreign rule hardened around this kernel of Christian faith. With the invention

Christianity in Armenia

Byzantine Emperorship

This mosaic from the San Vitale church in Ravenna, Italy, depicts Justinian surrounded by his civil, military, and ecclesiastic officials—a clear effort to project the emperor's identity as head of both state and church. The mosaic was commissioned in around 550 not by Justinian, however, but by Maximian, archbishop of Ravenna in Italy, the only figure labeled by the artist. (Giraudon/ Bridgeman Art Library.)

of the Armenian alphabet in around 400 came a distinctive Armenian literary heritage of Christian teachings. Christianity had become the hallmark of Armenian independence, and the Armenian clergy also repelled Justinian's attempts to impose religious orthodoxy.

Sasanid Toleration of Christianity

Except in Armenia, where Christians suffered political persecution, the Sasanids generally tolerated Christianity, which along with Judaism was well entrenched in Mesopotamia. The Nestorian church enjoyed a privileged position at the Sasanid capital of Ctesiphon (TEH-suh-fahn), south of modern Baghdad, and a number of Nestorian clergy attained high office at court. Nestorian Christians celebrated the Sasanid seizure of Jerusalem from Constantinople in 618 as a triumph over heresy. Nestorian missionaries traveled eastward and established churches along the trade routes leading from Persia to Central Asia. Merchants from the caravan settlements of Sogdia carried their adopted Nestorian faith eastward along the Silk Road as far as China, as we will see in Chapter 10. In this way, Sasanid political policies and economic connections facilitated the growth and spread of a distinctive form of Christianity.

Christianity also gained a foothold in Ethiopia, at the northern end of the Rift Valleys in eastern Africa, and once again trade played a key role. Long a bridge between sub-Saharan Africa and the Mediterranean, Ethiopia also became the main channel of trade and cultural contact between the Roman world and the Indian Ocean. Both Jewish and Christian merchants settled in the Ethiopian towns that served this trade, chief of which was Axum (AHK-soom).

Rise and Fall of Axum

By the first century C.E., Axum was a thriving metropolis connected to the Mediterranean trade network through the Red Sea port of Adulis (ah-DOOL-iss). Axum was the chief marketplace for exotic African goods such as ivory, gold, precious stones, and animal horns and skins. Although the majority of the population consisted of herders and farmers, townsmen made pottery, worked leather and metal, and carved ivory. The use at the Axum court of Greek and Syriac, along with Ge'ez (geeze), the native written language of Ethiopia, reflected the multinational character of the merchant and official classes.

Commercial wealth led to the creation of a powerful monarchy. During the early fourth century the rulers of Axum officially recognized Christianity as their state religion. Intolerance of other creeds hardened as the pace of conversion to Christianity accelerated.

Axum's Jews emigrated farther inland, where they formed the nucleus of their own independent state, which would later be known as Falasha.

But the Islamic conquests in the seventh century disrupted the lucrative trade on which Axum's vitality depended. Trade routes shifted away from the Red Sea to Syria, and Damascus became the new commercial capital of the eastern Mediterranean. When the Axum monarchy declined, a class of warrior lords allied with Christian monasteries gained both economic and legal control of the agrarian population. As in Europe, most of the population was reduced to servile status, and much of the produce of the land supported Christian monasteries, which remained the repositories of learning and literate culture. In this way, trade brought Christianity to Axum and created the wealth that built its Christian monarchy. When regional trade patterns changed, Christianity in Axum changed as well.

In the twelfth and thirteenth centuries, new royal dynasties arose in the highlands of Ethiopia that became great patrons of Christianity. These dynasties claimed direct descent from the ancient kings of Israel, but they also drew legitimacy from African traditions of sacred kingship. Ethiopia endured as a Christian stronghold down to modern times, although hemmed in by the hostile pastoral nomads of the coastal lowlands, who converted to Islam. Not surprisingly, isolated as it was from the larger Christian world, the Ethiopian church developed its own distinctive Christian traditions.

Ethiopia, Christian Stronghold

Christian Communities in Western Europe

While the Christian movements in Asia and Africa strove to maintain their independence from Constantinople, the collapse of the imperial order in the west posed different challenges for the Christian faithful. In the absence of the patronage (and interference) of the Byzantine emperors, a variety of distinctive Christian cultures emerged throughout the former western provinces. With imperial Rome in ruins, local communities and their leaders were free to rebuild their societies on the pillars of Christian beliefs and practices. When the Frankish king Charlemagne achieved military supremacy in western Europe at the end of the eighth century, his contemporaries heralded their new emperor as having been chosen by God "to rule and protect the Christian people."[3]

When imperial Rome fell, Christianity in the west was largely an urban religion. Amid ongoing warfare and violence, the beleaguered Christian towns in Gaul and Spain turned for leadership to provincial notables—great landowners and men of the old senatorial class. The bishops of Rome proclaimed their supreme authority in doctrinal matters as popes (from *papa*, or "grand old man"), the successors of St. Peter, who represented the universal ("Catholic") church. But Christian communities in the provinces of western Europe entrusted their protection to local men of wealth and family distinction, whom they elected as bishops. Bred to govern in the Roman style, these aristocrats took firm control of both secular and religious affairs. Although many of these men had been born to luxury and comfort, they embraced the austerity of monastic life, which further enhanced their aura of holiness. In time, with the assistance of zealous Christian missionaries, they negotiated settlements with their new Germanic overlords—the Franks in Gaul, the Visigoths in Spain, and the Saxons in Britain—that fully welcomed the Christian religion.

Bishops of the West

In an increasingly uncertain and violent world, the bishops of the west rallied their followers around collective religious ceremonies and the cults of saints. From at least the second century, Christians had commemorated beloved and inspiring martyrs and bishops as saints. Later, hermits, monks, and outstanding laypeople, both men and women, were also honored as saints. Christians viewed saints as their patrons, persons of power and influence who protected the local community and interceded on its behalf for divine blessings. They regarded the bodily remains of saints as sacred relics endowed with miraculous potency. Thus, worship of saints at the sites of their tombs became a focal point of Christian life. Just as Christian communities turned to provincial elites for protection, Christians looked to the saints to keep them safe in a hostile world.

Pope Gregory I

Pope Gregory I exercised firm personal leadership over the Latin Christian church through his voluminous correspondence with bishops, missionaries, and noble laypeople. At least twenty thousand letters were dispatched from Rome under his name during the fourteen years of his papacy. This ivory carving shows the pope at his writing desk, with scribes below copying his writings. (Erich Lessing/Art Resource, NY.)

In the 460s, the bishop of Tours built a huge and ornate basilica at the site of the grave of the martyr St. Martin (335–397). Its reputation swelled by a flood of reports of miracles, it became a fortress of Christian faith and attracted pilgrims from throughout Gaul and beyond. When the Frankish king Clovis challenged the Visigoth ruler Alaric for control of southern Gaul in 507, he sought (and reportedly received) divine blessing at St. Martin's shrine. After defeating the Visigoths, Clovis returned to Tours laden with booty that he donated to the shrine. Similar cults and networks of pilgrimage and patronage sprung up around the relics of other saints.

Pope Gregory I (540–604) typified the distinctive style of leadership in the western Christian church. Born into a prominent Roman aristocratic family, Gregory entered the imperial service in 573 as the governor of Rome. Pulled by a strong religious calling, however, he soon retired to become a monk. After achieving fame for his devotion to learning and ascetic lifestyle, Gregory yielded to repeated summons to return to public service. He spent a decade as the papal envoy to the Byzantine court before returning to Rome upon his election as pope in 590. Keenly aware of the divisions within the Christian world, Gregory strove to make the papacy the centerpiece of a church administration that stretched from Britain to North Africa. Mindful, too, of the limited penetration of Christian religion in the countryside, he worked tirelessly to instill a sense of mission among the Christian clergy. "The art to end all arts is the governing of souls," wrote Gregory, insisting that the contemplative life of the monastery must be joined to the pastoral duty of saving sinners.[4]

Slowly but surely, Gregory's vision of the Christian clergy as the spiritual rulers of the humble peasantry gained converts. By the eighth century, social life in the western European countryside revolved around the village church and its liturgies. Christian sacraments marked the major stages of the individual's life from birth (baptism) to death (last rites), and the religious calendar, with high points at the celebrations of Christ's birth (Christmas) and resurrection (Easter), introduced a new rhythm to the cycle of the seasons.

Still, Latin Christendom was far from united. Distinctive regional Christian churches and cultures had emerged in Italy, Gaul, Britain, and Spain; indeed, we can think of these as a cluster of micro-Christendoms clinging to the fragments of the former Roman Empire. During the eighth century, however, the rise of the Carolingian dynasty and its imperial aspirations would bring these regional Christendoms into a single European form.

Social and Political Renewal in the Post-Roman World   400–850

FOCUS

What major changes swept the lands of the former Roman Empire in the four centuries following the fall of imperial Rome?

The Byzantine emperors in the east and the Germanic chieftains who ruled the empire's former western European provinces shared a common heritage rooted in the Roman imperial past and Christian religion. The Byzantine Empire faced a profound crisis in the sixth and seventh centuries. Protracted wars with the Sasanids, the Slavs, and the Avars were followed by the loss of two-thirds of Byzantium's realm to the rapid advance of Muslim Arab armies. Yet the Byzantine Empire survived, thanks to the revitalization of the imperial state and a resilient economy. Byzantine political institutions and especially its distinctive version of Christianity also exerted a powerful influence on the Slavic peoples and led to the formation of the first Rus state. Although Byzantium regained its political and cultural vigor in the ninth century, their fellow Christians, the Frankish empire of the Carolingian dynasty, proved to be more a rival than an ally.

Crisis and Survival of the Byzantine Empire

Justinian I's conquests in Italy and North Africa had once again joined Constantinople and Rome under a single sovereign, but this union was short-lived. Lengthy wars and the enormous costs of Justinian's building programs sapped the fiscal strength of the empire. Although the Byzantine forces repulsed a Sasanid-led attack on Constantinople in 626, this victory was eclipsed within fifteen years by the loss of Syria, Palestine, and Egypt to Muslim armies, as we shall see. By 700 the Byzantine Empire was a shrunken vestige of Justinian's realm, consisting essentially of Constantinople and its immediate environs, a few territories in Greece, and Anatolia. Once-flourishing commercial cities lost much of their population and were rebuilt as smaller, fortified towns to defend the local bishop and his church.

Constantinople alone stood out as a thriving crossroads of trade, learning, and aristocratic culture. Home to a dense mosaic of languages and nationalities united by the Christian faith, Constantinople numbered five hundred thousand inhabitants at its peak in Justinian's age. Social frictions frequently ignited outbursts of violence, such as the Nika (Greek for "conquer") Revolt of 532, a weeklong protest against Justinian's high-handed officials that left nearly half of the city burned or destroyed. To soothe these tensions, the emperors staged an elaborate cycle of public rituals—military triumphs, imperial birthdays, and Christian festivals—that showcased their essential role in fostering unity and common purpose among Constantinople's populace.

Accompanying Byzantium's declining power and prestige were worsening relations with Rome. Emperor Justinian II (r. 685–695) convened a council of bishops at Constantinople in 692 that granted the emperor greater control over the church and its clergy. The council rejected Latin customs such as priestly celibacy and affirmed the independence of the patriarch of Constantinople from the Roman pope in matters of religious doctrine. This rupture between the emperor and the pope was partially mended in the later years of Justinian II's reign, but over the course of the eighth century the religious **schism** widened. The Frankish king Charlemagne's coronation as emperor by Pope Leo III in 800 in effect declared Charlemagne to be the protector of the church, usurping the Byzantine emperor's role. Although Charlemagne negotiated a compromise in 813 that recognized the Byzantine monarch as "emperor of the Romans" and pledged friendship between the two rulers, Latin Christendom had clearly emerged as a separate church.

Within Byzantium, debate raged over the proper conduct of life and religion in a Christian society, especially concerning the veneration of icons—painted images of Jesus, Mary, and the saints. The powerful new faith of Islam denounced any representation of the divine in human form as idolatry. This radical **iconoclasm** (Greek for "image-breaking") struck a responsive chord among the many Byzantines who saw the empire's political reversals as evidence of moral decline. Throughout the eighth century a bitter struggle divided Byzantium. On one side were the iconoclasts, who sought to match Muslim religious fervor by restoring a pristine faith rooted in Old Testament values. On the other side were the defenders of orthodoxy, who maintained that the use of explicitly Christian images of Jesus and Mary was an essential component of the imperially ordained liturgy on which social unity depended. In the mid-ninth century the proponents of orthodoxy prevailed over the iconoclasts. Henceforth Byzantine Christianity became known as the Orthodox Church, in which religious authority became tightly interwoven with imperial power.

In the second half of the ninth century the Muslim threat abated, and the Byzantine Empire enjoyed a rebirth. Resurgent economic strength at home fueled military success against the Muslims and the Slavs. The church and the army supported efforts to enhance the power and authority of the emperor and the central state. Yet as the leading classes of Byzantine society rallied around a revitalized imperial institution, the estrangement between the churches of Constantinople and Rome intensified. The split between the two churches was about more than conflicts over theology and church hierarchy. The peoples of the Latin west and the Greek east, who had once shared a common history and culture as subjects of the Roman Empire, were moving in different directions.

Schism Between Constantinople and Rome

The Iconoclastic Controversy

schism A split in any organized group (especially a church or religious community) resulting in a formal declaration of differences in doctrine or beliefs.

iconoclasm Literally, "destruction of images"; the word originates with the movement against the veneration of images in the Byzantine Empire in the eighth and ninth centuries.

Christ Pantokrator

Following the final defeat of iconoclasm, images of Christ Pantokrator (Greek for "ruler of all") became a standard feature of Byzantine church decoration. Typically placed on vaulted domes, these images emphasized Jesus's transcendent divinity. This version of the Pantokrator, which portrays Jesus as a teacher, was created in 1148 by Byzantine mosaic artists hired by Roger II, king of Sicily, to decorate his newly built Cefalu Cathedral. (Corbis.)

The Germanic Successor States in Western Europe

At the peak of the Roman Empire, its northern frontier stretched three thousand miles, from the British Isles to the Black Sea. From the vantage point of Rome, this frontier marked a sharp boundary between civilized and barbarian peoples. But as we saw in Chapter 7, provincial Romans had frequent social and economic interactions with their Celtic and Germanic neighbors. Many Germanic chieftains who became overlords of the empire's western provinces in the fifth and sixth centuries had previously served as mercenaries defending the territories they now ruled. In a sense, they were at least partially Romanized before they conquered Rome (see Map 9.2).

Livelihoods of the Germanic Peoples

Similar patterns of livelihood prevailed among the Germanic peoples—and indeed among all the peoples of northern and eastern Europe. In most of the region, small, patriarchal farming communities predominated, in which men had full authority over members of their families or clans. The most important crop was barley, which was consumed as porridge, bread, and beer. Cattle-raising also was important, both to feed the community and as an index of positions in the social hierarchy. The number of cattle a household possessed determined its wealth and prestige, and acquiring cattle was a chief objective of both trade and warfare.

Valor and success in warfare also conferred prestige. Village communities organized themselves into warrior bands for warfare and raiding, and at times these bands joined together to form broad confederations for mutual defense and campaigns of plunder. These groups were primarily political alliances, and thus they constantly dissolved and reformed as the needs and interests of their constituent tribes shifted. Kinfolk found solidarity in their common genealogical descent, but marriage ties, gift giving, and sharing food and drink at feasts helped nurture bonds of fellowship and loyalty. Contact with the Roman world, through both trade and war, magnified the roles of charismatic military leaders, men skilled at holding together their fragile coalitions of followers and negotiating with the Roman state. As we saw in Chapter 7, Rome's eagerness to obtain the military services of these confederations further encouraged the militarization of Germanic society.

The Goths

One such confederation, the Goths, arrived in Italy and Gaul as refugees, driven westward by the invasions of the Hun nomads from Central Asia in the fifth century (see Chapter 7).

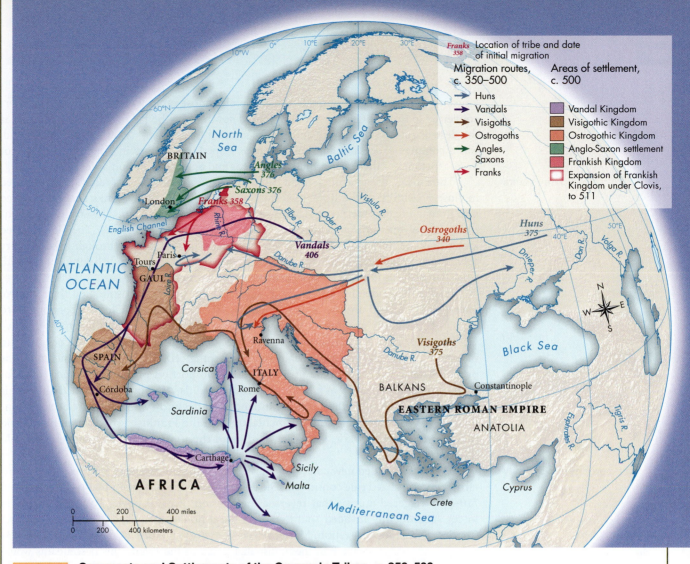

MAP 9.2 **Conquests and Settlements of the Germanic Tribes, c. 350–500**

The Germanic peoples had long inhabited the lands along the Roman Empire's frontiers in northern and eastern Europe. In the fourth and fifth centuries, as Rome's authority disintegrated, Germanic chieftains led their followers to invade and occupy Roman territories. The new Germanic rulers such as the Franks and the Goths cultivated alliances with local leaders and the Christian church and restored a measure of stability.

Expelled from their homeland in the lower Danube region, the Visigoths (Western Goths) followed their king Alaric into the Balkans and Italy. Driven more by desperation and hunger than by greed, Alaric's army captured and plundered Rome in 410. In 418 the Visigoths negotiated an alliance with the Byzantine emperor that allowed them to occupy southern Gaul—the first Germanic people to complete the transition from confederation to kingdom.

The Ostrogoths (Eastern Goths) emerged as an independent force in the late fifth century, following the death of the Hun leader Attila, whom the Ostrogoths loyally served. After Attila's empire disintegrated, the Ostrogoths shifted their allegiance to Constantinople. In 488 the Byzantine emperor dispatched the Ostrogoth leader Theodoric to subdue Odoacer, the German king who had seized Rome and deposed its last emperor in 476. Theodoric conquered the Italian peninsula in 493 but refused to relinquish control to Constantinople. The Ostrogoths ruled Italy until they were overwhelmed by Justinian's armies in 553.

Only a small number of the Goths entered Gaul and Italy as members of the warrior ruling elite, entitled to the privileges of "Gothic freedom." Most were farmers whose livelihood scarcely differed from that of their Roman neighbors. Sensational images of "barbarian invasions" obscure the fact that many Germans wanted to assimilate into the Roman world. The Romans likewise welcomed the peace and security brought by the German kings. Acceptance of "barbarian" rule accelerated most rapidly where the German rulers converted to Roman Christianity. We should not think of the fall of the western empire as the destruction of one culture and its replacement by another. What took place, instead, was a complex process of cultural exchange shaped by changes in the political and economic fortunes of the empire and by the needs and ambitions of nomadic peoples.

The Franks

The Franks, a league of German tribes in the lower Rhine River Valley, had long lived in close proximity to the Roman world. So thoroughly had the Franks been assimilated into Roman life that their own legends about their ancestry had faded by 600, the approximate date of the earliest Latin accounts of their history and origins. The "long-haired kings"—as the Romans called them—of the Franks gained power through loyal military service to the empire. When the Roman state collapsed, the Frankish kings allied with Christian bishops in the interest of preserving local order.

Under the leadership of Clovis (r. 482–511), the Franks consolidated their control over the Rhineland and Gaul. Although the circumstances of Clovis's conversion to Roman Christianity are murky, we have seen that he credited to St. Martin his decisive victory in 507 over the Visigoths in southern Gaul. Clovis also issued a law code, Roman in form but German in substance, of rules governing crime and property, including the principle, later widely adopted in Europe, that "no portion of the inheritance [of land] shall come to a woman."[5] When Clovis died in 511, his kingdom was divided among his four sons, including Clothar, future husband of Radegund (whom we met at the beginning of this chapter). But the fundamental unity of the Frankish kingdom endured, held together by Frankish law, Christian faith, and the unwavering allegiance of the old Roman aristocrats.

The Carolingian Dynasty

The Franks added new conquests during the sixth and seventh centuries, but the pattern of decentralized rule continued. The lightning conquest of Spain by Muslim armies in 710–711 triggered a crisis that reversed this erosion of royal power. When the Muslim forces subsequently invaded southern Gaul, local nobles turned to a Frankish warlord, Charles Martel, for protection. Martel's decisive victory over the Muslims at Tours in 732 made him the undisputed leader of the Franks; his descendants would rule as the Carolingian (from *Carolus*, Latin for "Charles") dynasty of kings.

Frankish political power reached its height under Martel's grandson Charlemagne (r. 768–814). Drawing on the Roman Empire as a model, Charlemagne's conquests added substantial territories to the Frankish empire, extending from the Baltic Sea to the Adriatic Sea. Charlemagne incorporated these new dominions into his empire by sharing power with local rulers and allowing their peoples to be governed in accordance with their own laws and customs. This policy also allowed colonists who migrated to newly conquered regions of the empire to preserve their distinct legal status and autonomy. Thus the Carolingian Empire created new ethnic identities among its diverse subjects.

Charlemagne sought to elevate himself and his empire to the imperial dignity enjoyed by Byzantium. He made protection of the pope and Roman orthodoxy an essential component of his mandate. The culmination of his efforts took place on Christmas Day, 800, when Pope Leo III placed a crown on Charlemagne's head and proclaimed him Augustus, the title of the first Roman emperor. Although recognition of Charlemagne and his successors as "emperors" only partially reversed the political fragmentation of post-Roman Europe, it forged a lasting bond between the papacy and the secular rulers of Latin Christendom. Compared with Byzantium, church and state remained more independent of each other in western Europe. Nonetheless, Charlemagne established a new ideology of Christian kingship.

Empire of Charlemagne, 814

- Frankish Kingdom, 768
- Areas conquered by Charlemagne, to 814
- Tributary peoples
- Byzantine Empire

Economic Contraction and Renewal in Christendom

The Manorial Order

Although the Franks preserved the rural aristocracy's control over the land and patronized the Christian church and monasteries, the urban culture of the Roman world withered. The nobility retreated to the security of their rural estates, and the great monasteries in the countryside, enriched by royal land grants, began to overshadow the urban bishops. The Carolingian monarchs, too, abandoned the old Roman towns, preferring to hold court at rural villas such as Charlemagne's capital at Aachen, along the modern border between Germany and Belgium. Both secular lords and monastic abbeys built up vast estates; for labor, they subjected the rural population to increasingly servile status. Throughout the Carolingian realm this new institution, the **manor**, was widely adopted. The tenants became **serfs**, tied to the land and subject to the legal authority of the lord. The obligations of serfs could vary significantly, but in general they owed labor services to the lord, as well as rents and fees for the right to graze animals and collect firewood. Women provided labor as well, either in the manor's workshops or by making cloth in their own homes.

Decline of Towns and Commerce

Whereas the expansion of the Carolingian Empire stimulated commercial exchange with Saxon lands in Britain and Denmark, elsewhere industry and trade diminished. Towns and commerce in Europe declined in part from the rise of the new rural manors, but more fundamental was the contraction of the international trading system centered on Constantinople. A terrible plague that swept across the Mediterranean from Egypt to Europe in 541–542 dealt a devastating blow to the urban network of the Roman world, which had survived the decline of the empire itself. Byzantine officials reported that 230,000 died in Constantinople alone, and Mediterranean cities from Antioch to Alexandria also suffered huge losses. Slav and Avar raids decimated the once-thriving cities of the Balkans, and the Sasanid and Muslim conquests of the seventh century deprived the empire of its richest domains. These cumulative demographic and territorial losses greatly reduced economic productivity. Egypt no longer delivered the ample grain tribute upon which the Byzantine state depended to feed its cities and armies, and in much of Anatolia farmland reverted to sheep pasture for lack of labor to grow cereal crops.

Political setbacks, the decline of towns, and the shrinking population led to a downturn in the Byzantine economy. The circulation of money slowed and in many parts of the empire disappeared altogether between the mid-seventh and early ninth centuries. Yet the Byzantine state still appropriated a significant share of agricultural surpluses, which it distributed as salaries to its officials and soldiers. Hit hardest by the waning economic fortunes of the empire was the provincial landowning aristocracy. Peasants who owned their own land increased in numbers and importance, and the state benefited from the taxes they paid.

Economic Recovery in Byzantium

Yet even as it hit bottom, the Byzantine economy displayed far more vigor than that of the Germanic kingdoms. During the sixth and seventh centuries, the Italian cities under Byzantine rule were the major exception to the pervasive decline of urban population and economic activity throughout Europe. Throughout the empire, political stability rekindled population growth in both town and countryside, especially in the long-settled coastal regions. By 800 unmistakable signs of economic prosperity had reappeared: the demand for coinage increased, new lands were put under the plow, and reports of famine became less frequent and less desperate. The Mediterranean trade network centered on Constantinople began to recover as tensions with Islamic rulers eased. A Muslim scholar writing in around 850 listed among Baghdad's imports from the Byzantine Empire "gold and silver wares, coins of pure gold, medicinal plants, gold-woven textiles, silk brocade, spirited horses, female slaves, rare copperware, unpickable locks, lyres, hydraulic engineers, agrarian experts, marble workers, and eunuchs."[6]

The quickening prosperity of the Byzantine economy promoted commerce across the Mediterranean. Silks produced in Constantinople's workshops ranked among the most prized luxury goods in the Carolingian world (see Lives and Livelihoods: Constantinople's

manor A great estate, consisting of farmlands, vineyards, and other productive assets, owned by a lord (which could be an institution, such as a monastery) and cultivated by serfs.

serf A semifree peasant tied to the land and subject to the judicial authority of a lord.

Constantinople's Silk Producers

During the heyday of the Roman Empire, when silk was said to be worth its weight in gold, Romans depended entirely on imports of silk from China. According to the historian Procopius, sericulture—the raising of silkworms to make silk—first appeared in the Byzantine Empire in his own time, during the reign of Emperor Justinian I (r. 527–565). Several Indian monks arrived at Constantinople offering to reveal the secrets of sericulture:

> When the Emperor questioned them very closely and asked how they could guarantee success in the business, the monks told him that the agents in the production of silk were certain caterpillars, working under nature's teaching, which continually urged them to their task. To bring live caterpillars from that country would be impracticable indeed, but . . . it was possible to hatch their eggs long after they had been laid by covering them with dung, which produced sufficient heat for the purpose.[1]

The monks delivered the eggs as promised, and silk manufacture subsequently became a pillar of the Byzantine economy.

Since Roman times, silk clothing had become a conspicuous mark of wealth and social distinction. The Byzantine government issued numerous decrees restricting the wearing of certain kinds of silk to the nobility. Purple-dyed silks—the "royal purple," a pigment derived from a tropical sea snail—were reserved for the emperor alone. Silk also served as a valuable tool of diplomacy. The Byzantine emperors regularly sent gifts of silk fabrics to the Frankish kings and the Islamic caliphs. In the Carolingian Empire, Byzantine silks were coveted luxury goods, flaunted by male aristocrats and well-born nuns no less than by royal princesses. The prominence of silk garments, furnishings, and liturgical vestments in wills, dowry and marriage contracts, and church inventories attests to both their economic value and their social prestige.

Emperor Justinian I restricted silk manufacture to imperial workshops, but the Islamic conquests deprived the Byzantine state of its monopoly on silk production. Muslim

Byzantine Silk Shroud
Byzantine silk fabrics were highly prized in Latin Christendom. Tradition has it that this piece was placed in the tomb of the Frankish ruler Charlemagne after his death in 814. The design features a charioteer—probably an emperor—driving a four-horse chariot. Attendants in the background hold out crowns and whips; those at the bottom pour coins onto an altar. (Erich Lessing/Art Resource, NY.)

entrepreneurs took over the flourishing silk industry in Syria and introduced sericulture to Sicily and Spain. Then, as the demand for luxury silk goods surged, in the ninth century the Byzantine court allowed private merchants to manufacture and trade silk. At the same time the imperial government imposed tight controls on the private silk trade. These laws have been preserved in the *Book of the Prefect*, a set of commercial regulations issued by the chief magistrate of Constantinople in around 912.

Silk manufacture involves a complex series of operations, ranging from low-skilled tasks such as raising silkworms and reeling yarn to those requiring high technical proficiency, such as weaving, dyeing, and embroidery. In late Roman times, imperial textile workers, both men and

Silk Producers). Significant economic growth, however, would not return to the European heartland until the late tenth century, well after the expansion of the Byzantine economy was under way.

Origins of the Slavs and the Founding of Rus

During its crisis of the sixth and seventh centuries, the Byzantine empire confronted a new people on its borders, the Slavs. Today nearly 300 million people in Eastern Europe

women, had been reduced to hereditary occupational castes. By Justinian's day, the standing of skilled silk artisans had risen appreciably, and government employment was considered a privilege, not a burden. In the tenth century shortages of skilled labor grew so acute that the government prohibited private merchants from offering artisans wage advances or contracts of more than one month's duration. The intent behind this rule was to ensure that all firms had competitive access to the best craftsmen. Further, the government required these private craftsmen to belong to one of five separate guilds.

This kind of intervention in the marketplace exemplified the Byzantine state's economic philosophy. By splitting the private silk industry into separate guilds, the state enforced a strict division of labor that prevented a few large firms from consolidating control over silk manufacture and trade. Thus, the reeling workshops had to purchase raw silk from middlemen dealers rather than from the producers themselves; after the raw silk was reeled into yarn, it had to be sold back to the middlemen, who in turn marketed the yarn to the silk clothiers. The clothiers produced finished cloth but could sell it only to wholesale merchants, not directly to retail customers.

Yarn production was largely a family business. The silk clothiers, in contrast, combined weaving, dyeing, and tailoring workshops under one management, relying mostly on hired labor but employing household slaves as well. Slaves also operated workshops as agents for their masters. Government workshops employed skilled craftsmen divided into guilds of clothiers, purple dyers, and gold embroiderers, who made richly decorated fabrics for the emperor and his officials. Menial tasks were relegated to servile labor, including foreign slaves.

Although keen to profit from the high prices its silks commanded in foreign markets, the Byzantine government also sought to protect the domestic industry from international competition. The Byzantine rulers kept foreign silk importers, chiefly Muslims and Jews, under close surveillance. After depositing their goods in a government warehouse, foreign merchants were sequestered in special lodgings, where they were permitted to remain for a maximum of three months. Domestic silk importers could not deal directly with foreign merchants. Instead, they negotiated collectively for the purchase of imported wares. This practice, too, ensured that all firms, small and large, had some access to imported products.

The Byzantines also feared the loss of trade secrets to foreign competitors. Foreign merchants were prohibited from taking certain silk goods and unsewn fabrics out of Constantinople, and their cargoes were carefully inspected before they could leave the city. The city magistrate decreed that "every dyer who sells a slave, a workman, or a foreman craftsman to persons alien to the city or the Empire shall have his hand cut off."[2] But these efforts to monopolize technological know-how proved futile. By 1000, technical mastery of silk manufacture had become widely disseminated. Surviving silk specimens show that Byzantine and Muslim artisans freely borrowed weaving techniques, artistic motifs, and color patterns from each other, to the point where it is nearly impossible to distinguish their handiwork.

---

1. Procopius, *The History of the Wars*, 4:17.
2. *Book of the Eparch*, Chapter 8, in E. H. Freshfield, *Roman Law in the Later Roman Empire: Byzantine Guilds, Professional, Commercial; Ordinances of Leo VI, c. 895, from The Book of the Eparch* (Cambridge, U.K.: Cambridge University Press, 1938), 26.

QUESTIONS TO CONSIDER

1. Did the Byzantine government's measures to regulate the silk industry stimulate or discourage competition among producers?

2. Did guild organizations in the Byzantine silk industry exist primarily to promote the interests of artisans, merchants, or the government?

For Further Information:
Laiou, Angeliki E., and Cécile Morrison. *The Byzantine Economy*. Cambridge, U.K.: Cambridge University Press, 2007.
Laiou, Angeliki E., ed. *The Economic History of Byzantium from the Seventh Through the Fifteenth Century*. 3 vols. Washington, DC: Dumbarton Oaks Research Library and Collections, 2002.

and Russia speak a Slavic language. They trace their ancestry back to peoples known as *Sclavenoi* in Greek, who first appear in sixth-century Byzantine chronicles. As the Goths migrated westward into the former Roman territories, they abandoned their homelands to the Slavs, small, independent communities who rejected the imperial order of Byzantium. As contact with the Roman world declined, the material culture beyond the eastern frontiers of the old empire became more impoverished. Early Byzantine accounts classified the Slavs, together with the Avars and the Goths, as pagan savages and mortal enemies of Christendom. Between the fifth and tenth centuries, however, Byzantine interaction with

Slavic Territories in Eastern Europe, c. 900

Legend:
- Slavic settlement
- Rus, c. 900

both settled and nomadic Slavic populations led to the crystallization of an identifiable Slavic culture with its own written languages and to the assimilation of the Slavs into a larger Christian civilization.

Like the Germanic peoples, most Slavs lived in small farming settlements consisting of several extended related families: "each living with his own clan on his own lands," in the words of a Russian chronicler.[7] The Slavs practiced shifting cultivation, regularly moving into wilderness areas and cutting down virgin forest to plant barley and millet, using the nitrogen-rich ash of burnt trees as fertilizer. Procopius portrayed the Slavs as leading "a primitive and rough way of life. . . . They are neither dishonorable nor spiteful, but simple in their ways, like the Huns."[8] Another Byzantine writer complimented Slavic women as "chaste beyond all measure," willing to kill themselves upon the death of their husbands because they "regard widowhood as no life at all."[9]

Social stratification increased by the eighth century; chiefs and their retinues crowned the social order, and hilltop strongholds with timber fortifications proliferated. Distinctive Slavic forms of pottery and silver jewelry appeared, but the material culture of the forest-dwelling Slavs was dominated by wood products and has mostly vanished. Trading posts for bartering furs and slaves sprang up near major crossroads, and craftsmen such as blacksmiths and silversmiths wandered from place to place offering their services.

Slavic Conversion to Christianity

In the ninth and tenth centuries the Slavic peoples were strongly influenced by Byzantine and Frankish models of government, law, and religion. The uniform Slavic culture divided into separate societies and political allegiances, leading to the emergence of Serb, Croat, Polish, and other Slavic national identities. The most far-reaching change was the conversion of most Slavic peoples to Christianity. Slav rulers, pressured by hostile Christian adversaries, were the first to convert. The Slavic adoption of Christianity only heightened frictions between Rome and Constantinople, however, because the southern and eastern Slavs adhered to Byzantine rites and beliefs, whereas Latin teachings prevailed among western Slavs.

Emergence of Rus

According to later (and not wholly reliable) Russian chronicles, the first state of Rus was formed in 862 when Scandinavian communities in the Novgorod region elected a Viking chieftain as their ruler. But a Rus confederation of Viking settlements engaging in slave raiding and fur trading had already emerged some decades before. Lured by the riches of the Mediterranean world, the Rus pushed southward toward the Black Sea along the Dnieper and the Volga rivers. A major assault by the Rus on Constantinople in 911 forced the Byzantine emperor to sue for peace by conceding generous trading privileges. At some point, probably in the 930s, the Rus princes shifted their capital to Kiev in the lower Dnieper valley.

By the late tenth century Kievan Rus had emerged as the dominant power in the Black Sea region. Prince Vladimir (r. 980–1015) consolidated Rus into a more unified state and adopted the Christian religion of Byzantium. Conversion to Christianity and deepening commercial and diplomatic ties with Byzantium marked a decisive reorientation of Rus away from its Scandinavian origins. Drawn south by Byzantine wealth, Rus invaders did not destroy the culture they encountered but instead became part of it, adding their own cultural heritage to that of the eastern Christian world.

Thus the middle centuries of the first millennium C.E. saw both the growth and the splintering of Christianity, as competing visions of Christianity emerged. This competition would soon become more complex with the arrival of a new religion. Although the Latin and Orthodox churches continued to win new converts in eastern and northern Europe, the sudden emergence of Islam in the seventh century transformed the religious landscape of the Mediterranean world. Even though large Christian communities persevered under Muslim rule in regions such as Syria, Iran, and Spain, the Mediterranean Sea took on new significance as a boundary between religious faiths.

The Rise and Spread of Islam 610–750

In the early seventh century, the Arab prophet Muhammad (c. 570–632) founded what became a new religion, Islam, rooted in the Judaic and Christian traditions but transformed by the divine revelations he proclaimed. Muhammad was more than a religious teacher, however. He envisioned the community of believers as a tight-knit movement dedicated to propagating the true faith, and his successors fashioned Islam into a mighty social and political force. Within a century of Muhammad's death in 632 an Islamic empire had expanded beyond Arabia as far as Iran to the east and Spain to the west. As in Christendom, tensions arose between political rulers and religious authorities. During the tenth century the united Islamic empire fractured into a commonwealth of independent states. Yet the powerful inspiration of Muhammad's teachings and Islam's radical egalitarian ideals sustained a sense of community that transcended political and ethnic boundaries.

> **FOCUS**
>
> In what ways did Islam instill a sense of common identity among its believers?

The Prophet Muhammad and the Faith of Islam

Muhammad's call for a renewal of religious faith dedicated to the one true God must be seen in the context of social and religious life in the Arabian peninsula. The harsh desert environment of Arabia could sustain little more than a nomadic pastoral livelihood. Domestication of the camel since about 1000 B.C.E. allowed small, clan-based groups known as Bedouins to raise livestock. During the summer the Bedouins gathered at oases to exchange animal products for grain, dates, utensils, weapons, and cloth. Some of these oases eventually supported thriving commercial towns, of which the most prosperous was Mecca.

The Arabian Background

The Bedouin (BED-uh-wuhn) tribes regularly came to Mecca to pay homage at the Ka'aba (KAH-buh) shrine, which housed the icons of numerous gods worshiped throughout the region. Mecca thus served as a sanctuary where different tribes could gather to worship their gods in peace. The religious harmony that prevailed at Mecca also offered opportunities to settle disputes and conduct trade. The Meccan fairs gave birth to a common culture, language, and social identity among the leading clans of Arabia.

Building on its status as an Arabian crossroads, Mecca developed economic connections with the larger world. During the sixth century, it blossomed into a major emporium of international trade between the Mediterranean and the Indian Ocean. Yet urban growth was accompanied by social tensions. Clan solidarity remained paramount, and the gap between rich and poor widened. No single ruler presided over Mecca, and economic inequality sowed dissension. It was here that Muhammad, the founder of Islam, was born in around the year 570.

Muhammad belonged to a once-prominent clan whose fortunes were in decline. As a young man he worked as a caravaner for a woman named Khadija, a rich widow older than Muhammad, whom he married when he was twenty-five. Although Muhammad seemed to have gained a secure livelihood, moral doubts and growing contempt for what he regarded as the arrogance and greed of his fellow Meccans deeply troubled him. Beginning in around 610 he experienced visions of a single, true God ("Allah") who did not cater to the worldly wishes of worshipers as the pagan gods of his countrymen did but instead imposed an uncompromising moral law upon all peoples. Muhammad's revelations were suffused with a deep sense of sin inspired by Christianity. From Judaism Muhammad incorporated devotion to the one true God, a sense of personal mission as a prophet sent to warn the world against impiety, and a regimen of ritual prayer intended to instill rightful thought and conduct. Thus Muhammad's message was shaped by both the social and economic conflicts of his day and the long religious history of the region.

Muhammad's Life and Message

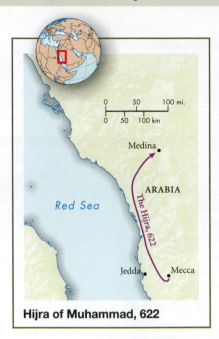

Hijra of Muhammad, 622

Initially, Muhammad communicated his visions only to a small group of confidants. In 613, however, a revelation instructed him to "rise and warn," and he began to preach publicly. Muhammad's egalitarian vision, in which all believers were equal before God, directly challenged tribal loyalties and clan leaders. Like Jesus, his teachings won favor among the lower classes, the poor and propertyless, while making him a pariah among the affluent and powerful clans. Persecution forced Muhammad and his followers to seek sanctuary in Medina, a nearby oasis town, in 622. Muhammad's move to Medina, known as the *hijra* (HIJ-ruh) ("migration"), subsequently marked the beginning of the Muslim calendar.

In Medina, Muhammad's reputation for holiness and fairness and his vision of a united community bound by a single faith elevated him to a position of leadership. The primary obstacle to the consolidation of his power in Medina was the town's large Jewish population, which rejected Muhammad's claims of prophethood and allied with his Meccan enemies. Muhammad began to issue new revelations accusing the Jews of breaking the covenant with God and declaring that he himself was the direct successor of the first and greatest prophet, Abraham. Muhammad vowed that his own creed of Islam ("submission") would supersede both Judaism and Christianity. Backed by Medina's clan leaders, Muhammad executed or exiled the town's leading Jewish citizens, thereby securing unchallenged authority in political as well as spiritual matters.

Subsequently Muhammad and his followers warred against Mecca—the first instance of a *jihad* ("struggle") of the sword, a holy war fought against those who persecute believers. In 630, the Meccans surrendered their city to Muhammad, who destroyed the idols of pagan gods in the Ka'aba and instead established it as the holiest shrine of Islam. Most Bedouin tribes soon capitulated to Muhammad as well. Preparing in 632 for an invasion of Syria, Muhammad was struck down by an illness and died in Medina. By the time of his death, he had created the basis for a new political order founded on a universal religion and a faith in the oneness of God that transcended clan, ethnic, and civic identities.

The Five Pillars of Islam

The revelations of Muhammad were written down in Arabic in the **Qur'an**, which Muslims regard as the completion of earlier revelations from God set down in the Jewish Torah and the Christian Gospels. The Qur'an elaborates the "five pillars of faith": (1) bearing witness to the unity of God and the prophethood of Muhammad; (2) daily prayers while facing the direction of Mecca; (3) fasting during Ramadan, the ninth month of the Islamic calendar; (4) giving alms to the poor; and (5) for those physically able and with the financial means, the obligation to make a pilgrimage (*hajj*) to Mecca. Performance of the "five pillars" gave public expression to membership in the **umma**, the community of the faithful. The daily regimen of prayer, the annual observation of Ramadan, and the duty to complete the hajj at least once during one's lifetime transformed the rhythms and purpose of life for herders and townfolk alike. All of these practices were joyous public ceremonies that served as visible symbols of submission to divine will. In the absence of a formal priesthood, the **ulama**—scholars and teachers steeped in study of the Qur'an—acted as the custodians and interpreters of divine teachings.

Several principles set Islam apart from the earlier monotheistic traditions of Judaism and Christianity: the stress on complete subjugation to God's commands—the fundamental tenet of Islam; the subordination of all other identities and loyalties to the community of believers; and dedication to defending the community and spreading the true religion. Although the Qur'an modified some of the prevailing norms of Bedouin society—for example, by recognizing women and children as individuals with their own needs and some limited rights—on the whole it reinforced the patriarchal traditions of clan society (see Reading the Past: Women and Property in Islam). At the same time, the charismatic leadership of clan elders yielded to the higher authority of divine will. Aspects of Islam were rooted in Bedouin culture, but the

hijra Muhammad's move from Mecca to Medina in 622, which marks year 1 of the Islamic calendar.

jihad Literally, "struggle"; a key concept in the Qur'an, which can refer to the individual's spiritual effort to follow "the path of God" (jihad of the soul) or to a holy war (jihad of the sword) against those who persecute Islam.

Qur'an The book recording the revelations of the Prophet Muhammad; regarded as the most sacred scripture in Islam.

umma The worldwide community of believers in Islam.

ulama Scholars learned in Islamic scripture and law codes who act as arbiters of Islamic teachings.

Women and Property in Islam

Under laws that prevailed in Latin Christendom until the nineteenth century, women had no right to inherit property, even from their deceased husbands. The Jewish legal tradition allowed only limited inheritance rights to women, generally for unmarried daughters or to perpetuate the family line when a man had no male heirs. Islamic law, by contrast, explicitly granted women certain property rights and control over their own earnings. In practice, however, the property rights of Islamic women and their access to gainful employment have been shaped and in some cases curtailed by social practices and scriptural interpretation.

Islam establishes men as the guardians of women, responsible for both their material welfare and their moral conduct, obligations that entail the right to punish women for their moral failings. At the same time, in keeping with the commandment against coveting the wealth and property of others, women are entitled to whatever earnings they receive from their work, trade, or property.

> Men are the ones who support women since God has given some persons advantages over others, and because they should spend their wealth on them. Honorable women are steadfast, guarding the Unseen just as God has it guarded. Admonish them, foresake them in beds apart, and beat them if necessary. If they obey you, do not seek any way to proceed against them.
> Qur'an, 4.34

> In no way covet those things in which God has bestowed his gifts more freely on some of you than on others: to men is allotted what they earn, and to women what they earn.
> Qur'an, 4.128

In both the Jewish and Islamic traditions, at the time of marriage the husband must provide the wife with a dowry that becomes her irrevocable personal property. Whereas the husband has free use of this property during the marriage under Jewish law, Islamic law places the dowry entirely at the disposal of the wife. The Qur'an also guarantees women an inheritance from their parents and close kin, though their share is usually less than the portion received by male heirs.

> [Upon marriage], give women their dowry as a free gift. If they of their own good wish remit any part of it to you, take it and enjoy it with good cheer.
> Qur'an, 4.4

> From what is left by parents and near relatives there is a share for men and a share for women, whether the property be small or large.
> Qur'an, 4.7

> God instructs you concerning your children's inheritance: a son should have a share equivalent to that of two daughters: if you have only daughters, two or more, their combined share is two-thirds of the inheritance; if only one, her share is a half.
> Qur'an, 4.11

Under Jewish law, both men and women could initiate a divorce, but one of the radical reforms of Christianity was to abolish divorce. Islamic law granted the right of divorce to men but not to women. The Qur'an allows the husband to divorce a wife without her consent, but it also requires that he provide financial support for a divorced wife, as well as a widow. Following a period of mourning, widows are free to leave their husband's household together with their property and remarry if they wish.

> A divorce may be pronounced twice [to give the parties a chance to reconcile]: after that, the parties should either hold together on equitable terms, or separate with kindness.
> Qur'an 2.229

> Those of you who die and leave widows should bequeath for their widows a year's maintenance and residence.
> Qur'an, 2.240

> For divorced women, maintenance should be provided on a reasonable scale.
> Qur'an, 2.241

EXAMINING THE EVIDENCE

1. Did Islamic law strengthen or weaken women's economic dependence on men?

2. Did Islamic laws on divorce and women's property correspond more closely to Jewish or to Christian precedents?

Divorce Hearing

Although permitted under Islamic law, divorce was regarded as a last resort. In this illustration from *The Assemblies* of al-Hariti, dated 1237, a man accompanied by his several wives pleads his case before the judge, who sits on a raised platform in front of a curtain of authority. Both the husband and the accused wife are portrayed as stubborn; the judge dismisses the case by giving each a gold coin. (Bibliothèque nationale de France.)

Factions Within Islam

caliph The designated successor to Muhammad as leader of the Muslim faithful in civil affairs.

imam The supreme leader of the Islamic community (especially in the Shi'a tradition), the legitimate successor to Muhammad; or any Islamic religious leader.

Shi'a A branch of Islam that maintains that only descendants of Muhammad through his cousin and son-in-law Ali have a legitimate right to serve as caliph.

Sunni The main branch of Islam, which accepts the historical succession of caliphs as legitimate leaders of the Muslim community.

religion pointed toward a new understanding of community in which membership was defined not by kinship or geography but by assent to a common set of religious principles.

The Islamic Empire of the Umayyad Caliphs 661–743

Muhammad's stature as the Prophet made him unique in the Islamic community. After his death the community faced the thorny problem of choosing his successor. Although Kadijah is said to have borne Muhammad four daughters and two sons, only two of his daughters outlived him. Eventually a compromise was reached that recognized Muhammad's father-in-law, Abu Bakr (AH-boo BOCK-ear), as **caliph** (KAY-luhf) ("deputy"). The caliph would inherit Muhammad's position as leader of the Islamic community, but not his role as prophet. As caliph, Abu Bakr led the community in wars of conquest and submission. The Byzantine and Sasanid empires, weakened by three decades of wars against each other, were no match for the Arabs. The Arabs decisively defeated the Byzantine army in Palestine in 634 and proceeded to capture Syria, Mesopotamia, and Egypt by 641. The Byzantine Empire lost most of its territories in the east but survived. The Sasanid Empire, however, utterly collapsed after Arab armies seized its capital of Ctesiphon in 637.

Abu Bakr and his immediate successors as caliphs ruled by virtue of their close personal relationships to the Prophet Muhammad, but disputes over succession persisted. The third caliph, Uthman (r. 644–656), a Meccan aristocrat of the Umayya (oo-MY-uh) clan, sought to resolve the succession problem by creating a family dynasty. Uthman's grab for power provoked civil war, however, and he was assassinated in 656. Ali, Muhammad's cousin and husband of his daughter Fatima, was elected to replace Uthman, but he failed to unite the warring Arab tribes. In 661 Ali, too, was assassinated. Mu'awiya (moo-AH-we-yuh) (r. 661–680), a cousin of Uthman and governor of Syria, emerged as the most powerful Muslim leader and succeeded in establishing a hereditary dynasty of Umayyad caliphs. Hence politics shaped Islam during Muhammad's lifetime and continued to affect its development long after his death. Just as the expansion of Christianity brought with it divisions and conflicts, Islam's success undermined its unity as factions formed within the Islamic world.

Although Mu'awiya cemented dynastic control over the caliphate and built up an imperial government in his new capital of Damascus, the wounds opened by the succession dispute failed to heal. When Mu'awiya died in 680, Ali's son Husayn (hoo-SANE) launched an insurrection in an attempt to reclaim the caliphacy. The Umayyads defeated the rebels, and Husayn was captured and killed. Nonetheless, a faction of Muslims remained who contended that the only rightful successors to the caliphate were Ali and his descendants, known as the *imam* ("leaders"). This group, which became known as the **Shi'a**, regarded Husayn as a great martyr. Another group, the Khariji, had turned against Ali because of his vacillating leadership and perceived moral failings. The Khariji rejected hereditary succession to the office of caliph in favor of election, insisting that religious devotion and moral purity were the only proper criteria for choosing the caliph. Both the Shi'a and the Khariji emphasized the role of the caliph as an infallible authority in matters of religious doctrine. Supporters of the Umayyad caliphs, known as the **Sunni**, instead regarded the caliph primarily as a secular ruler. Although the Sunni believed that the chief duty of the caliph was to protect and propagate Islam, they turned to the ulama rather than the caliph for interpretation of Islamic doctrine and law. Thus the divisions in Islam that grew out of disputes over the succession evolved into divergent understandings of the nature of the Islamic community and Islamic institutions.

When Abd al-Malik (r. 685–705), following a bloody struggle, assumed the office of Umayyad caliph in 685, the Muslim world was in disarray after a half century of astonishingly rapid expansion. Abd al-Malik succeeded in quelling uprisings by Shi'a and Khariji dissidents and restoring the caliph's authority over Arabia and Iran. He retained much of the administrative system of the Byzantine and Sasanid states, while substituting Arabic for Greek and Persian as the language of government. He also enacted currency reform, replacing images of human rulers with quotations from scripture, thereby providing another powerful symbol of Islamic unity. Abd al-Malik upheld the supremacy of Arabs in

Umayyad Reform and Expansion

government as well as faith, but bureaucratic office and mastery of the written word displaced martial valor as marks of leadership. He thus succeeded in creating a powerful monarchy supported by a centralized civilian bureaucracy.

Abd al-Malik and his successors continued to pursue vigorous expansion of **dar-al-Islam** ("the House of Belief") through military conquest, extending the Umayyad realm across North Africa and into Central Asia. In 710–711 a coalition of Arab and Berber forces from Morocco invaded the Iberian peninsula and quickly overran the Visigoth kingdom, stunning Latin Christendom. This invasion marked the beginning of a conflict between Christians and Muslims in the Iberian peninsula that would continue for centuries.

At first, to preserve the social unity of the conquerors, the Arabs ruled from garrison cities deliberately set apart from older urban centers. The Arabs thus became an elite military class based in garrison cities such as Basra and Kufa (both in Iraq), Fustat (modern Cairo), and Qayrawan (KYE-rwan) (in Tunisia), living off taxes extracted from farmers and merchants. Regarding Islam as a mark of Arab superiority, they made little effort to convert their non-Arab subjects. "Peoples of the Book"—Jews, Christians, and Zoroastrians, collectively referred to as **dhimmi** (DEE-me)—were permitted to practice their own religions, which the Arabs regarded as related but inferior versions of Islam, but under certain restrictions (see Reading the Past: The Pact of Umar). The dhimmi also had to pay a special tax (*jizya*) in return for the state's protection.

The segregation of Arabs from the conquered peoples could not be sustained indefinitely, however. Settlement in garrison towns transformed the lifestyle of the nomadic Arabs, and interactions with native populations led to assimilation, especially in Iran, far from the Arabian homeland. After a century of trying to maintain a distinct Arab-Muslim identity separate from local societies, the Umayyad caliphs reversed course and instead began to promote Islam as a unifying force. Caliph Umar II (r. 717–720) encouraged conversion of local rulers, merchants, and scholars. Although most people remained faithful to their ancestral religions, many members of the local elites were eager to ally with their Arab rulers. They converted to Islam, adopted the Arabic language, and sought places in the military and government service as equals to Arabs on the basis of their shared religion.

From Unified Caliphate to Islamic Commonwealth 750–1000

Umar II's efforts to erase the distinctions between Arabs and non-Arabs and create a universal empire based on the fundamental equality of all Muslims stirred up strong opposition from his fellow Arabs. Although the creation of a unified Islamic state fostered the emergence of a

dar-al-Islam Literally, "the House of Belief"; the name given to the countries and peoples who profess belief in Islam; in contrast to *dar-al-harb* ("the House of War"), where Islam does not prevail and Muslims cannot freely practice their religion.

dhimmi The Arabic term for "peoples of the book" (i.e., the Bible), namely Jews and Christians, who are seen as sharing the same religious tradition as Muslims.

> **FOCUS**
>
> How did the tensions between the ulama and the Abbasid caliphs weaken a unified Islamic empire?

READING THE PAST

The Pact of Umar

The Pact of Umar purports to be a letter from a Christian community in Syria seeking a truce with their Muslim overlords after the caliph Umar I conquered Syria in 637. Most scholars doubt that this document actually was written by Christians of that era. Rather, it was probably composed in the ninth century by Islamic jurists who wished to prescribe the conditions under which Muslims would tolerate the dhimmi communities, Jews as well as Christians, under their rule. But at least some of these regulations were enacted by the Abbasid caliphs. It has also been suggested that the restrictions on religious activities derived from Sasanid policies toward religious minorities within their empire. Regardless of its true origins, Muslim rulers frequently invoked the Pact of Umar as a model for regulating the conduct of Christians and Jews.

This is a letter to the servant of God Umar, Commander of the Faithful, from the Christians of [specific city]. When you came against us, we asked you for safe-conduct for ourselves, our descendants, our property, and the people of our community, and we undertook the following obligations toward you:

We shall not build, in our cities or in their neighborhood, new monasteries, churches, convents, or monks' cells, nor shall we repair, by day or by night, such of them as fall in ruins or are situated in the quarters of the Muslims.

We shall keep our gates wide open for passersby and travelers.

We shall give board and lodging to all Muslims who pass our way for three days.

We shall not give shelter in our churches or in our dwellings to any spy, nor hide him from the Muslims.

We shall not teach the Qur'an to our children.

We shall not manifest our religion publicly nor convert anyone to it. We shall not prevent any of our kin from entering Islam if they wish it.

We shall show respect toward the Muslims, and we shall rise from our seats when they wish to sit. We shall not seek to resemble the Muslims by imitating any of their garments, the qalansuwa [a fez-like cap], the turban, footwear, or the parting of the hair.

We shall not speak as they do, nor shall we adopt their kunyas [honorific names].

We shall not mount on saddles, nor shall we gird swords nor bear any kind of arms nor carry them on our persons.

We shall not engrave Arabic inscriptions on our seals. We shall not sell fermented drinks. . . . We shall not display our crosses or our books in the roads or markets of the Muslims.

We shall use only clappers [percussion instruments to accompany singing] in our churches very softly.

We shall not raise our voices when following our dead.

We shall not show lights on any of the roads of the Muslims or in their markets. We shall not bury our dead near the Muslims.

We shall not take slaves who have been allotted to Muslims.

We shall not build houses overtopping the houses of the Muslims.

(When I brought the letter to Umar, may God be pleased with him, he added, "We shall not strike a Muslim.")

We accept these conditions for ourselves and for the people of our community, and in return we receive safe-conduct. If we in any way violate these undertakings for which we ourselves stand surety, we forfeit our covenant, and we become liable to the penalties for contumacy [falsehood] and sedition [treason].

Source: A. S. Tritton, *The Caliphs and Their Non-Muslim Subjects*, by A. S. Tritton (1930): "The Pact of Umar." By permission of Oxford University Press.

EXAMINING THE EVIDENCE

1. In what ways were Christians expected to show deference to the superiority of Islam? Why were these visible expressions of subjugation considered important?

2. What Christian religious activities and symbols were deemed offensive to Muslims? Why?

cosmopolitan society and culture, rebellions by Bedouin tribes and Shi'a and Khariji communities caused the collapse of the Umayyad regime in 743. A new lineage of caliphs, the Abbasids, soon reestablished a centralized empire. But by 850, Abbasid power was in decline, and regional rulers and religious leaders began to challenge the caliphs' authority (see Map 9.3).

Rise of the Abbasid Caliphs

In 747, the Abbasids (ah-BASS-id), a branch of Muhammad's clan that had settled in Khurasan in northern Iran, seized the caliphate in their own name. They based their legitimacy on their vow to restore the caliphacy to the imams descended from Muhammad, a vow that won them the crucial support of Shi'a Muslims. Once securely in power, however, the Abbasids revived Umar II's vision of a pan-Islamic empire. Proclaiming the universal equality of all Muslims, the Abbasids stripped the Arabs of their military and economic privileges while recruiting non-Arab officers and administrators loyal to the new dynasty.

The Abbasid dynasty perpetuated the image of the caliph as a universal sovereign and supreme defender of Islam. When the Abbasid caliph al-Mansur (r. 754–775) began building his new capital of Baghdad on the banks of the Tigris River, near the former Sasanid capital of Ctesiphon, in 762, he claimed to be fulfilling a prophecy that a city would be built at this spot, at "the crossroads of the whole world."[10] Baghdad soon mushroomed into a giant complex of palaces, government offices, military camps, and commercial and industrial quarters.

The New Capital of Baghdad

At the heart of Baghdad, al-Mansur built the so-called Round City, more than a mile in diameter, which housed the caliph's family and the offices of government. At the center of the Round City, the green-domed palace of the caliph and the city's Grand Mosque stood together in the middle of a large open plaza, accentuating the unique majesty of the caliph's authority

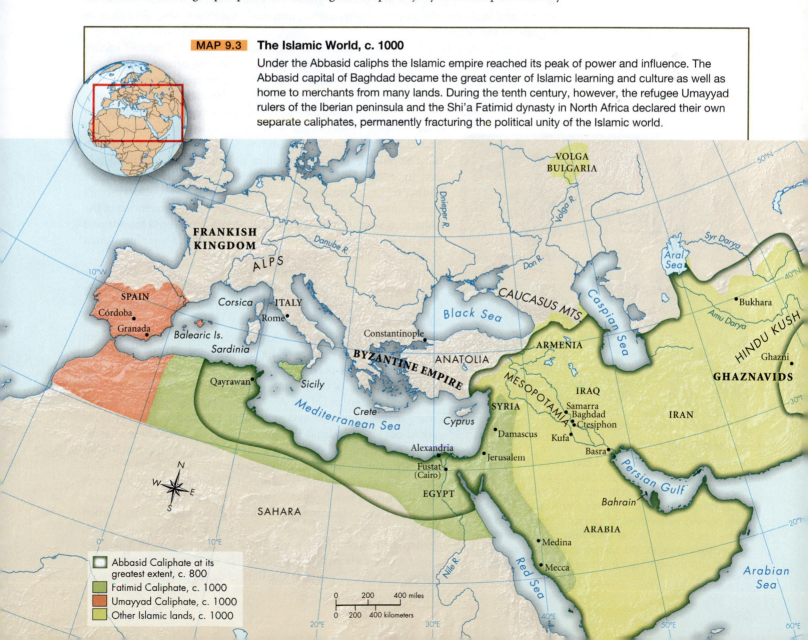

MAP 9.3   **The Islamic World, c. 1000**

Under the Abbasid caliphs the Islamic empire reached its peak of power and influence. The Abbasid capital of Baghdad became the great center of Islamic learning and culture as well as home to merchants from many lands. During the tenth century, however, the refugee Umayyad rulers of the Iberian peninsula and the Shi'a Fatimid dynasty in North Africa declared their own separate caliphates, permanently fracturing the political unity of the Islamic world.

- Abbasid Caliphate at its greatest extent, c. 800
- Fatimid Caliphate, c. 1000
- Umayyad Caliphate, c. 1000
- Other Islamic lands, c. 1000

over both civil and religious affairs. In Baghdad, as in other Islamic cities, the mosques, bazaars, and public baths became the centers of community life. Baghdad was divided into numerous residential neighborhoods, which acquired some measure of informal autonomy. The caliphs entrusted many tasks of municipal government to quasi-autonomous judicial, police, and fiscal officials, while the ulama dispersed across the city's neighborhoods performed informal but vital roles as community leaders. Well-regarded professionals, such as jewelers, perfumers, and booksellers, opened shops adjacent to the mosques, whereas those in dirty industries, such as tanners and butchers, were banished to the city's outskirts. House architecture and the winding, narrow city streets were designed to render women invisible to the public eye. Open public spaces such as squares and parks were notably absent. But Islamic rulers seldom imposed residential segregation based on ethnicity or religion.

Baghdad's Cosmopolitan Culture

The merchant communities of Baghdad and other cities included a mix of Jews, Christians, Persians, and Central Asians, as well as Muslims. Abbasid policies favoring conversion to Islam isolated Christians and Jews, turning them into ethnic minorities. Nonetheless, Jews and Nestorian Christians enjoyed better opportunities to earn a living and practice their religions in the Muslim world than they had under Byzantine rule.

The Abbasid rulers cultivated a cosmopolitan court life that blended Persian culture and Islamic faith. The court and wealthy officials and merchants in Baghdad became great patrons of scholars, physicians, and poets. Baghdad's scholars translated numerous Greek, Persian, and Indian works on philosophy, science, and medicine into Arabic, the common language of the Islamic world.

Alongside its officials, scholars, merchants, soldiers, and artisans, Baghdad society included a significant number of slaves. According to Islamic law, Muslims could not enslave their fellow Muslims. Thus, slaves were mostly obtained by purchase from Central Asia, the Slavic lands, and Africa. Elite households employed slaves as domestic servants, concubines, guards, and entertainers. Despite their legal status as slaves, they could acquire some measure of social rank in Muslim society, as the example of Arib al-Ma'muniya (797–890) shows. Sold as a young girl to a high Abbasid official, Arib was trained in singing and music, talents that were in great demand in the elite homes of Baghdad. Arib became a leading figure in the capital's musical and literary salons. Through these contacts and her love affairs with high-ranking members of the Abbasid government and army, she acquired powerful friends and patrons. By the end of her life Arib had become a wealthy woman who owned and trained her own slave singers.

The rise of the Abbasid caliphate drew the Islamic world farther from its roots in Arabia. The Umayyad caliphs had been tied to the culture and society of the Arabian deserts. After the founding of the Abbasid caliphate, however, Arabia was no longer at the center of the Islamic world. Mecca and Medina remained the holy cities, where pilgrims from every corner of the Muslim world gathered and intermingled. But religious leadership, like political and economic power, shifted to Baghdad and other commercial centers such as Damascus, Basra, and Cairo.

Iraq, the heartland of the Abbasid caliphate, experienced extraordinary economic and urban development. Building on improvements carried out by the Sasanid Empire, the Abbasid government invested heavily in the irrigation works needed to sustain agriculture. Muslim landowners in southern Iraq imported slaves from the nearby East African region of Zanj to work on sugar cane plantations and to convert the salt marshes into farmland. Foreign trade introduced both exotic goods and new manufacturing technologies. Papermaking, learned from China, displaced the practice of writing on papyrus leaves. Cotton textile manufacture and sugar refining emerged as major industries using techniques imported from India. The Muslim world became part of a vast global trading network, with Baghdad at its center.

Abbasid Court Culture

The Abbasid caliphs favored a cosmopolitan cultural style drawn from Persian and Greek, as well as Islamic, traditions. Frescoes from the ruins of the Abbasid palace at Samarra in Iraq—such as this scene of two dancing girls pouring wine—celebrate hunting, feasting, and the pleasures of court life. But after the caliphs' power began to decline in around 900, human figures disappeared almost entirely from Islamic art for centuries. (bpk/Art Resource, NY.)

Rise of the Religious Scholars

Whereas the power of the caliphs rested on their wealth, their legitimacy ultimately derived from their role as defenders of Islamic orthodoxy. Yet the caliphs did not inherit Muhammad's stature as prophet, and the Qur'an remained the indisputable testament of religious wisdom. Through their commentaries on scripture, the ulama taught how to apply the Qur'an to the conduct of social life. Religious teachers also compiled records of the deeds and words of Muhammad, known as *hadith*, as guides to the proper fulfillment of divine commandments. The caliphs thus occupied an ambiguous space in Islamic religious life. It was their job to defend Islamic orthodoxy, but they lacked the power to define that orthodoxy.

Their position was made even more difficult by the proliferation of scriptural commentaries and hadith, which widened the scope for individual interpretation of Islamic doctrine. In response, the caliphs sought to ensure orthodoxy by creating formal legal codes (*shari'a*) and law courts that combined religious and civil authority. Schools of law sprang up in major seats of Islamic learning such as Baghdad, Basra, Fustat, and Medina (see Chapter 13). However, because no consistent body of law could be applied uniformly throughout the caliphate, this initiative only added to the profusion of scriptural commentary and legal opinion that threatened to splinter the unity of Islamic teachings.

Faced with the potential fracturing of Islam, the ulama largely reconciled themselves to the caliphs' authority to maintain unity and order. Yet beneath this acceptance of Abbasid rule simmered profound discontent. "The best ruler is he who keeps company with scholars," proclaimed a leading religious teacher, "but the worst scholar is he who seeks the company of kings."[11] For the ulama, the special privileges and riches of the caliph and his courtiers betrayed Islam's most basic principles. The fundamental conflict remained. The caliphs sought to merge political and religious authority in a centralized state. The ulama, in contrast, worked to redefine the role of the caliph to establish clear limits to the caliph's power. In their view, the role of the caliph was not to determine Islamic law but rather to ensure the just administration of the shari'a for the benefit of all.

Relations between the caliphate and the ulama sank to their lowest point during the reign of al-Mamum (r. 813–833). Confronted with fierce opposition among the leading ulama and civil officials, al-Mamum launched a harsh campaign to force the ulama to acknowledge the caliph's higher authority in theological matters. His heavy-handed tactics failed, however. The spiritual leadership of the ulama rested securely on the unswerving allegiance of ordinary citizens, which the caliph was powerless to usurp.

Islamic Teachings and Law Schools

Tensions Between the Caliphs and the Ulama

Collapse of the Unified Caliphate

Unable to command the loyalty of its subjects and with its very legitimacy in question, the Abbasid regime grew weaker and ultimately collapsed. Al-Mamum's brother and successor as caliph, al-Mutasim (r. 833–842), faced growing dissent among both his officials and the ulama. He withdrew from Baghdad and took up residence at a new capital he built at Samarra, seventy miles to the northwest. Al-Mutasim also made the fateful decision to recruit Turkish slaves from Central Asia to form a new military force loyal to the caliphate. The slave soldiers soon ousted civil officials from the central government and provincial posts. In 861 a regiment of Turkish troops revolted and murdered the caliph, plunging the caliphate into anarchy. In 868 a renegade imam roused the Zanj slaves and other disaffected people in southern Iraq to revolt, promising "to give them slaves, money, and homes to possess for themselves."[12] The Zanj rebellion lasted fifteen years, claiming many thousands of lives and draining the fiscal and military resources of the Abbasid regime. Some measure of stability was restored in 945, when a Persian military strongman took control of Baghdad, reducing the Abbasid caliph to a mere figurehead. But by then rulers in Spain and North Africa had claimed the mantle of caliph for themselves.

In the early years of the Abbasid caliphate, the sole survivor of the Umayyad clan, Abd al-Rahman (ahbd al-rah-MAHN) (r. 756–788), had assembled a coalition of Berber and Syrian forces and seized power in Muslim Spain. Too far removed from the Muslim heartland

Rival Caliphates

to pose a threat to the Abbasids, the Umayyad regime in Spain coexisted uneasily with the Baghdad caliphate. In 931, as Abbasid authority ebbed, the Umayyad ruler Abd al-Rahman III (r. 912–961) declared himself the rightful caliph in the name of his forebears.

Another claim to the caliphacy arose in North Africa, a stronghold of a messianic Shi'a movement known as the Ismaili. The Ismaili believed that soon the final prophet, the true successor to Muhammad and Ali, would appear in the world to usher in the final judgment and the resurrection of the faithful. Hounded from Baghdad, Ismaili evangelists had instigated secessionist movements in North Africa, Bahrain, and the Caspian region. In 909, an Ismaili leader in Algeria proclaimed himself caliph, founding what came to be called (in homage to Muhammad's daughter Fatima) the Fatimid dynasty. In 969 the Fatimids captured Egypt and made Cairo the capital of their caliphate.

Flowering of Islamic Culture

By the middle of the tenth century, then, the unified caliphate had disintegrated into a series of regional dynasties. The collapse of political unity, however, did not lead to decline of Islamic social and cultural institutions. On the contrary, the tenth century was an age of remarkable cultural flowering in the Islamic world. The sharpening doctrinal disputes of the age produced an outpouring of theological scholarship and debate, and conversion of non-Arabs to Islam accelerated. Sufism, a mystical form of Islam based on commitment to a life of spirituality and self-denial, acquired a large following (see Chapter 13). Despite its political fragmentation, the Islamic world retained a collective identity as a commonwealth of states united by faith. The networks of travel and communications formed during the heyday of the Umayyad and Abbasid caliphates continued to help the circulation of people, goods, ideas, and technology throughout the Islamic lands.

COUNTERPOINT
The Norse Vikings: The New Barbarians

FOCUS

How did the Vikings' society and culture contrast with those of the settled societies of Europe?

The Norse Vikings ("sea raiders") who terrified Latin Christendom for more than two centuries can be seen as the maritime equivalent of the steppe nomads of Central Asia. The Vikings operated as independent bands of pirates and rarely acknowledged any authority other than the captains of their ships. Their Nordic homelands did not shift to formal centralized authority until the mid-eleventh century. Ultimately, however, the Vikings, like the nomadic peoples of the Central Asian steppes, were transformed by their interactions with the settled peoples whose goods they coveted.

The Viking Raids 790–1020

The earliest record of the Vikings relates that in the year 793 strange omens appeared in the skies over northeastern England, followed by a dire famine; then, "on June 8th of the same year, merciless heathens laid waste the Church of God in Lindisfarne [in northeast England], with plundering and killing."[13] By 799 the Vikings were launching raids along the coast of France. They would return to plunder the peoples to their south virtually every spring thereafter until the early eleventh century. The leaders of Christendom were aghast at what they interpreted as a brutal assault on the church and true religion. The Vikings were not, however, motivated by hatred of Christianity. They wanted money, goods, and slaves, and they were just as likely to prey on their fellow pagans as on Christians.

The Viking marauders originated from the Nordic, or Scandinavian, lands ringing the Baltic and North seas, whose thick forests, thin soils, and long winters discouraged agriculture (see Map 9.4). Like the Germans, the Norse prized cattle. Pasture was scarce, though, and in many places overgrazing had forced the inhabitants to replace cattle with less demanding sheep. Given this harsh and unpromising environment, it is not surprising that many Vikings turned to military raids to acquire what they could not produce themselves.

MAP 9.4

Viking Homelands, Raids, and Settlements, 790–1020

The Viking raiders were primarily interested in plunder and booty. But some Norse chieftains also led expeditions of conquest and settlement to England, France, Iceland, and the Baltic coast. Viking bands seeking the riches of Byzantium and the Islamic world also opened trade routes extending from the Baltic to the Black Sea.

Viking Warriors

Warfare had a long history in this region, but Nordic settlements rarely were fortified. The object of war was booty rather than seizing land, and the evolution of Viking military technology reflected this goal. Instead of developing the castles and stone fortifications that proliferated in northern Europe, the Vikings concentrated on improving their ability to launch seaborne raids. Between the fifth and eighth centuries, Norse shipbuilders developed larger and more seaworthy longboats, equipped with keels and powered by sails and by crews of thirty to sixty oarsmen. Using these vessels, roving Viking bands crossed the North Sea to pillage the unsuspecting coastal communities of Britain and France.

During the eighth century local chieftains all around the Nordic coasts constructed great halls, the "mead halls" celebrated in *Beowulf*, a tenth-century epic recounting the feats of a heroic Norse warrior. (Mead is a potent alcoholic beverage made from fermented honey and water.) Yet the great halls typically housed no more than thirty warriors and their families, and outfitting a single longboat required recruiting additional men beyond the chieftain's immediate retinue. For raiding expeditions, convoys of longboats were assembled under the leadership of a king, or paramount chief. Although these alliances were often renewed from season to season, the captains of these expeditions exercised little control over the subordinate chieftains, except in war and plunder. Such alliances did not reflect permanent connections among Viking groups or the beginnings of durable political institutions. Rather, they were arrangements of convenience, kept in place only as long as all involved profited from them.

Viking Kings

As a result, amid the conflict and rivalries of this warrior class few families could uphold their claim to royal authority for more than a couple of generations. The Christian missionary Ansgar, traveling in southern Sweden in around 865–875, observed that although the king at Uppsala led armies overseas and conducted diplomatic negotiations with the Franks, in civil matters he deferred to an assembly of chieftains and landowners. The anonymous author of *Beowulf* boasted of a mighty Danish king who "shook the halls, took mead-benches, taught encroaching foes to fear him . . . until the clans settled in the seacoasts neighboring over the whale-road all must obey him and give tribute."[14] Yet outside of the epics and sagas, few kings commanded such awe and allegiance.

The Norse kings did not levy taxes in coin or grain. The king's role was not to accumulate wealth, but to distribute it. Extravagant banqueting in the mead halls—occasions of majesty in lands of meager and monotonous diets—lay at the heart of social and ritual life. Feasting enabled kings and chieftains to renew friendships and allay rivalries, while bestowing gifts of gold and other treasures allowed them to display their liberality and lordship.

In contrast to the settled peoples of Christendom and the Islamic world, the Vikings were indifferent town builders and traders. Few merchants ventured into hostile Viking waters. Those who did briefly disembarked at seaside trading posts during the summer but did not settle permanently in the region. In the ninth and tenth centuries a few of these seasonal markets—including Ribe and Hedley in Denmark and Birka in Sweden—grew into towns, with their own Christian bishops and mints, and attracted colonies of foreign merchants. But these towns remained small enclaves of at most two thousand inhabitants. Only after 1000 did Nordic iron, furs, and slaves gain a foothold in European markets.

Islamic silver coins imported from the Black Sea began to appear in the Baltic region at the close of the eighth century. Silver was made into jewelry, used to pay legal fines, and offered as gifts to win allies and favors. The abundance of Islamic coins found in Viking hoards should not be taken as a measure of commercial activity, however. The richest hoards of Islamic coins have been discovered on the island of Gotland, midway between Latvia and Sweden. Yet Gotland lacked good harbors and towns. Most likely the islanders obtained their troves of silver from piracy rather than trade. Despite their treasure, they rigidly adhered to their traditional ways of life, to judge by the evidence of their small farms and the conservative dress and ornaments of their women.

Norse Emigration and Colonization

In the ninth century the Norse chieftains began to conduct expeditions aimed at conquest and colonization. Danish marauders seized lands in eastern England and imposed their own laws and customs on the Anglo-Saxons. By about 1000, the Danes had extended their control to parts of Norway, Sweden, and, under King Cnut (Keh-NEWT) (r. 1017–1035), all of England. Vikings also occupied parts of Ireland and coastal lands on the European continent from Normandy to Denmark.

Legends relate that the island of Iceland was first colonized during 870–930 by hundreds of families fleeing the tyranny of the Norwegian king Harald Fair-haired. More likely the immigrants were driven by hunger for land. Iceland, with its relatively mild winters, ample pasture for cattle, and abundant game, must have seemed a windfall. But human settlement soon upset the island's fragile ecology. Forests and fields were ruined by timber cutting, erosion, and overgrazing, while the game was hunted to extinction. By 1000 the settlers were desperately short of fuel and timber, and fishing had become the staple of their livelihood.

In around 980 Icelanders in search of virgin territories made landfall on Greenland, only to discover that this new world was even less well endowed with forests, pasture, and arable land. Subsequent foraging expeditions took them to Newfoundland, but there, too, the prospects for farming and stock raising were dim, and settlements were short-lived.

The maritime conquests of the Vikings proved to be more fleeting than the far-flung empires of the Central Asian nomads. Prolonged contact with Latin Christendom eventually eroded the Viking way of life. From about 1000 on, towns and merchants proliferated, local chieftains yielded to the rule of royal dynasties, and kings submitted to baptism and the Christian church's authority. As these new forms of economic, religious, and political

Viking Memorial Stone

Viking picture stones such as this eighth-century one from the island of Gotland off the coast of Sweden are believed to have been memorials dedicated to dead warriors and chiefs. Scholars disagree about the precise meaning of the scenes shown on this stone. One interpretation suggests that the stone depicts the death of a warrior in battle and his final journey to the underworld on the Viking longboat at bottom. (Courtesy of The Bunge Museum, an open air museum in Gotland, Sweden, displaying 8th century picture stones, and allowing visits to 17th, 18th and 19th century homes, mills, gardens, and workshops. www.bungemuseet.se.)

life permeated the Nordic world, the Vikings' plundering ceased. Yet even as the Norse peoples were pulled into the orbit of Latin Christendom, their songs and legends continued to celebrate the deeds of their pagan ancestors.

Conclusion

By the year 1000 the classical civilizations of western Eurasia had been reshaped by their new dominant religious cultures, Christianity and Islam. Christianity had spread throughout the European provinces of the old Roman Empire, whereas Islam prevailed in the heartlands of the ancient Persian and Egyptian empires and among the pastoral desert tribes of Arabia and North Africa. Christianity and Islam both flourished most vigorously in the cities. By 1000 the Christian church had made a concerted effort to extend its reach into village society through its legions of parish priests, and monastic orders ranked among the greatest landowners of Europe. The penetration of Islam into the countryside in long-settled areas such as Syria, Iraq, and Iran came more slowly.

The Christian communities allied with their secular rulers, whether they were Roman aristocrats, German chieftains, or the Byzantine emperor. From its inception, Islam became a political force as well as a religious movement, and the Umayyad caliphs created a vast Islamic empire. Despite efforts by the Byzantine emperors and the Muslim caliphs to impose religious orthodoxy, however, both Christendom and the Islamic empire fractured into competing religious traditions and a multitude of states.

At the same time, these religious faiths advanced into new frontiers. German kings and warriors followed in the footsteps of our chapter-opening heroine Radegund in embracing Christianity. Cultural, economic, and political interaction with the Byzantine Empire brought most Slavic peoples into the Christian fold. The arrival of Christianity in the Norse lands of northern Europe brought an end to the Viking menace. Although the prospects for a unified Muslim empire receded, Islamic religion and culture had become deeply implanted in a vast territory stretching from Iran to Spain. Starting in around 1000, Islam again underwent rapid expansion, notably in Africa and Asia, where, as we shall see in the next chapter, the Indian religions of Buddhism and Hinduism had shaped many diverse societies.

NOTES

1. Jo Ann McNamara and John E. Halborg, eds. and trans., *Sainted Women of the Dark Ages* (Durham, NC: Duke University Press, 1992), 65, 72, 75.
2. Procopius, *The Secret History*, trans. G. A. Williamson (London: Penguin, 1966), 106.
3. Alcuin, "Letter 8" (to Charlemagne), in Stephen Allott, *Alcuin of York, c. A.D. 732 to 804: His Life and Letters* (York, U.K.: Sessions, 1974), 11.
4. Gregory, *Pastoral Care*, 1.1, trans. Henry Davis, in *Ancient Christian Writers* (New York: Newman Press, 1950), 11:21.
5. Roy Cave and Herbert Coulson, eds., *A Source Book for Medieval Economic History* (New York: Biblo and Tannen, 1965), 336.
6. Al Djahiz, *A Clear Look at Trade*, quoted in Michael McCormick, *Origins of the European Economy: Communications and Commerce, A.D. 300–900* (Cambridge, U.K.: Cambridge University Press, 2001), 591.
7. S. H. Cross and O. P. Sherbovitz-Wetzor, *The Russian Primary Chronicle, Laurentian Text* (Cambridge, MA: Mediaeval Academy of America, 1953), 53, referring to the Poliane people inhabiting modern-day Ukraine.
8. Procopius, *History of the Wars*, trans. H. B. Dewing (Cambridge, MA: Harvard University Press, 1924), 7:14, 22–30.
9. Pseudo-Maurice, *Strategikon*, 11.4, quoted in P. M. Barford, *The Early Slavs: Culture and Society in Early Medieval Eastern Europe* (London: British Museum Press, 2001), 68.
10. Quoted in Gaston Wiet, *Baghdad: Metropolis of the Abbasid Caliphate* (Norman: University of Oklahoma Press, 1971), 11.
11. Sufyan al-Thawri, quoted in Francis Robinson, ed., *The Cambridge Illustrated History of the Islamic World* (Cambridge, U.K.: Cambridge University Press, 1996), 22.
12. *The History of al-Tabari* (Albany: State University of New York Press, 1992), vols. 36, 38.
13. Charles Plummer, ed., *Two of the Saxon Chronicles* (Oxford: Clarendon Press, 1892), 57.
14. *Beowulf*, lines 4–11, from *Beowulf: A Verse Translation*, trans. Michael Alexander (London: Penguin, 1973), 3.

RESOURCES FOR RESEARCH

Multiple Christianities, 400–850

Spearheaded by the pathbreaking work of Peter Brown, scholars now emphasize the continuation of the culture and institutions of the Roman Empire in the worlds of both Latin and Byzantine Christianity, as well as the multitude of distinct forms that Christianity took in different societies. MacMullen and the essays in Kreuger's volume focus on the religious experiences of ordinary people.

Brown, Peter. *The Rise of Western Christendom*, 2d ed. 2003.

Burstein, Stanley, ed. *Ancient African Civilizations: Kush and Axum*, rev. ed. 2009.

Kreuger, Derek, ed. *Byzantine Christianity*. 2006.

MacMullen, Ramsay. *Christianity and Paganism in the Fourth to the Eighth Centuries*. 1997.

McNamara, Jo Ann, and John E. Halborg, eds. and trans. *Sainted Women of the Dark Ages*. 1992.

Social and Political Renewal in the Post-Roman World, 400–850

In contrast to the conventional images of the Germans and Slavs as alien barbarians, recent studies—such as Geary's work—emphasize the fluidity of social and cultural identity and the dynamic interactions among peoples in post-Roman Europe. Angold provides a brief but compelling portrait of the early Byzantine Empire in relation to both Latin Christendom and the Islamic world.

Angold, Michael. *Byzantium: The Bridge from Antiquity to the Middle Ages*. 2001.

(Byzantium): Byzantine Studies on the Internet. http://www .fordham.edu/halsall/byzantium/index.html.

Franklin, Simon, and Jonathan Shepard. *The Emergence of Rus, 750–1200*. 1996.

Geary, Patrick J. *Before France and Germany: The Creation and Transformation of the Merovingian World*. 1988.

McKitterick, Rosamond, ed. *The Early Middle Ages: Europe, 400–1000*. 2001.

Treadgold, Warren. *A History of the Byzantine State and Society*. 1997.

Worlds of Late Antiquity. http://www9.georgetown.edu/faculty/ jod/wola.html.

The Rise and Spread of Islam, 610–750

Gordon's highly accessible text is a useful introduction to the origins and early history of the Islamic movement. Berkey's book combines narrative and thematic approaches to the development of Islam in the Middle East before modern times. Muhammad remains an elusive biographical subject; Rodinson's study, though dated (originally published in 1961), is still regarded as reliable.

Berkey, Jonathan. *The Formation of Islam: Religion and Society in the Near East, 600 to 1800*. 2003.

Bulliet, Richard. *Islam: The View from the Edge*. 1994.

Crone, Patricia. *Meccan Trade and the Rise of Islam*. 1987.

Gordon, Matthew S. *The Rise of Islam*. 2005.

Rodinson, Maxime. *Muhammad*, 2d ed. 1996.

From Unified Caliphate to Islamic Commonwealth, 750–1000

Lapidus's encyclopedic survey is especially valuable for its detailed regional-focused reviews of the varieties of Islamic society and culture. Hodgson remains a classic work in terms of both its erudition and its emphasis on the world-historical context of the rise and development of Islam. Daftary provides an authoritative introduction to the history, doctrines, and practice of one of the most important branches of Shi'a Islam.

(Byzantium): Byzantine Studies on the Internet. http://www .fordham.edu/halsall/islam/islamsbook.html.

Daftary, Farhad. *A Short History of the Ismailis: Traditions of a Muslim Community*. 1998.

Hodgson, Marshall. *The Venture of Islam: Conscience and History in a World Civilization*. Vol. 1, *The Classical Age of Islam*. 1974.

Kennedy, Hugh. *The Court of the Caliphs: The Rise and Fall of Islam's Greatest Dynasty*. 2004.

Lapidus, Ira M. *A History of Islamic Societies*, 2d ed. 2002.

Lewis, Bernard, ed. *Islam: From the Prophet Muhammad to the Capture of Constantinople*. 2 vols. 1974.

COUNTERPOINT: The Norse Vikings: The New Barbarians

Recent archaeological research—as exemplified by Christiansen's meticulous study—challenges many of the prevailing assumptions about the Vikings' society and livelihood. The Sawyers chronicle the transformation of Norse life and culture after the conversion to Christianity. Jochens, drawing primarily on Icelandic sources, argues that conversion brought few changes to the lives of Norse women.

Christiansen, Eric. *The Norsemen in the Viking Age*. 2002.

Jochens, Jenny. *Women in Old Norse Society*. 1995.

Logan, F. Donald. *The Vikings in History*, 3d ed. 2005.

Page, R. I. *Chronicles of the Vikings: Records, Memorials, and Myths*. 1995.

Sawyer, Birgit, and Peter Sawyer. *Medieval Scandinavia: From Conversion to Reformation, circa 800–1500*. 1993.

▶ **For additional primary sources from this period**, see *Sources of Crossroads and Cultures.*

▶ **For Web sites, images, and documents related to topics in this chapter**, see Make History at bedfordstmartins.com/smith.

REVIEW

The major global development in this chapter ▶ The spread of Christianity and Islam and the profound impact of these world religions on the societies of western Eurasia and North Africa.

IMPORTANT EVENTS

410	Visigoth sack of Rome
431	Council of Ephesus denounces Nestorianism as heresy
507	Clovis defeats Visigoth invaders and converts to Christianity
527–565	Reign of Justinian I as Byzantine emperor
570–632	Life of Muhammad, founder of Islam
589	Conversion of Visigoths to Roman Christianity
590–604	Papacy of Gregory I
622	Muhammad's hijra to Medina, marking the beginning of the Islamic calendar
661–743	Umayyad caliphate
680	Split between Shi'a and Sunni Islam
710–711	Muslim invasion and conquest of Visigoth-ruled Spain
732	Charles Martel halts Muslim advance into Europe
747–1258	Abbasid caliphate
793	Earliest record of Viking raids on Britain
800	Coronation of Charlemagne as emperor by Pope Leo III
868–883	Zanj revolt against the Abbasid regime
870–930	Vikings colonize Iceland
909	Fatimid dynasty founded
988	Vladimir, the Rus prince of Kiev, converts to Christianity

KEY TERMS

caliph (p. 292)	**Qur'an** (p. 290)
dar-al-Islam (p. 293)	**schism** (p. 281)
dhimmi (p. 293)	**serf** (p. 285)
hijra (p. 290)	**Shi'a** (p. 292)
iconoclasm (p. 281)	**Sunni** (p. 292)
imam (p. 292)	**ulama** (p. 290)
jihad (p. 290)	**umma** (p. 290)
manor (p. 285)	

CHAPTER OVERVIEW QUESTIONS

1. How and why did the development of the Christian church differ in the Byzantine Empire and Latin Christendom?

2. In what ways did the rise of Christianity and Islam challenge the power of the state?

3. Conversely, in what ways did the spread of these faiths reinforce state power?

4. Why did Christianity and Islam achieve their initial success in towns and cities rather than in the rural countryside?

SECTION FOCUS QUESTIONS

1. In what ways did Christianity develop and spread following its institutionalization in the Roman Empire?

2. What major changes swept the lands of the former Roman Empire in the four centuries following the fall of imperial Rome?

3. In what ways did Islam instill a sense of common identity among its believers?

4. How did the tensions between the ulama and the Abbasid caliphs weaken a unified Islamic empire?

5. How did the Vikings' society and culture contrast with those of the settled societies of Europe?

MAKING CONNECTIONS

1. How did the political institutions and ideology of the Islamic empire of the Umayyad and Abbasid caliphates differ from those of the Roman Empire (see Chapter 7)?

2. In what ways did the spiritual authority of the Islamic ulama differ from that exercised by the Christian popes and bishops?

3. How does the Islamic conception of the community of the faithful compare with Jewish and Christian ideas of community?

4. What were the causes and effects of the Viking raids and invasions in Europe in the eighth through tenth centuries, and how did these compare with the early invasions of the Roman Empire by the Germanic peoples (see Chapter 7)?

AT A CROSSROADS ▲

The Chinese monk Xuanzang's epic journey to India epitomized the cross-cultural exchanges that took place across Asia during the heyday of the Silk Road. In this Japanese painting commemorating Xuanzang's life, the pilgrim monk parades in triumph through the Chinese capital of Chang'an, preceded by horses bearing the precious Buddhist scriptures he brought back from India. The painting was commissioned in around 1300 by the Kofukuji Monastery in Nara, the headquarters of a Buddhist school dedicated to Xuanzang's teachings. (From the Collection of the Fujita Museum, Osaka, Japan. First section, tenth chapter of the painted scroll, *Genjo sanzo e* (Japanese National Treasure).)

Religion and Cross-Cultural Exchange in Asia

400–1000

In 642, a Chinese Buddhist pilgrim named Xuanzang (shoo-wen-zhang) (c. 602–664) was enjoying a leisurely stay at the court of the king of Assam, in the Himalayan foothills of northern India. Thirteen years before, Xuanzang had left China, where he had studied Buddhist scriptures and Indian languages at Chang'an, capital of the recently founded Tang dynasty (618–907). As his studies progressed, however, Xuanzang concluded that he could obtain authentic scriptures that preserved the Buddha's original teachings only by traveling to India, homeland of the Buddha, "the Awakened One." Defying an imperial decree that forbade travel abroad, Xuanzang embarked across the deserts and mountain ranges of Central Asia and spent years retracing the footsteps of the Buddha. It was these travels that had brought him to the court of Assam.

Xuanzang's visit, however, was interrupted by an urgent summons from King Harsha (r. 606–647), the most powerful Indian monarch at the time. During his time in India, Xuanzang had acquired a reputation as a great philosopher and skilled orator, and he had come to the attention of King Harsha, a pious man and an earnest patron of both Hindu Brahman priests and Buddhist monks. "He divided the day into three parts," commented Xuanzang, "the first devoted to affairs of state, and the other two to worship and charitable works, to which he applied himself tirelessly, as there were not enough hours in the day to complete his ministrations."[1] Harsha now wished to host a grand philosophical debate featuring his Chinese guest.

On the appointed day King Harsha led a vast procession of princes, nobles, soldiers, and priests to a parade ground on the banks of the Ganges River. Xuanzang wrote, "In the

BACKSTORY

In China as in the Roman world, invasions and migrations by "barbarian" peoples followed the collapse of the empire. After the Han Empire fell in the third century C.E. (see Chapter 6), endemic fighting among regional warlords weakened China and made it possible for steppe nomads to conquer the north China heartland in the early fourth century. Pressure from central Eurasian nomads also contributed to the demise of the Gupta Empire in northern India at the end of the fifth century (see Chapter 6). Yet political turmoil and the fragmentation of India and China into smaller rival kingdoms did not breed isolation. On the contrary, the Silk Road flourished as a channel of trade and cultural exchange during these centuries. Traversing both overland and overseas trade routes, missionaries and merchants carried Indian religions to China and Southeast Asia, where they profoundly influenced not only religious beliefs and practices but political and social institutions as well.

Steppe Peoples and Settled Societies of Central Asia

FOCUS What strategies did nomadic steppe chieftains and the rulers of agrarian societies apply in their dealings with each other?

The Shaping of East Asia

FOCUS How did the spread of Buddhism transform the politics and societies of East Asia?

The Consolidation of Hindu Society in India

FOCUS Why did the religious practices of Hinduism gain a broader following in Indian society than the ancient Vedic religion and its chief rival, Buddhism?

The Diffusion of Indian Traditions to Southeast Asia

FOCUS What aspects of Indian religions had the greatest influence on the societies and cultures of Southeast Asia?

COUNTERPOINT: Sogdian Traders in Central Asia and China

FOCUS How did the social and economic institutions of the Sogdian merchant network differ from those of the nomadic confederations and the agrarian empires?

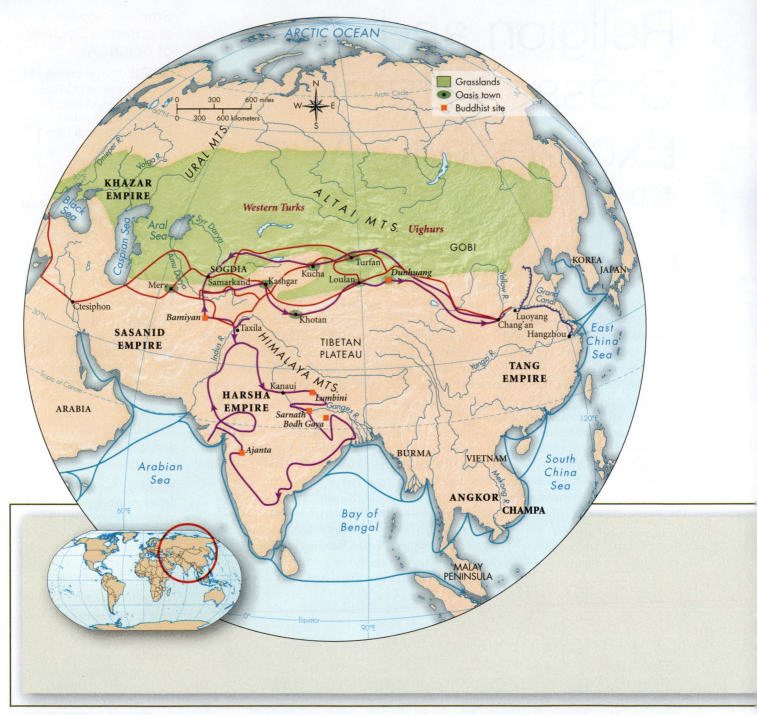

386–534 Northern Wei dynasty in north China and Mongolia

581–618 Sui dynasty in China

c. 670 ▪
The Khazars conquer and supplant the Bulgar khanate

552–603 First Turkish empire

618–907 Tang dynasty in China

400 **500** **600** **700**

Prince Shōtoku reorganizes the
Yamato kingdom in Japan **604 ▪**

690 ▪
Empress Wu declares the founding
of her Zhou dynasty in China

606–647 Reign of King Harsha as
paramount ruler of north India

629–645 Journey of the Chinese
Buddhist monk Xuanzang to India

Unification of the Korean peninsula under the rule of the Silla kingdom **668 ▪**

center strode a huge, elaborately caparisoned elephant bearing a golden statue of the Buddha more than three feet high. On the left went King Harsha, dressed as [the Hindu god] Indra and holding aloft a jeweled parasol, while on the right was the King of Assam, wearing the regalia of [the Hindu god] Brahma and grasping a white fly-whisk."[2] The theological tournament lasted five days, during which the rhetorical clashes grew increasingly fierce. When Harsha declared Xuanzang the victor, his Brahman opponents allegedly set fire to the shrine housing the Buddha's image, and one of them tried to assassinate the king. Harsha, keen to avert religious strife among his subjects, punished the ringleader but pardoned the rest of the disgruntled Brahmans.

Four months later, Xuanzang departed for home. Although he had left China illegally, he returned in triumph. The Tang emperor anointed him "the jewel of the empire" and built a magnificent monastery to house the precious Buddhist icons, relics, and books that he had brought back from India. A legend in his own lifetime, Xuanzang devoted the last twenty years of his life to translating Buddhist texts and to seeking refuge from his admirers.

Xuanzang's remarkable experiences were part of the larger pattern of cross-cultural encounters and exchanges that shaped Asia in the second half of the first millennium C.E. Since the inception of the Silk Road route in the first century C.E. (see Chapter 6), Buddhist missionaries had accompanied the caravans setting out from the frontiers of India to seek the fabled silks of China. As we will explore in this chapter, in later centuries others traveled between India and China bearing goods and ideas that fertilized cross-cultural exchange, including nomad warriors from Central Asia, long-distance traders such as the Sogdians, and missionaries and pilgrims. A similar interweaving of commerce and evangelism also drew Southeast Asia into sustained contact with India, and to a lesser extent with China.

The resulting spread of Buddhism and Hinduism from India provided the foundations for distinctive regional cultures across Asia. Political and social crises in China and India prompted serious questioning in those countries of traditional beliefs and values, creating a climate more receptive to new ideas. At the same time, the leaders of newly emerging states

MAPPING THE WORLD

Cross-Cultural Exchange in Asia

Both goods and ideas flowed across the Silk Road, the name given by a nineteenth-century German geographer to the network of caravan routes crossing Central Asia from China to Iran. During the peak of the Silk Road from the fourth to the eighth century C.E., Sogdian merchants dominated East-West trade. Buddhist missionaries journeyed from India to China by following the overland Silk Road, as did the Chinese monk Xuanzang on his pilgrimage to India in the early seventh century.

ROUTES ▼

— Silk Road, c. 600

— Maritime trade route, c. 600

➜ Travels of Xuanzang, 629–645

755–763 A Lushan rebellion in north China severely weakens the Tang dynasty

▪ **802** Consolidation of the Angkor kingdom in Cambodia by Jayavarman II

▪ **939** Vietnam achieves independence from China

800　　**900**　　**1000**

▪ **c. 760** Sailendra kings in Java begin construction of the Borobudur monument

▪ **965** Rus invaders destroy the Khazar khanate

▪ **861** Conversion of the Khazars to Judaism

▪ **792** Kyoto established as Japan's new capital

in East and Southeast Asia looked toward China and India for models of political institutions and cultural values. A common civilization inspired by Chinese political, philosophical, and literary traditions and permeated by Buddhist beliefs and practices emerged in East Asia. In Southeast Asia, a more eclectic variety of societies and cultures developed, one that blended Indian influences with native traditions. In time, the emergence of new societies throughout Asia would give rise to new trade patterns. By the tenth century the maritime realm stretching from Korea and Japan to Java and Malaysia had supplanted the overland Silk Road as the major channel of economic and cultural interaction within Asia.

OVERVIEW
QUESTIONS

The major global development in this chapter: The cultural and commercial exchanges during the heyday of the Silk Road that transformed Asian peoples, cultures, and states.

As you read, consider:

1. In what ways did Asian societies respond to cross-cultural interaction during the period 400–1000?

2. What strategies did pastoral nomads adopt in their relations with settled societies, and why?

3. What patterns of political and cultural borrowing characterized the emerging states in East and Southeast Asia?

4. Why did India and China experience different outcomes following the collapse of strong and unified empires?

Steppe Peoples and Settled Societies of Central Asia

FOCUS

What strategies did nomadic steppe chieftains and the rulers of agrarian societies apply in their dealings with each other?

Neither the fall of the Han dynasty in China in the early third century nor the collapse of the Roman Empire in the West in the fifth century resulted directly from invasions by pastoral nomads from the steppes of Central Asia. In both cases, imperial decline was the cause rather than the consequence of nomadic invasions. Political instability following the demise of the Han encouraged raids by nomadic groups on China's northern frontiers. During the fifth century, one of these groups, the Tuoba confederation, gradually occupied nearly all of northern China, as well as Manchuria and Mongolia.

Despite the political instability on the Eurasian steppe in this era, trade and cultural exchange flourished as never before. The heyday of the Silk Road between the fifth and the eighth centuries witnessed major changes in the societies and cultures of Asia. No group was more deeply affected by these changes than the pastoral nomads of the Central Asian steppe. The empires of the Tuoba, the Turks, and the Khazars marked a new stage in state formation among the nomadic tribes. The military ingenuity and political skills these nomad confederations developed would later make possible the greatest nomad conquerors of all, the Mongols.

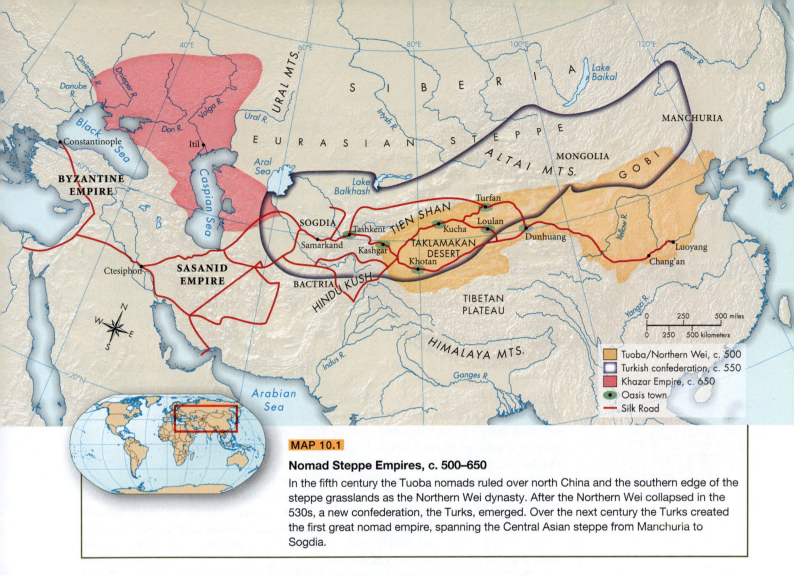

MAP 10.1

Nomad Steppe Empires, c. 500–650

In the fifth century the Tuoba nomads ruled over north China and the southern edge of the steppe grasslands as the Northern Wei dynasty. After the Northern Wei collapsed in the 530s, a new confederation, the Turks, emerged. Over the next century the Turks created the first great nomad empire, spanning the Central Asian steppe from Manchuria to Sogdia.

Nomad Conquerors of China: The Northern Wei 386–534

China had a frontier stretching thousands of miles along the border of the steppe grasslands. Throughout the more than four hundred years of the Han dynasty (202 B.C.E.–220 C.E.), steppe nomads had shifted between a "hard" strategy of invading China and extorting tribute during times of strength and a "soft" strategy of allying with Chinese rulers and symbolically acknowledging their overlordship during times of weakness. The nomads were primarily interested in obtaining scarce resources they could not produce themselves, such as grain. They also sought precious goods, notably gold, metal wares, and silk cloth, which they needed to cement the alliances that held their confederations together. Nomad chieftains had no desire to conquer the agrarian states and adopt their lifestyle. They preferred to acquire the goods they desired through tribute and trade rather than direct rule.

The demise of the Han dynasty in 220 ushered in a century of civil wars that sapped the empire's defenses and left China vulnerable to foreign invasion. In 311, steppe invaders sacked Luoyang (LWAUGH-yahng), the capital of the reigning Jin dynasty. The Jin emperor fled with his court to the Yangzi River delta, leaving the Chinese heartland in the north at the mercy of marauding armies. For the next three centuries, a series of foreign rulers controlled north China; some were wise, and many were rapacious. Then, in the late fourth century, a measure of stability was restored to north China by the rulers of a new confederation of steppe peoples, the Tuoba (TWAUGH-bah).

Nomad Conquest of North China

The rise of the Tuoba marked the first attempt by steppe nomads to build enduring institutions for governing agrarian China, rather than merely seeking to extract booty from it. In 386 the Tuoba declared their imperial ambitions by adopting a Chinese-style dynastic name, Northern Wei (way). From 430, when the Tuoba captured the former Han capital of Chang'an, down to the 530s, the Northern Wei reigned virtually unchallenged across a wide swath of Asia from Manchuria to Bactria (see Map 10.1).

Northern Wei State

To reinforce their legitimacy and further their imperial ambitions, the Northern Wei promoted cross-cultural exchange between themselves and their Chinese subjects. The Northern Wei rulers avidly embraced the Buddhist faith that, as we will see, had spread throughout Central Asia. Emperor Xiaowen (SHIAW-when) (r. 471–499) encouraged inter-marriage between the Tuoba nobility and the leading Chinese aristocratic clans, as well as adoption of Chinese language, dress, and customs. Xiaowen sought to create a hybrid ruling class that combined the martial traditions of the steppe with the cultural prestige and administrative acumen of imperial China. Ultimately, however, his policies divided the "sinified" Tuoba—those who adopted Chinese ways—within China from the Tuoba nobles based in the steppe grasslands, who staunchly resisted Chinese habits and values. This split widened when purist Tuoba chiefs from the steppes revolted in 524. The Northern Wei state crumbled ten years later. A cultural policy meant to unify the Tuoba and the Chinese and thereby cement Northern Wei rule ended up creating fatal divisions among the Tuoba themselves.

Rise of the Turks

The return of tribal strife to the eastern steppe gave charismatic leaders among the pastoral nomads a chance to forge new coalitions. In Mongolia, a chieftain named Bumin (BOO-min) (d. 552) emerged as the *khan* ("lord") of a new confederation called the Heavenly Turks. Bumin initially allied with the purist Tuoba chiefs, but he soon became their overlord. Bumin's successors extended the Turkic conquests eastward to Manchuria, but they were content to exact tribute from, rather than conquer, the Tuoba-Chinese states that had succeeded the Northern Wei in north China.

Turkic Warriors   Technology played a role in the Turks' rise to prominence. Recent innovations in warfare, such as the use of stirrups, had become widespread in the eastern steppe in the fifth century. The stirrup gave horse-riding archers a steadier posture from which to shoot. Turkic warriors cloaked themselves in mailed armor and wielded large bows and curved sabers. Thus equipped, the Turkic cavalry transformed themselves into a far more deadly force than the mounted warriors of the past.

The Turks' most dramatic advance occurred in the western steppe. They swallowed up the oasis towns and principalities of the Silk Road, reaching as far west as the Black Sea, and negotiated a marriage alliance with the Sasanid king. Like earlier steppe confedera-

Central Asian Horse Riders

The invention of the metal stirrup marked an important advance in warfare, enabling riders to wield bows and swords more effectively. By 200 C.E. Chinese craftsmen were making iron and bronze stirrups like the ones shown in this mural from the tomb of a Chinese general. Widely adopted by the steppe nomads of eastern Asia by 400, the stirrup spread westward and reached Europe in the eighth century. (Shaanxi Museum/ChinaStock.)

khan The Turkish word for "lord," used especially for rulers of the nomad empires of the central Eurasian steppes.

tions, the Turks preferred tribute and trade as means of obtaining booty. The merchants of Sogdia, in modern Uzbekistan, became key advisers and agents of the Turkic leaders. Control of the entire length of the Silk Road by a single power was a boon to trade, and the Sogdian capital of Samarkand (SAM-mar-kand) flourished as a great crossroads for merchant caravans (see Counterpoint: Sogdian Traders in Central Asia and China). This robust commercial activity also stimulated trade along the lower reaches of the Volga River and opened a route that the Vikings would later exploit.

Breakup of the Turkic Confederation

In diplomatic negotiations with the autocratic empires of Iran and China, the Turkic khans presented themselves as supreme monarchs. Nevertheless, the Turkic confederation remained a loose band of tribes whose chieftains retained considerable autonomy. When, as we will see, a strong empire reemerged in China under the Sui dynasty in the late sixth century, the Turks lacked effective leadership to counter a resurgent China. By 603 the Sui captured the eastern portion of the Silk Road corridor, splitting the Turks into separate eastern and western groups.

A Turkic Khanate in the West: The Khazars

Khazar Expansion

Following the division of the Turkic Empire in 603, local tribal identities once again came to the fore in the western part of the former empire, where few people were of Turkic ancestry. The Khazars (hus-ahr), based in the Caucasus region between the Black and Caspian seas, emerged as an independent khanate allied with the Byzantines against the Sasanids. In around 650 the Khazars conquered the rival Bulgar khanate that had been established northeast of the Black Sea (see again Map 10.1). Later, in the tenth century, the Khazars drove the Magyar chieftains westward into the Danube River basin, where they established a durable state, Hungary, and converted to Christianity.

Following their triumph over the Bulgars, the Khazars moved their capital to Itil in the Volga River delta. In the mid-eighth century the Khazars developed close diplomatic and commercial relations with the Abbasid caliphs. Although Itil consisted of little more than a massed array of felt tents, the Khazar capital attracted merchants from distant regions. Many Muslims resided there, along with a sizable community of Jewish merchants who had fled Constantinople because of the anti-Jewish policies of the Byzantine government. Commercial exchange with the Muslim world was fed by the rich mines of the Caucasus region, the tribute of furs collected from Slavs in the Dnieper River Valley, and the steady flow of slaves seized as war captives. Despite the Khazars' nomadic lifestyle, their capital became a crossroads for trade and cultural exchange.

Conversion to Judaism

This openness was dramatically demonstrated when, in around 861, the reigning Khazar khan abruptly converted to Judaism, reportedly after listening to debates among a Muslim mullah, a Christian priest, and a Jewish rabbi. The khan adopted the Jewish Torah as the legal code of the Khazars, although Christians and Muslims continued to be judged according to their own laws. Hebrew became the primary written language of government and religion. Subsequently the head of the Jewish community gained effective power over political affairs, relegating the khan to the role of a symbolic figurehead. The Khazar khanate did not long survive this dramatic shift. In 965 Rus armies overran Itil and other Khazar towns, bringing the khanate to an end and opening the region to settlement by Christian Slavs.

The Shaping of East Asia

The culture and technology of the Chinese Empire—and of course its political and military muscle—could not fail to have a powerful impact on its neighbors. Chinese agriculture and metalworking were adopted in the Korean peninsula from the eighth century B.C.E. and in the Japanese archipelago after the fourth century B.C.E. Rapid advances in agricultural production and the rise of local and regional chiefdoms followed.

FOCUS

How did the spread of Buddhism transform the politics and societies of East Asia?

The imposition of direct Chinese rule on part of the Korean peninsula and on Vietnam during the Han dynasty left a deep imprint on these regions. Independent Korean states arose after the Han Empire collapsed in the early third century C.E., but Vietnam remained under Chinese rule until the tenth century. In the Japanese islands, contact and exchange with the continent stimulated the progress of state formation beginning in the third century.

Although both Korea and Japan preserved their independence from the resurgent Sui (581–618) and Tang (618–907) empires in China, the societies of both the peninsula and the archipelago were shaped by Chinese political and cultural models and traditions. The farthest-reaching cultural transformation of this era was the adoption of a foreign tradition, Buddhism, as the dominant religion within China, and subsequently in the rest of East Asia. With the waning of Tang imperial might after the mid-eighth century, however, Japan and Korea shifted away from Chinese models and developed their own distinctive political and social identities. After Vietnam gained independence in the early tenth century, the multistate system of modern East Asia assumed definitive form.

The Chinese Transformation of Buddhism

From the first century C.E., Buddhist missionaries from India had crossed the steppe grasslands of Central Asia and reached China. The rise of the kingdom of the Kushans, great patrons of Buddhism, at the intersection of the trade routes linking China with India and Iran had stimulated the spread of Buddhism along these thoroughfares (see Chapter 6). Although the Kushan kingdom disintegrated in the second century, the rulers and inhabitants of the oasis towns of central Eurasia had converted to Buddhism, creating a neat path of stepping-stones for the passage of Buddhist monks and doctrines from India to China.

The collapse of the Han Empire and subsequent foreign invasions prompted many Chinese to question their values and beliefs and to become receptive to alternative ideas and ways of life. Buddhism was well known in Chinese philosophical circles by the third century, but it was not until the fifth century that this nonnative religion began to penetrate deeply into Chinese society.

In its original form, Buddhism could not be readily assimilated into the Chinese worldview. Its rejection of the mundane world and its stress on a monastic vocation conflicted with the humanist goals and family-centered ethics of Confucianism. As we saw in Chapter 6, however, the **Mahayana** school of Buddhism maintained that laypeople in any walk of life had equal potential for achieving enlightenment and salvation. The figure of the **bodhisattva** (boh-dihs-SAHT-vah), an enlightened being who delays entry into nirvana to aid the faithful in their own religious quests, exemplified the Mahayana ideal of selfless compassion and provided a model for pious laypeople and clergy alike. The Mahayana vision of a multitude of Buddhas (of whom the historical Buddha was only one) and bodhisattvas as divine saviors also encouraged the prospect of gaining salvation within a person's present lifetime, rather than after many lives of suffering. It was the Mahayana school of Buddhism, therefore, that made broad inroads in China.

Mahayana Buddhism's compatibility with existing Chinese cultural and intellectual traditions was crucial to its acceptance. The Buddhist doctrine of *karma*—the belief that the individual's good and evil actions determine one's destiny in the next reincarnation—was revised to allow people to earn merit not just for themselves but also for their parents and children. The pursuit of merit and eradication of sin became a collective family endeavor rather than a solitary, self-centered enterprise.

Buddhist Family Shrine
Although the Buddha had presented the pursuit of enlightenment as an individual quest, Mahayana Buddhists in China promoted devotional acts intended to earn karmic merit for the entire family. This stone stele, dated 562, features carvings of numerous Buddhas and bodhisattvas. The name of the donor is inscribed alongside each image. Nearly all the donors were surnamed Chen, suggesting that the monument was a collective family project. (Collected in Shanxi Museum.)

This understanding of karma fit well with the Chinese practice of ancestor worship and the emphasis on the family as the fundamental moral unit. Moreover, the Buddhist regimen of mastery of scripture, lavish donations to support the clergy, and ritual observances governing all aspects of daily life fit readily into the lifestyles of the educated, wealthy, and ritual-bound upper classes in China. Indeed, the lay religious practices of Buddhism served to confirm the Chinese aristocracy's own sense of social superiority. Not surprisingly, Buddhist missionaries in China initially directed their conversion efforts at the rulers and aristocrats, whose faith in Confucianism had been badly shaken by the collapse of the Han.

During the fifth century, devotion to Buddhism spread swiftly among the ruling classes in both north and south China. The Tuoba rulers of the Northern Wei dynasty had long been familiar with Buddhism. Several Northern Wei emperors converted to Buddhism and became avid patrons of Buddhist institutions. Buddhism also served useful political purposes. In a world fractured by warfare and political instability, the universalist spirit of Buddhism offered an inclusive creed that might ease social and ethnic frictions among the Chinese and the diverse foreign peoples who had settled within China. The Northern Wei rulers were especially attracted to the Buddhist ideal of the *chakravartin* (chuhk-ruh-VAHR-tin), the "wheel-turning king" (controller of human destiny) who wages righteous wars to bring the true religion to the unenlightened peoples of the world. The chakravartin ideal was founded on the historical precedent of Ashoka (see Chapter 6), the great Mauryan king of the third century B.C.E., whose imperial dominion was closely tied to his support and patronage of Buddhism.

Chinese rulers in the south also became patrons of Buddhism. The desire to earn religious merit through acts of faith and charity spurred Chinese aristocrats to donate land, money, and goods to support the Buddhist clergy. The profusion of domestic shrines and devotional objects illustrates the saturation of upper-class life in China by Buddhist beliefs and practices.

In the sixth century, two interrelated developments profoundly altered the evolution of Buddhism in East Asia. First, Chinese monastic communities and lay congregations created their own forms of Buddhist theology and religious discipline, forms that were more closely attuned to the concerns of their Chinese audience. Second, these new movements reached well beyond the elite and led to the emergence of Buddhism as a religion of the masses. As a reaction against the exclusivity of earlier forms of Buddhism, two new forms of Buddhism developed—Pure Land Buddhism and Chan (Zen) Buddhism.

Pure Land Buddhism first emerged as a coherent religious movement in China during the sixth century. Born amid the incessant war and deepening poverty that afflicted the Chinese world after the collapse of the Northern Wei state in 534, Pure Land expressed deep pessimism about mortal existence. The formidable burden of sins accumulated over countless lifetimes made the possibility of attaining salvation through one's own merit-earning actions appear hopelessly remote. Yet people of sincere faith could obtain rebirth in the Pure Land, a celestial paradise, through the aid of savior figures such as Amitabha (Ah-MEE-tah-bah), the presiding Buddha of the Pure Land, or Guanyin (GWAHN-yin), the bodhisattva of compassion.

Like the later Protestant Reformation of Christianity, Pure Land Buddhism emphasized salvation through faith alone rather than good works. One did not achieve nirvana by making large donations to Buddhist monasteries, but by fully committing oneself to a spiritual life. Thus, it offered the hope that through sincere piety all persons, no matter how humble, might attain salvation within their present lifetimes. Originating among lay congregations alienated by the luxury and splendor that increasingly enveloped the monastic establishments, Pure Land teachings found favor among poor and illiterate people. Its devotions focused on simple rituals, such as chanting the names of Amitabha and Guanyin, that did not require wealth, learning, or leisure. Because of the universal appeal of its message, the Pure Land movement transformed Chinese Buddhism into a mass religion focused on the worship of compassionate savior figures.

From an Elite to a Mass Religion

Mahayana A major branch of Buddhism that emphasizes the potential for laypeople to achieve enlightenment through the aid of the Buddha and bodhisattvas.

bodhisattva In Mahayana Buddhism, an enlightened being who delays entry into nirvana and chooses to remain in the world of suffering to assist others in their quest for salvation.

chakravartin In Indian political thought, the "wheel-turning king," a universal monarch who enjoys the favor of the gods and acts as a defender of religious orthodoxy.

Pure Land A school of Mahayana Buddhism, originating in China, that emphasizes the sinfulness of the human condition and the necessity of faith in savior figures (the Buddha and bodhisattvas) to gain rebirth in paradise.

Eleven-Headed Guanyin

Guanyin, the bodhisattva of compassion, became the most popular figure in East Asian Buddhism. This tenth-century banner depicts Guanyin with eleven heads and six arms, symbolizing Guanyin's role as a savior. Guanyin is surrounded by scenes from the *Lotus Sutra* in which the bodhisattva rescues devout followers from perils such as fire and bandits. The donor, dressed as a Chinese official, appears at bottom right. (Arthur M. Sackler Museum, Harvard University Art Museums/Bequest of Grenville L. Winthrop/Bridgeman Art Library.)

China's Grand Canal

Like Pure Land, **Chan Buddhism**—better known by its Japanese name, Zen—reacted against the unseemly wealth and privileges enjoyed by the clergy. Also like Pure Land, Chan Buddhists rejected a religious life centered on what they perceived to be rote recitation of scripture and performance of complex rituals. Chan instead embraced strict discipline and mystical understanding of truth as the genuine path of enlightenment. But in contrast to Pure Land, Chan Buddhism continued to honor the monastic vocation, and as the ultimate goal of its religious quest it emphasized sublime spiritual mastery of Buddhist teachings rather than rebirth in a paradise of material comfort. The Chan movement gained a widespread following among the clergy beginning in the eighth century and subsequently became the preeminent monastic tradition throughout East Asia.

Reunification of the Chinese Empire: The Sui Dynasty 581–618

The collapse of the Northern Wei in 534 once again plunged northern China into anarchic warfare. In 581, Yang Jian (d. 604), a member of the mixed-blood Tuoba-Chinese aristocracy, staged a bloody coup in which he deposed and killed his own grandson and installed himself as emperor. As iron-fisted ruler of the Sui dynasty (581–618), Yang Jian quickly reasserted military supremacy. In 589 he conquered southern China and restored a unified empire.

Yang Jian was determined to resurrect the grandeur of the Han by rebuilding a centralized bureaucratic state. He immediately abolished the entitlements to political office enjoyed by aristocratic families during the centuries of disunion. Although the inner circle of his government would still be drawn from the hybrid aristocracy fostered by the Northern Wei, high office was a privilege the emperor could bestow or take away as he saw fit.

Yang also retained the system of state landownership that the Northern Wei had put in place. The Northern Wei rulers, descended from nomad chiefs, had introduced policies designed to simplify the task of administering the unfamiliar agrarian world of China. Under the **equal-field system**, the Northern Wei government allocated landholdings to individual households according to formulas based on the number of able-bodied adults the household had to work the land and how many mouths it had to feed. Each household was expected to have roughly equal productive capabilities, so that the state could collect uniform taxes in grain, cloth, and labor or military service from all households. Although aristocratic families largely preserved their extensive landholdings, this system of state landownership provided the Northern Wei with dependable sources of tax revenues and soldiers.

Yang Jian's son and successor, Yang Guang (r. 604–618), further centralized control over resources by building the Grand Canal. This artificial waterway connected the Sui capital at Chang'an in northwestern China with the rice-growing regions of the Yangzi River delta. With the Grand Canal, the central government could tap the burgeoning agricultural wealth of southern China to feed the capital and the military garrisons surrounding it. As we have seen in previous chapters, ancient cities originally depended on their immediate surrounding rural areas for food and other products. The construction of the Grand Canal was important, because it allowed Chang'an to draw resources from further away in the countryside with greater ease, thereby increasing its size and power.

The Sui rulers differed sharply from their Han predecessors in their commitment to Buddhism rather than Confucianism. Unlike the uniform culture of the Han rooted in Confucian traditions, the Sui realm encompassed a heterogeneous collection of peoples divided by ancestry, language, and customs. A devout believer in Buddhism since childhood, Yang Jian recognized Buddhism's potential to aid him in rebuilding a universal empire. Buddhism was equally entrenched in all of China and could provide a set of common values that would unite his subjects. Yang Jian cultivated his self-image as a chakravartin king and imitated the example of Ashoka by building hundreds of Buddhist shrines and monasteries throughout the empire.

Yet the Sui dynasty ended as abruptly as it began. Foreign affairs, rather than domestic problems, proved the dynasty's undoing. From the outset the Sui had tempestuous relations with their Korean neighbors. In 612 Yang Guang launched an invasion of the Korean peninsula that ended in disastrous defeat. When the emperor insisted on preparing a new offensive, his generals revolted against him, and he was assassinated in 618. One of his former generals, Li Yuan (565–635), declared himself emperor of a new dynasty, the Tang.

The Power of Tang China 618–907

The coup that brought the Tang dynasty to power was only the latest in a series of coups led by the Tuoba-Chinese aristocratic clans dating back to the fall of the Northern Wei. Yet unlike its predecessors, the Tang fashioned an enduring empire, the wealthiest and most powerful state in Asia (see Map 10.2). Given their roots in both the Chinese and Tuoba nobilities, the Tang rulers laid equal claim to the worlds of the steppe nomads and settled peoples. They extended Chinese supremacy over the oasis city-states of the eastern steppe, which further fragmented the Turkic confederation. Within China, they revived Confucian traditions while building on the institutional foundations of the Northern Wei and Sui to reestablish a strong bureaucratic state.

At the pinnacle of its political supremacy in the late seventh century, the Tang dynasty was beset by a jarring crisis. During the reign of the sickly emperor Gaozong (r. 650–683), the empress Wu Zhao (625–705) took an increasingly assertive role in governing the empire. Fierce opposition from the aristocrats who dominated the Tang court provoked Empress Wu to unleash a campaign of terror against her enemies. At the same time she carefully nurtured support among lesser aristocrats, expanding the use of civil service examinations to broaden access to bureaucratic office.

In 690 Wu Zhao set aside the Tang dynasty and declared her own Zhou dynasty, becoming the only woman ever to rule as emperor of China. Although Confucian historians depicted her in the harshest possible light, there is little evidence that the empire's prosperity diminished during her reign. Shortly before her death in 705, however, Empress Wu was forced to abdicate, and the Tang dynasty was restored.

The Tang capital of Chang'an had been built by the Sui founder, Yang Jian, near the site of the ancient Han capital. The Chinese conceived of their capital not only as the seat of government but also as the axis of cosmological order. The capital's design—laid out as a nearly perfect square, with its main gate facing south—expressed the principles of order and balance that imperial rule was expected to embody. Imperial palaces, government offices, marketplaces, and residential areas were symmetrically arranged along a central north-south avenue in checkerboard fashion. Two great marketplaces, enclosed by walls and gates, were laid out in the city's eastern and western halves. The bustling Western Market, terminus of the Silk Road, teemed with foreign as well as Chinese merchants. The more sedate Eastern

Sui Patronage of Buddhism

Chan Buddhism A Buddhist devotional tradition, originating in China, that emphasizes salvation through personal conduct, meditation, and mystical enlightenment; also known as Zen Buddhism.

equal-field system A system of state-controlled landownership created by the Northern Wei dynasty in China that attempted to allocate equitable portions of land to all households.

A	Imperial Palace	—	Wall
B	Administrative City	▨	Imperial building
C	Western Market	▨	Government building
D	Eastern Market	▨	Market
E	Daming Palace and Park	▨	Residential district
F	Hibiscus Gardens and Serpentine Lake		

Chang'an, c. 700

The Imperial Capital of Chang'an

Market catered to an elite clientele of officials and aristocrats. The cosmopolitan styles of life and culture radiating from Chang'an reverberated throughout East Asia, shaping tastes in fashion, furnishings, and pastimes, as well as music, dance, and art (see Lives and Livelihoods: Tea Drinkers in Tang China). Chang'an was an economic and cultural crossroads of immense importance not just to China, but to all of Asia.

Demise of Tang Power

Yet the gilded glory of Tang civilization masked deepening political and economic divisions. In some ways, the Tang were victims of their own success. Aristocratic factions jockeyed for control of the court and the riches and privileges at its disposal. Economic prosperity and commercial growth unleashed market forces that eroded the foundations of the equal-field landownership system and jeopardized the state's financial stability. The gravest challenge to Tang rule came in 755, when An Lushan (ahn loo-shahn), a Sogdian general who commanded the Tang armies along the northeastern frontier, revolted. Convinced that he was about to fall victim to court intrigues, An rallied other generals to his side and marched on Chang'an. The emperor was forced to abandon the capital and seek sanctuary in the remote southwest. The dynasty survived, but probably only because An Lushan was assassinated—by his son—in 757. The rebellion finally was suppressed in 763, thanks to the crucial aid of Turkic Uighur mercenaries from Central Asia.

Although the Tang dynasty endured for another 150 years, it never recovered from the catastrophe of the An Lushan rebellion. The court ceded much military and civil authority to

MAP 10.2   East Asia, c. 650

The early Tang emperors sought to reassert Chinese dominion over the eastern steppe, including Manchuria and Korea. Tang military assistance helped the Korean kingdom of Silla to topple Koguryo, long the most powerful of the Korean states, in 668. Although Tang China exerted a powerful cultural influence on its East Asian neighbors, Silla and the newly christened emperors of Japan retained their political independence.

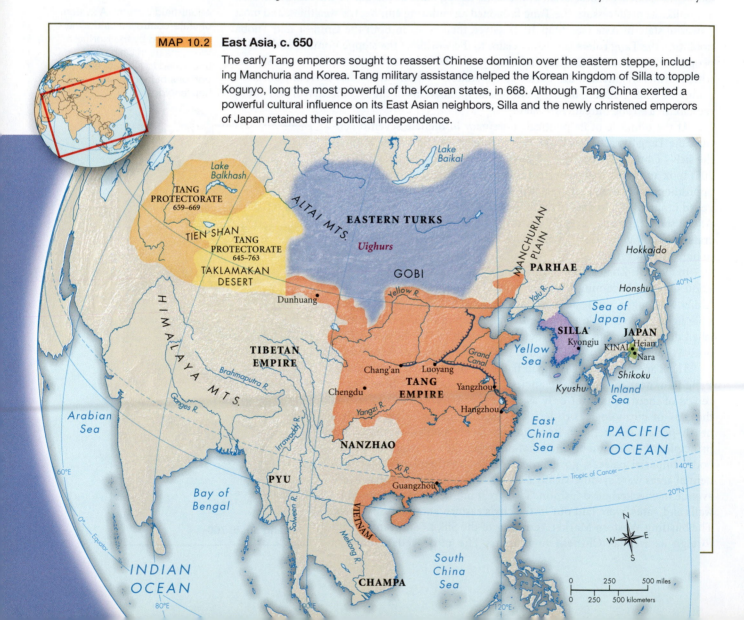

provincial warlords. The rebellion wrecked the empire's finances by forcing the government to abandon the equal-field system and relinquish its control over landholdings. Many of the millions of peasants displaced by marauding armies took refuge in the south, which escaped much of the devastation suffered by the north China heartland. The aristocratic families who had dominated government and society since the Han dynasty were perhaps the major casualties of the rebellion. Tethered to the weakened Tang court, their estates lying in ruin, the old aristocracy clung to its prestige but never regained its power.

China and Its Neighbors

At the height of its power in the late second century B.C.E., the Han Empire had annexed portions of the Korean peninsula and Vietnam and established colonial rule over the native peoples of these regions. The introduction of the Chinese written language, as well as China's political institutions and cultural heritage, exerted a lasting influence on Korea and Vietnam, and later on Japan as well. The rise and fall of the Sui and Tang empires gave birth to East Asia as a common civilization divided into separate national states. Although each state had a unique identity and aggressively asserted its independence, Chinese policies and influences profoundly shaped how each of them developed. Elites in Korea, Vietnam, and Japan all looked to China for political and cultural models, adapting Chinese practices to suit local conditions.

Vietnam

Local rulers continued to resist foreign domination after the Han Empire conquered northern Vietnam in 111 B.C.E. In 40 C.E. a Viet queen, Trung Trac, and her sister led a revolt against the tribute demands of the Han officials. A Han general ruthlessly crushed the rebellion, executed the Trung sisters, and imposed more direct Chinese control over local society. He also erected a pair of bronze pillars along Vietnam's central coast to mark the boundary of Chinese rule—and by extension to symbolize the limits of civilization itself. Vietnam remained under Chinese dominion after the fall of the Han dynasty, but actual authority passed to a landlord class of mixed Chinese and Vietnamese ancestry linked by cultural and literary traditions to the Chinese world.

Korea

Chinese rule in Korea continued until the nomad invasions that overran north China in the early fourth century C.E. In 313 the Chinese-ruled territories in Korea were seized by Koguryo (koh-goo-ryuh), a recently formed confederation based in southern Manchuria. Pressure from nomad invaders soon forced Koguryo out of Manchuria. Koguryo moved its capital to the site of modern Pyongyang, but it became embroiled in conflict with the states of Paekche (pock-CHAY) and Silla (SHEE-lah), which had sprung up in the southern peninsula.

Japan

The earliest reference to the Japanese islands in Chinese records refers to an embassy dispatched to the Chinese court in 238 by Himiko (hee-mee-KOH), queen of the Japanese Wa people. Himiko was described as a spinster sorceress whom the Wa had elected as ruler to instill unity and curb the violent disorder that had wracked the archipelago for generations. Himiko's stature as supreme ruler reflected a pattern of dual-gender rulership that was a distinctive feature of early states in Japan.

At the time that Himiko's envoys arrived in China, influences from the mainland had only recently set in motion what would become a profound transformation in the economy and society of the Japanese islands. Settled agriculture based on rice cultivation had developed in Japan only since the fourth century B.C.E. Bronze and iron wares—chiefly weapons and prestige goods such as bronze mirrors—appeared together in the archipelago, probably in the first century C.E. During the first four centuries C.E., the population of the Japanese islands grew rapidly, in part because of immigration from the continent.

During the fourth century the Yamato kingdom in Kinai, the region around the modern city of Osaka, gained dominance in the Japanese islands. The Yamato "great kings" may or may not have descended from the Wa lineage of Himiko, but their power clearly derived from their success as warrior chiefs. Although the Yamato won the Chinese court's

Tea Drinkers in Tang China

Tea Drinking and Buddhist Hospitality

During the Tang dynasty tea drinking became an indispensable part of Chinese social life. This painting is a sixteenth-century copy of one attributed to the Tang artist Yan Liben (d. 673). It illustrates the story of a scholar who visits an elderly monk, intending to steal a famous work of calligraphy for the Tang emperor. After the monk and the scholar devote several days to lofty talk of art, the monk finally shows the treasured heirloom to his guest, who snatches it away. Here the scholar and the monk converse while two servants prepare tea for them. (National Palace Museum, Taiwan, Republic of China.)

The wild tea plant is native to the mountainous borderlands between China and India. References to drinking an infusion of fresh tea leaves in hot water date back to the first century B.C.E., but the vogue for drinking tea made from roasted leaves became widespread during the Tang dynasty. In the mid-eighth century a Tang scholar-official named Lu Yu wrote *The Classic of Tea*, which became so widely celebrated as a handbook of connoisseurship that tea merchants made porcelain statues of Lu Yu and worshiped him as their patron deity.

In Lu Yu's estimation, the finest teas were produced in Sichuan in western China and in the hilly region south of the Yangzi River, along China's eastern coast. Tea plants flourished best in a humid climate and in stony, well-drained soils on mountain slopes. After the outbreak of the An Lushan rebellion in 755, many peasants fled war-torn northern China and settled in the upland valleys of the south, where the rugged terrain was far better suited to tea cultivation than to rice agriculture. Over the next four centuries, as the popularity of tea drinking rose, tea cultivation

recognition as rulers of Japan, they only gradually extended their authority over the heterogeneous local chiefdoms scattered across the archipelago.

Warrior Rule in Korea and Japan

Meanwhile, in the Korean peninsula, the practice of mounted warfare developed by steppe nomads such as the Tuoba upset the balance of power. Koguryo had quickly imitated the Tuoba style of mounted warfare, in which both warriors and horses were clad in full body armor. At the start of the fifth century, Koguryo decisively defeated the combined armies of Paekche and their Yamato allies. The Paekche king abandoned his capital near modern Seoul and resettled in the southwestern corner of the peninsula. The militarization of the Yamato state in the fourth and fifth centuries was accompanied by a sharp increase in the incidence of warfare in the Japanese islands, fueled by imports of iron weapons from Korea. As in Korea, a warrior aristocracy now dominated in Japan.

spearheaded settlement of the interior provinces of southern China.

Tea was harvested in the spring. Although large tea plantations hired both men and women, in peasant households the task of tea picking fell almost exclusively to women, of all ages. "Tea comes in chopped, loose, powdered, and brick varieties, but in all cases the tea leaves are simply picked, steamed, roasted, pounded, and sealed in a ceramic container,"[1] Lu wrote, but he scrupulously differentiated many types of tea and methods of preparation. In Lu Yu's day, roasted tea leaves usually were pressed into bricks for ease of storage and transport. Fragments of these bricks were crushed or ground into a fine powder before brewing.

Originally, drinking tea was a leisurely pastime of the elite, but over the course of the Tang dynasty, tea became a common staple in all social classes. Lu Yu greatly esteemed tea for its medicinal value:

> Because tea is of "cold" nature it is most suitable as a beverage. A person who ordinarily is moderate in disposition and temperament but feeling hot and dry, melancholic, or suffering from headaches, soreness of the eyes, aching in the four limbs, or pains in the hundred joints should take four or five sips of tea. Its flavor can compare favorably with the most buttery of liquors, or the sweetest dew of Heaven.[2]

Feng Yan, a contemporary of Lu Yu, attributed the rising popularity of tea to Chan Buddhist monks, who drank tea to remain wakeful and alert during their rigorous meditation exercises. Monastic regulations prohibited monks from eating an evening meal but allowed them to drink tea while fasting. The diary of the Japanese Buddhist monk Ennin, who traveled throughout China on a pilgrimage between 838 and 847, contains many references to tea as a courtesy provided to guests, as a gift, and as an offering placed on the altars of Buddhist divinities and saints.

The habit of tea drinking also spread beyond the borders of China. Feng Yan reported that "Uighur Turks who came to the capital bringing herds of fine horses for sale would hasten to the marketplace and buy tea before returning home."[3] The stock-raising nomads of Central Asia and Tibet flavored their tea with butter or fermented milk.

Lu Yu's commentary bristles with sharply worded judgments about the aesthetics of preparing and drinking tea. For example, he observed that it was common to "stew tea together with finely chopped onion, fresh ginger, orange peel, or peppermint, which is boiled until a glossy film forms, or the brew turns foamy."[4] But in Lu's view such vile concoctions were "like water tossed into a ditch."[5] In choosing tea bowls Lu favored the celadon (sea green) hue of the Yue porcelains of eastern China as a fitting complement to the greenish color of tea. Later generations of tea connoisseurs in China and Japan developed complex tea ceremonies that became fixtures of refined social life.

---

1. Translated from Lu Yu, *The Classic of Tea*, Chapter 6.
2. Ibid., Chapter 1.
3. Translated from Feng Yan, *Master Feng's Record of Things Seen and Heard*, Chapter 6.
4. Lu, *The Classic of Tea*, Chapter 6.
5. Ibid.

QUESTIONS TO CONSIDER

1. How did Buddhist religious practices promote tea drinking?

2. Why did the cultivation of tea in China increase dramatically during the Tang dynasty?

For Further Information:

Evans, John C. *Tea in China: The History of China's National Drink*. New York: Greenwood Press, 1992.

Sen Shōshitsu XV. *The Japanese Way of Tea: From Its Origins in China to Sen Rikyū*. Honolulu: University of Hawaii Press, 1998.

Buddhism first arrived in Korea in the mid-fourth century. The Koguryo kings lavishly supported Buddhist monasteries and encouraged the propagation of Buddhism among the people. Paekche and Silla adopted Buddhism as their official religion in the early sixth century. In 552 a Paekche king sent a letter to the Yamato ruler in Japan urging him to adopt Buddhism, which "surpasses all other doctrines," adding that in Korea "there are none who do not reverently receive its teachings."[3] Koguryo and Silla also dispatched Buddhist monks to Japan, and it was a Koguryo monk, Hyeja (tee ay-JUH), who after his arrival in Japan in 595 became tutor to the regent Prince Shōtoku (SHOW-toe-koo) (573–621). Shōtoku subsequently sent missions to China, and their reports inspired him to imitate both the Sui system of imperial government and its fervent devotion to Buddhism. In both Korea and Japan, Buddhist monasteries became far more

Spread of Buddhism to Korea and Japan

Korea, c. 600

powerful institutions than in China, but they still looked to China for innovations in religious doctrines and practices.

The fall of the Sui dynasty did not resolve the tense confrontation between the Chinese empire and Koguryo. The Tang rulers formed an alliance with Silla, the rising power in the southern part of the Korean peninsula. With Chinese support, Silla first defeated Paekche and then in 668 conquered Koguryo, unifying Korea under a single ruler for the first time. Although the Tang court naively assumed that Silla would remain a client state under Tang imperial dominion, the Silla kings quickly established their independence.

The growing power of the Tang was witnessed with great trepidation at the Yamato court. In 645, after a violent succession dispute, sweeping political reforms recast the Yamato monarchy in the image of Tang imperial institutions. Efforts to strengthen the hand of the Yamato king and his government intensified after the Tang-Silla alliance heightened fears of invasion from the mainland. The court issued a law code, based on that of the Tang, that sought to adapt Chinese institutions such as the equal-field landownership system to Japanese circumstances. At the same time, the Japanese court remade its national identity by replacing the dynastic title Yamato with a Chinese-inspired name, Nihon (nee-HOHN) ("Land of the Rising Sun"). Although their concepts of rulership were partly borrowed from Chinese models, the Japanese emperors (as they now called themselves) also asserted their independence from and equality with the Tang Empire.

Tang Influence on East Asian Neighbors

In the early eighth century, Tang China reached the height of its influence on its East Asian neighbors. In Korea, Japan, and Vietnam alike, the Chinese written language served as the *lingua franca*, or common language, of government, education, and religion. Adoption of Chinese forms of Buddhism reinforced Tang China's cultural preeminence. In northern Vietnam, Chinese ways of life became deeply implanted in the fertile plains of the Red River delta around modern Hanoi. Although the Vietnamese inhabitants of the plains chafed under Tang rule, their adoption of rice farming and settled livelihoods in-

Horyuji Monastery
After gaining the patronage of rulers and aristocrats in China in the fourth century C.E., Buddhism soon spread to Korea and Japan. The Horyuji monastery, founded by Japan's Prince Shōtoku in the seventh century, was built in a Chinese architectural style adjacent to the prince's palace. The five-story pagoda, believed to be the world's oldest wooden building, houses a statue of the bodhisattva Guanyin (known in Japan as Kannon). (Vanni/Art Resource, NY.)

creasingly alienated them from the forest-dwelling highland peoples, the ancestors of the modern Hmong (mahng). Thus Chinese culture created connections between all of the states of East Asia. Elites in China, Korea, Vietnam, and Japan were bound together by a common language, similar political ideas and institutions, and shared religious beliefs. East Asian elites outside of China had something else in common, however: they were united in resisting Chinese rule.

By the early tenth century, the political boundaries of East Asia had assumed contours that would remain largely intact down to the present. Silla (supplanted by the new Koryo dynasty in 935) ruled over a unified Korea. Most of the Japanese archipelago acknowledged the sovereignty of the emperor at Kyoto, the new capital modeled on the design of Chang'an and founded in 792. In 939, after the Tang dynasty was finally deposed, local chieftains in Vietnam ousted their Chinese overlords and eventually formed their own Dai Viet kingdom. Although Korea, Japan, and Vietnam achieved lasting political independence, they remained within the gravitational pull of a common East Asian cultural sphere centered on China. At the same time, the decline of the Silk Road caravan trade and the waning popularity of Buddhism in the land of its origin loosened the ties between China and India. Henceforth, the cultural worlds of East Asia and South Asia increasingly diverged.

East Asian Political Boundaries and Common Culture

The Consolidation of Hindu Society in India

The period of the Gupta Empire (c. 320–540) often is regarded as India's classical age. Indian historians portray the Guptas as the last great native rulers of India—a dynasty under which a revived Vedic religion surpassed the appeal of the dissident religions of Buddhism and Jainism. Yet the power of the Gupta monarchs was less extensive than that of the Mauryan emperors they claimed as their forebears. Gupta rule was largely confined to the Ganges River Valley heartland, and by the 480s the Hun invasions had already dealt the dynasty a mortal blow (see Chapter 6).

> **FOCUS**
>
> Why did the religious practices of Hinduism gain a broader following in Indian society than the ancient Vedic religion and its chief rival, Buddhism?

The demise of the Gupta Empire, like that of the Roman Empire in Europe, resulted in the fragmentation of political power and the formation of a system of regional states. Unlike in China, however, political disunity remained the norm in India for centuries to come. Not until the rise of the Mughal Empire in the sixteenth century would India be unified again. The absence of a unified state did not deflect the emerging cultural and social trends of the Gupta era, however. On the contrary, in post-Gupta India, as in post-Roman Europe, common values, social practices, and political institutions penetrated more deeply into all corners of the subcontinent.

Land and Wealth

The Chinese pilgrim Xuanzang, whom we met at the start of this chapter, arrived in India during the heyday of King Harsha (r. 606–647), perhaps the most powerful of the post-Gupta monarchs (see Map 10.3). Yet Harsha's kingdom depended on his own charismatic leadership, and it perished soon after his death. Other dynasties survived longer, but their authority was confined to the ruling families' regional power base. Nonetheless, a strikingly uniform political culture spread throughout India. In addition, regional states expanded their reach into hinterland territories, bringing neighboring hill and forest tribes under their sway and assimilating them to the norms of caste society. Thus, although political ties among Indian peoples were weak, the cultural connections were increasingly strong.

The Gupta monarchs, recognizing that their control over local societies was limited, had started awarding royal lands to their officials and Brahman priests. The Gupta expected the recipients to take charge of settling and cultivating these lands. In post-Gupta

Land Grants and Village Society

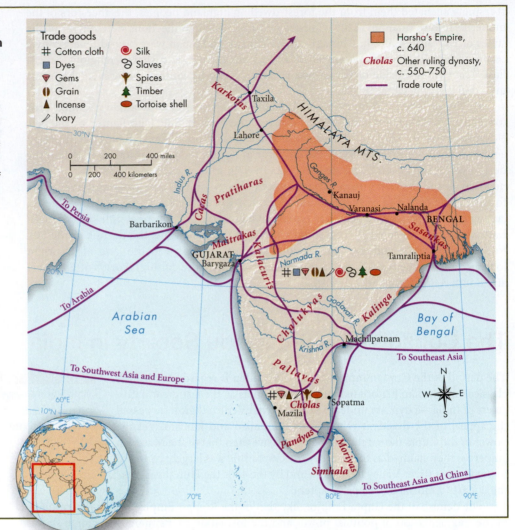

MAP 10.3

The Indian Subcontinent in the Age of Harsha, c. 640

A century after the demise of the Gupta Empire, King Harsha succeeded in restoring unified rule over most of the Gupta territories in northern India. Although tolerant of all religious faiths, Harsha became a devoted follower of Buddhism and patron to the Chinese pilgrim Xuanzang. After Harsha's death in 647, his empire disintegrated into numerous small states.

times, such land grants were often bestowed on corporate bodies such as temples, monasteries, and Brahman communities. Xuanzang observed that "the royal lands are divided into four parts: one portion provides for the needs of the court and sacrificial offerings; the second portion is given as compensation to officers and ministers for their service; the third is awarded to men of intelligence, learning, and talent; and the fourth establishes charitable endowments for religious institutions."[4] In some cases the grants included whole villages and their populations, and the peasants fell under the administrative and legal jurisdiction of the grant recipients (see Reading the Past: A Copper-Plate Land Grant Inscription).

This system of royal land grants stabilized the agricultural base of society and the economy while fostering a landlord class of Brahmans who combined religious authority, caste prestige, and landed wealth. Yet nothing like the large manors or serfdom characteristic of Latin Christendom at this time appeared in India. The peasant household remained the basic unit of work and livelihood. Rural society, especially in the south, typically was governed by village assemblies that enjoyed some measure of independence from their lords.

The practice of royal land grants transferred most wealth to temples and Brahman landlords. These landowners dominated the local economy, garnering tribute from the lands and peasants attached to them and controlling enterprises such as mills, oil presses, and moneylending. Beginning in the tenth century, temples dedicated to gods such as Shiva and Vishnu were built on an unprecedented monumental scale, symbolizing the

A Copper-Plate Land Grant Inscription

This inscription from 753 records a land grant made by the king of the Pallava dynasty in southern India to the king's religious teacher, a local Brahman. The grant was recorded on eleven copper plates that were strung together on a copper wire and stamped with the Pallava royal seal—a bull and the phallic symbol associated with the god Shiva.

The inscription begins with a eulogy written in Sanskrit lauding the king. Details of the land grant, written in the local language, Tamil, follow. This passage from the Tamil portion defines the relationship between the land grant recipient and the local village community.

> Having seen the order . . . we, the inhabitants, went to the boundaries which the headman of the district pointed out, walked around the village from right to left, and planted milk-bushes and placed stones around it. . . . The recipient shall enjoy the wet land and the dry land included within these four boundaries, wherever the iguana runs and the tortoise crawls, and shall be permitted to dig river channels and irrigation channels. . . . Those who take and use the water in these channels by pouring out baskets, by cutting branch channels, or by employing small levers shall pay a fine to be collected by the king. The recipient and his descendants shall enjoy the houses, house gardens, and so forth, and shall have the right to build houses and halls of burnt tiles. The land included

within these boundaries we have endowed with all exemptions. The recipient shall enjoy the exemptions obtaining in this village without paying for the oil-mill and looms, the hire of the well-diggers, the share of the Brahmans of the king, the share of shengodi [a plant], the share of figs, the share of lamp black, the share of corn-ears, the share of the headman, the share of the potter, the sifting of [rice] paddy, the price of ghee [clarified butter], the price of cloth, the share of cloth, the hunters, messengers, dancing-girls, the grass, the best cow and the best bull, the share of the district, cotton-threads, servants, palmyra molasses, the fines to the accountant and the minister.

Source: Kasakkudi Plates of Nandivarman, *South Indian Inscriptions,* Archaeological Survey of India, vol. 2, part 3 (Madras: Government Press, 1896), 360–362.

EXAMINING THE EVIDENCE

1. What services—supported by the taxes and fees explicitly exempted from this land grant—did the village community provide to its members?

2. Why did rights to water figure so prominently in this grant?

dominance of the temple over community life. In this way, royal land grants established a connection between local elites and institutions and the king, even as they increased the wealth and power of land grant recipients.

Devotional Worship in Hinduism

Beginning in Gupta times, Brahmanical religion regained its primacy, while competing religious movements such as Buddhism and Jainism retreated to the margins of Indian society. The resurgence of Brahmanical religion during this period—in the form now called **Hinduism**—stemmed both from changes in religious practice and from the wealth and power Brahman groups obtained through royal patronage.

The farthest-reaching change in Hindu practice was displacement of the sacrificial rituals only Brahmans could perform by forms of worship all ranks of society could participate in. Personal devotion to gods such as Shiva and Vishnu—whose cults took many distinct forms, depending on regional traditions and even individual imagination—replaced Brahmanical rituals as the core of religious life.

Devotional worship, or *bhakti*, was celebrated as the highest form of religious practice in religious texts known as the **Puranas**. The Puranas instructed believers in the proper forms for worshiping a specific god. Hinduism, like Buddhism and Jainism, centered on the salvation of the individual, regardless of one's caste. At the same time, Hinduism fostered collective worship of the gods enshrined at local village temples. Bhakti worship also encouraged more active participation by women, who previously had been excluded from religious life.

Hinduism The name given (first by Muslims) to the body of religious teachings, derived from the Brahmanical religion of the Vedic era, that developed in response to the challenge of Buddhism.

Puranas Religious writings, derived from oral tradition and written down during the first millennium C.E., that recount the legends of the gods and serve as the canonical texts of popular Hinduism.

Proliferation of Hindu Temples and Deities

Hindu temples joined religious piety to political power. The Puranas constructed genealogical ties between ancient heroes and gods and present-day rulers. Royal inscriptions also celebrated the close relationship between kings and the gods, in some cases asserting that the king was an incarnation of a god such as Shiva or Vishnu.

The focus on worshiping images of the gods that accompanied the spread of Hinduism accelerated the trend of founding temples through royal land grants. Temples grew in size and splendor. Major temples employed large retinues of Brahman priests, students, and caretakers. Many temples also maintained troupes of female attendants—known as *devadasis*—who were "married" to the local god. The devadasis performed rituals that combined music and dance and served as temple wardens. Devadasis at major temples often were highly educated and accomplished artists, respected in local society and accorded a freedom from social convention denied to married women. At poorly endowed temples, however, devadasis sometimes had no choice but to sell their sexual services to support themselves.

The rapid growth of local temples and bhakti devotion spurred intense adoration of a multitude of new or transformed deities. The proliferation of deities resulted from the absorption of local cults into Hindu religion. People worshiped the principal Hindu gods, Shiva and Vishnu, in many different incarnations. Krishna, an incarnation of Vishnu, appeared both as the wise philosopher-warrior of the celebrated philosophical poem *Baghavad Gita* ("Song of the Lord") and as a rustic herdsman, the patron of cowherds and devoted lover of the milkmaid Radha. Kings and warriors particularly venerated Shiva, an icon of sovereign authority and wielder of terrible powers of destruction. The elephant-headed god Ganesh was recast as the offspring of Shiva and his elegant consort (or spouse) Parvati.

Worship of goddesses who originated in local fertility cults marked a significant departure in Hinduism from the older Vedic tradition. Consort goddesses were seen as necessary complements to male gods such as Shiva, whose power and energy could be activated only through union with a female. Yet goddesses such as Lakshmi, the consort of Vishnu, and Shiva's many wives also attracted their own personal followings. Brahman priests condoned these goddess cults, which became a distinctive feature of Hinduism.

As he traveled about India, Xuanzang was appalled by the decayed state of Buddhism in its homeland. Monuments lay in ruin; once-grand monasteries stood desolate. Arriving at Varanasi (the modern city of Benares in northern India), which Buddhists revered as the site of the Buddha's first sermon, the Chinese pilgrim found "a densely crowded city teeming with rich and prosperous inhabitants, their houses filled with great wealth and rare goods." But "few of them revered Buddhist teachings. . . . Of Deva [Hindu] temples there were more than a hundred, and more than ten thousand adherents of the non-Buddhist sects, the great majority professing devotion to Shiva."[5] Popular devotion to Buddhism was fading, and by the thirteenth century it would vanish altogether.

New Economic and Social Trends

The land grant system and the temple-centered economy it spawned stimulated the expansion of agriculture and village settlement into frontier areas. New irrigation and fertilization techniques also promoted the growth of the agricultural economy. The encroaching agrarian states with their caste-based social order incorporated many tribal groups in the forests and hills. An inscription dated 861 celebrated the conquest of a frontier area in western India by a king of the Pratihara dynasty, boasting that he had made the land "fragrant with the leaves of blue lotuses and pleasant with groves of mango and *madhuka*-fruit trees, and covered it with leaves of excellent sugarcane."[6]

The prominence of the temple-centered economy in these centuries also reflected the decline of towns and trade. Xuanzang sadly observed that people had abandoned many of the great cities in which Buddhism had thrived in the past. Archaeological research confirms

The Many Faces of Shiva
Hindus worship the god Shiva in many forms, as both a creator and a destroyer. The faces on this sculpture—which include a bust of Shiva's consort Parvati, the embodiment of feminine composure and wifely devotion—portray Shiva as both a fierce exterminator and a serene ascetic. The four faces encircle a *linga*, an erect phallus symbolizing Shiva's powers of fertility and procreation. (Erich Lessing/Art Resource, NY.)

the decline of urban centers in the Ganges Valley between the seventh and tenth centuries. Circulation of coins ceased in many areas. The proliferation of land grants attests to the growing importance of wealth in the form of landed property and goods rather than money.

As local agricultural economies became more important, international trade declined. Arab seafarers frequented the western coast of the peninsula to obtain spices, pepper, gems, and teak in exchange for horses, but India was largely severed from the lucrative Central Asian caravan trade now in the hands of hostile Turkic and Muslim neighbors. Itinerant traders and local merchants remained active, however, supplying agricultural produce, ghee (clarified butter), betel leaves (a popular stimulant), and cotton cloth to ordinary villagers and procuring ritual necessities and luxury goods for temples and royal courts.

As Brahman religion and social norms became more deeply entrenched in village society and the frontier tribal regions, the structure of caste society underwent profound changes. Many of the upstart regional dynasties came from obscure origins. Although these ruling families strove to invent a noble ancestry in the *Kshatriya* (warrior) caste, status in court society depended more on personal relations and royal favor than caste standing.

The rigid formal hierarchy of the four major caste groups—Brahmans (priests), Kshatriyas (warriors), Vaishyas (merchants and farmers), and Shudras (servile peoples)—could not contain the growing complexity of Indian society, especially with the inclusion of pastoral nomads and forest-dwelling tribes. Social status based on occupation—known as *jati*—often superseded ancestral birth, at least on the lower rungs of the caste hierarchy. Jatis developed their own cultural identities, which were expressed in customs, marriage rules, food taboos, and religious practices. Merchant and artisan jati groups acquired an institutional identity as professional guilds. Leaders of wealthy jatis sometimes became temple wardens and persons of distinction in local society.

Yet the status of merchants and artisans often varied from place to place. In some localities, certain craftsmen jati—for example, butchers, shoemakers, and cloth fullers—were required to live outside the town walls, like Untouchables and other social groups deemed ritually unclean. Blacksmiths and carpenters formed special organizations in an effort to raise their social standing. The court also granted special privileges to groups of artisans who worked for it, such as copperplate engravers, weavers in the employ of the royal family, and masons building royal temples and palaces.

The rights and privileges of women, like those of men, differed according to caste and local custom. As in most cultures, writers and artists often idealized women, but they did so in terms that distinguished feminine from masculine qualities. Whereas the ideal man was described in strongly positive language—emphasizing, for example, ambition, energy, mastery of knowledge and spiritual paths, and skill in poetry and conversation—female virtues were often conveyed through negative constructions, such as absence of jealousy, greed, arrogance, frivolity, and anger. These characterizations reflect prevailing notions of women's weaknesses.

Women were encouraged to marry young and remain devoted to their husbands throughout their lives. The earliest reference to the practice of *sati*, in which a widow commits suicide following the death of her husband, dates from the sixth century. Yet only women of the Kshatriya caste were expected to perform sati, primarily when the husband had died heroically in battle. But the fate of a widow in this patriarchal society was often grim. Unable to inherit her husband's property or to remarry, a widow depended on her husband's family for support. However, women who chose not to marry, such as nuns and devadasis, were accepted as normal members of society.

Court Society and Culture

The gradual unraveling of the Gupta Empire left a multitude of local kings. Each claimed exalted ancestry and strove to shore up his social base by awarding land grants. In this political world—referred to as the "circle of kings" in the *Arthashastra* ("The Science of Material Gain"), a renowned treatise on statecraft—each ruler pursued his advantage through complex maneuvers over war and diplomacy involving numerous enemies and

jati In India, a caste status based primarily on occupation.

The Lure of Court Life

The sumptuous splendor of Indian court life drew sharp criticism from Buddhist and Jain ascetics. At the left of this mural, created in around 500 to represent a Buddhist legend, King Mahajanaka, wearing a crown and garlanded with pearls, sits in a stately palace. His wife and palace ladies fail to persuade him to continue his life of ease and luxury, however—at the right the king rides away from the palace, having renounced worldly pleasures. (Frédéric Soltan/Corbis.)

allies. Kings achieved political dominance by gaining fealty and tribute, not by annexing territory, as was usual in China, for example. The consequence was that connections between rulers were of paramount importance.

Given the treachery and uncertainty of the "circle of kings," rulers eagerly sought divine blessings through lavish patronage of temples and their gods. They portrayed themselves as devoted servants of the supreme gods Shiva and Vishnu, and they demanded similar reverence and subservience from their courtiers and subjects. The rituals of the royal court gave monarchs an opportunity to display their majesty and affirm their authority over lesser lords. As we also see in Europe and the Islamic world at this time, royal courts became the main arenas of political intercourse, social advancement, and cultural accomplishment.

Attendance at court and participation in its elaborate ceremonial and cultural life was crucial to establishing membership in the ruling class. Marrying a daughter to a powerful king was the surest means of securing a family's social and political eminence. Important kings had numerous wives, each with her own residence and retinue. Relations within royal households were governed by the same strategies of alliance, rivalry, and intrigue that characterized the political realm of the "circle of kings." In both cases, personal connections played a central role in the distribution and exercise of power.

Kama Sutra
The lifestyle of the courtly elite was exemplified in the *Kama Sutra* ("The Art of Pleasure"), composed during the Gupta period. Most famous for its frank celebration of sexual love, the *Kama Sutra* was intended as a guidebook to educate affluent men in the rules of upper-class social life. It is addressed to a "man about town" who has received an education, obtained a steady source of wealth (whether from land, trade, or inheritance), established a family, and settled in a city populated by other men of good birth and breeding. The book enumerates sixty-four "fine arts" that a cultivated man should master, from dancing and swordsmanship to skill in conversation and poetry. The *Kama Sutra* also dwells on the protocols of courtship and erotic love, although only one of its seven books is devoted to sexual techniques. Above all, the *Kama Sutra* exalts mastery of the self: only through discipline of the mind and senses can a man properly enjoy wealth and pleasure while avoiding the pitfalls of excess and indulgence.

The *Kama Sutra* describes an urbane lifestyle that imitated the worldly sophistication and conspicuous consumption of the king and his court. It dismisses rural society, in contrast, as boorish and stultifying. Village life dulls one's sensibilities and coarsens manners and speech. Village youths, complained a contemporary poet, "cannot grasp facial expressions, nor do they have the intelligence to understand subtle meanings of puns and innuendos."[7] Despite such assertions that a vast cultural gulf separated the court from the countryside, courtly culture and its values permeated the entire ruling class, including local lords and Brahman landowners.

The post-Gupta era witnessed steady cultural integration throughout the Indian subcontinent, even in the absence of political unity. Non-Brahman religions and social values were increasingly marginalized, and by the tenth century Hindu religious culture, as well as the norms of caste society, prevailed in almost all regions.

Cultural Integration

The Diffusion of Indian Traditions to Southeast Asia

Indian culture and religions spread to Southeast Asia before the emergence of indigenous states or literary and philosophical traditions, in a process resembling how China influenced its East Asian neighbors. Thus Indian traditions had a powerful effect on the development of Southeast Asian ideas about kingship and social order and provided a new vocabulary to express cultural and ethical values.

FOCUS

What aspects of Indian religions had the greatest influence on the societies and cultures of Southeast Asia?

Southeast Asian religious beliefs and practices integrated aspects of two Indian religions, Hinduism and Buddhism. As in East Asia, Mahayana Buddhist teachings were readily adapted to local cultures. Hinduism, with its roots in Indian social institutions, especially the caste system, proved less adaptable. Yet some elements of Hinduism, such as bhakti devotional cults and the worship of Shiva, also flourished in Southeast Asia. Given the Brahman priesthood's prominent role in Southeast Asia—despite the absence there of caste societies—it would be more appropriate to refer to this tradition as **Brahmanism** than as Hinduism. Across the mainland and islands of Southeast Asia, aspects of both Buddhism and Brahmanism would intermingle in novel ways, fusing with ancient local traditions to produce distinctive religious cultures (see Map 10.4).

Commerce and Religious Change in Southeast Asia

The spread of Indian religions and cultural traditions to Southeast Asia occurred gradually beginning in the early centuries C.E. Indian influence did not result from conquest or large-scale migration and colonization. Rather, it was carried by Indian merchants and missionaries following the maritime routes from the Bay of Bengal to the South China Sea. Buddhist missionaries were crossing the Southeast Asian seas to China by the second and third centuries C.E. Brahmans, in contrast, lacked the evangelical zeal of Buddhist monks, and Indian law prohibited Brahmans from traveling abroad for fear of jeopardizing their purity of body and spirit. Brahmanism was disseminated to Southeast Asia, therefore, largely via Indian merchant colonies, and also by Southeast Asian natives who traveled to India for study and training and returned as converts.

Historians find evidence for the diffusion of Brahmanism to Southeast Asia in Funan, the first identifiable state in the region, and in Java during the early centuries C.E. The Funan state, based in the lower Mekong River Valley (in present-day Vietnam and Cambodia), flourished during the first to fourth centuries C.E. as the principal trading center between India and China. Contemporary Chinese observers noted that Indian beliefs and practices were prevalent in Funan, as was the use of Indic script in writing. Local lore even attributed the ancestry of the Funan rulers to the marriage of a local princess with an Indian Brahman.

Brahmanism also flourished in central Java, as attested by the presence of Brahman monastic communities and the adoption of many Indian gods into local religion. The

Brahmanism in Funan and Java

Brahmanism The distinctive Hindu religious tradition of Southeast Asia, in which the Brahman priesthood remained dominant despite the absence of a caste system.

MAP 10.4 **States in Southeast Asia, c. 800**
Many Southeast Asian states, such as Angkor in the lower Mekong River Valley and the Sailendra dynasty in Java, were based in fertile agricultural regions. But the Champa and Srivijaya confederations ruled the seas and derived their power from the profits of trade. During its heyday from the seventh to the twelfth centuries, Srivijaya dominated the maritime trade routes linking China with India and the Islamic world.

Brahmanism in Champa

Brahmanism and Buddhism in Angkor

earliest inscriptions in Old Javanese, dating from the late fourth to early fifth centuries, refer to gifts of cattle and gold to Brahman priests and to royal ceremonies apparently derived from Indian precedents.

As in India, local rulers in Southeast Asia appropriated Hindu religious ideas and motifs that meshed with their own worldviews and grafted them onto ancient local traditions. In Champa (along Vietnam's central coast), the cult of Shiva, centered on the worship of stone phalli, resembled older fertility rituals in which people presented offerings to rough stone icons of local gods. In Java, the high gods of Hinduism came to be identified with the island's fearsome volcanoes, which the inhabitants regarded as the homes of the gods. Mountain symbolism is also striking in the architecture of the Buddhist monument of Borobudur (booh-roe-boe-DOOR) in central Java, and in the temple complexes of Angkor in Cambodia (see Seeing the Past: Borobudur: The World's Largest Buddhist Monument, page 331).

Religion and the Constitution of State Power

From the beginning, Southeast Asia's borrowing of religious ideas from India was closely linked to the ambitions of Southeast Asian rulers. Indian traditions that related kingship to all-powerful gods had obvious appeal to local chieftains seeking to augment their authority and power. Both Buddhism and Brahmanism provided models for divine blessing of royal authority. In the Buddhist tradition, the universal monarch, the chakravartin, achieved supremacy through lavish acts of piety and devotion. In the Brahmanical tradition, by contrast, the king partook of divine power by identifying with the high gods, above all Shiva, and received worship from his subjects much as the gods did. This association of the king with the gods sanctified the king's role as ruler and protector of his people. Although the gods might lend aid to the king, ultimately it was the king's personal charisma that endowed him with sovereign power.

The earliest appearance of the worship of Shiva in Southeast Asia is found in Champa, where a loose confederation of local rulers shared power under a weak royal overlord (see again Map 10.4). One Champa king instituted a Shiva cult at the royal shrine at Mi-son, the ritual center of the Champa confederation, in the fourth century. Yet the Champa chiefdoms never coalesced into a centralized state, perhaps because the small coastal plains yielded only meager agricultural surpluses. The Champa chieftains instead relied on piracy and plunder to obtain wealth. Thus Indian political and religious ideas alone were not enough to create a powerful king. Without the resources to pay soldiers and officials and reward allies, kings could never be powerful enough to dominate their wealthiest subjects.

However, where ample resources were combined with a compelling political ideology, powerful kings did emerge. For example, worship of Shiva aided consolidation of state power in the broad plains around the Tonle Sap Lake in the lower Mekong River Valley. The founder of the Angkor kingdom, Jayavarman (JUH-yuh-vahr-mon) II, was pro-

Angkor's Oldest Temple
The earliest kings in Southeast Asia often claimed to be avatars, or incarnations, of the Hindu god Shiva. Upon moving his capital to the new site of Angkor, the Khmer king Yasovarman I (r. 889–910) built Phnom Bahkeng, a temple dedicated to Shiva, on a hill overlooking the city. In the shape of a six-tiered pyramid, the temple symbolizes Mount Meru, the home of the Hindu gods. (Hervé Champollion/ akg-images.)

claimed universal monarch by his Brahman advisers in 802; he consolidated his dominion over the region's local lords by combining devotion to Shiva with homage to himself as deva-raja (divine lord).

During the early phase of the Angkor state, kings delegated control over the land and its inhabitants to officials assigned to temples established throughout the realm by royal charter. The Brahman priesthood managed the administrative affairs as well as the ritual ceremonies of these temples. Not until a century later did one of Jayavarman's successors, Yasovarman (YAH-suh-vahr-mon) I (r. 889–c. 910), consolidate royal authority by establishing his capital at Angkor and building the first of its numerous temple complexes. The many temples he founded at Angkor and elsewhere were dedicated primarily to Shiva, Vishnu, and Buddha. Depending on individual inclinations, later Angkor kings sometimes favored worship of Vishnu—the chief deity at Angkor's most famous temple complex, Angkor Wat—or patronage of Mahayana Buddhism, and their temple-building projects reflected these personal religious allegiances.

Apart from Brahmanism, Mahayana Buddhism was the other Indian religious tradition that initially attracted devotion and patronage in Southeast Asia. Chinese pilgrims in the seventh century described the Pyu and Mon city-states of lower Burma, which had ready access by sea to the great Mahayana monasteries in Bengal, as "Buddhist kingdoms." Burmese ambassadors to the Tang court in the ninth century reported that all children were required to spend some time as novices in Buddhist monasteries. Mahayana Buddhism was also enthusiastically welcomed by Malay chiefs in Sumatra, who had begun to capitalize on a major reorientation of maritime trade routes that occurred between the fourth and sixth centuries.

Mahayana Buddhism in Burma and Sumatra

Previously, merchants had avoided the monsoon winds that dictated the rhythms of seafaring in the Southeast Asian seas. Instead of sailing around the Malay peninsula,

Maritime Trade

ships would land at the Kra Isthmus, the narrowest point along the peninsula. From there, they would carry their goods overland to the Gulf of Siam before setting sail again for the Indochina peninsula. Funan used its strategic location on the more protected eastern shore of the Gulf of Siam to become the major crossroads where merchants from the Indian Ocean could meet those from China. Beginning in the fourth century, however, Malay navigators pioneered an all-sea route through the Straits of Melaka, bypassing the Gulf of Siam altogether. Funan's prosperity abruptly ended, and the ports of southeastern Sumatra replaced Funan as the linchpin of maritime trade (see again Map 10.4).

Trade routes shifted in part because of the growing importance of Southeast Asian products in international trade. Earlier, trade between India and China consisted largely of exchanging Chinese silk for products from western Asia (frankincense, myrrh, and other substances used to make perfume and incense). Gradually, cheaper local substitutes, such as Sumatran camphor and sandalwood from Timor, began to enter this trade, and by the seventh century both Arab and Chinese merchants had become avid buyers of Sumatran pepper and the fine spices (cloves, nutmeg, and mace) from the Molucca Islands far to the east. The Sumatran ports were ideally situated to capture this trade.

The Buddhist Kingdoms of Srivijaya and Sailendra

In the late seventh century, the ruler of the Sumatran port of Palembang founded the first of a series of kingdoms known collectively as Srivijaya (sree-vih-JUH-yuh). Our first image of a ruler of Srivijaya comes from an inscription of 683, which tells how the king celebrated his conquest of a rival city-state and gravely admonished his vanquished foe to accept Buddhism. The rulers of Srivijaya became great patrons of Mahayana Buddhism. The large international community of monks that gathered at Palembang included novices from China seeking instruction from Indian monks.

The rise of Srivijaya was soon followed by the emergence of a lineage of kings in the Kedu Plain of central Java. Known as the Sailendra (SIGH-len-drah) dynasty, these monarchs were equally dedicated to Mahayana Buddhism. Although boasting a rich rice agriculture, the Kedu Plain was isolated from the coast by a ring of mountains, and thus did not have direct access to the maritime commercial world. Nonetheless, in the mid-eighth century the Sailendra kings achieved dominance over the Kedu Plain by borrowing heavily from Indian religious and political traditions, probably through the cordial relations they cultivated with Srivijaya.

The Sailendra kings used Sanskrit sacred texts and administrative language to construct a network of religious and political allegiances under their leadership. They also founded many Buddhist shrines, which attracted monks from as far away as Bengal and Gujarat. The massive monument of Borobudur in central Java testifies to the Sailendra kings' deep faith in Mahayana Buddhism (see Seeing the Past: Borobudur: The World's Largest Buddhist Monument).

Allied to Srivijaya by their common faith and intermarriage between the royal families, the Sailendra dynasty flourished from 750 to 850. In around 850, however, the Sailendra were suddenly expelled from Java by an upstart rival devoted to Shiva. The royal house fled to Sumatra, where they joined their Srivijaya kin. Bereft of Sailendra patronage, the Buddhist monasteries in Java plunged into irreversible decline. Henceforth, Brahmanism predominated in Java until a wave of conversions to Islam began in the fifteenth century.

Indian Religions in Southeast Asia: A Summing-up

Indian religions were assimilated in Southeast Asia as the existing cultural and social frameworks adapted foreign ideas. The potent ideologies of the Sanskrit literary heritage and the organizational skills of Buddhist and Brahman holy men stimulated the formation of states based on divinely sanctioned royal authority. Both the Brahmanical and Buddhist traditions contributed to the rise of monarchies in the maritime realm, in the rice-growing plains of the great river valleys, and in central Java. The Angkor kingdom

Borobudur: The World's Largest Buddhist Monument

The Monument at Borobudur (Luca Tettoni/Corbis.)

The Sailendra kings never built palaces or cities for themselves. Instead they devoted their wealth and resources to building vast monuments displaying their devotion to the Buddhist faith. The massive stone edifice they erected at Borobudur in central Java rises from a fertile plain ringed by imposing volcanoes. Construction of Borobudur began in around 760 and took seventy years to complete.

The exact purpose of the Borobudur monument, which was neither a temple nor a monastery, continues to provoke scholarly debate. Borobudur consists of ten concentric terraces of decreasing size crowned by a bell-shaped stupa, a Buddhist shrine used as a repository for relics or other sacred objects. The terraces are adorned with carved reliefs depicting many episodes from the basic scriptures of Mahayana Buddhism and with more than five hundred statues of Buddhas. The carved reliefs provide a virtual encyclopedia of Mahayana teachings. But they also include many scenes from court life, which spoke more directly of the royal majesty of the Sailendras. Some scholars have suggested that the mountainlike edifice celebrated the Sailendras' exalted stature as "Lords of the Mountains" and marked the dynasty's original home.

By visiting Borobudur, the Buddhist faithful could pass physically and spiritually through the ten stages of devotion necessary to attain enlightenment. Entering from the eastern staircase, they would proceed slowly around each terrace, studying and absorbing the lessons told by the carved reliefs before passing to the next level. To see all the reliefs one must walk around the monument ten times, a distance of three miles. Reliefs at the lower levels retell well-known stories from the life of the Buddha and other holy figures. The higher levels are devoted to the pilgrim Sudhana, who visited 110 teachers in his quest for enlightenment. On the upper levels the narrow galleries of the lower levels give way to three round open terraces surmounted by numerous latticelike stupas enclosing life-size statues of Buddhas. The devotee's ascent of the monument symbolized a spiritual progress from the world of illusion to the realm of enlightenment.

Source: John Miksic, *Borobudur: Golden Tales of the Buddhas* (Hong Kong: Periplus, 1990).

EXAMINING THE EVIDENCE

1. How can we see the architectural design of Borobudur as a physical representation of the world, which in Buddhist cosmology is depicted as a series of circular oceans and continents surrounding a sacred mountain at the center?

2. In what ways does the monument reflect Buddhism's renunciation of worldly life?

represents the most striking case of simultaneous patronage of both Brahmanism and Mahayana Buddhism, but to a lesser degree this eclectic adoption of Indian religions occurred throughout Southeast Asia.

Royal temples and monuments became focal points for amassing wealth in service to the gods, while also serving as testaments to the kings' piety. Local temples likewise accumulated landholdings and stores of treasure, serving as both the economic and the ceremonial hubs of community life. In contrast to Islam, which exercised a powerful centralizing pull and created a common brotherhood of faith across national, ethnic, and cultural boundaries, Indian religions in Southeast Asia—as in India itself—spawned a diverse array of regional religious cultures.

COUNTERPOINT
Sogdian Traders in Central Asia and China

FOCUS

How did the social and economic institutions of the Sogdian merchant network differ from those of the nomadic confederations and the agrarian empires?

The heyday of the overland caravan routes of Central Asia—the Silk Road—was between the fifth and the eighth centuries. Chinese and Persian emperors, nomad chieftains, and kings of oasis city-states all struggled to capture a share of the lucrative Silk Road trade. Yet the great length of the trade routes and the harsh deserts and mountains through which they passed made it impossible for any single political power to dominate the Silk Road. Instead, rulers great and small had to cultivate close ties with those who, in the words of a Moroccan spice merchant turned Christian monk, "to procure silk for the miserable gains of commerce, hesitate not to travel to the uttermost ends of the earth."[8] The Sogdian merchants who linked the steppe lands of the nomads with Asia's great agrarian empires did so through economic enterprise rather than military might or political power.

A Robust Commercial Economy

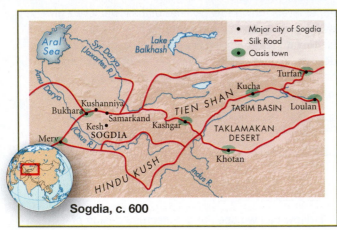

Sogdia, c. 600

Sogdia (SUGG-dee-yah) (now divided between Uzbekistan and Tajikistan) was a fertile agricultural region surrounded by the grassland habitat of the central Eurasian nomads. Persian in language and religion, Sogdian culture was also enriched by contact with the Indian and Greek worlds. Alexander the Great conquered the region in the fourth century B.C.E.

Sogdia's commercial economy began to develop slowly beginning in the first century C.E. Sogdian merchants achieved success by leaving their homeland and traveling to distant regions, especially eastward to China. The dispersion of Sogdian merchants took the form of a **trade diaspora** (*diaspora* was the Greek word for scattering grain), a network of merchant settlements spread throughout foreign lands. These communities remained united by their common origins, religion, and language, as well as by family ties and business partnerships (see Reading the Past: Letters from a Sogdian Castaway).

Nomad incursions in the fifth and sixth centuries ruined many cities in Central Asia, as the Chinese pilgrim Xuanzang observed. Sogdia's city-states were largely spared this devastation and began to enjoy unprecedented prosperity. Agriculture and trade supported ambitious building projects, including an extensive system of irrigation canals and long walls to fend off both nomad attacks and encroaching desert sands.

Sogdian-Turkic Alliance

The creation of the Turkic nomad empire in the mid-sixth century catapulted Sogdian merchants to dominance over the Silk Road trade. Sogdian merchants forged an alliance with the Turks and entered the administration, army, and diplomatic service of the Turkic khan. When the Sasanid king rebuffed the Turkic khan's offer of trade, a Byzantine historian tells us, it was "Maniakh, the leader of the Sogdians" who advised the khan "that it would be better for the Turks to cultivate the friendship of the Romans [i.e., the Byzantines] and send their raw silk for sale to them, because they made more use of it than other people."[9]

trade diaspora A network of merchants from the same city or country who live permanently in foreign lands and cooperate with one another to pursue trading opportunities.

Prominent Sogdians intermarried with the Turks, and the Turks adopted the written language of the Sogdians. Under the umbrella of Turkic military power, Sogdian merchant colonies sprouted in Mongolia and on the frontiers of China, and they spread westward as far as the Black Sea. Sales contracts found at Turfan, the principal hub of the Silk Road,

Letters from a Sogdian Castaway

In 1907, while surveying the ruins of a guardhouse near Dunhuang, the westernmost outpost of the Tang Empire, the British explorer Aurel Stein found a post bag that had been lost in transit. The letters, written in Sogdian and dating from the early fourth century, perhaps had been confiscated by Chinese border officials. Among the contents were two letters written by Miwnay, a Sogdian woman living in Dunhuang—one to her husband, a traveling merchant, and the other to her mother in Loulan, a desert town hundreds of miles farther west.

In the letter to her husband, Nanai-dhat, Miwnay complains that it had been three years since he abandoned her and her daughter in Dunhuang. She implores him to return. Miwnay had appealed to Artivan, a relative of her husband, and Farnkhund, apparently one of his business associates, as well as the leaders of the Sogdian community at Dunhuang, but they refused her requests for help. Here Miwnay describes her plight to her mother:

> I am very anxious to see you, but have no luck. I petitioned the councilor Sagharak, but the councilor says, "Here there is no other relative closer to [my husband] than Artivan." And I petitioned Artivan, but he says: "Farnkhund is . . . [missing text], and I refuse to hurry, . . ." And Farnkhund says, "If [Artivan] does not consent that you should go back to your mother, how should I take you? Wait until . . . comes; perhaps Nanai-dhat will come." I live wretchedly, without clothing, without money. I ask for a loan, but no one consents to give me one, so I depend on charity from the priest. He

said to me, "If you go, I will give you a camel, and a man should go with you, and on the way I will look after you well." May he do so for me until you send me a letter!

In a postscript to the letter to the husband, Miwnay's daughter adds that Farnkhund had run away and the Chinese authorities were holding her mother and herself liable for Farnkhund's debts. Miwnay's closing words convey her bitterness toward her husband:

> I obeyed your command and came to Dunhuang. I did not observe my mother's bidding, nor that of my brothers. Surely the gods were angry with me on the day when I did your bidding! I would rather be wife to a dog or pig than to you!

Source: Nicholas Sims-Williams, "Towards a New Edition of the Sogdian Ancient Letters: Ancient Letter 1," in Étienne de la Vaissière and Eric Trombert, eds., *Les Sogdiens en Chine* (Paris: École française d'Extrême Orient, 2005), 185–187.

EXAMINING THE EVIDENCE

1. What does Miwnay's predicament tell us about the status of women in Sogdian society?

2. What do these letters reveal about the role of the family in the organization of the Sogdian merchant network?

---

show Sogdian merchants buying and selling silk, silver, gold, perfume, saffron, brass, medicines, and cane sugar. Horses ranked first among the goods they brought to China, while slaves, Siberian furs, and gems and spices from India filled the markets of Samarkand and other Sogdian cities.

The dominance of Sogdians over Silk Road commerce fed stereotypes about their immense wealth and shallow morals. Xuanzang, who passed through Samarkand in 630, pronounced the Sogdians "greedy and deceitful," snidely observing that "fathers and sons scheme for profit, because everyone, noble and commoner alike, regards wealth as the measure of distinction."[10] At the same time, Sogdian merchants living in Chinese cities occupied a prominent place in the cosmopolitan cultural world of Tang China. The popularity of Persian fashions, music, dance, and sports such as polo at the Tang court can be attributed to the influence of Sogdians who settled in Chang'an. Sogdian merchants' homes, as well as temples dedicated to Persian religions, clustered around the Tang capital's Western Market, the gateway to the Silk Road.

The Sogdian émigré communities in Central Asia and China drew strength from their strong communal bonds, but as the generations passed, many Sogdians in China began to assimilate to the cosmopolitan Chinese culture. The Sogdian silk merchant He Tuo, who settled in China in the mid-sixth century, joined the entourage of a Chinese prince and

Sogdian Communities in Central Asia and China

amassed a great fortune. His eldest son and nephew became experts at cutting gemstones, and the Sui emperor Yang Jian placed the nephew in charge of the imperial jewelry workshop. The He family is credited with introducing the techniques of glassmaking to China. Another of He Tuo's sons had a brilliant career as a Confucian scholar in service to the Sui court. The Tang emperors also frequently employed Sogdians in important civil and military offices, most notoriously the general An Lushan, whose rebellion nearly brought down the Tang dynasty.

Breakdown of the Trade Network

Muslim Takeover of Sogdia

The Muslim conquest of Sogdia in the early eighth century marked the beginning of the end of Sogdian prosperity. When Samarkand surrendered to an Islamic army in 712, the city's population was forced to pay an indemnity of two million silver coins and three thousand slaves and agreed to submit annual tribute of two hundred thousand silver coins. Unlike many of their neighbors, however, the Sogdians stubbornly resisted both their new Arab overlords and Islamic religion. As a result Sogdia remained isolated from the commercial and cultural worlds of the Islamic empire.

Impact of An Lushan Rebellion

The An Lushan rebellion of 755–763 dealt another major blow to the Sogdian trade network. It severely damaged the Chinese economy, and after the rebels were defeated many Sogdians in China disguised their ancestry and abandoned their culture out of fear of persecution.

Rise of Asian Maritime Trade

Finally, with the rise of maritime trade routes connecting the Islamic world and China, overland traffic across the Silk Road dropped off steeply. By the late tenth century, the Sogdian language and culture were on the verge of extinction in Sogdia itself, and the scattered Sogdian communities had blended into the foreign societies they inhabited. Samarkand, however, would enjoy a brilliant revival in the fourteenth century under the Turkic emperor Timur, when the city was reborn as an Islamic metropolis (see Chapter 15).

Conclusion

Commercial and cultural exchanges across the Silk Road during the first millennium C.E. linked the distant agrarian empires of China, India, and Iran. The interactions that resulted transformed the peoples and cultures along the Central Asian trade routes. Nomad chieftains, for example, developed the political acumen to knit together tribal confederations and pursue profits through trade, plunder, and conquest. The Tuoba, the Turks, and the Khazars all transcended their original predatory purposes by creating empires that spanned both the pastoral nomadic and the settled agrarian worlds. In each case, however, these empires failed to create political institutions that might have perpetuated their dominion over settled societies. The Sogdian merchant communities forged very different commercial and cultural linkages across Asia, but these networks, too, proved vulnerable to shifts in political fortunes and trade patterns.

The movement across the Silk Road of goods and of people such as the Buddhist pilgrim Xuanzang fostered unprecedented cosmopolitan cultural intercourse throughout Asia. The complex intermingling of peoples, cultures, and religious faiths peaked with the rise of the Sui and Tang empires in China. The spread of Buddhism to China and from there to Korea, Japan, and Vietnam provided the foundation for a common East Asian culture. The political dominance of the Chinese empires also spread China's written language, literary heritage, and social values among its neighbors. Correspondingly, the demise of Tang power after the An Lushan rebellion in the mid-eighth century undermined China's cultural dominance. Subsequently a new order of independent states emerged in East Asia that has persisted down to the present.

In India, too, a cosmopolitan culture and a more homogeneous ruling class formed during the first millennium C.E., despite the absence of political unity. This elite culture was based on Gupta political institutions and Hindu religious beliefs and social values expressed through the new lingua franca, or common language, of Sanskrit. Some scholars have dubbed it "the Sanskrit cosmopolis." The royal lineages and noble classes that founded the first states in Southeast Asia during this period participated fully in creating this cosmopolitan culture. Yet by the tenth century, as in East Asia, the common elite culture encompassing South and Southeast Asia had begun to fragment into more distinctive regional and national traditions.

Between the fifth and tenth centuries, regional cultures in East and South Asia were formed by the movement of people and goods across trade routes, the mixture of religious and political ideas, and the spread of common forms of livelihood. The same forces were also at work in the formation of regional societies in the very different worlds of the Americas and the Pacific Ocean, as we will see in the next chapter.

NOTES

1. Translated from Xuanzang, *Record of the Western Regions*.
2. Ibid., Book 5.
3. Translated from *The Chronicles of Japan*, Chapter 19.
4. Translated from Xuanzang, *Western Regions*, Book 2.
5. Ibid., Book 7.
6. Translated in Munshi Debiprasad, "Ghatayala Inscription of the Pratihara Kakkuka of [Vikrama-]Samvat 918," *Journal of the Royal Asiatic Society* (1895): 519–520.
7. Quoted in Daud Ali, *Courtly Culture and Political Life in Early Medieval India* (Cambridge, U.K.: Cambridge University Press, 2004), 197.
8. Cosmas Indicopleustes, *Christian Topography* (c. 547–550) (London: Hakluyt Society, 1897), Book II, 47.
9. R. C. Blockley, *The History of Menander the Guardsman* (Liverpool, U.K.: Cairns, 1985), 115.
10. Translated from Xuanzang, *Western Regions*, Book 1.

RESOURCES FOR RESEARCH

Steppe Peoples and Settled Societies of Central Asia

The centrality of Central Asia to world history has been analyzed from a variety of perspectives. Bentley focuses on the spread of world religions, Beckwith on political interactions and the formation of empires, and Christian on the movements of peoples and social transformations. Liu offers a lively discussion of cultural life across the Silk Road.

Barfield, Thomas. *The Perilous Frontier: The Nomadic Empires and China*. 1989.

Beckwith, Christopher I. *Empires of the Silk Road: A History of Central Eurasia from the Bronze Age to the Present*. 2009.

Bentley, Jerry H. *Old World Encounters: Cross-Cultural Contacts and Exchanges in Pre-Modern Times*. 1993.

Christian, David. *A History of Russia, Central Asia, and Mongolia*. Vol. 1, *Inner Eurasia from Prehistory to the Mongol Empire*. 1998.

Liu, Xinru, *The Silk Road in World History*. 2010.

The Shaping of East Asia

Although he overstates the degree of Chinese influence, Holcombe provides a succinct digest of the formation of a shared East Asian civilization. Adshead likewise exaggerates China's cultural dominance, but his detailed comparison of Chinese, Islamic, Indian, and both Latin and Byzantine Christian civilizations contains many important insights. Farris and Pai offer sure-handed guidance through the thorny debates over foreign influence and cultural identity that have dominated the study of the emergence of the Japanese and Korean states, respectively.

Adshead, S. A. M. *T'ang China: The Rise of the East in World History*. 2004.

Benn, Charles. *Daily Life in Traditional China: The Tang Dynasty*. 2002.

Farris, William Wayne. *Sacred Texts and Buried Treasures: Issues in the Historical Archaeology of Ancient Japan*. 1998.

Holcombe, Charles. *The Genesis of East Asia, 221 B.C.–A.D. 907.* 2001.

Pai, Hyung-Il. *Constructing "Korean" Origins: A Critical Review of Archaeology, Historiography, and Racial Myth in Korean State-Formation Theories.* 2000.

A Visual Sourcebook of Chinese Civilization. http://depts .washington.edu/chinaciv/.

The Consolidation of Hindu Society in India

In contrast to earlier studies that defined post-Gupta India in terms of political and economic regression, recent work argues that the Indian economy and society continued to be vital despite political fragmentation. Thapar's encyclopedic yet accessible survey caps a distinguished career as the most important interpreter of India's early history. Ali's illuminating investigation of court society reconceptualizes the nature of kingship in Indian culture.

Ali, Daud. *Courtly Culture and Political Life in Early Medieval India.* 2004.

Basham, A. L. *The Origins and Development of Classical Hinduism.* 1989.

Champakalakshmi, R. *Trade, Ideology, and Urbanization: South India, 300 B.C. to A.D. 1300.* 1996.

Chattopadhyaya, Bradjadulal. *The Making of Early Medieval India.* 1994.

Thapar, Romila. *Early India: From the Origins to A.D. 1300.* 2002.

The Diffusion of Indian Traditions to Southeast Asia

Hall provides a comprehensive introduction to the impact of maritime trade on the political, economic, and religious transformations of the region during this formative era. Wolters's collection of essays examines conceptual approaches for the study of this highly diverse region. Higham, an archaeologist, admirably synthesizes current scholarship on Angkor.

Hall, Kenneth R. *A History of Early Southeast Asia: Maritime Trade and Societal Development, 100–1500.* 2011.

Higham, Charles. *The Civilization of Angkor.* 2002.

Shaffer, Lynda. *Maritime Southeast Asia to 1500.* 1996.

Tarling, Nicholas, ed. *Cambridge History of Southeast Asia.* Vol. 1, Part 1. 1992.

Wolters, O. W. *History, Culture, and Region in Southeast Asian Perspectives.* 1999.

COUNTERPOINT: Sogdian Traders in Central Asia and China

Little scholarship on Sogdia and its merchants is available in English, but the translation of de la Vaissière's landmark study helps to remedy this omission. Schafer catalogues the impact of the rich material culture of Central Asia on Tang culture and literature.

Schafer, Edward. *The Golden Peaches of Samarkand: A Study in T'ang Exotics.* 1963.

de la Vaissière, Étienne. *Sogdian Traders: A History.* 2005.

▶ **For additional primary sources from this period**, see *Sources of Crossroads and Cultures.*

▶ **For Web sites, images, and documents related to topics in this chapter**, see Make History at bedfordstmartins.com/smith.

REVIEW

Online Study Guide
bedfordstmartins.com/smith

The major global development in this chapter ▶ The cultural and commercial exchanges during the heyday of the Silk Road that transformed Asian peoples, cultures, and states.

IMPORTANT EVENTS

386–534	Northern Wei dynasty in north China and Mongolia
552–603	First Turkish empire
581–618	Sui dynasty in China
604	Prince Shōtoku reorganizes the Yamato kingdom in Japan
606–647	Reign of King Harsha as paramount ruler of north India
618–907	Tang dynasty in China
629–645	Journey of the Chinese Buddhist monk Xuanzang to India
668	Unification of the Korean peninsula under the rule of the Silla kingdom
c. 670	The Khazars conquer and supplant the Bulgar khanate
690	Empress Wu declares the founding of her Zhou dynasty in China
755–763	An Lushan rebellion in north China severely weakens the Tang dynasty
c. 760	Sailendra kings in Java begin construction of the Borobudur monument
792	Kyoto established as Japan's new capital
802	Consolidation of the Angkor kingdom in Cambodia by Jayavarman II
861	Conversion of the Khazars to Judaism
939	Vietnam wins independence from China
965	Rus invaders destroy the Khazar khanate

KEY TERMS

bodhisattva (p. 312)
Brahmanism (p. 327)
chakravartin (p. 313)
Chan Buddhism (p. 314)
equal-field system (p. 314)
Hinduism (p. 323)

jati (p. 325)
khan (p. 310)
Mahayana (p. 312)
Puranas (p. 323)
Pure Land (p. 313)
trade diaspora (p. 332)

CHAPTER OVERVIEW QUESTIONS

1. In what ways did Asian societies respond to cross-cultural interactions during the period 400–1000?

2. What strategies did pastoral nomads adopt in their relations with settled societies, and why?

3. What patterns of political and cultural borrowing characterized the emerging states in East and Southeast Asia?

4. Why did India and China experience different outcomes following the collapse of strong and unified empires?

SECTION FOCUS QUESTIONS

1. What strategies did nomadic steppe chieftains and the rulers of agrarian societies apply in their dealings with each other?

2. How did the spread of Buddhism transform the politics and societies of East Asia?

3. Why did the religious practices of Hinduism gain a broader following in Indian society than the ancient Vedic religion and its chief rival, Buddhism?

4. What aspects of Indian religions had the greatest influence on the societies of Southeast Asia?

5. How did the social and economic institutions of the Sogdian merchant network differ from those of the nomadic confederations and the agrarian empires?

MAKING CONNECTIONS

1. How and why did the spread of Buddhism from India to China and Southeast Asia differ from the expansion of Islam examined in Chapter 9?

2. Do you think that the invasions of Germanic peoples into the Roman Empire had more lasting consequences (see Chapter 9) than the invasions in China by steppe nomad peoples? Why or why not?

3. Compare the main values of Hinduism in the post-Gupta period with those of the ancient Vedic religion (see Chapter 3). How had the goals of religious practice changed, and what effect did these changes have on Indian society?

AT A CROSSROADS ▶

The Mesoamerican ball-game, which spread as far as northeastern North America, was charged with powerful ritual and religious meaning. Maya myths associate the ballgame with the Hero Twins' triumph over the gods of the underworld and with the gift of agriculture. This stone disk, which dates from about 590 and once marked the site of a ball court in the modern Mexican province of Chiapas, displays a ballplayer striking the ball with his hip. The headdress and inscriptions suggest that the ballplayer is a royal figure reenacting the feats of the Hero Twins. (Giraudon/Bridgeman Art Library.)

Societies and Networks in the Americas and the Pacific

300–1200

When Holy Lord Eighteen Rabbit (r. 695–738) became king of the Maya city-state of Copán (co-PAHN) in today's western Honduras, his society was at the peak of its wealth and strength. Eighteen Rabbit's building projects reflected Copán's power. He commissioned an impressive series of stone monuments, adding major new temples in the heart of the city and laying out a Great Plaza to the north. He rebuilt Copán's magnificent ball court, where the warriors reenacted the Maya myth of creation as a gladiatorial contest culminating in the blood sacrifice of captured nobles. At the entrance to the Great Plaza, Eighteen Rabbit erected a stone pillar commemorating his accession as king, and the plaza itself was studded with carved stelae depicting Eighteen Rabbit as a multifaceted deity. One stele shows him as a mighty warrior holding up the sky; others portray him dressed as the Maize God and the spirit of the planet Venus.

After ruling Copán for forty-three years, Eighteen Rabbit was betrayed by one of his followers. In 725 he had installed a man named Cauac (kah-WOK) Sky as ruler of the nearby city of Quiriga (kee-REE-gah). In 738 Cauac Sky captured Eighteen Rabbit and carried the Copán king back to Quiriga, where he was killed as a sacrificial victim. Copán preserved its independence after Eighteen Rabbit's execution; Cauac Sky made no attempt

BACKSTORY

As we saw in Chapter 8, during the first millennium B.C.E. signs of growing social complexity and a hierarchy of villages and towns emerged in both the Olmec culture on Mexico's Atlantic coast and the Chavín culture along Peru's Pacific coast. By 200 B.C.E., however, the Olmec and Chavín societies had been eclipsed by the rising city-states of the Maya and Moche, respectively. These city-states concentrated political and military power by mobilizing massive amounts of labor to build monumental cities and irrigation systems for agriculture. Meanwhile, in North America, agriculture and settled societies did not appear until the first millennium C.E., when native peoples began to adopt Mesoamerican food crops and farming techniques. In the Pacific Ocean, once the Lapita migrations ceased in around 200 B.C.E., many islands remained undisturbed by human occupation. Colonization of the Pacific Islands would not resume until after 500 C.E.

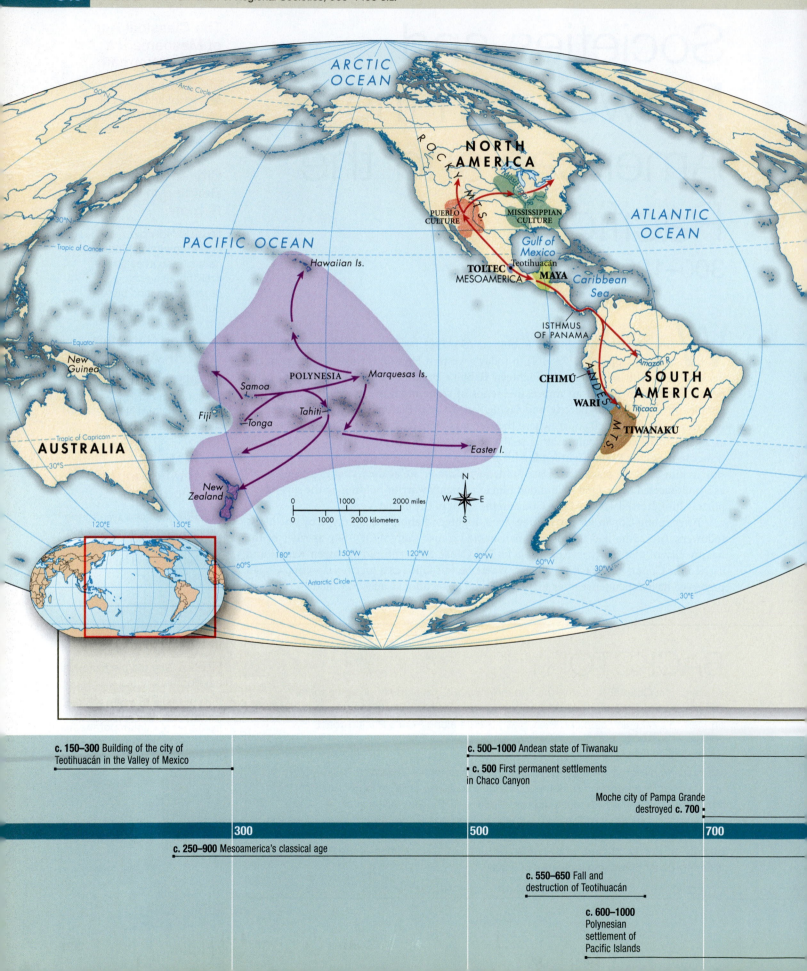

c. 150–300 Building of the city of
Teotihuacán in the Valley of Mexico

c. 500–1000 Andean state of Tiwanaku

c. 500 First permanent settlements
in Chaco Canyon

Moche city of Pampa Grande
destroyed **c. 700**

| | 300 | | 500 | | 700 |

c. 250–900 Mesoamerica's classical age

c. 550–650 Fall and
destruction of Teotihuacán

c. 600–1000
Polynesian
settlement of
Pacific Islands

to occupy Copán or destroy its monuments. In fact, Eighteen Rabbit's successor as Copán's ruler completed one of his predecessor's most ambitious projects, a pyramid staircase that set down in stone the history of his dynasty. The inscription carved into the staircase steps reaffirmed the power of Copán by celebrating the accomplishments of its ancient warrior kings. The seated sculptures of earlier rulers placed at ascending intervals include an image of Eighteen Rabbit. His death—"his breath expiring in war"—was duly noted, but only as an unfortunate episode in an otherwise heroic history. He received full honors as a noble martyr and sacred ancestor.

The life and death of Eighteen Rabbit recorded in his city's monuments exemplify the obsession with dynastic continuity that was so central to the Maya kings' identity. The rulers of the Maya city-states devoted enormous resources to asserting their godlike power to command their subjects' labor and wealth. Their monuments wove together history and myth to tell the story of conquests, captives, slain enemies, and military alliances. Yet this wealth of historical documentation speaks in a single uniform voice. It is the speech of kings and nobles and sheds little light on the lives of the commoners who toiled under their rule.

As we saw in Chapter 8, the scarcity of written records, especially in comparison to Eurasia, complicates scholars' efforts to recover the histories of peoples of the Americas, the Pacific Islands, and most of sub-Saharan Africa. Only in Mesoamerica, stretching from central Mexico to Honduras, do we find substantial indigenous writings, which are as yet only partly deciphered. But the absence of documentary evidence does not indicate social or cultural isolation. Throughout the period from 300 to 1200, movements of peoples, goods, and ideas had far-reaching influences on these regions of the world. As in Eurasia, cross-cultural interaction played a significant role in shaping peoples and cultures.

The intensity of interaction and degree of cultural convergence varied with time and place. In Mesoamerica, cross-cultural interactions created a set of institutions and ideologies that knitted together local societies and cultures from the highland plateaus of central Mexico to the tropical rain forests of the Maya world. In the Andean region of South

MAPPING THE WORLD

Formation of Regional Societies in the Americas and the Pacific

In the Americas and the Pacific—as in Eurasia and Africa during this era—migration and trade promoted cultural exchange and the formation of regional societies. Complex states based on intensive agriculture arose in Mexico, the Maya region, and the Andes, but the southwestern deserts and eastern woodlands of North America fostered sharply distinct societies. The Polynesian migrations spawned a remarkable cultural unity across the central and eastern Pacific Ocean.

ROUTES ▼

→ Spread of maize cultivation, c. 1000 B.C.E.–700 C.E.

→ Polynesian migration, c. 300–1000 C.E.

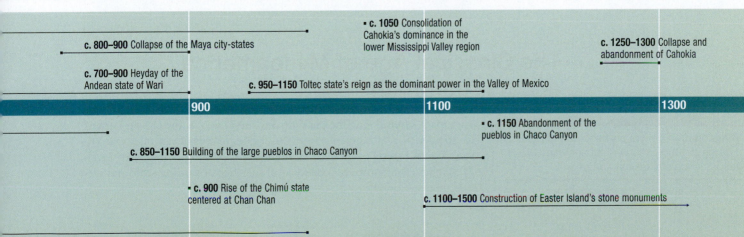

- **c. 1050** Consolidation of Cahokia's dominance in the lower Mississippi Valley region

c. 800–900 Collapse of the Maya city-states

c. 1250–1300 Collapse and abandonment of Cahokia

c. 700–900 Heyday of the Andean state of Wari

c. 950–1150 Toltec state's reign as the dominant power in the Valley of Mexico

900   **1100**   **1300**

- **c. 1150** Abandonment of the pueblos in Chaco Canyon

c. 850–1150 Building of the large pueblos in Chaco Canyon

- **c. 900** Rise of the Chimú state centered at Chan Chan

c. 1100–1500 Construction of Easter Island's stone monuments

America, too, inhabitants of the coastal plains and the highlands developed common political and cultural institutions. In contrast, cross-cultural influences touched virtually all of the local societies of North America without producing a shared cultural and political identity. In the Pacific Islands, migration, trade, and social interchange produced both the high degree of cultural uniformity of Polynesia and the remarkable cultural diversity found on the single island of Bougainville.

Equipped only with stone tools, these peoples faced formidable obstacles in their efforts to create stable agricultural economies. Landscapes as diverse as the alpine plateaus of the Andes, the barren deserts of southwestern North America, and the volcanic islands of the Pacific posed daily challenges to farming folk. Their success produced larger surpluses, greater social stratification, and more hierarchical political systems than before. In North America and the Pacific Islands, political and religious authority was dispersed among numerous hereditary chiefs. But in Mesoamerica and the Andean region, where irrigated agriculture supported denser populations, large states emerged. A distinct ruling class governed these states; their authority rested on an ideology that defined the cosmic order and explained the rights and obligations of all members of society, as well as the special status of the ruling class. The rulers of these states, such as Eighteen Rabbit, expressed their ideologies not only in words but in the design of their settlements and cities, in monumental architecture and sacred objects, and in rituals performed on behalf of both their deceased ancestors and their living subjects.

OVERVIEW
QUESTIONS

The major global development in this chapter: The formation of distinctive regional cultures in the Americas and the Pacific Islands between 300 and 1200.

As you read, consider:

1. How did these societies, equipped with only Stone Age technologies, develop the social and political institutions and the patterns of exchange to tame often hostile environments and build complex civilizations?

2. How did differences in environment and habitat foster or discourage economic and technological exchanges among adjacent regions?

3. What were the sources of political power in the societies discussed in this chapter, and how were they similar or dissimilar?

4. How did differences in urban design reflect distinctive forms of political and social organization?

The Classical Age of Mesoamerica and Its Aftermath

FOCUS

What common beliefs and social and political patterns did the various local societies of Mesoamerica's classical age share?

Historians often define the period from 250 to 900 as the classical era of Mesoamerica, which extends from the arid highlands of central Mexico to the tropical forests of modern Honduras and Nicaragua (see Map 11.1). Mesoamerica encompassed many local societies of varying scale and dif-

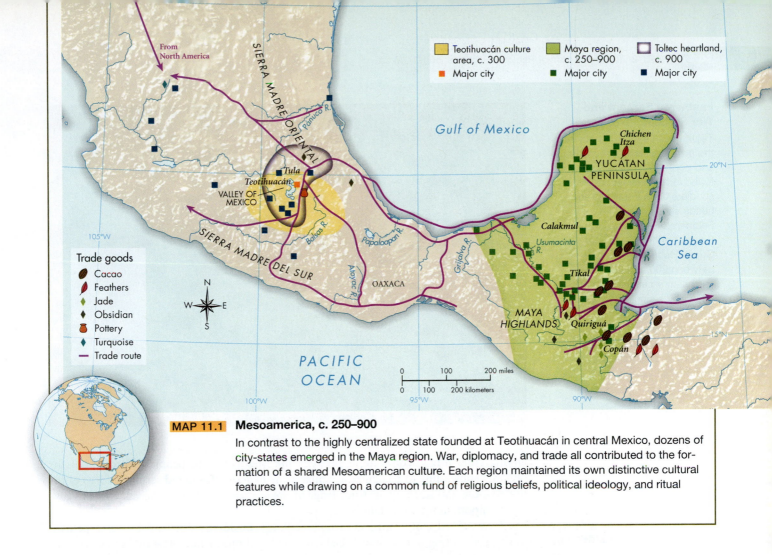

MAP 11.1 Mesoamerica, c. 250–900

In contrast to the highly centralized state founded at Teotihuacán in central Mexico, dozens of city-states emerged in the Maya region. War, diplomacy, and trade all contributed to the formation of a shared Mesoamerican culture. Each region maintained its own distinctive cultural features while drawing on a common fund of religious beliefs, political ideology, and ritual practices.

ferent degrees of integration and complexity. What united it as a regional society was a set of shared ideas about the operation of the cosmos. This common ideology produced similar patterns of elite status, political power, and economic control.

Between the first and ninth centuries, Mesoamerica underwent a remarkable cycle of political consolidation and disintegration. At the beginning of this period, Mesoamerica was home to numerous **chiefdoms**, in which a hereditary chief exercised political and religious authority and military leadership over a group of tribes or villages. By the third century, more complex and more steeply stratified political orders—**city-states**—dominated both the highlands and the lowlands by extracting labor and tribute from their subjects.

Bronze and iron metallurgy were unknown in Mesoamerica during this period. Yet despite the limitations of Stone Age technology, the people built great cities, and their skilled craft industries flourished. Highly productive agriculture based on maize, beans, squash, and chili peppers supported some of the world's densest populations.

The monumental metropolis of Teotihuacán (teh-o-tee-WAH-kahn) in central Mexico and the dozens of Maya city-states testify to the strong control the rulers wielded over their subjects' lives. As was true of the classical ages of Eurasia and Africa, the classical era of Mesoamerica was a time of strife and crisis as well as expanding economic and cultural interchange.

Political Power and Ideology in Mesoamerica

Scholars have traced the origins of Mesoamerican cultural and political traditions to the ancient Olmec civilization (see Chapter 8). Powerful Mesoamerican city-states emerged during the first centuries C.E., and cross-cultural exchange intensified as trade and warfare

chiefdom A form of political organization in which a hereditary leader, or chief, holds both political and religious authority and the rank of members is determined by their degree of kinship to the chief.

city-state A small independent state consisting of an urban center and the surrounding agricultural territory.

343

Feathered Serpent and War Serpent

Teotihuacán's monuments lack the prolific historical records and portraits of royal figures found in the Maya world. But scholars think the sculpted heads shown here of the Feathered Serpent and the War Serpent on the Temple of Queztalcoatl, constructed between 200 and 250, may represent an expression of power by a single ruler or dynasty. Many of these images were defaced in the fourth century, perhaps as a warning against royal ambitions. (Photolibrary.)

Sources of Political Power and Ideology

obsidian A hard volcanic stone used to sharpen cutting tools and thus one of the most valuable natural resources for Stone Age peoples.

prestige good A rare or exotic item to which a society ascribes high value and status.

Tollan In Mesoamerican myths, the name of the place where the gods created human beings, and thus the place of origin for all of humanity.

among cities forged connections between the Mesoamerican peoples. Throughout the region, people came to recognize a similar array of gods—feathered serpents, lords of the underworld, and storm gods. Knowledge of the Mesoamerican calendar and writing gave rulers important tools for state-building.

In the absence of bronze and iron metallurgy, **obsidian**—a hard volcanic stone used to sharpen cutting tools—was crucial to agricultural production. The two sources of obsidian in the region, the northern part of the Valley of Mexico and highland Guatemala, emerged as early centers of economic exchange and state formation. Poor transportation limited the reach of political control, however; in the absence of draft animals (domesticated beasts of burden) and wheeled vehicles, people could transport only what they could carry on their backs. Long-distance exchange was therefore difficult, and it was restricted to the most highly desired goods. Political power was based more on controlling labor than on accumulating property. Yet the possession of rare and exotic **prestige goods** gave rulers awesome authority, and so items such as jade, gold, jaguar skins, feathers, and cacao seeds (for making chocolate) acquired great value. Rulers of the Mesoamerican city-states constantly warred against each other, vying for control of labor resources and prestige goods and exacting tribute from their defeated enemies.

Mesoamerican political power was explained and legitimated by a political ideology that many scholars argue was rooted in memories of the great rulers and cities of antiquity. The people collectively associated these memories with a mythical city known as **Tollan** ("the place of reeds"), which they saw as a paradise of fertility and abundance, the place where human and animal life began. They believed Tollan was the earthly abode of the god Feathered Serpent (whom the Aztecs would later name Quetzalcoatl [kate-zahl-CO-ah-tal]), the creator and patron of humanity. Mesoamerican myths associated the Feathered Serpent with elemental forces such as wind and fire, and also with the planet Venus, the "morning star" that heralds the arrival of the life-giving sun. Mythological lore credited the Feathered Serpent with creating the sun and moon, inventing the calendar and thus the cycles of time, and bestowing basic necessities such as maize, their staple food.

But Mesoamerican concepts of cosmic order, in which cycles of time are punctuated by violence and death, required that the Feathered Serpent sacrifice his own life to renew the creative powers of the universe. Human rulers in turn could acquire and maintain political power only through offering frequent blood sacrifices to the gods. These blood sacrifices involved both the execution of war captives and bloodletting rituals by rulers and priests, who used needles of obsidian, bone, or stingray spines to pierce their tongues and ears and extract blood. Human rulers embodied the divine powers of the Feathered Serpent and reenacted his heroic exploits through ritual performance.

Mesoamericans believed that all humans originally spoke a common language and lived under the benign rule of the Feathered Serpent. Gradually, though, groups of people developed their own languages, customs, and beliefs and went their separate ways. By building temples and cities, rulers sought to renew the common community of the original Tollan. Claiming the heritage of Tollan gave legitimacy to new rulers and dynasties and provided a rationale for accepting foreign conquerors. Thus political power in Mesoamerica was rooted in a shared cultural heritage and a vision of cultural unity.

The City-State of Teotihuacán

The rise of Teotihuacán, about thirty miles northeast of present-day Mexico City, as the dominant center in the Valley of Mexico was due largely to its location near the region's major obsidian mines and irrigated farmland. Only a few fragments of Teotihuacán writing have survived, so we have far less direct evidence of Teotihuacán's history than we do for the Maya city-states. We know that in the first two centuries C.E., Teotihuacán's founders constructed a magnificent city with wide avenues, numerous walled residential complexes, and a massive open plaza anchored by giant pyramids and temples.

Most of the population of the valley, farmers and craftsmen alike, lived in this vast city. To house all these people, apartment-like stone buildings—the first apartment compounds in world history—were constructed. These compounds housed an average of fifty to one hundred persons in a series of apartments built around a central patio, which in some cases had its own ritual mound. The apartments usually housed members of a single kinship group, but some were for craftsmen working in the same trade. This residential pattern suggests that the city's people were divided into groups (probably based on kinship) that shared everyday life, collective rituals, and in some cases specialized trade and craft occupations.

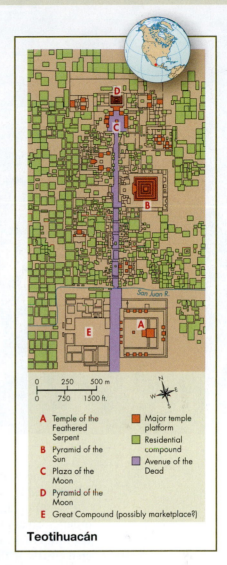

Teotihuacán

0   250   500 m
0   750   1500 ft.

A Temple of the Feathered Serpent
B Pyramid of the Sun
C Plaza of the Moon
D Pyramid of the Moon
E Great Compound (possibly marketplace?)

■ Major temple platform
■ Residential compound
■ Avenue of the Dead

San Juan R.

Social and Economic Organization

These groups may also have been the basic units of the city's economy. Although the scale of Teotihuacán's buildings and monuments shows that the state could command vast amounts of labor, there is little evidence that its rulers exercised direct control over the inhabitants' ordinary working lives. Even the obsidian tool–making industry, the mainstay of the city's economic dominance, was dispersed among hundreds of small domestic workshops, not centralized in large state-run industrial enterprises.

Priestly Rule and Ritual

Despite the extensive centralization of the Teotihuacán state, scholars have not found evidence of a hereditary dynasty of kings. Most believe that in its formative stages, Teotihuacán—like the city-states of Mesopotamia discussed in Chapter 2—was ruled by a cadre of priests rather than a military elite. Ritual action, including blood offerings, dominates the art and imagery of Teotihuacán, but warriors and scenes of warfare rarely appear until the fourth century C.E. Human sacrifice was a notable aspect of Teotihuacán's public culture. Nearly two hundred sacrificial victims, bound and dressed in war regalia, were

Teotihuacán

At its peak between 250 and 350, Teotihuacán was one of the largest cities in the world. The Avenue of the Dead stretches for 3 miles from the Pyramid of the Moon (foreground) to the Temple of Queztalcoatl and the residences of the elite; the Pyramid of the Sun stands to the left. Some two thousand apartment compounds housing the city's ordinary inhabitants lined both sides of the avenue. (©Herb Lingl/aerialarchives.com.)

buried beneath the Temple of the Feathered Serpent, the hub of government, when it was constructed in the early third century.

Teotihuacán's precise gridlike layout reflects a paramount desire to impose human order on an unpredictable natural world. The city's planners aligned its pyramids and plazas with crucial astronomical phenomena to provide a consecrated space to perform sacred rituals at the proper times. The Temple of the Feathered Serpent was flanked by twelve platforms, which served as stages for elaborate seasonal rites to ensure abundant harvests, cosmic balance, and social stability. The technologies of architecture, astronomy, and calendrical calculation were essential to maintain the orderly structure of the cosmos. Above all, the city's builders intended Teotihuacán to be seen as the Tollan of its day, a ceremonial complex dedicated to perpetuating the power and authority of its ruling class through awesome public rituals. It was for this reason that centuries later, the Aztecs named the city's massive ruins Teotihuacán, "the place where men become gods." In every way, the city was designed to function as a place of connection between the human and the divine.

Teotihuacán's Power and Influence

By 500 C.E. Teotihuacán's population had swelled to as many as two hundred thousand inhabitants, surpassed probably only by Constantinople among contemporary cities worldwide. The rise of Teotihuacán signaled the ascendancy of the central Mexican highlands as the dominant economic, political, and cultural region in Mesoamerica. Yet Teotihuacán's rulers pursued imperial expansion only fitfully, if at all. The area under their direct control seems to have been fairly limited, perhaps just the Valley of Mexico. Nevertheless, the city's influence radiated to the entire region through the prestige of its artifacts and culture, both of which were widely imitated throughout Mesoamerica. Visiting merchants and diplomatic missions from the Oaxaca (wah-HAH-kah) highlands, the Gulf Coast, and the Maya region inhabited their own special quarters in Teotihuacán. These foreigners' barrios (neighborhoods) were crossroads of cultural and economic exchange that helped disseminate sacred knowledge, ritual culture, political intelligence, and prestige goods throughout Mesoamerica.

By the fifth century, the Teotihuacán state exerted a far-reaching influence over the Mesoamerican world through its splendid monuments, its grand public ceremonies, and the abundant output of its craft workshops. At the same time, Teotihuacán's leaders took a more aggressive stance toward rival chiefs and foreign states. This shift would have crucial consequences for the Maya city-states.

The Maya City-State Network

The Maya city-states developed before the rise of Teotihuacán in central Mexico. Like other Mesoamerican cultures, the Maya inherited many features of the ancient Olmec civilization of the Gulf coast, including its monumental architecture, social institutions, calendar, and ritual art. In contrast to the Mexican highlands, however, where the massive scale of Teotihuacán dwarfed all other cities and polities, the Maya region never had a single dominant power.

In both the highlands near the Pacific coast and the lowland rain forests to the north, the early phase of Maya political and economic expansion was suddenly interrupted in the second and third centuries C.E. Major cities were abandoned, especially in the Pacific highlands, and new building and settlement came to a halt. The causes of this disruption are unknown, but its pervasive effects have led scholars to speculate that it resulted from some ecological catastrophe, perhaps a volcanic eruption. This catastrophe did not bring an end to Maya society, but it did alter the political landscape. By the time economic and demographic growth recovered at the beginning of the fourth century, political power had shifted decisively from the highlands to the city-states of the lowlands, such as Copán and Tikal (tee-KAHL).

Contraction and Recovery

The period from 250 to 900, the classical age of Maya civilization, witnessed the founding of nearly forty city-states. During these centuries the **Holy Lords**, as the Maya rulers called themselves, engaged in prodigious building of cities and monuments. But this era was also marked by succession struggles, dynastic changes, and perpetual political insecurity. The Holy Lords of powerful city-states frequently resorted to war to subdue neighbors and rivals. Victors rarely established direct rule over vanquished enemies, however. Unlike the Eurasian rulers we studied in earlier chapters, Maya elites did not dream of creating vast empires.

Warring City-States of the Classical Age

Instead, they were more likely to seek booty and tribute, and above all to seize war captives. Conquerors often brought back skilled craftsmen and laborers to their home city, reserving captives of high rank, such as the unfortunate Eighteen Rabbit, for blood sacrifices. Maya ceramic art often depicts tribute bearers offering cloth, foodstuffs, feathers, and cacao to enthroned rulers. Thus the Maya nobility may have conceived of war as a sacred ritual, but one that also furthered their ambitions for wealth and power. At the same time, armed conflict resulted in the exchange of people and goods among Maya city-states, contributing to the Maya region's cultural uniformity.

Maya myths about the origins of the gods and humanity have been preserved in the *Popol Vuh*, or "Book of Council." The descendants of a former Maya royal family wrote down these legends in the Latin alphabet after the Spanish conquest of Mesoamerica in the sixteenth century (see Reading the Past: The Maya Hero Twins Vanquish the Lords of the Underworld). The *Popul Vuh* portrays humans as the servants of the all-powerful gods who created them. In return for the gods' gifts of maize and timely rains, humans were obliged to build monuments to glorify the gods, to offer them sacrifices (especially human blood), and to regulate their own lives according to a sacred calendar. The Maya believed that all human beings possess a sacred essence, *ch'ulel* (choo-LEL), which is found in blood. The exalted status of kings and nobles endowed them with more potent ch'ulel, and so they were especially prized as blood sacrifices. Although the Maya kings depicted themselves as

Myths of Origins in the *Popol Vuh*

Holy Lord The title given by the Maya to the rulers of their city-states.

ch'ulel In Maya belief, the sacred essence contained in human blood that made it a potent offering to the gods.

The Maya Hero Twins Vanquish the Lords of the Underworld

The *Popol Vuh* records the myths about the world's creation and the origins of human society as handed down by the Quiché, a late Maya people. Central to the mythology of the Popol Vuh is the struggle between the gods and the Xibalba (shee-BAHL-ba), the lords of the underworld. The narrative focuses mostly on the exploits of the Hero Twins, whose father had been defeated by the Xibalba in a ball-game contest and decapitated. The Hero Twins travel to the underworld, outwit the Xibalba, and avenge their father's death.

In the following passages from the *Popol Vuh*, the Hero Twins inform the defeated Xibalba that as punishment for their heinous deed they will no longer receive blood sacrifices—and thus they will lose their power over mortals. Then the Hero Twins resurrect their father and assure him that in the future he will receive worship from the as-yet-unborn humans. Their triumph complete, the twins become transformed into the sun and moon (or, in other versions, the planet Venus), whose daily progressions through the heavens remind humanity of the triumph of the gods over the lords of death.

Passage 1:

"Here then is our word that we declare to you. Hearken, all you of Xibalba; for never again will you or your posterity be great. Your offerings also will never again be great. They will be reduced to croton [a shrub] sap. No longer will clean blood be yours. Unto you will be given only worn-out griddles and pots, only flimsy and brittle things."

"You shall surely eat only the creatures of the grass and the creatures of the wastelands. No longer will you be given the children of the light, those begotten in the light. Only things of no importance will fall before you." . . . Thus began their devastation, the ruin of their being called upon in worship. . . .

Here now is the adornment of their father by them. . . . His sons then said to him: "Here you will be called upon. It shall be so." Thus his heart was comforted.

"The child who is born to the light, and the son who is begotten in the light shall go out to you first. Your name shall not be forgotten. Thus be it so," they said to the father when they comforted his heart.

"We are merely the avengers of your death and your loss, for the affliction and misfortune that were done to you." Thus was their counsel when they had defeated all Xibalba.

Then [the Hero Twins] arose as the central lights. They arose straight into the sky. One of them arose as the sun, and the other as the moon.

Passage 2:

Now when they came from Tulan Zuyva [Tollan], they did not eat. They fasted continuously. Yet they fixed their eyes of the dawn, looking steadfastly for the coming forth of the sun. They occupied themselves in looking for the Great Star, called Icoquih [Venus], which appears first before the birth of the sun. The face of this Green Morning Star always appears at the coming forth of the sun.

When they were there at the place called Tulan Zuyva, their gods came to them. But it was surely not then that they received their ultimate glory or their lordship. Rather it was where the great nations and the small nations were conquered and humiliated when they were sacrificed before the face of Tohil. They gave their blood, which flowed from the shoulders and armpits of all the people.

Straightaway at Tulan came the glory and the great knowledge that was theirs. It was in the darkness, in the night as well, that they accomplished it. . . .

[Tohil spoke to them]: "You shall first give thanks. You shall carry out your responsibilities first by piercing your ears. You shall prick your elbows. This shall be your petition, your way of giving thanks before the face of god."

"Very well," they said. Then they pierced their ears. They wept as they sang of their coming from Tulan.

Source: Allen J. Christenson. Popol Vuh, *The Sacred Book of the Maya,* translated by Allen Christenson. Copyright © 2003 by O Books. University of Oklahoma Press, 2007. Used by permission of the publisher.

EXAMINING THE EVIDENCE

1. Why did the Maya believe that human beings must offer blood sacrifices to the gods?

2. Why might the Maya have been so deeply interested in the movements of the sun, moon, and planets?

gods, they attained immortality only after death, and the natural death of a king was considered a necessary sacrifice to ensure the renewal of divine blessings. Women of high birth also participated in the political and ceremonial life of the Maya ruling class, and Maya inscriptions record that several women ruled as Holy Lords. Maya elites thus occupied a unique position at the intersection of the human and the divine, ensuring the world's continuity both by demanding labor and sacrifices from the Maya population and by becoming sacrifices themselves.

The Mesoamerican ballgame, which dates back at least to Olmec times, was no mere spectator sport. On important ritual occasions, the ballgame became a solemn restaging of the mythical contest in which the Hero Twins triumphed over the lords of the underworld. When Eighteen Rabbit renovated Copán's ball court, he made it the city's ceremonial centerpiece, surrounding it with the greatest temples and monuments. The object of the ballgame, played by two teams of up to four players each, was to keep a rubber ball up in the air without using hands or feet. The slope-sided arenas represented the crack in the earth leading to the underworld. Allowing the ball to strike the ground risked incurring the wrath of the underworld gods. After the outcome was decided, the ball court became a sacrificial altar where the losers' heads were impaled on a skull rack alongside the court. These blood sacrifices not only commemorated the victory of the Hero Twins but also renewed the life-giving power of the gods.

The intricate Maya calendar determined the timing of war, sacrifice, agricultural work, and markets and fairs. The Maya believed that time and human history moved in elaborate cycles determined by the movements of the sun, moon, and planets—especially Venus, which in Maya belief governed sacrifice and war. To ensure a favorable outcome, the Maya people sought to align major actions in the present, such as attacks on enemies, with heroic events and accomplishments in the past. Thus the Maya took great care to observe and record astronomical phenomena. Maya astronomers calculated eclipses and the movements of planets with astonishing precision: their charts of the movements of Venus, which survive in bark-paper books, are accurate to within one day in five hundred years.

Bloodletting by a Maya Queen

Blood sacrifices offered to the gods occupied a central place in Mesoamerican political life. This stone monument shows the king of Yaxchilan holding a torch over the head of his queen, who is performing a ritual bloodletting by passing a spiked cord through her tongue. The ritual celebrated the birth of the king's son in 709. (Erich Lessing/Art Resource.)

Maya society revolved around the activities of the king and the royal clan. Beneath this ruling elite existed a multitiered social order based on class, residence, and kinship. As in many early Eurasian cultures, astrologers, diviners, and especially scribes occupied privileged positions in Maya society. These groups possessed the knowledge crucial to maintaining the royal mystique and to carrying out the tasks of government. The cities also housed large groups of specialized craftworkers in trades such as pottery manufacture, stone and wood carving, weaving, toolmaking, and construction. Urban artisans who made luxury goods for the nobility lived in larger dwellings near the cities' ceremonial centers, which indicates that they had higher socioeconomic status. At Tikal one artisans' compound was reserved for dentists who specialized in inlaying the teeth of the nobility with jade and other precious stones.

In the countryside, three to four families, probably kinfolk, lived in a common compound, each family in its own one-room building. The residential compound included a common kitchen and storage facilities, which they all shared. Clusters of residential compounds formed hamlets of several hundred persons. The considerable differences in the richness of burial goods suggest that the size, wealth, and prestige of the kin groups of commoners varied widely.

Maya Social Order

Larger outlying settlements, where powerful noble families resided, had paved plazas, pyramids, and temples but lacked the altars and ball courts of royal cities. These local nobles governed the surrounding population and organized the delivery of tribute and labor demanded by the supreme Holy Lords. The burden of labor service—to construct cities and to serve in the military—weighed heavily on the subject population. Like other ancient city-states we have studied, Maya city-states turned to the surrounding area for resources and labor and thereby became local crossroads for people, goods, and ideas.

Maya Family Life   Written records from the Maya classical age say little about family life. Although descriptions of Maya society compiled by the Spanish conquerors in the sixteenth century suffer from biases and misrepresentations, they reveal aspects of Maya culture that cannot be gleaned from archaeological evidence. According to these accounts, children were considered members of their fathers' lineage and took their surnames, but they also acquired "house names" from their mothers. Property and status passed from parents to children: sons inherited from fathers, and daughters inherited from mothers. Upon marriage, the husband usually moved in with his wife's family for a period of service lasting six or more years. Thereafter the couple might live with the husband's family or set up their own separate household.

Maize, usually made into steamed cakes known as *tamales*, was the staple of the Maya diet. The lowland Maya practiced both dry-land and intensive wet-land agriculture, growing maize, cotton, beans, squash, chili peppers, root crops, and many other vegetables. Hunting also provided food, but the only domestic animals the Maya possessed were dogs and turkeys. Maya rulers also received fish and shellfish as tribute from coastal areas.

Population Growth and Long-Distance Exchange   During the prosperous classical era the Maya population grew rapidly. In a pattern we have seen repeated around the world, population growth stimulated regular contact and communication throughout the region, and also the specialized production of agricultural and craft goods. The urban ruling elites, while continuing to war against one another, exchanged prestige goods over long distances. The unusual uniformity in spoken languages and pottery manufacture suggests that ordinary people also interacted frequently.

Influence of Teotihuacán   It was during the classical age, too, that Teotihuacán's influence left a clear imprint on the Maya world. Obsidian tools, ceramics, stone pyramid architecture, and other artifacts imported into Maya city-states show that cultural interaction and trade with Teotihuacán were well established (see again Map 11.1). Long-distance trade between the central Mexican highlands and the Maya lowlands was complemented by reciprocal gift giving and the dispatch of emissaries among rulers. The circulation of exotic goods charged with sacred power—feathers, pelts, and precious stones—reinforced elite status and helped spread religious practices.

In the fourth century Teotihuacán also became a major political force in the Maya region. Teotihuacán trade and diplomatic missions made forays into Maya lands and cultivated local clients, who reaped political and economic benefits from allying with Teotihuacán. The sudden appearance of Teotihuacán building styles, pottery, and tomb goods suggests that some cities, particularly in the coastal plains and highlands of Pacific Guatemala, fell under the rule of governors dispatched from Teotihuacán. At the very least, some Maya elites, especially upstart contenders for power seeking to unseat established royal dynasties, emulated certain features of Teotihuacán's political ideology. At Tikal and Copán, mysterious figures identified as "Lords of the West" overthrew previous rulers and founded new royal dynasties. These foreign regimes quickly assimilated into the native ruling elites of their cities. Economic ties to Teotihuacán, and perhaps adoption of Teotihuacán's more centralized system of administration and tribute collection, enriched Tikal and Copán. Both cities developed their own networks of client cities and exercised at least informal dominance over their local regions.

The Passing of Mesoamerica's Classical Age

Destruction of Teotihuacán   Between 550 and 650 Teotihuacán was destroyed. Sacred monuments were cast down, civic buildings were burned, and at least some portion of the population was slaughtered, leaving little doubt that the destruction was politically motivated. Historians do not know whether the razing of Teotihuacán resulted from foreign invasion or domestic political strife. Clearly, the perpetrators aimed not merely to overthrow the current regime but to obliterate the city's sacred aura. Most of Teotihuacán's population scattered, and the city never regained its preeminence. No successor emerged as the dominant power. For the next three or more centuries, the Valley of Mexico was divided among a half-dozen smaller states that warred constantly against one another.

From Ruin to Recovery in Tikal

In 562 an alliance of rival states vanquished Tikal, the most powerful Maya city-state, and sacrificed its king. As was Maya practice, however, the allies did not attempt to establish direct rule over Tikal, and by 700 it had recovered and its kings once again became the paramount lords of an extensive network of allies and trading partners. Interestingly, Maya royal monuments of the eighth century at Tikal (and at Copán during the reign of Eighteen Rabbit and his successors) feature a great revival of Teotihuacán imagery, even though the Mexican city had long been reduced to ruin. The reverence shown to Teotihuacán as a royal capital illustrates the lasting appeal of its ideas and institutions throughout Mesoamerica.

Collapse of the Maya City-States

The brilliant prosperity that Tikal and other Maya city-states enjoyed in the eighth century did not last. Over the course of the ninth century, monument building ceased in one Maya city after another. Although there is evidence of internal struggles for power and of interstate warfare, scholars believe that population pressure or an ecological disturbance triggered a more profound economic or demographic crisis. The collapse of the Maya city-state network not only ended individual ruling dynasties but also dismantled the basic economy of the region. Cities and cultivated fields were abandoned and eventually disappeared into the encroaching jungle. The region's population fell by at least 80 percent. New—but much more modest—cities arose along the Gulf coast of the Yucatan peninsula in the following centuries, but the cities of the Maya classical age never recovered.

The crumbling of the entire region's political and economic foundations reveals the tight web of interdependence within the Maya city-state network. The Maya peoples were more culturally uniform than peoples in other parts of Mesoamerica, sharing common languages, material culture, ritual practices, aesthetic values, and political institutions. Their diversified regional economy promoted specialized production and reliance on exchange to meet subsistence needs. Yet the competition among many roughly equal city-states also produced an unstable political system rife with conflict. Sharp reversals in political fortunes, booms in monument building followed by busts of destruction and abandonment, and frequent changes of ruling dynasties (which court historians took great pains to conceal) shaped the Maya world. Ultimately the political instability of the Maya city-state network eroded its infrastructure of production, labor, transport, and exchange.

Post-Classical Mesoamerica: The Toltecs and Chichen Itza

By 900, with the passing of both Teotihuacán and the Maya city-states, Mesoamerica's classical age had ended. Yet the region's cosmopolitan heritage endured in the Toltec state that dominated the central Mexican highlands from around 950 to 1150 (see again Map 11.1). Although descended from nomadic foragers from Mexico's northern deserts, the Toltecs resurrected the urban civilization, craft industries, and political culture of Teotihuacán. The Toltec capital of Tula became the new Tollan. According to Toltec annals written shortly after the Spanish conquest, the founder of Tula bore the name Quetzalcoatl (Feathered Serpent). Images of the Feathered Serpent frequently recur among Tula's ruins. Once again, in a pattern we have seen in other parts of the world, a nomadic people had inherited the culture of an urban society.

This era also produced a remarkable synthesis of Mexican and Maya traditions. Chichen Itza (chuh-chen uht-SAH), in the heart of the Yucatan peninsula, dominated the northern Maya region in the tenth century. The art and architecture of Chichen Itza so closely resembles that of Tula that some scholars believe Chichen Itza was a colony of the Toltec state. But Chichen Itza's major monuments are older than those of Tula. Relief carvings on the temples surrounding Chichen Itza's ball court depict the lords of Itza (the name means "sorcerer of water") summoning the Feathered Serpent, who grants them the right to rule this land. Although it is unlikely that the Toltecs ruled over Chichen Itza, there is little doubt that both cities were conceived as reincarnations of ancient Tollan and shared a political ideology centered on the Feathered Serpent. The striking similarities between Tula and Chichen Itza offer compelling evidence of the growing cultural integration of Mesoamerica.

City and State Building in the Andean Region

FOCUS

How did environmental settings and natural resources shape livelihoods, social organization, and state building in the Andean region?

At the height of Mesoamerica's classical age, a series of rich and powerful states, centered on spectacular adobe and stone cities, sprouted in both the northwestern coastal lowlands and the Andean highlands of South America (see Map 11.2). But the narrow land bridge of the Isthmus of Panama, covered by thick tropical forests, hampered communication between North and South America. Despite similarities in art, architecture, ritual, and political ideology, there is scant evidence of sustained contact between Mesoamerican and Andean societies during this era. Indeed, their differences are striking. Metalworking, already highly refined in the Andean region in the first millennium B.C.E., was unknown in Mesoamerica until the seventh century C.E. The massive irrigation systems of the Andean region had no parallel in Mesoamerica, and urbanization and trade networks were far more extensive in Mesoamerica than in the Andes. And although the Andean region was characterized by strong states and powerful rulers, they did not develop the traditions of writing and record keeping that became vital to political life in the Maya city-states.

All along the Pacific coast of South America, the abrupt ascent of the Andean mountain chain creates a landscape of distinctive ecological zones. Low coastal deserts give way to steep valleys and high mountain ranges interspersed with canyons and plateaus. Marked differences in climate and resources within relatively short distances led local populations to practice a variety of subsistence strategies, while also encouraging cooperation and exchange. Still, the formidable geographical barriers and uneven distribution of resources favored social and cultural diversity and inhibited imperial control by highly centralized states.

Nonetheless, Andean rulers strove to forge regional connections, promoting economic integration by bringing together diverse groups, resources, and technologies. These efforts met with some success. Careful use of the region's material wealth produced impressive achievements, most spectacularly in the monumental cities built in both the highlands and lowlands. Yet the challenges of the Andean environment and the resulting fragility of its agriculture continually threatened the social and political institutions that produced these achievements.

States and Societies in the Coastal Lowlands

Demise of the Moche and Rise of the Chimu

As we saw in Chapter 8, the earliest Andean states, Chavín and Moche, were founded in the arid coastal valleys of northern Peru. Moche, which had supplanted the earlier Chavín cultures by the first century C.E., was dominated by a powerful warrior elite who mobilized large numbers of forced laborers to build monumental pyramids and irrigation systems. But Moche was beset by climatic and political upheavals. In the early seventh century the grand ceremonial complex at Cerro Blanco was abandoned. Evidence from tree rings indicates that in the late sixth century the region suffered a drought lasting more than thirty years, followed by decades of unusually heavy rains and severe flooding, which partly destroyed Cerro Blanco's great pyramids in around 635. Scholars speculate that the El Niño currents might have caused these climatic upheavals. The largest late Moche city,

Pampa Grande, was burned to the ground in around 700. Whether the city's destruction resulted from domestic unrest or foreign invasion is unclear.

In the late ninth century a new state, Chimú (chee-MOO), arose in the Moche valley. Chimú's rulers, like the Moche leaders, depicted themselves as godlike figures and dramatized their authority through rituals of human sacrifice. But Chimú achieved far more political control over the coastal region than Moche had. It would thrive for over five centuries before succumbing to the Incas.

At its peak, the Chimú capital of Chan Chan comprised a vast maze of adobe-walled enclosures covering eight square miles. The city included at least nine palace compounds, residences for members of the royal clan who shared paramount rulership. There were also some thirty smaller residences of minor nobility and state officials, and densely packed barrios where the city's artisans, laborers, and traders lived in cramped dwellings made of mud-covered cane. Caravansaries (inns with large courtyards and stables) at the city's center welcomed llama caravans bringing trade goods from the highlands, especially alpaca wool, gold, silver, and copper.

Chan Chan was built on a barren plain near the Peruvian coast. Its inhabitants, and the power of its rulers, were nourished by irrigated agriculture and the construction of a much more extensive network of canals than that of Moche. In the thirteenth and fourteenth centuries the Chimú state expanded into neighboring valleys to tap additional land and water supplies. Military conquest was undoubtedly important in this expansion, but the stability of the Chimú state owed much more to trade and economic integration. Local rulers enjoyed substantial autonomy, and they had access to an enormous range of fine prestige goods produced in Chan Chan's workshops. Centuries later, Inca conquerors relocated large numbers of Chan Chan artisans to their capital at Cuzco after annexing Chimú in the 1460s.

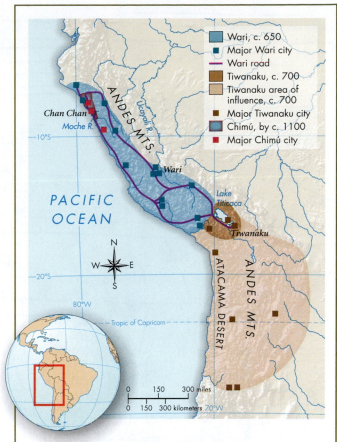

MAP 11.2   **Major Andean States, c. 600–1100**
Despite their radically different ecological habitats, both coastal and highland states of the Andean region relied on sophisticated—but fragile—systems of irrigated agriculture. Coastal Chimú and highland Tiwanaku each developed extensive networks of interregional trade. The highland Wari state, in contrast, imposed its military rule by building a series of fortified towns to control local populations.

States and Societies in the Andean Highlands

Inhabitants of the Andean highlands developed sophisticated agricultural systems to overcome the high altitude, erratic rainfall, and short growing season of the region. Indigenous crops, chiefly potatoes and quinoa (a native cereal), were the staples of the highland diet. Cultivation of raised fields constructed on cobblestone bases and fed by runoff of rain from the surrounding mountains began as early as 800 B.C.E.

Raised-field agriculture relied on an intricate system of irrigation but did not require complex technology, intensive labor, or large-scale organization. Local groups of farmers, known to the Inca as *ayllu* (aye-YOO), constructed the fields well before the appearance of complex political systems. The ayllu were essentially based on cooperative labor, though in some cases they relied on real or invented kinship ties to reinforce group solidarity. Ayllu typically owned lands in different locations and ecological zones (valley floors, hillsides, pasture) to minimize risk of crop failures. Groups of ayllu periodically pooled their labor to construct and maintain extensive networks of fields, canals, and causeways.

Raised-Field Farming

ayllu Groups of farmers (or other specialized occupations) in the Andean highlands who shared claims to common lands and a common ancestry.

Andean Agriculture

Farmers in the arid Andean highlands irrigated their fields with water stored in stone-lined reservoirs. The public benefits of irrigation encouraged the formation of cooperative labor groups known as ayllu. This depiction of Andean raised-field farming was included in a chronicle written by a native Peruvian in around 1615. (Photo: akg-images.)

In contrast to Mesoamerican peoples, who lacked economically useful domesticated animals, Andean peoples used the llama as a beast of burden and the alpaca as a source of meat and wool; the latter was especially important in this bitterly cold environment. Llama caravans traveled up and down the spine of the Andes ranges, trading in local specialties such as woolen cloth, pottery, and bone tools and utensils. Small towns near Lake Titicaca became trading posts that fed this growing interregional exchange. In the fifth century C.E. the city of Tiwanaku (tee-wah-NAH-coo), at the southern end of Lake Titicaca, became the dominant economic and political center of the region, serving as a crossroads connecting the environmentally diverse Andean communities (see again Map 11.2).

Tiwanaku included ceremonial centers with grand temples and public plazas, a large square stone-walled administrative center, and extensive residential barrios. At its peak between 500 and 800 the city may have housed as many as sixty thousand inhabitants, so it was roughly the same size as Chan Chan but less than one-third of Teotihuacán's maximum population. Some scholars believe that by this time Tiwanaku had developed from a major metropolis into a highly centralized state led by a small group of priestly clans or perhaps a royal dynasty. The power of the ruling elite rested on a highly ordered cosmology expressed through the precise spatial layout of the city and its lavish culture of rituals and feasting. The religious symbols and images of gods found at Tiwanaku were clearly ancestral to those of the Incas. As in Mesoamerica, public ceremony was central to religious and political life. The many drinking vessels and snuff tubes, spoons, and trays found among the ruins of Tiwanaku confirm that consumption of alcohol and hallucinogenic plants was important during these ceremonies. The prodigious drinking and eating at these events also provided occasions for rulers to demonstrate their generosity and to strengthen social and political bonds with their subjects (see Seeing the Past: Images of Power in Tiwanaku Art).

Tiwanaku's Broad Influence   The uniformity of Tiwanaku ceramic art and architecture, which came to be widely dispersed throughout the region, suggests that Tiwanaku's political ideology and craft traditions exercised a strong influence over local communities. Some scholars interpret Tiwanaku's pattern of development—intensification of agriculture, specialization of craft manufactures, road building, and resettlement of the population on farmland reclaimed from the lake bed—as evidence of strong state control. Others question the portrayal of Tiwanaku as a centralized empire whose rule rested on colonial domination and extraction of tribute. Although there is ample archaeological evidence of human sacrifice and display of decapitated enemies as trophies, Tiwanaku had no fortifications. Weapons and images of warfare are rare in Tiwanaku art, suggesting that the city's power derived more from its economic strength and religious ideology than from military aggression.

Wari's Militarized State   Tiwanaku was not the only significant political force in the Andean highlands. During the seventh and eighth centuries the city-state of Wari (WAH-ree), four hundred miles to the north, established a far-flung network of walled settlements in the highland valleys to its north and south, extending almost the entire length of modern Peru. In contrast to

Images of Power in Tiwanaku Art

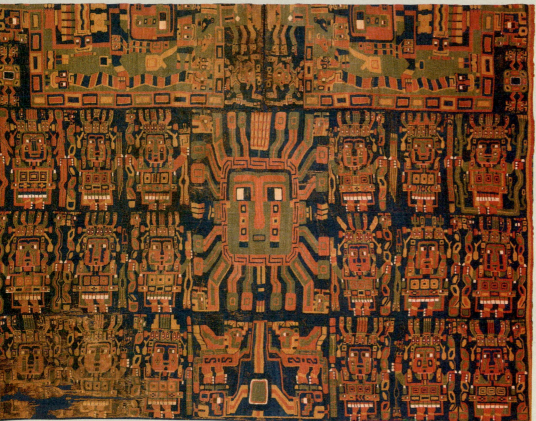

Wool Tunic from Tiwanaku, c. 200–400 (Private Collection.)

The lack of written records leaves us with many mysteries about the composition, character, and even the names of the ruling elites who lived in the sumptuous palaces of the city of Tiwanaku. But artistic and architectural evidence gives important clues about the self-image of Tiwanaku's rulers. Decorated wool garments and tapestries provide us with rich visual materials of a sort rarely found for other ancient civilizations. The extreme dryness of the Andean highland environment preserved organic materials such as textiles that would have quickly disintegrated in humid climates.

Scholars interpret the dense patterns on the wool tunic shown here as a representation of Tiwanaku and its ruling powers. The face of a god, shown as a many-rayed sun, dominates the center. Below the god's face is a stepped structure that resembles the principal shrine at Tiwanaku. On the lowest tiers of this structure stand two winged figures with feline faces (their heads turned back over their

shoulders) and gold ankle bracelets. These figures are probably priests wearing ritual costumes.

Flanking the central images on each side are rows of human figures in elaborate dress holding staffs, arrows, or plants. All of the figures, like the central deity, have vertically divided eyes, which are thought to be a mark of ancestral or divine status. Three upturned animal heads are attached to each headdress, and each figure wears three gold ornaments on its chest. Yet the great variety of headdress styles, facial markings, and garment patterns indicates that each figure represents a specific identity, most likely the heads of the ruling lineages of Tiwanaku or the leaders of subordinate towns and social groups. The array of images suggests a religious festival or procession in which the leaders of human society pay homage to the gods and ancestors.

The Incas who later ruled the Andean region believed that festivals were occasions when the living could connect with their ancestors and invoke divine power to bring life-giving rain to their fields and pastures. The dominant images in Tiwanaku art suggest that the Tiwanaku shared such beliefs.

Source: From Margaret Young-Sánchez, ed., *Tiwanaku: Ancestors of the Inca* (Lincoln: University of Nebraska Press, 2004), 47, Figure 2.26a.

EXAMINING THE EVIDENCE

1. The figures in the wool tunic hold staffs that take the form of hybrid creatures with serpent bodies and feline (perhaps jaguar) heads. Why do you think Tiwanaku's leaders chose these animals to represent their power?

2. What does the emphasis on symmetry and repetition in Tiwanaku art, architecture, and urban design suggest about their rulers' ideas of social and cosmic order?

Tiwanaku, the Wari state set up military outposts to control and extract tribute from local populations.

Wari was located on a plateau at a lower altitude than Tiwanaku, but the region was drier and more dependent on irrigation for agriculture. Wari farmers grew maize along with highland crops such as the mainstays, potato and quinoa, in terraced fields constructed on hillsides and watered by canals. Tiwanaku and Wari shared a common religious heritage but had markedly different forms of religious practice. Wari architecture suggests a more exclusive ceremonial culture restricted to private settings and a small elite, in contrast to the grand temples and public plazas of Tiwanaku.

Decline of the Highland States

Archaeological evidence reveals that by the ninth century Wari's colonial empire had collapsed and new building in the city had come to a halt. In around 1000 the same fate befell Tiwanaku. Prolonged drought had upset the fragile ecological balance of raised-field agriculture, and food production declined drastically. The city of Tiwanaku was abandoned, and political power came to be widely dispersed among local chieftains solidly entrenched in hilltop forts. Highland peoples continued some irrigated agriculture, but they relied heavily on animal herds for subsistence. Incessant warfare merely produced a political standoff among local chiefdoms, with no escalation into conquest and expansion until the rise of the Inca Empire in the fifteenth century.

Agrarian Societies in North America

FOCUS

How did the introduction of Mesoamerican crops transform North American peoples?

North America, like the Andean region, long remained isolated from developments in Mesoamerica. The deserts of northern Mexico impeded movement of peoples and technologies from the centers of Mesoamerican civilization to the vast landmass to the north. Although North American peoples cultivated some native plants as food sources as early as 2000 B.C.E., agriculture did not emerge as a way of life in North America until maize was introduced from Mesoamerica in around 1000 B.C.E. (see again Mapping the World, page 340).

Maize first appeared in North America's southwestern deserts, but the transition to agriculture in this arid region was gradual and uneven. The eastern woodlands had a greater variety of subsistence resources and a longer tradition of settled life, yet here, too, Mesoamerican crops eventually stimulated the emergence of complex societies and expanding networks of communication and exchange (see Map 11.3).

Pueblo Societies in the Southwestern Deserts

Shift to Settled Life

Mesoamerican agriculture penetrated the deserts of northern Mexico and the southwestern United States slowly. Farmers gradually adapted Mesoamerican crops to this hot, arid environment by carefully selecting seeds, soils, and naturally irrigated lands for cultivation. But it was only after 200 C.E. that yields from growing crops encouraged the southwestern desert peoples to abandon gathering and hunting in favor of settled agriculture. Clay pots used for food storage and cooking also first appeared in the Southwest at this time. Another important cause of the shift to farming was, ironically, the bow and arrow, introduced by bison hunters of North America's Great Plains, also in around 200 C.E. By providing more protein from game, use of the bow and arrow made it easier to adopt maize, which supplies ample calories but is very low in protein, as a staple food.

Early agricultural settlements in the southwestern deserts tended to be small, loose clusters of oval pit dwellings. But even these small villages contained special buildings used for ritual purposes. These buildings were the forerunners of the *kivas*, or large ceremonial rooms, of the later pueblo societies in which people lived in large complexes of adjoining adobe buildings.

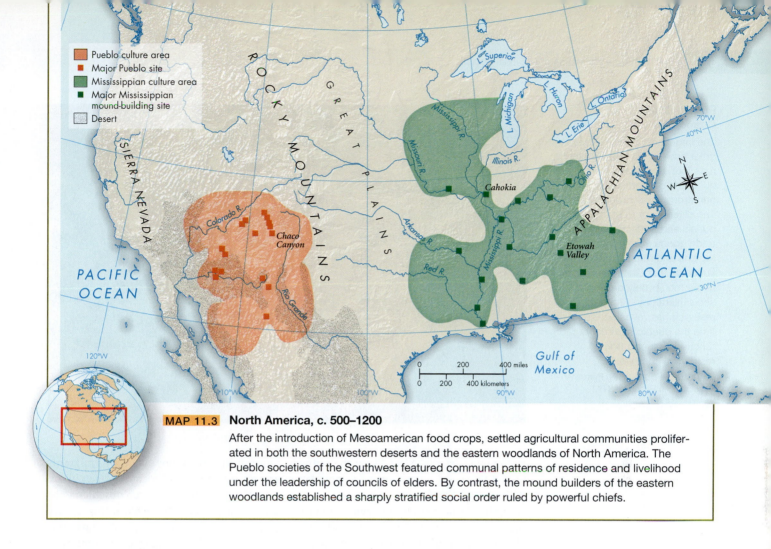

MAP 11.3 **North America, c. 500–1200**

After the introduction of Mesoamerican food crops, settled agricultural communities proliferated in both the southwestern deserts and the eastern woodlands of North America. The Pueblo societies of the Southwest featured communal patterns of residence and livelihood under the leadership of councils of elders. By contrast, the mound builders of the eastern woodlands established a sharply stratified social order ruled by powerful chiefs.

Pueblo Villages

The limited productivity of the land made self-sufficiency difficult. Farmers often traded to obtain food as well as salt, stone for toolmaking, and prestige goods, including hides and precious stones such as turquoise. After 700 C.E., population growth and increasing dependence on agriculture led to replacement of the pithouse villages with **pueblos**, in which hundreds or even thousands of people lived in contiguous buildings constructed of adobe clay or stone. By 900, pueblo villages had spread throughout much of the northern tier of the southwestern deserts, especially on the Colorado River plateau.

Chaco Canyon

Chaco Canyon, in northwestern New Mexico, dramatically illustrates the transformation of social life in the southwestern deserts as its agricultural livelihood matured. The first villages, along with maize and squash agriculture, appeared in the canyon in around 500 C.E. The largest of these early villages consisted of no more than twenty pithouses. Between 700 and 900, large pueblos replaced the pithouse villages. The dwelling spaces in the pueblos were arranged in semicircular arcs so that each multiroom family unit was equidistant from a central chamber, the **kiva** that served as the community's ceremonial nucleus.

During the tenth century, Chaco Canyon's population exploded. Much larger pueblos with more than two hundred rooms appeared. By the twelfth century the canyon had thirteen of these large pueblos housing a population of approximately six thousand people.

Both large and small settlements in Chaco Canyon contained turquoise workshops that manufactured a wide range of ritual ornaments. Because the nearest sources of turquoise were in the modern Santa Fe area, about one hundred miles to the east, craftsmen had to obtain their raw material through trade or possibly tribute. Exchange networks linked Chaco Canyon with at least seventy communities dispersed across more than ten thousand square miles throughout the Colorado River plateau. These outlying settlements also featured pueblo construction and were connected to Chaco Canyon by a network of

pueblo A communal village built by the peoples of southwestern North America, consisting of adjoining flat-roofed stone or adobe buildings arranged in terraces.

kiva A large ceremonial chamber located at the center of the pueblo.

Pueblo Bonito, Chaco Canyon

The largest of Chaco Canyon's great houses, Pueblo Bonito rose four stories and contained hundreds of rooms and numerous large circular kivas. The diversity of Pueblo Bonito's burials and artifacts—including trade goods from coastal regions and Mesoamerica—suggests that Chacoan society had a moderately developed social hierarchy. Archaeological research has revealed that over time the pueblo's primary function changed from residential complex to ceremonial center. (R. Perron/Art Resource, Art Resource, NY.)

rudimentary roads. Most likely the outlying communities were populated by emigrants forced to leave Chaco Canyon as population growth overburdened local food resources. Although Chaco Canyon may have served as a ritual hub for the entire web of settlements, centralized rule was absent even within the canyon's confines. Each pueblo seems to have pursued similar industrial, trade, and ceremonial activities. Historians generally have concluded that councils of elders coordinated these activities and managed relations with neighboring communities but that no privileged groups of families attained exclusive rights to political office. Hence in Chaco Canyon we see another example of the diversity of historical development. Agriculture led to population growth and large settlements, but, unlike in much of Eurasia, it did not lead to the emergence of kingship or empire building.

Abandonment of Chaco Canyon

In the early twelfth century prolonged drought weakened the canyon's fragile agricultural base. Many inhabitants migrated elsewhere, and others probably returned to foraging. Pueblo societies continued to flourish in other parts of the southwestern deserts where local conditions remained favorable to farming or trade. Although long-distance exchange continued, none of the other pueblo societies developed an integrated network of settlements like that of Chaco Canyon.

Some scholars believe that regional exchange and the founding of pueblo towns were stimulated by long-distance trade with merchants from the central Mexican highlands. Others contend that trade emerged in the southwestern deserts as a practical response to the unreliability of agriculture in this harsh environment. Environmental changes—especially soil exhaustion and increasingly irregular rainfall—may also have led to the abandonment of concentrated pueblo settlements and the return to more dispersed settlement beginning in the twelfth century. However, a similar trend toward concentration of political power and wider networks of exchange during the period 1000 to 1200, followed by a reversion to smaller and more isolated communities in the centuries before European contact, also occurred in the temperate woodlands of the Mississippi Valley, where livelihoods were less vulnerable to climatic change.

Mound-Building Societies in the Eastern Woodlands

Spread of Mesoamerican Agriculture

Beginning in around 700 C.E., the introduction of new technologies radically altered the evolution of eastern woodland societies in North America. The most important innovation was the cultivation of Mesoamerican food crops. The widespread cultivation of maize, perhaps prompted by greater control over labor and resources by a rising class of chiefs, revolutionized agriculture and transformed the woodlanders' economic livelihood. At the same time, the flint hoes that accompanied the spread of maize farming made it possible to construct mounds on a much larger scale, and the introduction of the bow and arrow from the Great Plains led to new hunting tactics.

The spread of Mesoamerican agriculture encouraged migration, regional exchange, and the formation of chiefdoms. Unlike the southwestern deserts, where the founding of settled communities followed the transition to agriculture, the eastern woodlands already had permanent villages. Still, population growth triggered by the capacity to produce more food led to greater occupational specialization and social complexity. Favorably located mound settlements conducted a lively trade in stone tools made from chert (a flintlike rock) and obsidian, marine shells from the Gulf of Mexico, and copper from the upper Great Lakes region, as well as salt, pottery, and jewelry. Population growth also caused friction among neighboring groups competing for land, and farmers displaced foragers from the river valleys best suited to agriculture.

As a result of these developments, the middle and lower reaches of the Mississippi River Valley experienced rapid economic and political changes. Scholars have given the name **Mississippian emergence** to the spread of common technologies, cultural practices, and forms of social and political organization among Mississippi Valley farming societies from the eighth century onward (see Lives and Livelihoods: The North American Mound Builders).

Although most Mississippian societies remained small, in some cases regional trading centers blossomed into powerful chiefdoms. The most famous is Cahokia (kuh-HOH-kee-uh), at the junction of the Illinois and Mississippi rivers just east of modern St. Louis. At its fullest extent, the settlement at Cahokia covered an area of eight square miles. Surrounded by four sets of wooden fortifications, it contained at least ten thousand people, and perhaps as many as thirty thousand. Cahokia's physical size and population thus were comparable to those of the city-states of ancient Mesopotamia, as well as Mesoamerica, in their formative stages of development.

Mound building at Cahokia began in around 900. From 1050 the pace of construction quickly accelerated, and by 1200 Cahokia's inhabitants had erected more than one hundred mounds surrounding a four-tiered pyramid set in the middle of four large plazas oriented north, south, east, and west. Five woodhenges (circles marked by enormous upright cedar posts) enclosed additional ceremonial sites.

Some of Cahokia's mounds were used for elite burials, but most served as platforms for buildings. The height of a mound was an index of prestige. The central pyramid, covering fourteen acres and rising over one hundred feet, was crowned by an enormous pole-and-thatch building covering five thousand square feet, which scholars believe was the residence of Cahokia's paramount chief. As was the case with the monuments of Mesoamerican cities, the placement of Cahokia's mounds was apparently determined by observations of crucial celestial events.

Also as in Mesoamerican cities, Cahokia's impressive mounds, plazas, and woodhenges displayed the power of its rulers to command labor and resources. The Grand Plaza of Cahokia served as a stage from which the chiefs presided over celebratory feasts, fiercely competitive games played with small stone disks known as chunkeys, and solemn death rites in which troops of young women, probably obtained as tribute from outlying areas, were sacrificed. Nonetheless, despite the similarity of Cahokia's plaza-and-pyramid

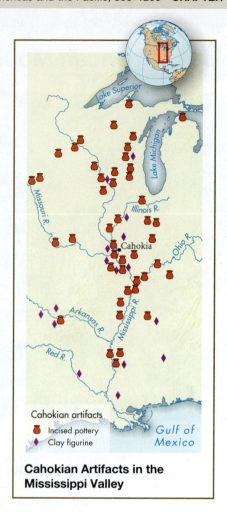

Cahokian Artifacts in the Mississippi Valley

Cahokia

Mississippian emergence The name scholars give to the spread of common technologies, cultural practices, and forms of social and political organization among a wide range of farming societies in the Mississippi Valley of North America, beginning in around 700 and peaking between 1000 and 1500.

The North American Mound Builders

Artist's Reconstruction of Cahokia
Compared to Chaco Canyon (see pages 357–358), Cahokia exhibited a more steeply graded social order. Moreover, in contrast to other mound-building societies—which gradually increased the size of their mounds—construction at Cahokia began with the massive pyramid and great plaza at its core. From the outset Cahokia's rulers displayed an ability to mobilize community labor on a scale unparalleled anywhere else in North America. (Richard Schlecht, National Geographic Image Collection.)

Scholars generally believe that the mounds built by North American woodlands societies symbolized the fertility of the earth and its inhabitants. The idea was that the act of building mounds renewed the fertility of the earth and the welfare of the community. Mound construction strengthened social solidarity by bringing people together in activities intended to ensure the prosperity of all. Moreover, mound building was accompanied by feasting that celebrated communal solidarity. Yet as the woodlands societies grew more complex and stratified, mound-building began to serve other purposes. Paramount chiefs and elite families often appropriated the mounds' symbolic power by reserving them as burial grounds for their exclusive use or by erecting temples on their summits to glorify their ancestors.

The Etowah (EE-toe-wah) River Valley in northwestern Georgia provides evidence of this process of social and political change. Here, as in many parts of the eastern

architecture to Mesoamerican prototypes, there is no evidence of direct Mesoamerican influence at Cahokia or other Mississippian mound-building sites. Indeed, archaeologists have not found imported Mesoamerican manufactured goods anywhere in the eastern woodlands. Although Mesoamerican beliefs and rituals may have had some influence on them, Cahokia's elite generated its own distinctive cosmology and ideology (see Seeing the Past: Symbols of Fertility in Cahokian Sculpture).

Cahokia's Influence   Following the abrupt and dramatic consolidation of power at Cahokia in around 1050, its influence radiated outward throughout the Mississippi Valley. A number of other regional centers, perhaps rivals of Cahokia, emerged from the area of modern Oklahoma to the Atlan-

woodlands, the adoption of maize agriculture led to greater social and political complexity. Etowah, which eventually boasted six mounds, became the region's major political center. It first achieved local prominence in the eleventh century, but over the next five centuries its history showed a cyclical pattern of development and abandonment.

In the eleventh century Etowah was a small settlement with residences, community buildings, and perhaps a small mound and plaza. Ritual life was confined to feasting, and there was a notable absence of prestige goods that would signify a strong social hierarchy. The earliest confirmed evidence of mound building dates from the twelfth century, when several other mound settlements appear in the Etowah Valley. Although these settlements were probably the capitals of independent chiefdoms, archaeological evidence of social ranking at this time is slim. Apparently these settlements were still organized around principles of community solidarity rather than hierarchy and stratification.

In the first half of the thirteenth century, the entire Etowah Valley was abandoned, for unknown reasons. When settlement resumed after 1250, a social transformation occurred. Over the next century mound building expanded dramatically, and a sharply stratified chiefdom emerged that exercised overlordship over at least four neighboring mound settlements. Monuments were built at the site, including a large ceremonial hall and a raised central plaza. In a burial mound reserved exclusively for Etowah's ruling elite, archaeologists have found prestige goods such as engraved shell ornaments, flint swords, embossed copper plates, and copper headdress ornaments. The wide dispersal of these items across the southeastern woodlands in the thirteenth and fourteenth centuries indicates that there were strong networks of regional exchange.

In Etowah and elsewhere in the region, wooden fortifications and ceremonial art featuring motifs of violence and combat testify to increasing political conflict and warfare. Copper plates depicting winged warriors found in Etowah burial mounds were almost certainly imported from the Mississippian heartland, if not from Cahokia itself.

The concentration of power that was evident in the Etowah chiefdom during the thirteenth and fourteenth centuries proved to be unstable. After 1375 Etowah and other large chiefdoms in the southeastern woodlands collapsed. The inhabitants again abandoned the site of Etowah. Regional trade networks became constricted, and the flow of prestige goods diminished. Whether chiefly authority was weakened by enemy attack or internal strife is uncertain. By the time the Spanish explorers arrived in 1540, another trend toward concentration of political power and expansion of territorial control was well under way. At this point, however, the capacity to organize mound building and the possession of prestige goods were no longer sufficient to claim political authority. Warfare had supplanted religious symbolism as the source of a chief's power.

For Further Information:

King, Adam. *Etowah: The Political History of a Chiefdom Capital*. Tuscaloosa: University of Alabama Press, 2003.

Reilly, F. Kent, III, and James F. Garber, eds. *Ancient Objects and Sacred Realms: Interpretations of Mississippian Iconography*. Austin: University of Texas Press, 2007.

tic coast. Local chiefs imitated the mound building and sacred ceremonies of the Mississippian culture. Control of prestige goods acquired through trade enhanced the charismatic authority of these chiefs. Still, the power of the paramount chiefs at Cahokia and elsewhere rested on their alliances with lesser chiefs, who were the heads of their own distinct communities, rather than on direct control of the settled population. Political power thus remained fragile—vulnerable to shifts in trade patterns, economic fortunes, and political loyalties.

Cahokia declined after 1250 as competition from rival chiefs grew and as its farming base shrank due to prolonged droughts and deforestation. After 1300, Cahokia's inhabitants abandoned its grand ceremonial center and dispersed. Other smaller Mississippian

Cahokia's Collapse

Symbols of Fertility in Cahokian Sculpture

Birger Figurine (Courtesy of the Illinois State Archaeological Survey, University of Illinois.)

Mississippian peoples rarely incorporated images of humans and their activities into their art. Scholars have therefore closely scrutinized a small number of flint clay sculptures in the form of human beings for clues to Mississippian ideas about themselves and their world. These figurines mostly depict men engaged in battle, beheading enemies, and making offerings to ancestors and gods. Only in a few rare cases, such as the so-called Birger figurine shown here, do they include images of women.

Unearthed at Cahokia, the Birger figurine dates to the early twelfth century, the peak of Cahokia's dominance. It depicts a woman kneeling on a coiled snake, her left hand resting on the serpent's feline head (perhaps a puma) and her right hand holding a hoe. On her back she wears a square pack. Vines entwine the woman's body and stretch up her spine, putting forth fruit resembling squash or gourds. The figurine, discovered at a mortuary temple reserved for priests and nobles, was apparently deliberately broken during a ritual dedicated to the dead.

The association with serpents and agricultural tools and crops is typical among the small number of female Mississippian flint clay figures. Scholars generally agree that these symbols link the fertility of women as childbearers to the fertility of the earth. The snake symbolizes the earth itself, which the woman cultivates with her hoe. The plants and fruit wrapped around the woman's body signify both the fertility of women and their prominent role in farming. Images of the land and farming appear only in connection with female figures in Mississippian art.

Some scholars go further to argue that the Birger figurine and similar objects express a mythology in which women are associated with an underworld (symbolized by the serpent) that is the source of water, fertility, and the power of water-dwelling monsters. Male chiefs and warriors, by contrast, appear together with signs of the heavens, such as the sun and birds. The imagery of the Birger figurine also suggests a connection to the Earth Mother or Corn Mother myths that recur frequently in the ceremonial traditions of later eastern woodland peoples. The Earth Mother symbolized the life-giving power of plants and women, as well as the cycles of regeneration in which crops sprung from seeds and the souls of the dead were reborn in children. The Earth Mother thus was a goddess of both life and death.

Mississippian art and mythology exhibit a profound dualism: the underworld associated with women and water is strictly divided from the upper world of men and its motifs of sun, fire, and birds. This rigid gender segregation undoubtedly reflects a society that sharply separated the spheres, activities, and powers of men and women.

Source: Birger Figurine: From Rinita A. Dalan et al., *Envisioning Cahokia: A Landscape Perspective* (DeKalb: Northern Illinois University Press, 2003), 202, Figure 47. (Courtesy of Illinois Transportation Archaeological Research Program, University of Illinois.)

EXAMINING THE EVIDENCE

1. In what ways do Mississippian ideas about female qualities and powers, as revealed in the Birger figurine, differ from the Mesoamerican conception of masculine power expressed by the "At a Crossroads" ballplayer illustration on page 338?

2. Why would the priests break objects such as this figurine during the rituals performed in honor of the dead?

chiefdoms persisted down to the first contacts with Europeans in the sixteenth century and beyond. But in the wake of Cahokia's collapse, long-distance economic and cultural exchanges waned, and the incidence of violence grew. The prevalence of warrior imagery, the concentration of the population in fortified towns, and the ample evidence of traumatic death from excavated cemeteries all point to the emergence of warfare as a way of life.

The scale and complexity of the settlements and ritual complexes at Cahokia were unique in North America. Yet its influence as a panregional cultural force is reminiscent of other urban centers in the Americas. As in Tiwanaku, feasting, sacrifice, and resettlement of rural inhabitants in the urban core forged a distinctive cultural identity at Cahokia. Also like Tiwanaku, Cahokia apparently served as a ritual center for a group of independent chiefdoms that for a time merged into a single political entity. At the peak of its power, Cahokia's culinary habits, pottery styles, and agricultural techniques spread over a vast area. In this sense, as an economic and political crossroads, Cahokia was central to the emergence of a distinctive Mississippian society.

Habitat and Adaptation in the Pacific Islands

The Lapita colonization (see Chapter 8) transformed the landscapes and seascapes of the western Pacific, or Near Oceania. After approximately 200 B.C.E., though, what historians call the "long pause" in transoceanic migrations set in. Subsequently the cultural unity spawned by the Lapita migrations fragmented as local groups adapted to their diverse island habitats. Trade networks collapsed, and pottery making declined everywhere.

> **FOCUS**
>
> In what ways did the habitats and resources of the Pacific Islands promote both cultural unity and cultural diversity?

The "long pause" may reflect not people's lack of effort, but rather their lack of success in making landfall on the smaller and far more widely dispersed islands of the central and eastern Pacific, or Remote Oceania. But in around 300 C.E. (some scholars would say even several centuries earlier), a new wave of migration began with a leap eastward of more than twelve hundred miles from Samoa to the Marquesas and Society Island archipelagoes. This second wave of exploration brought human colonists to virtually every habitable island in the Pacific Ocean by the year 1000 (see Map 11.4).

In Near Oceania, the interaction of the Lapita peoples with the native Papuan societies had generated extraordinary cultural diversity. In contrast, this second wave of migrations into the farthest reaches of Remote Oceania fostered a culturally unified set of islands known as Polynesia. Still, Polynesian settlers did modify their livelihoods and social and political institutions to suit the resources of their island habitats. **Human ecology**—the ways in which people adapt to their natural environment—was as flexible in the Pacific Islands as in the world's great continental landmasses.

Polynesian Expansion

The Pacific Islands are commonly divided into three parts: Melanesia ("Middle Islands"), Micronesia ("Small Islands"), and Polynesia ("Many Islands"). Yet Melanesia makes sense only as a geographic label, not as a social or cultural unit. In fact, the peoples of Melanesia (if we include New Guinea) make up the most diverse and complex assembly of peoples and cultures on earth. Similarly, Micronesia had at least two major language groups and was populated over the course of four separate periods of immigration.

Polynesian societies, in contrast, share a strong social and cultural identity. Polynesian culture emerged from the Lapita settlements of Tonga and Samoa in the first millennium B.C.E. Following the leap to the Marquesas and Society archipelagoes, Polynesians spread through a chain of migrations westward into Micronesia, northward to the Hawaiian Islands, and eastward as far as Easter Island.

human ecology Adaptation of people to the natural environment they inhabit.

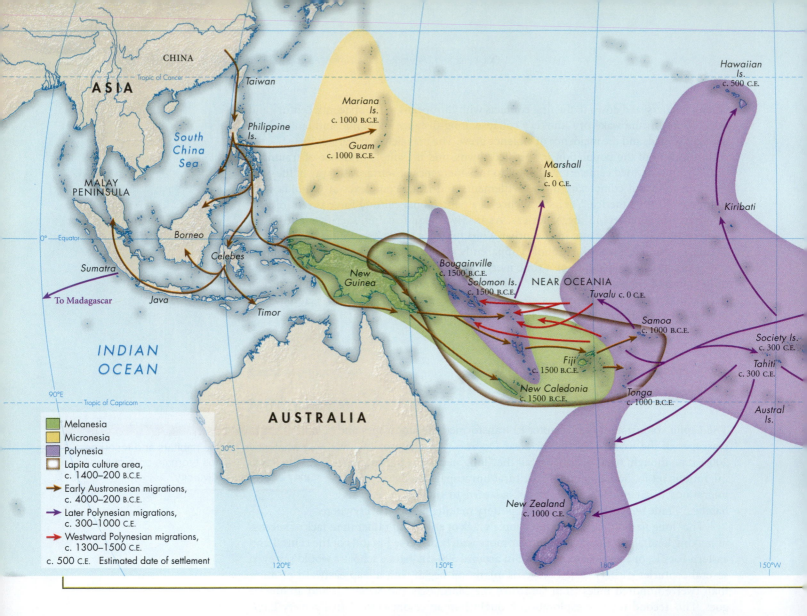

Polynesia's Cultural Unity

Like the Lapita colonization, the Polynesian expansion included a cycle of vigorous interisland interactions during the initial phase of colonization, followed by progressive isolation and interruption of communication and exchange. The most remote parts of Polynesia, such as Easter Island and the Hawaiian archipelago, became solitary worlds.

The distinctive character of Polynesian societies owes much to their isolation. Fiji was virtually unique in maintaining exchanges of goods, people, and cultural influences with Melanesian societies; Tonga and the rest of Polynesia lost all contact with Melanesia. But however isolated the Polynesian societies of the central Pacific became, their recent common ancestry gave them similar languages, social practices, and forms of livelihood. One striking feature of the Polynesian expansion was the widespread abandonment of pottery manufacture. In contrast to the Lapita peoples, who regarded elaborately decorated pottery as a sign of high social rank, pottery—for reasons still unknown—lost its status as a prestige good among the Polynesians. Pottery was also replaced by coconut shells and wooden bowls for utilitarian purposes such as storing and cooking food.

Although Polynesian settlers had reached all of the habitable Pacific Islands by 1000, migration among settled islands continued. In around the year 1300 Polynesian voyagers would begin to travel westward into Micronesia and the southern parts of Melanesia. On some small islands, such as Tikopia (TEE-co-pi-ah) in Melanesia, Polynesians would wholly replace the native population, but more commonly the migrants mixed with the native peoples to produce hybrid cultures. Micronesian peoples, living in unstable envi-

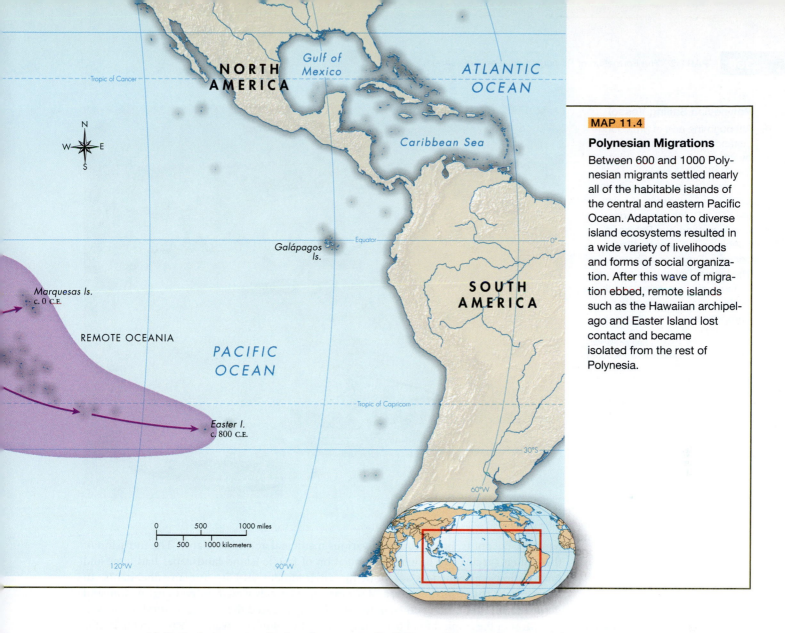

MAP 11.4

Polynesian Migrations
Between 600 and 1000 Polynesian migrants settled nearly all of the habitable islands of the central and eastern Pacific Ocean. Adaptation to diverse island ecosystems resulted in a wide variety of livelihoods and forms of social organization. After this wave of migration ebbed, remote islands such as the Hawaiian archipelago and Easter Island lost contact and became isolated from the rest of Polynesia.

ronments with limited resources, displayed enormous flexibility in changing their ways of life and welcoming strangers into their communities.

Distinctive ecosystems nurtured a wide range of livelihoods and political systems across the Polynesian Pacific. Larger islands with richer and more varied resources, among them Tahiti, Tonga, and Hawaii, gave rise to highly stratified societies and complex chiefdoms with tens of thousands of subjects. The rigid hierarchical structure of the Polynesian chiefdoms was based on command of economic resources. The vast majority in their populations were landless commoners. Local chiefs held title to cultivated lands but owed **fealty** (allegiance to a higher authority) and tribute to paramount chiefs, who wielded sacred power over entire islands (as we will see in Chapter 12's Counterpoint on the Hawaiian Islands, page 398).

Ecosystems and Social Stratification

Subsistence and Survival in the Pacific Islands

Counter to the romantic fantasies of nineteenth-century European travelers and twentieth-century anthropologists, the Pacific Islands were not pristine natural worlds undisturbed by their "primitive" human inhabitants. On the contrary, human hands had radically transformed the island ecosystems. For example, the islands of Remote Oceania originally lacked plant and animal species suitable for human food consumption. Polynesian settlers changed all that by bringing with them pigs, dogs, chickens, yams, taro, sugar cane,

fealty An expression of allegiance to a higher political authority, often verified by swearing an oath of loyalty, giving tribute, and other gestures of submission.

365

Polynesian Sailing Vessel

Although the age of great long-distance voyaging had ceased by the time Europeans reached the Pacific, Polynesians continued to make open-ocean journeys of hundreds of miles. In 1616 a Dutch mariner drew this illustration of a Polynesian double-hulled canoe sailing between Tonga and Samoa. The largest Polynesian canoes were roughly the same length as the sailing vessels of the European explorers. (*A Chronological History of the Voyages & Discoveries in the South Sea or Pacific Ocean*, London: Lake Hansard & Sons.)

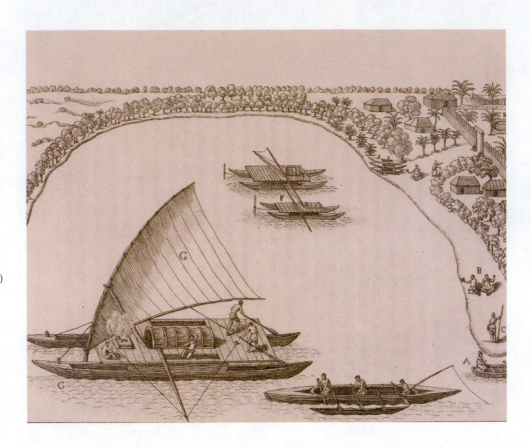

**Environmental
Transformation and
Population Growth**

bananas, coconuts, breadfruit, and various medicinal and fiber plants. The intrusion of these alien species and human manipulation of fragile island landscapes had large and long-lasting consequences for both the environment and its human inhabitants. In many places native bird, turtle, and sea mammal species were hunted to extinction, and **deforestation**, the cutting down of forests, sharply reduced the islands' natural resources.

Most of the tropical food plants transported by colonizers readily thrived in the Pacific Islands. Settlers practiced horticulture (the cultivation of fruits and vegetables), planting orchards of coconuts and bananas around their villages while cutting down rain forests to make room for root and tuber crops that required little care. As in Iceland's early history (see Chapter 9), explosive population growth typically followed initial settlement on uninhabited islands. Settlers had a compelling reason—fear of extinction—to have enough children to attain populations large enough to maintain their societies. Population densities on many islands reached 250 persons per square mile. Ecological constraints, however, ultimately curbed unrestricted population growth.

Micronesia's low-lying atolls—rings of coral surrounding a central lagoon—presented the most challenging environments. Exposed to destruction by typhoons and tsunamis, lacking fresh water other than rainfall, with just sand and crushed coral for soil, atolls offered only slender footholds for human colonists. Because cultivating taro and breadfruit was impossible on many coral atolls, coconut trees were essential to human survival. In addition to depending on coconuts for food, atoll dwellers used coconut leaves for textile fiber and for construction material. Lacking ceramics and metals, the atoll peoples fashioned utensils and tools from coconuts, seashells, and fish bones.

On many islands, population pressure began to strain resources after 1100. Where possible, islanders applied more laborious agricultural methods, building irrigation canals and terraced or walled garden plots. In the Marquesas, swelling population growth increased competition and warfare. More fortified villages were built, and the authority of warrior chiefs rose. Settlement became concentrated in the island interiors, which afforded

deforestation The cutting down of forests, usually to clear land for farming and human settlement.

not only protection from sea raiders but lands more suitable for intensive cultivation. A similar pattern of intensified agriculture and warfare in response to population pressure appeared in Fiji. The growing diversity of local ceramic styles in Fiji also suggests a greater demarcation of ethnic groups and political boundaries. Here, too, constant warfare shifted the basis of chiefship from priestly duties to military leadership.

Increased Competition and Warfare

The most striking example of the fragility of island ecosystems and the risk of demographic catastrophe is Easter Island. When Polynesian voyagers originally settled Easter Island sometime after 600 C.E., the island was well endowed with fertile soils and abundant forests. These rich resources supported a population that at its peak numbered ten thousand people. Easter Island's famous stone monuments—thirty-ton sculptures believed to be images of ancestors who were transformed into gods—were carved and installed on more than two hundred temple platforms across the island between 1100 and 1500. But the clearing of forests for agriculture depleted fuel and construction resources, and erosion and exposure to wind and surf ruined soil fertility. After 1500, the island was plunged into incessant raiding and warfare, accompanied by ritual cannibalism. Construction of stone monuments halted. As the once plentiful flora and fauna of Easter Island were decimated, its human population dwindled to a mere several hundred persons subsisting mainly on fishing, the Pacific Ocean's most reliable resource.

Easter Island

COUNTERPOINT
Social Complexity in Bougainville

Bougainville (bow-gahn-VEEL), one of the chain of islands stretching in a long arc southeastward from New Guinea, typifies the phenomenon of **ethnogenesis**, the formation of separate ethnic groups from common ancestors. In contrast to the underlying social and cultural unity of many of the societies studied in this chapter, the long-settled islands of Melanesia display extraordinary social and cultural diversity. The complexity of the Melanesian world presents an important challenge for any theory of the evolution of human societies. Here the progress of history fostered not closer interaction and cross-cultural borrowing but rather more acute social differences and strong ethnic boundaries.

> **FOCUS**
>
> Why did the historical development of the Melanesian island of Bougainville depart so sharply from that of contemporaneous societies in the Americas and the Pacific?

Bougainville's Diverse Peoples

Situated slightly below the equator, Bougainville has a tropical climate with virtually no seasonal variation, enabling the island's farmers to cultivate food crops, mainly taro, year-round. Yet with four active volcanoes, Bougainville is one of the most geologically unstable places on earth. Volcanic eruptions have periodically covered major portions of the island with ash and forced the inhabitants to relocate, at least temporarily. The island, roughly the size of Puerto Rico, is sparsely populated even today. The mountainous interior remains virtually uninhabited. Settlements are concentrated along streams on the relatively flat terrain of the northern coast and in the southern interior.

Twenty different languages are spoken on Bougainville today. Scholars classify twelve of these languages as Austronesian (AW-stroh-NEE-zhuhn), the language group of the seafarers who settled in the islands of Southeast Asia and the Pacific during the Lapita colonization. Linguists broadly define the rest as Papuan (PAH-poo-en), the languages spoken by the ancient inhabitants of New Guinea, although their relationship to the other Papuan languages is uncertain. Four of Bougainville's languages are so idiosyncratic that the associations among them confound linguists.

Linguistic and Cultural Diversity

ethnogenesis The formation of separate ethnic groups from common ancestors.

Bougainville

Beyond the striking language differences, Bougainville's inhabitants also vary so much in stature, body type, and biological chemistry that Bougainville islanders rank among the most genetically diverse populations on the planet. Cultural variation is similarly striking. Although pottery manufacture on Bougainville dates back to the pre-Lapita era, some groups apparently have never made pottery and rarely sought ceramic wares from those who did.

What accounts for such remarkable diversity within the confines of this one island? One popular theory is that the kind of tropical agriculture practiced in Bougainville is relatively rich and reliable, and so the islanders have not had to build trading networks or other kinds of connections between communities to meet their needs. Traditions of matrilineal descent and local **endogamy**— marriage within the group—reinforced this pattern of isolated village life. The social isolation of individual villages also tended to raise language barriers over time. With two exceptions, the geographical range of the languages spoken on Bougainville does not exceed fifteen miles in diameter. Further, as modern biological research shows, small populations are more likely to experience large genetic fluctuations from one generation to the next, which fosters more, not less, genetic diversity. Not surprisingly, genetic variation among Bougainville's modern populations correlates strongly with language groups.

The Historical Roots of Social Difference

Yet the diversity of Bougainville's languages did not result from a long period of isolation. The island probably experienced a number of separate immigrations both before and after the Lapita era. The island's Austronesian speakers did not simply all arrive together at the time of the Lapita migrations. There is clear evidence that some coastal regions were resettled by Austronesian speakers after volcanic eruptions displaced the previous inhabitants.

The Siwai and the Buin: A Case Study

Further, it is not possible to make neat distinctions between the cultures of "native" Papuan speakers and "immigrant" Austronesian speakers. The Siwai (sih-why), a Papuan-speaking community in southern Bougainville, is noted in anthropological theory as a model **big man society**. According to the American anthropologist Marshall Sahlins, so-called big man societies are characterized by an egalitarian social structure and strong communal identity based on sharing and reciprocal exchange. The role of the big man is to redistribute wealth among members of the community to ensure the well-being of all, but the big man does not hold a position above the rest of society. Sahlins has contrasted Melanesian big man societies with the sharply stratified social hierarchy of Polynesian chiefdoms, in which a hereditary elite of chiefs monopolized political power and the control of economic resources. Near the Siwai in southern Bougainville, however, is another Papuan-speaking group, the Buin (boo-een), whose society developed the high degree of stratification and inherited rank and privilege typical of Polynesian chiefdoms.

Environmental adaptation does not explain the different social structures of the Siwai and the Buin: the two groups occupy virtually identical habitats, practice similar forms of irrigated taro agriculture, and speak closely related languages. Despite their similar livelihoods, the Siwai and Buin embraced different notions of prestige and status. For example, the Buin regarded pottery making as women's work, whereas the Siwai, uniquely among Melanesian societies, reserve pottery making exclusively for men. Scholars have explained this peculiar feature of Siwai culture as a consequence of the unusually cloistered life of Siwai women. According to this theory, knowledge of pottery making was acquired by men, who, unlike women, could travel outside the village, and it became a mark of their superior status.

This contrast underscores one important difference between the Buin and their Siwai neighbors. The Buin had access to the coast and, unlike the Siwai, interacted with peoples in neighboring islands. They learned their techniques of pottery making from Austronesian-speaking inhabitants of the nearby Shetland Islands in around 1000. Indeed, immigrants

endogamy Marriage within a defined group, such as a village or a kinship network.

big man society In modern anthropological theory, an egalitarian society in which a chosen leader, the "big man," supervises the distribution of the community's collective wealth and resources.

from the Shetlands probably arrived in southern Bougainville at that time and may have been absorbed into Buin society.

Yet differences in contact with the outside world cannot fully explain the variations in social practices among Bougainville societies. Some scholars have suggested that in the past, a more pronounced social hierarchy was common in Melanesian societies. In their view, the egalitarian big man societies for which Melanesia became the model were not ancient or primitive forms of social organization; rather, they resulted from the profound changes set in motion by contact with Europeans, including population losses from disease. At the very least, we can no longer attribute the complex human ecology of Melanesia in general, and of Bougainville in particular, to the former historical interpretation of unchanging island cultures cut off from the march of history by the encircling ocean.

Conclusion

During the period 300 to 1200, distinctive regional cultures coalesced in many parts of the Americas and the Pacific Islands. As in Latin Christendom and East Asia, the spread and intensification of agriculture, expanding networks of trade and cultural exchange, and the founding of cities and states led to the formation of common civilizations.

This period marked the classical age in Mesoamerica and the Andean region. There, the development of urban societies and states generated lasting traditions concerning knowledge, livelihoods, and social organization. Rulers such as the Maya Holy Lord Eighteen Rabbit built monumental cities and conducted elaborate public rituals to display their supreme power and bind their subjects to their will.

Permanent towns and long-distance networks of exchange also developed in North America. The spread of prestige goods and ritual art in the eastern woodlands and the southwestern deserts also indicates active cross-cultural borrowing in these regions, at least among elites.

The rapid peopling of the islands of Remote Oceania between 600 and 1000 gave this vast region a common cultural identity as Polynesia. Similar political and social structures and forms of livelihood took root across Polynesia, even though many island populations, such as those of the Hawaiian archipelago and Easter Island, lost contact with the outside world.

Striking, too, are patterns of regional diversity. Different types of social order evolved as new crops and technologies diffused and were adopted, people adjusted social and political institutions and forms of livelihood to new or transformed habitats, and notions of prestige, status, and authority changed. In all of these regions—even among the small village societies of Bougainville, which mostly shunned contact and interaction with their neighbors—social identities and community boundaries changed constantly. Ethnogenesis was a dynamic, continuous, and open-ended process.

By the year 1200, many of these societies were suffering from economic decline and political fragmentation. Scholars have attributed the collapse of the Maya city-state network in the ninth century, the disintegration of the Tiwanaku state in around 1000, and the abandonment of Chaco Canyon and Cahokia in the twelfth and thirteenth centuries primarily to ecological causes: either some climatic catastrophe, or the inability of the existing agricultural technologies and political systems to provide for their growing populations. The collapse of these societies reminds us of the fragility of their agricultural systems, still limited to Stone Age technologies, and their vulnerability to long-term ecological and climatic changes. As we shall see in the next chapter, advances in agricultural and industrial technology and the development of new economic institutions in Eurasia during the eleventh to thirteenth centuries laid the foundations for more sustained economic and demographic growth.

RESOURCES FOR RESEARCH

General Works

Our knowledge of the history of all the societies in this chapter except the Maya depends on research in fields such as archaeology and linguistics rather than written sources. The essays in Quilter and Miller use broad comparative and interdisciplinary analysis to survey the Americas as a whole in the era before the arrival of Europeans. Diamond's provocative analysis of human responses to ecological crises and the collapse of social systems includes case studies of Easter Island, the southwestern deserts of North America, and the Maya.

Diamond, Jared. *Collapse: How Societies Choose to Fail or Succeed.* 2004.

Quilter, Jeffrey, and Mary Miller, eds. *A Pre-Columbian World.* 2006.

Renfrew, Colin, and Steven Shennan, eds. *Peer Polity Interaction and Socio-Political Change.* 1986.

The Classical Age of Mesoamerica and Its Aftermath

The scholarship on the Maya is especially rich. Drew provides an excellent overview of both Maya civilization and the development of scholarship on the Maya. Carrasco's study of the Feathered Serpent is a pioneering investigation of the common cultural heritage of Mesoamerica as a whole.

Carrasco, David. *Quetzalcoatl and the Irony of Empire: Myth and Prophecies in the Aztec Tradition*, rev. ed. 2000.

Drew, David. *The Lost Chronicles of the Maya Kings.* 1999.

Pasztory, Esther. *Teotihuacan: An Experiment in Living.* 1997.

Schele, Linda, and Peter Mathews. *The Code of Kings: The Language of Seven Sacred Maya Temples and Tombs.* 1998.

Sharer, Robert J. *Daily Life in Maya Civilization*, 2d ed. 2009.

City and State Building in the Andean Region

Recent studies have sought to trace the social and political evolution of precolonial Andean societies through comparative studies of archaeological remains. Kolata's study remains the most thorough examination of Tiwanaku's archaeological record. Janusek proposes new models for understanding the formation of social identity and political power in the Andean region in a very accessible fashion.

Janusek, John Wayne. *Ancient Tiwanaku.* 2008.

Janusek, John Wayne. *Identity and Power in the Ancient Andes: Tiwanaku Cities Through Time.* 2004.

Kolata, Alan. *The Tiwanaku: Portrait of an Andean Civilization.* 1993.

Stanish, Charles. *Ancient Titicaca: The Evolution of Complex Society in Southern Peru and Northern Bolivia.* 2003.

von Hagen, Adriana, and Craig Morris. *The Cities of the Ancient Andes.* 1998.

Agrarian Societies in North America

Reconstruction of the history of North American societies during this period relies especially heavily on the fruits of archaeological research. Fagan's skill at weaving up-to-date coverage of new archaeological evidence into a compelling narrative is displayed in both his textbook survey of North American societies and his Chaco Canyon volume.

Emerson, Thomas E. *Cahokia and the Archaeology of Power.* 1997.

Fagan, Brian. *Ancient North America: The Archaeology of a Continent*, rev. ed. 2005.

Fagan, Brian. *Chaco Canyon: Archaeologists Explore the Lives of an Ancient Society.* 2005.

Milner, George R. *The Moundbuilders: Ancient Peoples of Eastern North America.* 2005.

Pauketat, Timothy R. *Ancient Cahokia and the Mississippians.* 2004.

Habitat and Adaptation in the Pacific Islands

Kirch's 2000 book provides the most comprehensive survey of settlement and social development in the Pacific Islands, and the essays in Howe focus on voyaging and exploration. Challenging the idea of universal stages of social evolution, Earle marshals evidence from case studies of Denmark, Hawaii, and the Andes to distinguish the sources of power in chiefdom societies.

Earle, Timothy. *How Chiefs Come to Power: The Political Economy in Prehistory.* 1997.

Howe, K. R., ed. *Vaka Moana, Voyages of the Ancestors: The Discovery and Settlement of the Pacific.* 2007.

Kirch, Patrick V. *The Evolution of the Polynesian Chiefdoms.* 1984.

Kirch, Patrick V. *On the Road of the Winds: An Archaeological History of the Pacific Islands Before European Contact.* 2000.

Terrell, John. *Prehistory in the Pacific Islands: A Study of Variation in Language, Customs, and Human Biology.* 1986.

COUNTERPOINT: Social Complexity in Bougainville

Since the 1930s anthropologists have considered Melanesia, and Bougainville in particular, as a laboratory for the study of social evolution. The classic works by Sahlins and Service drew on extensive cross-cultural comparisons to develop highly influential models of the emergence of complex social organization and political hierarchy in human societies.

Sahlins, Marshall. *Social Stratification in Polynesia.* 1958.

Service, Robert. *Origins of the State and Civilization: The Process of Cultural Evolution.* 1975.

Spriggs, Matthew. *The Island Melanesians.* 1997.

▶ **For additional primary sources from this period**, see *Sources of Crossroads and Cultures.*

▶ **For Web sites, images, and documents related to topics in this chapter**, see Make History at bedfordstmartins.com/smith.

The major global development in this chapter ▶ The formation of distinctive regional cultures in the Americas and the Pacific Islands between 300 and 1200.

IMPORTANT EVENTS

c. 150–300	Building of the city of Teotihuacán in the Valley of Mexico
c. 250–900	Mesoamerica's classical age
c. 500	First permanent settlements in Chaco Canyon
c. 500–1000	Andean state of Tiwanaku
c. 550–650	Fall and destruction of Teotihuacán
c. 600–1000	Polynesian settlement of Pacific Islands
c. 700	Moche city of Pampa Grande destroyed
c. 700–900	Heyday of the Andean state of Wari
c. 800–900	Collapse of the Maya city-states
c. 850–1150	Building of the large pueblos in Chaco Canyon
c. 900	Rise of the Chimú state centered at Chan Chan
c. 950–1150	Toltec state's reign as the dominant power in the Valley of Mexico
c. 1050	Consolidation of Cahokia's dominance in the lower Mississippi Valley region
c. 1100–1500	Construction of Easter Island's stone monuments
c. 1150	Abandonment of the pueblos in Chaco Canyon
c. 1250–1300	Collapse and abandonment of Cahokia

KEY TERMS

ayllu (p. 353)
big man society (p. 368)
chiefdom (p. 343)
ch'ulel (p. 347)
city-state (p. 343)
deforestation (p. 366)
endogamy (p. 368)
ethnogenesis (p. 367)
fealty (p. 365)

Holy Lord (p. 347)
human ecology (p. 363)
kiva (p. 357)
Mississippian emergence (p. 359)
obsidian (p. 344)
prestige good (p. 344)
pueblo (p. 357)
Tollan (p. 344)

CHAPTER OVERVIEW QUESTIONS

1. How did these societies, equipped with only Stone Age technology, develop the institutions and patterns of exchange to tame often hostile environments and build complex civilizations?

2. How did differences in environment foster or discourage exchanges among adjacent regions?

3. What were the sources of political power in the societies discussed in this chapter, and how were they similar or dissimilar?

4. How did differences in urban design reflect distinctive forms of political and social organization?

SECTION FOCUS QUESTIONS

1. What common beliefs and social and political patterns did the various local societies of Mesoamerica's classical age share?

2. How did environmental settings and natural resources shape livelihoods, social organization, and state building in the Andean region?

3. How did the introduction of Mesoamerican crops transform North American peoples?

4. In what ways did the habitats and resources of the Pacific Islands promote both cultural unity and cultural diversity?

5. Why did the historical development of Bougainville depart so sharply from that of contemporaneous societies in the Americas and the Pacific?

MAKING CONNECTIONS

1. Why were the human populations of the regions covered in this chapter more vulnerable to ecological changes than the settled societies of Eurasia?

2. How did the political and social organization of North American chiefdoms compare with those of the Maya city-states?

3. Although North America's eastern woodlands farmers began to cultivate the same food crops as Mesoamerican peoples during the Mississippian emergence, their societies developed in different ways. What might explain these variations?

12

AT A CROSSROADS ▶

Arabs and Persians dominated the Indian Ocean trade routes, but by the eleventh century Indian and Malay mariners also plied Asian seas from Africa to China. This thirteenth-century illustration depicts a dhow, the most common type of Indian Ocean sailing vessel, on a voyage from East Africa to Basra, the great port linking Mesopotamia to the Persian Gulf. Indian Ocean trade vastly expanded cultural as well as economic exchange: although the passengers are Arabs, the crew appears to be Indian. (Bibliothèque Nationale, Paris, France/Bildarchiv Preussischer Kulturbesitz/Art Resource, NY.)

The Rise of Commerce in Afro-Eurasia

900–1300

Early in the twelfth century, the Jewish merchant Allan bin Hassun wrote home from Aden, in Yemen on the coast of the Arabian Sea, upon his return from India. Allan had been sent to Yemen by his father-in-law, a prominent Cairo cloth merchant, to sell the purple-dyed cloth that was the father-in-law's specialty. But the cloth had proved unprofitable, so Allan persuaded his reluctant father-in-law to supply him with coral and perfume for a trading venture to India. The journey to India and back had been long and dangerous, and Allan's return had been delayed repeatedly by local uprisings, storms, and accidents.

Upon finally reaching Aden, Allan reported, "I sold the iron for a good price, 20 gold dinars a *bahar* [one bahar equaled 300 pounds]. I had with me 72 bahars and 50 separate pieces, 30 *mann* [one mann equaled 2 pounds] of spices, and 40 mann of cloves. After customs I had obtained 1500 dinars and a lot in other currencies." Allan had intended to return to Cairo, but the high prices that pepper fetched in Aden instead spurred him to immediately set out for India again.

Only fragments of Allan's correspondence survive today, and we do not know how he fared during his return voyage to India. But however successful he was as a businessman, Allan's long sojourns took their toll on his family. In a letter his wife sent to Allan in North

Agricultural Innovation and Diffusion

FOCUS Which groups took the most active role in adopting new agricultural technologies in the different regions of Eurasia during the centuries from 900 to 1300?

Industrial Growth and the Money Economy

FOCUS How did the composition and organization of the industrial workforce change in different parts of Eurasia during this period?

Merchants and Trade Networks in Afro-Eurasia

FOCUS How did the commercial revival of 900 to 1300 reorient international trade routes across Afro-Eurasia?

COUNTERPOINT: Production, Tribute, and Trade in the Hawaiian Islands

FOCUS How did the sources of wealth and power in the Hawaiian Islands differ from those of market economies elsewhere in the world?

BACKSTORY

The collapse of the Han Empire in China and the Western Roman Empire ended a prolonged era of growth in agriculture and trade in the agrarian heartlands of Eurasia (see Chapters 6 and 7). The steppe nomad invasions devastated many cities in China, India, and the Roman Empire's former territories. Political disunity hindered efforts to revive agriculture and commerce. Yet the rise of steppe empires such as that of the Turks also fostered trade and cultural exchange across the caravan routes of Central Asia.

In the seventh century, the formation of a vast Islamic empire and the reestablishment of a unified empire in China by the Sui and Tang dynasties created stable political and social foundations for economic recovery (see Chapters 9 and 10). Latin Christendom remained divided into many kingdoms and city-states, and here the reinvigoration of trade and industry came later. The expanding Islamic world also began to reach across the seas and deserts to bring parts of sub-Saharan Africa into its orbit.

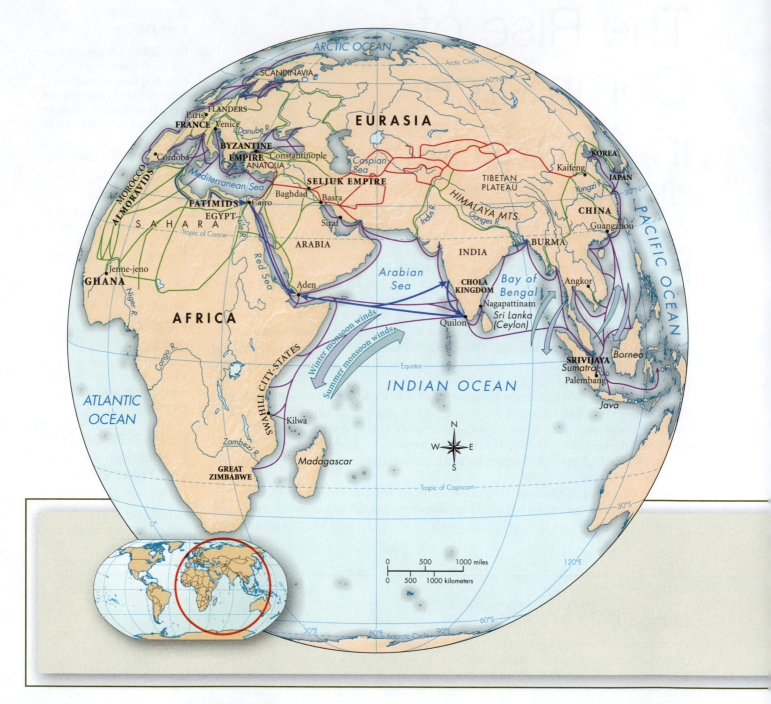

850–1267 Chola kingdom in southern India

c. 1120–1150 Construction of Angkor Wat begins

• **969** Fatimids conquer Egypt

| 900 | 1000 | 1100 | 1200 |

960–1279 Song dynasty in China

• **1024** The Song dynasty issues the first paper money in world history

• **1127** The Jurchen conquer north China; the Song dynasty retains control of southern China

• **1055** Seljuk Turks capture Baghdad

Africa, she bitterly chided him for his absence: "We are in great distress, owing to bad health and loneliness." Caring for their sick infant had forced her to sell furniture and rent out the upper story of their house to pay for doctors and medicines. Lamenting that her father was abroad on business at the same time, the wife urged her husband, "By God, do not tarry any longer . . . we remain like orphans without a man."

Allan's last surviving letter, written when he was an old man about to embark on another expedition to India, warned his adult sons not to abandon their families as he had done. He advised his sons, merchants themselves, to form a partnership that would spread the burdens of travel among them, and admonished them to take good care of their families and one another. His letter conveyed heartfelt regrets about the personal costs of his life as a merchant: "Had I known how much I would be longing after you, I would not have undertaken this voyage altogether."[1]

Merchants such as Allan bin Hassun faced formidable challenges: slow and frail modes of transportation, unfamiliar and sometimes dishonest clients and competitors, and the constant threat of bandits, pirates, and greedy rulers. To overcome these obstacles they devised new business organizations and practices. Allan, an Arabic-speaking Jew from Cairo who roamed westward to Spain and eastward to India, epitomized this cosmopolitan merchant class.

In Allan bin Hassun's day, a sustained economic expansion was spreading across Eurasia and Africa. Favorable climatic conditions, improved agricultural efficiency and output, increases in population and growth of cities, and new patterns of consumption led to rapid expansion of the money economy, culminating in a veritable commercial revolution. Long-distance merchants such as Allan opened new trade routes that connected Europe and the Mediterranean with the Islamic lands and the Indian Ocean. Vigorous commercial growth in China stimulated an unprecedented flowering of maritime trade between East Asia and the Indian Ocean world. The thirst for gold brought parts of sub-Saharan Africa into these trade networks as well. In all of these places, commercial wealth reshaped social and political power.

MAPPING THE WORLD
Commercial Crossroads in Afro-Eurasia, c. 900–1300

After 900, the maritime routes across the Mediterranean Sea and the Indian Ocean eclipsed the overland Silk Road as the great avenues of Eurasian trade. The shift in trade patterns led to the rise of new centers of international trade: Venice became the gateway to Europe, Cairo replaced Baghdad as the commercial capital of the Islamic world, and Nagapattinam, the chief port of the Chola kingdom, flourished as the main crossroads of the Indian Ocean.

ROUTES ▼

— Old Silk Road
— Other land trade route
— Maritime trade route
➜ Voyages of
   Allan bin Hassun, c. 1115

1250–1517 Mamluk dynasty in Egypt

c. 1150–1300 Heyday of the Champagne fairs

| 1300 | 1400 | 1500 |

1323–1325 Pilgrimage to Mecca of Musa Mansa, ruler of Mali

1258 The Italian city-states of Florence and Genoa mint the first gold coins issued in Latin Christendom

c. 1400–1450 Great Zimbabwe in southern Africa reaches peak of prosperity

1230–1255 Reign of Sunjata, founder of the Mali Empire in West Africa

c. 1200–1400 Formation of first chiefdoms in the Hawaiian Islands

Although the pace and dynamics of economic change varied from region to region, the underlying trends were remarkably consistent. Similarly, in the fourteenth century this surge in economic prosperity suddenly ended across all of Eurasia, from Spain to China. This cycle of economic growth and decline was powered by the progressive integration of local economies into regional and cross-cultural networks of exchange. Parts of the world, however, were still cut off from this web of economic connections. In relatively isolated places such as the Hawaiian Islands, more intensive exploitation of economic resources also had important social and political consequences, but with strikingly different results.

OVERVIEW
QUESTIONS

The major global development in this chapter: The sustained economic expansion that spread across Afro-Eurasia from 900 to 1300.

As you read, consider:

1. How did agricultural changes contribute to commercial and industrial growth?

2. What technological breakthroughs increased productivity most significantly?

3. What social institutions and economic innovations did merchants devise to overcome the risks and dangers of long-distance trade?

4. In what ways did the profits of commerce translate into social and economic power?

5. Above all, who benefited most from these economic changes?

Agricultural Innovation and Diffusion

FOCUS

Which groups took the most active role in adopting new agricultural technologies in the different regions of Eurasia during the centuries from 900 to 1300?

Commercial growth, the most robust feature of economic change during these centuries, was rooted in an increasingly productive agrarian base. The invention, adaptation, and diffusion of new farming techniques raised yields and encouraged investment in agriculture and specialization of production. Rulers, landowners, and peasants all contributed innovations and more intense agricultural production. As urban demand for foodstuffs and industrial raw materials increased, it became more rewarding to produce goods for sale than for household consumption. Increased agricultural production transformed patterns of rural life and community, and changed the relationship between peasants working the land and the lords and states that commanded their loyalty and labor.

Retrenchment and Renewal in Europe and Byzantium

serf A peasant who was legally bound to the land and who owed goods, labor, and service to the lord who owned the land.

The third-century collapse of the unified Roman Empire disrupted economic life in the cities, but it had little direct impact on work and livelihoods in the countryside. In subsequent centuries great lords and peasant smallholders alike concentrated on growing food for their own consumption. Even in the tenth and eleventh centuries, when political stability had restored some measure of economic prosperity in the Byzantine Empire and Latin Europe, self-sufficiency was the goal. Kekaumenos, an eleventh-century Byzantine official, instructed his sons that proper household management meant minimizing expenses, diversifying assets, and avoiding dependence on the market. His first priority was to ensure that the family had "an abundance of wheat, wine, and everything else, seed and livestock, edible and movable." In addition, Kekaumenos advised, "Make for yourself things that are 'self-working'—mills, workshops, gardens, and other things as will give you an annual return whether it be in rent or crop."[2] Vineyards, olives, and fruit trees would yield steady income year after year with the least amount of effort or expenditure. The greatest danger was debt, and the worst evil was to lose one's property to moneylenders.

Manorial Lords and Serfs

Great landowners were the main agents of agricultural development and innovation in Europe. Although the population of Europe rose in the tenth and eleventh centuries, labor remained scarce. After the death of Charlemagne in 814, the imperial authority of the Frankish kings declined, and power was largely privatized. The warrior nobility and monastic establishments founded manorial estates that reduced the rural population to the condition of **serfs**, who were bound to the soil they tilled as well as to their masters' will. The spurt of castle-building that swept across western Europe beginning in the late tenth century remade the landscape. Lords gathered their serfs into compact villages and subjected them to their laws as well as the rules of parish priests. Although free smallholder farmers were probably still the majority, they too sought the protection of local lords.

As lordship came to be defined in terms of control over specific territories and populations, the nobility took greater interest in increasing their revenue. Landowners began to invest in enterprises such as watermills, vineyards, and orchards that required large initial outlays of capital but would yield steady long-term returns. In addition to owing their lords numerous dues and services, serfs were obliged to grind their grain at their master's mill, bake their bread in their master's ovens, and borrow money from their master.

Manorial lords also introduced other new technologies, such as the wheeled moldboard plow. Pulled by horses rather than oxen, this device was better than the light Mediterranean-style plow at breaking up northern Europe's heavy, clayey soils. Monasteries and manorial lords also promoted grape cultivation and wine making. Still, some fundamental aspects of European agriculture continued unchanged in both the Latin west and the Byzantine east. Wheat and barley remained the dominant crops. Farmers combined livestock-raising with cereal cultivation, providing more protein in European diets. The large amount of land needed to pasture animals kept population densities relatively low, however.

Agricultural innovation had less impact in the Byzantine Empire than in western Europe. For example, waterwheels were conspicuously absent, perhaps because Byzantine peasants, unlike European serfs, were not compelled to use the mills of the great landowners, who thus had less incentive to invest in expensive machinery. The recovery of Byzantium's political fortunes in the tenth and eleventh centuries led to renewed economic growth. Cultivation of olives, grapes, and figs expanded throughout the Mediterranean

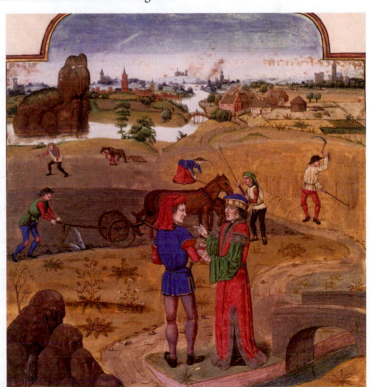

A Managerial Landlord

In this illustration from a fifteenth-century French handbook on farming, a landowner personally supervises the agricultural work on his estate. The laborers are engaged in various tasks, including plowing, sowing, and harvesting. The team of horses is pulling a wheeled moldboard plow, which allowed farmers to till the heavy soils of northern Europe more efficiently. (HIP/Art Resource, NY.)

lands. In Anatolia (modern Turkey), however, the scarcity of labor prompted landowners to replace agriculture with stock-raising—a trend that accelerated when the Seljuk (SEL-juk) Turks, nomadic Muslim warriors from Central Asia, conquered most of Anatolia in the late eleventh century.

Agricultural Transformation in the Islamic World

Emergence of Landed Estates

The Arab conquerors of Syria, Iraq, and Iran initially were confined to towns, and thus had little immediate impact on the already well-developed agricultural systems in these regions. Undeveloped areas were another matter, however. The new rulers awarded wilderness lands to Arab governors to reduce the fiscal burdens of the caliphate's far-flung empire. The governors were expected to convert the wastelands to agriculture and use the revenues to defray the costs of public administration. In the ninth and tenth centuries, as the caliphate began to lose its grip over the provinces, local governors turned to slave armies to maintain control. They allocated landed estates, *iqta* (ihk-ta), to military commanders for the upkeep of these slave forces. Under the rule of the Seljuk Turks, first in Iran and subsequently in the central Muslim lands, most of the land was held as iqta estates to support the slave armies.

New Crops and Farming Practices

Islamic agriculture was transformed by new crops and farming practices. The burgeoning trade with Asia (discussed later in this chapter) introduced into Islamic domains a host of new crops—including rice, cotton, sugar cane, sorghum, and citrus fruits—from the lands surrounding the Indian Ocean. Cultivating these tropical imports as summer crops in the arid Middle East and North Africa required more elaborate irrigation systems. Thus, the spread of Asian crops in Syria, Egypt, and Spain was accompanied by irrigation technologies originally developed in India and Iran.

By 1200, Asian tropical crops had been domesticated throughout the Islamic world, from Iran to Spain (see Map 12.1, page 380). In addition to providing a more diverse diet and better nutrition, the new imports spurred industrial production and trade. New processing industries such as cotton textile manufacture and sugar refining emerged, primarily in Egypt and Syria.

Surprisingly, Europeans adopted few of the new crops and farming practices that were spreading throughout the Islamic world. One exception was hard wheat (durum), a variety developed in North Africa in about 500 to 600. Muslims introduced hard wheat, used to make pasta and couscous (and now pizza crust), to Spain and Italy. The earliest mention of pasta making in Italy dates from the thirteenth century, but it is unclear whether this was an Italian novelty or a Muslim export.

In northern Europe, climate prevented cultivation of most warm-weather crops. Yet prevailing habits and food preferences also figured significantly in Europeans' lack of interest in Muslim innovations, as the experience of Spain shows. Rice, citrus fruits, and sugar cane were widely grown in Muslim-ruled Spain, whose rulers also invested heavily in irrigation projects. But in the wake of the Christian reconquest of Spain in the thirteenth and fourteenth centuries (discussed in Chapter 14), the new landowners converted the wheat and cotton fields to pasture for sheep and allowed the irrigated rice fields to revert to swamps.

Retreat to Pastoral Livelihoods

The Seljuk conquests disrupted the agrarian basis of the Islamic world's economic prosperity. As nomadic warriors, the Seljuks were ill suited to maintaining the fragile ecology of intensive irrigated farming in these arid regions. Moreover, unlike in the manorial order of Western Europe, possession of an iqta estate gave the owner no political or legal powers over the peasants who worked it. Further, the estates could not be sold, leased, or passed on to one's heirs. Lacking ownership of the land and control over the peasants' labor, estate holders had little incentive to try to improve the efficiency of agriculture. Economic regression was most severe in Iraq and Anatolia. Neglect of irrigation systems and heavy taxation prompted massive peasant flight, leading to depopulation and a retreat from farming to pastoralism.

iqta In the Islamic world, grants of land made to governors and military officers, the revenues of which were used to pay for administrative expenses and soldiers' salaries.

Rice Economies in Monsoon Asia

Between 700 and 1200, an agricultural revolution also transformed economic life and livelihoods throughout monsoon Asia. Earlier Asian farmers had mainly grown dry land cereals such as wheat and millet. Beginning in the eighth century, however, Asian agriculture shifted to irrigated rice as the main staple food. The high efficiency and yields of irrigated rice agriculture, which can feed six times as many people per acre as wheat, generated substantial surpluses and fostered rapid population growth.

Nowhere was the scale of this agricultural transformation greater than in China. The An Lushan rebellion in the mid-eighth century had devastated the north China plain, the traditional Chinese heartland (see Chapter 10). Refugees fleeing the war-torn north resettled in the south, especially in the well-watered plains of the Yangzi River Valley. Massive investment of labor and capital in dikes, canals, and irrigation channels made it possible to control the annual Yangzi floods and reclaim land in the Yangzi Delta. Man-made canals, along with the abundant natural waterways of southern China, also encouraged mobility and trade. Southern products such as tea, sugar, porcelain, and later cotton led to new industries and new patterns of consumption. The unprecedented growth of cities and towns widened the circulation of goods and made it possible to acquire great fortunes through landowning and commerce. Yet the imperial state, which gained renewed strength under the Song dynasty (960–1279), strictly limited the social and legal powers exercised by the landed elite. In contrast to other parts of Eurasia during this era, in China small property owners drove agricultural expansion and economic growth.

Water conservation, irrigation technologies such as pedal-powered water pumps, and the construction of terraced fields along hillsides dramatically increased the amount of land under rice cultivation. The introduction of faster-ripening, drought-resistant rice varieties from Southeast Asia allowed Chinese farmers to develop a double-cropping rotation. Fields were planted with rice during the summer, and then reused to cultivate winter crops such as wheat, barley, and soybeans. Yangzi Delta farmers also planted mulberry trees, whose leaves provided fodder for silkworms, on the embankments dividing the rice paddies.

Growing exchanges between town and countryside also altered dietary and consumption habits. The brisk market activity in the Yangzi Delta countryside deeply impressed one thirteenth-century visitor from another province. He observed that peasants coming to town to sell rice returned home "arms laden with incense, candles, paper money offerings for the ancestors, cooking oil, salt, soy sauce, vinegar, flour, noodles, pepper, ginger, and medicines."[3] The introduction of irrigated rice cultivation thus had consequences well beyond the production of more food for rural families. The surplus food made possible by rice cultivation helped create new connections between rural and urban peoples, changing both city and country life in the process.

In mainland Southeast Asia, wet rice cultivation became common probably in the first centuries C.E., and it had spread to Java by the eighth century. Fish and coconuts (a source of fruit, sugar, oil, and wine) also were important staple foods in tropical agriculture. Dried or fermented fish could be stored for lengthy periods, and coconut trees typically yielded fruit four times a year. Tuber crops such as taro and yams provided alternative sources of subsistence.

Women Making Pasta

The Chinese made noodles from millet flour as early as 3000 B.C.E., but pasta was introduced to Europe from the Islamic world much later. A twelfth-century Muslim geography mentions that *itriya*—long, thin noodles like those being made by the women in this fourteenth-century Italian illustration—was manufactured in Sicily and exported throughout Muslim and Christian lands around the Mediterranean. (Alinari/Art Resource, NY.)

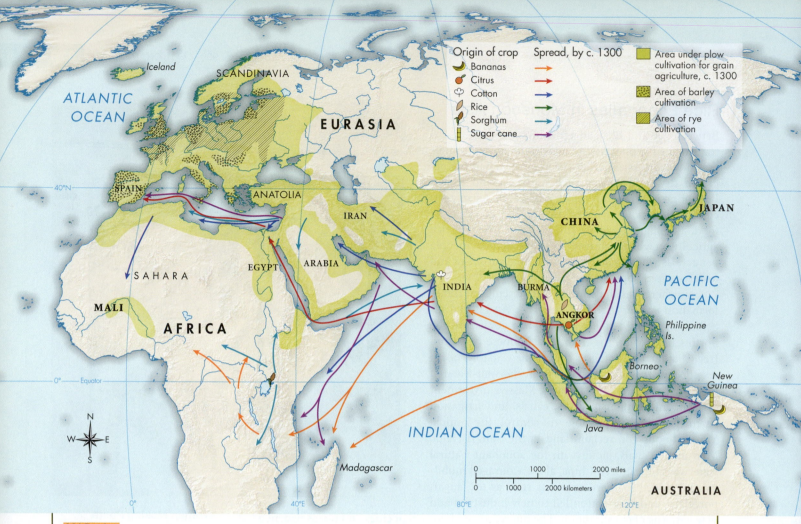

MAP 12.1

Principal Crops of Afro-Eurasia, c. 1300

The commercial prosperity of this era rested on the population growth made possible by the rising productivity of agriculture. New staple crops expanded the frontiers of agriculture: irrigated rice in Southeast Asia, rye and barley in northern Europe, and bananas in tropical Africa. Techniques of sugar and cotton production developed in India spread west to the Middle East and east to China.

Rise of Powerful Monarchies in Southeast Asia

The development of irrigated rice agriculture from the eighth century onward laid the economic foundations for the rise of powerful monarchies, most notably Angkor in Cambodia. In contrast to Chinese traditions, the Khmer kings of Angkor never created a centralized bureaucratic state. Instead, they extended their overlordship by recruiting local landowning elites as allies. The Angkor kings established networks of royal temples supported by ample land endowments. In addition to revenue from landholdings, royal and aristocratic patrons gave temples donations of rice, cattle, goats, coconut palms, fruit trees, betel nuts, and clothing. The temples became storehouses of goods shared with the whole community. Java and Burma had similar patterns of intensive rice cultivation, organized by allocating land and labor rights to temple networks. Hence, in Angkor, Java, and Burma, temples acted as local crossroads, functioning as hubs for the collection and distribution of resources and as points of connection between rural communities and the king.

In keeping with Indian political traditions, the Angkor monarchs portrayed themselves as servants of the gods and custodians of their temples. The kings ceded neither sacred authority nor temple administration to an independent priesthood, however. Even without a centralized bureaucracy, the Angkor kings retained control over temples and the land and wealth attached to them. The revenues that flowed to Angkor from the temple network financed massive construction projects, including irrigation works and new temple complexes. The power and wealth of Angkor reached its peak during the twelfth cen-

Annual Cycle of Rice Cultivation
Highly productive rice agriculture fueled Song China's dramatic economic growth. Irrigated rice fields could feed six times as many people per acre as dry-land crops such as wheat or maize. This twelfth-century painting depicts the annual cycle of rice farming in the Yangzi Delta (clockwise from top): sowing, irrigation with pedal-powered water pumps, harvesting, threshing, husking, and storing the husked grain in a granary. (The Palace Museum, Beijing/ChinaStock.)

tury, when Angkor Wat was built. The world's largest religious monument, it was originally covered in gold leaf. Designed to represent the world in miniature, it served both as a shrine dedicated to the Hindu god Vishnu and as a royal mausoleum.

In Japan, too, land reclamation efforts organized by aristocratic and religious estates fostered the spread of rice cultivation. Because most large landowners lived in the capital at Kyoto, actual cultivation of the land was divided among tenant farmers and serflike laborers working under the direction of a village headman. The estate economy remained highly localized and self-sufficient until the early fourteenth century, when double-cropping (combining, as in China, a winter harvest of wheat or soybeans with the summer rice crop) and other technical improvements raised rural incomes. Peasants began to sell their surplus produce at rural markets. Although traders still conducted most exchange through barter, imported Chinese coins began to appear in local markets as well.

Estate-Based Economy in Japan

Favorable climatic trends also contributed to agricultural expansion across Eurasia. After 900 warmer temperatures set in, lengthening growing seasons and boosting yields. With rising agricultural productivity, farmers could feed more people, leading to population expansion and the growth of cities. Increasing commercial ties between the countryside and the towns brought more people into the market economy: rural inhabitants obtained more of their daily necessities from markets and fairs, while urban merchants and artisans developed new products to satisfy the mounting consumer demand.

Industrial Growth and the Money Economy

Economic growth during these centuries was driven by rising agricultural productivity, population increases, and the expansion of markets, rather than revolutionary changes in industrial organization and technology. A world in which labor was cheap and often unfree offered little incentive for investing in labor saving technology. Although no "industrial revolution" occurred, important strides in technological progress stimulated expansion of manufacturing and transport. In both technical innovation and scale of output, textiles,

FOCUS

How did the composition and organization of the industrial workforce change in different parts of Eurasia during this period?

metallurgy, and shipbuilding were the leading industries. As the volume of transactions increased, so did the demand for money and credit. Money became the lifeblood of urban society and an increasingly important measure of social status.

Technological Change and Industrial Enterprise

Human and animal power continued to serve as the main sources of energy in both agriculture and industry. However, water and windmills, first used in Europe in Roman times, proliferated rapidly from the tenth to the thirteenth centuries. People used mills primarily to grind grain, but they also adapted milling techniques to industrial purposes such as crushing ore, manufacturing woolen cloth, and pressing oil seeds.

Increased Iron Production

The production of iron expanded in Europe during these centuries, though no significant technological breakthrough occurred until blast furnace technology using water-driven bellows emerged in Germany sometime after 1300. In China, innovations such as piston-driven blast furnaces and the use of coke (refined coal) as fuel made vigorous growth in iron and steel output possible. In the eleventh century China produced perhaps as much as 125,000 tons of iron per year, more than twice the entire output of Europe. The loss of China's chief iron mines after the Jurchen conquest of the north in 1127 severely slowed iron production, however, and even led to regression to more primitive iron-making techniques.

Advances in Shipbuilding and Navigation

Probably the farthest-reaching technological advances during this era came in shipbuilding and navigation. Arab seafarers had conquered the monsoon winds of the Indian Ocean by rigging their ships (known as *dhows*) with lateen sails, which allowed them to sail against the wind. By the thirteenth century, Arabian ships were equipped with stern-post rudders that greatly enhanced their maneuverability. Because of the dhow's relatively flimsy hull, though, its range was limited to the placid waters of the Indian Ocean (see At a Crossroads, page 372).

The Chinese were slow to develop seagoing vessels, for reasons we will consider in Chapter 15. But by the twelfth century, Chinese merchants were sailing to Korea, Japan, and Southeast Asia in "Fuzhou ships," which featured deep keels, stern-post rudders, nailed planking, and waterproofed bulkheads. The magnetic compass had been known in China since ancient times, but the earliest mention of its use as a navigational aid at sea refers to Arab and Persian vessels in the Indian Ocean in the eleventh century.

Important innovations in seafaring and navigation came somewhat later in Europe. The traditional Mediterranean galley, powered by oars, was designed for war rather than commerce, and had little space for cargo. Beginning in the late thirteenth century, the Venetians developed more capacious galleys specifically designed as cargo vessels. In addition, a new kind of sailing ship known as the "cog" was introduced from northern Europe in the early fourteenth century. Equipped with square-sail rigging and stern-post rudders, the cogs could be built on a much larger scale, yet they required only one-fifth the crew needed to man a galley.

Equally important to the expansion of European maritime trade were innovations in navigation. The nautical compass came into use in the Mediterranean in around 1270. At around the same time, European navigators began to compile sea charts known as "portolans" that enabled them to plot courses between any two points. The combination of compass, portolans, and the astrolabe—introduced to Europe via Muslim Spain—vastly broadened the horizons of European seafarers. Mediterranean mariners began to venture beyond the Straits of Gibraltar into the Atlantic Ocean. A Genoese ship made the first voyage from Italy to Flanders in 1277, the initial step in the reorientation of European trade away from the Mediterranean and toward the Atlantic.

Expansion of Textile Manufacture

In addition to metallurgy and shipbuilding, textile manufacture—the most important industrial enterprise in every premodern society—was also transformed by technological innovation. Egypt, renowned for its linen and cotton fabrics, continued to produce high-quality cloth that was sold across the Islamic world and in Europe as well. Egyptian cloth-making techniques were copied in many other Muslim societies. Knowledge of silk manufacture, brought to Iran from China by the seventh century, was later passed on to Syria and Byzantium. Woolen cloth manufacture was the largest industry in Europe. The expansion of textile weaving sparked the rise of industrial towns in Flanders (modern Belgium), while Italian cities such as Milan and Florence specialized in dyeing and finishing cloth.

Innovations such as spinning wheels, treadle-operated looms, and water mills sharply increased productivity at virtually every step in textile manufacturing. The new technologies also encouraged a more distinct division of labor. As textile manufacture shifted from a household or manorial activity to an urban, market-oriented industry, skilled tasks such as weaving and dyeing became the exclusive preserve of male artisans. Women were relegated to the low-skilled and laborious task of spinning yarn.

In the twelfth century the Chinese silk industry underwent momentous changes. Previously, silk production had been almost exclusively a northern industry, carried out in state-run workshops or by rural women working at home. However, in 1127 the Jurchen Jin kingdom in Manchuria seized north China, forcing the Song court to take refuge at a new capital at Hangzhou (hahng-jo) in the Yangzi Delta. Subsequently China's silk industry shifted permanently to the Yangzi Delta, where the humid climate was more conducive to raising silkworms (see Map 12.2, page 394). New machinery such as the silk spinning reel and the treadle-operated loom greatly increased the output of silk yarn and cloth.

Like woolen manufacture in Europe, silk production in China steadily ceased to be a cottage industry and moved into urban industrial workshops. Instead of weaving cloth themselves, peasant households increasingly specialized in producing raw silk and yarn for sale to weaving shops. Although state-run silk factories continued to employ some women, private workshops hired exclusively male weavers and artisans.

Indeed, as the role of the market in the household economy grew, men began to monopolize the more skilled and better-paid occupations throughout Eurasia. In European cities especially, women found their entry barred to occupations that had formerly been open to them. Moreover, for urban women throughout Eurasia, public participation in social and economic activities became a mark of lower-class status.

Cultural preconceptions about the physical, emotional, and moral weaknesses of women aroused anxieties about their vulnerability in the public realm. The Muslim philosopher and

Exclusion of Women from the Workforce

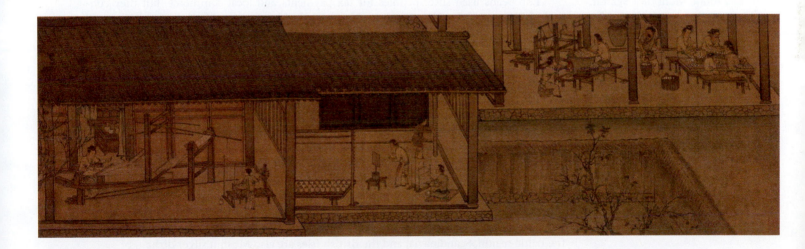

Chinese Silk Weaving
Growing demand for luxury silks with fancy weaves stimulated technological innovations in the Chinese silk industry. This thirteenth-century scroll painting shows various stages of silk production, including sorting cocoons, extracting the silk filaments (right background), and winding yarn on a silk reeling machine (center foreground). At left a female weaver operates a treadle-powered loom. Peasant women could not afford such expensive equipment, however; most stopped weaving and concentrated on raising silkworms and producing raw silk.
(Attributed to Liang Kai (Chinese). Sericulture (The Process of Making Silk), early 13th Century. Handscroll, ink and color on silk. 27.3x93.5 cm. The Cleveland Museum of Art. John L. Severance Collection 1977.5.)

jurist Ibn Hazm (994–1064) warned that men preyed on women working outside the home: "Women plying a trade or profession, which gives them ready access to people, are popular with lovers [men looking for sexual partners]—the lady broker, the coiffeuses, the professional mourner, the singer, the soothsayer, the school mistress, the errand girl, the spinner, the weaver, and the like."[4] At the same time, the segregation of women in Muslim societies conferred high status on women doctors and midwives, which were considered necessary and honorable professions. Muslim women's control over their dowries enabled them to invest in moneylending, real estate, and other commercial activities.

Hazm's list of occupations that exposed women to public scrutiny provides a glimpse of women's jobs in his home city, Córdoba in Muslim Spain. Household surveys conducted in Paris in around 1300 show that female taxpayers were represented in more than a hundred trades at all levels of income. Many worked as independent artisans, although nearly three-quarters were employed as servants, in preparing and selling food, and in the textile and clothing industries. But the urban economy of Paris was relatively open. Elsewhere, merchant and artisan guilds (see page 388) almost always excluded women. By the fifteenth century, independent wage-earning women had virtually disappeared from European cities, even in Paris. The majority of women who earned wages were domestic servants. Married women typically worked at family businesses—as innkeepers, butchers, bakers, and clothiers—serving as helpers to their husbands.

Expanding Circulation of Money

Before 1000, most parts of Eurasia suffered from acute shortages of money. The use of money in Latin Christendom sharply contracted after the demise of the Roman Empire. Local rulers began to issue their own coins, but their circulation was limited. With gold scarce, the Frankish kings minted silver coins known as pennies. Kings and princes across Europe also frequently granted coinage privileges to various nobles and clerical authorities, and a great profusion of currencies resulted. Silver pennies were still relatively high in value, though, and their use was largely restricted to the nobility and merchants. The great majority of European peasants paid their lords in goods and services rather than money.

Byzantine Monetary System   Europeans used silver pennies for tax payments and local commerce, but they conducted international trade using the gold coins issued by the Byzantine emperors. The gold *nomisma* (nom-IHS-mah) coin, the cornerstone of Byzantine monetary and fiscal systems, ruled supreme throughout the Mediterranean world from Justinian's time until the end of the eleventh century. The Byzantine state collected taxes in gold coins, which it spent on official salaries, public works, foreign subsidies, the ecclesiastic establishment, and above all its standing army. Payment of soldiers' salaries in gold coin ensured their wide dispersal throughout the empire. Byzantium's prominence as the main trading partner of Italy's mercantile cities established the nomisma as the monetary standard in Italy as well.

Islamic Monetary System   The Umayyad caliph Abd al-Malik's currency reforms in the 690s had established the silver *dirham* (DEER-im) as the monetary standard for the Islamic world (see Seeing the Past: Imitation and Innovation in Islamic Coinage). The ease with which merchants circulated throughout the Islamic world is demonstrated by a hoard of nine hundred dirhams buried in Oman in around 840, which included coins issued by fifty-nine different mints from Morocco to Central Asia. Most of the coins found in Viking hoards scattered across the Baltic region, Scandinavia, and the British Isles are also Muslim silver dirhams.

The Islamic world suffered from shortages of gold until, as we will see, the rise of trans-Saharan trade in the ninth century. North African rulers reaped enormous profits from minting this gold into coins known as *dinars*. The Arab geographer Ibn Hawqal reported that the king of Sijilmasa (sih-jil-MAS-suh), in southern Morocco, obtained annual revenues of 400,000 gold dinars, equivalent to 1.9 tons of gold, from commercial tolls and his mint.

European Monetary System   The revival of gold coinage in Italy in the mid-thirteenth century, first by Florence and Genoa in 1258 and later by Venice, confirms Italian merchants' growing supremacy over Mediterranean trade. The dominance of Venice and Genoa in trade with Byzantium enabled the Italian city-states to supply their mints with gold imported from Constantinople. Italian merchants also obtained an increasing portion of the African gold crossing the Sahara. The Venetian gold ducat, introduced in 1284, soon established itself as the new monetary standard of Mediterranean commerce. Although gold coins filled the purses of nobles and great merchants throughout Europe, artisans continued to receive their wages in silver coin, and so-called black money (silver debased with lead and other cheap metals that gave it a black color) was widely used for everyday purchases and almsgiving.

Chinese Monetary System

The Chinese Empire developed an entirely different monetary system based on low-value bronze coins rather than precious metals. Shortages of bronze coins had forced the Tang government to collect taxes in grain, bolts of cloth, and labor services, with only a few commercial duties paid in coin. In the early eleventh century the Song dynasty launched an ambitious policy of monetary expansion. By the 1020s, the output of Song mints already far surpassed that of earlier dynasties, and it soared to nearly 6 billion coins per year (requiring ninety-six hundred tons of copper) in the 1070s. Yet even this level of coinage failed to satisfy the combined needs of the state and the private market. Beginning in the early eleventh century, the Song government introduced paper money to expand the money supply and facilitate the movement of money across long distances.

Credit and the Invention of Paper Money

Despite the influx of African gold, shortages of gold and silver coin persisted in the Mediterranean world. These shortages, coupled with the high risk and inconvenience of shipping coin over long distances, encouraged the development of credit and the use of substitutes for metallic currency, including bank money, deposit certificates, and bills of exchange. The growing sophistication of business skills and commercial practices during this period was the product of pragmatic solutions to the problems of long-distance trade.

Genoese Bankers

The Christian church's ban on usury clashed with the financial needs of Europe's rising merchant class. In his *Treatise on the Seven Vices* (c. 1320), an Italian nobleman chose to portray the sin of greed with an illustration of the counting house of a Genoese banker. Genoa's bankers were pioneers in the development of bills of exchange and interest-bearing deposit accounts. (© 2011 The British Library Add. 27695, f.8.)

Imitation and Innovation in Islamic Coinage

Since their invention in the sixth century B.C.E., metallic coins have served a variety of purposes. The first goal of Eurasian rulers who issued the coins was to facilitate trade, but coins were also used to pay taxes, and in many cultures coins played an important role in religious ritual and offerings to the gods. Coins also possessed symbolic significance. The stamp or design on a coin became synonymous with the authority of the ruler or state that minted it. Coins thus became vehicles for expressing sovereign power and political and religious beliefs.

During its rapid expansion in the seventh and eighth centuries C.E., the Islamic realm spread over two distinct monetary zones: the Mediterranean region, where Byzantine gold coins prevailed as the international monetary standard, and the former Sasanid Empire in Iran and Mesopotamia, where Sasanid silver coins known as *drachm* dominated. At first Muslim rulers imitated the design, weight, and metallic content of Byzantine and Sasanid coins. Thus the first Muslim coins minted in Iran (known as *dirham*, an Arabic rendering of *drachm*) continued to display a bust of the Sasanid king on one side and a fire altar, the centerpiece of the Zoroastrian religion, on the reverse; the words "In the name of God" in Arabic were added along the edge. In 661 the first Umayyad caliph, Mu'awiya, issued a new coin that retained the imagery of the Sasanid king's bust and the fire altar, but a Persian inscription identified the ruler as Mu'awiya.

Similarly, the first Umayyad gold coins (dinars) portrayed the caliphs in the style of Byzantine emperors (A), but they removed the cross that Byzantine coins prominently displayed atop the tiered platform (B). Moreover, the legend encircling the image of the caliph defiantly proclaims that "Muhammad is the Prophet of God whom He sent with guidance and the religion of truth that he may make it victorious over every other religion" (Qur'an IX: 33).

A   **B**

(© The Trustees of the British Museum/Art Resource, NY.)

Provoked by this religious broadside, in 692 the Byzantine emperor Justinian II radically changed the design of Byzantine coins. He replaced the emperor's bust with an image of Jesus Christ and made the Christian cross even more obvious.

Overcoming Bans Against Usury

In Muslim and Christian societies, merchants had to overcome strong religious objections to profiting from commercial enterprise, especially the prohibitions against **usury**, the practice of charging interest on debts. The Qur'an, which took shape within the commercial world of Mecca, devotes much attention to codifying ethical principles for merchants. The Qur'an firmly forbids usury, but later Islamic jurists devised means of permitting buying and selling on credit as well as investments aimed at earning a profit. Christian merchants evaded similar prohibitions against usury by drawing up contracts that disguised interest payments as fees or fines. In cases such as loans for overseas trading expeditions, where the borrower was obligated to repay the loan only if the ship and its cargo returned safely, clerical authorities allowed lenders to collect interest as compensation for the high risk.

The global connections created by long-distance trade required institutional support, mechanisms to facilitate the exchanges of goods and wealth between peoples from distant parts of the world. Thus, every major trading city had moneychangers to handle the diverse assortment of coins in use. Rudimentary banks that acted primarily as safe deposits but also transferred funds to distant cities were operating in China and the Islamic world by the ninth century and appeared in Genoa and Venice by the early twelfth century.

Long-distance merchants also benefited from new forms of credit such as the **bill of exchange**. The bill of exchange was a written promise to pay or repay a specified sum of money at a future time, which enabled a merchant to deposit money with a bank in one place and collect payment from the bank's agent in another place. Bills of exchange were

usury The practice of charging interest on loans, forbidden under Christian and Muslim legal codes.

bill of exchange A paper note that allowed the bearer to receive money in one place and repay the debt in another currency at another place at a later date.

In response, the caliph Abd al-Malik introduced a change in 696, one that would establish the style for Islamic coins for centuries to come. Abd al-Malik removed all images, including the depiction of the ruler, and replaced them with quotations from the Qur'an (C, D).

C   **D**

(© The Trustees of the British Museum/Art Resource, NY.)

The main face of the coin shown here (C) bears the Islamic declaration of faith (*shahada*): "There is no god but God; there is no partner with him." In addition to other quotations from the Qur'an, such coins often state the name of the caliph or provincial governor who issued them. This change reflected Muslim clerics' growing concern that the images of rulers on coins violated the Muslim prohibition against idolatry.

Later Muslim rulers modified this basic model to reflect their political or doctrinal independence. The Fatimid rulers in Egypt, for example, issued coins with legends testifying to their Shi'a affiliation. Thanks to their control over the trans-Saharan gold trade, the Fatimids and the Almoravid dynasty in Morocco began to issue gold dinars in such

great quantities that they displaced the Byzantine coin as the international monetary standard of the Mediterranean. Some Christian rulers in Iberia and Italy issued their own copies of Islamic dinars. The gold coin struck by King Alfonso VIII (r. 1158–1214) of Castile imitated the style of the Almoravid dinar, but replaced the shahada with professions of Christian faith (still written in Arabic) and the image of a cross (E, F).

E   **F**

(Courtesy of the American Numismatic Society.)

EXAMINING THE EVIDENCE

1. Why did Muslim rulers at first retain the images of Byzantine and Sasanid rulers on their own coins?

2. How did Muslim and Christian rulers differ in expressing their religious commitments and values through the images on their coins?

used in the Islamic world by the tenth century, when we hear of a Moroccan merchant using one to remit a payment of 42,000 gold dinars to a client in a Saharan oasis town. In Europe, traders at the Champagne fairs, which, as we will see, began in the twelfth century, conducted most of their business on the basis of credit. But not until the fourteenth century, about three hundred years later than financiers in Baghdad and Cairo, did European bankers begin to issue bills of exchange that were payable on demand.

Development of Credit

The flood of African gold into the Fatimid capital of Cairo in the tenth and eleventh centuries made that city the first great international financial center. The Arab geographer Al-Muqaddasi, writing in about 985, boasted that Cairo "has superseded Baghdad and is the glory of Islam, and is the marketplace for all mankind."[5] Muslim, Jewish, and Christian merchants in Cairo did business with each other and frequently cooperated in business deals, money transfers, and information sharing. The Cairo Exchange acted as a clearinghouse for moneychanging and the settlement of debts for merchants from Morocco to Persia. The guiding principle of trade was to keep one's capital constantly at work. "Do not let idle with you one dirham of our partnership, but buy whatever God puts into your mind and send it on with the very first ship sailing," wrote a Spanish merchant in Lebanon to his partner in Cairo.[6]

Cairo, a Commercial Crossroads

In China, too, merchants used letters of credit to transfer funds to distant regions. In the late tenth century, private merchants in western China began to issue their own bills of exchange. In 1024 the Song government replaced these private bills with its own official

Invention of Paper Money in China

ones, creating the world's first paper money. By the thirteenth century paper money had become the basic currency of China's fiscal administration, and it was widely used in private trade as well. At the same time merchants carried great quantities of Chinese bronze coin overseas to Japan, where by 1300 nearly all Japanese paid their rent and taxes and conducted business using imported Chinese coin.

The flow of money across borders and oceans testified to the widening circulation of goods. Few villagers would ever see a gold coin. Yet the demand for gold, luxury goods, and industrial raw materials drew many peasants—however unwittingly—into networks of long-distance trade.

Merchants and Trade Networks in Afro-Eurasia

FOCUS

How did the commercial revival of 900 to 1300 reorient international trade routes across Afro-Eurasia?

During the period 900 to 1300, major trading centers across Eurasia and Africa came to be linked in a series of regional and international networks of exchange and production. To be sure, the great majority of rural inhabitants remained largely disengaged from the commercial life of the cities and toiled strictly to feed their families and fulfill their obligations to their lords. Yet if the channels of commerce remained narrow, they were far more extensive than ever before, reaching from China to Europe and from southern Africa to the Mediterranean.

Much of this trade consisted of luxury goods such as spices, silk, and gold intended for a select few—rulers, nobles, and urban elites. Yet bulk products such as grain, timber, and metal ores also became important commodities in maritime trade, and processed goods such as textiles, wine, vegetable oils, sugar, and paper became staple articles of consumption among the urban middle classes. Although the movement of goods would seem sluggish and sporadic to modern eyes, the volume of trade and its size relative to other forms of wealth grew enormously. Genoa's maritime trade in 1293 was three times greater than the entire revenue of the kingdom of France.

Merchant Partnerships and Long-Distance Trade

Long-distance merchants venturing far from their homelands had to overcome the hazards of travel across dangerous seas and alien lands; cultural barriers created by different languages, religions, and laws; and the practical problems of negotiating with strangers. The expansion of trade required new forms of association and partnership and reliable techniques for communication, payment, credit, and accounting. Notable advances in all of these spheres of trade and finance were made during the "commercial revolution" of the twelfth and thirteenth centuries.

Guild System

Not all innovations in commercial institutions promoted open access to trade. The **guild** system that took root in European towns during this period reflected the corporate character of urban government and merchant society. Guilds were granted extensive authority to regulate crafts and commerce, restrict entry to a trade, and dictate a wide array of regulations ranging from product specifications to the number of apprentices a master might employ. In the name of guaranteeing a "just" price and goods of uniform quality, the guild system also stifled competition and technical innovation. In China and the Islamic world, by contrast, guilds were formed chiefly to supply goods and services to the government, and they had no authority to regulate and control trade. Muslim rulers appointed market inspectors to supervise commerce and craftsmen. These officials upheld Islamic law, adjudicated disputes, and collected taxes and fees.

guild An association of merchants or artisans organized according to the kind of work they performed.

Merchants who engaged in international trade usually operated as individuals, carrying with them their entire stock of goods and capital, although they often traveled in caravans and convoys for protection against bandits and pirates. As in the case of the Jewish trader Allan bin Hassun, whose story opened this chapter, a family firm might dispatch its members to foreign markets, sometimes permanently, to serve as agents. But as the volume of trade grew, more sophisticated forms of merchant organization emerged.

Islamic legal treatises devoted much attention to commercial partnerships. Muslim law permitted limited investment partnerships in which one partner supplied most of the capital, the other traveled to distant markets and conducted their business, and the two shared the profits equally. Apparently caravan traders of the Arabian deserts first developed such cooperative agreements in pre-Islamic times. Italian merchants later imitated this type of partnership in what became known as the *commenda* (coh-MEHN-dah) (see Reading the Past: The Commenda Partnership Among Venetian Merchants). Artisans such as bakers, tailors, silversmiths, and pharmacists as well as entrepreneurs in industrial enterprises such as weaving, metalworking, wine making, and sugar refining also formed investment partnerships. Chinese merchants likewise created joint trading ventures in the form of limited partnerships for both domestic and international trade.

Commercial Partnerships

READING THE PAST

The Commenda Partnership Among Venetian Merchants

New institutions and business practices to raise capital for conducting long-distance trade facilitated the expansion of Mediterranean trade in the eleventh century. One new practice was the *commenda*, a form of partnership in which one partner provides investment capital and the other partner acts as business agent. Byzantine and Jewish merchants in the Mediterranean developed similar partnerships, but the precise model for the commenda was the Muslim *qirad* contract, which appeared in Islamic law codes by the eighth century. The following commenda contract drawn up in Venice is the earliest known example from Latin Christendom.

> In the year . . . 1073, in the month of August . . . I, Giovanni Lissado of Luprio, together with my heirs, have received in partnership from you, Sevasto Orefice, son of Ser Trudimondo, and from your heirs, the amount of £200 [Venetian]. And I myself have invested £100 in it. And with this capital we have acquired two shares in the ship of which Gosmiro da Molino is captain. And I am under obligation to bring all of this with me on a commercial voyage to Thebes [in Greece] in the ship in which the aforesaid Molino sails as captain. Indeed, by this agreement and understanding of ours I promise to put to work this entire sum and to strive the best way I can. Then, if the capital is preserved, we are to divide whatever profit the Lord may grant us from it by exact halves, without fraud and evil device. And whatever I can gain with those goods from any source,

I am under obligation to invest all of it in the partnership. And if all these goods are lost because of the sea or of people [pirates], and this is proved—may this be averted—neither party ought to ask any of them from the other. If, however, some of them remain, in proportion as we invested so shall we share. Let this partnership exist between us so long as our wills are fully agreed.

But if I do not observe everything just as is stated above, I together with my heirs then promise to give and to return to you and your heirs everything in the double, both capital and profit, out of my land and my house or out of anything that I am known to have in this world. [signed by Lissado, two witnesses, the ship captain, and the clergyman who acted as notary]

Source: Robert S. Lopez and Irving W. Raymond, eds., *Medieval Trade in the Mediterranean World: Illustrative Documents* (Cambridge, U.K.: Cambridge University Press, 1955), 176–177.

EXAMINING THE EVIDENCE

1. What did these Italian merchants regard as the greatest risks in investing in maritime trade?

2. In what ways was the commenda partnership different from modern business organizations such as corporations?

Joint Stock Companies

The commenda partnerships were the forerunners of permanent **joint stock companies**, which were first founded in Italian cities in the thirteenth century. These companies, in which investors pooled their capital for trading ventures, engaged in finance as well as trade and often maintained their own fleets and branch offices in foreign cities. The merchant banks of Florence and other cities of northern Italy gradually became involved in fund transfers, bills of exchange, and moneychanging. Bardi, the largest Florentine bank, had over three hundred agents stationed throughout Europe and the Mediterranean in 1340, and its capital resources were more than four times as large as the annual income of the English crown, one of its main customers. Apart from trade and banking, such firms provided insurance for maritime trading expeditions; insuring such expeditions became a common practice after 1350.

Karimi Merchant Associations

In the late twelfth century, merchants based in Egypt created a commercial association known as the *karimi* (KUH-ree-mee) to organize convoys for trading expeditions in the Indian Ocean. Cairo's karimi merchants became a powerful **cartel**—a commercial association whose members join forces to fix prices or limit competition—that squeezed small entrepreneurs out of the lucrative spice trade. The karimi merchants cooperated closely with the sultans of Egypt, especially under the Mamluk dynasty (1250–1517), generating substantial tax revenue for the state in exchange for their trade privileges. By 1300 Cairo's two-hundred-plus karimi merchants had become the chief middlemen in trade between Asia and Europe.

Merchants and Rulers

The sumptuous wealth and rising social stature of merchant groups such as the Italian bankers and Cairo's karimi inevitably altered relationships between government and commerce. Rulers who had formerly depended almost exclusively on revenue from the land increasingly sought to capture the scarcely imaginable profits of the money economy. In places as far removed as England and Japan, landowners and governments began to demand payments in money rather than agricultural products or labor services. In Europe the expanding availability of credit was an irresistible temptation to monarchs whose ambitions outgrew their resources. Italian bankers became the chief lenders to the papacy and to the kings and princes of Latin Christendom.

Merchant-Ruler Relations in Europe

The Italians took the lead in putting private capital to work in service to the state. Merchant communities became closely allied with political leaders in the Italian city-states, most notably in Venice. In the late twelfth century the Venetian government imposed a system of compulsory loans that required contributions from every citizen. In 1262, the city's magistrates consolidated all of these debts into a single account. Public debt proved to be more efficient than taxation for raising revenue quickly to cope with war and other emergencies. Investment in state debt provided the men, fleets, and arms that enabled Venice to become the great maritime power of the Mediterranean.

As mercantile interests came to dominate the Venetian state, the government took charge of the republic's overseas trade. The state directed commercial expeditions, dictated which merchants could participate, built the vessels at its publicly funded shipyard, and regulated the prices of exports as well as crucial imports such as grain and salt. Venice was fortunate in its ability to maintain civic solidarity even as its mercantile oligarchy tightened its grip on the state and its resources.

Economic regulation was a powerful unifying force elsewhere in Europe as well. For example, the merchant communities of the trading cities along the Baltic seacoast formed an alliance known as the Hanseatic League. The League acted as a cartel to preserve its members' monopoly on the export of furs, grain, metals, and timber from the Baltic region to western Europe.

Efforts to merge commercial and political power did not, however, always result in increased prosperity and political strength. In Genoa,

• Principal Hanseatic League member
▲ Hanseatic trading partner

The Hanseatic League

antagonisms between the landed aristocracy and the city's rising merchant and financier families provoked frequent and sometimes bloody feuds that paralyzed the city's leadership. In the industrial cities of Flanders, fiscal policies and economic regulation that favored merchants over workers ultimately incited revolts that undermined Flanders' preeminence in the textile industry.

In most of the Islamic world, merchants—regardless of their religious commitments—enjoyed high status and close ties to the political authorities. The Fatimid government in Egypt largely entrusted its fiscal affairs to Coptic Christian officials, and Jewish merchant houses achieved prominence as personal bankers to Muslim rulers in Baghdad and Cairo. Private trade and banking were largely free of government interference during the Fatimid dynasty. But state intervention in commerce intensified under the Mamluk sultans, who came to power in Egypt after a palace coup in 1250.

The Mamluks' political and military strength rested on their slave armies, which were supported by revenues from iqta estates and commercial taxes. The karimi-controlled spice trade was an especially important source of income for the Mamluk state. Karimi merchants—most of whom were Jewish—also managed the fiscal administration of the Mamluk regime, helping to collect provincial revenues, pay military stipends, and administer state-run workshops and trade bureaus. Like European monarchs, the Mamluk sultans became heavily dependent on loans from private bankers to finance wars. And, again like their European counterparts, Mamluk sultans were always on the lookout for new sources of revenue. In the fifteenth century the Mamluk government took over many commercial enterprises, most notably the spice and slave trades and sugar refining, and operated them as state monopolies.

In China, the fiscal administration of the imperial state penetrated deeply into the commercial world. The revenues of the Song Empire far exceeded those of any other contemporary government. The state generated more than half of its cash revenue by imposing monopolies on the production of rice wine and key mineral resources such as salt, copper, and alum. Yet in the most dynamic commercial sectors—iron mining and metallurgy, silk textiles, and the emerging industries of south China such as tea, porcelain, paper, and sugar—private enterprise was the rule. The Song government mainly intervened in private commerce to prevent private cartels from interfering with the free flow of goods.

The Song thus effectively stifled the formation of strong merchant organizations such as the European guilds. The state also assumed major responsibility for famine relief, stockpiling grain in anticipation of periodic harvest failures. Foreign trade was strictly regulated, and the export of strategic goods such as iron, bronze coin, and books was prohibited. Still, Chinese officials recognized the value of international trade as a source of revenue and of vital supplies such as warhorses, and they actively promoted both official trade with foreign governments and private overseas trading ventures.

Merchants in China did not enjoy the social prestige accorded to their Italian or Muslim counterparts. Confucianism viewed the pursuit of profit with contempt and relegated merchants to the margins of respectable society. Yet Confucian moralists expressed even greater hostility toward government interference in the economy than to private profit-seeking. Moreover, Confucian values applauded the prudent management of the household economy and the accumulation of wealth to provide for the welfare of one's descendants. As a minor twelfth-century official named Yuan Cai (you-ahn tsai) wrote in his *Family Instructions*, "Even if the profession of scholar is beyond your reach, you still can support your family through recourse to the arts and skills of medicine, Buddhist or Daoist ministry, husbandry, or commerce without bringing shame upon your ancestors."[7] Like his Byzantine counterpart Kekaumenos, Yuan Cai counseled his peers to be frugal in spending, to invest wisely in land, moneylending, and business ventures, to diversify their assets, and to never become dependent on the goodwill and honesty of those with whom one does business (see Reading the Past: A Chinese Official's Reflections on Managing Family Property).

Despite their wealth, merchants led a precarious existence. Long-distance trade offered opportunities to make great profits, but the risks of failure were equally great. To lessen these risks, merchants built communities, negotiated alliances with ruling authori-

Merchant-Ruler Relations in the Islamic World

Merchant-Ruler Relations in China

joint stock company A business whose capital is held in transferable shares of stocks by its joint owners.

cartel A commercial association whose members join forces to fix prices or limit competition.

A Chinese Official's Reflections on Managing Family Property

In *Precepts for Social Life* (1179), Yuan Cai departed from the focus on personal ethics found in earlier Chinese writings on the family. A Chinese official living in a time of rapid economic change, Yuan concentrated on the practical problems of acquiring wealth and transmitting it to future generations. Yuan also adopted a more pragmatic attitude toward individual behavior in addressing the inevitable conflicts that arise within families. In the following selections, Yuan confronts the problem of disparities of wealth among relatives who live together as a joint family.

Wealth and liberality will not be uniform among brothers, sons, and nephews. The rich ones, only pursuing what's good for them, easily become proud. The poor ones, failing to strive for self-improvement, easily become envious. Discord then arises. If the richer ones from time to time would make gifts of their surplus without worrying about gratitude, and if the poorer ones would recognize that their position is a matter of fate and not expect charity, then there would be nothing for them to quarrel about. . . .

Some people actually start from poverty and are able to establish themselves and set up prosperous businesses without making use of any inherited family resources. Others, although there was a common family estate, did not make use of it, separately acquiring their individual wealth through their own efforts. In either case their patrilineal kinsmen will certainly try to get shares of what they have acquired. Lawsuits taken to the county and prefectural courts may drag on for decades until terminated by the bankruptcy of all parties concerned. . . .

When brothers, sons, and nephews live together, it sometimes happens that one of them has his own personal fortune. Worried about problems arising when the family divides the common property, he may convert his fortune to gold and silver and conceal it. This is perfectly foolish. For instance if he has one million cash [bronze coins] worth of gold and silver and used this money to buy productive property, in a year he would gain 100,000 cash; after ten years or so, he would have regained the one million cash and what would be divided among the family would be interest. Moreover, the one million cash could continue to earn interest. If it were invested in a pawnbroking business, in three years the interest would equal the capital. . . . What reason is there to store it in boxes rather than use it to earn interest for the profit of the whole family?

Source: Patricia Buckley Ebrey, *Family and Property in Sung China: Yuan Ts'ai's* Precepts for Social Life (Princeton, NJ: Princeton University Press, 1984), 197–200.

EXAMINING THE EVIDENCE

1. What did Yuan identify as the greatest threats to the preservation of the family's wealth and property?

2. What values did Yuan regard as crucial for gaining and maintaining wealth?

---

ties, and developed reliable methods of communication. Although some rulers coveted the profits of trade for themselves, and others treated merchants as pariahs, traders and rulers usually reached an accommodation that benefited both. The spread of new techniques and institutions for conducting trade strengthened the foundations of international commerce.

Maritime Traders in the Indian Ocean

The seventh century, when the Tang dynasty in China was at its height (see Chapter 10), marked the heyday of trade and travel along the Silk Road across Central Asia. As we have seen, however, overland commerce between India and China collapsed after the outbreak of the An Lushan rebellion in 755. By the time the Song dynasty was founded in 960, China's principal trade routes had shifted away from Central Asia to the maritime world (see Map 12.2).

Dominance of Muslim Merchants

Muslim merchants, both Arab and Persian, dominated Indian Ocean trade in the ninth century thanks to their superior shipbuilding and organizational skills. Travel across the Indian Ocean was governed by monsoon winds, which blew steadily from east to west in winter and from west to east in summer, making it impossible to complete a round trip between China and India in a single year. Initially, Muslim seafarers from Persian Gulf ports sailed all the way to China, taking two or three years to complete a round-trip voyage. A ninth-century Arab chronicler claimed that more than half of the two hundred thousand residents of Guangzhou (gwahng-joe) (Canton), southern China's principal port, were Arab, Persian, Christian, and Jewish traders, a testimony to the dense web of trading connections that had developed by this time.

By the tenth century, merchants more commonly divided the journey to China into shorter segments. By stopping at ports along the Strait of Melaka (Malacca), between Sumatra and the Malay peninsula, Muslim merchants could return to their home ports within a single year. The Srivijaya (sree-vih-JUH-yuh) merchant princes of Sumatra grew wealthy from their share of profits in this upsurge in trade between India and China.

In the eleventh century, however, new maritime powers arose to contest the dominance of Srivijaya and the Muslim merchants in Asian international commerce. The most assertive new entrant into the Indian Ocean trade was the Chola (chohz-ah) kingdom (907–1279), at the southeastern tip of the Indian peninsula. At first Chola nurtured cordial diplomatic and commercial relations with Srivijaya. The Chola port of Nagapattinam (Nah-gah-POT-tih-nahm) flourished as an international trading emporium under the patronage of both the Chola and Srivijaya rulers, who funded the construction of mosques, temples, and shrines for the city's expatriate merchant communities of Muslims, Jews, Christians, Parsis (Zoroastrian immigrants from Iran), and Chinese. Yet in 1025 Chola suddenly turned against Srivijaya, and its repeated attacks on Sumatran ports over the next fifty years fatally weakened the Srivijaya princes. But Chola's aggressiveness made many enemies, including the Sinhala kings of Sri Lanka, who stymied its attempt to succeed Srivijaya as the region's supreme maritime power.

Chola's Quest for Maritime Supremacy

Chola's foreign trade was controlled by powerful Tamil merchant guilds that mobilized convoys and founded trading settlements overseas. Tamil merchants carried cargoes of Indian pepper and cotton cloth and Sumatran ivory, camphor, and sandalwood to the southern Chinese ports of Guangzhou and Quanzhou (chwehn-joe). Numerous architectural and sculptural fragments from Hindu temples found in Quanzhou attest to the city's once-thriving Tamil merchant colony.

Tamil Merchants and the China Trade

Silk textiles had long been China's principal export commodity. After the tenth century, however, the growth of domestic silk industries in India and Iran dampened demand for Chinese imports. Although Chinese luxury fabrics such as brocades and satins still were highly prized, porcelain displaced silk as China's leading export. Maritime trade also transferred knowledge of sugar refining and cotton manufacture from India to China, leading to major new industries there.

During the twelfth century Chinese merchants began to mount their own overseas expeditions. Chinese commercial interests increasingly turned toward the Indonesian archipelago in search of fine spices such as clove and nutmeg (which grew only in the remote Moluccas, the so-called Spice Islands), and other exotic tropical products. Chinese merchants also imported substantial quantities of gold, timber, and sulfur (used in gunpowder and medicines) from Japan in exchange for silk, porcelain, and contraband bronze coin.

The advent of Muslim traders in Indian Ocean trade had stimulated commerce along the east coast of Africa as well. The Swahili peoples of the coasts of Tanzania and Kenya were descended from Bantu settlers who arrived in the region in around 500 C.E. The Swahili lived in coastal villages or on offshore islands, where they combined farming and fishing with small-scale trade. Beginning in the ninth century, Swahili merchants transformed the island towns of Shanga and Manda into major trading ports that functioned as regional crossroads, exporting ivory, hides, and quartz and other gems to the Islamic heartland in return for cotton, pottery, glass, and jewelry. When Swahili merchants ventured southward in search of ivory, they discovered an abundance of gold as well.

Swahili Merchants and East African Trading Cities

The reorientation of East African trade networks toward the export of gold had far-reaching political and economic repercussions. In the twelfth century, Mapungubwe

South African Gold Trade

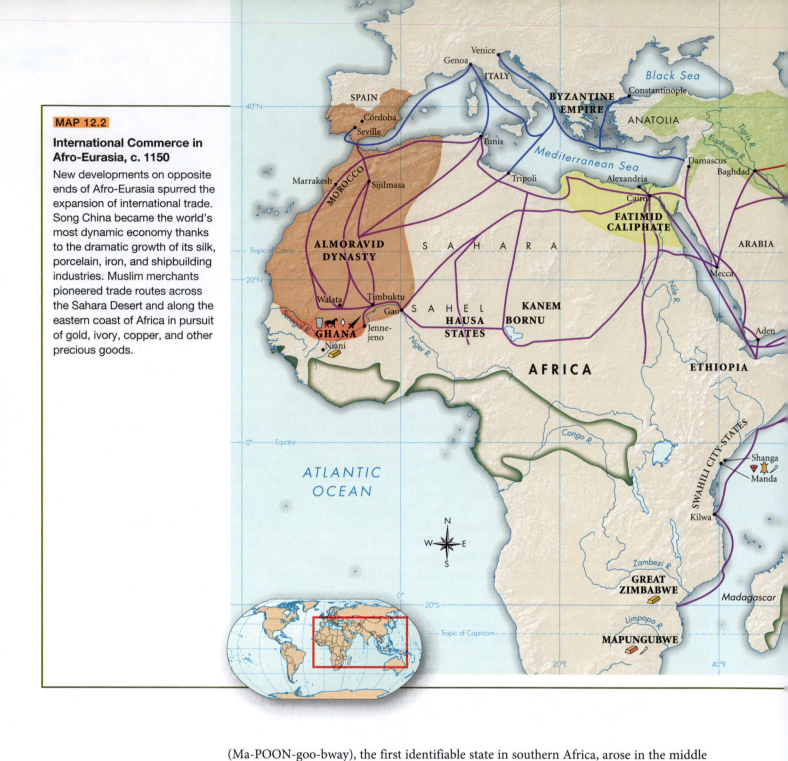

MAP 12.2

International Commerce in Afro-Eurasia, c. 1150

New developments on opposite ends of Afro-Eurasia spurred the expansion of international trade. Song China became the world's most dynamic economy thanks to the dramatic growth of its silk, porcelain, iron, and shipbuilding industries. Muslim merchants pioneered trade routes across the Sahara Desert and along the eastern coast of Africa in pursuit of gold, ivory, copper, and other precious goods.

Rise and Fall of Great Zimbabwe

(Ma-POON-goo-bway), the first identifiable state in southern Africa, arose in the middle Limpopo River Valley, at the junction of the trade routes bringing ivory and copper from the south and gold from the north. The monsoon winds allowed Arab merchants to sail as far south as Kilwa, which eclipsed the older towns of Shanga and Manda as the preeminent trading center along the East African coast (see again Map 12.2). Control of the gold trade greatly enriched the Muslim sultans, possibly of Arabian origin, who ruled Kilwa. By the early fourteenth century the city boasted stone palaces, city walls, a Muslim law school, and a domed mosque constructed in the Indian style. South of Kilwa trade goods were relayed by local merchants from the interior and the Swahili colonies along the coast.

The mid-thirteenth century brought the rise of another powerful state, Great Zimbabwe, that would exert direct control over the main goldfields and copper mines in the interior. The capital of Great Zimbabwe consisted of a large complex of stone towers and enclosures housing a warrior elite and perhaps as many as eighteen thousand inhabitants. Similar but smaller stone enclosures (known as *zimbabwe*), built to shelter livestock as

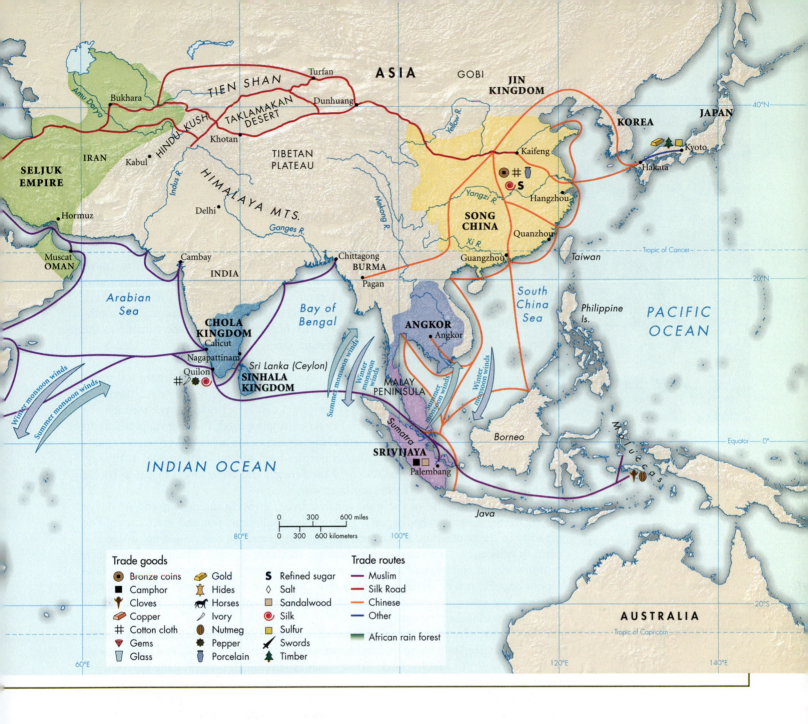

well as protect their inhabitants, sprang up throughout the region. The abandonment of Mapungubwe at around the same time can probably be attributed to the diversion of commercial wealth to Great Zimbabwe. Traders prized gold for its value as an export commodity and conducted local exchange using cross-shaped copper currency. The rich array of copper goods in royal and elite burials across southern Africa confirms the importance of copper as the chief sign of wealth and status. Textiles made of raffia palm fronds, bark cloth, and cotton were also important trade items in the continent's interior.

Great Zimbabwe's dominance over the export trade could not be sustained indefinitely. In the fourteenth century the copper and ivory trade routes shifted to the Zambezi River Valley to the north. The empire fashioned by the rulers of Great Zimbabwe disintegrated in the early fifteenth century, and the capital city was abandoned by the 1450s. Although no single dominant state emerged, trade continued to flourish. The great volume of Chinese coins and porcelain shards that archaeologists have found at Great Zimbabwe and sites along the coast documents East Africa's extensive trade across the Indian Ocean.

Kilwa

Located on an island off the coast of Tanzania, Kilwa grew rich and powerful thanks to its dominance over the trade in African gold and ivory. The large quantities of Chinese pearls, porcelains, and coins unearthed at Kilwa attest to its prominence in Indian Ocean trade as well. In this German engraving from 1572, the city's domed mosques stand out among a dense cluster of multistory buildings made from stone and coral. (The National Library of Israel, Shapell Family Digitization Project and The Hebrew University of Jerusalem, Department of Geography—Historic Cities Research Project.)

Trans-Saharan Traders

The vast Sahara Desert separated most of the African continent from the Mediterranean world, but the thirst for gold breached this seemingly impenetrable barrier in the wake of the Muslim conquest of North Africa. The conversion of the Berbers to Islam and their incorporation into the far-flung Muslim trading world during the seventh century provided the catalyst for the rapid escalation of trans-Saharan trade. Reports of the fabulous gold treasure of *al-Sudan* ("country of the blacks"), the Sahel belt of grasslands spanning the southern rim of the Sahara from the Atlantic to the Indian Ocean, lured Berber and Arab merchants across the desert.

Trade across the western Sahara was negligible before the second century C.E., when Berber camel caravans began to trek through the desert, bringing food and animal products to remote salt and copper mines. Salt, essential for sustaining life in arid climates, was a valuable commodity, so precious that Saharan peoples used salt rather than gold as money. Gold from the mines at the headwaters of the Senegal and Niger rivers began to trickle northward across the Sahara by the fourth century.

Well before the rise of the trans-Saharan trade, growing interaction and exchange among the Sahel societies had begun to generate social differentiation and stratification. The majority of the population, the farmers and herders, remained free people not assigned a caste. In villages, however, communities began to specialize in manufacturing activities such as ironworking, pottery, leather making, and cotton weaving. Many in these occupational groups began to marry only among themselves. Occupational specialization, residential segregation, and endogamy—marriage within a closed group of families—fostered the formation of castes of skilled tradesmen.

By 400 C.E., clusters of specialized manufacturing villages in the inland delta of the Niger River coalesced into towns trading in iron wares, pottery, copper, salt, and leather goods as well as foodstuffs and livestock. Towns such as Jenne-jeno preserved the independent character of its various artisan communities. But in other Sahelian societies, powerful warrior elites dominated. Originating as clan leaders, these warrior chiefs appropriated ideas of caste status to define themselves as an exclusive and hereditary nobility. They also drew on traditions of sacred kingship originating in the eastern Sudan, which exalted the king as a divine figure and required him to live a cloistered private life, rarely visible to his subjects.

Gold Trade and Ghana

The earliest Muslim accounts of West Africa, dating from around 800, report that a great king—whose title, Ghana, came to be applied to both the ruler's capital and his state—monopolized the gold trade. Ghana's exact location remains uncertain, but its ruler, according to Muslim merchants, was "the wealthiest king on the face of the earth because of his treasures and stocks of gold."[8] The Muslim geographer al-Bakri described the capital of Ghana as consisting of two sizable towns, one in which the king and his court resided and a separate Muslim town that contained many clerics and scholars as well as merchants. Although the king was a pagan, al-Bakri deemed him to have led a "praiseworthy life on account of his love of justice and friendship for Muslims."[9]

Advance of Islam

At first the impact of Islam on the indigenous peoples was muted. Berber caravans halted at the desert's edge, because camels had little tolerance for the humidity and diseases of the savanna belt. Confined to segregated enclaves within the towns, Muslim merchants depended on the favor of local chiefs or the monarchs of Ghana. Yet local rulers found the lucrative profits of trade in gold and slaves irresistible, and the wealth and literacy of Muslim merchants made them valuable allies and advisers. Trade also yielded access to coveted goods such as salt, glass, horses, and swords (see again Map 12.2). The kings of Ghana and other trading cities converted to Islam by the early twelfth century, and to varying degrees required their subjects to embrace the new religion as well. At the same time Muslim commercial towns displaced many of the older trading centers such as Jenne-jeno, which were abandoned. Thus, the desire to engage in trade was a major stimulus for cultural exchange and adaptation in West Africa.

Rise of Mali

During the twelfth century Ghana's monopoly on the gold trade eroded, and its political power crumbled as well. In the thirteenth century a chieftain by the name of Sunjata (r. 1230–1255) forged alliances among his fellow Malinke to create a new empire known as Mali. Whereas Ghana probably exercised a loose sovereignty within the savanna region, Mali enforced its dominion over a much larger territory by assembling a large cavalry army equipped with horses and iron weapons purchased from Muslim traders. Unlike Ghana, Mali exercised direct control over the gold mines.

The kings of Mali combined African traditions of divine kingship with patronage of the Islamic faith. The Mali monarch Mansa Musa (MAHN-suh MOO-suh) (r. 1312–1337) caused a great sensation when he visited Cairo on his pilgrimage to Mecca in 1325. According to a contemporary observer, "Musa flooded Cairo with his benefactions, leaving no court emir nor holder of a royal office without a gift of a load of gold. . . . They exchanged gold until they depressed its value in Egypt and caused its price to fall."[10] The visit provided evidence of both the power and wealth of Mali and the increasing cultural connections between West Africa and the rest of the Muslim world.

Trade and industry flourished under Mali's umbrella of security. Muslim merchants formed family firms with networks of agents widely distributed among the oasis towns and trading posts of the Sahara. Known as *Juula* (meaning "trader" in Malinke), these Muslim merchants also extended their operations into the non-Muslim states of the rainforest belt and brought a variety of new goods, such as kola nuts, textiles, and brass and copper wares, into the Saharan trading world. Like other town-dwelling craftsmen and specialists, such as the blacksmiths and leatherworkers, the Juula became a distinct occupational caste and ethnic group whose members lived in separate residential quarters and married among themselves (see Lives and Livelihoods: The Mande Blacksmiths).

Mediterranean and European Traders

Revival of Towns

The contraction of commerce that followed the fall of the western Roman Empire persisted longer in Europe than did the economic downturn in Asia and the Islamic world. By the twelfth century, however, the rising productivity of agriculture and population growth in western Europe had greatly widened the horizons for trade. Lords encouraged the founding of towns by granting **burghers**—free citizens of towns—certain legal liberties as well as economic privileges such as tax exemptions, fixed rents, and trading rights. In England and Flanders a thriving woolen industry developed—the towns of Flanders, notably Bruges, Ghent, and Ypres, became highly specialized in weaving cloth using raw wool imported from Britain. Merchant guilds in both England and Flanders grew so powerful that they chose their own city councils and exercised considerable political autonomy. In northern Europe, repeating a dynamic we have seen before in other parts of the world, commercial expansion altered the political landscape (see Map 12.3, page 399).

Growing Power of the Italian City-States

The prosperity of the woolen industry made Flanders the wealthiest and most densely urbanized region in twelfth-century northern Europe, yet the Flemish towns were dwarfed by the great cities of Italy. Although social tensions often flared between the landed aristocracy and wealthy town-dwellers, the political fortunes of the Italian city-states remained firmly wedded to their mercantile interests. The city-states of Pisa, Genoa, and Venice aggressively pursued trade opportunities in the Mediterranean, often resorting to force to seize trade routes and ports from Muslim, Greek, and Jewish competitors. By the twelfth century Italian navies and merchant fleets dominated the Mediterranean, with Genoa paramount in the west and Venice the major power in the east.

burgher In Latin Christendom, a free citizen residing in a town who enjoyed certain legal privileges, including the right to participate in town governance.

Champagne Trade Fairs

Economic revival in northern and western Europe breathed new life into the long-defunct Roman commercial network. In the county of Champagne, southeast of Paris, a number of towns located at the intersections of Roman roads had continued to serve as local markets and sites of periodic fairs. In the twelfth century the counts of Champagne offered their protection and relief from tolls to the growing number of merchants who traveled between the textile manufacturing towns of Flanders and Italy's commercial centers. They established an annual cycle of six two-month fairs that rotated among the towns. Champagne's location midway between Flanders and Italy enhanced its stature as the major crossroads of international commerce and finance in western Europe. Merchants adopted the coins and weights used at the fairs as international standards.

Champagne's heyday as a medieval version of a free-trade zone came to an end in the early fourteenth century. Political tensions between Champagne's counts and the French monarchy frequently interrupted the smooth flow of trade. The Champagne fairs were also victims of their own success: the innovations in business practices spawned by the Champagne fairs, such as transfers of goods and money via agents and bills of exchange, made actual attendance at the fairs unnecessary. Champagne would regain fame after the seventeenth century, when its famous sparkling wine was invented, but trade and finance shifted to the rising commercial cities of northern Europe such as Antwerp and London.

COUNTERPOINT
Production, Tribute, and Trade in the Hawaiian Islands

FOCUS

How did the sources of wealth and power in the Hawaiian Islands differ from those of market economies elsewhere in the world?

During the period of this chapter, rulers everywhere sought to regulate the exchange of goods to both preserve the existing social structure and enhance their own authority. In the temple- and estate-based economies of India, Southeast Asia, Japan, and western Europe, payments in goods and services prevailed over market exchange. These payments took the form of **tribute**, obligations social inferiors owed to their superiors; thus, by its very nature tribute reinforced the hierarchical structure of society. Yet in all of these societies markets played some role in meeting people's subsistence needs. Expansion of the market economy provided access to a wider range of goods and allowed entrepreneurs to acquire independent wealth. Both the circulation of goods and the new concentrations of commercial wealth threatened to subvert the existing social hierarchy.

In societies that lacked market exchange, such as the Hawaiian Islands, rulers maintained firmer control over wealth and social order. During the thirteenth and fourteenth centuries, when hierarchical chiefdoms first formed in Hawaii, investment in agricultural production remained modest. Intensive agricultural development took off after 1400, however, as chiefs consolidated their control over land and labor. The construction of irrigation systems further strengthened the chiefs' authority, allowing them to command more resources, mobilize more warriors, and expand their domains through conquest. Complex systems of tribute payment—from commoners to local chiefs and ultimately to island-wide monarchs—facilitated the formation of powerful states.

tribute Submission of wealth, labor, and sometimes items of symbolic value to a ruling authority.

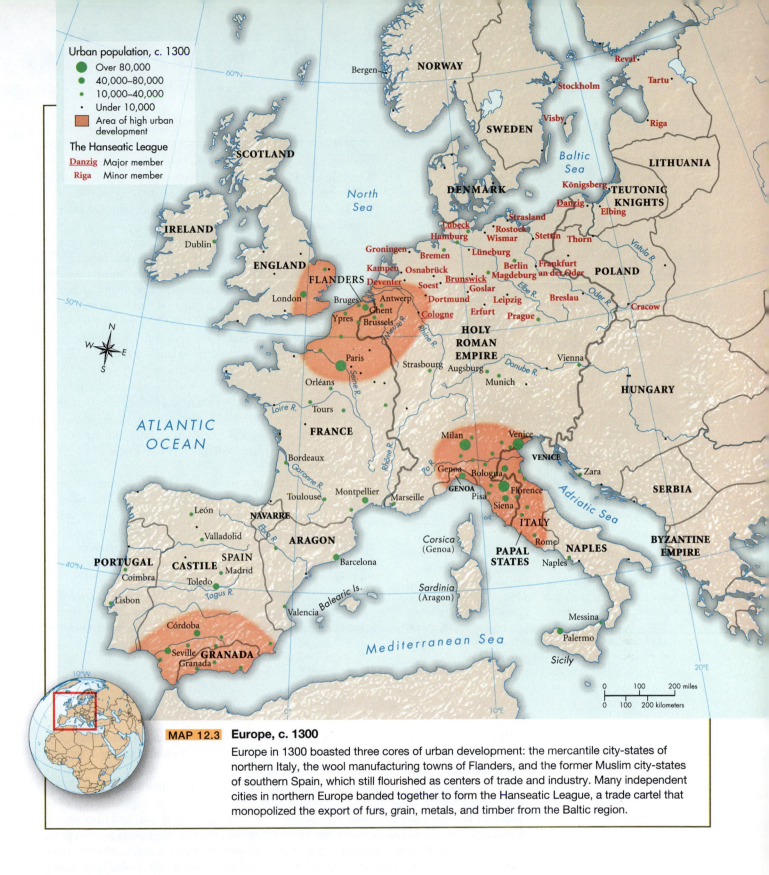

Urban population, c. 1300
- ● Over 80,000
- ● 40,000–80,000
- ● 10,000–40,000
- · Under 10,000
- ▨ Area of high urban development

The Hanseatic League
- **Danzig** Major member
- *Riga* Minor member

MAP 12.3 **Europe, c. 1300**

Europe in 1300 boasted three cores of urban development: the mercantile city-states of northern Italy, the wool manufacturing towns of Flanders, and the former Muslim city-states of southern Spain, which still flourished as centers of trade and industry. Many independent cities in northern Europe banded together to form the Hanseatic League, a trade cartel that monopolized the export of furs, grain, metals, and timber from the Baltic region.

Settlement and Agriculture

Humans first arrived in the Hawaiian Islands during the great wave of Polynesian voyaging of the first millennium C.E. (see Chapter 11). The dating of the initial settlement of Hawaii is disputed, with scholarly opinion ranging from as early as 300 C.E. to as late as 800. The early colonists maintained contact with distant societies in the Marquesas (the most likely origin

The Mande Blacksmiths

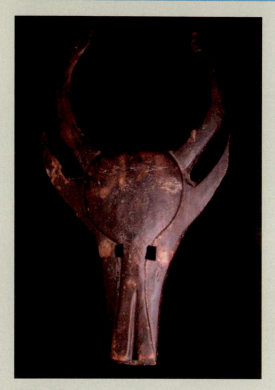

Komo Mask

Among the Mande peoples of West Africa, komo associations governed many aspects of community life, such as the secret rites of passage that inducted young males into adulthood. The komo associations may date back to the period 700 to 1100, when blacksmiths first emerged as a powerful social caste. Blacksmiths, who worked with wood as well as metal, carved the animal masks used in komo religious rituals. (Barakat Gallery.)

In West Africa, ironworking was far more than a useful technology for manufacturing tools and weapons. It also became a fearsome instrument of symbolic power, especially among the Mande peoples inhabiting the Sahelian savanna between the Senegal and Niger river valleys. Mande society was divided into three principal groups: free persons (including both commoners and the warrior nobility); specialized professional castes (*nyamakala*) such as blacksmiths, leatherworkers, and storytelling bards; and slaves. This three-tiered structure had taken shape at least by the time of the Mali Empire in the thirteenth and fourteenth centuries. But the unique status of blacksmiths in Mande society clearly had more ancient origins.

The nyamakala possessed closely guarded knowledge of technical arts, and this knowledge was tinged with supernatural power. It gave them special abilities that set them apart from the rest of society. The nyamakala were considered alien peoples who married only with their own kind. The right to practice their craft was a hereditary monopoly.

An aura of mystery surrounded the blacksmiths in particular, whose work involved transforming rock into metal through the sublime power of fire. Ordinary people regarded them with a mixture of dread and awe. Similarly, the women of blacksmith clans had the exclusive right to make pottery. Like iron metallurgy, pottery making required mastery of the elemental force of fire.

Armed with secret knowledge and "magical" powers, blacksmiths occupied a central place in the religious life of the community. The right to perform circumcision, a solemn and dangerous ritual of passage to adulthood, was

Agriculture and Ecological Change

of the Hawaiians) and Society Islands. But long-distance voyaging ceased in around 1300. For the next five centuries, until the British explorer Captain Cook arrived in 1788, the Hawaiian archipelago remained a world unto itself.

The original settlers, probably numbering no more than a few hundred persons, introduced a wide range of new plants and animals, including pigs, dogs, and chickens, tuber crops (taro and yams), banana, coconut, and a variety of medicinal and fiber plants. Colonists soon hunted some native species to extinction, notably large birds such as geese and ibis, but the human impact on the islands' ecology remained modest until after 1100. Between 1100 and 1650, however, the human population grew rapidly, probably doubling every century. Agricultural exploitation intensified, radically transforming the natural environment. In the geologically older western islands, the inhabitants constructed irrigated taro fields fed by stone-lined canals on the valley floors and lower hillsides. But irrigation was not practicable on the large eastern islands of Hawaii and Maui because they were largely covered by lava flows. As a result agriculture in the eastern islands lagged behind that of the western islands.

entrusted to blacksmiths. Blacksmiths also manufactured ritual objects, such as the headdresses used in religious ceremonies. They were believed to have healing powers, too. Together with leatherworkers, they made amulets (charms) for protection against demonic attack.

The social distance that separated blacksmiths from the rest of Mande society enhanced their reputation for fairness. Blacksmiths commonly acted as mediators in disputes and marriage transactions. Mande peoples often swore oaths upon a blacksmith's anvil. Most important, only blacksmiths could hold leadership positions in *komo* associations, initiation societies composed mostly of young men and charged with protecting the community against human and supernatural enemies. The ritual masks used by komo associations in their religious ceremonies were carved by blacksmiths, whose occult powers imbued the masks with magical potency.

The caste status of blacksmith clans affirmed their extraordinary powers, but it simultaneously relegated them to the margins of society. In Mande origin myths, blacksmiths appear as a powerful force to be tamed and domesticated. The Mande epics trace the founding of the Mali Empire to an intrepid warrior hero, the hunter Sunjata (see page 397), who is said to have overthrown the "blacksmith king" Sumanguru (soo-mahn-guh-roo) in the mid-thirteenth century. Sumanguru is depicted as a brutal tyrant. Sunjata's triumph over Sumanguru enabled him to gain mastery of spiritual forces without being polluted and corrupted by them. In the new social order of the Mali Empire, the dangerous powers of the blacksmiths were contained by marginalizing them as an occupational caste that was excluded from warfare and rulership and forbidden to marry outside their group. Despite their crucial importance to economic and religious life, the caste identity of the blacksmiths branded them as inferior to freeborn persons in Mande society.

QUESTIONS TO CONSIDER

1. Why did Mande society regard blacksmiths as exceptional?

2. In what ways was the caste system of West African peoples such as the Mande different from the caste system in India discussed in Chapter 6?

3. Why did the rulers of Mali perceive the Mande blacksmiths as a threat?

For Further Information:
McIntosh, Roderick. *The Peoples of the Middle Niger: The Island of Gold.* Oxford, U.K.: Blackwell, 1998.
McNaughton, Patrick R. *The Mande Blacksmiths: Knowledge, Power, and Art in West Africa.* Bloomington, IN: Indiana University Press, 1988.

Population growth and the building of irrigation systems reached their peak in the fifteenth and sixteenth centuries. This was also the period when the *ahupua'a* (ah-HOO-poo-ah-hah) system of land management developed. The ahupua'a consisted of tracts of land running down from the central mountains to the sea, creating wedge-shaped segments that cut across different ecological zones. Each ahupua'a combined a wide range of resources, including forests, fields, fishponds, and marine vegetation and wildlife.

In other Polynesian societies, kinship groups possessed joint landownership rights, but in Hawaii the land belonged to powerful kings. These rulers claimed descent from the gods and sharply distinguished themselves from the rest of society. The kings distributed the ahupua'a under their control to subordinate chiefs in return for tribute

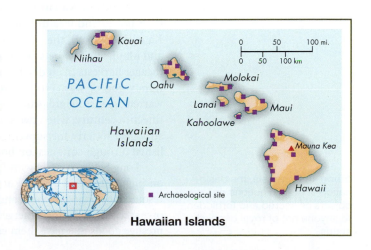

Hawaiian Islands

Hawaiian Landscape

The first European visitors to Hawaii were impressed by the intensive agriculture practiced by the Hawaiian islanders. This sketch of a Hawaiian village was drawn by a member of the expedition led by the British explorer George Vancouver, who landed at Hawaii in 1792. Cultivated fields lined with stone irrigation channels can be seen in the background. (Bishop Museum Library & Archives.)

and fealty, especially in times of war. Local chiefs in turn allocated rights to land, water, and fishing grounds to commoners, who were obliged to work on the personal lands of the chief and to pay tribute in produce. These rights were etched into the landscape by the construction of stone walls that lined fields, ponds, and canals.

Exchange and Social Hierarchy

Social Stratification

Strict rules of descent and inheritance determined social rank in Hawaiian society, and an elaborate system of **taboos** reinforced social stratification. Taboos also regulated gender differences and boundaries. Women were forbidden to eat many foods, including pork, bananas, and certain kinds of fish, and had to cook their food in separate ovens and eat apart from men. Chiefs proclaimed their exalted status through temple construction, ritual performances, and personal dress. Specialized craftsmen directly under the control of the chief class fashioned the elaborate feather cloaks, capes, and helmets worn by rulers that signified their divine status.

Omnipotent Kings

In the genealogical lore of Hawaii, the oldest royal lineages were in the densely populated islands of Kauai (kah-WAH-ee) and Oahu. The ruling elites of these islands drew their power and wealth from irrigated agriculture and focused their religious worship on Kane (KAH-nay), the god of flowing waters and fertility. On the larger islands of Hawaii and Maui, where chiefs and kings derived their power from military might rather than the meager harvests from dry-land farming, their devotion centered instead on Ku, the bloodthirsty god of war. From 1400 onward the local rulers in Hawaii and Maui incessantly warred against neighboring rivals. Temple-building on Maui escalated dramatically in the fifteenth century, when two regional chiefdoms formed on opposite ends of the island and struggled bitterly for supremacy. By 1650, single, island-wide kingdoms would be established through conquest on both Maui and Hawaii.

taboo In Polynesia, the designation of certain actions or objects as sacred and forbidden to anyone not of royal or chiefly status.

Long before contact with Europeans, then, Hawaiian rulers forged powerful states based on highly stratified systems of social ranking. Private property did not exist. All land and resources belonged to chiefs and kings, who were regarded as gods. In the absence of the kind of market networks that emerged in Eurasia and Africa, rulers could effectively monopolize the prestige goods that gave them exalted status. Through their monopoly of not only productive resources but the exchange and use of goods, Hawaiian rulers gained full command over the wealth of their realm and the labor of their subjects. Taboos served above all to regulate consumption and to enforce the sharp social divide between rulers and commoners.

Conclusion

Beginning in the tenth century, agricultural growth and commercial integration generated a sustained economic expansion across much of Eurasia and Africa. A warmer global climate and the introduction of new crops increased agricultural productivity in both the ancient centers of civilization of the Mediterranean, India, and China and the newly developing areas of settlement such as northern and eastern Europe and mainland Southeast Asia. Larger and more stable food supplies nourished population growth in cities and the countryside alike.

The farthest-reaching transformations in economic life and livelihood were the expansion of trade networks and the growing sophistication of commercial practices. Cairo, Venice, Quanzhou, and other leading commercial cities served as the crossroads for enterprising merchants such as Allan bin Hassun; their trade ventures linked the Mediterranean and the Middle East to sub-Saharan Africa, the Indian Ocean, and China. The cosmopolitan merchant communities of these cities were the forefathers of this "commercial revolution" and the new forms of business organization and banking that it spawned. In contrast to places such as Hawaii, where wealth remained yoked to political power, the dynamic market economy threatened to subvert the existing social order. Commercial cities harbored new centers of education and intellectual inquiry, too, and these also posed challenges to established political and cultural authority, as we will see in the next chapter.

Dramatic as the changes in economic life were during these centuries, we should remember their limitations. Population growth eventually outpaced increases in productivity. The profits generated by commerce accrued mainly to merchants and their fellow investors—including religious establishments and landowning aristocrats—rather than producers. Hunger was a constant threat, and the poor had to survive on the last dregs of grain and chaff in the final months before the new harvest.

By 1300, the capacities of existing agricultural and commercial systems were reaching their limits. Under the intensifying strain of population growth, natural disasters, and political pressures, the commercial networks spanning Eurasia and Africa began to break down, ushering in an age of crisis and economic contraction that we will consider in Chapter 15.

NOTES

1. Quotations from S. D. Goitein, "Portrait of a Medieval India Trader: Three Letters from the Cairo Geniza," *Bulletin of the School of Oriental and African Studies,* 50, no. 3 (1987): 461; S. D. Goitein, *A Mediterranean Society: The Jewish Communities of the World as Portrayed in the Documents of the Cairo Geniza* (Berkeley: University of California Press, 1978–88), 3:194; 5:221.

2. Kekaumenos, *Strategikon,* quoted in Angeliki E. Laiou, "Economic Thought and Ideology," in Angeliki E. Laiou, ed., *The Economic History of Byzantium from the Seventh Through the Fifteenth Century* (Washington, DC: Dumbarton Oaks Research Library and Collection, 2002), 3:1127.

3. Quotation from Fang Hui (1227–1307), cited in Richard von Glahn, "Towns and Temples: Urban Growth and Decline in the Yangzi Delta, 1100–1400," in Paul Jakov Smith and Richard von Glahn, eds., *The Song Yuan-Ming Transition in Chinese History* (Cambridge, MA: Harvard University Council on East Asian Studies, 2004), 182.

4. Ibn Hazm, *The Ring of the Dove: A Treatise on the Art and Practice of Arab Love* (London: Luzac, 1953), 74.

5. Al-Muqaddasi, *The Best Divisions for Knowledge of the Regions,* trans. Basil Anthony Collins (Reading, U.K.: Garnet Publishing, 1994), 181.

6. Quoted in Goitein, *A Mediterranean Society,* 1:200.

7. Translation adapted from Yuan Ts'ai, *Family Instructions for the Yuan Clan,* quoted in Patricia Buckley Ebrey, *Family and Property in Sung China* (Princeton, NJ: Princeton University Press, 1984), 267.

8. Ibn Hawqal, *The Picture of the Earth*, translated in N. Levtzion and J. F. P. Hopkins, eds., *Corpus of Early Arabic Sources for West African History* (Cambridge, U.K.: Cambridge University Press, 1981), 49.

9. Al-Bakri, *Kitab al masalik wa-'l-mamalik*, translated in Levtzion and Hopkins, eds., *Corpus of Early Arabic Sources*, 79.

10. Al-Umari, "The Kingdom of Mali and What Appertains to It" (1338), cited in Levtzion and Hopkins, eds., *Corpus of Early Arabic Sources*, 270–271.

RESOURCES FOR RESEARCH

Agricultural Innovation and Diffusion

The diffusion of crops and the invention of new technologies gave impetus to major advances in agricultural productivity across Eurasia between 900 and 1300. Duby's classic work on the early medieval European economy remains unsurpassed, but Verhulst, who reviews the large historiography on this topic and the growing body of archaeological evidence, provides a valuable supplement for the early part of this period.

Bray, Francesca. *The Rice Economies: Technology and Development in Asian Societies*. 1986.

Chaudhuri, K. N. *Asia Before Europe: Economy and Civilization of the Indian Ocean from the Rise of Islam to 1750*. 1990.

Duby, Georges. *The Early Growth of the European Economy: Warriors and Peasants from the Seventh to the Twelfth Century*. 1974.

Verhulst, Adriaan. *The Carolingian Economy*. 2002.

Watson, A. M. *Agricultural Innovation in the Early Islamic World: The Diffusion of Crops and Farming Techniques, 700–1100*. 1983.

Industrial Growth and the Money Economy

Technological innovation was also a key stimulus to industrial growth, especially in China. Lopez was the pioneer in establishing the now widely accepted idea of a "commercial revolution" in medieval Europe. Herlihy and Bray are landmarks in the study of women, work, and the domestic economy.

Bray, Francesca. *Technology and Gender: Fabrics of Power in Late Imperial China*. 1997.

Epstein, Steven A. *An Economic and Social History of Later Medieval Europe, 1000–1500*. 2009.

Herlihy, David. *Opera Muliebria: Women and Work in Medieval Europe*. 1990.

Laiou, Angeliki E., and Cécile Morrison. *The Byzantine Economy*. 2007.

Lombard, Maurice. *The Golden Age of Islam* (rpt.). 2004.

Lopez, Robert S. *The Commercial Revolution of the Middle Ages, 950–1350*. 1976.

Merchants and Trade Networks in Afro-Eurasia

We have much more abundant documentary evidence of the increasingly far-flung activities of merchants than we have for those of farmers and industrialists. Abu-Lughod provides the most comprehensive synthesis of the development of cross-cultural exchange and commercial practices in this era. Favier and Constable both marshal impressive bodies of evidence on the merchant world of western Europe.

Abu-Lughod, Janet. *Before European Hegemony: The World System, A.D. 1250–1350*. 1989.

Constable, Olivia Remie. *Trade and Traders in Muslim Spain: The Commercial Realignment of the Iberian Peninsula, 900–1500*. 1994.

Coquery-Vidrovitch, Catherine. *The History of African Cities South of the Sahara: From the Origins to Colonization*. 2005.

Favier, Jean. *Gold and Spices: The Rise of Commerce in the Middle Ages*. 1998.

Sen, Tansen. *Buddhism, Diplomacy, and Trade: The Realignment of Sino-Indian Relations, 600–1400*. 2003.

COUNTERPOINT: Production, Tribute, and Trade in the Hawaiian Islands

Through painstaking archaeological research, the major developments in land use and economic life in the Pacific Islands before European contact are gradually becoming clear. Kirch is the foremost authority on the archaeology of the Hawaiian Islands and Polynesia generally. Earle's study of the different types of chiefdom societies emphasizes the crucial importance of economic power in the formation of Hawaiian chiefdoms.

Earle, Timothy. *How Chiefs Come to Power: The Political Economy in Prehistory*. 1997.

Kirch, Patrick V. *Feathered Gods and Fishhooks: An Introduction to Hawaiian Archaeology and Prehistory*. 1985.

Kirch, Patrick V., and Jean-Louis Rallu, eds. *The Growth and Collapse of Pacific Island Societies: Archaeological and Demographic Perspectives*. 2007.

▶ **For additional primary sources from this period**, see *Sources of Crossroads and Cultures*.

▶ **For Web sites, images, and documents related to topics in this chapter**, see Make History at bedfordstmartins.com/smith.

The major global development in this chapter ▶ The sustained economic expansion that spread across Afro-Eurasia from 900 to 1300.

IMPORTANT EVENTS

850–1267	Chola kingdom in southern India
960–1279	Song dynasty in China
969	Fatimids conquer Egypt
1024	The Song dynasty issues the first paper money in world history
1055	Seljuk Turks capture Baghdad
c. 1120–1150	Construction of Angkor Wat begins
1127	The Jurchen conquer north China; the Song dynasty retains control of southern China
c. 1150–1300	Heyday of the Champagne fairs
c. 1200–1400	Formation of first chiefdoms in the Hawaiian Islands
1230–1255	Reign of Sunjata, founder of the Mali Empire in West Africa
1250–1517	Mamluk dynasty in Egypt
1258	The Italian city-states of Florence and Genoa mint the first gold coins issued in Latin Christendom
1323–1325	Pilgrimage to Mecca of Musa Mansa, ruler of Mali
c. 1400–1450	Great Zimbabwe in southern Africa reaches peak of prosperity

KEY TERMS

bill of exchange (p. 386) serf (p. 376)
burgher (p. 397) taboo (p. 402)
cartel (p. 390) tribute (p. 398)
guild (p. 388) usury (p. 386)
iqta (p. 378)
joint stock company
(p. 391)

CHAPTER OVERVIEW QUESTIONS

1. How did agricultural changes contribute to commercial and industrial growth?

2. What technological breakthroughs increased productivity most significantly?

3. What social institutions and economic innovations did merchants devise to overcome the risks and dangers of long-distance trade?

4. In what ways did the profits of commerce translate into social and economic power?

5. Above all, who benefited most from these economic changes?

SECTION FOCUS QUESTIONS

1. Which groups took the most active role in adopting new agricultural technologies in the different regions of Eurasia during the centuries from 900 to 1300?

2. How did the composition and organization of the industrial workforce change in different parts of Eurasia during this period?

3. How did the commercial revival of 900 to 1300 reorient trade routes across Afro-Eurasia?

4. How did the sources of wealth and power in the Hawaiian Islands differ from those of market economies elsewhere in the world?

MAKING CONNECTIONS

1. In what ways did the spread of new crops and farming technologies during this period have a different impact in the Islamic world and in Asia?

2. How had the principal east-west trade routes between Asia and the Mediterranean world changed since the time of the Han and Roman empires (see Chapters 6 and 7)?

3. To what extent did the Christian, Jewish, and Muslim merchant communities of the Mediterranean adopt similar forms of commercial organization and business practices during the "commercial revolution" of 900 to 1300? How can we explain the differences and similarities among these groups?

13

AT A CROSSROADS ▲

Schools in Latin Christendom organized the learning of ancient Greece and Rome into the seven liberal arts. The trivium (Latin for "three roads") of logic, rhetoric, and grammar endowed the student with eloquence; the quadrivium ("four roads") of arithmetic, geometry, astronomy, and music led to knowledge. This detail from a mural composed between 1365 and 1367 for a Franciscan chapel in Florence depicts the trivium (at right in first row) and the quadrivium (at left) in the persons of the ancient scholars credited with their invention; behind each scholar sits his muse, represented in female form. (Scala/Art Resource, NY.)

Centers of Learning and the Transmission of Culture

900–1300

In her masterful novel of court life in Heian Japan, *The Tale of Genji*, Murasaki Shikibu (c. 973–1025) sought to defend the art of fiction and women as readers of fiction. Murasaki's hero, Genji, finds his adopted daughter copying a courtly romance novel and mocks women's passionate enthusiasm for such frivolous writings. Genji protests that "there is hardly a word of truth in all of these books, as you know perfectly well, but here you are utterly fascinated by such fables, taking them quite seriously and avidly copying every word." At the end of his speech, though, Genji reverses his original judgment. Romance novels, he concludes, may be fabricated, but they have the virtue of describing "this world exactly as it is."[1]

Many of Murasaki's contemporaries shared Genji's initial low opinion of the content of courtly romances, but they also rejected such works at least in part because they were written in vernacular Japanese—the language of everyday speech. In Lady Murasaki's day, classical Chinese was the language of politics and religion at the Heian court. Writing in the Japanese vernacular was considered at best a trifling skill, acceptable for letters and diaries but ill-suited to the creation of literature or art.

Lady Murasaki had been born into an aristocratic family of middling rank. She was a quick study as a child and, she tells us, far more proficient at Chinese than her brother.

BACKSTORY

As we saw in Chapters 9 and 10, from 400 to 1000 religious traditions consolidated in the main centers of civilization across Eurasia. Christianity prevailed in many parts of the former Roman Empire, but divisions deepened between the Greek church, which was closely allied with the Byzantine Empire, and the Latin church of Rome. Islam was fully established as the official religion across a vast territory extending from Spain to Persia. In India, the classical Brahmanic religion, recast in the form of Hinduism, steadily displaced Buddhism from the center of religious and intellectual life. In contrast, the Mahayana tradition of Buddhism enjoyed great popularity at all levels of society in East Asia. In China, however, Buddhist beliefs clashed with the long-cherished secular ideals of Confucian philosophy. In all of these regions, the study of scripture—and the written language of sacred texts—dominated schooling and learning.

Church and Universities in Latin Christendom

FOCUS What political, social, and religious forces led to the founding of the first European universities?

Students and Scholars in Islamic Societies

FOCUS To what extent did Sunni and Sufi schools foster a common cultural and religious identity among Muslims?

The Cosmopolitan and Vernacular Realms in India and Southeast Asia

FOCUS What political and religious forces contributed to the development of a common culture across India and Southeast Asia and its subsequent fragmentation into regional cultures?

Learning, Schools, and Print Culture in East Asia

FOCUS To what extent did intellectual and educational trends in Song China influence its East Asian neighbors?

COUNTERPOINT: Writing and Political Power in Mesoamerica

FOCUS How did the relationship between political power and knowledge of writing in Mesoamerica differ from that in the other civilizations studied in this chapter?

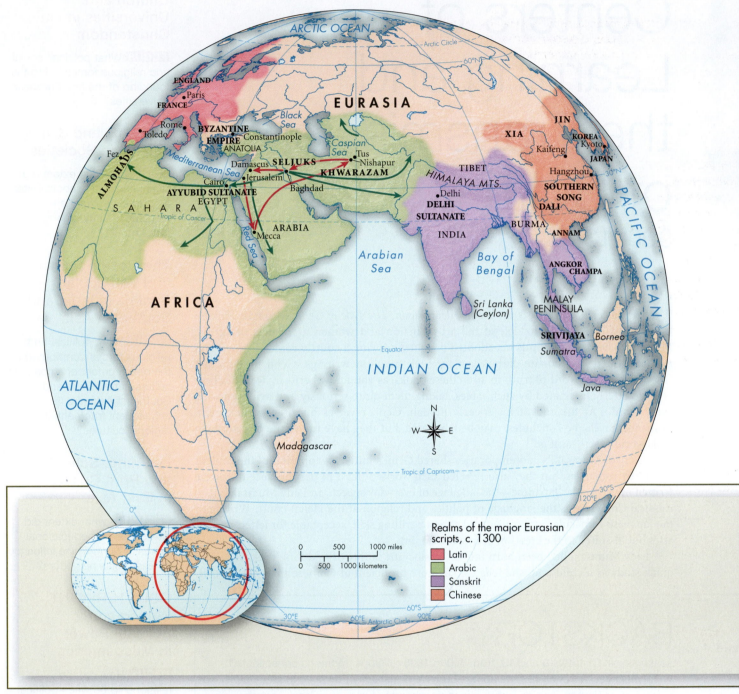

Realms of the major Eurasian scripts, c. 1300

- Latin
- Arabic
- Sanskrit
- Chinese

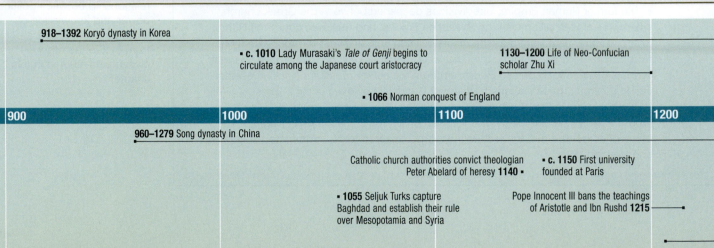

918–1392 Koryŏ dynasty in Korea

- c. 1010 Lady Murasaki's *Tale of Genji* begins to circulate among the Japanese court aristocracy

1130–1200 Life of Neo-Confucian scholar Zhu Xi

- 1066 Norman conquest of England

900 | 1000 | 1100 | 1200

960–1279 Song dynasty in China

Catholic church authorities convict theologian Peter Abelard of heresy 1140 ▪

- c. 1150 First university founded at Paris

- 1055 Seljuk Turks capture Baghdad and establish their rule over Mesopotamia and Syria

Pope Innocent III bans the teachings of Aristotle and Ibn Rushd 1215

Knowledge of Chinese was considered unbecoming in a woman, however. Calligraphy (brush writing), poetry, and music were deemed appropriate subjects for female education. Like many women of her class, Murasaki was also fond of romance tales, which typically revolved around the lives, loves, and marriages of court women. Widowed in her twenties, Murasaki had already acquired some fame as a writer when she was summoned in around 1006 to serve as lady-in-waiting to the empress. During her years at the court Murasaki completed her *Tale of Genji*. Manuscript copies circulated widely among court women in Murasaki's lifetime and captivated a sizable male readership as well. From Murasaki's time forward, fiction and poetry written in the Japanese vernacular gained distinction as serious works of literature.

Yet Chinese remained the language of officials, scholars, and priests. The role of Chinese as the language of public discourse and political and religious authority throughout East Asia paralleled that of Latin in western Europe, of Arabic in the Islamic world, and of Sanskrit in South and Southeast Asia. Between the tenth and the fourteenth centuries these cosmopolitan languages—languages that transcended national boundaries—became deeply embedded in new educational institutions, and as a result their intellectual and aesthetic prestige grew. Although writing in vernacular languages gained new prominence as well, the goal was not to address a wider, nonelite audience. Rather, the emergence of vernacular literature was often closely tied to courtly culture, as in Murasaki's Japan. Authors writing in the vernacular still wrote for elite, learned readers.

Choosing to write in the vernacular was both a political and an artistic statement. The turn toward the vernacular was undoubtedly related to the ebbing authority of vast multinational empires and the rise of national and regional states. But the emergence of vernacular literary languages did not simply reflect existing national social and political identities; they were instrumental in inventing regional and national identities. Thus, both cosmopolitan and vernacular languages helped create new cultural connections, the former by facilitating the development of international cultural communities, and the latter by broadcasting the idea that nations were defined, in part, by the shared culture of their inhabitants.

MAPPING THE WORLD

The Major Written Languages of Eurasia, c. 1300

The use of a common written language fostered cultural unity within each of the four major regional societies of Eurasia. The spread of the four "classical" languages—Latin, Arabic, Sanskrit, and Chinese—resulted from their prominent role as the written word of religious scriptures. After 1000, a shift toward vernacular, or everyday, written languages occurred in all of these regions, but the classical languages retained their cultural authority, especially in religion and higher education.

ROUTES ▼

→ Spread of Sufi orders, 1150–1300

→ Travels of Abu Hamid al-Ghazali, 1091–1111

1392–1910 Yi dynasty in Korea

▪ **1273** Publication of Thomas Aquinas's *Summa Theologica*

1300   **1400**   **1500**

1313–1321 Dante Alighieri composes his epic poem *Divine Comedy*

▪ **1382** Ibn Khaldun becomes professor of Islamic law at Cairo

1206–1526 Delhi Sultanate in India

OVERVIEW QUESTIONS

The major global development in this chapter: The expansion of learning and education across Eurasia from 900 to 1300 and its relationship to the rise of regional and national identities.

As you read, consider:

1. Did the spread of higher learning reinforce or undermine established political and religious authority?

2. How did educational institutions reshape social hierarchy and elite culture?

3. What were the different uses of cosmopolitan languages (which transcended national boundaries) and vernacular (everyday) languages, and to what degree did they broaden access to written knowledge?

4. How did the different technologies of writing affect the impact of the written word?

Church and Universities in Latin Christendom

FOCUS

What political, social, and religious forces led to the founding of the first European universities?

Between the tenth and the fourteenth centuries, Latin Christendom witnessed the emergence of a unified learned culture. The values and self-images of clergy and knights increasingly converged. For knights, chivalric virtue and dedication to defense of the Christian faith replaced the wanton lifestyle of the Germanic warriors. At the same time, the clergy became more militant in their promotion of orthodoxy, as reform-minded religious orders devoted themselves to spreading the faith and stamping out heresy.

Schooling created a common elite culture and a single educated class. The career of Peter Abelard (1079–1142) captures this transformation. Abelard's father, a French knight, engaged a tutor to educate young Peter in his future duties as a warrior and lord. Abelard later recalled that "I was so carried away by my love of learning that I renounced the glory of a soldier's life, made over my inheritance and rights of the elder son to my brothers, and withdrew from the court of Mars [war] in order to kneel at the feet of Minerva [learning]."[2] Abelard's intellectual daring ultimately provoked charges of heresy that led to his banishment and the burning of his books. In the wake of the Abelard controversy, kings and clerics wrestled for control of schools. Out of this contest emerged a new institution of higher learning, the university.

Monastic Learning and Culture

cathedral school In Latin Christendom, a school attached to a cathedral and subject to the authority of a bishop.

rhetoric The art of persuasion through writing or speech.

From the time of Charlemagne (r. 768–814), royal courts and Christian monasteries became closely allied. Royally sponsored monasteries grew into huge, wealthy institutions whose leaders came from society's upper ranks. Many monks and nuns entered the cloisters as children, presented (together with their inheritances) by their parents as gifts to the church. Kings and local nobles safeguarded monasteries and supervised their activities.

Devoted to the propagation of right religion and seeking educated men to staff their governments, Charlemagne and his successors promoted a revival of classical learning consistent with the established doctrines of Latin Christianity. Charlemagne summoned famous scholars to his court and gave them the tasks of reforming ecclesiastic practices and establishing an authoritative text of the Bible. Although he never realized his hope that schooling would be widely available, local bishops began to found **cathedral schools**— schools attached to a cathedral and subject to a bishop's authority—as a complement to monastic education.

Cathedral Schools

Elementary schools trained students to speak and read Latin. Advanced education in both monasteries and cathedral schools centered on the "liberal arts," particularly the Roman *trivium* (TREE-vee-um) (Latin for "three roads") of grammar, rhetoric, and logic. Roman educators had championed **rhetoric**—the art of persuasion through writing or speech—and especially oratorical skill as crucial to a career in government service. Monastic teachers likewise stressed the importance of rhetoric and oratory for monks and priests. Unlike the Romans, however, the clergy deemphasized logic; they sought to establish the primacy of revelation over philosophical reasoning. Similarly, the clergy separated the exact sciences of the Greeks—the *quadrivium* (kwo-DRIV-ee-uhm) ("four roads") of arithmetic, geometry, music, and astronomy—from the core curriculum of the trivium and treated these fields as specialized subjects for advanced study.

Emphasis on Liberal Arts

Bishops appointed "master scholars" to take charge of teaching at the cathedral schools. The masters in effect had a monopoly on teaching within their cities. Individuals who ventured to teach without official recognition as a master faced excommunication. The privileged status of these masters and their greater receptivity to logic and the quadrivium caused friction between cathedral schools and monasteries.

The revival of learning encouraged by Charlemagne and the Germanic kings led to a dramatic increase in book production, including theological works, biblical commentaries, encyclopedias, and saints' lives. The kings distributed manuscripts to monasteries, where scribes and artists made copies. By the eleventh century many religious texts were created as lavish works of art featuring copious illustration and expensive materials such

Boom in Book Production

Deluxe Illustrated Manuscript
Monastic communities in Latin Christendom created many beautifully illustrated copies of the Gospels, the accounts of the life of Christ. The first page of this *Gospel of Matthew*, produced at a German monastery in around 1120 to 1140, shows Saint Matthew writing with a quill pen and sharpening knife. On the next page the first line of the Gospel begins with a large letter *L* (the beginning of the word *liber*, "book"), nested among golden vines against a background resembling the luxurious Byzantine silks highly prized in Europe. (The J. Paul Getty Museum, Los Angeles, Ms. Ludwig II 3, fol.10, Decorated Incipit Page, ca.1120-1140, Temera colors, gold and silver on parchment, Leaf: 9 × 6½ in.)

Medical Professionals of Latin Christendom

Economic revival and urban growth in Europe after 1000 spurred major changes in the practice and study of medicine. The rising urban commercial and professional classes increasingly demanded academically trained physicians. The cathedral schools, and later the universities, added medicine as an advanced subject of study. The institutionalization of medicine as an academic discipline transformed learned doctors into a professional class that tightly regulated its membership, practices, and standards.

In around 1173, the Jewish traveler Benjamin of Tudela described Salerno, in southern Italy, as the home of "the principal medical university of Christendom." By *university* Benjamin meant an organized group of scholars, not a formal educational institution. By the tenth century Salerno had already achieved renown for its skilled doctors. Many hailed from the city's large Jewish and Greek communities and were familiar with Arabic and Byzantine medical traditions. Beginning in the eleventh century, Salerno's learned doctors produced many medical writings that profoundly influenced medical knowledge and training across Latin Christendom.

Among the notable scholars at Salerno was Constantine the African, a Muslim who arrived from North Africa, possibly as a drug merchant, in around 1070. Constantine converted to Christianity and entered the famed Montecassino monastery north of Salerno. His translations of Muslim, Jewish, and Greek works on medicine became the basis of medical instruction in European universities for centuries afterward.

Salerno's doctors also contributed important writings on gynecology and obstetrics. A local female healer named Trota became a famed authority on gynecology ("women's medicine"). A Salerno manuscript falsely attributed to Trota justified singling out women's illnesses as a separate branch of medicine:

Trota Expounds on the Nature of Women

The *Trotula*, a set of three treatises on gynecology and women's health, was probably composed in Salerno in the twelfth century. All three works were attributed to Trota, a healer acclaimed as an authority on female physiology, although only one is likely to have come from her hand. In this illustration from a fourteenth-century French encyclopedia on natural science, Trota sits before a large open book and instructs a clerk in "the secrets of nature." (Bibliothèque de Rennes Métropole, MS593, folio 532.)

Because women are of a weaker nature than men, so more than men they are afflicted, especially in childbirth. It is for this reason also that more frequently diseases abound in them than in men, especially around the organs assigned to the work of nature. And because only with shame and embarrassment do they confess the fragility of the condition of their diseases that occur around their secret parts, they do not dare reveal their distress to male physicians. Therefore,

as gold leaf. A strikingly different style of creating manuscripts, however, was developed by the Cistercians, a new religious order that spread like wildfire across Europe within fifty years of its founding in 1098 (see Chapter 14). The Cistercians rebelled against the opulent lifestyle of wealthy monastic communities and dedicated themselves to lives of simplicity and poverty. In keeping with its principles of frugality, the Cistercian order produced great numbers of religious texts without elaborate decoration. Cistercian clergy also abhorred the growing importance of reasoning and logic in the cathedral schools, instead emphasizing religious education based on memorization, contemplation, and spiritual faith. Thus, the expansion of learning created both new connections and new divisions in Europe's intellectual and cultural elite.

their misfortune, which ought to be pitied, and especially the sake of a certain woman, moved me to provide some remedy for their above-mentioned diseases.[1]

The author attributed women's infirmity to their physical constitution and the trauma of childbirth, but also noted that women were less likely to seek treatment from male doctors. Local authorities, however, typically prohibited women other than midwives from treating patients.

Despite its outpouring of medical treatises, Salerno had no formal institution for medical training until the thirteenth century. By that time the universities of Bologna and Paris had surpassed Salerno as centers of medical learning. Bologna, for example, revived the study of anatomy and surgery and introduced human dissection as part of the curriculum. At the universities, students studied medicine only after completing rigorous training in the liberal arts.

The growing professionalization of medicine nurtured a new self-image of the doctor. Guy de Chauliac, a surgeon trained at Paris in the fourteenth century, wrote:

> I say that the doctor should be well mannered, bold in many ways, fearful of dangers, that he should abhor the false cures or practices. He should be affable to the sick, kindhearted to his colleagues, wise in his prognostications. He should be chaste, sober, compassionate, and merciful: he should not be covetous, grasping in money matters, and then he will receive a salary commensurate with his labors, the financial ability of his patients, the success of the treatment, and his own dignity.[2]

The emphasis on high ethical standards was crucial to the effort to elevate medicine's stature as an honorable occupation given the popular image of doctors and pharmacists as charlatans who, in the English poet Chaucer's mocking words, "each made money from the other's guile."[3]

This professional class of doctors steeped in rigorous study and guided by Christian compassion largely served the upper classes, however. Care of the poor and the rural populace was left to uneducated barber-surgeons, bonesetters, and faith healers.

---

1. Monica H. Green, ed. and trans., *The Trotula: An English Translation of the Medieval Compendium of Women's Medicine* (Philadelphia: University of Pennsylvania Press, 2002), 65.
2. Guy de Chauliac, "Inventarium sive chirurgia magna," quoted in Vern L. Bullough, *The Development of Medicine as a Profession: The Contribution of the Medieval University to Modern Medicine* (New York: Hafner Publishing, 1966), 93–94.
3. Geoffrey Chaucer, "Prologue," *The Canterbury Tales* (Harmondsworth, U.K.: Penguin), 30.

QUESTIONS TO CONSIDER

1. What kind of education and personal characteristics were considered necessary to become a professional physician?

2. Why did the public hold doctors in low regard? How did university education aim to improve that image?

For Further Information:

Bullough, Vern L. *The Development of Medicine as a Profession: The Contribution of the Medieval University to Modern Medicine*. New York: Hafner Publishing, 1966.
Siraisi, Nancy. *Medieval and Early Renaissance Medicine: An Introduction to Knowledge and Practice*. Chicago: University of Chicago Press, 1990.

The Rise of Universities

During the eleventh and twelfth centuries, demand for advanced education rose steadily. Eager young students traveled to distant cities to study with renowned masters. Unable to accommodate all of these students by themselves, masters began to hire staffs of specialized teachers who taught medicine, law, and theology in addition to the liberal arts. Certain schools acquired international reputations for excellence in particular specialties: Montpellier and Salerno in medicine, Bologna in law, Paris and Oxford in theology. These schools also applied higher learning to secular purposes. Montpellier and Salerno incorporated Greek and Arabic works into the study of medicine (see Lives and Livelihoods: Medical Professionals of Latin Christendom). At Bologna separate schools were established for civil and church law.

Increased Demand for Advanced Education

Influence of Greek and Muslim Learning

Christian conquests of Muslim territories in Spain and Sicily in the eleventh century reintroduced Greek learning to Latin Christendom via translations from Arabic. In 1085, King Alfonso VI (r. 1072–1109) of Castile captured Toledo, a city renowned as a center of learning where Muslims, Jews, and Christians freely intermingled. He made it his capital, and he and his successors preserved its multicultural heritage and spirit of religious toleration. In the twelfth century Toledo's Arabic-speaking Jewish and Christian scholars translated into Latin the works of Aristotle and other ancient Greek writers as well as philosophical, scientific, and medical writings by Muslim authors. Access to this vast body of knowledge had a profound impact on European intellectual circles. The commentaries on Aristotle by the Muslim philosopher Ibn Rushd (IB-uhn RUSHED) (1126–1198), known in Latin as Averröes (uh-VERR-oh-eez), sought to reconcile the paradoxes between faith and reason. They attracted keen interest from Christian theologians grappling with similar questions.

Ibn Rushd's insistence that faith is incomplete without rational understanding, for which he was persecuted and exiled, added new fuel to the intellectual controversies that flared up in Paris in the 1120s. Peter Abelard, who based his study of theology on the principle that "nothing can be believed unless it is first understood," attracted thousands of students to his lectures. Abelard's commitment to demonstrating the central tenets of Christian doctrine by applying reason and logical proof aroused heated controversy. Church authorities in 1140 found Abelard guilty of heresy and exiled him from Paris. He died a broken man two years later.

The First European Universities

The dispute over the primacy of reason or faith continued after Abelard's death. Paris's numerous masters organized themselves into guilds to defend their independence from the local bishop and from hostile religious orders such as the Cistercians, who had led the campaign against Abelard. The popes at Rome, eager to extend the reach of their own authority, placed Paris's schools of theology under their own supervision. In 1215 Pope Innocent III (1198–1216) formally recognized Paris's schools of higher learning as a **university**—a single corporation including masters and students from all the city's schools—under the direction of the pope's representative. Universities at Oxford and Bologna soon gained similar legal status.

In the end, though, chartering universities as independent corporations insulated them from clerical control. European monarchs, eager to enlist educated men in government service, became ardent patrons of established schools and provided endowments to create new ones. Consequently, during the thirteenth century more than thirty universities sprang up in western Europe (see Map 13.1). Royal patrons gave the universities leverage against local bishops and municipal councils. In some places, such as Oxford in England, the university became the dominant institution in local society, thanks to its substantial property holdings and control over both ecclesiastic and civil courts.

Among all the university towns, Paris emerged as the intellectual capital of Latin Christendom in the thirteenth century. Despite a papal ban on teaching Aristotle's works on natural science, the city swarmed with prominent teachers espousing Aristotle's ideas and methods. Even conservative scholars came to recognize the need to reconcile Christian doctrine with Greek philosophy. Thomas Aquinas (c. 1225–1274), a theologian at the University of Paris, incorporated Abelard's methods of logical argument into his great synthesis of Christian teachings, *Summa Theologica*. It stirred turbulent controversy, and much of it was banned until shortly before Aquinas's canonization as a saint in 1323. Academic freedom in the universities, to the extent that it existed, rested on an insecure balance among the competing interests of kings, bishops, and the papacy for control over the hearts and minds of their students.

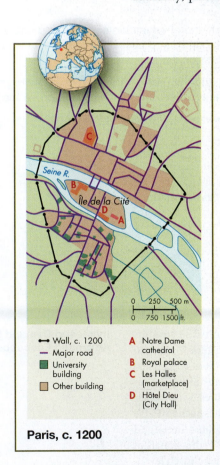

Seine R.

Île de la Cité

0   250   500 m
0   750   1500 ft.

⌒● Wall, c. 1200
— Major road
▪ University building
▪ Other building

A Notre Dame cathedral
B Royal palace
C Les Halles (marketplace)
D Hôtel Dieu (City Hall)

Paris, c. 1200

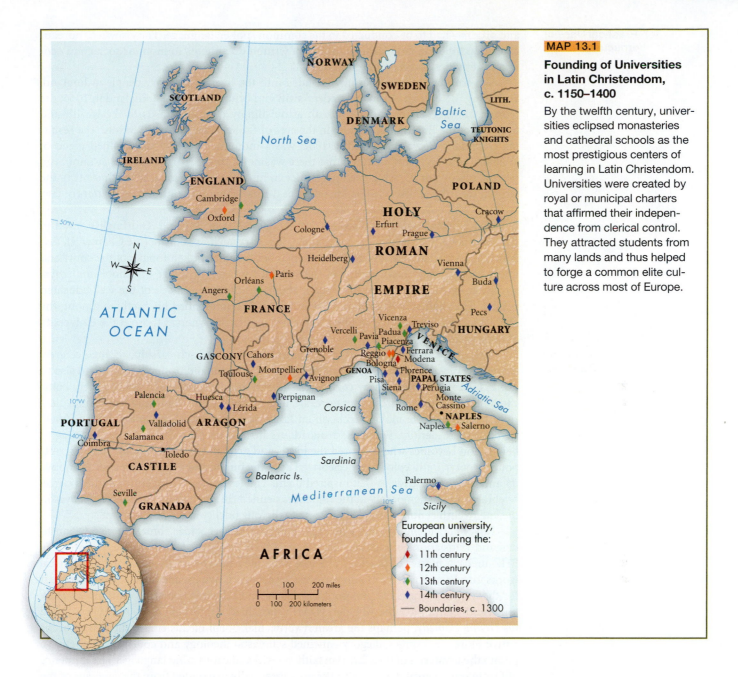

MAP 13.1

Founding of Universities in Latin Christendom, c. 1150–1400

By the twelfth century, universities eclipsed monasteries and cathedral schools as the most prestigious centers of learning in Latin Christendom. Universities were created by royal or municipal charters that affirmed their independence from clerical control. They attracted students from many lands and thus helped to forge a common elite culture across most of Europe.

European university, founded during the:
- ♦ 11th century
- ♦ 12th century
- ♦ 13th century
- ♦ 14th century
- — Boundaries, c. 1300

Vernacular Language and Literature

The growing need for literacy was a driving force behind the expansion of schooling and the founding of universities in Latin Europe. The mental agility and practical knowledge obtained by mastering the liberal arts curriculum had wide applications in bureaucratic and ecclesiastic office, professional careers, and private business. Schooling based on literacy in Latin fostered a unified elite culture across western Europe, well beyond national boundaries. At the same time, however, the practical needs of government and business and changes in the self-image of the rising administrative and commercial classes encouraged writing in a **vernacular language**—the language of everyday speech.

Despite the dominance of Latin in formal education, commercial growth and political expansion demanded more practical forms of literacy. The everyday business of government—recording disputes and judicial settlements, collecting vital statistics, transmitting warrants

university In Latin Christendom, a single corporate body that included teachers and students from a range of different academic disciplines.

vernacular language The language of everyday speech, in contrast to a language that is mainly literary.

Practical Uses of Vernacular Writing

and orders—had to be conducted in the common spoken language. The growth of bureaucracy developed in tandem with the use of written documents to monitor social and economic activities and control resources.

Government most powerfully intruded into the lives of ordinary people in England. Following the French Norman invaders' swift and brutal conquest of England in 1066, the Norman king William I undertook an astonishingly detailed census of the wealth and property of the English population. In the eyes of the vanquished Anglo-Saxons, the resulting *Domesday Book*, completed in 1087, was a monument to the unrestrained greed of William, who "was not ashamed that there was not a single [parcel of land] . . . not even one ox, or cow, or pig which escaped notice in his survey."[3] By the thirteenth century the written record had displaced oral memory as the indispensable authority in matters of law, business, and government.

The Norman conquest also transformed language in England. Old English, used to compose the Anglo-Saxon law codes and epic poetry such as *Beowulf* (see Chapter 9), disappeared as a written language, while French became the spoken tongue of the court and upper-class society. Latin served as the standard written language of schools and royal government. Mastery of the three main languages became a mark of the well-educated person. The mathematician Roger Bacon (d. 1294) commended his brethren among the Oxford faculty for teaching in English, French, and Latin, whereas those at the University of Paris exclusively used Latin.

Vernacular Literary Traditions

Although Latin prevailed as the language of liturgy and scholarship, acceptance grew for the use of vernacular languages to manage government and business affairs, and also to express emotion. Enriched by commercial wealth and land revenues, court society cultivated new fashions in dress, literature, art, and music. Yet the Bible and the Roman classics offered few role models with whom kings and princes, let alone knights and merchants, could identify. Poets and troubadours instead used vernacular speech to sing of heroes and heroines who mirrored the ideals and aspirations of their audiences. An outpouring of lyric and epic poetry celebrated both the public and private virtues of the nobility and the chivalric ideals that inspired them. The legends of King Arthur and his circle, celebrated most memorably in the romances penned (in French) by Chrétien de Troyes in the late twelfth century, mingled themes of religious fidelity and romantic love.

Royal and noble patrons who eagerly devoured vernacular romances also began to demand translations of religious and classical texts. Scholars such as Nicole Oresme (or-EHZ-meh), a master of theology at Paris, welcomed the challenge of translating classical works into French as a way to improve the vernacular language and enable people to use it for the higher purposes of philosophical debate and religious contemplation. In the early fourteenth century, Dante Alighieri (DAHN-tay ah-lee-JIHR-ee) (1265–1321), composed his *Divine Comedy*, perhaps the greatest vernacular poem of this era, in the dialect of his native Florence. Dante's allegory entwined scholastic theology and courtly love poetry to plumb the mysteries of the Christian faith in vivid and captivating language. The influence of Dante was so great that modern Italian is essentially descended from the language of the *Divine Comedy*. Thus, even as the rise of universities promoted a common intellectual culture across Latin Christendom, the growth of vernacular languages led to the creation of distinctive national literary traditions.

Students and Scholars in Islamic Societies

FOCUS

To what extent did Sunni and Sufi schools foster a common cultural and religious identity among Muslims?

In contrast to Latin Christendom, in the Islamic world neither the caliphs nor dissenting movements such as Shi'ism sought to establish a clergy with sacred powers and formal religious authority. Instead, the task of teaching the faithful about matters of religion fell to the *ulama* (oo-leh-MAH), learned persons whose wisdom and holiness earned them the respect of their peers. But the ulama did not claim any special relationship to God.

The ulama remained immersed in the secular world because Islam disdained the celibacy and monastic withdrawal from society that were so central to Latin Christianity. Ulama could be found in all walks of life, from wealthy landowners and government officials to ascetic teachers and humble artisans and shopkeepers. Some ulama earned their living from official duties as judges, tax collectors, and caretakers of mosques. But many were merchants and shopkeepers; the profession of religious teacher was by no means incompatible with pursuit of personal gain.

During the heyday of Abbasid power in the eighth and ninth centuries (discussed in Chapter 9), educated professional men such as bureaucrats, physicians, and scribes—often trained in Persian or Greek traditions of learning—competed with theologians for intellectual leadership in the Islamic world. Following the decline of caliphal authority in the tenth century, religious scholars regained their privileged status. The ulama codified what became the Sunni orthodoxy by setting down formal interpretations of scriptural and legal doctrine, founding colleges, and monopolizing the judgeships that regulated both public and private conduct.

The Rise of Madrasas

During the Umayyad and Abbasid caliphates, scriptural commentators sought to apply Muhammad's teachings to social life as well as religious conduct. Scholars compiled anthologies of the sayings and deeds of Muhammad, known as *hadith* (hah-DEETH), as guidelines for leading a proper Muslim life. The need to reconcile Islamic ethical principles with existing social customs and institutions resulted in the formation of a comprehensive body of Islamic law, known as *shari'a* (sha-REE-ah). Yet the formal pronouncements of hadith and shari'a did not resolve all matters of behavior and belief.

During the eighth and ninth centuries four major schools of legal interpretation emerged in different parts of the Islamic world to provide authoritative judgments on civil and religious affairs. These schools of law essentially agreed on important issues. Yet as in Latin Christendom, the tension between reason and revelation—between those who emphasized rational understanding of the divine and the free will of the individual and those who insisted on the incomprehensible nature of God and utter surrender to divine will—continued to stir heated debate. The more orthodox schools of law—Hanafi, Maliki, and Shafi'i—were receptive to the rationalist orientation, but the Hanbali tradition firmly rejected any authority other than the revealed truths of the Qur'an and the hadith.

These schools of law became institutionalized through the founding of *madrasas* (MAH-dras-uh), formal colleges for legal and theological studies. Commonly located in mosques, madrasas received financial support from leading public figures or the surrounding community. In addition, charitable foundations often subsidized teachers' salaries, student stipends, and living quarters and libraries. In the twelfth and thirteenth centuries, donations to construct madrasas became a favorite form of philanthropy.

Higher education was not confined to the madrasas. The world's oldest university, in the sense of an institution of higher education combining individual faculties for different subjects, is Al-Qarawiyyin, founded at Fez in Morocco in 859 by the daughter of a wealthy merchant. In 975, the Fatimid dynasty established Al-Azhar University, attached to the main mosque in their new capital at Cairo, as a Shi'a theological seminary. Al-Azhar grew into a large institution with faculties in theology, law, grammar, astronomy, philosophy, and logic. In the twelfth century, Saladin, after ousting the Fatimids (see Chapter 14), reorganized Al-Azhar as a center of Sunni learning, which it remains today.

Islamic education revolved around the master-disciple relationship. A madrasa was organized as a study circle consisting of a single master and his disciples. Most madrasas were affiliated with one of the four main schools of law, but students were mainly attracted by the master's reputation rather than school affiliation. "One does not acquire learning nor profit from it unless one holds in esteem knowledge and those who possess it," declared a thirteenth-century manual on education.[4] Several assistants might instruct students in subjects such as Qur'an recitation and Arabic grammar, but Islamic schools had

Hadith and Shari'a

Varying Interpretations of Islamic Law

Founding of Madrasas

ulama Deeply learned teachers of Islamic scripture and law.

hadith Records of the sayings and deeds of the Prophet Muhammad.

shari'a The whole body of Islamic law—drawn from the Qur'an, the hadith, and traditions of legal interpretation—that governs social as well as religious life.

madrasa A school for education in Islamic religion and traditions of legal interpretation.

Firdaws Madrasa

The proliferation of madrasas beginning in the eleventh century strengthened the dominance of Sunni teachings in Islamic intellectual circles. Far from being cloistered enclaves of students and scholars, however, madrasas served as the centers of religious life for the whole community. Aleppo in Syria reportedly had forty-seven madrasas, the grandest of which was the Firdaws madrasa, built in 1235. (Photograph by K.A.C. Creswell, © The Creswell Photographic Archive, Ashmolean Museum of Art and Archaeology, University of Oxford.)

no fixed curriculum like the trivium and quadrivium of Latin Europe. Knowledge of hadith and shari'a law and insight into their application to social life were the foundations of higher education. Because learning the hadith was a pious act expected of all Muslims, schools and study circles were open to all believers, whether or not they were formally recognized as students. Although madrasas rarely admitted women as formal students, women often attended lectures and study groups. In twelfth-century Damascus, women took an especially active role as patrons of madrasas and as scholars and teachers as well.

Under the Seljuk sultans (1055–1258), who strictly enforced Sunni orthodoxy and persecuted Shi'a dissidents, the madrasas also became tools of political propaganda. The Seljuks lavishly patronized madrasas in Baghdad and other major cities (see Map 13.2). The Hanafi school became closely allied with the sultanate and largely dominated the judiciary. The Hanbalis, in contrast, rejected Seljuk patronage and refused to accept government positions. The Hanbalis' estrangement from the Seljuk government made them popular among the inhabitants of Baghdad who chafed under Seljuk rule. Charismatic Hanbali preachers frequently mustered common people's support for their partisan causes and led vigilante attacks on Shi'a "heretics" and immoral activities such as drinking alcohol and prostitution.

Role of the Ulama

Turkish military regimes such as the Seljuks in Mesopotamia and Syria, and later the Mamluks in Egypt, came to depend on the cooperation of the ulama and the schools of law to carry out many government tasks and to maintain social order. Yet the authority of the ulama was validated by their reputation for holiness and their personal standing in the community, not by bureaucratic or clerical office. Urban residents were considered adherents of the school of law that presided over the local mosque or madrasa and were subject to its authority. The common people often turned to the neighborhood ulama for counsel, protection, and settlement of disputes, rather than seeking recourse in the official law courts. Ulama were closely tied to their local communities, yet at the same time the ulama's membership in a school of law enrolled them in fraternities of scholars and students spanning the whole Muslim world.

The proliferation of madrasas between the tenth and thirteenth centuries promoted the unification of Sunni theology and law and blurred the boundaries between church and state. The Islamic madrasas, like the universities of Latin Christendom, helped to forge a common religious identity. But to a much greater degree than the Christian universities, the madrasas merged with the surrounding urban society and drew ordinary believers, including women, into their religious and educational activities.

Sufi Mysticism and Sunni Orthodoxy

In addition to the orthodox schools of law and the tradition of revelation expressed in hadith, an alternative tradition was **Sufism** (SOO-fiz-uhm)—a mystical form of Islam that emphasizes personal experience of the divine over obedience to scriptures and Islamic law. Sufis cultivated spiritual and psychological awareness through meditation, recitation, asceticism, and personal piety. Over the course of the ninth century Sufi masters elaborated comprehensive programs of spiritual progress that began with intensely emotional expressions of love of God and proceeded toward a final extinction of the self and mystical union with the divine. Some Sufis spurned the conventions of ordinary life, including the authority of the Qur'an and hadith, instead claiming to directly apprehend divine truth. This version of Sufism, deeply unsettling to political authorities, thrived in the distant regions of

Sufism A mystical form of Islam that emphasizes personal experience of the divine over obedience to the dictates of scripture and Islamic law.

MAP 13.2

Postimperial Successor States in the Islamic World

By 1000 the Islamic world had fragmented into many regional states, and upstart regimes such as the Shi'a Fatimids in North Africa vied with the Sunni Abbasid caliphs based in Baghdad for supremacy. Nomadic Turkish warriors such as the Seljuks became fierce champions of Islam in Central Asia. After the Seljuk conquest of Baghdad in 1055, the Abbasids ceded political authority to the Seljuk sultans, who strictly upheld Sunni teachings.

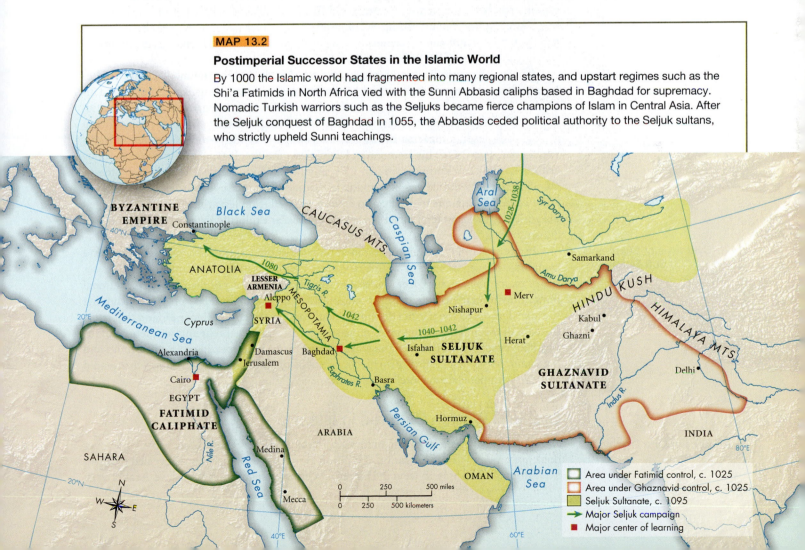

Iran and Central Asia. A more sober-minded form of Sufism, endorsing practical virtue and conformity to Islamic law, flourished in Baghdad and the central Islamic lands.

Sufism's Broad Appeal

Originating as a quest for personal enlightenment, Sufism evolved into a broad social movement. Sufis, like the madrasas, reached out to the common faithful. In their public preaching and missionary work, Sufis addressed everyday ethical questions and advocated a life of practical morality and simplicity. The Sufi ethic of personal responsibility, tolerance and sympathy toward human failings, and moderation in enjoyment of worldly pleasures, had broad appeal among all social classes.

Revered as holy persons with a special relationship to God, Sufi masters acquired an aura of sainthood. Tombs of renowned Sufi masters became important pilgrimage sites that drew throngs of believers from near and far, helping forge a sense of community among like-minded devotees. Women played a more prominent role in Sufism than in other Islamic traditions. One of the earliest Sufi teachers, Rabi'a al-'Adawiyya (717–801), attracted many disciples, chiefly men, with her fierce asceticism and her insistence that God should be loved for God's own sake, not out of fear of punishment or desire for reward. In the words of her biographer, Rabi'a was "on fire with love and longing, enamored of the desire to approach her Lord," and men accepted her "as a second spotless Mary."[5]

By the eleventh century the Sufi masters' residences, known as *khanaqa* (CON-kah) had developed into lodges where religious teachers lived, taught their disciples, and provided accommodations for traveling Sufis. Relationships between master and disciple became more formalized, and Sufis expected each student to submit wholeheartedly to the master's instruction and guidance. In the early thirteenth century Sufis began to form brotherhoods that integrated groups of followers into far-flung religious orders. Bonds of Sufi brotherhood cut across national borders and parochial loyalties, restoring a measure of unity sorely lacking in the Islamic world since the Abbasid caliphate's decline. Muslim rulers warmly welcomed leading Sufi masters as spiritual counselors. Yet the khanaqas and the tombs of Sufi saints—centers of congregational devotion and religious instruction—remained the heart of the Sufi movement.

Ongoing tensions between reason and faith sharply divided the intellectual world of Islam. This dilemma was epitomized by the personal spiritual struggle of Abu Hamid al-Ghazali (AH-boo hah-MEED al-gahz-AHL-ee) (1058–1111), the greatest intellectual figure in Islam after Muhammad himself. Al-Ghazali was appointed to a senior professorship at Baghdad's leading madrasa in 1091, at the young age of thirty-three. Although he garnered great acclaim for his lectures on Islamic law and theology, al-Ghazali was beset by self-doubt and deep spiritual crisis. In 1095, al-Ghazali found himself "continuously tossed about between the attractions of worldly desires and the impulses toward eternal life" until "God caused my tongue to dry up and I was prevented from lecturing."[6] He then resigned his position and spent ten years as a wandering scholar exploring the mystical approach of Sufism.

Synthesis of Sunni and Sufi Teachings

In the end, al-Ghazali's immersion in Sufism restored his faith in Muslim beliefs and traditions. In the last years of his life, al-Ghazali returned to the academy and wrote a series of major philosophical treatises that reaffirmed the primacy of revelation over rational philosophy in matters of faith and morals. According to al-Ghazali, a proper Muslim life must be devoted to the purification of the soul and the direct experience of God that lay at the core of the Sufi quest. But he also insisted that the personal religious awakening of individuals must not violate the established principles of Islam set down in the Qur'an and the hadith. Al-Ghazali's ideas provided a synthesis of Sunni and Sufi teachings that would come to dominate Islamic intellectual circles.

Oral and Written Cultures in Islam

Primacy of Oral Traditions

As the teaching methods of the madrasas reveal, oral instruction took precedence over book learning in Islamic education. Tradition holds that the Qur'an was revealed orally to Muhammad, who was illiterate. The name *Qur'an* itself comes from the Arabic verb "to recite," and recitation of the Qur'an became as fundamental to elementary education as it was to religious devotion. Moreover, the authority of any instruction rested on the reputation of the teacher, which in turn was validated by chains of transmission down through generations of scholars. Sufism reinforced this emphasis on direct person-to-person oral instruction. The persistence of ambivalent attitudes toward written documents is also evident in the priority Islamic law gives to the oral testimony of trustworthy witnesses over documents that could be easily forged or altered. Nonetheless, by the eleventh century books were regarded as indispensable aids to memorization and study, though learning solely from books was dismissed as an inferior method of education (see Reading the Past: Ibn Khaldun on Study and Learning). This preference for oral communication would ensure that the connections between individuals formed by Islamic schooling would be direct and deeply personal.

Primacy of Arabic Language

As the sacred language of scripture, Arabic occupied an exalted place in Islamic literary culture. To fulfill one's religious duty one had to master the Qur'an in Arabic. Arabic

READING THE PAST

Ibn Khaldun on Study and Learning

Ibn Khaldun (ee-bin hal-DOON) (1332–1406), born in Tunis in North Africa, was one of the greatest Islamic historians and philosophers. Khaldun served various Muslim rulers in North Africa before devoting himself to study and teaching. He spent the last twenty-four years of his life in Cairo, where he completed his monumental *Universal History*.

In the prologue of his *Universal History* Khaldun discusses the proper methods of study and learning. Like other Muslim scholars, he valued oral instruction over mere book learning. A good scholar was expected to be well traveled, seeking insight from a variety of teachers. Citing Muhammad bin Abdallah (1077–1148), Khaldun urges that education begin with the study of Arabic and poetry.

Human beings obtain their knowledge and character qualities and all their opinions and virtues either through study, instruction, and lectures, or through imitation of a teacher and personal contact with him. The only difference here is that habits acquired through personal contact with a teacher are more strongly and firmly rooted. Thus, the greater the number of authoritative teachers, the more deeply rooted is the habit one acquires.

When a student has to rely on the study of books and written material and must understand scientific problems from the forms of written letters in books, he is confronted by the veil that separates handwriting and the form of the letter found in writing from the spoken words found in the imagination.

Judge Abdallah places instruction in Arabic and poetry ahead of all other sciences: "Poetry is the archive of the Arabs. . . . From there, the student should go on to arithmetic and study it assiduously, until he knows its basic norms. He should then go to the study of the Qur'an, because with his previous preparation it will be easy for him." He continues, "How thoughtless are our compatriots in teaching children the Qur'an when they are first starting out. They read things they do not understand. . . . He also forbids teaching two disciplines at the same time, save to the student with a good mind and sufficient energy."

Source: Ibn Khaldun, *The Muqaddimah: An Introduction to History*, trans. Franz Rosenthal (Princeton, NJ: Princeton University Press, 1967), 426, 431, 424.

EXAMINING THE EVIDENCE

1. Why did Ibn Khaldun value oral instruction over reading books?

2. To what extent was the curriculum proposed by Ibn Khaldun parallel to the study of the liberal arts found in the cathedral schools and universities of Latin Christendom?

Basra Library

Although Islamic scholars esteemed oral instruction by an outstanding teacher over book learning, libraries served as important places for intellectual exchange as well as repositories of knowledge. In this illustration to a story set in the Iraq seaport of Basra—a city renowned as a seat of scholarship—a group of well-dressed men listen to a lecture on Arabic poetry delivered by the figure at right. In the background, leather-bound books are stacked on their sides in separate cupboards. (Bibliothèque Nationale, Paris, France; Scala/White Images/Art Resource, NY.)

Revival of Persian Literature

became the language of government from Iran to Spain. The Sunni orthodoxy endorsed by the Abbasid caliphs and the Seljuk sultans was also based on codification in Arabic of religious teachings and laws. Thus, the Arabic language came to occupy an important place in the developing Islamic identity.

Book collecting and the founding of libraries helped expand book learning in Islamic society. The size of Muslim libraries dwarfed the relatively small libraries of Latin Christendom. The most eminent Christian monasteries in France and Italy had libraries of about four hundred to seven hundred volumes, and an inventory of the University of Paris collections from 1338 lists about two thousand books. By contrast, the House of Knowledge, founded by an Abbasid official at Baghdad in 991, contained over ten thousand books. The Islamic prohibition against the worship of images discouraged the use of illustrations in books, but Arabic calligraphy became an extraordinarily expressive form of art (see Seeing the Past: A Revolution in Islamic Calligraphy).

The breakup of the Abbasid caliphate and the rise of regional states fractured the cultural and linguistic unity of the Islamic world. In the ninth century, Iranian authors began to write Persian in the Arabic script, inspiring new styles of poetry, romance, and historical writing. The poet Firdausi (fur-dow-SEE) (d. c. 1025), for example, drew from Sasanid chronicles and popular legends and ballads in composing his *Book of Kings*. This sprawling history of ancient monarchs and heroes has become the national epic of Iran. The Persian political heritage, in which monarchs wielded absolute authority over a steeply hierarchical society, had always clashed with the radical egalitarianism of Islam and the Arabs. But the reinvigorated Persian poetry of Firdausi and others found favor among the upstart Seljuk sultans.

Court poets and artists drew from the rich trove of Persian literature—ranging from the fables of the sailor Sinbad to the celebrated love story of Warqa and Gulshah—to fashion new literary, artistic, and architectural styles that blended sacred and secular themes. The Seljuks absorbed many of these Persian literary motifs into a reinvented Turkish language and literature, which they carried with them into Mesopotamia and Anatolia. Persian and Turkish gradually joined Arabic as the classical languages of the Islamic world. Following the founding of the Muslim-ruled Delhi Sultanate in the early thirteenth century (discussed later in this chapter), Persian and Turkish literary cultures expanded into India.

In the absence of a formal church, the Islamic schools of law, madrasas, and Sufi khanaqa lodges transmitted religious knowledge among all social classes, broadening the reach of education to a wider spectrum of society than the schools and universities of Latin Christendom. The schools of law and madrasas helped to unify theology and law and to forge a distinct Sunni identity.

Nevertheless, regional and national identities were not completely subsumed by the overarching Islamic culture. Moreover, although most religious teachers harbored a deep

A Revolution in Islamic Calligraphy

Early Kufic Script on Parchment (©The Trustees of the Chester Beatty Library, Dublin.)

Calligraphy of Ibn al-Bawwab (©The Trustees of the Chester Beatty Library, Dublin.)

During the early centuries of Islam, the sacredness of the Qur'an was reflected in the physical books themselves. Early manuscripts of the Qur'an, like this example, are invariably written in an Arabic script known as Kufic on parchment. The introduction of paper into the Islamic world from China in the late eighth century led to an explosion in the output of Qur'an manuscripts. Legal and administrative texts, poetry, and works on history, philosophy, geography, mathematics, medicine, and astronomy also began to appear in great numbers in the tenth century. At the same time professional copyists developed new cursive styles of script, easier to write as well as to read, that revolutionized the design and artistry of the Qur'an and other sacred texts.

A leading figure in this revolution in Islamic calligraphy, Ibn al-Bawwab (ih-bihn al-bu-wahb) (d. 1022), had worked as a house decorator before his elegant writing launched him into a career as a manuscript illustrator, calligrapher, and librarian. Only six specimens of Ibn al-Bawwab's calligraphy have survived, the most famous being a complete Qur'an in 286 folio sheets, one of which is shown here. The writing—a graceful and flowing script, with no trace of the ruling needed for parchment—is more compact than the Kufic script, but also more legible. Unlike Kufic, Ibn al-Bawwab's writing is composed in strokes of uniform thickness, with each letter equally proportioned. On this page, which contains the opening verses of the Qur'an, the first two chapter headings appear in large gold letters superimposed on decorative bands with dotted frames. By contrast,

the parchment Qur'an simply marks the end of chapters by inserting small decorative bands without text. Ibn al-Bawwab also indicated the beginning of each of the Qur'an's 114 chapters with large, colored roundels in the margin. The roundels are generally floral designs, such as the lotus in the bottom roundel shown here, but no two are exactly alike. Smaller roundels in the margins mark every tenth verse and passages after which prostrations should be performed.

This copy lacks a dedication, and scholars believe that it was made for sale rather than on commission from a mosque or other patron. Ibn al-Bawwab reportedly made sixty-four copies of the Qur'an in his lifetime.

EXAMINING THE EVIDENCE

1. How does the design of Ibn al-Bawwab's Qur'an make it easier to use for prayer than the parchment manuscript?

2. How does the style of decoration of Ibn al-Bawwab's Qur'an differ from that of the Latin Christian Gospel pages shown on page 411? What religious and aesthetic values might account for these differences?

suspicion of the "rational sciences" of the ancient Greeks, in the Islamic world—as in Latin Christendom—the tension between reason and revelation remained unresolved. The Sunni ulama were also troubled by the claims of Sufi masters to intuitive knowledge of the divine, and by the tendency of Sufis to blur the distinction between Islam and other religions. Nowhere was the Sufi deviation from orthodox Sunni traditions more pronounced than in India, where Sufism formed a bridge between the Islamic and Hindu religious cultures.

The Cosmopolitan and Vernacular Realms in India and Southeast Asia

FOCUS

What political and religious forces contributed to the development of a common culture across India and Southeast Asia and its subsequent fragmentation into regional cultures?

Between the fifth and the fifteenth centuries, India and Southeast Asia underwent two profound cultural transformations. In the first phase, from roughly 400 to 900, a new cultural and political synthesis emerged simultaneously across the entire region. Local rulers cultivated a common culture reflecting a new ideology of divine kingship. Sanskrit became a cosmopolitan language for expressing rulers' universal claims to secular as well as sacred authority. In the second phase, from 900 to 1400, rulers instead asserted sovereign authority based on the unique historical and cultural identity of their lands and peoples. The spread of diverse vernacular cultures fragmented the cosmopolitan unity of Sanskrit literary and political discourse. The growing differentiation of India and Southeast Asia into regional vernacular cultures after 900 received added impetus from the Turkish conquests and from the founding of the Delhi Sultanate in 1206.

The Cosmopolitan Realm of Sanskrit

Beginning in about the third century C.E., Sanskrit, the sacred language of the Vedic religious tradition, became for the first time a medium for literary and political expression as well. The emergence of Sanskrit in secular writings occurred virtually simultaneously in South and Southeast Asia. By the sixth century a common cosmopolitan culture expressed through Sanskrit texts had become fully entrenched in royal courts from Afghanistan to Java. The spread of Sanskrit was not a product of political unity or imperial colonization, however. Rather, it came to dominate literary and political discourse in the centuries after the demise of the Gupta Empire discussed in Chapter 6, when the Indian subcontinent was divided into numerous regional kingdoms (see Map 13.3).

Sanskrit and Political Ideology

Sanskrit's movement into the political arena did not originate with the Brahman priesthood. Instead, the impetus came from the Central Asian nomads, notably the Kushan, who, as we saw in Chapter 6, ruled over parts of Afghanistan, Pakistan, and northwestern India from the first century B.C.E. to the fourth century C.E. The Kushan kings patronized Buddhist theologians and poets who adopted Sanskrit both to record Buddhist scriptures and to commemorate their royal patrons' deeds in inscriptions and eulogies. Later, the Gupta monarchs used Sanskrit to voice their grand imperial ambitions. The Gupta state collapsed in the mid-fifth century, but subsequent rulers embraced its ideology of kingship centered on the ideal of the *chakravartin*, or universal monarch.

This conception of kingship connected political authority to the higher lordship of the gods, above all Shiva and Vishnu. Temples became not only centers of community life but also places for individual worship. Modest acts of devotion—offerings of food presented to a deity's image, vows and fasting, and pilgrimages to temples—complemented Brahmanic rituals. Thus the egalitarian ethic and more personal relationship to the divine espoused by Buddhism left a lasting legacy in the devotional cults dedicated to the Hindu gods.

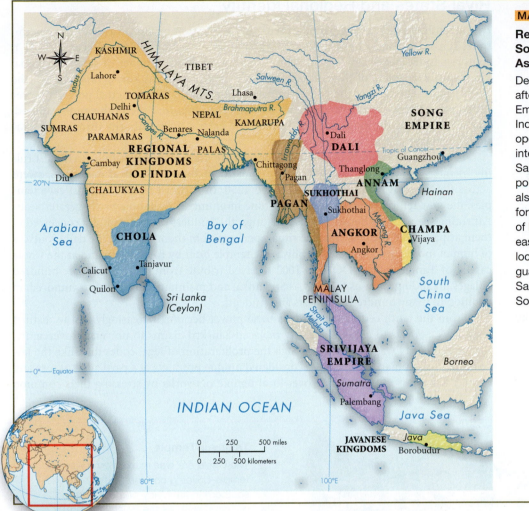

MAP 13.3

Realm of Sanskrit in South and Southeast Asia, c. 1100

Despite its political disunity after the collapse of the Gupta Empire in around 540, the Indian subcontinent developed a common literary and intellectual culture based on Sanskrit texts. Religious and political writings in Sanskrit also gave impetus to state formation and the expansion of Indian religions into Southeast Asia. After 900, however, local vernacular written languages began to displace Sanskrit in both India and Southeast Asia.

Brahmanic colleges attached to temples and Buddhist and Jain monasteries provided formal schooling. These colleges were open to anyone from the "twice-born" (that is, ritually pure) castes of Brahmans, warriors, and *Vaishya* (herders, farmers, and merchants). Beginning in the eighth century, hostels known as *mathas*, often devoted to the worship of a particular deity, became important as meeting places where students, scholars, and pilgrims gathered for religious discussion. Above all, royal courts served as the centers of intellectual life and literary production. The cultural realm of Sanskrit lacked a single paramount center such as the capitals of the Roman or Chinese empires, but through borrowing and imitation, political ideology and royal government assumed remarkably similar forms in many lands.

The predominance of Sanskrit was equally strong in the Angkor state in Cambodia and in the Javanese kingdoms. Public display of royal power and virtue through monumental architecture and Sanskrit inscriptions took forms in Angkor identical to those found in the Indian subcontinent. Although Khmer (kih-MAY) served as the language of everyday life, used to record matters such as land grants, tax obligations, and contracts, Sanskrit prevailed as the language of politics, poetry, and religion in Cambodia down to the seventeenth century.

Sanskrit's rise as a cosmopolitan language thus allowed local rulers and intellectual elites to draw on a universal system of values and ideas to establish their claims to authority. Royal mystique was expressed symbolically through courtly epics, royal genealogies, and inscriptions that depicted the ruler as a divinely ordained monarch.

Centers of Sanskrit Learning

Sanskrit Culture in Southeast Asia

Rival States and Regional Identity

By the tenth century, a long period of economic expansion produced a series of powerful states across the Sanskrit realm. Most prominent were Angkor in Cambodia and Chola in southern India (see again Map 13.3), but there were also a number of smaller regional kingdoms. The rulers of these states deemed themselves "great kings" (*maharajas*), the earthly representatives of the gods, particularly Shiva and Vishnu. Actual political power rested on the growing interdependence between the kings and the Brahman priesthood. At the same time, the kings sought to affirm and extend their authority through ostentatious patronage of gods and their temples.

Temple architecture most strikingly reveals the maharajas' (mah-huh-RAH-juh) ruling ideology. A wave of temple-building, most of it funded by royal donations, swept across the Sanskrit realm between 1000 and 1250. In contrast to the Buddhist cave temples, the new temples were freestanding stone monuments built on a vastly greater scale. Affirming the parallels between gods and kings, the builders of these temples conceived of them as palaces of the gods, but the rituals performed in them imitated the daily routines of human monarchs. Dedicated to Shiva, the temple built by royal command at the Chola capital of Tanjavur (tan-JOOR) in 1002 received tribute from more than three hundred villages, including some as far away as Sri Lanka, and maintained a staff of six hundred, in addition to many hundreds of priests and students.

Rising Regional Identity   From the tenth century onward, as royal power became increasingly tied to distinct territories, appeals to regional identity replaced Sanskrit claims to universal sovereignty. Regional identity was expressed through the proliferation of legal codes that, like the law codes of post-Roman Europe, were considered unique products of a particular culture and people. Kings asserted their rule over local temple networks by stressing their common

Tanjavur Temple

The Chola era was marked by a wave of temple-building on a grand scale across southern India. Many of these building projects, such as the Rajarajeshvara temple at the Chola capital of Tanjavur seen here, benefited from royal donations intended to underscore the connections between divine authority and kingship. But Hindu temples also attracted patronage from merchant and artisan guilds and obtained revenues from their landholdings, commercial activities, and contributions by village assemblies. (Bob Krist/CORBIS.)

identity with a distinct territory, people, and culture. Consequently the cosmopolitan cultural community based on Sanskrit writings no longer suited their political goals.

The displacement of Sanskrit by vernacular languages accompanied this political transformation. Between the tenth and fourteenth centuries, political boundaries increasingly aligned with linguistic borders. By the tenth century royal inscriptions began to use local vernacular languages rather than Sanskrit. The Chola kings, for example, promoted a Tamil cultural identity defined as "the region of the Tamil language" to further their expansionist political ambitions. Royal courts, the major centers of literary production, also championed a rewriting of the Sanskrit literary heritage in vernacular languages. The first vernacular versions of the *Mahabharata* epic (discussed in Chapter 6) appeared in the Kannada (kah-nah-DAH) language of southwestern India in the tenth century and in the Telugu (tehl-oo-JOO) and Old Javanese languages in the eleventh century. The poet Kamban composed his celebrated Tamil version of the *Ramayana* at the Chola court at the same time. These vernacular versions of the epics were not merely translations, but a rewriting of the classic works as part of local history rather than universal culture. Although Sanskrit remained the language of Brahmanic religion (and many sacred scriptures were never translated into vernacular languages), after 1400 Sanskrit all but disappeared from royal inscriptions, administrative documents, and courtly literature. The turn toward vernacular literary languages did not broaden the social horizons of literary culture, however. Vernacular literatures relied heavily on Sanskrit vocabulary and rhetoric and were intended for learned audiences, not the common people.

Displacement of Sanskrit by Vernacular Languages

Sufism and Society in the Delhi Sultanate

In the late twelfth century Muhammad Ghuri, the Muslim ruler of Afghanistan, invaded India and conquered the Ganges Valley. After Ghuri's death in 1206, a Turkish slave-general declared himself sultan at Delhi. Over the next three centuries a series of five dynasties ruled over the Delhi Sultanate (1206–1526) and imposed Muslim rule over much of India. By about 1330 the Delhi Sultanate reached its greatest territorial extent, encompassing most of the Indian peninsula.

The Delhi sultans cast themselves in the mold of Turko-Persian ideals of kingship, which affirmed the supremacy of the king over religious authorities. Nonetheless, like their Turkish predecessors, the Delhi sultans cultivated close relations with Sufi masters. Sufism affirmed the special role of the saint or holy man as an earthly representative of God, insisting that it was the blessing of a Sufi saint that conferred sovereign authority on monarchs. A leading Iranian Sufi proclaimed that God "made the Saints the governors of the universe . . . and through their spiritual influence [Muslims] gain victories over the unbelievers."[7] Implicitly recognizing the practical limits of their authority, the Delhi sultans sought to strengthen their control over their Indian territories by striking an alliance between the Turkish warrior aristocracy and the revered Sufi masters.

Initially the Delhi sultans staffed their government with Muslims, recruiting ulama and Sufis, mostly from Iran and Central Asia. The sultans also founded mosques and madrasas to propagate Islamic teachings, but the ulama and their schools had little impact on the native Hindu population. Instead, it was the missionary zeal of the Sufi orders that paved the way for Islam's spread in South Asia.

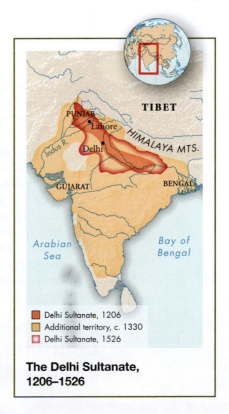

Delhi Sultanate, 1206
Additional territory, c. 1330
Delhi Sultanate, 1526

The Delhi Sultanate, 1206–1526

In the wake of Muslim conquests, the Sufi orders established khanaqa lodges in the countryside as well as in the cities, reaching more deeply into local society. United by total devotion and obedience to their master, the Sufi brotherhoods formed tightly knit networks whose authority paralleled that of the sultans, and in some respects surpassed it.

Sufi Influence in the Sultanate

Sufi masters presided over the khanaqas much like princes over their courts. For example, they welcomed local people seeking justice, dispute mediation, and miraculous cures. Learned dignitaries, both Muslim and Hindu, sought out Sufi masters for spiritual counsel and instruction. The monumental tombs of renowned saints became cultural and religious crossroads as they attracted steady streams of both Hindu and Muslim worshipers and pilgrims.

Sufis used vernacular language to address local audiences. In the Delhi region they adopted Hindi as a spoken language, and it was Sufis who developed Urdu, a literary version of Hindi, as the common written language among Muslims in South Asia. In the fifteenth century, as the political fortunes of the Delhi Sultanate waned, provincial Muslim regimes promoted the integration of Hindu and Muslim cultures and the use of vernacular literary languages. For example, the independent sultans of Bengal sponsored translations of the epics and other Sanskrit classics into Bengali, and they also patronized Bengali writers. A Chinese visitor to Bengal in the early fifteenth century reported that although some Muslims at the court understood Persian, Bengali was the language in universal use.

Sufi-Hindu Accommodation

Leading Sufis often sought spiritual accommodation between Islamic and Hindu beliefs and practices. In their quest for a more direct path to union with the divine, many Sufis were attracted to the ascetic practices, yoga techniques, and mystical knowledge of Hindu yogis. Similarly, Hindus assimilated the Sufi veneration of saints into their own religious lives without relinquishing their Hindu identity. Most important, the Sufi ethic of practical piety in daily life struck a responsive chord among Hindus. Sufis, like Brahmans, valued detachment from the world but not rejection of it. They married, raised families, and engaged in secular occupations. Nizam al-Din Awliya (1236–1325), an eminent Sufi master, ministered to the spiritual needs of Hindus as well as Muslims. His message—forgive your enemies, enjoy worldly pleasures in moderation, and fulfill your responsibilities to family and society—was closely aligned with the basic principles of Hindu social life. Thus, Sufism served as a bridge between the two dominant religious traditions of India.

Relations Between Muslim Leaders and Hindu Subjects

Although some sultans launched campaigns of persecution aimed at temples and icons of the Hindu gods, most tolerated the Hindu religion. Particularly in the fourteenth century, after the Delhi Sultanate extinguished its major Hindu rivals, the sultans adopted more lenient religious and social policies. They also made greater efforts to recruit Brahmans for government office. Sultans and regional governors even bestowed patronage on major Hindu shrines as gestures of magnanimity toward their non-Muslim subjects.

Despite this growing political accommodation, Muslim and Hindu elites preserved separate social and cultural identities. Both groups, for example, strictly forbade intermarriage across religious lines. Nonetheless, the flowering of regional cultures and inclusion of non-Muslim elites into government and courtly culture foreshadowed the synthesis of Islamic and Indian cultures later patronized by the Mughal Empire, which replaced the Delhi sultans as rulers of India in 1526 (see Chapter 19).

Learning, Schools, and Print Culture in East Asia

FOCUS

To what extent did intellectual and educational trends in Song China influence its East Asian neighbors?

Compared to the worlds of Christendom and Islam, in East Asia learning and scholarship were much more tightly yoked to the state and its institutions. Beginning with the Song dynasty (960–1279), the civil service examination system dominated Chinese political life and literary culture. At the same time the political and social rewards of examination success led to a proliferation of schools and broader access to education (see Map 13.4).

The Print Culture of East Asia, c. 1200

Chinese literary and philosophical works and Buddhist scriptures written in Chinese provided the foundations of a common East Asian intellectual culture. The prestige of Chinese culture remained intact despite the conquest of north China by the Jin dynasty in 1127. The proliferation of private academies and the greater availability of printed books contributed to the rise of Neo-Confucianism in Southern Song China.

The invention and spread of printing transformed written communication and intellectual life in China. Neither the state nor the Confucian-educated elite played a significant role in the invention and early development of printing. Yet throughout the Song dynasty, the period when Confucian education and examination success became the marks of elite status in China, the emerging culture of the educated classes dominated printing and publishing. Elsewhere in East Asia, however, the spread of printing and vernacular writing had a much more limited impact on government and social hierarchy. In Japan and Korea, literacy and education remained the preserve of the aristocratic elites and the Buddhist clergy.

Civil Service Examinations and Schooling in Song China

Chinese civil service examinations were a complex series of tests based on the Confucian classics, history, poetry, and other subjects. They served as the primary method for recruiting government officials from the eleventh century onward. Their use starting in the Song

Institution of Civil Service Exams

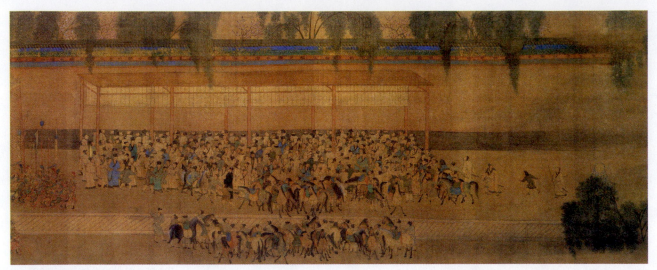

Examination Candidates

No institution exercised a more powerful influence on the culture and lifestyle of China's ruling class than the civil service examinations. Success in the examinations not only opened the path to a political career but also conferred prestige and privileges on the whole family. In this sixteenth-century painting, a crowd of men dressed in scholars' robes anxiously scan the lists of successful candidates posted outside the examination hall. (National Palace Museum, Taiwan, Republic of China.)

State Schools

Neo-Confucianism The revival of Confucian teachings beginning in the Song dynasty that firmly rejected Buddhist religion and reasserted the Confucian commitment to moral perfection and the betterment of society.

dynasty transformed not only the composition and character of the political elite, but the educational system and strategies for social success. The examinations also played a crucial role in establishing **Neo-Confucianism**, a revival of Confucian teachings that firmly rejected Buddhism and reasserted the Confucian commitment to moral perfection and the betterment of society, as an intellectual orthodoxy. Finally, the system helped produce a more uniform ruling class of people connected by their common educational experiences and mastery of the examination subject matter.

Prior to the Song, China's imperial governments recruited their officials mostly through a system of recommendations. Local magistrates nominated promising candidates on the basis of subjective criteria such as literary talent and reputation for virtue. Prominent families had enough influence to ensure that their sons received preferential consideration. Family pedigree, secured through wealth, marriage connections, and a tradition of office-holding, was the key to continued access to political office. Fewer than 10 percent of officials were chosen through competitive written examinations.

From the start, however, the Song dynasty was determined to centralize both military and civil power in the hands of the emperor and his ministers. To restore the supremacy of civil authority, the early Song emperors greatly expanded the use of civil service examinations. They sought to create a skilled, ideologically cohesive cadre of officials whose chief loyalty would be to the state rather than to their families. Competitive tests diminished the influence of family prestige in the selection of government officials. The impulse behind the civil service examinations was less democratic than autocratic, however: the final choice of successful candidates rested with the emperor.

By the mid-thirteenth century four hundred thousand men had taken the civil service examinations. Of this number, only eight hundred were selected for appointment to office. The enormous number of examination candidates reflected the crucial importance of government office to achieving social and political success. It also testified to the powerful influence of schooling in shaping the lives and outlook of the ruling class. The Song government set up hundreds of state-supported local schools, but budget shortfalls left many of them underfunded. For the most part, primary education was limited to those who could afford private tutors.

At every level of schooling, the curriculum mirrored the priorities of the civil service examinations. Although the central government constantly tinkered with the content of the examinations, in general the examinations emphasized mastery of the Confucian classics, various genres of poetry, and matters of public policy and statecraft. Over time the prominence of poetry diminished, and the application of classical knowledge to public policy and administrative problems grew in importance.

Critics of the civil service examinations complained that the impartiality of the evaluation procedures did not allow for proper assessment of the candidates' moral character. They advocated replacing the examinations with a system of appointment based on promotion through the state school system, in which student merit would be judged on the basis of personal qualities as well as formal knowledge. Other critics condemned the examination system and government schools for stifling intellectual inquiry. In their view, the narrow focus of the curriculum and the emphasis on rote knowledge over creative thinking produced petty-minded pedants rather than dynamic leaders.

These various criticisms spurred the founding of private academies. Moreover, many leading scholars rejected political careers altogether. This trend received a major boost from Zhu Xi (jew she) (1130–1200), the most influential Neo-Confucian scholar, who reordered the classical canon to revive humanistic learning and infuse education with moral purpose. Zhu mocked the sterile teaching of government schools, instead engaging his students (and critics) in wide-ranging philosophical discussions, often held under the auspices of private academies. Zhu Xi championed the private academy as the ideal environment for the pursuit of genuine moral knowledge. His teachings inspired the founding of at least 140 private academies during the twelfth and thirteenth centuries. Nevertheless, many students enrolled at private academies out of the self-serving conviction that studying with a renowned scholar would enhance their prospects for success in the examinations.

Private Academies

Ironically, later dynasties would adopt Zhu Xi's philosophical views and interpretations of the classics as the official orthodoxy of the civil service examinations. Consequently, his Neo-Confucian doctrines were more influential even than Thomas Aquinas's synthesis of Greek philosophy and Christian revelation, or al-Ghazali's contributions to Islamic theology.

Influence of Zhu Xi's Neo-Confucianism

For educated men, the power of the examination system was inescapable. Only a few rare individuals would ever pass through, as contemporaries put it, "the thorny gate of learning." Yet examination learning defined the intellectual and cultural values not only of officials, but of the educated public at large. In a poem, a Song emperor exhorted young men to apply themselves to study:

> To enrich your family, no need to buy good land;
> Books hold a thousand measures of grain.
> For an easy life, no need to build a mansion;
> In books are found houses of gold.
> When traveling, be not vexed at the absence of followers;
> In books, carriages and horses form a crowd.
> When marrying, be not vexed by lack of a good matchmaker;
> In books there are girls with faces of jade.
> A boy who wants to become somebody
> Devotes himself to the classics, faces the window, and reads.[9]

The average age of men who passed the highest level of the civil service examinations was thirty-one. Thus China's political leaders commonly underwent a long apprenticeship as students that lasted well into their adult life.

The Culture of Print in Song China

Just as papermaking originated in China (see Chapter 6), the Chinese invented the technology of printing, probably in the early eighth century. The Chinese had long used carved stone, bronze, and wood seals to make inked impressions on silk, and the process of using carved wooden blocks to print on paper probably derived from this practice.

Invention of Printing

The earliest known example of woodblock printing is a miniature Buddhist charm dating from the first half of the eighth century. Chinese inventors devised movable type by the mid-eleventh century, but this technology was not widely used. Chinese is a **logographic** language that uses symbols to represent whole words, not sounds. Given the large number of Chinese logographs in common use, printers found that carving entire pages of

logographic A system of writing that uses symbols to represent whole words, not sounds (as in the case of alphabetic writing systems).

Chinese Woodblock Printing

The religious merit earned for spreading Buddhist teachings appears to have been the motivating force behind the invention of printing in China. Nearly all early printed Chinese books are Buddhist scriptures and other religious works. This copy of the *Diamond Sutra*, a popular digest of Mahayana Buddhist teachings, bears the date 868, making it the oldest known dated example of block printing. (©2011 The British Library Or.8210.)

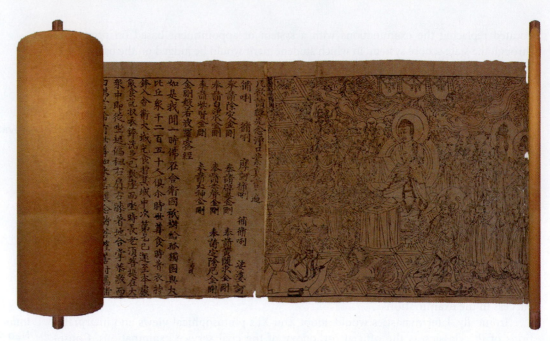

a book was less laborious than producing fonts that would require tens of thousands of individual pieces of type.

Mass Production of Books

By the ninth century printing had developed into a substantial industry in China. Printers produced a wide range of written materials, ranging from single-sheet almanacs to poetry anthologies and commentaries on the Confucian classics. But the most important use of print was to reproduce Buddhist scriptures and other religious texts. Buddhists regarded the dissemination of scriptures as an important act of piety that earned karmic merit for the sponsor. Mass production of religious texts and icons was very probably the original motivation behind the invention of printing.

Song Sponsorship

The founding of the Song dynasty marked the ascendancy of government-sponsored printing. Just as the Song took the lead in education to reinforce their rule, the Song government used printing to help disseminate official ideas and values. In the 970s the Song emperor ordered government workshops to print encyclopedias, dictionaries, literary anthologies, and official histories of all earlier dynasties, in addition to the Confucian classics. One of the government's largest printing projects was an official edition of the Buddhist canon, consisting of 1076 titles, published in 983. This project required the carving of 130,000 woodblocks and took twelve years to complete.

Before the twelfth century, the Song government dominated the world of publishing. The state printed collections of statutes, laws, and government procedures and works on medicine, astronomy, and natural history, as well as standard editions of classics, histories, and literary anthologies. Many of these works were sold through private booksellers or donated to government schools. In the twelfth century, however, private publishers, including schools as well as commercial firms, surpassed the Song government as the main source of printed books. Schools and academies had the intellectual and financial resources to publish fine-quality, scrupulously edited editions (see again Map 13.4).

Commercial firms usually issued cheaply printed texts that catered to market tastes, especially demand for a wide variety of aids to prepare students for the civil service exams. These works included classical commentaries by famous scholars, dictionaries, school primers, writing manuals, phrase books, collections of examination essays by the highest-ranked candidates, and—most notorious of all—so-called kerchief albums, crib sheets that candidates could fold like a kerchief and smuggle into the examination hall. Books largely for personal enjoyment, such as poetry and prose anthologies by famous authors and works of drama and fiction, also became staples of commercial publishing, along with medical and divination texts purveying practical knowledge.

Despite the advantages of printing as a means of mass reproduction, the technology of printing spread slowly. Elsewhere in East Asia, state and religious institutions monopolized printing. Although Muslims were aware of printing by the eleventh century, they felt deep reverence for the handwritten word and fiercely opposed mechanical reproduction of the sacred words of the Qur'an and other religious texts. No printing presses were established in the Islamic world before the eighteenth century. The printing press invented by the goldsmith Johannes Gutenberg in the German city of Mainz in the 1440s appears to have been a separate invention unrelated to Chinese printing technology.

Printing Outside China

Classical and Vernacular Traditions in East Asia

Just as Latin endured as the common literary language of Latin Christendom, the classical Chinese language unified East Asian intellectual life. Since the logographic forms of written Chinese could not be adapted to represent sounds in other languages, Korean and Japanese writers at first composed their works in classical Chinese. Even in China the written language had long been divorced from vernacular speech.

The earliest writings that use vernacular Chinese are all Buddhist works, especially translations of Indian texts but also sermons, hymns, and parables, written by monks in China to make the foreign religion more familiar and comprehensible to ordinary Chinese. Although works of popular entertainment such as drama and fiction begin to include colloquial speech during the Song period, classical Chinese prevailed as the dominant literary language of East Asia down to modern times.

China

In Korea, mastery of Chinese literary forms, especially poetry, became an essential mark of accomplishment among aristocrats. The advent of the Koryŏ (KAW-ree-oh) dynasty (918–1392), which brought the Korean peninsula under unified rule in 935, signaled the dominance of Confucianism in Korean political culture. The Koryŏ state preserved aristocratic rule, but it also instituted civil service examinations. Schooling and the examination system were highly centralized in the capital of Kaesong, and they were largely restricted to aristocratic families. From the mid-eleventh century, eminent officials and scholars encouraged the study of Confucian ideas at private academies. Although Buddhism continued to enjoy public and private patronage, study at a private academy became a badge of honor for sons of the aristocracy.

Korea

Confucian culture became even more deeply entrenched in the ruling class during the succeeding Yi dynasty (1392–1910). The Yi monarch Sejong (SAY-johng) (r. 1418–1450) took the initiative in creating a native writing system, known as *han'gul* (HAHN-goor), to enable his people to express themselves in their everyday tongue. But the Korean aristocracy, determined to preserve its monopoly over learning and social prestige, resisted the new writing system. As in Japan, it was women of aristocratic families who popularized the native script by using it extensively in their correspondence and poetry.

In Japan, too, Chinese was the learned, formal, written language of public life. Aristocratic men studied the Chinese classics, history, and law and composed Chinese poetry. By 850 the Japanese had developed a phonetic system for writing Japanese, but they rarely used it in public life. The Japanese kana script instead was relegated to the private world of letters and diaries; it became so closely associated with women writers that it was called "woman's hand." Women of the Heian aristocracy were expected to be well versed in poetry and composition, and this era witnessed a remarkable outpouring of great literature by women writing vernacular Japanese. In fact, women composed much of the memorable writing of this era. Men confined themselves to writing in Chinese, whereas gifted women of the Japanese aristocracy used the full resources of their native language to express themselves in the frank and evocative styles found in outstanding works such as the *Pillow Book* of Sei Shōnagon (SAY SHON-nah-gohn) and Lady Murasaki's *Tale of Genji*. Although the world immortalized by Murasaki was narrowly self-centered, she and her fellow women writers gave birth to Japanese as a written language, and in so doing gave Japanese literature its distinctive genius (see Reading the Past: Lady Murasaki on Her Peers Among Women Writers).

Japan

The heyday of women's literature in Japan had no parallel elsewhere in the premodern world, but it was short-lived. By 1200 the Japanese court had been reduced to political impotence, and a rising class of warrior lords seized political power (as we will see in Chapter 15). New cultural forms replaced both Chinese literary fashions and the courtly romances of the Heian era. Prose narratives chronicled not the love affairs of courtiers but the wars and political rivalries among warrior brotherhoods. Women often strode onto the political stage in the era of the shoguns, but they were no longer at the center of its literary culture.

To different degrees, the spread of vernacular writing broadened access to written knowledge throughout East Asia. In China, the classical language retained its preeminence as a literary language, but the early development of printing and public schools fostered a relatively high level of literacy. In Mesoamerica, by contrast, writing remained a jealously guarded prerogative of the ruling class.

READING THE PAST

Lady Murasaki on Her Peers Among Women Writers

In addition to her great novel *Tale of Genji*, Lady Murasaki composed a memoir, covering a brief period from 1008 to 1010, that reflects on events and personalities at the Heian court. Among its more personal elements are Murasaki's observations about other women writers of her day, such as Izumi Shikibu (EE-zoo-mee SHEE-kee-boo), who earned the scorn of many for the frankly amorous tone of her poems and her flamboyant love affairs, and Sei Shōnagon, the renowned author of the *Pillow Book*, a collection of writings on taste and culture. Murasaki's tart judgments reveal the intense rivalry for literary fame among women in the court's status-conscious circles.

Now someone who did carry on a fascinating correspondence was Izumi Shikibu. She does have a rather unsavory side to her character but she has a talent for tossing off letters with ease and seems to make the most banal statement sound special. Her poems are most interesting. Although her knowledge of the canon and her judgments of other people's poetry leave something to be desired, she can produce poems at will and always manages to include some clever phrase that catches the attention. Yet when it comes to criticizing or judging the works of others, well, she never really comes up to scratch—the sort of person who relies on a talent for extemporization, one feels. I cannot think of her as a poet of the highest rank.

Sei Shōnagon, for instance, was dreadfully conceited. She thought herself so clever and littered her writings with Chinese words; but if you examined them closely, they left a great deal to be desired. Those who think of themselves as being superior to everyone else in this way will inevitably suffer and come to a bad end.[1]

Yet Murasaki is no less harsh in her self-appraisal:

Thus do I criticize others from various angles—but here is one who has survived this far without having achieved anything of note. . . . Pretty yet shy, shrinking from sight, unsociable, fond of old tales, conceited, so wrapped up in poetry that other people hardly exist, spitefully looking down on the whole world—such is the unpleasant opinion that people have of me.[2]

---

1. Ivan Morris, *The World of the Shining Prince: Court Life in Ancient Japan* (New York: Knopf, 1964), 251.
2. *The Diary of Lady Murasaki*, trans. Richard Bowring (London: Penguin, 1996), 53–54.

EXAMINING THE EVIDENCE

1. Although women writers such as Murasaki did not compose their major works in Chinese, they still held literary skill in Chinese in high regard. Why?

2. Why might Lady Murasaki have believed that a woman writer's talent was best expressed by poetry? (Consider the chapter narrative as well as this excerpt in formulating your response.)

COUNTERPOINT
Writing and Political Power in Mesoamerica

The Greeks coined the word *hieroglyph* (priestly or sacred script) for the Egyptian language, whose signs differed radically from their own alphabetic writing. In ancient societies such as Egypt, writing and reading were skills reserved for rulers, priests, and administrators. Writing was both a product and an instrument of political control. Because of their sacred character or strategic importance, written records were closely guarded secrets. Rulers denied ordinary people access to books and other forms of written knowledge.

FOCUS

How did the relationship between political power and knowledge of writing in Mesoamerica differ from that in the other civilizations studied in this chapter?

This monopoly over the written word vanished in the major civilizations of Eurasia and Africa during the first millennium B.C.E. Subsequently the evangelical zeal of Buddhists, Christians, and Muslims encouraged the spread of literacy and written knowledge. The desire to propagate Buddhist scriptures appears to have been the catalyst for one of the most significant technological milestones of human history, the invention of printing. But in more isolated parts of the world, such as Mesoamerica, writing, like ritual, served to perpetuate the profound social gulf that separated the rulers from the common people.

Mesoamerican Languages: Time, History, and Rulership

In Mesoamerica, written languages took the form of symbols with pictorial elements, much like the hieroglyphs of ancient Egypt. Mesoamerican texts also display many parallels with Egyptian writings. Writing was a product of the violent competition for leadership and political control. Most surviving texts are inscriptions on monuments that commemorate the great feats and divine majesty of rulers. Knowledge of astronomical time-keeping, divination and prophecy, and rituals intended to align human events with grand cycles of cosmic time were indispensable to political power.

The earliest writing in Mesoamerica was the Zapotec (sah-po-TEHK) script of the Monte Alban state in southern Mexico, which was in use at least as early as 400 B.C.E. The Zapotec language achieved its mature form in 300–700 C.E., the Monte Alban state's heyday. Unfortunately, the Zapotec language remains undecipherable: the ancient written language does not correspond to modern spoken Zapotec. Nonetheless, Zapotec inscriptions display many of the same themes found in later Mesoamerican literary traditions. For example, the earliest Zapotec monuments with writing depict slain enemies and captives, a common motif in Maya monuments. Like Maya texts, too, Zapotec inscriptions apparently focus on diplomacy and war.

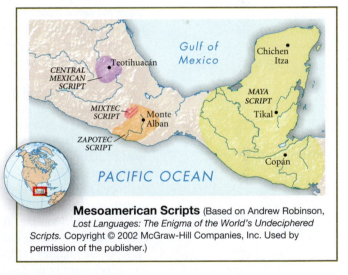

Mesoamerican Scripts (Based on Andrew Robinson, *Lost Languages: The Enigma of the World's Undeciphered Scripts.* Copyright © 2002 McGraw-Hill Companies, Inc. Used by permission of the publisher.)

Zapotec Script

Classic Maya Script

Maya rulers wielded the written word to consolidate their power, using it to display both divine approval of their reign and the fixed course of human history. Maya scribes used calendrical calculation to create genealogical histories organized around the crucial events and persons—birth, marriage, ancestors, offspring—in the lives of royal and noble persons. Maya inscriptions also commemorated the rulers' accomplishments by portraying them as reenacting the triumphs of ancient heroes (see Reading the Past: The Maya Hero Twins Vanquish the Lords of the Underworld, page 348). Creating new monuments gave rulers opportunities to rewrite history, but only within the framework of a set interpretation of the past that affirmed the social order of the present. The regular destruction of monuments

Maya Scribe

In the Maya classical age, the power of the pen often was mightier than that of the sword. Court scribes combined writing ability, artistic skill, and esoteric knowledge of such fields as calendrical science to create the monuments and artifacts that perpetuated the authority of Maya royalty. Scribes were also associated with divine figures, as in this painted vase from the period 600 to 900 C.E., which depicts a scribe in the guise of the maize god. (Photograph K1185 ©Justin Kerr.)

testifies to the power of the visible word in Mesoamerican societies. The Zapotecs at Monte Alban plastered over or reused old monuments in new construction. The Maya frequently defaced, sawed, buried, or relocated monuments of defeated enemies or disgraced persons.

In addition to stone inscriptions on monuments, temples, and dwellings, a handful of Maya bark-paper books have survived. Whereas stone monuments served as public propaganda, the bark-paper books contained the technical knowledge of astronomy, calendrical science, divination, and prophecy that governed the lives of the Maya elite.

The tradition of monument-building lapsed almost entirely after the demise of the classic Maya city-states in the ninth and tenth centuries. Yet the nobility preserved knowledge of the Maya script down to the Spanish conquests in the sixteenth century. Early Spanish accounts observed that although only noble Maya could read, they instructed the commoners in history through storytelling and song. Spanish missionaries deliberately destroyed nearly all of the bark-paper books, which they condemned as works of the devil. In their place the Spanish taught the Maya to write their language using the Roman alphabet. The *Popul Vuh*, the "Book of Council" that has served as a rich mine of information about Maya mythology and religion, was composed in Roman script in the mid-sixteenth century (see Chapter 11). After an alphabet was adopted, however, knowledge of the Maya hieroglyphic script died out.

The Legacy of Mesoamerican Languages

Although the classical Maya language became extinct, scholars today can decipher as much as 80 percent of surviving Maya texts. Linguists have found that the political institutions and cultural values embedded in the Maya literary legacy also appear, in altered form, in the later written records of the Mixtecs and Aztecs of central Mexico. All of these languages, as well as Zapotec, were part of a broader Mesoamerican tradition that used writing and calendrical science to create histories designed to enhance rulers' prestige and power. Although command of writing was restricted to a tiny elite, Mesoamerican rulers addressed the mass of the populace through public monuments, which were intended to convey a sense of the immobility of history and the permanence of the present-day social order. Here, as in many cultures, the sacred and imperishable character of writing, in contrast to the fleeting nature of ordinary speech, endowed the ruler's words with a powerful aura of truth.

Yet it was precisely because of such tight control that written languages like classic Maya became extinct once the social and political systems that created them disappeared. In the cosmopolitan civilizations of Eurasia, by contrast, rulers and religious authorities failed to maintain a monopoly over the power of the written word, especially when vernacular tongues displaced classical languages as the chief media of written communication.

Conclusion

The tenth to the fourteenth centuries witnessed a remarkable expansion of learning and schooling across Eurasia. This expansion of knowledge and education was fostered by the growing penetration of religious institutions and values in local society and by the creation of formal institutions of higher learning. The languages of sacred texts and religious instruction—Latin, Arabic, Sanskrit, and Chinese—achieved new prominence in higher education and intellectual discourse. The growing prestige of these cosmopolitan languages led them to be adopted in government and literary expression as well.

The deepening infusion of religious faith into traditions of learning thus produced more distinct and coherent cultural identities in each of the major civilizations of Eurasia. At the same time the friction between sacred and secular learning—between faith and reason—intensified. In Latin Christendom, struggles erupted among the Roman church, monarchs and city councils, and guilds of masters, each seeking to dictate the structure and content of university education. In the Islamic world, in the absence of a centralized religious authority or even an ordained clergy, individual ulama and madrasas aligned themselves with one of several separate traditions of Islamic law and theological study. Sufis proposed a radically different understanding of Islam. In China, a resurgent, secular Neo-Confucianism dominated public discourse through the state-run civil service examinations and schools, pushing Buddhism to the margins of intellectual life. In the Maya world, by contrast, the rulers' monopoly of the written word ensured their domination over all aspects of political, social, and religious life.

The unity of learned culture was increasingly undercut by the emergence of vernacular literary languages. Writing in the vernacular was stimulated by political fragmentation and rivalry, governments' desire to intrude more deeply into the everyday lives of their subjects, and the flowering of local and regional literary and artistic expression in an era of vigorous economic prosperity. By the tenth century the cosmopolitan Sanskrit culture had fragmented into a chain of regional literary cultures across South and Southeast Asia. In the eleventh century Japanese authors, notably elite women such as Lady Murasaki, fashioned a new national literary culture written in the Japanese vernacular. In much of the Islamic world, Arabic persevered as the dominant written and spoken language, but Persian and Turkish achieved new stature in religion, government, and literature. Despite this proliferation of vernacular literatures, however, the cultural and social gulf between the literate and the illiterate remained as wide as ever.

The intense struggles over the definition of religious truth and social values in the major regions of Eurasia during these centuries aggravated conflicts between different civilizations and ways of life. As we will see in the next chapter, the launch of the Crusades and the Mongol conquests inflamed the already smoldering tensions between Christians and Muslims and between nomadic and settled peoples.

NOTES

1. Lady Murasaki, *The Tale of Genji*, quoted in Ivan Morris, *The World of the Shining Prince: Court Life in Ancient Japan* (New York: Knopf, 1964), 308–309.
2. *The Letters of Abelard and Heloise*, trans. Betty Radice (Harmondsworth, U.K.: Penguin, 1974), 58.
3. *The Anglo-Saxon Chronicle*, trans. G. N. Garmonsway (London: J. M. Dent, 1954), 216.
4. Burhan ad-Din Az-Zarnuji, *Ta'lim al-Muta'allim-Tariq at-Ta'allum, Instruction of the Student: The Method of Learning*, trans. G. E. von Grunebaum and Theodora M. Abel (New York: King's Crown Press, 1947), 32.
5. Farid al-Din Attar, *Tadhkirat al-Awliya*, quoted in Margaret Smith, *Rabi'a the Mystic and Her Fellow Saints in Islam* (Cambridge, U.K.: Cambridge University Press, 1928), 3–4.

6. W. Montgomery Watt, *The Faith and Practice of al-Ghazali* (London: George Allen & Unwin, 1967), 57.

7. Ali Hujwiri, *The Kashf al-Mahjūb: The Oldest Persian Treatise on Sufism*, trans. Reynold A. Nicholson (rpt. ed.; London: Luzac & Co., 1976), 213.

8. *The Itinerary of Rabbi Benjamin of Tudela*, trans. A. Asher (New York: Hakesheth Publishing, n.d.), 43.

9. Quoted in Ichisada Miyazaki, *China's Examination Hell: The Civil Service Examinations of Imperial China* (New Haven, CT: Yale University Press, 1981), 17.

RESOURCES FOR RESEARCH

Church and Universities in Latin Christendom

Scholars regard the rediscovery of Greek philosophy and science via translations from Arabic and the rise of the universities as the catalysts for a "twelfth-century renaissance" in European intellectual life. Moore's examination of the emergence of a distinctive European ruling culture provides historical background for assessing the political and social influence of higher learning. Cobban's classic study highlights the distinctive characters of the major European universities.

Clanchy, M. T. *Abelard: A Medieval Life*. 1997.

Cobban, A. B. *The Medieval Universities: Their Development and Organization*. 1975.

Ferruolo, Steven. *The Origins of the University: The Schools of Paris and Their Critics, 1100–1215*. 1985.

Moore, R. I. *The First European Revolution, c. 970–1215*. 2000.

Pedersen, Olaf. *The First Universities:* Studium Generale *and the Origins of University Education in Europe*. 1997.

Students and Scholars in Islamic Societies

Much scholarship has been devoted to the educational and legal institutions that shaped Islamic intellectual and cultural life. In recent years, scholars such as Chamberlain and Ephrat have examined the role of knowledge and teaching in the social life of the ulama and urban society in general. Trimingham remains the basic work on the social history of Sufism.

Berkey, Jonathan. *The Transmission of Knowledge in Medieval Cairo: A Social History of Islamic Education*. 1992.

Chamberlain, Michael. *Knowledge and Social Practice in Medieval Damascus, 1190–1350*. 1994.

Ephrat, Daphna. *A Learned Society in a Period of Transition: The Sunni Ulama of Eleventh-Century Baghdad*. 1995.

Makdisi, George. *The Rise of Colleges: Institutions of Learning in Islam and the West*. 1981.

Trimingham, J. S. *The Sufi Orders in Islam*. 1971.

The Cosmopolitan and Vernacular Realms in India and Southeast Asia

After the demise of the Gupta Empire, India's intellectual and political culture initially remained unified, but the Muslim conquests fostered strong regional diversity in vernacular languages and literary cultures. Pollock's seminal work on "the Sanskrit cosmopolis" has dramatically enhanced our understanding of the relationship between language and political and cultural authority.

Asher, Catherine B., and Cynthia Talbot. *India Before Europe*. 2006.

Eaton, Richard M., ed. *India's Islamic Traditions, 711–1750*. 2003.

Pollock, Sheldon. *The Language of the Gods in the World of Men: Sanskrit, Culture, and Power in Premodern India*. 2006.

Talbot, Cynthia. *Precolonial India in Practice: Society, Religion, and Identity in Medieval Andhra*. 2001.

Wink, André. *Al-Hind: The Making of the Indo-Islamic World*, 2d ed. 1997.

Learning, Schools, and Print Culture in East Asia

Civil government by officials selected through competitive examinations shaped the distinctive political, social, and cultural traditions not only of China but of East Asia as a whole. Chaffee provides a succinct institutional history of the Song civil service examinations that focuses on the question of social mobility, while Miyazaki offers a lively social history spanning the late imperial era. Morris remains the most engaging introduction to the literary culture of Heian Japan.

Bol, Peter K. *Neo-Confucianism in History*. 2008.

Chafee, John. *Thorny Gates of Learning in Song China: A Social History of Examinations*, 2d ed. 1995.

Chia, Lucille. *Printing for Profit: The Commercial Publishers of Jianyang, Fujian (11th–17th Centuries)*. 2002.

Miyazaki, Ichisada. *China's Examination Hell: The Civil Service Examinations of Imperial China*. 1981.

Morris, Ivan. *The World of the Shining Prince: Court Life in Ancient Japan*. 1964.

COUNTERPOINT: Writing and Political Power in Mesoamerica

Scholars' painstaking efforts to decode the Maya language have now yielded impressive results. Schele and Mathews combine archaeology, art history, and linguistic analysis to retrieve the history and meaning of key Maya monuments. Tedlock's study provides translations of a wide range of Maya literary texts down to modern times.

Coe, Michael D. *Breaking the Maya Code*, rev. ed. 1999.

Marcus, Joyce. *Mesoamerican Writing Systems: Propaganda, Myth, and History in Four Ancient Civilizations*. 1992.

Schele, Linda, and Peter Mathews. *The Code of Kings: The Language of Seven Sacred Maya Temples and Tombs*. 1998.

Tedlock, Dennis. *2000 Years of Mayan Literature*. 2010.

► **For additional primary sources from this period**, see *Sources of Crossroads and Cultures*.

► **For Web sites, images, and documents related to topics in this chapter**, see Make History at bedfordstmartins.com/smith.

The major global development in this chapter ▶ The expansion of learning and education across Eurasia from 900 to 1300 and its relationship to the rise of regional and national identities.

IMPORTANT EVENTS

918–1392	Koryŏ dynasty in Korea
960–1279	Song dynasty in China
c. 1010	Lady Murasaki's *Tale of Genji* begins to circulate among the Japanese court aristocracy
1055	Seljuk Turks capture Baghdad and establish their rule over Mesopotamia and Syria
1066	Norman conquest of England
1130–1200	Life of Neo-Confucian scholar Zhu Xi
1140	Catholic church authorities convict theologian Peter Abelard of heresy
c. 1150	First university founded at Paris
1206–1526	Delhi Sultanate in India
1215	Pope Innocent III bans the teachings of Aristotle and Ibn Rushd
1273	Publication of Thomas Aquinas's *Summa Theologica*
c. 1313–1321	Dante Alighieri composes his epic poem *Divine Comedy*
1382	Ibn Khaldun becomes professor of Islamic law at Cairo
1392–1910	Yi dynasty in Korea

KEY TERMS

cathedral school (p. 410)
hadith (p. 417)
logographic (p. 431)
madrasa (p. 417)
Neo-Confucianism (p. 430)
rhetoric (p. 410)
shari'a (p. 417)
Sufism (p. 419)
ulama (p. 417)
university (p. 415)
vernacular language (p. 415)

CHAPTER OVERVIEW QUESTIONS

1. Did the spread of higher learning reinforce or undermine established political and religious authority?

2. How did educational institutions reshape social hierarchy and elite culture?

3. What were the different uses of cosmopolitan languages and vernacular languages, and to what degree did they broaden access to written knowledge?

4. How did the different technologies of writing affect the impact of the written word?

SECTION FOCUS QUESTIONS

1. What political, social, and religious forces led to the founding of the first European universities?

2. To what extent did Sunni and Sufi schools foster a common cultural and religious identity among Muslims?

3. What political and religious forces contributed to the development of a common culture across India and Southeast Asia and its subsequent fragmentation into regional cultures?

4. To what extent did intellectual and educational trends in Song China influence its East Asian neighbors?

5. How did the relationship between political power and knowledge of writing in Mesoamerica differ from that in the other cultures in this chapter?

MAKING CONNECTIONS

1. In what ways did the cathedral schools and universities of Latin Christendom modify the classical traditions of learning of ancient Greece and Rome?

2. How did the madrasas of the Islamic world differ from European universities in their curricula, their teachers, and their relationships with political and religious authorities?

3. How can we explain the failure of printing technology to spread from China to neighboring societies such as Japan, India, or the Islamic world until centuries later?

AT A CROSSROADS ▶

Qubilai, grandson of the great conqueror Chinggis, cemented his claim as Great Khan of all the Mongols only after winning a bloody struggle against one of his brothers. In his single-minded quest to make himself the first foreign emperor of China, Qubilai turned his back on the Mongols' steppe homeland. His success in conquering China came at the cost of undermining the unity of the Mongol Empire, which fragmented into four separate khanates. (The Art Archive.)

Crusaders, Mongols, and Eurasian Integration

1050–1350

"The empire can be won on horseback, but it cannot be ruled from horseback." Reciting this old Chinese proverb, Yelu Chucai, a Chinese-educated adviser, delivered a tart rebuke to the Mongol Great Khan Ogodei (ERG-uh-day). A council of Mongol princes had just chosen Ogodei (r. 1229–1241) to succeed his father, Chinggis (CHEEN-gihs). The Mongol armies had overrun much of the territory of the Jin kingdom that then ruled north China. Now the princes urged Ogodei to massacre the defeated population and turn their farmlands into pasture for the Mongol herds. But Yelu Chucai persuaded Ogodei that preserving China's agricultural way of life would generate far greater rewards.

Yelu Chucai had served as a Jin official until the Mongols captured him in 1215. Three years later Yelu accompanied Chinggis (Genghis was the Persian version of his name) on his campaigns in western Asia, serving the Mongol khan as scribe, astrologer, and confidential adviser. Upon gaining the confidence of Ogodei, Yelu in effect became chief minister of the Mongol Empire and began to construct a strong central government based on Chinese models. But Yelu made many enemies among the Mongol princes, who distrusted his promotion of Chinese ways. After initially approving Yelu's plans, Ogodei withdrew his support.

BACKSTORY

By the twelfth century, economic revival and commercial integration had begun to stimulate unprecedented cultural contact and exchange across Eurasia (see Chapters 12 and 13). But economic prosperity did not necessarily translate into political strength. The weakened Abbasid caliphs, already challenged by rival caliphates in Egypt and Spain, had become pawns of the Seljuk Turks, invaders from Central Asia. In China, the Song dynasty was also vulnerable to invasion by its northern neighbors. In 1127 Jurchen Jin invaders from Manchuria seized the northern half of the empire, forcing the Song court to flee to the south. Within Christendom, the division between the Latin West and the Byzantine East widened into outright hostility, and the Roman and Byzantine churches competed against each other to convert the pagan peoples of eastern Europe and Russia to Christianity.

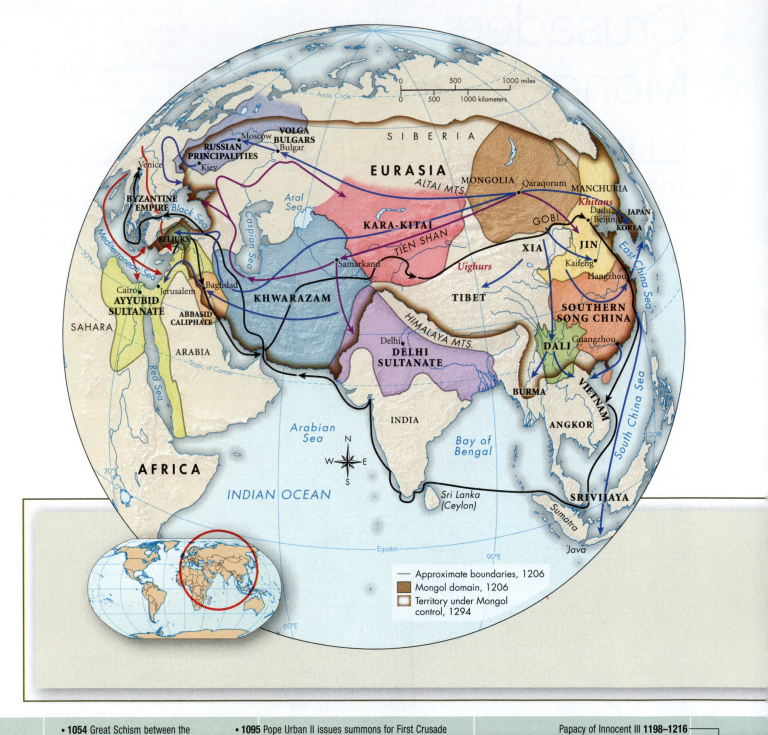

Approximate boundaries, 1206

Mongol domain, 1206

Territory under Mongol control, 1294

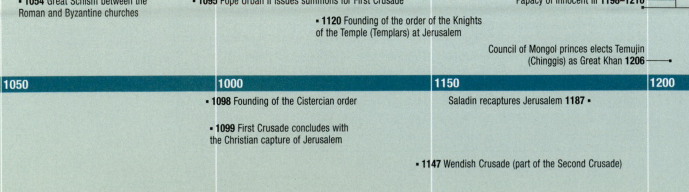

- **1054** Great Schism between the Roman and Byzantine churches

- **1095** Pope Urban II issues summons for First Crusade

Papacy of Innocent III **1198–1216**

- **1120** Founding of the order of the Knights of the Temple (Templars) at Jerusalem

Council of Mongol princes elects Temujin (Chinggis) as Great Khan **1206**

| 1050 | 1000 | 1150 | 1200 |

- **1098** Founding of the Cistercian order

Saladin recaptures Jerusalem **1187**

- **1099** First Crusade concludes with the Christian capture of Jerusalem

- **1147** Wendish Crusade (part of the Second Crusade)

Following Ogodei's death in 1241 and Yelu Chucai's death two years later, Mongol leaders dismantled Yelu's efforts to remake the Mongol Empire in the likeness of China. Wracked by conflict among the sons and grandsons of Chinggis, the empire fragmented into a series of independent regional khanates. Two decades later, many features of Yelu's vision of bureaucratic government were adopted by Qubilai (KOO-bih-lie) Khan, who made himself emperor of China. But by then the unified Mongol Empire had ceased to exist.

The Mongol conquests dominate the history of Eurasia in the thirteenth century. From humble origins among the nomadic herders of Central Asia, the Mongols became world conquerors. They terrified settled peoples from Korea to Hungary, laid waste to dozens of cities, and toppled many rulers. Yet they also unified Eurasia in unprecedented ways. Merchants and missionaries, groups who received special favor from the Mongols, moved with ease from the Mediterranean to China. The Mongol Empire exerted a powerful influence on the histories of China, Russia, and the Islamic world.

A century before the Mongol armies swept across Eurasia, another clash of civilizations, the Crusades, had erupted—this one in the Mediterranean world. In this conflict, the tense hostility that had divided Christians and Muslims exploded into a succession of religious wars. Although the Crusaders ultimately failed to turn the Holy Land into a Christian stronghold, the Crusades marked a crucial moment in the definition of Europe as the realm of Latin Christendom. At the same time, centralization of administrative control and theological orthodoxy within the Latin church brought about a final rupture between Rome and the Christian churches of Byzantium and Asia. But the papacy's drive to create a united Latin Christendom under clerical leadership collapsed, and national monarchies enhanced their power throughout Europe.

For all of the destruction they caused, both the Mongol conquests and the Crusades expanded the horizons of cross-cultural contact and influence. Exotic goods whetted new appetites—elites in Europe and China alike craved the pepper grown in India. The Mongols introduced knowledge of gunpowder and cannon to the Islamic world, from whence it spread to Europe. Christian missionaries journeyed to the courts of the Mongol khans,

MAPPING THE WORLD
Eurasian Integration, c. 1050–1350

Although the Mongol conquests caused much devastation and loss of life, they also stimulated an unprecedented surge of people and goods across Eurasia. The Venetian Marco Polo, who after traveling overland to the court of Qubilai Khan returned to Italy via maritime routes through Southeast Asia and the Indian Ocean, exemplified this new mobility. The Crusades intensified religious and political tensions between Christians and Muslims, but also led to greater economic interaction between Europe and the Middle East.

ROUTES ▼

→ Mongol campaigns under Chinggis, 1206–1227

→ Later Mongol campaigns, 1229–1295

→ General routes of the Crusades, 1096–1291

→ Travels of Marco Polo, 1271–1295

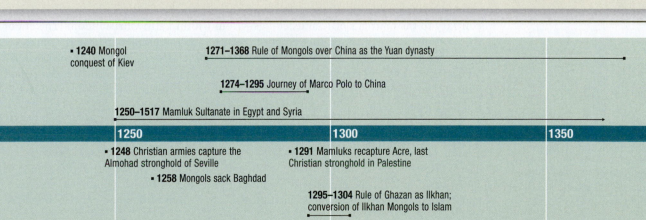

- 1240 Mongol conquest of Kiev

1271–1368 Rule of Mongols over China as the Yuan dynasty

1274–1295 Journey of Marco Polo to China

1250–1517 Mamluk Sultanate in Egypt and Syria

| 1250 | 1300 | 1350 |

- 1248 Christian armies capture the Almohad stronghold of Seville

- 1258 Mongols sack Baghdad

- 1291 Mamluks recapture Acre, last Christian stronghold in Palestine

1295–1304 Rule of Ghazan as Ilkhan; conversion of Ilkhan Mongols to Islam

seeking converts and allies in their holy war against Islam. The Mongols, rulers of the largest contiguous land empire in human history, built bridges that connected diverse civilizations rather than walls that divided them. But ultimately the contradictions between the political and cultural traditions of the nomadic Mongols and the settled lives of the peoples they conquered proved too great, and the Mongol empires collapsed. By 1400 Europe and Asia had once again grown distant from each other.

OVERVIEW
QUESTIONS

The major global development in this chapter: The Eurasian integration fostered by the clashes of culture known as the Crusades and the Mongol conquests.

As you read, consider:

1. In what ways did the growing economic and cultural unity of Latin Christendom promote the rise of powerful European national monarchies?

2. To what degree did the expansion of Latin Christendom remake eastern Europe in the image of western Europe?

3. In what ways did the Mongol conquests foster cultural and economic exchange across Eurasia?

4. How and why did the Mongol rulers of China, Iran, and Russia differ in their relationships with the settled societies they ruled?

The Crusades and the Imperial Papacy 1050–1350

FOCUS

In what ways did the Roman popes seek to expand their powers during the age of the Crusades?

The **Crusades** are generally understood as an effort to reclaim control of the sacred sites of the Christian religion from Muslim rule. More broadly, the Crusades developed into an evangelical movement to Christianize the world. The summons to rescue Jerusalem from the "heathen" Muslims, announced at a church council in 1095, escalated to include campaigns to recover Islamic Spain; to impose orthodox Christianity on the pagan Celtic, Slavic, and Baltic peoples of Europe; and to eradicate heresy—doctrines contrary to the church's official teachings—from within Latin Christendom. The era of the Crusades also witnessed the temporary rise of an "imperial" papacy as administrative reforms within the church broadened the Roman popes' authority over secular affairs as well as the spiritual life of the Christian faithful. Both "Christendom" and "Europe" acquired more precise meaning: the lands of the Christian peoples subject to the spiritual commands of the Roman pope.

Crusades The series of military campaigns instigated by the Roman papacy with the goal of returning Jerusalem and other holy places in Palestine to Christian rule.

The Papal Monarchy

The transformation of Latin Christendom that led to the crusading movement began with initiatives to reform the church from within. In the eyes of both lay and clerical critics, abuses such as violations of celibacy and the sale of church offices had compromised the clergy's moral authority. The reformers also sought to renew the church's commitment to spread the teachings of Christ to all peoples of the world. Pope Gregory VII (r. 1073–1085) was the staunchest advocate of the primacy of the pope as the leader of all Christian peoples. Within the church, Gregory campaigned to improve the moral and educational caliber of the clergy by holding the priesthood to high standards of competence, and also—especially in matters of sexual behavior—to stringent standards of conduct. Gregory also demanded strict conformity to the standard religious services authorized by the church hierarchy and the use of Latin as the universal language of Christianity. Thus, under Gregory VII, the movements for clerical reform and centralization of authority within the church merged. As a result, clerical reform became a force for the religious and cultural unification of Europe.

Great Schism of the Christian Churches

Long before Gregory VII's papacy, the rivalry between the Roman and Byzantine churches had resulted in bitter division in the Christian world. The Roman pope's claim to supreme authority over all Christians rankled both the Byzantine emperor and the patriarch at Constantinople. Half-hearted efforts at reconciliation came to an end in 1054, when the Roman pope and the patriarch at Constantinople expelled each other from the church. This mutual excommunication initiated a formal break between the Latin and Orthodox churches that came to be known as the **Great Schism**. As the split between the Christian leadership widened, Rome and Constantinople openly competed for the allegiance of new converts in eastern Europe and Russia.

Investiture Controversy

The leaders of the Orthodox church were not the only powerful figures who challenged the supremacy of the Roman popes. In their efforts to assert and consolidate their authority, the popes faced competition from within Europe as well as from without. Secular leaders in many parts of Europe had the right to make appointments to key church positions in their domains. In effect, this gave them control over church lands and officials. Pope Gregory demanded an end to such secular control, seeing it as a threat to the papacy's dominion over Latin Christendom. In a deliberately public disagreement with the Holy Roman Emperor Henry IV (r. 1056–1106) known as the **investiture controversy** (*investiture* refers to the appointment of church officials), Gregory challenged the emperor's authority to appoint bishops within his domains. The struggle for control of the church pitted the most powerful secular and sacred rulers of Christendom against each other. Gregory invalidated Henry's right to rule over his territories, provoking the emperor's enemies among the German princes to rise against him. Henry was forced to prostrate himself before the pope and beg forgiveness. Ultimately, a compromise gave kings and princes some say in appointments to major church offices in their territories but ceded leadership of the church to the papacy.

Deprived of control over the church, the Holy Roman emperors lost their primary base of support. The German princes consolidated their power over their own domains, reducing the emperorship to a largely ceremonial office. The Roman papacy, in contrast, increasingly resembled a royal government, with its own law courts, fiscal officers, and clerical bureaucracy.

Cistercian Religious Order

Although the assertion of papal authority was originally linked to the movement for clerical reform, ironically, papal success and the church's growing immersion in worldly affairs gave rise to a new round of calls for change within the church. The Cistercian order, founded in France in 1098, epitomized the renewed dedication to poverty, chastity, and evangelism among the Latin clergy. Within half a century the Cistercians had more than three hundred affiliated monasteries stretching from Spain to Sweden—even while refusing to admit female convents into their order. Although the Cistercians preserved the tradition that monks must confine themselves to their monastery for life, the order developed elaborate networks of communication to coordinate their activities. Passionate defenders of Roman orthodoxy, the Cistercians worked tirelessly to uproot what they perceived as the heresies of their fellow Christians. It was the Cistercians who secured the papal condemnation that ended the career of the Parisian theologian Peter Abelard in 1140 (discussed in Chapter 13).

Great Schism The separation of the Latin Catholic and Greek Orthodox churches following the mutual excommunication by the Roman pope and the Byzantine patriarch in 1054.

investiture controversy Conflict between the pope and the Holy Roman emperor over who had the authority to appoint bishops and other church officials.

Crusaders Voyaging to Holy Land

Pope Urban's summons for a crusade to recapture Jerusalem was directed at knights and other men experienced in war. Nonetheless, people of all walks of life—including women and the urban poor—rallied to the Crusader cause. This Spanish illustration from 1283 shows the Crusaders embarking for the Holy Land aboard galleys powered chiefly by oars, the typical type of warship used in the Mediterranean Sea. (Biblioteca Monasterio del Escorial, Madrid/Giraudon/Bridgeman Art Library.)

The Crusades 1095–1291

The First Crusade

Upon receiving an appeal from the Byzantine emperor for aid against the advancing armies of the Seljuk Turks in 1095, Pope Urban II (r. 1088–1099) called upon "the race of Franks [Latin Christians] . . . beloved and chosen by God" to "enter upon the road to the Holy Sepulcher; wrest that land from the wicked race, and subject it to yourselves."[1] Urban II's summons for a crusade to liberate Jerusalem drew inspiration from the reform movements within the church, and from a desire to transform the warrior rulers of Latin Christendom, constantly fighting among each other, into a united army of God. A papal dispensation granted to the Crusaders by Urban II transformed participation in the crusade into a form of penance, for which the Crusader would receive a full absolution of sins. This helped create enthusiasm for crusading among the knightly class, which saw the crusade as a means of erasing the heavy burden of sin that inevitably saddled men of war and violence.

The Crusader forces, more a collection of ragtag militias under the command of various minor nobles than a united army, suffered setbacks, yet achieved surprising success in capturing Jerusalem in 1099 (see Map 14.1). To some extent this success reflected the disunity prevailing in the Islamic world. The Seljuk sultans of Baghdad had ceded control of Palestine and Syria to the emirs of individual towns, who had failed to join forces for common defense. Yet the victors also lacked strong leadership and failed to follow up their initial success by establishing unified political and military institutions. Spurning the Byzantine emperor's claims to sovereignty, the Crusaders divided the conquered territories among themselves and installed a French duke as king of Jerusalem and defender of the Holy Land. Perhaps the greatest beneficiaries of the crusading movement were Venice and Genoa, whose merchants rushed to secure trading privileges in the Crusader kingdoms along the eastern shores of the Mediterranean. The capture of the Holy Land also prompted the founding of **military orders** that pledged themselves to the defense of the Holy Land (see Counterpoint: The "New Knighthood" of the Christian Military Orders). But in the long run, lack of coordination and unity of purpose among the leaders of

military order One of the new monastic orders, beginning with the Knights of the Temple founded in 1120, that combined the religious vocation of the priesthood with the military training of the warrior nobility.

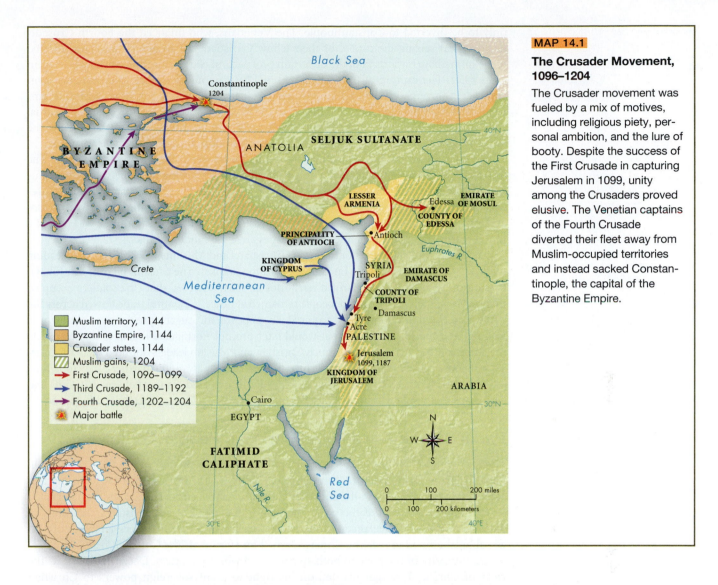

MAP 14.1

The Crusader Movement, 1096–1204

The Crusader movement was fueled by a mix of motives, including religious piety, personal ambition, and the lure of booty. Despite the success of the First Crusade in capturing Jerusalem in 1099, unity among the Crusaders proved elusive. The Venetian captains of the Fourth Crusade diverted their fleet away from Muslim-occupied territories and instead sacked Constantinople, the capital of the Byzantine Empire.

Crusader kingdoms, merchants, and military orders would doom Christian aspirations for permanent domination of the Holy Land.

At first Muslims did not understand the religious aspirations of the Crusaders and failed to rally against the Christian invaders. Nearly a century elapsed before a serious challenge arose to Christian rule over Jerusalem. In 1169 the Seljuk emir of Damascus dispatched one of his lieutenants, Saladin (c. 1137–1193), to Egypt to shore up defenses against a possible Christian attack. Saladin soon seized power from the much-weakened Fatimid caliphate and declared himself an independent sultan. He sought to muster support by declaring a holy war against the Christian occupiers of Jerusalem. In 1187 Saladin conquered Jerusalem and most of the Crusader principalities.

This unexpected reversal prompted Christendom's leading monarchs—the kings of England and France and the Holy Roman emperor—to join together in what became known as the Third Crusade (1189–1192). Dissension among the Christian kings hobbled the military campaign, however, and the crusade ended with a truce under which the Christian armies withdrew in exchange for a Muslim pledge to allow Christian pilgrims access to holy sites.

Over the next century new crusades were repeatedly launched, with little success. Moreover, the original religious motivations of the Crusaders came to be overshadowed by political and economic objectives. The riches of Egypt beckoned but proved to be an elusive prize. The army mustered under the banner of the Fourth Crusade initially set sail for Egypt,

Saladin's Recapture of Jerusalem

Failure of the Later Crusades

only to be diverted to Constantinople. The Venetians, who financed the Fourth Crusade, decided that seizing the capital of their fellow Christian, the Byzantine emperor, offered more immediate rewards than the uncertain prospects of war against the Muslims (see again Map 14.1). The capture of Constantinople in 1204 catapulted Venice to dominance over commerce throughout the eastern Mediterranean and the Black Sea. The Byzantine emperor recovered his capital in 1260 thanks to the naval support of Genoa, Venice's perennial rival. After the Venetian seizure—with the pope's tacit approval—of Constantinople, the schism between the Roman Catholic and Greek Orthodox churches became irreparable.

The Crusades also intensified the cultural divide between Christians and Muslims. The militant rhetoric and propaganda of holy war rendered any lasting peace between Christians and Muslims inconceivable. Chronicles from both sides are filled with grotesque caricatures and misconceptions of each other's beliefs and customs. The proliferation of new *madrasas* and Sufi lodges following the Muslims' humiliating defeat in the First Crusade was part of a moral rearmament of the Islamic community against the infidel "Franks."

In reality, not all interactions between Christians and Muslims were hostile (see Reading the Past: A Muslim Courtier's Encounters with the Franks). The Muslim pilgrim Ibn Jubayr, passing through the Crusader-ruled territories in 1184, observed that "the soldiers occupied themselves in their war, while the people remained at peace."[2] Plentiful trade flowed across the battle lines, and the Crusaders acquired an appetite for sugar (previously unknown in Europe) and the spices of Asia that would later prompt Portuguese seafarers to seek a new maritime route to Asia. However much Christian and Muslim leaders admired their adversaries' religious zeal and courage in battle or valued each other as trading partners, they took little interest in each other's cultures or ideas. Indeed, the increased contact between Muslims and Christians that resulted from the Crusades only intensified religious and ethnic differences.

Papal Supremacy and the Christian People

Expansion of Papal Authority

The reorientation of the Crusades toward political aims originated within the papacy itself. Pope Innocent III (r. 1198–1216) tried to capitalize on the crusading spirit to strengthen papal authority both within the church and over secular society. The Crusaders had rallied together under the sign of the cross, the common symbol of all Christians regardless of national origins and allegiances. Innocent likewise invoked the Crusaders' language of universal brotherhood to redefine Christendom as an empire of "the Christian people" subject to the authority of the pope in both spiritual and worldly matters. Declaring himself "the vicar of Christ," Innocent insisted on his right to grant sovereign powers to Christian kings and princes. Legislation enacted at Innocent's instigation created a more centralized Christian church and deprived bishops of much of their independence. Civil matters such as marriage now fell under church jurisdiction. Innocent also established a judicial body, the **Inquisition**, to investigate and punish anyone who challenged the pope's supreme authority. The Inquisition expanded, with the eager support of lay monarchs, into a broad-based campaign directed against heretics and nonbelievers alike. Thus, it became, in many ways, an internal Crusade. In the view of European elites, just as military expeditions to the Holy Land would strengthen Christendom by bringing sacred sites outside of Europe under Christian control, the Inquisition would strengthen Christendom by eliminating religious diversity within Europe.

Persecution of Jews

Jewish communities in Christian Europe were early targets of Innocent's Inquisition. Many Christians regarded Jews as an alien race whose presence corrupted Christian society. Jews had suffered various kinds of legal discrimination since Roman times, but their persecution intensified from the eleventh century onward. Christian rulers prohibited Jews from owning land, forcing them to take up occupations as urban craftsmen and merchants. Jews were often vilified because of their prominence in trades such as moneylending, which tainted them with the stigma of usury. In many places Jews lacked legal protections and were subject to the arbitrary whims of kings and princes. Innocent's new orders, which compelled Jews to wear distinctive forms of dress such as special badges or hats, were intended to reinforce existing laws forbidding marriage between Christians and Jews.

Inquisition A system of courts and investigators set up by the Roman papacy in the early thirteenth century to identify and punish heretics.

A Muslim Courtier's Encounters with the Franks

Usamah ibn Mundiqh (1095–1188) was a Muslim courtier in the entourage of Mu'in ad-Din Unur, a general in command of Damascus. Usamah fought in numerous battles against the Crusaders, but he also frequently visited Christian-ruled Jerusalem on diplomatic business and had cordial relations with some Christians. He wrote his *Learning by Example*, a book of moral advice and instruction, as a gift to Saladin, who conquered Jerusalem four years later.

> Among the Franks—God damn them!—no quality is more highly esteemed in a man than military prowess. The knights have a monopoly of the positions of honor and importance among them, and no one else has any prestige in their eyes. . . .
>
> The Franks are without any vestige of a sense of honor and jealousy. If one of them goes along the street with his wife and meets a friend, this man will take the woman's hand and lead her aside to talk, while the husband stands by waiting until she has finished the conversation. . . .
>
> I was present myself when one of them came up to the emir Mu'in ad-Din—God have mercy on him—in the Dome of the Rock and said to him: "Would you like to see God as a baby?" The emir said he would, and the fellow proceeded to show us a picture of Mary with the infant Messiah on her lap. "This," he said, "is God as a baby." Almighty God is greater than the infidels' concept of him! . . .
>
> [Upon entering a Christian church I found] about ten old men, their bare heads as white as combed cotton. They were facing the east, and wore on their breasts staves ending in crossbars turned up like the rear of a saddle. They took their oath of this sign, and gave hospitality to those who needed it. The sight of their piety touched my heart, but at the same time it displeased and saddened me, for I had never seen such zeal and devotion among the Muslims. . . . One day, as Mu'in ad-Din and I were passing the Peacock House, he said to me, "I want to dismount and visit the Old Men.". . . [Inside] I saw about a hundred prayer-mats, and on each a Sufi, his face expressing peaceful serenity, and his body humble devotion. This was a reassuring sight, and I gave thanks to Almighty God that there were among the Muslims men of even more zealous devotion than those Christian priests. Before this I had never seen Sufis in their monastery, and was ignorant of the way they lived.

Source: Usamah ibn Mundiqh, *The Book of Learning by Example*, quoted in Francesco Gabrieli, ed., *Arab Historians of the Crusades* (Berkeley: University of California Press, 1969), 73, 77, 80, 84.

EXAMINING THE EVIDENCE

1. What virtues did Usamah admire in the Christians, and why?

2. Why did Usamah find the picture of Mary and the child Jesus offensive?

Efforts to impose religious conformity on Latin Christendom received further impetus from the formation of new religious orders, most notably the Franciscans and the Dominicans. Like the Cistercians, these new orders dedicated themselves to the principles of poverty and evangelism. Unlike the Cistercians, who remained confined to their monasteries, Franciscan and Dominican friars traveled widely, preaching to the populace and depending on almsgiving for their livelihood. The new preaching orders sought to carry out the church's mission to regulate and reform the behavior of lay believers. The Dominicans assumed a conspicuous role in leading the Inquisition. The Franciscan and Dominican orders were also in the forefront of campaigns to convert the non-Christian peoples of eastern Europe.

Franciscan and Dominican Religious Orders

During the thirteenth century the precarious position of the Christian outposts along the coast of Palestine and Syria became dire. The rise of a powerful Islamic state under the Mamluk dynasty in Egypt (discussed later in this chapter) after 1250 sealed the fate of the crusading movement. In 1291 the Mamluks captured Acre, the last Christian stronghold in Palestine. Dissension among the leaders of Christendom, especially between the pope and the French king, made it impossible to revive an international alliance to recapture the Holy Land.

End of the Crusades

The Making of Christian Europe 1100–1350

FOCUS

How did the efforts to establish Christianity in Spain and eastern Europe compare with the Crusaders' quest to recover Jerusalem?

Despite their ultimate failure, the Crusades had profound consequences for the course of European history. Among the most important was their role in consolidating the social and cultural identity of Latin Christendom. Even as the movement to retake the Holy Land from the Muslim occupiers foundered and sank, the crusading spirit provided the crucial momentum for Christendom to expand into northern and eastern Europe.

The crusading ideal also encouraged assimilation of the warrior class into the monastic culture of the Christian church. This merger produced the culture of **chivalry**—the knightly class's code of behavior, which stressed honor, piety, and devotion to one's ideals. The code of chivalry confirmed the moral as well as social superiority of the warrior nobility. Knights played at least as great a role as clerical evangelists in spreading Christian culture.

We can see the connection between the Crusades and the expansion of Latin Christendom in the use of the term "Franks," the term both Christian and Islamic chroniclers used to refer to the Crusaders. Along the frontiers of Latin Christendom, the term assumed a special meaning. "Frankish" knights were aggressive colonizers who combined ambitions for conquest with the missionary zeal of the Roman church. In the thirteenth and fourteenth centuries such kings and knights conquered and colonized territories from Spain in the west to the Baltic Sea in the east. Europe took form out of the processes of military conquest, migration, and cultural colonization that would later also characterize European expansion into the Americas.

The Reconquest of Spain 1085–1248

Under its Umayyad dynasty (756–1030), Muslim-ruled Spain had enjoyed relative religious peace. Although religious toleration was often compromised by sharp differences in social standing among Muslims, Jews, and Christians, the Umayyad rulers fostered a tradition of mutual accommodation. Yet the subjection of Christian peoples to Muslim rulers in Spain, as in Palestine and Syria, became increasingly intolerable to Christian rulers and church leaders alike. At the same time that he issued his summons for the First Crusade, Pope Urban II urged Christian rulers in northern Spain to take up arms against their Muslim neighbors. The *Reconquista* ("reconquest" of Spain) thus became joined to the crusading movement.

Muslim Rule in Spain

In its heyday the Umayyad caliphate in Spain was the most urbanized and commercially developed part of Europe. In the early eleventh century, however, the Umayyad caliphate disintegrated, and Muslim-ruled Spain splintered into dozens of feuding city-states. The conquest of Toledo, Spain's second-largest city, by King Alfonso of Castile in 1085 lifted Castile into a preeminent position among Spain's Christian kingdoms. The Muslim emirs turned to the Almoravid (al-moe-RAH-vid) rulers of North Africa for protection. The Almoravids, fervently devoted to the cause of holy war, halted the Christian advance but imposed their own authoritarian rule over the Muslim territories in Spain.

The Almohad (AHL-moh-had) dynasty, which supplanted the Almoravids in North Africa and Spain in 1148, was even more fiercely opposed to the Umayyad heritage of tolerance toward non-Muslims. Almohad policies, which included the expulsion of all Jews who refused to convert to Islam, were highly unpopular. Despite a major victory over Castile in 1195, the Almohads were unable to withstand intensified Christian efforts to "reconquer" Spain. Between 1236 and 1248 the major Muslim cities of Spain—Córdoba, Valencia, and finally Seville—fell to Castile and its allies, leaving Granada as the sole remaining Muslim state in Spain.

After capturing Toledo in 1085, the kings of Castile made the city their capital. Toledo was renowned as a cultural and intellectual crossroads and, despite the rhetoric of holy war, the Castilian kings preserved Toledo's multicultural character. Toledo's large

chivalry The code of behavior, stressing honor, piety, and devotion to one's ideals, of the knightly class of medieval Europe.

Arabic-speaking Christian and Jewish communities epitomized this spirit of religious pluralism. During the twelfth century, Toledo prospered as Europe's brightest intellectual center, a city in which Arabic and Jewish culture and learning flourished under Christian rule.

But Toledo's intellectual and religious tolerance steadily eroded as the Reconquista advanced. Christian monarchs expelled most of the Muslims from the cities and awarded Muslim lands and dwellings to Christian princes, bishops, and military orders. The religious toleration that the kings of Castile had extended to Muslim and Jewish minorities gradually dissipated. At first, the Christian kings allowed their Muslim subjects, known as Mudejars (mu-DAY-hahr), to own property, worship in mosques, and be judged by Islamic law before *qadi* jurists. After 1300, however, judicial autonomy eroded, and Mudejars accused of crimes against Christians were tried in Christian courts under Christian law. Christian rulers also converted the great mosques of Córdoba, Seville, and Toledo into Christian cathedrals.

The place of Jews also deteriorated in a European world that had come to define itself as the realm of "the Christian people." Attacks on Jews escalated dramatically with the onset of the Crusades. In the 1230s, when the Inquisition began a deliberate persecution of Jews, many fled from France, England, and Germany to seek sanctuary in Spain. Yet in Spain, too, Jews occupied an insecure position. In the fourteenth century, as in other parts of Latin Christendom, violence against Jews swept Spain. Anti-Jewish riots in Toledo in 1370, encouraged by the Castilian king, wiped out the city's Jewish population almost overnight. In 1391 wholesale massacres of Jews in Spain's major cities dealt a catastrophic blow to Jewish communities from which they never recovered. Rigid intolerance had replaced the vibrant multiculturalism of Umayyad Spain.

Reconquest of Spain, 1037–1275

Christianizing Eastern Europe 1150–1350

In issuing a summons in 1145 for the Second Crusade to recover territories retaken by the Muslims, Pope Eugene III also invited the knights of Christendom to launch a crusade against the non-Christian populations of northern and eastern Europe—collectively referred to as the Wends. The pope acted at the instigation of his teacher Bernard of Clairvaux (d. 1153), the Cistercian abbot who had put Peter Abelard on trial for heresy. Bernard had urged Christian knights to take up arms against pagan peoples everywhere "until such a time as, by God's help, they shall be either converted or wiped out" (see Reading the Past: Bernard of Clairvaux's Summons to the Wendish Crusade).[3] In the three centuries following the Wendish Crusade of 1147, Latin Christendom steadily encroached upon the Baltic and Slavic lands. Latin Christendom incorporated northern and eastern Europe through a combination of conquest and colonization that transformed political, cultural, and economic life.

Wendish Crusade

The fissure that split the Latin and Greek Christian churches also ran through eastern Europe. In the tenth and eleventh centuries, the rulers of Poland and Hungary had chosen to join the Roman church, but Christian converts in the Balkans such as the Serbs and Bulgars as well as the Rus princes had adopted the Greek Orthodoxy of Constantinople. In subsequent centuries, Latin and Greek clerics waged war against each other for the allegiance of the eastern European peoples along a frontier stretching from the Adriatic Sea to the Baltic Sea (see Map 14.2).

Freebooting nobles enthusiastically joined the Wendish Crusade and were the first to profit from its military successes. The lightly armed Wendish foot soldiers and cavalry were no match for the mounted Frankish knights, clad in heavy armor, and their superior siege weapons. Small groups of knights subjugated the Wendish peoples in piecemeal fashion, built stoutly fortified castles to control them, and recruited settlers from France

Bernard of Clairvaux's Summons to the Wendish Crusade

In March 1147, the Cistercian abbot Bernard of Clairvaux came to Frankfurt to promote what would become the Second Crusade. Few German knights expressed enthusiasm for a new crusade in the east, but they clamored to attack their pagan Slav and Balt neighbors in eastern Europe. Eager to capitalize on this fervor, Bernard secured the pope's permission to launch the part of the Second Crusade known as the Wendish Crusade. In this letter—addressed "to all Christians"—Bernard seeks to drum up recruits for the Wendish Crusade.

[Satan] has raised up evil seed, wicked pagan sons, whom, if I may say so, the might of Christendom has endured too long, shutting its eyes to those who with evil intent lie in wait, without crushing their poisoned heads under its heel. . . . Because the Lord has committed to our insignificance the preaching of this crusade, we make known to you that at a council of the king, bishops, and princes who had come together at Frankfurt, the might of Christians was armed against them, and that for the complete wiping out or, at any rate, the conversion of these peoples, they have put on the Cross, the sign of our salvation. And we by virtue of our authority promised them the same spiritual privileges as those enjoy who set out toward Jerusalem. Many

took the Cross on the spot, the rest we encouraged to do so, so that all Christians who have not yet taken the Cross for Jerusalem may know that they will obtain the same spiritual privileges by undertaking this expedition, if they do so according to the advice of the bishops and princes. We utterly forbid that for any reason whatsoever a truce should be made with these peoples, either for the sake of money or for the sake of tribute, until such a time as, by God's help, they shall be either converted or erased. . . . The uniform of this army, in clothes, in arms, and in all else, will be the same as the uniform of the other, for it is fortified with the same privileges.

Source: Bernard of Clairvaux, *Letters*, trans. Bruno Scott James (London: Burns, Oates, 1953), 466–468.

EXAMINING THE EVIDENCE

1. In Bernard's view, who is the real enemy of the Christian faithful?

2. How and why does Bernard link the Wendish Crusade to the original crusading goal of capturing Jerusalem?

and the Low Countries to clear the forests for cultivation. The colonists were accompanied by missionaries, led by the Cistercians, seeking to "civilize" the Slavs by converting them to Latin Christianity. Thus, from the start the goal of the Frankish conquerors was to remake the east in the image of Latin Christendom.

Colonization and Conversion in Eastern Europe

Many Slavic princes opted to embrace Latin Christianity and to open their lands to settlement by immigrants from the west. Conversion not only preserved the political independence of native rulers but offered material rewards: willing settlers knowledgeable about advanced farming techniques, more reliable revenues from the land, and a retinue of Christian clerics determined to impose discipline on their subjects using the long arm of church law. For their part, Christian missionaries believed that the salvation of the pagan peoples required changing their work habits as well as ministering to their souls. A poem penned by a Cistercian monk in the early fourteenth century depicted Poland at the time his predecessors first arrived there as backward and poverty-stricken:

The land lacked cultivators and lay under wood
And the Polish people were poor and idle,
Using wooden ploughs without iron to furrow the sandy soil,
Knowing only how to use two cows or oxen to plough.
There was no city or town in the whole land,
Only rural markets, fallow fields, and a chapel near the castle.

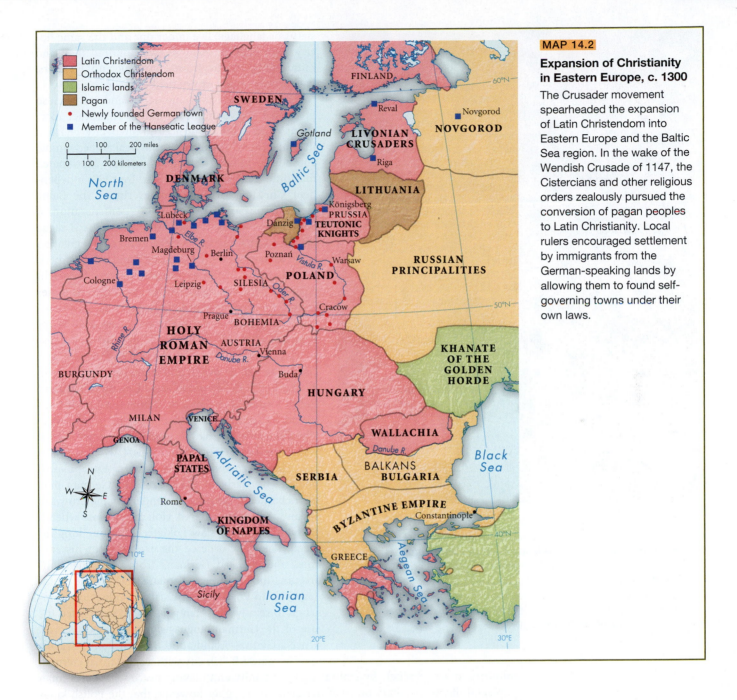

MAP 14.2

Expansion of Christianity in Eastern Europe, c. 1300

The Crusader movement spearheaded the expansion of Latin Christendom into Eastern Europe and the Baltic Sea region. In the wake of the Wendish Crusade of 1147, the Cistercians and other religious orders zealously pursued the conversion of pagan peoples to Latin Christianity. Local rulers encouraged settlement by immigrants from the German-speaking lands by allowing them to found self-governing towns under their own laws.

Neither salt, nor iron, nor coinage, nor metal,
Nor good clothes, nor even shoes
Did that people have; they just grazed their flocks.
  These were the delights that the first monks found.[4]

Hence, remaking the east would require more than the religious conversion of its people. It would require the reordering of the region's society and economy. With this belief in mind, princes, bishops, and monks often took the lead in recruiting farmers and craftsmen from the west to settle newly opened territories in the east. To attract settlers, local lords usually exempted homesteaders from feudal obligations and the legal condition of serfdom. For example, a charter issued by the king of Hungary in 1247 to new settlers in a sparsely populated corner of his realm declared, "Let the men gathered there, of whatever

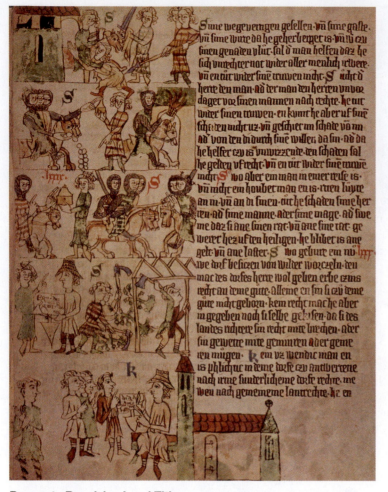

Peasants Receiving Land Title

New peasant settlers brought fresh labor and superior farming technology that transformed the landscape of eastern Europe. The legal and economic privileges granted to immigrants created conditions favorable for economic development. This illustration from the *Sachsenspiegel* (c. 1220), the first major law code written in German rather than Latin, shows homesteaders receiving titles of ownership to the lands they cleared for farming. (akg-images.)

status or language, live under one and the same liberty."[5] Perhaps as many as two hundred thousand immigrants, mostly from Germany and Flanders, had already settled east of the Elbe River by 1200.

Local princes, both conquerors and natives, also promoted the founding of cities. To attract merchants and artisans, princes granted city charters that guaranteed considerable political and economic autonomy. Lübeck, founded in 1159, dominated maritime trade in the Baltic Sea. By 1300, independent Christian trading colonies ringed the Baltic (see again Map 14.2). In 1358, a confederation of commercial cities formed the Hanseatic League discussed in Chapter 12. In addition to regulating trade among its more than one hundred members, the Hanseatic League provided a counterweight against rulers seeking to extort heavy customs duties from traders passing through their lands.

Throughout eastern Europe, cities and towns became oases of foreign colonists who differed sharply from the rural inhabitants in language and culture as well as wealth and status. For example, in 1257 a Polish duke reestablished Cracow, an ancient Polish fortress, as a center of international trade populated by German immigrants whom he recruited. The duke forbade Poles to reside in the town, which was governed by German municipal law.

This Germanization of eastern Europe provoked a backlash. In 1312, Cracow's German burghers backed a German contender for the crown of Poland, but they suffered violent reprisals when a native Pole, Wladyslaw Lokieteck, became king instead. Lokieteck ordered the execution of his enemies and expelled Germans from their mansions fronting the city's market square, turning the buildings over to Poles. Lokieteck also conducted a campaign to remove German priests and prohibited the use of the German language in municipal records. Once a German island amid a sea of Poles, Cracow now became a Polish city with a substantial German minority. It was precisely by embracing Christianity and making peace with the Roman pope and the new military order of the Teutonic Knights, however, that the Polish kings could establish themselves as independent monarchs within the expanding realm of Christendom.

Rise of National Monarchies   By 1350, Latin Christianity was firmly implanted in all parts of Europe except the Balkan peninsula. But the rise of strong national monarchies had thwarted the Roman popes' ambitions to create a unified Christendom under papal rule. The vigorous commercial expansion during this era discussed in Chapter 12 had swelled royal treasuries. Kings and princes increased their demands for tax revenue, extended the jurisdiction of royal courts, and convened assemblies (known as "parliaments") of leading nobles, clergy, and townsmen to rally support for their policies. Europe's patchwork of feudal domains and independent cities began to merge into unified national states, especially in England and France. The French philosopher Nicole Oresme (c. 1323–1382) expressed the spirit of his age when he rejected a "universal monarchy" as "neither just nor expedient."[6] Instead,

Oresme argued, practical necessity dictated that separate kingdoms, each with its own laws and customs, should exercise sovereign power over their own people.

Neither did the Muslims' success in repelling the Crusaders restore unity to the Islamic world. After enduring for sixty years, the Ayyubid dynasty founded by Saladin was overthrown in 1250 by Turkish slave soldiers. At that same time, the Islamic world faced a new challenge, the Mongol invasions, that would have a far more lasting impact on the development of Islamic societies than did the Crusades.

The Mongol World-Empire 1100–1368

The era of Mongol domination marked a watershed in world history. Although the Mongols drew on long-standing traditions of tribal confederation, warfare, and tribute extraction, the Mongol Empire was unprecedented in its scope and influence. Historians give much of the credit for the Mongols' swift military triumphs and political cohesion to the charismatic authority of the empire-builder Chinggis Khan. Later generations of Mongol rulers built upon Chinggis's legacy, seeking to adapt steppe traditions of rulership to the complex demands of governing agrarian societies.

> **FOCUS**
>
> How did the organization of Mongol society and government change from the time of Chinggis Khan to that of his grandson Qubilai, the ruler of China?

Despite the brutality and violence of the Mongol conquests, the Mongol Empire fostered far-reaching economic and cultural exchanges. The Mongols encouraged the free movement of merchants throughout their domains and embraced religious and intellectual diversity. Wherever they went the Mongols sought to impose their own political, social, and military institutions, but the Mongol conquerors of Iran and central Asia adopted the Islamic religion of their subjects. The Mongol courts also became flourishing centers of artistic, literary, and religious patronage. The Mongols transformed the world—and were themselves transformed by the peoples they subjugated.

Rise of the Mongols

In the several centuries before the rise of the Mongols, the dynamics of state formation in the Eurasian steppe underwent dramatic transformation. The Turkish and Uighur confederations had depended on control of the lucrative Silk Road trade routes and extraction of tribute from the settled empires of China and Iran (see Chapter 10). In the aftermath of the Tang dynasty in 907, the Khitans (kee-THANS) of eastern Mongolia annexed Chinese territories around modern Beijing and established a Chinese-style dynasty, Liao (lee-OW) (937–1125). The new dynasty was a hybrid state that incorporated elements of Chinese bureaucratic governance, including the taxation of settled farmers, while retaining the militarized tribal social structure and nomadic lifestyle of the steppe.

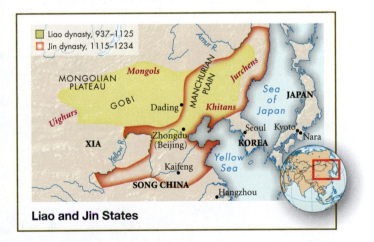

Liao and Jin States

In the 1120s the Jurchens, a seminomadic group from northern Manchuria, overran the Liao and the rest of northern China and founded their own state of Jin (1115–1234). The Jin state largely retained the dual administrative structure of the Liao. But in contrast to the Liao, the Jin conquerors were dwarfed by the enormous Chinese population under their rule. The Jin rulers struggled to preserve their cultural identity in the face of overwhelming pressures to assimilate to Chinese ways.

Temujin (teh-MU-jihn) (c. 1167–1227), the future Chinggis Khan, was born into one of the numerous tribes living in eastern Mongolia, on the margins of the Jin realm. Tribal affiliations were unstable, however, and at that time the "Mongol people" was not a clearly

Steppe Society

Mongol Women in the Household Economy and Public Life

The prominent roles of women in the social and economic life of the pastoral nomads of the Eurasian steppe contrasted starkly with women's reclusive place in most settled agrarian and urban societies. Under Chinggis Khan's permanently militarized society, nearly all adult men had to embark on lengthy campaigns of conquest far from home. The women left behind were compelled to shoulder even the most arduous tasks. Kinship and gender relations among the pastoral nomads also differed in many ways from the practices of settled societies. Mongol women remained subservient to their husbands, but royal and noble women participated vigorously in public life and political affairs.

European travelers to the Mongol domains expressed surprise at women's key roles in the pastoral economy. John of Plano Carpini, a papal envoy dispatched to the Mongol court in 1245, claimed that productive labor fell entirely to the Mongol women:

> The men do not make anything at all, with the exception of arrows, and they sometimes tend the flocks, but they hunt and practice archery. . . . Their women make everything, including leather garments, tunics, shoes, and everything made of leather. They also drive the carts and repair them. They load the camels, and in all tasks they are very swift and energetic. All the women wear breeches, and some of them shoot like the men.[1]

Marco Polo agreed that Mongol women "do all the work that is needed for their lords and family and themselves" while the men "trouble themselves with nothing at all but with hunting and with feats of battle and of war and with hawking [falconry]."[2]

Despite women's vital contributions to the family's economic welfare, however, Mongol society was based on a patrilineal system of inheritance in which men controlled property and wealth. Mongol women had no property of their own. Women who lacked the protection of a husband often found themselves abandoned and destitute. Such was

Mongol Empress Chabi

Mongol leaders often had multiple wives, each of whom took charge of her own household. Chabi, the second of Qubilai's four wives, became one of the most powerful figures at the Mongol court after Qubilai's election as Great Khan. Her ambition to become empress of China rather than merely the wife of a tribal chieftain was a driving force behind Qubilai's conquest of the Southern Song. (National Palace Museum, Taiwan, Republic of China.)

defined group. Family and clan were the basic units of Central Asian nomadic societies. Tribal allegiances grew out of political expediency, providing the means for mobilizing isolated groups for common purposes ranging from herding and migration to trade and war.

The pastoral livelihood of the steppe nomads was vulnerable to catastrophic disruptions, such as prolonged drought, severe winters, and animal diseases. Scarcity of resources often provoked violent conflict among neighboring tribes. Raiding to steal livestock, women, slaves, and grazing lands was common. The constant violence of the steppe produced permanently militarized societies. For most of the male population, warfare became a regular profession, and women took charge of tending herds and other activities usually reserved for men in the premodern world (see Lives and Livelihoods: Mongol Women in the Household Economy and Public Life).

the fate that befell Chinggis's mother, Hoelun, whose husband was murdered when Chinggis was nine years old. Deserted by her husband's kinfolk, Hoelun doggedly raised her sons on her own, at times forced to forage for roots and berries to survive.

Nonetheless, royal Mongol women were outspoken figures whose voices carried much weight in court deliberations. When Ogodei died in 1241, his widow ruled over the Mongol confederation for five years before ceding power to one of her sons. Qubilai's mother, Sorqaqtani-Beki, likewise played a decisive role in the history of the Mongol Empire. The pastoral nomads of the Eurasian steppe commonly protected widows by remarrying them to younger male relatives of their deceased husbands, and when Sorqaqtani-Beki's husband, Tolui, died in 1232, Ogodei offered to marry her to one of his sons. She firmly declined Ogodei's proposal and instead demanded a fiefdom to provide for her upkeep. Ogodei reluctantly granted her a fief of eighty thousand households in northern China, which Sorqaqtani-Beki insisted on governing herself. In keeping with the policies of Ogodei's minister Yelu Chucai, Sorqaqtani-Beki instituted a Chinese-style civil administration and engaged Chinese scholars to tutor her sons. Qubilai's upbringing thus turned his attention, and the direction of the Mongol Empire, away from the Mongols' steppe homeland and toward China.

Sorqaqtani-Beki proved to be a shrewd politician who earned wide admiration among Mongols and foreigners alike. She had converted to Nestorian Christianity, but promoted toleration of all of the major faiths of the subject peoples. The Ilkhan historian Rashid al-Din, a Muslim, wrote that "in the care and supervision of her sons and in the management of their affairs and those of the army and the people, Sorqaqtani-Beki laid a foundation that would have been beyond the capability of any crowned head."[3]

In 1251, her popularity and political agility paid off when she succeeded in elevating her son Mongke to the position of Great Khan, displacing the lineage of Ogodei. Sorqaqtani-Beki died the following year, but the supreme authority of the Great Khans remained with her sons, including Qubilai, the future emperor of China.

1. Christopher Dawson, ed., Mission to Asia: Narratives and Letters of the Franciscan Missionaries of Mongolia and China in the Thirteenth and Fourteenth Centuries (New York: Harper & Row, 1966), 18.
2. Marco Polo: The Description of the World, eds. A. C. Moule and Paul Pelliot (London: George Rutledge & Sons, 1938), 1:169.
3. Rashiduddin Fazullah's Jami'u't-tawarikh (Compendium of Chronicles): A History of the Mongols, trans. W. M. Thackston (Cambridge, MA: Harvard University, Department of Near Eastern Languages and Civilizations, 1999), Part II, 400–401.

QUESTIONS TO CONSIDER

1. How did the division of household work in pastoral societies such as the Mongols differ from that found among settled farming peoples?

2. How might the role of women in the Mongol household economy explain the power they wielded in tribal affairs?

For Further Information:

Lane, George. Daily Life in the Mongol Empire. Westwood, CT: Greenwood Press, 2006.
Rossabi, Morris. Khubilai Khan: His Life and Times. Berkeley: University of California Press, 1988.

The instability of steppe life worked against social stability, but it also created opportunities for new leadership. Personal charisma, political skills, and prowess in war counted far more than hereditary rights in determining chieftainship. We see this fluidity of Mongol society reflected in Temujin's rise to power. Orphaned at age nine and abandoned by his father's tribe, Temujin gained a following through his valor and success as a warrior. Building on this reputation, he proved extraordinarily adept at constructing alliances among chiefs and transforming tribal coalitions into disciplined military units. By 1206 Temujin had forged a confederation that unified most of the tribes of Mongolia, which recognized him as Chinggis (meaning "oceanic"), the **Great Khan**, the universal ruler of the steppe peoples.

Chinggis Khan

Great Khan "Lord of the steppe"; the Great Khan of the Mongols was chosen by a council of Mongol chiefs.

Creation and Division of the Mongol Empire 1206–1259

Maintaining unity among the fractious coalition of tribal leaders required a steady stream of booty in the form of gold, silk, slaves, and horses. Thus, once installed as Great Khan, Chinggis led his army in campaigns of plunder and conquest. Initially he set his eye on the riches of China and aimed at conquering the Jin kingdom. But in 1218, Chinggis's attention turned toward the west after the Turkish shah of Khwarazam (in Transoxiana) massacred a caravan of Muslim merchants traveling under the Mongol khan's protection. Enraged, Chinggis laid waste to Samarkand, the shah's capital, and other cities in Transoxiana and eastern Iran in what was perhaps the most violent of the Mongol campaigns. After deposing the Khwarazam shah, Chinggis returned to the east and renewed his campaign to conquer China.

By the time of Chinggis's death in 1227, Mongol conquests stretched from eastern Iran to Manchuria. Up to this point, the impact of the Mongol invasions had been almost wholly catastrophic. Solely interested in plunder, Chinggis had shown little taste for the daunting task of ruling the peoples he vanquished (see Map 14.3).

Chinggis's Successors   Throughout Central Asian history the death of a khan almost always provoked a violent succession crisis. But Chinggis's charisma sufficed to ensure an orderly transition of power. Before he died, Chinggis parceled out the Mongol territories among his four sons or their descendants, and he designated his third son Ogodei to succeed him as Great Khan.

The Mongol state under Chinggis Khan was a throwback to the Turkish-Uighur practice of allowing conquered peoples to maintain their own autonomy in exchange for tribute. Ogodei, in contrast, began to adopt features of the Liao-Jin system of dual administration under the direction of the Khitan statesman Yelu Chucai, whom we met at the start of this chapter. Creating an enduring imperial system required displacing tribal chiefs with more centralized political and military control. Thus Ogodei also established a permanent capital for the Mongol Empire at Qaraqorum.

Formation of Independent Mongol Khanates   Under Ogodei's leadership the Mongols steadily expanded their dominions westward into Russia, and they completed the conquest of the Jin. Mongol armies had invaded Hungary and Poland and were threatening to press deeper into Europe when Ogodei's death in 1241 halted their advance. After Ogodei's nephew Mongke was elected Great Khan in 1252, he radically altered Chinggis's original allocation of Mongol territories, assigning the richest lands, China and Iran, to his brothers Qubilai and Hulegu. Mongke's dispensation outraged the other descendants of Chinggis. By the end of his reign, the Mongol realm had broken into four independent and often hostile khanates (see again Map 14.3).

Qubilai Khan and the Yuan Empire in China 1260–1368

Conquest of China   The death of Mongke in 1259 sparked another succession crisis. After four years of bitter struggle Mongke's brother Qubilai secured his claim as Great Khan. Qubilai devoted his energies to completing the conquest of China. In 1271 he adopted the Chinese-style dynastic name Yuan and moved the Great Khan's capital from Mongolia to China, where he built a massive city, Dadu, at the former capital of Zhongdu (modern Beijing). Five years later, Mongol armies captured the Southern Song capital of Hangzhou, and by 1279 Chinese resistance to Mongol rule had ceased. The Yuan Empire (1271–1368) would last only about one hundred years, but for the first time all of China had fallen under foreign rule.

Qubilai was not content with the conquest of China. In 1281, he mustered a great armada, carrying forty-five thousand Mongol soldiers and their horses, for an invasion of Japan. Most of the Mongol fleet was destroyed by a typhoon, which the Japanese gratefully saluted as the *kamikaze*, the "divine wind" that defended them from the Mongol onslaught. The would-be invaders abandoned their effort to take over Japan. Qubilai's army captured the central plains of Burma in 1277, but attempts to conquer Vietnam and naval invasions of Java and Sumatra failed. After 1285, when one of his favorite sons died fighting in Vietnam, Qubilai halted his campaigns of conquest.

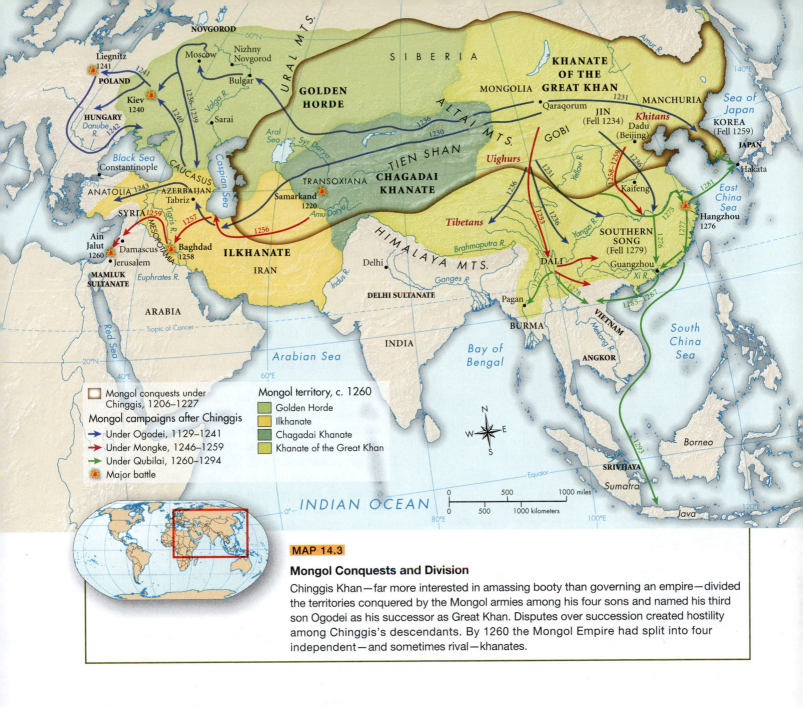

MAP 14.3

Mongol Conquests and Division

Chinggis Khan—far more interested in amassing booty than governing an empire—divided the territories conquered by the Mongol armies among his four sons and named his third son Ogodei as his successor as Great Khan. Disputes over succession created hostility among Chinggis's descendants. By 1260 the Mongol Empire had split into four independent—and sometimes rival—khanates.

Qubilai as Chinese Emperor

Qubilai envisioned himself not merely as first among the Mongol princes but also as an exalted "Son of Heaven" in the style of the Chinese emperors. He surrounded himself with foreign advisers, including Muslims, Uighurs, and Chinese, and laid the foundations for permanent Mongol rule over China. Building on the precedents of the Liao and Jin states, Qubilai created a highly centralized administration designed to extract the maximum revenue from China's land, people, and commerce. The Venetian merchant Marco Polo (1254–1324), astonished at the splendor of the Great Khan's capital, proclaimed that Qubilai was "the most powerful man in people and in lands and in treasure that ever was in the world or that now is from the time of Adam our first father till this moment."[7]

Although Qubilai was a conscientious and diligent ruler, his successors gave little attention to the tasks of maintaining the infrastructure of the agrarian economy or protecting people's welfare. Instead, they relied on a system of **tax farming** that delegated tax collection privileges to private intermediaries, mostly Muslim merchants. Many of these tax farmers abused their authority and demanded exorbitant payments from an increasingly disgruntled agrarian population.

tax farming The assignment of tax collection powers to private individuals or groups in exchange for fixed payments to the state.

At the same time, however, the Mongols strongly encouraged commerce, and international trade flourished. The Mongols created a vast network of post stations and issued passports to merchants to ensure safe passage throughout the Mongol realm. The chief beneficiaries of expanding trans-Eurasian trade were the Uighur and Muslim merchants who acted as commercial agents for their Mongol patrons.

The Yuan Empire maintained the Central Asian tradition of a social structure based on tribal loyalties. Political, legal, and economic privileges rested on an ethnic hierarchy that favored the Mongol tribes and the so-called "affiliated peoples"—non-Chinese who had served the Mongols since the time of Chinggis, including Turks, Tibetans, Persians, and above all Uighurs. Former Chinese subjects of the Jin state, designated "Han people," occupied the third rung of this social hierarchy. "Southerners" (former subjects of the Southern Song), who composed more than 80 percent of the Yuan population, were relegated to the bottom. The Yuan state largely drew its administrators from merchants and scholars among the "affiliated peoples" and barred "southerners" from high office. The Mongols also forbade Chinese to possess firearms, ride horses, learn the Mongol language, or intermarry with Mongols.

Qubilai aspired to be a truly universal monarch. In his quest for an appropriate model, he turned to Phags-pa (pak-pa) Lama (1235–1280), the spiritual leader of the Saskya sect of Tibetan Buddhism. As a transnational faith, Buddhism helped unite the diverse peoples of eastern Asia under Mongol rule. At the same time, Qubilai's support enabled Phags-pa and the Saskya Lamas to gain supreme authority over Tibet, a position they would hold until the rival lineage of Dalai Lamas displaced them in the sixteenth century.

Religious Tolerance   Even as Qubilai declared Phags-pa the head of the Buddhist church, the Mongols accorded full tolerance to all religions. Muslim, Jewish, and Nestorian Christian communities flourished in China under Mongol rule. John of Montecorvino, a Franciscan missionary dispatched by the pope, arrived at the Yuan capital in 1294. John erected a church near the khan's palace, translated the New Testament into Chinese and Uighur, and by his own estimate attracted six thousand converts—mostly non-Chinese—to Christianity. Pleased with John's reports of the progress of his missionary work, in 1308 the pope consecrated him as the first Latin bishop of Beijing.

Under Qubilai's leadership the Mongol Empire in China departed from the practices of the early steppe empires, which relied on plunder and extraction of tribute from settled societies. Instead the Yuan state, like its Liao and Jin predecessors, developed institutions for imposing direct rule on its Chinese subjects, even if it did not penetrate local society to the extent that native Chinese empires had. At the same time, the Mongols in China turned their backs on their steppe homeland. By 1300 the Yuan emperors were raised exclusively within the confines of the capital at Dadu and had largely severed their connections with the independent Mongol khanates in central and western Asia.

Mongol Passport

The Mongols established a comprehensive network of post stations to maintain communications with their far-flung armies. Only those with proper authorization, in the form of metal or wooden paiza tablets, were allowed use of the lodgings, supplies, and horses provided at these post stations. The Mongolian inscription on this silver paiza reads, "By the power of the Eternal Heaven, may the name of Mongke Khan be sacred. He who does not honor it shall perish and die." (© The State Hermitage Museum/photo by Vladimir Terebenin, Leonard Kheifets, Yuri Molodkovets.)

The Mongol Khanates and the Islamic World 1240–1350

In 1253 the Great Khan Mongke assigned his brother Hulegu (HE-luh-gee) responsibility for completing the Mongol conquest of Iran and Mesopotamia. In 1258 Baghdad fell to Hulegu's army, and the last Abbasid caliph was reportedly wrapped in a carpet and trampled to death, to avoid spilling royal blood on the ground. In their hunger for booty, the Mongol victors utterly destroyed the city of Baghdad, the official capital of Islam. By Hulegu's own estimate, two hundred thousand people perished. Survivors of the Mongol conquest fled to Cairo, where the Mamluk (MAM-luke) sultanate, a regime of military slave origins, had overthrown the dynasty of Saladin and was consolidating its power over Egypt and Syria. The Mamluks became the new political leaders of the Islamic world, rallying their fellow Muslims to the cause of holy war against the Mongol onslaught.

The conquest of Baghdad was the last great campaign conducted jointly by the Mongol princes. As we have seen, by the time of Qubilai's succession in 1263 as Great Khan, rivalry among Chinggis's heirs had fractured the Mongol Empire into four independent khanates: the Golden Horde along the frontiers of Russia; the Chagadai (shah-gah-TY) khanate in Central Asia; the Ilkhanate based in Iran; and the khanate of the Great Khan in China (see again Map 14.3).

FOCUS

In what respects did the Turkish Islamic states of the Mamluks and Ottomans pursue policies similar to those of the Mongol regimes in Iran and Russia?

Mongol Rule in Iran and Mesopotamia

After conquering Iran and Mesopotamia, Hulegu's army suffered a decisive defeat at the hands of the Mamluks in Palestine in 1260 and withdrew. At around this time Hulegu adopted the Turkish title of *Ilkhan* ("subordinate khan"), implying submission to his brother Qubilai, the Great Khan. Hulegu and his successors as Ilkhan (il-con) also made diplomatic overtures to the Christian monarchs of Europe with the goal of forming an alliance against their common enemy, the Mamluks. In 1287 the Ilkhanate sent Rabban Sauma, a Nestorian Christian monk from China, as an envoy to the courts of England, France, and the Roman pope to enlist their aid against the Mamluks, to no avail.

The Ilkhans ruled over their domains from a series of seasonal capitals in Azerbaijan, a region in the northwestern corner of Iran where good pastureland was plentiful. Unlike Qubilai in China, the Ilkhans did not build a fixed, monumental capital in the style of their subjects. Instead they followed the nomadic practice of moving their camps in rhythm with the seasonal migrations of their herds. The Mongol conquests of Iran and Mesopotamia had caused immense environmental and economic harm. Abandonment of farmlands and the deterioration of irrigation systems

Mongol Siege of Baghdad

The Mongol conquest of Baghdad in 1258 ended the caliphate, the main political institution of the Islamic world since the death of Muhammad. In this illustration of the siege of Baghdad, a group of Mongols at lower right beat a flat drum; the archers and soldiers are all in Persian dress. At upper left the last Abbasid caliph makes a futile attempt to escape by boat. (Bildarchiv Preussischer Kulturbesitz/ Art Resource.)

sharply curtailed agricultural production. Much land was turned over to pasture or reverted to desert.

As in China, Mongols composed a tiny minority of the Ilkhanate's population. Even in the Ilkhan armies, Turks far outnumbered Mongols. Like the Yuan state, the Ilkhanate initially recruited its administrative personnel from foreigners and members of minority groups. Christian communities, notably the Nestorians and Armenians, had been quick to side with the Mongol invaders against their Muslim overlords. Christians hoped that their connections to the Ilkhan court—Hulegu's queen was a Christian, and a number of Christians rose to high positions in the Ilkhanate government—might win official endorsement of their religion. Instead, the Mongols in Iran increasingly turned toward the faith of the Muslim majority. The proselytizing efforts of Sufi sheikhs attracted many converts, especially among the Mongol and Turkish horsemen who were the backbone of the Ilkhanate's military strength. Muslim advisers became influential in the ruling circles of the Ilkhanate as well.

By the late thirteenth century, escalating religious tensions and the familiar pattern of violent succession disputes among the Mongol leaders threatened to tear apart the Ilkhan state. The ascension of Ghazan (haz-ZAHN) (r. 1295–1304) as Ilkhan revived the Ilkhanate and marked a decisive turning point in Mongol rule in Iran.

Ghazan's Reforms

A convert to Islam, Ghazan took pains to show his devotion to the faith of the great majority of his subjects. Ghazan reduced Christians and Jews to subordinate status and banished Buddhist monks from the Ilkhan realm. He also placed the Ilkhanate government on sounder footing by reforming the fiscal system, investing greater resources in agriculture, instituting a new currency system, and reducing taxes. Ghazan broke with the practice of seasonal migration and constructed a permanent capital at Tabriz appointed with palaces, mosques, Sufi lodges, a grand mausoleum for himself, and baths and caravanserais to accommodate traveling merchants. Tabriz quickly developed into a major center of international trade and artistic production.

Rashid al-Din (ra-SHEED al-DEEN) (1247–1318), a Jewish doctor who converted to Islam, served as chief minister and architect of Ghazan's program of reform. Rashid al-Din also carefully embellished Ghazan's image as ruler, forging a new ideology of sovereignty that portrayed Ghazan as a devout Muslim, a Persian philosopher-king, and a second Alexander the Great. Ghazan ceased to refer to himself as Ilkhan, a title that implied subordination to the rulers of Yuan China, and adopted the Turkish and Persian royal titles sultan and *shah*. Under Rashid al-Din's direction, court scholars compiled the *Compendium of Chronicles*, a history of the world that glorified the Mongol rulers as rightful heirs to the legacies of the Persian kings and the Abbasid caliphate.

Patronage of Arts and Letters

The Ilkhans became great patrons of arts and letters. Rashid al-Din boasted that "in these days when, thank God, all corners of the earth are under our rule and that of Chinggis Khan's illustrious family, philosophers, astronomers, scholars, and historians of all religions and nations—Cathay and Machin (North and South China), India and Kashmir, Tibetans, Uighurs, and other nations of Turks, Arabs, and Franks—are gathered in droves at our glorious court."[8] Manuscript painting, luxury silks, architectural decoration, metalworking, and ceramics all reflected the impact of new aesthetic ideas and motifs, with Chinese influences especially prominent. Prolific production of luxury editions of the Qur'an and lavish decoration of mosques, shrines, and tombs also attest to the vitality of the religious art promoted by the Muslim Ilkhans.

Under Rashid al-Din's stewardship, the ideological basis of the Ilkhanate shifted away from descent from Chinggis Khan and toward the role of royal protector of the Islamic faith. Nonetheless, diplomatic ties and cultural and economic exchanges with China became even closer. In the early fourteenth century, a renewal of cordial relations among the leaders of the four Mongol khanates eased the passage of caravans and travelers across the Silk Road. Conversion to Islam did not alienate their fellow Mongols, but neither did it repair the breach with the Mamluk regime.

Sultan, Poet, and Courtiers
The Mongol elite of the Ilkhanate quickly became ardent patrons of Islam after Ghazan's conversion in 1295. In addition to building religious monuments and establishing charitable foundations, Mongol leaders commissioned numerous lavishly illustrated manuscripts attesting to their Muslim faith. In this illustration from a poetry anthology copied in 1315, a poet holding a scroll recites poetry before a seated Mongol ruler surrounded by his courtiers. (©2011 The British Library I.O. Islamic 132.)

End of the Ilkhanate

Ghazan's reforms failed to ensure the long-term stability of the Ilkhanate regime, however. Ghazan's attempt to recast the Ilkhanate as a monarchy in the tradition of the Islamic caliphate ran into strong opposition among Mongol leaders accustomed to tribal independence and shared sovereignty. The reign of Ghazan's nephew Abu Said (r. 1316–1335) was wracked by factional conflicts that sapped the Ilkhan leadership and cost Rashid al-Din his life. After Abu Said died without an heir in 1335, the Ilkhanate's authority steadily disintegrated. In 1353 members of a messianic Shi'a sect murdered the last Ilkhan.

The Golden Horde and the Rise of Muscovy

Founding of the Golden Horde

The Golden Horde in Central Asia and Russia proved more durable than the Ilkhanate. In 1237 a Mongol army led by Chinggis's grandson Batu conquered the Volga River Valley and sacked the main cities of the Bulgars and the Rus princes, including the fortified outpost of Moscow. In 1240 Kiev succumbed to a Mongol siege, and the Mongol armies quickly pushed westward into Poland and Hungary, prompting the Roman pope to declare a crusade against this new menace. But feuding among the Mongol princes after the death of Ogodei in 1241 halted the Mongol advance into Europe. Instead, Batu created an independent Mongol realm known as the **Golden Horde**, with its capital at Sarai in the lower Volga River Valley (see again Map 14.3).

Batu's successor, Berke (r. 1257–1267), was the first of the Mongol khans to convert to Islam. A fierce rivalry erupted between Berke and the Ilkhan Hulegu for control over the Caucasus region. Berke allied with the Mamluks against the Ilkhanate and opposed the election of Hulegu's brother Qubilai as Great Khan. Political and commercial competition with the Ilkhanate also prompted the khans of the Golden Horde to seek close ties with Genoese merchant colonies around the shores of the Black Sea and with the Byzantine emperors.

Indirect Rule in Russia

In the Rus lands, as in Iran, the Mongols instituted a form of indirect governance that relied on local rulers as intermediaries. The Mongols required that the Rus princes conduct censuses, raise taxes to support the Mongol army, maintain post stations, and personally appear at the khan's court at Sarai to offer tribute. The Golden Horde and the Ilkhanate both adopted the Persian-Turkish institution of *iqta*, land grants awarded to military officers to feed and supply the soldiers under their command. The administrative structure of the Golden Horde and its system of military estates were subsequently adopted by the expanding Muscovy state in the fifteenth century.

Rus's Commercial Growth and Religious Independence

As elsewhere in the Mongol realms, the khans of the Golden Horde strongly encouraged commerce, and their favorable policies toward merchants increased the volume of trade passing through Rus lands. The Rus princes and the Christian church benefited enormously from the profits of commerce. Moscow flourished as the capital of the fur trade. As a result of this commercial prosperity, the first Grand Prince of Muscovy, Ivan I (r. 1328–1340), nicknamed "Moneybags" by his subjects, was able to build the stone churches that became the heart of the Kremlin, the seat of future Russian governments. New commercial towns were founded, most importantly Nizhny Novgorod (1358), populated by German and Scandinavian merchants from the Baltic region. The wealth accumulated by the Orthodox Christian clerics and the protection they enjoyed under the traditional Mongol respect for religious institutions strengthened the church's position in Rus society and fostered greater independence from the Byzantine patriarch.

The Golden Horde and the Mongol Heritage

Despite its commercial expansion, Rus was marginal to the khanate, which focused its attention instead on controlling the steppe pasturelands and trade routes. In contrast to the Yuan dynasty and the Ilkhanate, the Golden Horde retained its connections to the steppe and the culture of pastoral nomadism. Nor did conversion to Islam bring about substantial changes in the Golden Horde culture comparable to those that occurred in the Ilkhanate. Berke's conversion to Islam arose from personal conviction and was not accompanied by a mandate to adopt the new faith. Not until the 1310s did the Golden Horde adopt Islam as its official religion. Although conversion to Islam pulled the Mongols of the Golden Horde more firmly into the cultural world of their Turkish subjects (and away from that of Christian Rus), it did not lead them to abandon their pastoral way of life.

Retrenchment in the Islamic World: The Mamluk and Ottoman States

The fall and destruction of Baghdad in 1258 delivered a devastating blow to the Islamic world—even greater than the shock that reverberated across Latin Christendom when Jerusalem fell to Saladin in 1187. The sack of Baghdad and the execution of the Abbasid caliph left the Islamic confederacy leaderless and disorganized. Out of this political crisis emerged two new dynastic regimes, the Mamluks in Egypt and the Ottomans in Anatolia (modern Turkey). Together, these two dynasties restored order to the Islamic lands of the eastern Mediterranean and halted further Mongol advances (see Map 14.4). Both the Mamluks and the Ottomans were warrior states, but they owed their political longevity to their ability to adapt to the requirements of governing large settled populations. The Mamluk Sultanate ruled from 1250 to 1517, nearly three times as long as the Yuan dynasty. The Ottoman Empire would prove to be one of the most enduring in world history, stretching from its origins in the late thirteenth century to final eclipse in 1923, following World War I.

Rise of the Mamluk Sultanate

In 1250 the Mamluks, a regiment of Turkish slave soldiers, overthrew the Ayyubid dynasty in Egypt and chose one of their officers as sultan. The Mamluk regime gained enormous stature among Muslims when it repelled the Mongol incursions into Syria in 1260. Its prestige was further burnished after it expelled the last of the Crusader states from Palestine in 1291.

The Mamluk elite consisted solely of foreigners, predominantly Turks, who had been purchased as slaves and raised in Egypt for service in the Mamluk army or administrative corps. Sons of Mamluk soldiers were excluded from government and military service, which therefore had to be replenished in each generation by fresh slave imports from the steppe. The Mamluk soldiers and administrators were bound to the state by personal allegiance to their officers and the sultan. Except from 1299 to 1382, when a form of hereditary succession prevailed, the sultans were chosen by the officer corps.

The Mamluk regime devoted itself to promoting the Islamic faith and strengthening state wealth and power. Although barred from the overland caravan trade by the Ilkhans, Mamluk Egypt sat astride the maritime routes connecting the Mediterranean to the Indian Ocean. Revenues from the burgeoning commerce with Asia, driven especially by Europeans' growing appetite for spices such as pepper and ginger, swelled the coffers of the Mamluk treasury. To offset the Ilkhanate's partnership with Byzantium and the Genoese merchants, the Mamluk regime cultivated close commercial and political ties with Venice—evidence that the Mamluks, like the Ilkhans, were willing to set aside intense religious differences with their Christian allies to further their own political and commercial interests.

Relations with the Ilkhanate thawed, however, after Ghazan's conversion to Islam. In 1322 the Mamluks concluded a commercial treaty with the Ilkhans that ensured free movement of slave caravans from the Black Sea through Ilkhan territories to Egypt. Although the Ilkhan regime would unravel during the next several decades, the Mamluk state now enjoyed peace and prosperity.

Despite the stability of the Mamluk regime, membership in the ruling class was insecure. Not only were sons of the slave-soldiers excluded from military and government service, but family fortunes were often vulnerable to confiscation amid the factional conflicts that beset the Mamluk court. Sultans and other affluent notables sought to

Stability Under Mamluk Rule

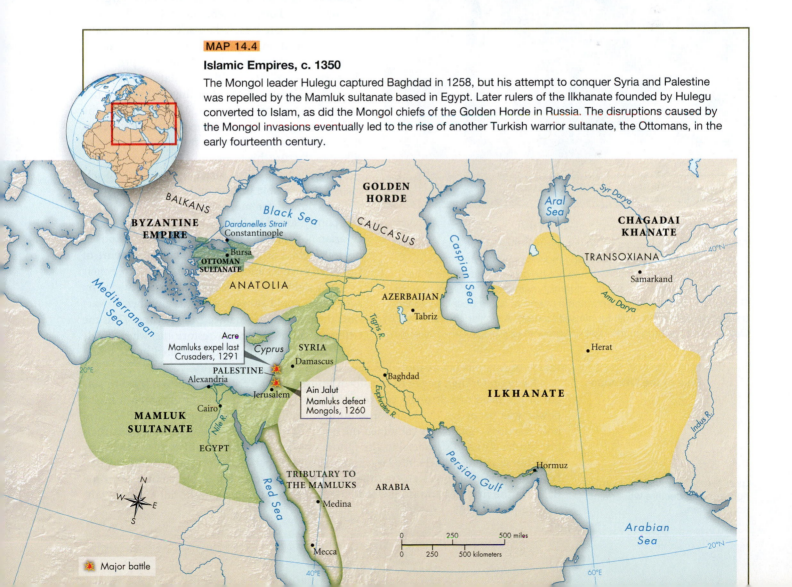

MAP 14.4

Islamic Empires, c. 1350

The Mongol leader Hulegu captured Baghdad in 1258, but his attempt to conquer Syria and Palestine was repelled by the Mamluk sultanate based in Egypt. Later rulers of the Ilkhanate founded by Hulegu converted to Islam, as did the Mongol chiefs of the Golden Horde in Russia. The disruptions caused by the Mongol invasions eventually led to the rise of another Turkish warrior sultanate, the Ottomans, in the early fourteenth century.

Qala'un Complex in Cairo

Since the Mamluk leaders could not pass on their status and privileges to their sons, they turned to creating monuments and charitable foundations—whose property could not be confiscated by the state—that remained under the control of family members. The Mamluk sultan Qala'un (r. 1280–1290) incorporated a madrasa and a hospital into the ornate mausoleum he built for himself (center). A similar complex built by Qala'un's son stands in the right foreground. (akg-images/Gerard Degeorge.)

preserve control of their wealth by establishing charitable trusts that were exempt from such seizures. The founding patrons often used the resources of these trusts to build large ceremonial complexes that housed a variety of religious and charitable institutions, including mosques, madrasas, elementary schools, hospitals, and Sufi hospices, as well as their own tombs.

Another Islamic warrior state, one that would ultimately contest the Mamluks' leadership within the Islamic world, emerged in Anatolia. The Ottomans traced their origins to Osman (d. 1324), who arose as the leader of an expanding confederation of nomadic warriors in the late thirteenth century. In Osman's day, Anatolia was the frontier between the Byzantine Empire and the Ilkhanate (see again Map 14.4). There, tribes of Muslim herders competed with Christian farmers and pagan nomads for lands and followers. Like other nomadic confederations, the Ottoman alliance was based on political expediency rather than permanent ethnic allegiances, and Osman's first invasions targeted neighboring Turks. Then, in 1302, after bad weather decimated their herds, Osman's warriors turned against the Byzantine towns of Anatolia. Osman's victories over the Byzantines prompted the surrender of much of the population of western Anatolia, Christians and Muslims alike. Osman's son and successor Orkhan (r. 1324–1362) led the Ottoman army in conquests of the major cities of Anatolia and made Bursa, a prosperous center of silk manufacture, his capital in 1331.

Although the tribal society of the Turkish nomads was a flexible institution in which loyalty and service counted far more than lineage and faith, it was poorly suited to the needs of governing a large agrarian population. Osman granted pasturelands to his followers, but he also cultivated the support of Christian farmers and town folk and protected their property rights. The stable revenue base provided by agriculture could support a greater number of warriors than the booty obtained from raiding. Thus the Ottoman rulers sought to restore the wheat fields and olive orchards that had flourished in the fertile valleys of Anatolia before the Seljuk invasions in the eleventh century.

Rise of the Ottomans

Early on Orkhan began to transform himself from a tribal chief into a Muslim sultan at the head of a strongly centralized state. The rapid growth of Ottoman military power was propelled by the incorporation into the army's ranks of bands of Muslim holy warriors—**gazi**, who combined the qualities of frontier bandits and religious zealots. Under Orkhan's leadership the Ottoman army also underwent a metamorphosis from horse-riding archers into large infantry units capable of sophisticated siege tactics. In 1354, Ottoman forces crossed the Dardanelles to seize Byzantine territories in the Balkans, the first step toward the conquest of Constantinople and the fall of the Byzantine Empire in 1453.

gazi "Holy warriors"; in Islam, fighters who declare war against nonbelievers.

COUNTERPOINT
The "New Knighthood" of the Christian Military Orders

Following the success of the First Crusade, a new church institution was formed: the military orders, religious orders that combined the vocations of monk and warrior. Inspired by new international monastic orders dedicated to the spread of the Christian faith, such as the Cistercians, these armed monks redefined both the monastic calling and the ideals of knighthood.

FOCUS

In what ways did the self-image and mission of the Christian military orders resemble or differ from those of the papal and royal leaders of the Crusades?

Their movement began with the Knights of the Temple, an order founded in 1120 to protect Christian pilgrims and merchants; it was named after their headquarters near the site of the ancient Temple of Solomon in Jerusalem. Subsequently, the Templars (as they were commonly known) and other military orders spearheaded the militant Christian expansionism that resulted in the "reconquest" of Spain and the conversion of much of eastern Europe to Latin Christianity. Yet in the end Christian monarchs and the papacy turned against the military orders, annihilating the Templars and sharply restricting other military orders' activities. The ideal of an international brotherhood united in faith and in arms—the Crusader ideal—was swept away by the rising tide of national monarchies.

The Templar Model and the Crusading Movement

The Templar knights were expected to maintain equal fidelity to both the code of chivalry and monastic rules. Like the Cistercians, the Templars took vows of poverty, chastity, and obedience. The Cistercian abbot Bernard of Clairvaux praised what he called the "new knighthood" of the Templars for its steadfast commitment to combating both the evil within—the temptations of the devil—and the external enemy, the Muslims.

The Templars and Their Followers

Critics of the military orders voiced misgivings about their unseemly combination of religious devotion with armed violence. Nonetheless, donations to the orders, strongly encouraged by the church, led to rapid expansion of their ranks. Within thirty years the Templars had taken proprietorship of scores of estates and castles throughout western Europe and in the Crusader states. The outpouring of patronage for the Templar order encouraged imitation. Two new military orders based on the Templar model, the Hospitallers and the Teutonic Knights, were formed to tend to the poor and infirm among the pilgrims to the Holy Land. In the late twelfth century a number of military orders also sprang up in Spain to aid the cause of the "reconquest."

Members of the military orders committed themselves to lifelong service. Strict rules imbued the military orders with the discipline and solidarity that other Crusaders lacked. The knights' brave defense of the Christian enclaves against the Muslim counterattack led by Saladin earned them high regard from the enemy as well as from their fellow Christians. After vanquishing Christian armies, Saladin ordered the immediate beheading of captured Templars and Hospitallers, whom he regarded as the backbone of the Christian defenders.

Despite Jerusalem's fall to Saladin in 1187, the military orders continued to attract new recruits and donations. Pope Innocent III staunchly supported the military orders, which he regarded as crucial allies in his campaign to create an imperial papacy. But the Mamluks' final expulsion of Latin Christians from Acre in 1291 deprived the military orders of their reason for existence. Moreover, the Templars had powerful enemies, especially the French king Philip IV (r. 1285–1314), who resented their autonomy and coveted

Destruction of the Templars

Domains of the Teutonic Knights, 1309–1410

their wealth. With the cowardly consent of a weak pope, Philip launched a campaign of persecution against the order. The officers of the Inquisition found the Templars guilty of heresy. Hundreds of knights were burned at the stake, and in 1312 the pope disbanded the Templar order.

The Teutonic Knights and Christian Expansion in Eastern Europe

In contrast to the Templars, the Teutonic military order gained renewed life after the failure of the Crusades. In the late 1220s a Polish duke recruited members of the Teutonic order (so called because nearly all its members were German) to carry out a crusade against his rivals among the pagan lords of Prussia. Anticipating sharing in the spoils of victory, German princes and knights rushed to join the new crusading enterprise in their own backyard. The popes claimed sovereign authority over Prussia and delegated the Teutonic order to rule the region on their behalf. In 1309 the Teutonic Knights relocated to Prussia and focused exclusively on building up their own territorial state in the Baltic region.

After 1370, when the Teutonic Knights defeated the pagan princes of Lithuania, new commercial towns affiliated with the Hanseatic League arose and the Baltic region was rapidly colonized. Town charters gave urban burghers considerable independence but reserved sovereign rights to the order, which possessed large rural estates and received annual tribute from town dwellers.

Marienburg Castle

After withdrawing from the Mediterranean, the Teutonic Knights found a new mission: spearheading the Christian advance among the pagan peoples of eastern Europe. From 1309 the order's leaders took up residence at a grand new headquarters at Marienburg on the Vistula River (now Malbork, Poland). The state created by the Teutonic order in the Baltic Sea region was considered a model of bureaucratic efficiency. (Photolibrary.)

Unschooled in Latin, the Teutonic order promoted Christianity through books, libraries, and schools in the German vernacular. The law codes adopted by the German overlords reminded the natives of their subordinate status by imposing various forms of legal discrimination. For example, the fine for killing a German was twice that for killing a native Prussian. Ethnic tensions were also evident in the rule that when drinking together, the Germans required the Prussians to drink first, for fear of poisoning.

End of the Teutonic State

When economic conditions worsened in the waning years of the fourteenth century, local landowners began to challenge the order's autocratic rule. The marriage of the Lithuanian king and the Polish queen in 1386 prompted Lithuanians to convert to Christianity, removing the last justification for the Teutonic order's holy war against paganism. During the fifteenth century the Prussian towns and rural lords gained independence from the order's rule. By the early sixteenth century the order had ceased to function as a sovereign state.

Demise of the Crusader Ideal

The Teutonic order was thus a victim of its own success. Once the order completed its mission of implanting Christianity through conquest, colonization, and conversion of pagans, the Knights no longer had a cause to serve. The military orders had represented the ideal of a universal Christian brotherhood championed by the Roman popes. Yet the dramatic expansion of Christendom to all corners of Europe between the twelfth and the fifteenth centuries had fostered national rivalry rather than political unity. With the failure of the Crusades and the demise of the military orders, the papacy's ambitions to rule over a united Christian people likewise perished.

Conclusion

The initial waves of the Mongol invasions spread fear and destruction across Eurasia, and the political and cultural repercussions of the Mongol conquests would resound for centuries. Adapting their own traditions to vastly different local settings, the Mongols reshaped the societies and cultures of Iran, Russia, and China as well as Central Asia. The Mongol legacy of steppe empires spanning the pastoral and settled worlds would inspire later empire-builders from Timur to the Mughals and the Manchus.

The Mongol incursions most profoundly affected the Islamic states and societies of Iran and Mesopotamia and the Rus lands. Many areas never recovered from the disruption of irrigated agriculture and reverted to pasture for stock raising, and in some cases even to barren desert. The Mongol invasions also erased the last of the Seljuk emirates, clearing the ground for the rise of new Turkish sultanates, the Mamluks and the Ottomans.

Like the Ilkhans in Iran, the Mongols of the Golden Horde converted to Islam, although their Rus subjects remained Christians. The rising Muscovy state would retain Mongol military and political institutions in building its own Russian empire. In China, by contrast, the Mongol legacy proved fleeting. Ignoring Yelu Chucai's warning that "the empire cannot be ruled on horseback," the Mongols failed to adapt their style of rule to the requirements of a large agrarian empire. The Yuan regime in China had badly deteriorated by the 1330s and collapsed into civil war and rebellion in the 1350s. As we will see in the next chapter, the founder of the Ming Empire (1368–1644) in China would seek to eliminate all traces of Mongol influence.

The Mongols brought the worlds of pastoral nomads and settled urban and agrarian peoples into collision, but a different kind of clash of civilizations had been triggered by the Crusades. Although the Crusaders failed to achieve their goal of restoring Christian rule over Jerusalem, the crusading movement expanded the borders of Latin Christendom by advancing the "reconquest" in Spain and by converting the Wendish peoples of eastern Europe.

The crusading movement and institutions such as the Christian military orders played a crucial role in the formation of Europe as the realm of "the Christian people" obedient to the Roman papacy. But the growing power of national monarchies frustrated the popes' efforts to establish supreme rule over secular as well as spiritual affairs. The unity imposed by the Mongol conquests also was short-lived. Although the creation of the Mongol Empire made possible an unprecedented movement of people, goods, and ideas throughout Eurasia, such cross-cultural exchanges vanished almost completely after the collapse of the Ilkhan and Yuan states in the mid-fourteenth century. By then, as the next chapter will reveal, both Europe and the Islamic lands had plunged into a new era of crisis following the devastating catastrophe of the Black Death.

NOTES

1. *The Deeds of the Franks and the Other Pilgrims to Jerusalem*, cited in James Harvey Robinson, ed., *Readings in European History* (Boston: Ginn & Co., 1904), 1:312.
2. Ibn Jubayr, "Relation de voyages," *Voyageurs arabes: Ibn Fadlan, Ibn Jubayr, Ibn Battuta et un auteur anonyme*, trans. Paul Charles-Dominique (Paris: Éditions Gallimard, 1995), 310.
3. Bernard of Clairvaux, *Letters*, trans. Bruno Scott James (London: Burns, Oates, 1953), 467.
4. Cited in Robert Bartlett, *The Making of Europe: Conquest, Colonization and Cultural Change, 950–1350* (Princeton, NJ: Princeton University Press, 1993), 154.
5. Cited in Bartlett, *The Making of Europe*, 132.
6. Nicole Oresme, "Le Livre de Politiques d'Aristotle," *Transactions of the American Philosophical Society*, new series, vol. 60, part 6 (1970), 292.
7. *Marco Polo: The Description of the World*, eds. A. C. Moule and Paul Pelliot (London: George Routledge & Sons, 1938), 1:192.
8. *Rashiduddin Fazullah's Jami'u't-tawarikh* (Compendium of Chronicles): *A History of the Mongols*, trans. W. M. Thackston (Cambridge, MA: Harvard University, Department of Near Eastern Languages and Civilizations, 1998), Part I, 6.

RESOURCES FOR RESEARCH

The Crusades and the Imperial Papacy, 1050–1350

The story of the Crusades has almost always been told from European and Christian perspectives. Hillenbrand's survey of Muslim attitudes helps to correct this bias. In his short, provocative study Tyerman challenges the conventional historiography and questions whether the Crusades constituted a coherent movement.

(Crusades: Introduction): http://www.theorb.net/encyclop/religion/crusades/crusade_intro.html.

France, John. *The Crusades and the Expansion of Catholic Christendom, 1000–1714.* 2005.

*Gabrieli, Francesco, ed. *Arab Historians of the Crusades.* 1969.

Hillenbrand, Carole. *The Crusades: Islamic Perspectives.* 2000.

Madden, Thomas F. *A Concise History of the Crusades.* 1999.

Tyerman, Christopher. *The Invention of the Crusades.* 1998.

The Making of Christian Europe, 1100–1350

Recent scholarship considers this the formative period for the emergence of a distinct European political and cultural identity. In Bartlett's view, this European identity was closely interwined with Latin Christendom's expansion and colonization of eastern and northern Europe and Spain. Nirenberg's pathbreaking work analyzes the culture of violence that led to persecution of Jews and other minorities.

Bartlett, Robert. *The Making of Europe: Conquest, Colonization, and Cultural Change, 950–1350.* 1993.

Christiansen, Eric. *The Northern Crusades: The Baltic and the Catholic Frontier, 1100–1525*, 2d ed. 1997.

Nirenberg, David. *Communities of Violence: Persecution of Minorities in the Middle Ages.* 1996.

Reilly, Bernard F. *The Medieval Spains.* 1993.

Reynolds, Susan. *Kingdoms and Communities in Western Europe, 900–1300.* 1984.

The Mongol World-Empire, 1100–1368

Despite the wealth of books on the Mongols, there is no comprehensive study of the Mongol Empire in its entirety. Lane and Morgan, both Islamic specialists, concentrate primarily on the Mongol domains in the west. Most treatments of the Mongols focus on the lives and deeds of the great khans, but Lane details many features of Mongol social life and customs.

Biran, Michal. *Chinggis Khan.* 2007.

Lane, George. *Daily Life in the Mongol Empire.* 2006.

Larner, John. *Marco Polo and the Discovery of the World.* 1999.

Morgan, David. *The Mongols.* 2d ed. 2007.

*Polo, Marco. *The Travels of Marco Polo.* 1958.

The Mongol Khanates and the Islamic World, 1240–1350

Revisionist scholars, while acknowledging the destructive effects of the Mongol conquests in Russia and Iran, have emphasized the transformative influences of Mongol rule as well. Lane rejects depictions of Ilkhan rule in Iran as a "dark age" and instead sees this period as one of cultural renaissance.

Allsen, Thomas. *Culture and Conquest in Mongol Eurasia.* 2001.

Kafadar, Cemal. *Between Two Worlds: The Construction of the Ottoman State.* 1995.

Lane, George. *Early Mongol Rule in Thirteenth-Century Iran: A Persian Renaissance.* 2003.

Morgan, David. *Medieval Persia, 1040–1797.* 1988.

Ostrowski, Donald. *Muscovy and the Mongols: Cross-Cultural Influences on the Steppe Frontier, 1304–1589.* 1998.

COUNTERPOINT: The "New Knighthood" of the Christian Military Orders

The history of the military orders is full of drama and controversy, and modern scholars have struggled to separate fact from fiction. Barber has written the definitive scholarly study of the Templar order, and the same can be said of Riley-Smith's work on the Hospitallers.

Barber, Malcolm. *The New Knighthood: A History of the Order of the Temple.* 1994.

(Military Orders: A Guide to On-line Resources): http://www .theorb.net/encyclop/religion/monastic/milindex.html .

Nicholson, Helen. *Templars, Hospitallers and Teutonic Knights: Images of the Military Orders, 1128–1291.* 1993.

Riley-Smith, Jonathan. *Hospitallers: The History of the Order of St. John.* 1987.

* Primary source.

▶ **For additional primary sources from this period**, see *Sources of Crossroads and Cultures*.

▶ **For Web sites, images, and documents related to topics in this chapter**, see Make History at bedfordstmartins.com/smith.

The major global development in this chapter ▶ The Eurasian integration
fostered by the clashes of culture known as the Crusades and the Mongol conquests.

IMPORTANT EVENTS

1054	Great Schism between the Roman and Byzantine churches
1095	Pope Urban II issues summons for First Crusade
1098	Founding of the Cistercian order
1099	First Crusade concludes with the Christian capture of Jerusalem
1120	Founding of the order of the Knights of the Temple (Templars) at Jerusalem
1147	Wendish Crusade (part of the Second Crusade)
1187	Saladin recaptures Jerusalem
1198–1216	Papacy of Innocent III
1206	Council of Mongol princes elects Temujin (Chinggis) as Great Khan
1240	Mongol conquest of Kiev
1248	Christian armies capture the Almohad stronghold of Seville
1250–1517	Mamluk Sultanate in Egypt and Syria
1258	Mongols sack Baghdad
1271–1368	Rule of Mongols over China as the Yuan dynasty
1274–1295	Journey of Marco Polo to China
1291	Mamluks recapture Acre, last Christian stronghold in Palestine
1295–1304	Rule of Ghazan as Ilkhan; conversion of Ilkhan Mongols to Islam

KEY TERMS

chivalry (p. 450)   Inquisition (p. 448)
Crusades (p. 444)   investiture controversy
gazi (p. 466)   (p. 445)
Great Khan (p. 457)   military order (p. 446)
Great Schism (p. 445)   tax farming (p. 459)

CHAPTER OVERVIEW QUESTIONS

1. In what ways did the growing economic and cultural unity of Latin Christendom promote the rise of powerful European national monarchies?

2. To what degree did the expansion of Latin Christendom remake eastern Europe in the image of western Europe?

3. In what ways did the Mongol conquests foster cultural and economic exchange across Eurasia?

4. How and why did the Mongol rulers of China, Iran, and Russia differ in their relationships with the settled societies they ruled?

SECTION FOCUS QUESTIONS

1. In what ways did the Roman popes seek to expand their powers during the age of the Crusades?

2. How did the efforts to establish Christianity in Spain and eastern Europe compare with the Crusaders' quest to recover Jerusalem?

3. How did the organization of Mongol society and government change from the time of Chinggis Khan to that of his grandson Qubilai, the ruler of China?

4. In what respects did the Turkish Islamic states of the Mamluks and Ottomans pursue policies similar to those of the Mongol regimes in Iran and Russia?

5. In what ways did the self-image and mission of the Christian military orders resemble or differ from those of the papal and royal leaders of the Crusades?

MAKING CONNECTIONS

1. How did the relationship between the Roman popes and the Christian monarchs of western Europe change from the reign of Charlemagne (see Chapter 9) to the papacy of Innocent III?

2. In what ways did the Crusades contribute to the definition of Europe as the realm of Latin Christendom?

3. To what extent were the policies of the Mongols similar to those of earlier Central Asian nomad empires such as the Khazars and the Turks (see Chapter 10)?

15

AT A CROSSROADS ▶

The fall of Constantinople to the Ottoman Turks in 1453 marked the end of the Byzantine Empire and heralded the coming age of gunpowder weapons. The Ottoman forces under Sultan Mehmed II breached the massive walls of Constantinople using massive cannons known as *bombards*. The Turkish cannons appear in the center of this book illustration of the siege of Constantinople, published in France in 1455. (The Art Archive/Bibliothèque Nationale Paris.)

Collapse and Revival in Afro-Eurasia

1300–1450

In August 1452, as the armies of the Ottoman sultan Mehmed II encircled Constantinople, the Byzantine emperor Constantine XI received a visit from a fellow Christian, a Hungarian engineer named Urban. Urban had applied metallurgical skills acquired at Hungary's rich iron and copper mines to the manufacture of large cannons known as *bombards*. He came to the Byzantine capital to offer his services to repel the Ottoman assault. But although Urban was a Christian, he was a businessman, too. When Constantine could not meet his price, Urban quickly left for the sultan's camp. Facing the famed triple walls of Constantinople, Mehmed promised to quadruple the salary Urban requested and to provide any materials and manpower the engineer needed.

Seven months later, in April 1453, Ottoman soldiers moved Urban's huge bronze bombards—with barrels twenty-six feet long, capable of throwing eight-hundred-pound shot—into place beneath the walls of Constantinople. Although these cumbersome cannons could fire only seven rounds a day, they battered the walls of Constantinople, which had long been considered impenetrable. After six weeks of siege the Turks breached the walls and swarmed into the city. The vastly outnumbered defenders, Emperor Constantine among them, fought to the death.

Urban's willingness to put business before religious loyalty helped tip the balance of power in the Mediterranean. During the siege, the Genoese merchant community at Constantinople—along with their archrivals, the Venetians—maintained strict neutrality. Although the Italian merchants, like Urban, were prepared to do business with Mehmed II, within a decade the Venetians and Ottomans were at war. Venice could not produce

Fourteenth-Century Crisis and Renewal in Eurasia

FOCUS How did the Black Death affect society, the economy, and culture in Latin Christendom and the Islamic world?

Islam's New Frontiers

FOCUS Why did Islam expand dramatically in the fourteenth and fifteenth centuries, and how did new Islamic societies differ from established ones?

The Global Bazaar

FOCUS How did the pattern of international trade change during the fourteenth and fifteenth centuries, and how did these changes affect consumption and fashion tastes?

COUNTERPOINT
Age of the Samurai in Japan, 1185–1450

FOCUS How and why did the historical development of Japan in the fourteenth and fifteenth centuries differ from that of mainland Eurasia?

BACKSTORY

In the fourteenth century, a number of developments threatened the connections among the societies of the Afro-Eurasian world. The collapse of the Mongol empires in China and Iran in the mid-1300s disrupted caravan traffic across Central Asia, diverting the flow of trade and travel to maritime routes across the Indian Ocean. Although the two centuries of religious wars known as the Crusades ended in 1291, they had hardened hostility between Christians and Muslims. As the power of the Christian Byzantine Empire contracted, Muslim Turkish sultanates—the Mamluk regime in Egypt and the rising Ottoman dynasty in Anatolia (modern Turkey)—gained control of the eastern Mediterranean region. Yet the Crusades and direct contact with the Mongols had also whetted European appetites for luxury and exotic goods from the Islamic world and Asia. Thus, despite challenges and obstacles, the Mediterranean remained a lively crossroads of commerce and cross-cultural exchange.

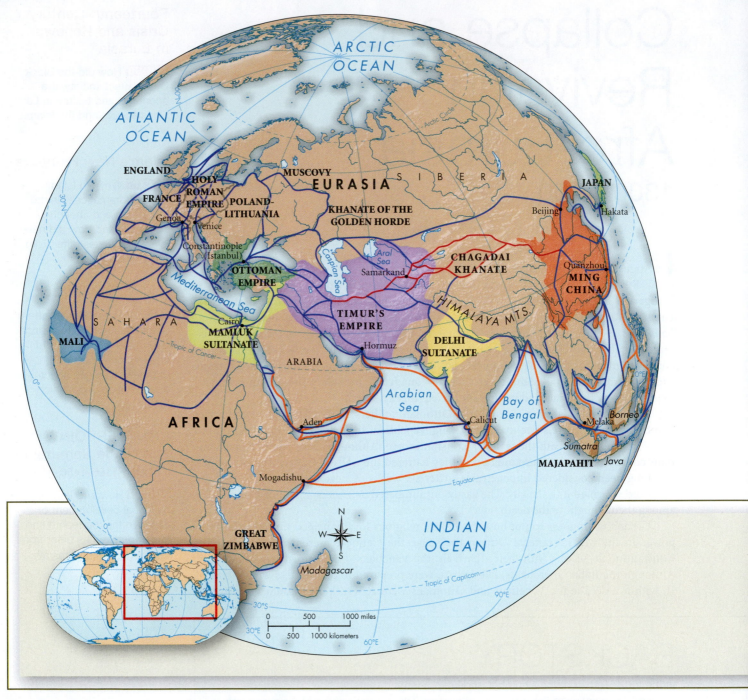

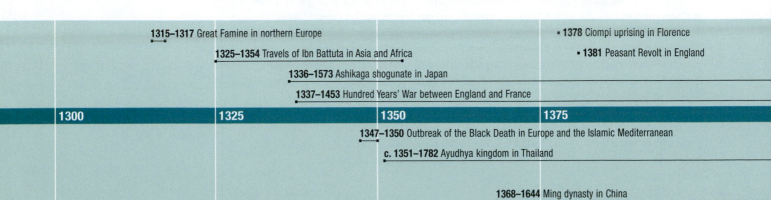

enough cannons to match the heavily armed Ottoman army and navy, which expelled the Venetians from the Black Sea in 1475. Although Venetian merchants still flocked to Constantinople, which Mehmed renamed Istanbul, to obtain spices, silks, and other Asian goods, the Ottomans held the upper hand and could dictate the terms of trade.

The fall of Constantinople to the Ottomans marks a turning point in world history. After perpetuating ancient Rome's heritage and glory for a thousand years, the Byzantine Empire came to an end. Islam continued to advance; in the fourteenth and fifteenth centuries, it expanded most dramatically in Africa and Asia. Italian merchants and bankers lost their dominance in the eastern Mediterranean and turned westward toward the Atlantic Ocean in search of new commercial opportunities. And this shift in commercial power and focus was not the only profound change that followed the Ottoman capture of Constantinople. The bombards cast by the Hungarian engineer for the Ottoman sultan heralded a military revolution that would decisively alter the balance of power among states and transform the nature of the state itself.

The new global patterns that emerged after Constantinople changed hands had their roots in calamities of the fourteenth century. The Ottoman triumph came just as Europe was beginning to recover from the previous century's catastrophic outbreak of plague known as the Black Death. The demographic and psychological shocks of epidemic disease had severely tested Europe's political and economic institutions—indeed, even its Christian faith.

The Black Death also devastated the Islamic world. Economic depression struck hard in Egypt, Syria, and Mesopotamia, the heartland of Islam. However, Europe's economy recovered more quickly. One consequence of the plague was the slow demise of serfdom, which contributed to the growing political and economic power of European monarchs and the urban merchant classes. By 1500 European merchants, bankers, and artisans had surpassed their Muslim counterparts in innovation and efficiency.

In Asia, the fourteenth century witnessed the rise and fall of the last Mongol empire, that of Timur (also known as Tamerlane). The end of the Mongol era marked the passing of nomadic rule, the resurgence of agrarian bureaucratic states such as Ming China and

MAPPING THE WORLD
Afro-Eurasia in the Early Fifteenth Century

After the Mongol Empire disintegrated, trans-Eurasian trade shifted from the overland Silk Road to the maritime routes stretching from China to the Mediterranean. Muslim merchants crossed the Sahara Desert and the Indian Ocean in pursuit of African gold, Chinese porcelain, and Asian spices. Although Chinese fleets led by Admiral Zheng He journeyed as far as the coasts of Arabia and Africa, the Ming rulers prohibited private overseas trade.

ROUTES ▼

— Major trade route
— Silk Road
— Voyages of Zheng He

1392–1910 Yi dynasty in Korea

▪ **1405** Death of Timur; breakup of his empire into regional states in Iran and Central Asia

▪ **1453** Ottoman conquest of Constantinople marks fall of the Byzantine Empire

1400   **1425**   **1450**

1405–1433 Chinese admiral Zheng He's expeditions in Southeast Asia and the Indian Ocean

▪ **1421** Relocation of Ming capital from Nanjing to Beijing

1428–1788 Le dynasty in Vietnam

the Ottoman Empire, and the shift of trade from the overland Silk Road to maritime routes across the Indian Ocean. Commerce attained unprecedented importance in many Asian societies. The flow of goods across Eurasia and Africa created new concentrations of wealth, fostered new patterns of consumption, and reshaped culture. The European Renaissance, for example, although primarily understood as a rebirth of the classical culture of Greece and Rome, also drew inspiration from the wealth of goods that poured into Italy from the Islamic world and Asia. By contrast, Japan remained isolated from this global bazaar, and this isolation contributed to the birth of Japan's distinctive national culture. For most Afro-Eurasian societies, however, the maritime world increasingly became the principal crossroads of economic and cultural exchange.

OVERVIEW
QUESTIONS

The major global development in this chapter: Crisis and recovery in fourteenth- and fifteenth-century Afro-Eurasia.

As you read, consider:

1. In the century after the devastating outbreak of plague known as the Black Death, how and why did Europe's economic growth begin to surpass that of the Islamic world?

2. Did the economic revival across Eurasia after 1350 benefit the peasant populations of Europe, the Islamic world, and East Asia?

3. How did the process of conversion to Islam differ in Iran, the Ottoman Empire, West Africa, and Southeast Asia during this period?

4. What political and economic changes contributed to the rise of maritime commerce in Asia during the fourteenth and fifteenth centuries?

Fourteenth-Century Crisis and Renewal in Eurasia

FOCUS

How did the Black Death affect society, the economy, and culture in Latin Christendom and the Islamic world?

No event in the fourteenth century had such profound consequences as the **Black Death** of 1347–1350. The unprecedented loss of life that resulted from this **pandemic** abruptly halted the economic expansion that had spread throughout Europe and the Islamic heartland in the preceding three centuries. Although the population losses were as great in the Islamic world as in Latin Christendom, the effects on society, the economy, and ideas diverged in important ways.

Largely spared the ravages of the Black Death, following the collapse of the Mongol empires in the fourteenth century Asian societies and economies faced different challenges. Expanding maritime trade and the spread of gunpowder weapons gave settled empires a decisive edge over nomadic societies, an edge that they never again relinquished. The founder of the Ming dynasty (1368–1644) in China rejected the Mongol model of "universal empire" and strove to restore a purely Chinese culture and social order. The prestige, stability, and ruling ideology of the Ming state powerfully influenced neighbors such as Korea and Vietnam—but had far less effect on Japan.

Black Death The catastrophic outbreak of plague that spread from the Black Sea to Europe, the Middle East, and North Africa in 1347–1350, killing a third or more of the population in afflicted areas.

pandemic An outbreak of epidemic disease that spreads across an entire region.

The "Great Mortality": The Black Death of 1347–1350

On the eve of the Black Death, Europe's agrarian economy already was struggling under the strain of climatic change. Around 1300 the earth experienced a shift in climate. The warm temperatures that had prevailed over most of the globe for the previous thousand years gave way to a **Little Ice Age** of colder temperatures and shorter growing seasons; it would last for much of the fourteenth century. The expansion of agriculture that had occurred in the Northern Hemisphere during the preceding three centuries came to a halt. The Great Famine of 1315–1317, when severe winters and overly wet summers brought on successive years of crop failure, killed 10 percent of the population in northern Europe and the British Isles. Unlike famine, though, the Black Death pandemic struck the ruling classes as hard as the poor. Scholars estimate that the Black Death and subsequent recurrences of the pandemic killed approximately one-third of the population of Europe.

Although the catastrophic mortality (death rates) of the Black Death is beyond dispute, the causes of the pandemic remain mysterious. The Florentine poet Giovanni Boccaccio (1313–1375), an eyewitness to the "great mortality," described the appearance of apple-sized swellings, first in the groin and armpits, after which these "death-bearing plague boils" spread to "every part of the body, wherefrom the fashion of the contagion began to change into black or livid blotches . . . in some places large and sparse, and in others small and thick-sown." The spread of these swellings, Boccaccio warned, was "a very certain token of coming death."[1]

Causes and Spread of the Black Death

The prominence of these glandular swellings, or buboes, in eyewitness accounts has led modern scholars to attribute the Black Death to bubonic plague, which is transmitted by fleas to rats and by rats to humans. Yet the scale of mortality during the Black Death far exceeds levels expected in plague outbreaks. Moreover, in Egypt the Black Death struck in winter, when bubonic plague is usually dormant, and the chief symptom was spitting blood rather than developing buboes, suggesting an airborne form of the plague. The pandemic killed as many livestock, especially cattle, as it did humans. Although it is difficult to identify the Black Death with any single modern disease, there is no doubt that the populations of western Eurasia had no previous experience of the disease, and hence no immunity to it. Outbreaks of plague continued to recur every decade or two for the next century, and intermittently thereafter.

Boccaccio and other eyewitnesses claimed that the Black Death had originated in Central Asia and traveled along overland trade routes to the Black Sea. The first outbreak among Europeans occurred in 1347 at the Genoese port of Caffa, on the Crimean peninsula. At that time Caffa was under siege by Mongols of the Golden Horde. Legend relates that the Mongols used catapults to lob corpses of plague victims over the city walls. Whether or not the Mongols really used this innovative type of germ warfare, the Genoese fled, only to spread the plague to the seaports they visited throughout the Mediterranean. By the summer of 1350 the Black Death had devastated nearly all of Europe (see Map 15.1).

The historian William McNeill has suggested that the Black Death was a byproduct of the Mongol conquests. He hypothesized that Mongol horsemen carried the plague bacillus from the remote highland forests of Southeast Asia into Central Asia, and then west to the Black Sea and east to China. The impact of the plague on China remains uncertain, however. The Mongol dynasty of Kubilai (Qubilai) (KOO-bih-lie) Khan already was losing its hold on China in the 1330s, and by the late 1340s China was afflicted by widespread famine, banditry, and civil war. By the time the Ming dynasty took control in 1368, China's population had fallen substantially. Yet Chinese sources make no mention of the specific symptoms of the Black Death, and there is no evidence of pandemic in the densely populated areas of South and Southeast Asia.

Demographic Consequences

The demographic collapse resulting from the Black Death was concentrated in Europe and the Islamic lands ringing the Mediterranean. In these regions population growth halted for over a century. England's population did not return to pre-plague levels for four hundred years.

Little Ice Age Name applied by environmental historians to periods of prolonged cool weather in the temperate zones of the earth.

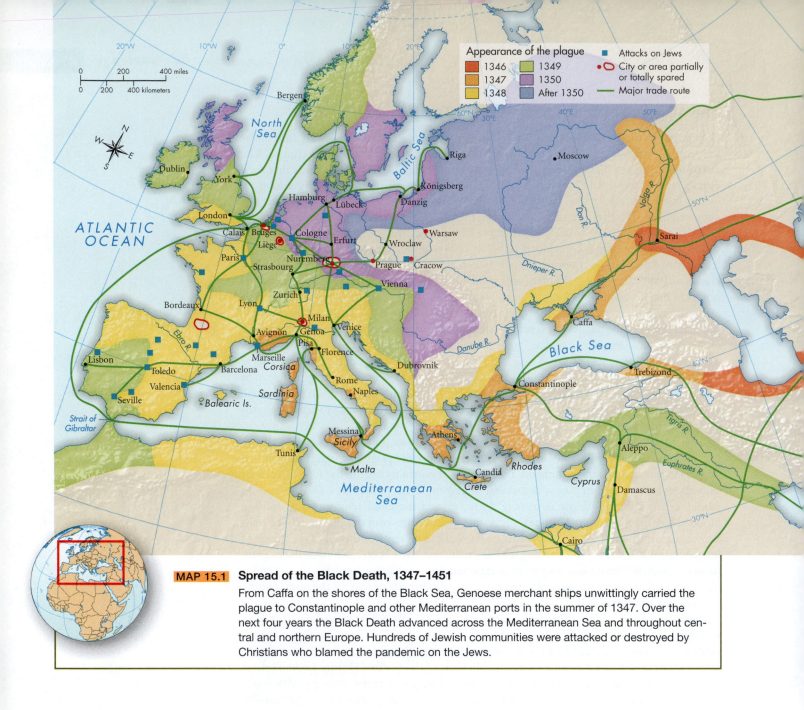

MAP 15.1 **Spread of the Black Death, 1347–1451**

From Caffa on the shores of the Black Sea, Genoese merchant ships unwittingly carried the plague to Constantinople and other Mediterranean ports in the summer of 1347. Over the next four years the Black Death advanced across the Mediterranean Sea and throughout central and northern Europe. Hundreds of Jewish communities were attacked or destroyed by Christians who blamed the pandemic on the Jews.

Population losses from the Black Death were equally devastating in the Islamic parts of the Mediterranean. Italian ships brought the plague to Alexandria in the autumn of 1347. The Egyptian historian al-Maqrizi (al-mak-REE-zee) recorded that twenty thousand people died each day in Cairo, then the most populous city in the world. Although this estimate surely is exaggerated, the plague probably did cause more than one hundred thousand deaths in Cairo alone. In the Islamic world, as in Europe, the loss of human lives and livestock seriously disrupted agriculture. While rural inhabitants flocked to the towns in search of food and work, urban residents sought refuge in the countryside from the contagion that festered in crowded cities.

Decline of the Mamluk Sultanate

The devastation of the plague dealt a serious blow to the agricultural economy of the Mamluk (MAM-luke) Sultanate, which ruled over Egypt and Syria. The scarcity of labor following the pandemic prompted a return to pastoral nomadism in many rural areas, and the urban working classes who survived benefited from rising wages. "The wages of skilled artisans, wage workers, porters, servants, stablemen, weavers, masons, construction workers, and the like have increased manyfold," wrote al-Maqrizi, who served as Cairo's market inspector from 1399 to 1405. But, he added, "of this class only a few remain, since most have died."[2]

The Mamluk Sultanate depended on agricultural wealth for its support, so population losses and declining agricultural production following the Black Death undermined the Mamluk government. A struggle for power broke out among rival factions. Bureaucratic mismanagement compounded the economic distress. Faced with decreasing revenues, the sultanate tried to squeeze more taxes from urban commerce and industry. But the creation of state monopolies in the spice trade and the sugar industry throttled private enterprise and undermined the commercial vitality of Cairo and Damascus. The impoverishment of the urban artisan and merchant classes further weakened the Mamluk regime, leading to its ultimate downfall at the hands of Ottoman conquerors in 1517. In the fall of the Mamluk Sultanate, we can see how the plague produced a chain of interconnected consequences. Population decline led to agricultural decline, which in turn produced economic problems, undermined political authority, and created the conditions for significant social, political, and military upheaval.

Although the horrific mortality caused by the Black Death afflicted Latin Christendom and the Islamic world in equal measure, their responses to the epidemic diverged in significant ways. Christians interpreted the plague as divine punishment for humanity's sins (see Reading the Past: A French Theologian's View of the Black Death). Acts of piety and atonement proliferated, most strikingly in the form of processions of flagellants (from *flagella*, a whip used by worshipers as a form of penance), whose self-mutilation was meant to imitate the sufferings of Christ. In many places Christians blamed vulnerable minorities—such as beggars, lepers, and especially Jews—for corrupting Christian society. Although the Roman Church, kings, and local leaders condemned attacks against Jews, their appeals often went unheeded. For example, the citizens of Strasbourg threw the municipal council out of office for trying to protect the city's Jewish population and then burned nine hundred Jews on the grounds of the Jewish cemetery. The macabre images of death and the corruption of the flesh in European painting and sculpture in the late fourteenth and fifteenth centuries vividly convey the anguish caused by the Black Death.

Christian Responses to the Black Death

Dance of Death

The scourge of the Black Death pandemic dramatically influenced attitudes toward death in Latin Christendom. Literary and artistic works such as this woodcut of skeletons dancing on an open grave vividly portrayed the fragility of life and the dangers of untimely death. For those unprepared to face divine judgment, the ravages of disease and death were only a prelude to the everlasting torments of hell. (akg-images/ Imagno.)

A French Theologian's View of the Black Death

This account of the Black Death comes from Jean de Venette (d. c. 1368), a monk and master of theology at the University of Paris who compiled, probably in the late 1350s, a chronicle of his own lifetime.

Some said that this pestilence was caused by infection of the air and waters. . . . As a result of this theory. . . . the Jews were suddenly and violently charged with infecting wells and water and corrupting the air. . . . In Germany and other parts of the world where Jews lived, they were massacred and slaughtered by Christians, and many thousands were burned everywhere, indiscriminately. . . . But in truth, such poisonings, granted that they actually were perpetrated, could not have caused so great a plague nor have infected so many people. There were other causes; for example, the will of God and the corrupt humors and evil inherent in air and earth. . . .

After the cessation of the epidemic, or plague, the men and women who survived married each other. There was . . . fertility beyond the ordinary. Pregnant women were seen on every side. . . . But woe is me! The world was not changed for the better but for the worse by this renewal of the population. For men were more avaricious and grasping than before, even though they had far greater possessions. They were more covetous and disturbed each other more frequently with suits, brawls, disputes, and pleas. Nor by the mortality

resulting from this terrible plague inflicted by God was peace between kings and lords established. On the contrary, the enemies of the king of France and of the Church were stronger and wickeder than before and stirred up wars on sea and on land. Greater evils than before pullulated everywhere in the world. And this factor was very remarkable. Although there was an abundance of all goods, yet everything was twice as dear, whether it were utensils, victuals, or merchandise, hired helpers or peasants and serfs, except for some hereditary domains which remained abundantly stocked with everything. Charity began to cool, and iniquity with ignorance and sin to abound, for few could be found in the good towns and castles who knew how or were willing to instruct children in the rudiments of grammar.

Source: Richard A. Newhall, ed., The Chronicle of Jean de Venette (New York: Columbia University Press, 1953), 50–51.

EXAMINING THE EVIDENCE

1. How did Venette's interpretation of the causes of the epidemic differ from those of his European contemporaries?

2. In Venette's view, what were the social and moral consequences of the Black Death?

Muslim Responses to the Black Death

Muslims did not share the Christian belief in "original sin," which deemed human beings inherently sinful, and so they did not see the plague as a divine punishment. Instead, they accepted it as an expression of God's will, and even a blessing for the faithful. The Muslim cleric Ibn al-Wardi (IB-unh al-wahr-dee), who succumbed to the disease in 1349, wrote that "this plague is for Muslims a martyrdom and a reward, and for the disbelievers a punishment and rebuke."[3] Most Muslim scholars and physicians rejected the theory that the pandemic was spread through contagion, counseling against abandoning stricken family members. The flagellants' focus on atonement for sin and the scapegoating of Jews seen in Christian Europe were wholly absent in the Islamic world.

Rebuilding Societies in Western Europe 1350–1492

Just as existing religious beliefs and practices shaped Muslim and Christian responses to the plague, underlying conditions influenced political and economic recovery in the two regions. Latin Christendom recovered more quickly than Islamic lands. In Europe, the death toll caused an acute labor shortage. Desperate to find tenants to cultivate their lands, the nobility had to offer generous concessions, such as release from labor services, that liberated the peasantry from the conditions of serfdom. The incomes of the nobility and the Church declined by half or more, and many castles and monasteries fell into ruin. The shortage of labor enabled both urban artisans and rural laborers to bargain for wage increases. Rising wages improved living standards for ordinary people, who began to consume more meat, cheese, and beer. At the same time, a smaller population reduced the demand for grain and manufactured goods such as woolen cloth. Many nobles, unable to find tenants, converted their agricultural land into pasture. Hundreds of villages were abandoned. In much of central Europe, cultivated land reverted back to forest. Thus, the plague redrew the economic map of Europe, shifting the economic balance of power.

Economic change brought with it economic conflict, and tensions between rich and poor triggered insurrections by rural peasants and the urban lower classes throughout western Europe. In the Italian city-states, the working classes of Florence, led by unemployed wool workers, revolted against the patricians (the wealthy families who controlled the city's government) in 1378. Their demand for a greater share of wealth and political rights alarmed the city's artisan guilds, which allied with the patricians to suppress what became known as the Ciompi revolt ("uprising by the little people"). While the revolt failed, it clearly demonstrated the awareness of Florence's working classes that the plague had undermined the status quo, creating an opportunity for economic and political change.

The efforts of elites to respond to the new economic environment could also lead to conflict. In England, King Richard II's attempt to shift the basis of taxation from landed wealth to a head tax on each subject incited the Peasant Revolt of 1381. Led by a radical preacher named John Ball, the rebels presented a petition to the king that went beyond repeal of the head tax to demand freedom from the tyranny of noble lords and the Christian Church:

> Henceforward, that no lord should have lordship but that there should be proportion between all people, saving only the lordship of the king; that the goods of the holy church ought not to be in the hands of men of religion, or parsons or vicars, or others of holy church, but these should have their sustenance easily and the rest of the goods be divided between the parishioners, . . . and that there should be no villeins [peasants subject to a lord's justice] in England or any serfdom or villeinage, but all are to be free and of one condition.[4]

In the end the English nobles mustered militias to suppress the uprising. This success could not, however, reverse the developments that had produced the uprising in the first place. High wages, falling rents, and the flight of tenants brought many estates to the brink of bankruptcy. Declining aristocratic families intermarried with successful entrepreneurs, who coveted the privileges of the titled nobility and sought to emulate their lifestyle. A new social order began to form, one based on private property and entrepreneurship rather than nobility and serfdom, but equally extreme in its imbalance of wealth and poverty.

Perhaps nowhere in Europe was this new social order more apparent than in Italy. In the Italian city-states, the widening gap between rich and poor was reflected in their governments, which increasingly benefited the wealthy. Over the course of the fifteenth century, the ideals and institutions of republican (representative) government on which the Italian city-states were founded steadily lost ground. A military despot wrested control of Milan in 1450. Venice's **oligarchy**—rule by an exclusive elite—strengthened its grip over the city's government and commerce. In Florence, beset by constant civil strife after the Ciompi uprising, the Medici family of bankers dominated the city's political affairs. Everywhere, financial power was increasingly aligned with political power.

In the wake of the Black Death, kings and princes suffered a drop in revenues as agricultural production fell. Yet in the long run, royal power grew at the expense of the nobility and the Church. In England and France, royal governments gained new sources of income and established bureaucracies of tax collectors and administrators to manage them. The rulers of these states transformed their growing financial power into military and political strength by raising standing armies of professional soldiers and investing in new military technology. The French monarchy, for instance, capitalized on rapid innovations in gunpowder weapons

Social Unrest and Rebellion

Rise of National States

oligarchy Rule by a small group of individuals or families.

to create a formidable army and to establish itself as the supreme power in continental Europe. Originally developed by the Mongols, these weapons had been introduced to Europe via the Islamic world by the middle of the fourteenth century.

Hundred Years' War

The progress of the Hundred Years' War (1337–1453) between England and France reflected the changing political landscape. On the eve of the Black Death pandemic, the war broke out over claims to territories in southwestern France and a dispute over succession to the French throne. In the early years of the conflict, the English side prevailed, thanks to the skill of its bowmen against mounted French knights. As the war dragged on, the English kings increasingly relied on mercenary armies, paid in plunder from the towns and castles they seized. By 1400, combat between knights conducted according to elaborate rules of chivalry had yielded to new forms of warfare. Cannons, siege weapons, and, later, firearms undermined both the nobility's preeminence in war and its sense of identity and purpose. An arms race between France and its rivals led to rapid improvements in weaponry, especially the development of lighter and more mobile cannons. Ultimately the French defeated the English, but the war transformed both sides. The length of the conflict, the propaganda from both sides, and the unified effort needed to prosecute the increasingly costly war all contributed to the evolution of royal governments and the emergence of a sense of national identity.

Consolidating State Power

To strengthen their control, the monarchs of states such as France, England, and Spain relied on new forms of direct taxation, as well as financing from bankers. The French monarchy levied new taxes on salt, land, and commercial transactions, wresting income from local lords and town governments. The kings of England and France promoted domestic industries such as textiles and metallurgy to enhance their national power. The marriage of Isabella of Castile and Ferdinand of Aragon in 1469 created a unified monarchy in Spain. This expansion of royal power in Spain depended heavily on loans from Genoese bankers, who also financed the maritime ventures of the Portuguese and Spanish monarchs into the Atlantic Ocean. Thus, in all three of these states, new economic conditions contributed to the growth of monarchical power (see Map 15.2).

Ultimately, consolidation of monarchical power in western Europe would create new global connections. In their efforts to consolidate power, Ferdinand and Isabella, like so many rulers in world history, demanded religious conformity. In 1492 they conquered Granada, the last Muslim foothold in Spain, and ordered all Jews and Muslims to convert to Christianity or face banishment. With the *Reconquista* (Spanish for "reconquest") of Spain complete, Ferdinand and Isabella turned their crusading energies toward exploration. That same year, they sponsored the first of Christopher Columbus's momentous transatlantic voyages in pursuit of the fabled riches of China.

Wheeled Cannon

The Hundred Years' War between England and France touched off an arms race that spurred major advances in the technology of warfare. Initially, gunsmiths concentrated on making massive siege cannons capable of firing shot weighing hundreds of pounds. By 1500, however, military commanders favored more mobile weapons, such as this wheeled cannon manufactured for the Holy Roman Emperor Maximilian I. (Erich Lessing/Art Resource.)

MAP 15.2

Europe and the Greater Mediterranean, 1453

The century following the Black Death witnessed the growth of royal power and territorial consolidation across Europe, most notably in England and France. But central Europe and Italy remained politically fragmented. The Ottoman conquest of Constantinople in 1453 extinguished the Byzantine Empire and sharpened the conflict between Christendom and the Islamic world in southeastern Europe.

Ming China and the New Order in East Asia 1368–1500

State building in East Asia, too, fostered the development of national states. The Yuan dynasty established in China by the Mongol khan Kubilai had foundered after his death in 1294. Kubilai's successors wrung as much tribute as they could from the Chinese population, but they neglected the infrastructure of roads, canals, and irrigation and flood-control dikes that the Chinese economy depended on. By the time the Mongol court at Dadu (modern Beijing) began to enlist the services of the Confucian-educated elite in the late 1330s, economic distress and social unrest already had taken a heavy toll. When peasant insurrections and civil wars broke out in the 1350s, the Mongol leaders abandoned China and retreated to their steppe homeland. After a protracted period of war and devastation, a Chinese general of peasant origin restored native rule, founding the Ming dynasty in 1368 (see Map 15.3).

MAP 15.3

The Ming Empire, 1449

After expelling the Mongols, the rulers of the Ming dynasty rebuilt the Great Wall to defend China from nomad invasions. Emperor Yongle moved the Ming capital from Nanjing to Beijing and launched expeditions commanded by his trusted aide Zheng He that voyaged throughout Southeast Asia and the Indian Ocean.

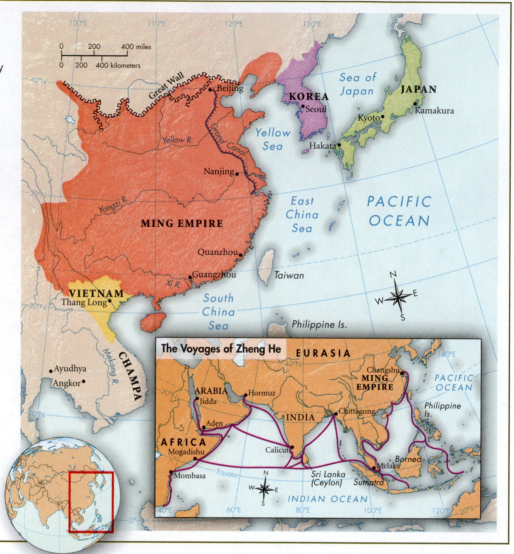

Ming Autocracy

The Ming founder, Zhu Yuanzhang (JOO yuwen-JAHNG) (r. 1368–1398)—better known by his imperial title, Hongwu (hoong-woo)—resurrected the basic Chinese institutions of civil government. But throughout his life Hongwu viewed the scholar-official class with suspicion. Born a peasant, Hongwu saw himself as a populist crusading against the snobbery and luxurious lifestyle of the rich and powerful. Once in command, he repeatedly purged high officials and exercised despotic control over his government. Hongwu reinstituted the civil service examinations system to select government officials, but he used the examinations and the state-run school system as tools of political indoctrination, establishing the teachings of twelfth-century Neo-Confucian philosopher Zhu Xi (JOO shee) as the standard for the civil service exams. Zhu shared the Neo-Confucian antipathy toward Buddhism as a foreign religion and sought to reassert the Confucian commitment to moral perfection and the betterment of society. **Neo-Confucianism** advocated a strict moral code and a patriarchal social hierarchy, and the Ming government supported it with the full force of imperial law. Thus, Hongwu drew on tradition and a belief in China's cultural superiority as he created a new state.

This strong sense of Chinese superiority can be seen in many of Hongwu's policies. Determined to eradicate any taint of Mongol customs, Hongwu rejected the Mongol model of a multiethnic empire and turned his back on the world of the steppe nomads. He located his

Neo-Confucianism The reformulation of Confucian doctrines to reassert a commitment to moral perfection and the betterment of society; dominated Chinese intellectual life and social thought from the twelfth to the twentieth centuries.

capital at Nanjing, on the south bank of the Yangzi River, far from the Mongol frontier. Foreign embassies were welcome at the Ming court, which offered trading privileges in return for tribute and allegiance to the Chinese emperor. But Hongwu distrusted merchants as much as he did intellectuals. In 1371 he forbade Chinese merchants from engaging in overseas commerce and placed foreign traders under close government scrutiny.

Hongwu's son, the Emperor Yongle (r. 1402–1424), reversed his father's efforts to sever China from the outside world. Instead, Yongle embraced the Mongol vision of world empire and rebuilt the former Mongol capital of Dadu, creating the modern city of Beijing. Throughout his reign Yongle campaigned to subdue the Mongol tribes along the northern frontier, but with little success. He also wanted to expand southward. In 1405 he launched a series of naval expeditions under Admiral Zheng He (JUNG-huh) that, as we will see, projected Chinese power deep into the Indian Ocean, and in 1407 he invaded and conquered Vietnam (see again Map 15.3). Nonetheless, Yongle's reign did not represent a complete break with that of Hongwu. Like his father, Yongle was an autocrat who promoted Neo-Confucian policies, even as he sought to reestablish some of the global connections Hongwu had tried to sever.

The impact of Hongwu's policies went far beyond the realms of court politics and international diplomacy. He envisioned his empire as a universe of self-sufficient and self-governing villages, where men worked in the fields and women remained at home. The Neo-Confucian ideology of Hongwu emphasized the patriarchal authority of the lineage, and his policies deprived women of many rights, including a share in inheritance. It outlawed the remarriage of widows. By the fourteenth century, many elite families practiced foot binding, which probably originated among courtesans and entertainers. From around age six the feet of young girls were tightly bound with bandages, deforming the bones and crippling them. The feet of adult women ideally were no more than three to four inches long; they were considered a mark of feminine beauty and a symbol of freedom from labor. Foot binding accompanied seclusion in the home as a sign of respectable womanhood.

Despite the strictures of patriarchal society, in the households of nonelite groups, women played an essential economic role. Women worked alongside men in rice cultivation and performed most tasks involved in textile manufacture. As national and international markets for Chinese silk expanded beginning in the twelfth century, male artisans in urban workshops took over skilled occupations such as silk weaving. But the spread of cotton, introduced from India in the thirteenth century, gave peasant women new economic opportunities. Most cotton was grown, ginned (removing the seeds), spun into yarn, and woven into cloth within a single household, principally by women. Confucian moralists esteemed spinning, weaving, and embroidery as "womanly work" that would promote industriousness and thrift; they became dismayed, however, when women displayed entrepreneurial skill in marketing their wares. Nevertheless, women did engage in commercial activities, suggesting that there were limits to the moralists' control of women's lives.

The Ming dynasty abandoned its designs for conquest and expansion after the death of Yongle in 1424. Yet the prestige, power, and philosophy of the Ming state continued to influence its neighbors, with the significant exception of Japan (see Counterpoint: Age of the Samurai in Japan, 1185–1450). Vietnam regained its independence from China in 1427, but under the long-lived Le dynasty (1428–1788), Vietnam retained Chinese-style bureaucratic government. The Le rulers oversaw the growth of an official class schooled in Neo-Confucianism and committed to forcing its cultural norms, kinship practices, and hostility to Buddhism on Vietnamese society as a whole. In Korea, the rulers of the new Yi dynasty (1392–1910) also embraced Neo-Confucian ideals of government. Under Yi rule the Confucian-educated elite acquired hereditary status with exclusive rights to political office. In both Vietnam and Korea, aristocratic rule and Buddhism's dominance over daily life yielded to a "Neo-Confucian revolution" modeled after Chinese political institutions and values.

Ming Patriarchal Society

Neo-Confucianism in Vietnam and Korea

Islam's New Frontiers

FOCUS

Why did Islam expand dramatically in the fourteenth and fifteenth centuries, and how did new Islamic societies differ from established ones?

In the fourteenth and fifteenth centuries, Islam continued to spread to new areas, including central and maritime Asia, sub-Saharan Africa, and southeastern Europe. In the past, Muslim rule had often preceded the popular adoption of Islamic religion and culture. Yet the advance of Islam in Africa and Asia came about not through conquest, but through slow diffusion via merchants and missionaries. The universalism and egalitarianism of Islam appealed to rising merchant classes in both West Africa and maritime Asia.

During this period, Islam expanded by adapting to older ruling cultures rather than seeking to eradicate them. Timur, the last of the great nomad conquerors, and his descendants ruled not as Mongol khans but as Islamic sultans. The culture of the Central Asian states, however, remained an eclectic mix of Mongol, Turkish, and Persian traditions, in contrast to the strict adherence to Muslim law and doctrine practiced under the Arab regimes of the Middle East and North Africa. This pattern of cultural adaptation and assimilation was even more evident in West Africa and Southeast Asia.

Islamic Spiritual Ferment in Central Asia 1350–1500

The spread of Sufism in Central Asia between 1350 and 1500 played a significant role in the process of cultural assimilation. **Sufism**—a mystical tradition that stressed self-mastery, practical virtues, and spiritual growth through personal experience of the divine—had already emerged by 1200 as a major expression of Islamic values and social identity. Sufism appeared in many variations and readily assimilated local cultures to its beliefs and practices. Sufi mystics acquired institutional strength through the communal solidarity of their brotherhoods spread across the whole realm of Islam. In contrast to the orthodox scholars and teachers known as *ulama*, who made little effort to convert nonbelievers, Sufi preachers were inspired by missionary zeal and welcomed non-Muslims to their lodges and sermons. This made them ideal instruments for the spread of Islam to new territories.

Timur   One of Sufism's most important royal patrons was Timur (1336–1405), the last of the Mongol emperors. Born near the city of Samarkand (SAM-ar-kand) when the Mongol Ilkhanate in Iran was on the verge of collapse, Timur—himself a Turk—grew up among Mongols who practiced Islam. He rose to power in the 1370s by reuniting quarreling Mongol tribes in common pursuit of conquest. Although Timur lacked the dynastic pedigree enjoyed by Chinggis Khan's descendants, like Chinggis he held his empire together by the force of his personal charisma.

From the early 1380s, Timur's armies relentlessly pursued campaigns of conquest, sweeping westward across Iran into Mesopotamia and Russia and eastward into India. In 1400–1401 Timur seized and razed Aleppo and Damascus, the principal Mamluk cities in Syria. In 1402 he captured the Ottoman sultan in battle. Rather than trying to consolidate his rule in Syria and Anatolia (modern Turkey), however, Timur turned his attention eastward. He was preparing to march on China when he fell ill and died early in 1405. Although Timur's empire quickly fragmented, his triumphs would serve as an inspiration to later empire builders, such as the Mughals in India and the Manchus in China. Moreover, his support of Sufism would have a lasting impact, helping lay the foundation for a number of important Islamic religious movements in Central Asia.

The institutions of Timur's empire were largely modeled on the Ilkhan synthesis of Persian civil administration and Turkish-Mongol military organization. Like the Ilkhans and the Ottomans, Timur's policies favored settled farmers and urban populations over pastoral nomads, who were often displaced from their homelands. While Timur allowed local princes a degree of autonomy, he was determined to make Samarkand a grand imperial capital.

Sufism A tradition within Islam that emphasizes mystical knowledge and personal experience of the divine.

He forcibly relocated artists, craftsmen, scholars, and clerics from many regions and put them into service in Samarkand (see Reading the Past: A Spanish Ambassador's Description of Samarkand). The citadel and enormous bazaar built by Timur have long since perished, but surviving mosques, shrines, and tombs illuminate Timur's vision of Islamic kingship: all-powerful, urbane and cosmopolitan, and ostentatious in its display of public piety.

After Timur's death in 1405, his sons carved the empire into independent regional kingdoms. Like Timur, his successors sought to control religious life in royal capitals such as Herat and Samarkand by appointing elders (*shayks*) and judges (*qadis*) to administer justice, supervise schools and mosques, and police public morality. Yet Sufi brotherhoods and the veneration of Sufi saints exerted an especially strong influence over social life and religious practice in Central Asia. Timur had lavished special favor on Sufi teachers and had strategically placed the shrines of his family members next to the tombs of important Sufi leaders. The relics of Timur in Samarkand, along with the tombs of Sufi saints, attracted pilgrims from near and far.

Elsewhere in the Islamic world, a number of religious movements combined the veneration of Sufi saints and belief in miracles with unorthodox ideas derived from Shi'ism, the branch of Islam that maintains that only descendants of Muhammad's son-in-law Ali have a legitimate right to serve as caliph. Outside the major cities, Islamic leadership passed to Sufis and popular preachers. One of the most militant and influential of these radical Islamic sects was the Safavid (SAH-fah-vid) movement founded by a Sufi preacher, Safi al-Din (SAH-fee al-dean) (1252–1334). Like other visionary teachers, Safi preached the need for a purified Islam cleansed of worldly wealth, urban luxury, and moral laxity. His missionary movement struck a responsive chord among the pastoral Turk and Mongol tribes of Anatolia and Iran. The Safavids roused their followers to attack Christians in the Caucasus region, but they also challenged Muslim rulers such as the Ottomans and Timur's successors. At the end of the fifteenth century, a charismatic leader, Shah Isma'il (shah IS-mah-eel), combined Safavid religious fervor with Shi'a doctrines to found a **theocracy**—a state subject to religious authority. It would rule Iran for more than two centuries and shape modern Iran's distinctive Shi'a religious culture.

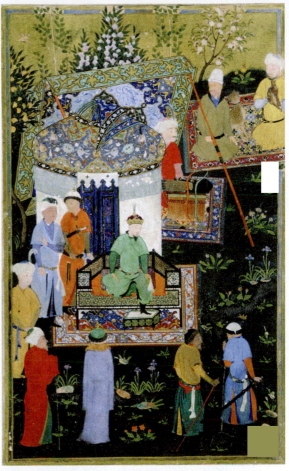

Timur Enthroned

We can glean some sense of Timur's self-image from the *Book of Victories*, a chronicle of Timur's campaigns commissioned by one of his descendants in the 1480s. This scene portrays the moment in 1370 when Timur declared himself successor to the Chagadai khans. (Rare Books and Manuscripts Department, The Sheridan Libraries, The Johns Hopkins University.)

Ottoman Expansion and the Fall of Constantinople   1354–1453

The spread of Islam in Central Asia would have profound consequences for the region. In the eyes of Europeans, however, the most significant—and alarming—advance was the Ottoman expansion into the Balkan territories of southeastern Europe. The Byzantine state was severely shaken by the Black Death, and in 1354 the Ottomans took advantage of this weakness to invade the Balkans. After a decisive victory in 1389, the Ottoman Empire annexed most of the Balkans except the region around Constantinople itself, reducing it to an isolated enclave.

The growing might of the Ottoman Empire stemmed from two military innovations: (1) the formation of the **janissary corps**, elite army units composed of slave soldiers, and (2) the use of massed musket fire and cannons, such as the bombards of Urban, the Hungarian engineer whom we met at the start of this chapter. In the late fourteenth century the Ottomans adopted the Mamluk practice of organizing slave armies that would be more reliably loyal to the sultan than the unruly *ghazi* ("holy warrior") bands that Osman

theocracy A state ruled by religious authorities.

janissary corps Slave soldiers who served as the principal armed forces of the Ottoman Empire beginning in the fifteenth century; also staffed much of the Ottoman state bureaucracy.

A Spanish Ambassador's Description of Samarkand

In September 1403, an embassy dispatched by King Henry III of Castile arrived at Samarkand in hopes of enlisting the support of Timur for a combined military campaign against the Ottomans. Seventy years old and in failing health, Timur lavishly entertained his visitors, but made no response to Henry's overtures. The leader of the Spanish delegation, Ruy Gonzalez de Clavijo, left Samarkand disappointed, but his report preserves our fullest account of Timur's capital in its heyday.

The city is rather larger than Seville, but lying outside Samarkand are great numbers of houses that form extensive suburbs. These lay spread on all hands, for indeed the township is surrounded by orchards and vineyards. . . . In between these orchards pass streets with open squares; these are all densely populated, and here all kinds of goods are on sale with breadstuffs and meat. . . .

Samarkand is rich not only in foodstuffs but also in manufactures, such as factories of silk. . . . Thus trade has always been fostered by Timur with the view of making his capital the noblest of cities; and during all his conquests . . . he carried off the best men to people Samarkand, bringing thither the master-craftsmen of all nations. Thus from Damascus he carried away with him all the weavers of that city, those who worked at the silk looms; further the bow-makers who produce those cross-bows which are so famous; likewise armorers; also the craftsmen in glass and porcelain, who are known to be the best in all the world. From Turkey he had brought their gunsmiths who make the arquebus. . . . So great therefore was the population now of all nationalities gathered together in Samarkand that of men with their families the number they said must amount to 150,000 souls . . . [including] Turks, Arabs, and Moors of diverse sects, with Greek, Armenian, Roman, Jacobite [Syrian], and Nestorian Christians, besides those folk who baptize with fire in the forehead [i.e., Hindus]. . . .

The markets of Samarkand further are amply stored with merchandise imported from distant and foreign countries. . . . The goods that are imported to Samarkand from Cathay indeed are of the richest and most precious of all those brought thither from foreign parts, for the craftsmen of Cathay are reputed to be the most skillful by far beyond those of any other nation.

Source: Ruy Gonzalez de Clavijo, *Embassy to Tamerlane, 1403–1406*, trans. Guy Le Strange (London: Routledge, 1928), 285–289.

EXAMINING THE EVIDENCE

1. What features of Timur's capital most impressed Gonzalez de Clavijo?

2. How does this account of Samarkand at its height compare with the chapter's description of Renaissance Florence?

(r. 1280–1324), the founder of the Ottoman state, had gathered as the core of his army. At first, prisoners and volunteers made up the janissary corps. Starting in 1395, however, the Ottomans imposed a form of conscription known as *devshirme* (dev-SHEER-may) on the Christian peoples of the Balkans to supplement Turkish recruits. Adolescent boys conscripted through the devshirme were taken from their families, raised as Muslims, and educated at palace schools for service in the sultan's civil administration as well as the army. The Mamluks purchased slaves from Central Asia, but the Ottomans obtained a cheaper and more abundant supply from within their empire. At the same time, they created a government and military wholly beholden to the sultan. Janissaries were forbidden to marry and forfeited their property to the sultan upon their death.

Practical concerns dictated Ottoman policies toward Christian communities. Where Christians were the majority of the population, the Ottomans could be quite tolerant. Apart from the notorious devshirme slave

Ottoman Expansion, c. 1200–1453

Ottoman territory
- By c. 1300
- By c. 1360
- By c. 1453
- Tributary state
- Major battle

WALLACHIA
Danube R.
Kosovo 1389
BALKANS
Black Sea
Constantinople (Istanbul) 1453
ANATOLIA

levy, the Ottoman impositions were less burdensome than the dues the Balkan peoples had owed the Byzantine emperor. The Ottomans allowed Balkan Christians freedom to practice their religion, and they protected the Greek Orthodox Church, which they considered indispensable to maintaining social order. In Anatolia and other places where Christians were a minority, however, the Ottomans took a much harder line, seeing such minorities as a potential threat to the Ottoman order. Muslim governors stripped Christian bishops of their authority, seized church properties and revenues, and curbed public worship. By 1500 Christian society in Anatolia had nearly vanished; most Christians had converted to Islam.

Like the Ming emperors of China, Ottoman rulers favored the creation of a stable peasant society that would serve as a reliable source of revenue. A married peasant with a plot of land that could be worked by two oxen became the basic unit of Ottoman society. The state controlled nearly all cultivated land, but peasant families enjoyed permanent rights to farm the land they occupied. The government sold the rights to collect land taxes (a practice known as tax farming) to merchants and other wealthy individuals, including non-Muslims such as Greeks and Jews. The practice of tax farming guaranteed revenues for the state, but it distanced Ottoman officials from their subjects.

Despite their own nomadic origins, the Ottomans regarded nomadic tribes, like religious minorities, as a threat to stability. Many nomads were forcibly deported and settled in the Balkans and western Anatolia, where they combined farming with stock raising. Due to heavy taxes imposed on animal herds, nomads had to earn additional income through transport, lumbering, and felt and carpet manufacture. The push toward such activities created by harsh Ottoman policies was matched by the pull of global trade connections. Strong demand from European customers and the imperial capital of Istanbul (the name Mehmed II gave to Constantinople) stimulated carpet weaving by both peasants and herders.

The patriarchal family, in which the wife is subject to her husband's control, was a pillar of Ottoman law, just as it was in Ming China. Although the Ottoman state barred women from owning cultivated land, it did not infringe on women's rights to a share of family inheritance, as prescribed in the Qur'an. Thus, although men usually controlled property in the form of land and houses, women acquired wealth in the form of money, furnishings, clothes, and jewelry. Women invested in commercial ventures, tax farming, and moneylending. Because women were secluded in the home and veiled in public—long-established requirements to maintain family honor and status in the central Islamic lands—women used servants and trusted clients to help them conduct their business activities.

The final defeat of the Byzantine Empire by Ottoman armies in 1453 shocked the Christian world. Mehmed II's capture of Constantinople also completed a radical transformation of the Ottoman enterprise. The Ottoman sultans no longer saw themselves as roving ghazi warriors, but as monarchs with absolute authority over a multinational empire at the crossroads of Europe and Asia: "ruler of the two seas and the two continents," as the inscription over Mehmed's palace gate proclaimed. A proudly Islamic regime, the Ottoman sultanate aspired to become the centerpiece of a broad cosmopolitan civilization spanning Europe, Asia, and Africa.

Commerce and Culture in Islamic West Africa

West African trading empires and the merchants they supported had long served as the vanguard of Islam in sub-Saharan Africa. The Mali Empire's adoption of Islam as its official religion in the late thirteenth century encouraged conversion to Islam throughout the West African savanna. Under Mali's protection, Muslim merchant clans expanded their activities throughout the towns of the savanna and the oasis trading posts of the Sahara. Islam continued to prosper despite the collapse of Mali's political dominion in the mid-fourteenth century.

Timbuktu Manuscript

Timbuktu became the hub of Islamic culture and intellectual life in the western Sahara. Scholars and students at Timbuktu assembled impressive libraries of Arabic texts, such as this twelfth-century Qur'an. Written mostly on paper imported from Europe, Timbuktu's manuscripts were preserved in family collections after the city's leading scholars were deported to North Africa by Moroccan invaders in 1591. (Candace Feit.)

Muslim Merchants and Scholars

The towns of Jenne and Timbuktu, founded along the Niger River by Muslim merchants in the thirteenth century, emerged as the new crossroads of trans-Saharan trade. Jenne benefited from its access to the gold mines and rain forest products of coastal West Africa. Timbuktu's commercial prosperity rose as trade grew between West Africa and Mamluk Egypt. Islamic intellectual culture thrived among the merchant families of Timbuktu, Jenne, and other towns.

As elsewhere in the Islamic world, West African trader families readily combined religious scholarship with mercantile pursuits. Thus, in West Africa, trade and Islamic culture went hand in hand. In fact, West Africa saw the development of a profitable trade *in* Islamic culture. Since the eleventh century, disciples of renowned scholars had migrated across the Sahara and founded schools and libraries. The Moroccan Muslim scholar and traveler Ibn Battuta (IB-uhn ba-TOO-tuh), who visited Mali in 1352–1353, voiced approval of the people's "eagerness to memorize the great Qur'an: they place fetters on their children if they fail to memorize it and they are not released until they do so."[5] Books on Islamic law, theology, Sufi mysticism, medicine, and Arabic grammar and literature were staple commodities of trans-Saharan trade. The Muslim diplomat Hasan al-Wazzan (hah-SAHN al-wah-zan), whose *Description of Africa* (published in Italian in 1550) became a best-seller in Europe, wrote that in Timbuktu "the learned are greatly revered. Also, many book manuscripts coming from the Berber [North African] lands are sold. More profits are realized from sales of books than any other merchandise."[6]

Muslim Clerics and Native Religious Leaders

Muslim clerics wielded considerable influence in the towns. Clerics presided over worship and festival life and governed social behavior by applying Muslim law and cultural traditions. Yet away from the towns the majority of the population remained attached to ancestral beliefs in nature spirits, especially the spirits of rivers and thunder. Healer priests, clan chiefs, and other ritual experts shared responsibility for making offerings to the spirits, providing protection from evil demons and sorcerers, and honoring the dead. Much to the chagrin of purists such as Ibn Battuta, West African rulers maintained their authority in rural areas by combining Muslim practices with indigenous rituals and traditions. Islam in West Africa was largely urban, and West African rulers knew that their control of the countryside depended on religious accommodation.

trade diaspora A network of merchants from the same city or country who live permanently in foreign lands and cooperate with one another to pursue trading opportunities.

Advance of Islam in Maritime Southeast Asia

Muslim Arab merchants had dominated maritime commerce in the Indian Ocean and Southeast Asia since the seventh century. Not until the thirteenth century, however, did Islam begin to gain converts in Malaysia and the Indonesian archipelago. By 1400 Arab and Gujarati traders and Sufi teachers had spread Islam throughout maritime Asia. The dispersion of Muslim merchants took the form of a **trade diaspora**, a network of merchant settlements dispersed across foreign lands but united by common origins, religion, and language, as well as by business dealings.

Political and economic motives strongly influenced official adoption of Islam. In the first half of the fourteenth century, the Majapahit (mah-jah-PAH-hit) kingdom (1292–1528), a bastion of Hindu religion, conquered most of Java and the neighboring islands of Bali and Madura and forced many local rulers in the Indonesian archipelago to submit tribute. In response, many of these rulers adopted Islam as an act of resistance to dominance by the Majapahit kings. By 1428 the Muslim city-states of Java's north coast, buoyed by the profits of trade with China, secured their independence from Majapahit. Majapahit's dominion over the agricultural hinterland of Java lasted until 1528, when a coalition of Muslim princes forced the royal family to flee to Bali, which remains today the sole preserve of Hinduism in Southeast Asia.

Cosmopolitan port cities, with their diverse merchant communities, were natural sites for religious innovation. The spread of Islam beyond Southeast Asia's port cities, however, was slow and uneven. Javanese tradition attributes the Islamization of the island to a series of preachers, beginning with Malik Ibrahim (mah-leek EE-bra-heem) (d. 1419), a Gujarati spice trader of Persian ancestry. Because merchants and Sufi teachers played a far greater role than orthodox ulama in the spread of Islam in Southeast Asia, relatively open forms of Islam flourished. The Arab shipmaster Ibn Majid (IB-uhn maj-jid), writing in 1462, bemoaned the corruption of Islamic marriage and dietary laws among the Muslims of Melaka (mah-LAK-eh): "They have no culture at all. The infidel marries Muslim women while the Muslim takes pagans to wife. . . . The Muslim eats dogs for meat, for there are no food laws. They drink wine in the markets and do not treat divorce as a religious act.[7] Enforcement of Islamic law often was suspended where it conflicted with local custom. Southeast Asia never adopted some features of Middle Eastern culture often associated with Islam, such as the veiling of women.

Local pre-Islamic religious traditions persisted in Sumatra and Java long after the people accepted Islam. The most visible signs of conversion to Islam were giving up the worship of idols and the consumption of pork and adopting the practice of male circumcision. In addition, the elaborate feasting and grave goods, slave sacrifice, and widow sacrifice (*sati*) that normally accompanied the burials of chiefs and kings largely disappeared. Yet Southeast Asian Muslims continued to honor the dead with prayers and offerings adapted to the forms of Islamic rituals. Malays and Javanese readily adopted veneration of Sufi saints and habitually prayed for assistance from the spirits of deceased holy men. Muslim restrictions on women's secular and religious activities met with spirited resistance from Southeast Asian women, who were accustomed to active participation in public life. Even more than in West Africa, Islam in Southeast Asia prospered not by destroying existing traditions, but by assimilating them.

In regions such as West Africa and Southeast Asia, then, Islam diffused through the activities of merchants, teachers, and settlers rather than through conquest. The spread of Islam in Africa and Asia also followed the rhythms of international trade. While Europe recovered slowly from the Black Death, thriving commerce across the Indian Ocean forged new economic links among Asia, Africa, and the Mediterranean world.

Politics of Conversion

Religious Diversity

The Global Bazaar

Dynastic changes, war, and the Black Death roiled the international economy in the fourteenth century. Yet even before the end of the century, trade and economic growth were reviving in many areas. The maritime world of the Indian Ocean, largely spared both pandemic and war, displayed unprecedented commercial dynamism. Pepper and cotton textiles from India, porcelain and silk from China, spices and

FOCUS

How did the pattern of international trade change during the fourteenth and fifteenth centuries, and how did these changes affect consumption and fashion tastes?

other exotic goods from Southeast Asia, and gold, ivory, and copper from southern Africa circulated through a network of trading ports that spanned the Indian Ocean, Southeast Asia, and China. These trading centers attracted merchants and artisans from many lands, and the colorful variety of languages, dress, foods, and music that filled their streets gave them the air of a global bazaar.

The crises of the fourteenth century severely disrupted the European economy, but by 1450 Italy regained its place as the center within Latin Christendom of finance, industry, and trade. Previously, European craftsmen had produced only crude imitations of Islamic luxury wares. By the early fifteenth century, however, mimicry had blossomed into innovation, and Italian production of luxury goods surpassed Islamic competitors' in both quantity and quality. Wealth poured into Italy, where it found new outlets in a culture of conspicuous consumption. In contrast, the Islamic heartlands of the Middle East never recaptured their former momentum. In sum, the crises of the fourteenth century did not destroy the shared economy and commerce of the Afro-Eurasian world, but they did re-shape them in profound and long-lasting ways (see Map 15.4).

Economic Prosperity and Maritime Trade in Asia 1350–1450

In Kubilai Khan's day, hostility among the Mongol khanates disrupted Central Asian caravan trade. Thus when the Venetian traveler Marco Polo returned home in 1292, he traveled by ship rather than retracing the overland route, known as the Silk Road, that had brought him to China two decades before. Polo's experience was a sign of things to come. After 1300 maritime commerce largely replaced inland trade over the ancient Silk Road. Asian merchants from India to China would seize the opportunities presented by the new emphasis on maritime commerce.

India: Cotton and Pepper

In India, improvements in spinning wheels and looms, and above all the invention of block printing of fabrics in the fourteenth century, led to a revolution in cotton textile manufacture. Using block printing (carved wooden blocks covered with dye), Indian weavers produced colorful and intricately designed fabrics—later known in Europe as chintz, from the Hindi *chint* ("many-colored")—that were far cheaper than luxury textiles such as silk or velvet. Gujarat in the northwest and the Tamil lands in southeastern India became centers of cotton manufacture and trade. Although cotton cultivation and weaving spread to Burma, Thailand, and China, Indian fabrics dominated Eurasian markets (see Lives and Livelihoods: Urban Weavers in India).

Along with textiles, India was famous for its pepper, for which Europeans had acquired a taste during the age of the Crusades. Muslim merchants from Gujarat controlled both cotton and pepper exports from the cities of Calicut and Quilon (KEE-lon). By 1500 Gujarati merchants had created a far-flung trade network across the Indian Ocean from Zanzibar to Java. Gujarati *sharafs* (from the Persian word for "moneylender") and Tamil *chettis* ("traders") acted as bankers for merchants and rulers alike in nearly every Indian Ocean port.

China: Silk and Porcelain

China's ocean-going commerce also flourished in the fourteenth century. The thriving trade between India and China deeply impressed Ibn Battuta, who found thirteen large Chinese vessels, or *junks*, anchored at Calicut when he arrived there in 1341. These junks, Battuta tells us, carried a complement of a thousand men and contained "four decks with rooms, cabins, and saloons for merchants; a cabin has chambers and a lavatory, and can be locked by its occupant, who takes along with him slave girls and wives."[8]

Silk had long dominated China's export trade, but by the eleventh century domestic silk-weaving was flourishing in Iran, the Byzantine Empire, and India. Because Iranian and Byzantine silk manufacturers were better positioned to respond to changing fashions in the Islamic world and Europe, China primarily exported raw silk rather than finished fabrics. At the same time, China retained its preeminent place in world trade by exporting porcelain, which became known as "chinaware."

Much admired for their whiteness and translucency, Chinese ceramics already had become an important item of Asian maritime trade in the tenth century. Bulky and fragile,

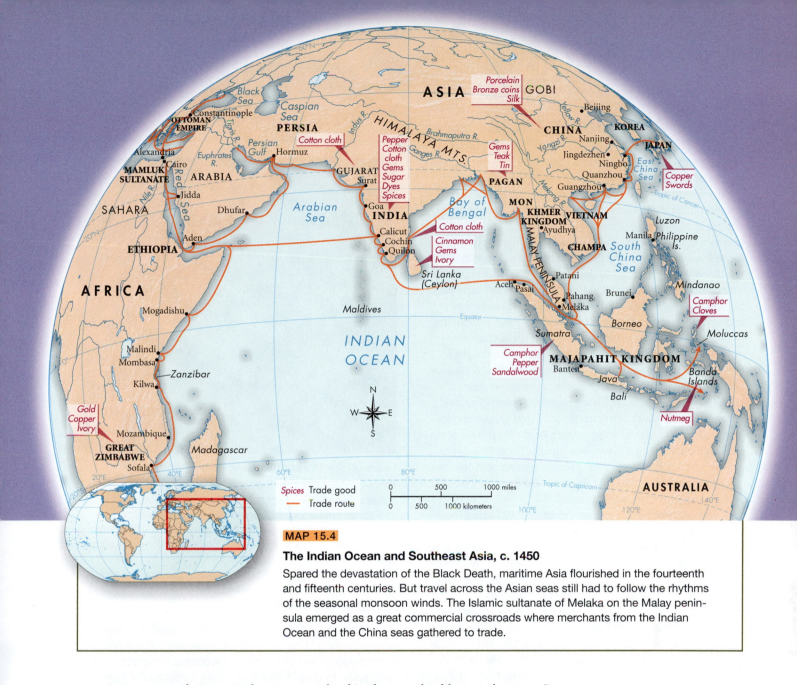

MAP 15.4

The Indian Ocean and Southeast Asia, c. 1450

Spared the devastation of the Black Death, maritime Asia flourished in the fourteenth and fifteenth centuries. But travel across the Asian seas still had to follow the rhythms of the seasonal monsoon winds. The Islamic sultanate of Melaka on the Malay peninsula emerged as a great commercial crossroads where merchants from the Indian Ocean and the China seas gathered to trade.

ceramic wares were better suited to transport by ship than overland by camel or cart. In the thirteenth century, artisans at Jingdezhen (JING-deh-JUHN) in southern China perfected the techniques for making true porcelains, which transform into glass the glaze and pigments, as well as the body of the piece. Porcelain wares, which were harder and whiter than previous types of ceramics, could be made into thin yet strong vessels. Although the Chinese preferred monochromatic (single-colored) porcelains that imitated the colors and texture of jade, consumers in the Islamic world prized intricate designs executed with the metallic pigments used by glassmakers. Muslim merchants introduced the cobalt blue pigment (which Chinese potters called "Mohammedan blue") used to create blue-and-white decorated porcelains. By 1400, Jingdezhen had become the largest manufacturing city in the world, housing more than one thousand kilns with some seventy thousand craftsmen engaged in several dozen specialized tasks. Thus, technological innovation and the demands of the international marketplace shaped both the production and decoration of Chinese ceramics.

The most avid consumers of Chinese porcelains were in the Islamic world, reflecting the global nature of the Chinese ceramics industry. Muslims used Chinese porcelains both as eating and drinking vessels and to decorate mosques, tombs, and other holy places. Imports of Chinese porcelain devastated local ceramic manufacturing in many parts of maritime Asia,

Urban Weavers in India

Industry and commerce in India, especially in textiles, grew rapidly beginning in the fourteenth century. Specialized craftsmen in towns and regional groups of merchants formed guilds that became the nuclei of new occupational castes, *jati* (JAH-tee). Ultimately these new occupational castes would join with other forces in Indian society to challenge the social inequality rooted in orthodox Hindu religion.

It was growth in market demand and technological innovations such as block printing that drove the rapid expansion of India's textile industries. Luxury fabrics such as fine silks and velvet remained largely the province of royal workshops or private patronage. Mass production of textiles, on the other hand, was oriented toward the manufacture of cheaper cotton fabrics, especially colorful chintz garments. A weaver could make a woman's cotton *sari* in six or seven days, whereas a luxury garment took a month or more. Domestic demand for ordinary cloth grew steadily, and production for export accelerated even more briskly. At the beginning of the sixteenth century, the Portuguese traveler Tomé Pires, impressed by the craftsmanship of Indian muslins and calicoes (named after the port of Calicut), observed that "they make enough of these to furnish the world."[1]

Weaving became an urban industry. It was village women who cleaned most of the cotton and spun it into yarn; they could easily combine this simple if laborious work with other domestic chores. But peasants did not weave the yarn into cloth, except for their own use. Instead, weaving, bleaching, and dyeing cloth were skilled tasks performed by professional urban craftsmen, or in some cases by artisans living in separate weavers' settlements in the countryside.

Like other trades in India, weaving was a hereditary occupation that conferred a distinct *jati* caste status and identity. Families of weavers belonged to one of a number of regional guilds with branches in different towns, and members married within their guilds. Unlike European guilds, Indian guilds did not have exclusive monopolies over their trades. A single town could include a number of different weaving guilds, which could become fierce economic and social rivals.

Indian Block-Printed Textile, c. 1500

Block-printed textiles with elaborate designs were in great demand both in India and throughout Southeast Asia, Africa, and the Islamic world. Craftsmen carved intricate designs on wooden blocks (a separate block for each color), which were then dipped in dye and repeatedly stamped on bleached fabric until the entire cloth was covered. This cotton fabric with geese, lotus flower, and rosette designs was manufactured in Gujarat in western India. (Ashmolean Museum, University of Oxford/ Bridgeman Art Library.)

Increased affluence brought further social and economic differentiation to the ranks of weavers. Although guild leaders negotiated orders from merchants and princes, artisans could freely sell their own wares through urban shops and country fairs. The most successful weavers became merchants and brokers, buying more looms and hiring others to work under their supervision. By the fourteenth century some weavers had begun to add the honorific title *chetti* (merchant) to their names.

Southeast Asia: Spices and Rain Forest Products

from the Philippines to East Africa. Chinese porcelains became potent prestige goods among the tribal societies of the Philippines and Indonesia, who attributed magical powers to them.

In mainland Southeast Asia, the shift in political power from the inland rice-growing regions toward coastal port cities reflected the new prominence of maritime trade in the region's economic life. Burma exported cotton to China as early as 1400 and became an important source of metals, gems, and teak for shipbuilding. The profits of maritime commerce fueled the emergence of Ayudhya (a-YOOD-he-ya) in Thailand as the dominant power in mainland Southeast Asia in the late fourteenth century. By 1400 Ayudhya was challenging Majapahit for control of the Southeast Asian trade routes between India and China.

The rising prosperity of weavers whetted their aspirations for social recognition. Amid the whirl and congestion of city life, it was far more difficult than in villages to enforce the laws governing caste purity and segregation. As a fourteenth-century poet wrote about the crowded streets of his hometown of Jaunpur in the Ganges Valley, in the city "one person's caste-mark gets stamped on another's forehead, and a brahman's holy thread will be found hanging around an untouchable's neck."[2] Brahmans objected to this erosion of caste boundaries, to little avail. Weaver guilds became influential patrons of temples and often served as trustees and accountants in charge of managing temple endowments and revenues.

In a few cases the growing economic independence of weavers and like-minded artisans prompted complete rejection of the caste hierarchy. Sufi preachers and *bhakti* (BAHK-tee)—devotional movements devoted to patron gods and goddesses—encouraged the disregard of caste distinctions in favor of a universal brotherhood of devout believers. The fifteenth-century bhakti preacher Kabir, who was strongly influenced by Sufi teachings, epitomized the new social radicalism coursing through the urban artisan classes. A weaver himself, Kabir joined the dignity of manual labor to the purity of spiritual devotion, spurning the social pretension and superficial piety of the brahmans ("pandits") and Muslim clerics ("mullahs"):

I abandoned kin and caste, I weave my threads at ease

I quarrel with no one, I abandoned the pandits and mullahs,

I wear what I have woven; forgetful of myself, I come close to God.[3]

In Kabir's mind, genuine piety was rooted in honest toil, devotion to family, and abstinence from sensual pleasure.

By the seventeenth century, such ideas had coalesced into a separatist religious movement, Sikhism, centered on a trinity of labor, charity, and spiritual devotion. The Sikhs, who gained a following principally among traders and artisans in the northwestern Punjab region, drew an even more explicit connection between commerce and piety. In the words of a hymn included in a sixteenth-century anthology of Sikh sacred writings:

The true Guru [teacher] is the merchant;

The devotees are his peddlers.

The capital stock is the Lord's Name, and

To enshrine the truth is to keep His account.[4]

Sikh communities spurned the distinction between pure and impure occupations. In their eyes, holiness was to be found in honest toil and personal piety, not ascetic practices, book learning, or religious rituals.

---

1. Tomé Pires, *The Suma Oriental of Tomé Pires*, ed. and trans. Armando Cortes (London: Hakluyt Society, 1944), 1:53.
2. Vidyapati Thakur, *Kirtilata*, quoted in Eugenia Vanina, *Urban Crafts and Craftsmen in Medieval India (Thirteenth–Eighteenth Centuries)* (New Delhi: Munshiram Manoharlal, 2004), 443.
3. Quoted in Vanina, *Urban Crafts and Craftsmen,* 149.
4. *Sri Guru Granth Sahib*, trans. Gophal Singh (Delhi: Gur Das Kapur & Sons, 1960), 2:427.

QUESTIONS TO CONSIDER

1. In what ways did the organization of textile production reinforce or challenge the prevailing social norms of Hindu society?

2. In what ways did religious ideas and movements reflect the new sense of dignity among prosperous Indian merchants and craftsmen?

For Further Information:
Ramaswamy, Vijaya. *Textiles and Weavers in Medieval South India*. Delhi: Oxford University Press, 1985.
Vanina, Eugenia. *Urban Crafts and Craftsmen in Medieval India (Thirteenth–Eighteenth Centuries)*. New Delhi: Munshiram Manoharlal, 2004.

Thus, China influenced patterns of international trade not only as a producer, as with ceramics, but as a market for exported goods large enough to shape production elsewhere in the world. China was the principal market for the international trade in pepper, and it was Chinese demand that drove the rapid expansion of pepper cultivation in Southeast Asia, in particular Sumatra, during the fifteenth century. In return for exports of pepper, sandalwood, tin and other metals, fine spices, and exotic products of the tropical rain forests, Southeast Asia imported cotton cloth from India and silks, porcelain, and bronze coins from China. In the wake of this trade boom, Indian and Chinese merchant communities sprouted across maritime Southeast Asia. The trade diasporas of Gujarati Muslims and Chinese from Guangzhou

Wedding Present of Chinese Porcelains

Avid demand in the Muslim world stimulated development of China's renowned blue-and-white porcelains. This Persian miniature from around 1480 illustrates the story of a Chinese princess who in a gesture of diplomacy is sent to marry a Turkish nomad chieftain. The dowry that accompanies the reluctant bride includes blue-and-white porcelains and brass wares of Turkestan design. (The Art Archive/Topkapi Museum Istanbul/ Gianni Dagli Orti.)

(Canton) and Quanzhou (CHYWAN-joe) created networks of cultural as well as economic influence, ultimately altering the balance of political power as well (see again Map 15.4).

China's Overseas Overture: The Voyages of Zheng He 1405–1433

The growth of South Asian maritime trade attracted the attention of the Chinese government, and in the early fifteenth century, the Ming dynasty in China took a more active role in maritime Southeast Asia, becoming a rival for political and economic supremacy. From the 1390s Malay princes in Sumatra appealed to the Ming court for protection against the demands of the Majapahit kings. In 1405 the Ming emperor Yongle decided to intervene by sending a naval expedition to halt the expansionist aggression of Majapahit and Ayudhya and to assert Chinese authority over the maritime realm.

Zheng He's Mission   Yongle entrusted the fleet to the command of a young military officer named Zheng He (1371–1433). Zheng was born into a Muslim family who had served the Mongol rulers of the Yuan dynasty. In 1383, Zheng He, then age twelve, was conscripted into the eunuch corps (castrated males employed as guardians of the imperial household) and placed in the retinue of the prince who would become Emperor Yongle. Zheng assisted the prince in the overthrow of his nephew that brought Yongle to the throne in 1402, and became his most trusted confidant.

For his mission to Southeast Asia, Yongle equipped Zheng He with a vast armada, a fleet of sixty-three ships manned by nearly twenty-eight thousand sailors, soldiers, and officials. Zheng's seven-masted flagship, more than four hundred feet long, was a marvel of Chinese nautical engineering. His fleet later became known as the "treasure ships" because of the cargoes of exotic goods and tribute they brought back from Southeast Asia, India, Arabia, and Africa. But Zheng's primary mission was political, not economic. Yongle, as we have seen, had a vision of world empire, in part borrowed from the Mongols, in which a multitude of princes would pay homage to Ming sovereignty. The constant flow of foreign embassies, the display of exotic tribute, and the emperor's pivotal role as arbitrator of disputes among lesser rulers were crucial to his sense of imperial dignity.

Departing in November of 1405, Zheng's fleet sailed first to Java in a show of force designed to intimidate Majapahit. He then traveled to Sumatra and Melaka and across the Indian Ocean to Ceylon and Calicut. No sooner had Zheng He returned to China in the

Renaissance A period of intense intellectual and artistic creativity in Europe, beginning in Italy in the fourteenth century as a revival of the classical civilization of ancient Greece and Rome.

humanism The study of the humanities (rhetoric, poetry, history, and moral philosophy), based on the works of ancient Greek and Roman writers, that provided the intellectual foundations for the Renaissance.

autumn of 1407 than Yongle dispatched him on another voyage. Yongle had recently launched his invasion of Vietnam, and the purpose of the second voyage was to curtail Ayudhya's aggression and establish a Chinese presence at strategic ports such as Melaka along the Straits of Sumatra. Altogether Yongle commissioned six expeditions under Zheng He's command. During the fourth and subsequent voyages, Zheng He sailed beyond India to Arabia and down the east coast of Africa.

The projection of Chinese power over the sea-lanes of maritime Asia led to far-reaching economic and political changes. The close relations Zheng He forged with rulers of port cities strengthened their political independence and promoted their commercial growth. Under the umbrella of Chinese protection, Melaka flourished as the great cross-roads of Asian maritime trade.

The Last of the Treasure Fleets

The high cost of building and equipping the treasure ships depleted the Ming treasury, however, and after Yongle's death in 1424, Confucian ministers at the Ming court prevailed on his young successor to halt the naval expeditions. In 1430, Yongle's successor nonetheless overcame bureaucratic opposition and dispatched Zheng He on yet another voyage, his seventh. After traveling once again to Africa, Zheng died during his return home. With the passing of the renowned admiral, enthusiasm for the expeditions evaporated. Moreover, the Ming court faced a new threat: a resurgent Mongol confederation in the north. In 1449 a foolish young Ming emperor led a military campaign against the Mongols, only to be taken captive. The Ming court obtained the emperor's release by paying a huge ransom, but its strategic priorities had been completely transformed. Turning its back on the sea, the Ming state devoted its energies and revenues to rebuilding the Great Wall, much of which had crumbled to dust, as a defense against further Mongol attacks. The Great Wall that survives today was largely constructed by the Ming dynasty.

The shift in Chinese policy did not mean the end of Chinese involvement in maritime trade. Chinese merchants continued to pursue trading opportunities in defiance of the imperial ban on private overseas commerce. Even though Muslim merchants dominated Asian maritime commerce, Chinese merchant colonies dotted the coasts of Southeast Asia. Melaka's rulers converted to Islam but welcomed merchants from every corner of Asia. The population probably reached one hundred thousand before Melaka was sacked by the Portuguese in 1511. The Portuguese, like the Chinese before them, were drawn to Southeast Asian waters by the tremendous wealth created by maritime trade. Spurred by the growing European appetite for Asian spices, the violent intrusion of the Portuguese would transform the dynamics of maritime trade throughout Asia.

Commerce and Culture in the Renaissance

European expansion in the late fourteenth and early fifteenth centuries was preceded and influenced by a period of dramatic cultural change. The century after the outbreak of the Black Death marked the beginning of a sweeping transformation in European culture known as the **Renaissance**. In its narrow sense *Renaissance* (French for "rebirth") refers to the revival of ancient Greek and Roman philosophy, art, and literature that originated in fourteenth-century Italy. Scholars rediscovered classical learning and began to emulate the language and ideas of Greek and Roman philosophers and poets; these individuals became known as humanists, students of the liberal arts or humanities. The new intellectual movement of **humanism** combined classical learning with Christian piety and dedication to civic responsibilities.

At the same time the Renaissance inaugurated dramatic changes in the self-image and lifestyle of the wealthy. The new habits of luxurious living and magnificent display diverged sharply from the Christian ethic of frugality. Innovations in material culture and aesthetic values reflected crucial changes in the Italian economy and its relationship to the international trading world of the Mediterranean and beyond. These transformations in turn led to a reorientation of Europe away from Asia and toward the Atlantic world.

Italy's Economic Transformation

The Black Death had hit the Italian city-states especially hard. Some contemporary observers claimed that the pandemic had radically reshaped the social order. Although artisan guilds became a powerful force in urban government for a time in Florence, Siena, and other cities, over the long term the patrician elite of wealthy merchants and landowners reasserted their oligarchic control. The rich became richer, and status and power were increasingly measured in visible signs of wealth.

Still, the economies of the Italian city-states underwent fundamental transformation. Diminishing profits from trade with the Islamic world prompted many Italian merchants to abandon commerce in favor of banking. Squeezed out of the eastern Mediterranean by the Turks and Venetians, Genoa turned its attention westward. Genoese bankers became financiers to the kings of Spain and Portugal and supplied the funds for their initial forays into the Atlantic in search of new routes to African gold and Asian spices. European monarchs' growing reliance on professional armies, naval fleets, and gunpowder weapons also stimulated demand for banking services, forcing them to borrow money to meet the rising costs of war.

Italy became the primary producer of luxury goods for Europe, displacing the Islamic world and Asia. Before 1400, Islamic craftsmanship had far surpassed that of Latin Christendom. The upper classes of Europe paid handsome sums to obtain silk and linen fabrics, ceramics, rugs, glass, metalwork, and jewelry imported from the Mamluk Empire. "The most beautiful things in the world are found in Damascus," wrote Simone Sigoli, a Florentine who visited the city in 1386. "Such rich and noble and delicate works of every kind that if you had money in the bone of your leg, without fail you would break it to buy these things. . . . Really, all Christendom could be supplied for a year with the merchandise of Damascus."[9] But the Black Death, Timur's invasions, and Mamluk mismanagement devastated industry and commerce in Egypt and Syria. According to a census of workshops in Alexandria recorded in 1434, the number of looms operating in the city had fallen to eight hundred, compared with fourteen thousand in 1395.

Seizing the opportunity these developments created, Italian entrepreneurs first imitated and then improved on Islamic techniques and designs for making silk, tin-glazed ceramics known as *maiolica* (my-OH-lee-kah), glass, and brassware. By 1450 these Italian products had become competitive with or eclipsed imports from Egypt and Syria. Italian firms captured the major share of the international market for luxury textiles and other finished goods, and the Islamic lands were reduced to being suppliers of raw materials such as silk, cotton, and dyestuffs.

A Culture of Consumption

Along with Italy's ascent in finance and manufacturing came a decisive shift in attitudes toward money and its use. The older Christian ethics of frugality and disdain for worldly gain gave way to prodigal spending and consumption. This new inclination for acquisition and display cannot be attributed simply to the spread of secular humanism. Indeed, much of this torrent of spending was lavished on religious art and artifacts, and the Roman papacy stood out as perhaps the most spendthrift of all. Displaying personal wealth and possessions affirmed social status and power. Civic pride and political rivalry fueled public spending to build and decorate churches and cathedrals. Rich townsmen transformed private homes into palaces, and artisans fashioned ordinary articles of everyday life—from rugs and furniture to dishes, books, and candlesticks—into works of art. Public piety blurred together with personal vanity. Spending money on religious monuments, wrote the fifteenth-century Florentine merchant Giovanni Rucellai (ROO-chel-lie) in his diary, gave him "the greatest satisfaction and the greatest pleasure, because it serves the glory of God, the honor of Florence, and my own memory."[10]

"Magnificence" became the watchword of the Renaissance. Wealthy merchants and members of the clergy portrayed themselves as patrons of culture and learning. Their private townhouses became new settings for refined social intercourse and conspicuous display. Magnificence implied the liberal spending and accumulation of possessions that advertised a person's virtue, taste, and place in society. "The magnificence of a building," the architect Leon Battista Alberti (1404–1472) declared, "should be adapted to the dignity of its owner."[11] Worldly goods gave tangible expression to spiritual refinement. The paintings of Madonnas and saints that graced Renaissance mansions were much more than objects of devotion: they were statements of cultural and social values. Thus, as with Islam in West Africa, changes in commerce and culture were closely linked. New commercial wealth created an expanded market for art, which was in turn shaped by the values associated with commerce.

Cultural Innovations

Again, as with Islam in West Africa, the intellectual ferment of the Renaissance was nurtured in an urban environment. Humanist scholars shunned the warrior culture of the old nobility while celebrating the civic roles and duties of townsmen, merchants, and clerics. Despite their admiration of classical civilization, the humanists did not reject Christianity. Rather, they sought to reconcile Christian faith and doctrines with classical learning. By making knowledge of Latin and Greek, history, poetry, and philosophy the mark of an educated person, the humanists transformed education and established models of schooling that would endure down to modern times.

Nowhere was the revolutionary impact of the Renaissance felt more deeply than in visual arts such as painting, sculpture, and architecture. Artists of the Renaissance exuded supreme confidence in the ability of human ingenuity to equal or even surpass the works of nature. The new outlook was exemplified by the development of the techniques of perspective, which artists used to convey a realistic, three-dimensional quality to physical forms, most notably the human body. Human invention also was capable of improving on nature by creating order and harmony through architecture and urban planning. Alberti advocated replacing the winding narrow streets and haphazard construction of medieval towns with planned cities organized around straight boulevards, open squares, and monumental buildings whose balanced proportions corresponded to a geometrically unified design.

Above all, the Renaissance transformed the idea of the artist. No longer mere manual tradesmen, artists now were seen as possessing a special kind of genius that enabled them to express a higher understanding of beauty. In the eyes of contemporaries, no one exemplified this quality of genius more than Leonardo da Vinci (1452–1519), who won renown as a painter, architect, sculptor, engineer, mathematician, and inventor. Leonardo's father, a Florentine lawyer, apprenticed him to a local painter at age eighteen. Leonardo spent much of his career as a civil and military engineer in the employ of the Duke of Milan, and developed ideas for flying machines, tanks, robots, and solar power that far exceeded the engineering capabilities of his time. Leonardo sought to apply his knowledge of natural science to painting, which he regarded as the most sublime art (see Seeing the Past: Leonardo da Vinci's *Virgin of the Rocks*).

The flowering of artistic creativity in the Renaissance was rooted in the rich soil of Italy's commercial wealth and nourished by the flow of goods from the Islamic world and Asia. International trade also invigorated industrial and craft production across maritime Asia and gave birth there to new patterns of material culture and consumption. In Japan, however, growing isolation from these cross-cultural interactions fostered the emergence of a national culture distinct from the Chinese traditions that dominated the rest of East Asia.

COUNTERPOINT
Age of the Samurai in Japan 1185–1450

In Japan as in Europe, the term *Middle Ages* brings to mind an age of warriors, a stratified society governed by bonds of loyalty between lords and vassals. In Japan, however, the militarization of the ruling class intensified during the fourteenth and fifteenth centuries, a time when the warrior nobility of Europe was crumbling. Paradoxically, the rise of the **samurai** (sah-moo-rye) ("those who serve") warriors as masters of their own estates was accompanied by the increasing independence of peasant communities.

In contrast to the regions explored earlier in this chapter, Japan became more isolated from the wider world during this era. Commercial and cultural exchanges with China reached a peak in the thirteenth century, but after the failed Mongol invasion of Japan in 1281, ties with continental Asia became increasingly frayed. Thus, many Japanese see this era as the period in which Japan's unique national identity—expressed most distinctly in the ethic of *bushidō* (boo-shee-doe), the "Way of the Warrior"—took its definitive form. Samurai warriors became the

> **FOCUS**
>
> How and why did the historical development of Japan in the fourteenth and fifteenth centuries differ from that of mainland Eurasia?

samurai Literally, "those who serve"; the hereditary warriors who dominated Japanese society and culture from the twelfth to the nineteenth centuries.

Leonardo da Vinci's *Virgin of the Rocks*

Virgin of the Rocks, c. 1483–1486
(Erich Lessing/Art Resource.)

Leonardo's Botanical Studies with Star-of-Bethlehem, Grasses, Crowfoot, Wood Anemone, and Another Genus,
c. 1500–1506 (The Royal Collection © 2011 Her Majesty Queen Elizabeth II/Bridgeman Art Library.)

the menacing darkness of the cavern; desire to see if there was any marvelous thing within."[1]

Fantastic as the scene might seem, Leonardo's meticulous renderings of rocks and plants were based on close observation of nature. The Star of Bethlehem flowers at the lower left of the painting, symbolizing purity and atonement, also appear in the nearly contemporaneous botanical drawing shown here. Geologists have praised Leonardo's highly realistic sandstone rock formations and his precise placement of plants where they would most likely take root.

Masterpieces such as the *Virgin of the Rocks* display Leonardo's careful study of human anatomy, natural landscapes, and botany. Although he admired the perfection of nature, Leonardo also celebrated the human mind's rational and aesthetic capacities, declaring that "we by our arts may be called the grandsons of God."[2]

While living in Milan in the early 1480s, Leonardo accepted a commission to paint an altarpiece for the chapel of Milan's Confraternity of the Immaculate Conception, a branch of the Franciscan order. Leonardo's relationship with the friars proved to be stormy. His first version of the painting (now in the Louvre), reproduced here, apparently displeased his patrons and was sold to another party. Only after a fifteen-year-long dispute over the price did Leonardo finally deliver a modified version in 1508.

In portraying the legendary encounter between the child Jesus and the equally young John the Baptist during the flight to Egypt, Leonardo replaced the traditional desert setting with a landscape filled with rocks, plants, and water. Leonardo's dark grotto creates an aura of mystery and foreboding, from which the figures of Mary, Jesus, John, and the angel Uriel emerge as if in a vision. A few years before, Leonardo had written about "coming to the entrance of a great cavern, in front of which I stood for some time, stupefied and uncomprehending. . . . Suddenly two things arose in me, fear and desire: fear of

1. Arundel ms. (British Library), p. 115 recto, cited in Martin Kemp, *Leonardo da Vinci: The Marvelous Works of Nature and Man* (Oxford: Oxford University Press, 2006), 78.
2. John Paul Richter, ed., *The Notebooks of Leonardo da Vinci* (rpt. of 1883 ed.; New York: Dover, 1970), Book IX, 328 (para. 654).

EXAMINING THE EVIDENCE

1. How does Leonardo express the connection between John (at left) and Jesus through position, gesture, and their relationships with the figures of Mary and the angel Uriel?

2. The friars who commissioned the painting sought to celebrate the sanctity and purity of their patron, the Virgin Mary. Does this painting achieve that effect?

patrons of new forms of cultural expression whose character differed markedly from the Chinese traditions cherished by the old Japanese nobility. A culture based on warriors, rather than Confucian scholars, created a different path for the development of Japanese society.

"The Low Overturning the High"

During the Kamakura period (1185–1333), the power of the **shogun**, or military ruler, of eastern Japan was roughly in balance with that of the imperial court and nobility at Kyoto in the west. Warriors dominated both the shogun's capital at Kamakura (near modern Tokyo) and provincial governorships, but most of the land remained in the possession of the imperial family, the nobility, and religious institutions based in Kyoto. The shoguns appointed low-ranking samurai among their retainers to serve as military stewards on local estates, with responsibility for keeping the peace.

After the collapse of the Kamakura government in 1333, Japan was wracked by civil wars. In 1336 a new dynasty of shoguns, the Ashikaga (ah-shee-KAH-gah), came to power in Kyoto. Unlike the Kamakura shoguns, the Ashikaga aspired to become national rulers. Yet not until 1392 did the Ashikaga shogunate gain uncontested political supremacy, and even then it exercised only limited control over the provinces and local samurai.

In the Kamakura period, the samurai had been vassals subordinated to warrior clans to whom they owed allegiance and service. But wartime disorder and Ashikaga rule eroded the privileges and power of the noble and monastic landowners. Most of their estates fell into the hands of local samurai families, who formed alliances known as *ikki* ("single resolve") to preserve order. The *ikki* brotherhoods signed pacts pledging common arbitration of disputes, joint management of local shrines and festivals, and mutual aid against outside aggressors.

Rise of the Samurai

Just as samurai were turning themselves into landowners, peasants banded together in village associations to resist demands for rents and labor service from their new samurai overlords. These village associations began to assert a right to self-government, claiming legal powers formerly held by the noble estate owners.

Like the *ikki* leagues, villages and districts created their own autonomous governments. Their charters expressed resistance to outside control while requiring strict conformity to the collective will of the community. As one village council declared, "Treachery, malicious gossip, or criminal acts against the village association will be punished by excommunication from the estate."[12] Outraged lords bewailed this reversal of the social hierarchy, "the low overturning the high," but found themselves powerless to check the growing independence of peasant communities.

Japan, 1185–1392

The political strength of the peasants reflected their rising economic fortunes. Japan's agrarian economy improved substantially with the expansion of irrigated rice farming. The village displaced the manorial estate as the basic institution of rural society. Rural traders, mostly drawn from the affluent peasantry, formed merchant guilds and obtained commercial privileges from local authorities. Japan in the fifteenth century had little involvement in foreign trade, and there were few cities apart from the metropolis of Kyoto, which had swelled to 150,000 inhabitants by midcentury. Yet the prosperity of the agrarian economy generated considerable growth in artisan crafts and trade in local goods.

The New Warrior Order

After the founding of the Ashikaga shogunate, provincial samurai swarmed the streets of Kyoto seeking the new rulers' patronage. Their reckless conduct prompted the shoguns to issue regulations forbidding samurai to possess silver swords, wear fine silk clothing, gamble, stage tea-drinking competitions, and consort with loose women—to little effect. In this world of "the low overturning the high," warriors enjoyed newfound wealth while much of the old nobility was reduced to abject poverty.

shogun The military commander who effectively exercised supreme political and military authority over Japan during the Kamakura (1185–1333), Ashikaga (1338–1573), and Tokugawa (1603–1868) shogunates.

Night Attack on the Sanjo Palace

The Heiji Revolt of 1159 marked a key turning point in the shift from aristocratic to warrior rule in Japan. This scene from a thirteenth-century scroll painting depicts the samurai rebels storming the imperial palace and taking the emperor hostage. Although the leaders of the insurrection were captured and executed, the revolt plunged Japan into civil wars that ended only when the Kamakura shogun seized power in 1185. (Werner Forman/Art Resource.)

Cultural and Social Life of the Samurai

While derided by courtiers as uneducated and boorish, the shoguns and samurai became patrons of artists and cultural life. The breakdown of the traditional social hierarchy allowed greater intermingling among people from diverse backgrounds. By the early fifteenth century the outlandish antics of the capital's samurai had been tempered by a new sense of elegance and refinement. The social and cultural worlds of the warriors and courtiers merged, producing new forms of social behavior and artistic expression.

In the early years of the Ashikaga shogunate, the capital remained infatuated with Chinese culture. As the fourteenth century wore on, however, this fascination with China was eclipsed by new fashions drawn from both the court nobility and Kyoto's lively world of popular entertainments. Accomplishment in poetry and graceful language and manners, hallmarks of the courtier class, became part of samurai self-identity as well. A new mood of simplicity and restraint took hold, infused with the ascetic ethics of Zen Buddhism, which stressed introspective meditation as the path to enlightenment.

The sensibility of the Ashikaga age was visible in new kinds of artistic display and performance, including poetry recitation, flower arrangement, and the complex rituals of the tea ceremony. A new style of theater known as *nō* reflected this fusion of courtly refinement, Zen religious sentiments, and samurai cultural tastes. The lyrical language and stylized dances of *nō* performances portrayed samurai as men of feeling rather than ferocious warriors. Thus, the rise of warrior culture in Japan did not mean an end to sophistication and refinement. It did, however, involve a strong focus on cultural elements that were seen as distinctly Japanese.

In at least one area, developments in Japan mirrored those in other parts of the world. The warriors' dominance over Ashikaga society and culture led to a decisive shift toward patriarchal authority. Women lost rights of inheritance as warrior houses consolidated landholdings in the hands of one son who would continue the family line. Marriage and sexual conduct were subject to stricter regulation. The libertine sexual mores of the Japanese aristocracy depicted in Lady Murasaki's *Tale of Genji* (c. 1010) gave way to a new emphasis on female chastity as an index of social order. The profuse output of novels, memoirs, and diaries written by court women also came to an end by 1350. Aristocratic women continued to hold positions of responsibility at court, but their literary talents were devoted to keeping official records rather than expressing their personal thoughts.

By 1400, then, the samurai had achieved political mastery in both the capital and the countryside and had eclipsed the old nobility as arbiters of cultural values. This warrior culture, which combined martial prowess with austere aesthetic tastes, stood in sharp contrast to the veneration of Confucian learning by the Chinese literati and the classical ideals and ostentatious consumption prized by the urban elite of Renaissance Italy.

Conclusion

The fourteenth century was an age of crisis across Eurasia and Africa. The population losses resulting from the Black Death devastated Christian and Muslim societies and economies. In the long run Latin Christendom fared well: the institution of serfdom largely disappeared from western Europe; new entrepreneurial energies were released; and the Italian city-states recovered their commercial vigor and stimulated economic revival in northern Europe. However, the once-great Byzantine Empire succumbed to the expanding Ottoman Empire and, under fire by Urban's cannon, came to an end in 1453. Although the Ottoman conquest of the Balkan peninsula threatened Latin Christendom, the central Islamic lands, from Egypt to Mesopotamia, never regained their former economic vitality. Still, the Muslim faith continued to spread, winning new converts in Africa, Central Asia, and Southeast Asia.

The fourteenth century also witnessed the collapse of the Mongol empires in China and Iran, followed by the rise and fall of the last of the Mongol empires, that of Timur. In China, the Ming dynasty spurned the Mongol vision of a multinational empire, instead returning to an imperial order based on an agrarian economy, bureaucratic rule, and Neo-Confucian values. New dynastic leaders in Korea and Vietnam imitated the Ming model, but in Japan the rising samurai warrior class forged a radically different set of social institutions and cultural values.

The Black Death redirected the course of European state-making. Monarchs strengthened their authority, aided by advances in military technology, mercenary armies, and fresh sources of revenue. The intensifying competition among national states would become one of the main motives for overseas exploration and expansion in the Atlantic world. At the same time, the great transformation in culture, lifestyles, and values known as the Renaissance sprang from the ruin of the Black Death. But the Renaissance was not purely an intellectual and artistic phenomenon. Its cultural innovations were linked to crucial changes in the Italian economy and the international trading world of the Mediterranean and beyond.

Asia was largely spared the ravages of the Black Death pandemic. Maritime Asia, from China to the east coast of Africa, enjoyed a robust boom in trade during the fifteenth century, in contrast to the sluggish economic recovery in much of Europe and the Islamic world. The intrusion of the Portuguese into the Indian Ocean in 1498 would upset the balance of political and economic power throughout Asian waters and dramatically alter Asia's place in what became the first truly global economy. But the arrival of the Europeans would have far more catastrophic effects on the societies of the Americas, which were unprepared for the political and economic challenges—and especially the onslaught of epidemic disease—that followed Columbus's landing in the Caribbean islands in 1492.

NOTES

1. Giovanni Boccaccio, *The Decameron* (New York: Modern Library, 1931), 8–9.
2. Quoted in Adel Allouche, *Mamluk Economics: A Study and Translation of Al-Maqrizi's* Ighathah (Salt Lake City: University of Utah Press, 1994), 75–76 (translation slightly modified).
3. Quoted in Michael W. Dols, "Ibn al-Wardi's *Risalah al-naba' 'an al'waba'*: A Translation of a Major Source for the History of the Black Death in the Middle East," in *Near Eastern Numismatics, Iconography, Epigraphy and History: Studies in Honor of George C. Miles*, ed. Dickran K. Kouymjian (Beirut, Lebanon: American University of Beirut, 1974), 454.
4. *Anonimalle Chronicle*, in *The Peasants' Revolt of 1381*, ed. R. B. Dobson (London: Macmillan, 1970), 164–165.
5. Ibn Battuta, "The Sultan of Mali," in *Corpus of Early Arabic Sources for West African History*, trans. J. F. P. Hopkins, ed. N. Levtzion and J. F. P. Hopkins (Cambridge, U.K.: Cambridge University Press, 1981), 296.
6. Leo Africanus, *History and Description of Africa*, trans. John Poy (London: Hakluyt Society, 1896), 3:825.
7. Shihab al-Din Ahmad ibn Majid, "Al'Mal'aqiya," in *A Study of the Arabic Texts Containing Material of South-East Asia*, ed. and trans. G. R. Tibbetts (Leiden, Netherlands: Brill, 1979), 206.

8. Ibn Battuta, *Travels in Asia and Africa, 1325–1354*, trans. H. A. R. Gibb (London: Routledge & Kegan Paul, 1929), 235.

9. Simone Sigoli, "Pilgrimage of Simone Sigoli to the Holy Land," in *Visit to the Holy Places of Egypt, Sinai, Palestine and Syria in 1384 by Frescobaldi, Gucci, and Sigoli*, trans. Theophilus Bellorini and Eugene Hoade (Jerusalem: Franciscan Press, 1948), 182.

10. Quoted in Lisa Jardine, *Worldly Goods: A New History of the Renaissance* (New York: Doubleday, 1996), 126.

11. Quoted in Richard A. Goldthwaite, *Wealth and the Demand for Art in Italy, 1300–1600* (Baltimore: Johns Hopkins University Press, 1993), 220.

12. Declaration of Oshima and Okitsushima shrine association, dated 1298, quoted in Pierre François Souyri, *The World Turned Upside Down: Medieval Japanese Society* (New York: Columbia University Press, 2001), 136.

RESOURCES FOR RESEARCH

Fourteenth-Century Crisis and Renewal in Eurasia

William McNeill's landmark work drew attention to the profound impact of epidemic diseases on world history. The exact cause of the Black Death remains a subject of debate, as the works of Cantor and Herlihy show, but few dispute that the pandemic had lasting consequences for European history. The influence of the Black Death in the Islamic world is less well studied, but Borsch's recent study seeks to explain why the economic depression it caused lasted longer in Egypt than in Europe.

Borsch, Stuart J. *The Black Death in Egypt and England: A Comparative Study*. 2005.

British History in Depth: The Black Death. http://www.bbc.co.uk/history/british/middle_ages/black_01.shtml

Brook, Timothy. *The Confusions of Pleasure: Commerce and Culture in Ming China*. 1998.

Cantor, Norman. *In the Wake of the Plague: The Black Death and the World It Made*. 2001.

Herlihy, David. *The Black Death and the Transformation of the West*. 1997.

McNeill, William H. *Plagues and Peoples*. 1976.

Islam's New Frontiers

The study of Islam in Africa has advanced rapidly in recent years. Robinson serves as a good overview; the essays in Levtzion and Pouwells provide comprehensive regional coverage. Imber provides the best introduction to the early history of the Ottoman Empire.

Dunn, Ross E. *The Adventures of Ibn Battuta: A Muslim Traveler of the 14th Century*. 1989.

Imber, Colin. *The Ottoman Empire, 1300–1650: The Structure of Power*, 2d ed. 2009.

Levtzion, Nehemia, and Randall L. Pouwells, eds. *The History of Islam in Africa*. 2000.

Manz, Beatrice Forbes. *The Rise and Rule of Tamerlane*. 1989.

Robinson, David. *Muslim Societies in African History*. 2004.

The Global Bazaar

New scholarship has erased the older image of this period as "the Dark Ages." The original understanding of the Renaissance as an intellectual and artistic movement centered in Italy has been broadened to include transformative changes in trade, industry, material culture, and lifestyles. Similarly, accounts of voyages of Zheng He—lucidly described by Levathes—have opened a window on the vigorous cultural and economic interchange across Asia; Reid examines this topic in greater detail.

Burke, Peter. *The European Renaissance: Centres and Peripheries*. 1998.

Finlay, Robert. *The Pilgrim Art: Cultures of Porcelain in World History*. 2010.

Goldthwaite, Richard A. *Wealth and the Demand for Art in Italy, 1300–1600*. 1993.

Jardine, Lisa. *Worldly Goods: A New History of the Renaissance*. 1996.

Levathes, Louise. *When China Ruled the Seas: The Treasure Fleet of the Dragon Throne, 1405–1433*. 1994.

Reid, Anthony. *Southeast Asia in the Age of Commerce, 1350–1750*. Vol. 1, *The Land Below the Winds*; Vol. 2, *Expansion and Crisis*. 1989, 1993.

COUNTERPOINT: Age of the Samurai in Japan, 1185–1450

Recent years have seen a wave of revisionist scholarship on medieval Japan. Souyri's work stands out for its finely detailed depiction of social diversity. *Tale of the Heike*, an account of the struggle between warlords that led to the founding of the Kamakura shogunate, provides a sharp contrast to earlier courtly literature such as Lady Murasaki's *Tale of Genji*.

Adolphson, Mikael S. *The Gates of Power: Monks, Courtiers, and Warriors in Premodern Japan*. 2000.

Mass, Jeffrey P., ed. *The Origins of Japan's Medieval World: Courtiers, Clerics, Warriors, and Peasants in the Fourteenth Century*. 1997.

McCullough, Helen Craig, trans. *Tale of the Heike*. 1988.

Souyri, Pierre-François. *The World Turned Upside Down: Medieval Japanese Society*. 2001.

Wakita, Haruko. *Women in Medieval Japan: Motherhood, Household Economy, and Sexuality*. 2006.

▶ **For additional primary sources from this period**, see *Sources of Crossroads and Cultures*.

▶ **For Web sites, images, and documents related to topics in this chapter**, see Make History at bedfordstmartins.com/smith.

REVIEW

The major global development in this chapter ► Crisis and recovery in fourteenth- and fifteenth-century Afro-Eurasia.

IMPORTANT EVENTS

1315–1317	Great Famine in northern Europe
1325–1354	Travels of Ibn Battuta in Asia and Africa
1336–1573	Ashikaga shogunate in Japan
1337–1453	Hundred Years' War between England and France
1347–1350	Outbreak of the Black Death in Europe and the Islamic Mediterranean
c. 1351–1782	Ayudhya kingdom in Thailand
1368–1644	Ming dynasty in China
1378	Ciompi uprising in Florence
1381	Peasant Revolt in England
1392–1910	Yi dynasty in Korea
1405	Death of Timur; breakup of his empire into regional states in Iran and Central Asia
1405–1433	Chinese admiral Zheng He's expeditions in Southeast Asia and the Indian Ocean
1421	Relocation of Ming capital from Nanjing to Beijing
1428–1788	Le dynasty in Vietnam
1453	Ottoman conquest of Constantinople marks fall of the Byzantine Empire

KEY TERMS

Black Death (p. 478) pandemic (p. 478)
humanism (p. 498) Renaissance (p. 498)
janissary corps (p. 489) samurai (p. 501)
Little Ice Age (p. 479) shogun (p. 503)
Neo-Confucianism Sufism (p. 488)
  (p. 486) theocracy (p. 489)
oligarchy (p. 483) trade diaspora (p. 492)

CHAPTER OVERVIEW QUESTIONS

1. How and why did Europe's economic growth begin to surpass that of the Islamic world in the century after the Black Death?

2. Did the economic revival across Eurasia after 1350 benefit the peasant populations of Europe, the Islamic world, and East Asia?

3. How did the process of conversion to Islam differ in Iran, the Ottoman Empire, West Africa, and Southeast Asia during this period?

4. What political and economic changes contributed to the rise of maritime commerce in Asia during the fourteenth and fifteenth centuries?

SECTION FOCUS QUESTIONS

1. How did the Black Death affect society, the economy, and culture in Latin Christendom and the Islamic world?

2. Why did Islam expand dramatically in the fourteenth and fifteenth centuries, and how did new Islamic societies differ from established ones?

3. What were the principal sources of growth in international trade during the fourteenth and fifteenth centuries, and how did this trade affect patterns of consumption and fashion tastes?

4. How and why did the historical development of Japan in the fourteenth and fifteenth centuries differ from that of mainland Eurasia?

MAKING CONNECTIONS

1. What social, economic, and technological changes strengthened the power of European monarchs during the century after the Black Death?

2. How and why did the major routes and commodities of trans-Eurasian trade change after the collapse of the Mongol empires in Central Asia?

3. In what ways did the motives for conversion to Islam differ in Central Asia, sub-Saharan Africa, and the Indian Ocean during this era?

4. In this period, why did the power and status of the samurai warriors in Japan rise while those of the warrior nobility in Europe declined?

PART 3

The Early Modern World

1450–1750

CH 16

CH 17

MAJOR GLOBAL CHANGES occurred between 1450 and 1750, as regional societies gave way to multiethnic empires, and horse-borne raiders gave way to cannon and long-distance sailing craft. Historians call this era "early modern" because it was marked by a general shift toward centralized, bureaucratic, monetized, and technologically sophisticated states. Yet nearly all of these "modern" states also clung to divine kingship and other remnants of the previous age, and most sought to revive and propagate older religious or philosophical traditions. Some states embraced mutual tolerance, but many others fought bitterly over matters of faith.

One of the most striking breaks with the past was the creation of new linkages between distant regions, most notably the Americas and the rest of the world. Early globalization accelerated changes in everything from demography to commerce to technology, allowing populations to grow and many individuals to get rich. Yet globalization also enabled the spread of disease, and some technical innovations increased the scale and deadliness of warfare; early modernity did not promise longer and better lives for everyone. The shift to modernity was not a uniquely Western phenomenon either, although western Europeans were key players in its spread, usually as traders, missionaries, or conquerors.

Beginning in around 1450, Iberians—the people of Spain and Portugal—used new ships and guns to venture into the Atlantic, where they competed in overseas colonization, trade, and conquest. They set out to claim new territories for their monarchs and to spread their Roman Catholic faith. They did both at the expense of many millions of native peoples, first in Africa and the East Atlantic and then throughout the Americas and beyond. Wherever they went, Iberians moved quickly from plunder to the creation of settled colonies, creating a new trading sphere that historians call the "Atlantic world." Other Europeans soon followed in the Iberians' wake, but the silver of Spanish America became the world's money.

Modernity affected Africa most deeply via the slave trade. The older flow of captive workers to the Muslim Middle East and Indian Ocean basin continued well into early modern times, but it was soon overshadowed by a more urgent European demand in the Atlantic. This desire for slaves to staff distant plantations and mines fueled

existing antagonisms within Africa even as it spawned new ones, each generating captives and refugees to be traded abroad for select commodities, including firearms, textiles, and metal ware. Europeans did not penetrate, much less conquer, sub-Saharan Africa at this time, however, in part due to their general lack of resistance to tropical disease.

In the vast Indian Ocean basin a freer model of interaction and integration developed. Islamic merchants had come to dominate these seas by 1450, not through imperial means but rather by establishing trading networks from East Africa to Southeast Asia. Luxury products from the African interior were traded abroad for spices, cloth, porcelain, and other compact valuables. Ships also carried bulk commodities and religious pilgrims. After 1500, European interlopers discovered that in such a thriving, diverse, and politically decentralized region, they would have to compete fiercely for space. This they did, first by establishing coastal trading forts, then by moving inland.

On the Eurasian mainland, with the aid of modern firearms, powerful Ottoman, Russian, Safavid, and Mughal leaders turned from regional consolidation to massive imperial expansion by the sixteenth century. Each combined religious fervor with considerable political ambitions, but several of these states, notably the Ottomans and Mughals, embraced religious diversity. Collecting tributes in cash and establishing the appropriate bureaucracies to collect them were shared objectives. Unlike the Safavids and Mughals, the Ottomans sought to extend their empire overseas, taking on Venice and the Habsburgs in the Mediterranean and the Portuguese in the Indian Ocean. Russia would venture abroad under Peter the Great.

Europe remained mostly embroiled in religious and political conflict. The religious schism known as the Protestant Reformation touched off over a century of bloody war after 1500, and doctrinal disputes would carry on well into modern times. Warfare itself was transformed from knightly contests and town sieges to mass infantry mobilization and bombardment of strategic fortresses. These models would be exported, along with armed sailing ships. Europe's political fractures enabled the rise of market economies as well, with more states sponsoring overseas colonizing ventures

CH 20

over time to augment their share of business. New forms of government emerged, and also a marked tendency to question ancient authorities. From this came a revolution in science, emphasizing physical observation and secular reasoning, and at the end of the early modern period, a new intellectual movement known as the Enlightenment.

In East Asia, by contrast, introversion rather than foreign engagement was the rule in early modern times. Although both China and Japan had strong seafaring traditions by 1450, state policies from the fifteenth to sixteenth centuries gradually discouraged external affairs. Despite official isolation, both regions proved to be extraordinarily dynamic. Political consolidation and population growth were matched with a general shift from tributary to money economies. In the Chinese Ming and Qing empires this led to a massive rise in demand for silver, stimulating global circulation of this mostly American-produced metal. Porcelain and silk, much of it produced by poor women working in the household, were sent abroad in exchange. With the patronage of newly wealthy merchants and bureaucrats, the arts flourished on a scale not seen before.

By 1700, the American colonies were not the neo-Europes their first colonizers had envisioned. Centuries of ethnic and cultural mixture, forced labor regimes, frontier expansion, and export-oriented economies all led to the formation of distinct societies. Native populations were recovering in some areas, and African and African-descended populations had grown to dominate whole regions. Europeans continued to migrate to the colonies in search of new livelihoods, but most soon adopted the nativist attitudes of earlier colonizers. In much of the Americas, the different outlooks of European colonizers and colonists would prove irreconcilable by the end of the early modern era.

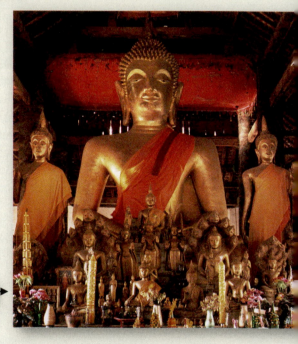

CH 21

	1400		1500	
Americas	1325–1521 Aztec Empire	1430–1532 Inca Empire Columbus reaches the Americas 1492 Portuguese reach Brazil 1500	Spanish conquest of Aztecs 1519–1521 Spanish conquest of Inca 1532–1536	Discovery of silver at Potosí 1545
Europe		1462–1505 Ivan III unites Russia Christian reconquest of Spain completed 1492 1473–1543 Copernicus	1517 Luther confronts Catholic Church, sparking the Protestant Reformation	
Middle East		1453 Ottoman conquest of Constantinople	Ottoman conquest of Egypt 1517	Battle of Lepanto 1571 1520–1566 Reign of Suleiman the Magnificent
Africa	First sub-Saharan Africans captured and taken to Portugal 1441	1450 Height of kingdom of Benin 1464–1492 Reign of Songhai emperor Sunni Ali	1506–1543 Reign of Afonso I of Kongo	
Asia and Oceania	1405–1433 Voyages of Ming admiral Zheng He 1421 Relocation of Ming capital to Beijing 1428–1788 Vietnamese Le dynasty		1498 Vasco da Gama reaches India Portuguese establish fort in Ceylon 1517	

Despite these profound transformations, many people remained largely unaffected by the currents of early modernity. Though not densely populated, most of North and South America, Polynesia, Oceania, central and southern Africa, and highland Asia remained beyond the zone of sustained contact with foreigners. New commodities and biological transfers were only beginning to be felt in many of these places at the end of the early modern period. As a result of their long isolation, inhabitants of these regions would be among the most drastically affected by modernity's next wave.

CH 22

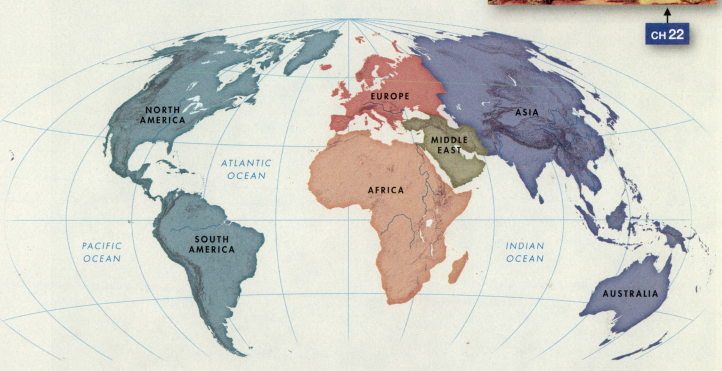

NORTH AMERICA

EUROPE

ASIA

MIDDLE EAST

ATLANTIC OCEAN

AFRICA

PACIFIC OCEAN

SOUTH AMERICA

INDIAN OCEAN

AUSTRALIA

1600	1700	1800

- **1625** Dutch settle New Amsterdam; English establish colony on Barbados
- **1607** English establish colony at Jamestown, Virginia
- **1608** French establish colony at Quebec City
- **1695–1800** Brazil's "gold rush"
- **1763** Rio de Janeiro becomes capital of Brazil

- **1588** English defeat Spanish Armada
- **1618–1648** Thirty Years' War
- **1643–1715** Reign of Louis XIV
- **1600** English East India Company founded
- **1642–1727** Newton
- **1688** England's Glorious Revolution
- **1712–1714** War of the Spanish Succession
- **1712** Peter the Great founds St. Petersburg
- **1700–1800** The Enlightenment

- **1600–1629** Peak of Safavid Empire
- Last Ottoman siege at Vienna defeated **1683**
- **1736–1747** Nadir Shah reunites Iran
- **1722** Fall of Safavid Empire

- **1591** Moroccan raiders conquer Songhai Empire
- **1624–1663** Reign of Queen Nzinga in Ndongo
- **1638–1641** Dutch seize São Jorge da Mina and Luanda
- **1680s** Rise of kingdom of Asante
- **1720s** Rise of kingdom of Dahomey
- **1750–1800** Height of Atlantic slave trade

- **1602–1867** Tokugawa Shogunate
- **1644** Manchu invasion of Beijing; Ming Empire replaced by Qing
- **1500–1763** Mughal Empire
- **1736–1799** Reign of Qing emperor Qianlong
- **1751** Qing annexation of Tibet

16

AT A CROSSROADS ▲

Perched on a granite ridge high above Peru's Urubamba River, the Inca site of Machu Picchu continues to draw thousands of visitors each year. First thought to be the lost city of Vilcabamba, then a convent for Inca nuns, Machu Picchu is now believed to have been a mid-fifteenth-century palace built for the Inca emperor and his mummy cult. It was probably more a religious site than a place of rest and recreation. (The Art Archive/Gianni Dagli Orti.)

Empires and Alternatives in the Americas

1430–1530

I n 1995, American archaeologist Johan Reinhard and his assistants discovered a tomb atop Mount Ampato, a peak overlooking the Peruvian city of Arequipa. Inside were the naturally mummified remains of a fourteen-year-old girl placed there some five hundred years earlier. Material and written evidence suggests she was an *aclla* (AHK-yah), or "chosen woman," selected by Inca priests from among hundreds of regional headmen's daughters. Most aclla girls became priestesses in temples and palaces dedicated to the Inca emperor or the imperial sun cult. Others became the emperor's concubines or wives. Only the most select, like the girl discovered on Mount Ampato, were chosen for the "debt-payment" sacrifice, or *capacocha* (kah-pah-KOH-chah), said to be the greatest honor of all.

According to testimonies collected soon after the Spanish conquest of the Incas in 1532 (discussed in the next chapter), the capacocha sacrifice was a rare and deeply significant event preceded by numerous rituals. First, the victim, chosen for her (and rarely, his) physical perfection, trekked to Cuzco, the Inca capital, to be feasted and blessed. The child's father brought gifts and sacred objects from his province and in turn received fine textiles from the emperor. Following an ancient Andean tradition, reciprocal ties between ruler and ruled were reinforced through such acts of ritualized gift exchange, feasting, and finally, sacrifice. The girl, too, received fine alpaca and cotton skirts and shawls, along with tiny gold and silver votive objects, a necklace of shell beads, and tufts of tropical bird feathers. These items adorned her in her tomb, reached after a long journey on foot from Cuzco.

As suggested by later discoveries in Chile and Argentina, at tomb-side the aclla girl was probably given a beaker filled with beer brewed from maize. In a pouch she carried coca leaves. The sacred coca, chewed throughout the Andes, helped fend off the headaches

BACKSTORY

By the fifteenth century, the Americas had witnessed the rise and fall of numerous empires and kingdoms, including the classic Maya of Mesoamerica, the wealthy Sicán kingdom of Peru's desert coast, and the Cahokia mound builders of the Mississippi Basin. Just as these cultures faded, there emerged two new imperial states that borrowed heavily from their predecessors. The empires treated in this chapter, the Aztec and Inca, were the largest states ever to develop in the Americas, yet they were not all-powerful. About half of all native Americans, among them the diverse peoples of North America's eastern woodlands, lived outside their realms.

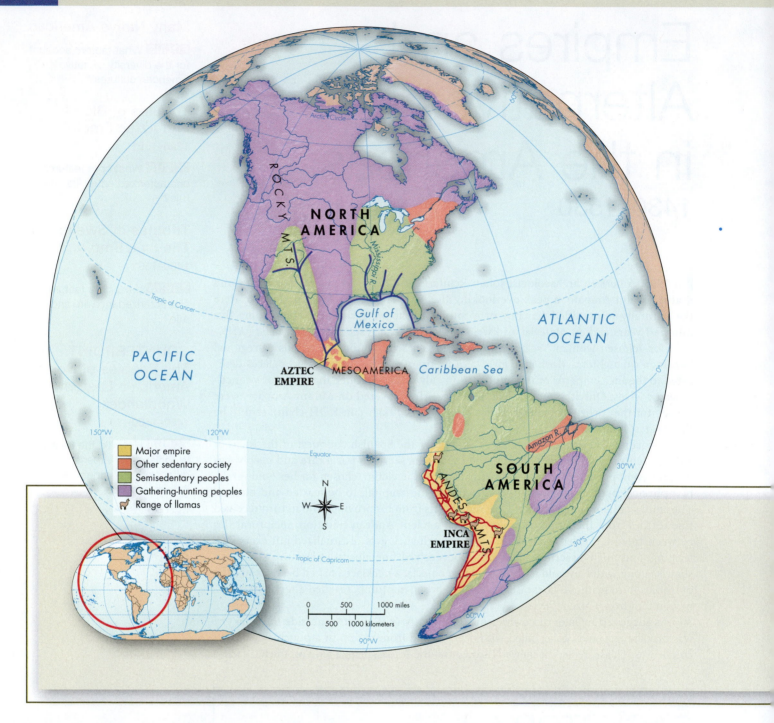

Major empire
Other sedentary society
Semisedentary peoples
Gathering-hunting peoples
Range of llamas

c. 900–1600 Late Woodland period of dispersed farming and hunting

c. 1100 Aztecs leave Aztlán

c. 1200 Incas move into Cuzco region

900   1000   1100   1200

and nausea brought on by oxygen starvation at high altitude, whereas the maize beer induced sleepiness. Barely conscious of her surroundings, the girl was lowered into her grass-lined grave, and, according to the forensic anthropologists who examined her skull, struck dead with a club. Other Inca sacrificial victims appear to have been buried alive and left to freeze to death, as described in postconquest accounts.

Why did the Incas sacrifice children, and why in these ways? By combining material, written, and oral evidence, scholars are beginning to solve the riddle of the Inca mountain mummies. From what is now known, it appears that death, fertility, reciprocity, and imperial links to sacred landscapes were all features of the capacocha sacrifice. Although macabre practices such as this may challenge our ability to empathize with the leaders, if not the common folk, of this distant culture, with each new fact we learn about the child mummies, the closer we get to understanding the Inca Empire and its ruling cosmology.

The Incas and their subjects shared the belief that death occurred as a process rather than in an instant, and that proper death led to an elevated state of consciousness. In this altered state a person could communicate with deities directly, and in a sense join them. If the remains of such a person were carefully preserved and honored, they could act as an oracle, a conduit to the sacred realms above and below the earth. Mountains, as sources of springs and rivers, and sometimes fertilizing volcanic ash, held particular spiritual significance.

In part, it was this complex of beliefs about landscape, death, and the afterlife that led the Incas to mummify and otherwise preserve respected ancestors, including their emperors, and to bury chosen young people atop mountains that marked the edges, or heights, of empire. Physically perfect noble children such as the girl found on Mount Ampato were thus selected for the role of communicants with the spirit world. Their sacrifice unified the dead, the living, and the sacred mountains, and also bound together a far-flung empire that was in many ways as fragile as life itself.[1]

MAPPING THE WORLD

The Western Hemisphere, c. 1500

Native Americans inhabited the entire Western Hemisphere from the Arctic Circle to the tip of South America. Their societies varied tremendously in density and political sophistication, largely as a result of adaptation to different natural environments. Empires were found only in the tropical highlands of Mesoamerica and the Andes, but large chiefdoms based on farming could be found in eastern Canada, the bigger Caribbean islands, and the lower Amazon Basin. Gatherer-hunters were the most widespread of all native American cultures, and despite their relatively small numbers they proved most resistant to conquest by settled neighbors.

ROUTES ▼

— Inca road
— Other trade route

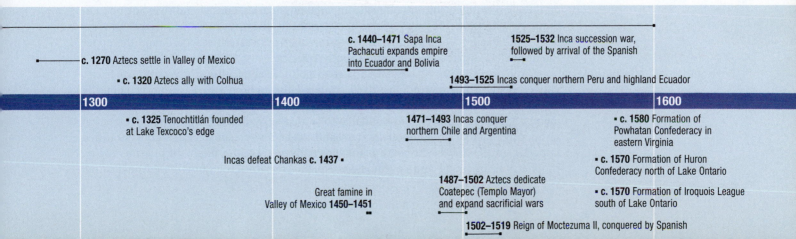

c. 1270 Aztecs settle in Valley of Mexico

■ c. 1320 Aztecs ally with Colhua

c. 1440–1471 Sapa Inca Pachacuti expands empire into Ecuador and Bolivia

1525–1532 Inca succession war, followed by arrival of the Spanish

1493–1525 Incas conquer northern Peru and highland Ecuador

1300 | 1400 | 1500 | 1600

■ c. 1325 Tenochtitlán founded at Lake Texcoco's edge

1471–1493 Incas conquer northern Chile and Argentina

■ c. 1580 Formation of Powhatan Confederacy in eastern Virginia

Incas defeat Chankas c. 1437 ■

■ c. 1570 Formation of Huron Confederacy north of Lake Ontario

Great famine in Valley of Mexico 1450–1451

1487–1502 Aztecs dedicate Coatepec (Templo Mayor) and expand sacrificial wars

■ c. 1570 Formation of Iroquois League south of Lake Ontario

1502–1519 Reign of Moctezuma II, conquered by Spanish

But this fragility was not evident to the people gathered at the capacocha sacrifice. By about 1480, more than half of all native Americans were subjects of two great empires, the Aztec in Mexico and Central America and the Inca in South America. In part by drawing on ancient religious and political traditions, both empires excelled at subduing neighboring chiefdoms through a mix of violence, forced relocation, religious indoctrination, and marriage alliances. Both empires demanded allegiance in the form of tribute. Both the Aztecs and Incas were greatly feared by their many millions of subjects. Perhaps surprisingly, these last great native American states would prove far more vulnerable to European invaders than their nonimperial neighbors, most of whom were gatherer-hunters and semisedentary villagers. Those who relied least on farming had the best chance of getting away.

OVERVIEW
QUESTIONS

The major global development in this chapter: The diversity of societies and states in the Americas prior to European invasion.

As you read, consider:

1. In what ways was cultural diversity in the Americas related to environmental diversity?

2. Why was it in Mesoamerica and the Andes that large empires emerged in around 1450?

3. What key ideas or practices extended beyond the limits of the great empires?

Many Native Americas

FOCUS

What factors account for the diversity of native American cultures?

Scholars once claimed that the Western Hemisphere was sparsely settled prior to the arrival of Europeans in 1492, but we now know that by the end of the fifteenth century the overall population of the Americas had reached some 60 million or more. Vast open spaces remained, but in places the landscape was more intensively cultivated and thickly populated than

Population Density

western Europe (see Map 16.1). Fewer records for nonimperial groups survive than for empire builders such as the Incas and Aztecs, but by combining archaeological, artistic, anthropological, linguistic, and historical approaches, scholars have shed much new light on these less-studied cultures. Outside imperial boundaries, coastal and riverside populations were densest. This was true in the Caribbean, the Amazon and Mississippi river basins, the Pacific Northwest, parts of North America's eastern seaboard, and the upper Río de la Plata district of southeastern South America.

Environmental and Cultural Diversity

Ecological diversity gave rise in part to political and cultural diversity. America's native peoples, or Amerindians, lived scattered throughout two vast and ecologically diverse continents. They also inhabited a variety of tropical, temperate, and icy environments that proved more or less suitable to settled agriculture. Some were members of wandering, egalitarian gatherer-hunter bands; others were subjects of rigidly stratified imperial states. In between were many alternatives: traveling bands of pilgrims led by prophets, as in Brazil and southeastern North America; chiefdoms based on fishing,

MAP 16.1

Main Settlement Areas in the Americas, c. 1492

Most native Americans settled in regions that supported intensive agriculture. In Mesoamerica and greater North America, maize, beans, and squash were key crops. Andean peoples also grew these crops, but they relied more on potatoes and related tubers, supplemented by quinoa. People throughout the tropical Americas grew cotton, and tobacco was even more widespread. The trade routes shown here linked peoples from very different cultures, mostly to exchange rare items such as shells, precious stones, gold dust, and bird feathers, but seeds for new crops also followed these paths.

Map labels:
ROCKY MTS.
NORTH AMERICA
Missouri R.
Mississippi R.
APPALACHIAN MTS.
Rio Grande
Gulf of Mexico
MESOAMERICA
Greater Antilles
Lesser Antilles
Caribbean Sea
ATLANTIC OCEAN
Tropic of Cancer
Orinoco R.
Amazon R.
ANDES MTS.
SOUTH AMERICA
PACIFIC OCEAN
Equator
Tropic of Capricorn
Paraná R.
Río de la Plata

Legend:

☐ Main areas of settlement, c. 1492
— Major trade route

Principal crops
- Amaranth
- Beans
- Cacao
- Chilies
- Cotton
- Maize
- Manioc
- Peanuts
- Potatoes, sweet potatoes
- Quinoa
- Squash, pumpkins, gourds
- Sunflowers
- Tobacco
- Tomatoes

0   500   1000 miles
0   500   1000 kilometers

whaling, or farming, as in the Pacific Northwest and Greater Antilles; large confederacies of chiefdoms as in highland Colombia and northeastern North America; commercially vibrant and independent city-states as in the Maya heartland of Central America. Others, such as the peoples of coastal Ecuador and the Lesser Antilles, had mastered the sea, routinely ferrying goods and ideas from one continent to the other, and throughout the Caribbean islands. Gold working and maize farming were among the many technologies that traversed American waters. Long-distance overland traders were equally important, carrying copper and tropical feathers from Central America to North America's desert Southwest in exchange for turquoise or, in South America, trekking between distant jungle, mountain, and coast settlements to trade gold and precious stones for seashells, animal pelts, and salt.

Political diversity was more than matched by cultural diversity. The Aztecs and Incas spread the use of imperial dialects within their empires, but elsewhere hundreds of distinct Amerindian languages could be heard. Modes of dress and adornment were even more varied, ranging from total nudity and a few tattoos to highly elaborate ceremonial dress. Arctic peoples had no choice but to bundle up, yet even their style choices distinguished one group from another. In imperial societies strict rules of dress and decorum separated elites from commoners, women from men, and juniors from seniors. Lip and ear piercing, tooth filing, and molding of the infant skull between slats of wood were but a few of the many ways human appearances were reconfigured. Architecture was just as varied, as were ceramics and other arts. In short, the Americas' extraordinary range of climates and natural resources both reflected and encouraged diverse forms of material and linguistic expression. Perhaps only in the realm of religion, where shamanism persisted, was a unifying thread to be found.

Shamanism

Not a formal ideology or doctrine but rather a broadly similar set of beliefs and practices, **shamanism** consisted of a given tribe's or chiefdom's reliance on healer-visionaries for spiritual guidance. In imperial societies shamans constituted a priestly class. Both male and female, shamans had functions ranging from fortuneteller to physician, with women often acting as midwives (see Lives and Livelihoods: The Aztec Midwife, page 528). Judging from material remains and eyewitness accounts, most native American shamans were males. In some Amerindian cultures the role of shaman was inherited; in others, select juniors announced their vocation following a vision quest, or lengthy ritual seclusion. This often entailed a solo journey to a forest or desert region, prolonged physical suffering, and controlled use of hallucinogenic substances. In many respects Amerindian shamanism reflected its Central Asian origins, and in other ways it resembled shamanistic practices in sub-Saharan Africa.

Often labeled "witch-doctors" or "false prophets" by unsympathetic Christian Europeans, shamans maintained and developed a vast body of esoteric knowledge that they passed along to juniors in initiations and other rituals. Some served as village or clan historians and myth-keepers. Most used powerful hallucinogens, including various forms of concentrated tobacco, to communicate with the spirits of predatory animals. Perhaps a legacy of the ancient era of great mammals and a sign of general human vulnerability, predators were venerated almost everywhere in the Americas. Animal spirits were regarded as the shaman's alter ego or protector, and were consulted prior to important occasions

Canadian War Club

This stone war club with a fish motif was excavated from a native American tomb in coastal British Columbia, Canada, and is thought to date from around 1200 to 1400 C.E. Such items at first suggest a people at war, but this club was probably intended only for ceremonial use. Other clubs from the same tomb share its overt sexual symbolism. Modern Tsimshian inhabitants of the region, who still rely on salmon, describe the exchange of stone clubs in their foundation myths. (National Museum of the American Indian, Smithsonian Institution. Catalog number: 5/5059. Photo by Katherine Fogden.)

shamanism Widespread system of religious belief and healing originating in Central Asia.

such as royal marriages, births, and declarations of war. Shamans also mastered herbal remedies for virtually all forms of illness, including emotional disorders. These rubs, washes, and infusions were sometimes highly effective, as shown by modern pharmacological studies. Shamans nearly always administered them along with complex chants and rituals aimed at expelling evil spirits. Shamans, therefore, combined the roles of physician and religious leader, using their knowledge and power to heal both body and spirit.

The many varieties of social organization and cultural practice found in the early modern Americas reflect both creative interactions with specific environments and the visions of individual political and religious leaders. Some Amerindian gatherer-hunters lived in swamplands and desert areas where subsistence agriculture was impossible using available technologies. Often such gathering-hunting peoples traded with—or plundered—their farming neighbors. Yet even farming peoples, as their ceramic and textile decorations attest, did not forget their past as hunters. As in other parts of the world, big-game hunting in the early modern Americas was an esteemed, even sacred activity among urban elites, marked by elaborate taboos and rituals.

Range of Livelihoods

Kwakiutl Culture Area, c. 1500

Just as hunting remained important to farmers, agriculture could be found among some of the Americas' least politically complex societies, again characterized by elaborate rituals and taboos. According to many early modern observers, women controlled most agricultural tasks and spaces, periodically making offerings and singing to spirits associated with human fertility. Staple foods included maize, potatoes, and manioc, a lowland tropical tuber that could be ground into flour and preserved. Agricultural rituals were central in most cultures, and at the heart of every imperial state. With the ebb and flow of empires, many groups shifted from one mode of subsistence to another, from planting to gathering-hunting and back again. Some, such as the Kwakiutl (KWAH-kyu-til) of the Pacific Northwest, were surrounded by such abundant marine and forest resources that they never turned to farming. Natural abundance combined with sophisticated fishing and storage systems allowed the Kwakiutl to build a settled culture of the type normally associated with agricultural peoples. Thus, the ecological diversity of the Americas helped give rise to an equally diverse array of native American cultures, many of which blurred the line between settled and nomadic lifestyles.

Tributes of Blood:
The Aztec Empire 1325–1521

Mesoamerica, comprised of modern southern Mexico, Guatemala, Belize, El Salvador, and western Honduras, was a land of city-states after about 800 C.E. Following the decline of ancient cultural forebears such as Teotihuacán (tay-oh-tee-wah-KAHN) in the Mexican highlands and the classic Maya in the greater Guatemalan lowlands, few urban powers, with the possible exception of the Toltecs, managed to dominate more than a few neighbors at a time.

FOCUS

What core features characterized Aztec life and rule?

This would change with the arrival in the Valley of Mexico of a band of former gatherer-hunters from a mysterious northwestern desert region they called Aztlán (ost-LAWN), or "place of cranes." As newcomers these "Aztecs," who later called themselves Mexica (meh-SHE-cah, hence "Mexico"), would suffer a number of humiliations at the hands of powerful city-dwellers centered on Lake Texcoco, now overlain by Mexico City. The Aztecs were at first regarded as coarse barbarians, but as with many conquering outsiders, in time they would have their revenge (see Map 16.2).

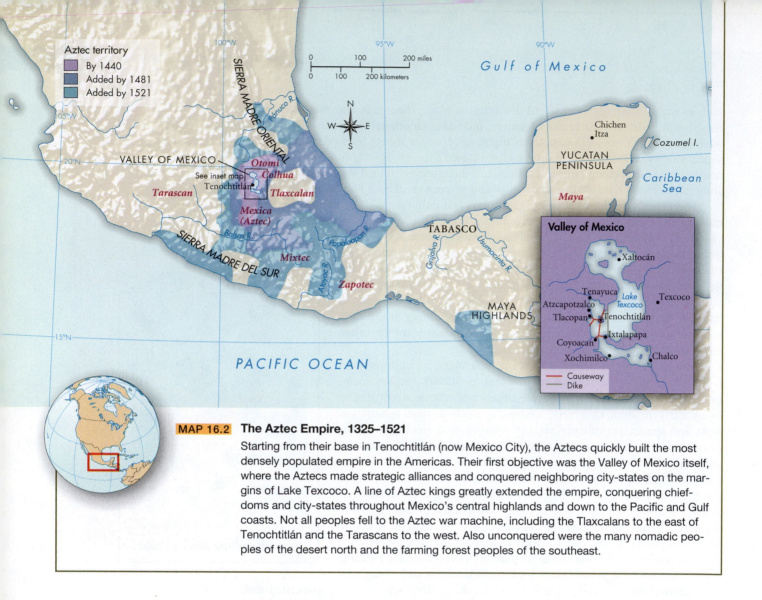

Aztec territory
- By 1440
- Added by 1481
- Added by 1521

Valley of Mexico
- Causeway
- Dike

MAP 16.2 **The Aztec Empire, 1325–1521**

Starting from their base in Tenochtitlán (now Mexico City), the Aztecs quickly built the most densely populated empire in the Americas. Their first objective was the Valley of Mexico itself, where the Aztecs made strategic alliances and conquered neighboring city-states on the margins of Lake Texcoco. A line of Aztec kings greatly extended the empire, conquering chiefdoms and city-states throughout Mexico's central highlands and down to the Pacific and Gulf coasts. Not all peoples fell to the Aztec war machine, including the Tlaxcalans to the east of Tenochtitlán and the Tarascans to the west. Also unconquered were the many nomadic peoples of the desert north and the farming forest peoples of the southeast.

Humble Origins, Imperial Ambitions

Unlike the classic Maya of preceding centuries, the Aztecs did not develop a phonetic writing system. They did, however, preserve key aspects of their history in a mix of oral and symbolic, usually painted or carved, forms. Aztec elders developed and maintained a series of chronicles of the kind historians call master narratives, or state-sponsored versions of the past meant to glorify certain individuals or policies. These narratives related foundation myths, genealogies, tales of conquest, and other important remembrances. Though biased, fragmentary, and otherwise imperfect, many Aztec oral narratives were preserved by dozens of young native scribes writing in Nahuatl (NAH-watt), the Aztec language, soon after the Spanish Conquest of 1519–1521 (discussed in the next chapter).

Historical Documentation

Why is it that the Spanish victors promoted rather than suppressed these narratives of Aztec glory? In one of history's many ironic twists, Spanish priests arriving in Mexico in the 1520s taught a number of noble Aztec and other Mesoamerican youths to adapt the Latin alphabet and Spanish phonetics to various local languages, most importantly Nahuatl. The Spanish hoped that stories of Aztec rule and religion, once collected and examined, would be swiftly discredited and replaced with Western, Christian versions. Not only did this quick conversion not happen as planned, but an unintended consequence of the information-gathering campaign was to create a vast and diverse body of Mesoamerican literature written in native languages.

Despite the agony of the immediate postconquest years, the Aztecs were a quick study in the production of written historical documents. Indeed, most of what we know of Aztec history relies heavily on these hybrid and often enigmatic sixteenth-century sources (see Seeing the Past: An Aztec Map of Tenochtitlán). Aside from interviews with the elders,

An Aztec Map of Tenochtitlán

Tenochtitlán, from the *Codex Mendoza* (The Granger Collection, New York.)

contains an illustrated history of Aztec conquests, crimes and punishments, and even a map of Tenochtitlán, the Aztec capital. This symbol-filled map is reproduced here.

According to legend, the Aztec capital came into existence when an eagle landed on a cactus in the middle of Lake Texcoco. This image, now part of the Mexican national flag, is at the center of the map. Beneath the cactus is a picture of a stone carving of a cactus fruit, a common Aztec symbol for the human heart, emblem of sacrifice. Beneath this is a third symbol labeled afterwards by a Spanish scribe "Tenochtitlán."

The city, or rather its symbol, marks the meeting of four horizontal, spatial quarters as well as a vertical axis linking the sky, earth, and watery underworld. In each quarter are various Aztec nobles, only one of whom, Tenochtli (labeled "Tenuch" on the map), is seated on a reed mat, the Aztec symbol of supreme authority. He was the Aztecs' first emperor; the name "Tenochtli" means "stone cactus fruit."

The lower panel depicts the Aztec conquests of their neighbors in Colhuacan and Tenayuca. Framing the entire map are symbols for dates, part of an ancient Mesoamerican system of time keeping and prophesying retained by the Aztecs. Finally, barely legible in the upper left-hand corner is the somewhat jarring signature of André Thevet, a French priest and royal cosmographer who briefly possessed the *Codex Mendoza* in the late sixteenth century.

Named for Mexico's first Spanish viceroy, the *Codex Mendoza* was painted by Aztec artists about a dozen years after the Spanish Conquest of 1519–1521. It was commissioned by the viceroy as a gift for the Holy Roman emperor and king of Spain, Charles V. After circulating among the courts of Europe, the *Codex Mendoza* landed in the Bodleian Library in Oxford, England, where it remains. Much of the document consists of tribute lists, but it also

EXAMINING THE EVIDENCE

1. What does this map reveal about the Aztec worldview?

2. How might this document have been read by a common Aztec subject?

several painted books, or codices, marked with precise dates, names, and other symbols, survive, along with much archaeological and artistic evidence. In combining these sources with Spanish eyewitness accounts of the conquest era, historians have assembled a substantial record of Aztec life and rule.

Aztec Origins

According to most accounts, the Aztecs arrived in the Valley of Mexico sometime in the thirteenth century, but it was not until the early fourteenth that they established a permanent home. The most fertile sites in the valley were already occupied by farmers who had no interest in making room for newcomers, but the Aztecs were not dissuaded; they had a reputation for being tough and resourceful. Heeding an omen in the form of an eagle perched on a cactus growing on a tiny island near the southwest edge of Lake Texcoco, the refugees settled there in 1325. Reclaiming land from the shallow lakebed, they founded a city called Tenochtitlán (teh-noach-teet-LAWN), or "cactus fruit place." Linked to shore by three large causeways, the city soon boasted imposing stone palaces and temple-pyramids.

The Aztecs quickly transformed Tenochtitlán into a formidable capital. By 1500 it was home to some two hundred thousand people, ranking alongside Nanjing and Paris among the world's five or six most populous cities at the time. At first the Aztecs developed their city by trading military services and lake products such as reeds and fish for building materials, including stone, lime, and timber from the surrounding hillsides. They then formed marriage alliances with regional ethnic groups such as the Colhua, and by 1430 initiated the process of imperial expansion.

Intermarriage with the Colhua, who traced their ancestry to the mighty Toltec warriors, lent the lowly Aztecs a new, elite cachet. At some point the Aztecs tied their religious cult, focused on the war god Huitzilopochtli (weetsy-low-POACH-tlee), or "hummingbird-on-the-left" to cults dedicated to more widely known deities, such as Tlaloc, a powerful water god. Also known to the distant Maya, the fearsome Tlaloc resembled a goggle-wearing crocodile, and was usually surrounded by shells and other marine symbols. A huge, multilayered pyramid faced with carved stone and filled with rubble, now referred to by archaeologists as the Templo Mayor, or "Great Temple," but called by the Aztecs Coatepec, or "Serpent Mountain," became the centerpiece of Tenochtitlán. At its top, some twenty stories above the valley floor, sat twin temple enclosures, one dedicated to Huitzilopochtli, the other to Tlaloc. Like many imperial structures, Coatepec was built to awe and intimidate. In the words of one native poet:

Lake Texcoco and Tenochtitlán, c. 1500

Legend		
Causeway	**A**	Great Temple
Major road	**B**	Ritual center
Major canal	**C**	Palace
Aqueduct	**D**	Assembly hall

Proud of itself
Is the City of Mexico-Tenochtitlán
Here no one fears to die in war
This is our glory

This is Your Command
Oh Giver of Life
Have this in mind, oh princes
Who could conquer Tenochtitlán?
Who could shake the foundation of heaven?[2] *

As these words suggest, the Aztecs saw themselves as both stagehands and actors in a grandscale cosmic drama centered on their great capital city.

---

* Miguel Leon-Portilla. *Pre-Columbian Literatures of Mexico*, by and Leon-Portilla, translated from the Spanish by Grace Lobanov. Copyright © 1969 by The University of Oklahoma Press. Used by permission of the publisher.

Enlarging and Supplying the Capital

Land Reclamation

With Tenochtitlán surrounded by water, subsistence and living space became serious concerns amid imperial expansion. Fortunately for the Aztecs, Lake Texcoco was shallow enough to allow an ingenious form of land reclamation called *chinampa* (chee-NAHM-pah). Still visible in a few Mexico City neighborhoods today, **chinampas** were long, narrow terraces built by hand from dredged mud, reeds, and rocks, bordered by interwoven sticks and live trees. Chinampa construction also created rows of deep canals, which served as waterways, or suburban "canoe roads." Because the Aztecs lacked iron or bronze metallurgy, wheeled vehicles, and draft animals, construction of large-scale agricultural works such as chinampas and massive temple-pyramids such as Coatepec absorbed the labors of many thousands of workers. Their construction, therefore, is a testimony to the Aztecs' ability to command and organize large amounts of labor.

Over time, Tenochtitlán's canals accumulated algae, water lilies, and silt. Workers periodically dredged and composted this organic material to fertilize maize, bean, and tomato plantings on the newly formed island-terraces. Established chinampa lands encompassing several square miles were eventually used for building residences, in part to help ease urban crowding. Always hoping not to anger Tlaloc, the fickle water god, by the mid-fifteenth century the Aztecs countered problems such as chronic flooding and high salt content at their end of the lake with dikes and other complex, labor-intensive public works.

Long-Distance Trade

Earlier, in the fourteenth century, an adjacent "twin" city called Tlatelolco (tlah-teh-LOLE-coe) had emerged alongside Tenochtitlán. Tlatelolco served as the Aztec marketplace. Foods, textiles, and goods from throughout Mesoamerica and beyond were exchanged here. Highly prized cocoa beans from the hot lowlands served as currency in some exchanges, and more exotic products, such as turquoise and the iridescent tail feathers of the quetzal bird, arrived from as far away as northern New Mexico and southern Guatemala, respectively. Though linked by trade, these distant regions fell well outside the Aztec domain. No matter how far they traveled, all products were transported along well-trod footpaths on the backs of human carriers. Only when they arrived on the shores of Lake Texcoco could trade goods be shuttled from place to place in canoes. Tlatelolco served as crossroads for all regional trade, with long-distance merchants, or *pochteca* (poach-TEH-cah), occupying an entire precinct. For the Aztecs, Tenochtitlán was the center of the political and spiritual universe. Tlatelolco was the center of Aztec commerce, connecting the peoples of the Valley of Mexico to diverse societies scattered across the Americas.

From City-State to Empire

Genuine Aztec imperial expansion began only in around 1430, less than a century before the arrival of Europeans. An auspicious alliance between Tenochtitlán and the neighboring city-states of Texcoco and Tlacopan led to victory against a third, Atzcapotzalco (otts-cah-poat-SAUL-coh). Tensions with Atzcapotzalco extended back over a century to the Aztecs' first arrival in the region, and these early slights were not forgotten. Whether motivated by revenge or something else, the Aztecs used the momentum of this victory to overtake their allies and lay the foundations of a regional, tributary empire. Within a generation they controlled the entire Valley of Mexico, exacting tribute from several million people representing many distinct cultures. The Nahuatl language helped link state to subjects, although many newly conquered and allied groups continued to speak local languages. These persistent forms of ethnic identification, coupled with staggering tribute demands, would eventually help bring about the end of Aztec rule.

Holy Terror: Aztec Rule, Religion, and Warfare

A series of six male rulers, or *tlatoque* (tlah-TOE-kay, singular *tlatoani*), presided over Aztec expansion. When a ruler died, his successor was chosen by a secret council of elders from among a handful of eligible candidates. Aztec kingship was sacred in that each tlatoani traced his lineage back to the legendary Toltec warrior-sages. For this, the incorporation of the Colhua lineage had been essential. In keeping with this Toltec legacy, the Aztec

chinampa A terrace for farming and house building constructed in the shallows of Mexico's Lake Texcoco by the Aztecs and their neighbors.

The Coyolxauhqui Stone

Coyolxauhqui Stone (The Art Archive/Museo del Templo Mayor Mexico/Gianni Dagli Orti.)

Like many imperial peoples, the Aztecs sought to memorialize their deities in stone. The Aztec war god Huitzilopochtli was central, but as in other traditions, so were his mother and other female relatives. Huitzilopochtli's mother was Coatlicue (kwat-lih-KWAY), "Serpent Skirt," a fearsome and not obviously maternal figure. Huitzilopochtli's birth was said to be miraculous; Coatlicue had been inseminated by downy feathers while sweeping a temple, a ruse of the trickster-creator god Tezcatlipoca (tess-caught-lee-POH-cah), "Smoking Mirror."

A daughter, Coyolxauhqui (coe-yole-SHAU-key), "She Who is Adorned with Copper Bells," was so outraged at her mother's suspicious pregnancy that she incited her four hundred siblings to attempt matricide. Coatlicue was frightened at the prospect, but her unborn child, Huitzilopochtli, spoke from the womb to calm her. Upon the arrival of the angry children, dressed for war and led by Coyolxauhqui, Huitzilopochtli burst out of his mother's womb fully grown. He quickly prepared for battle and confronted his sister, whom he dismembered with a fire serpent. Huitzilopochtli went on to rout his other siblings, running them down like a proper Aztec warrior, stripping and sacrificing each without mercy.

The circular stone shown here, discovered by electrical workers near Mexico City's cathedral in 1979, depicts Coyolxauhqui dismembered on the ground. Some ten feet across, this stone apparently sat at the base of the Aztec Templo Mayor. Sacrificed warriors from all over the Aztec Empire probably got a good look at it before climbing the temple stairs to their deaths. Although shown in defeat, Coyolxauhqui is the ideal woman warrior, her serpent belt buckled with a human skull. Earth Monster knee- and elbow-pads, as well as heel-cups, add to her fearsome appearance, as do serpent ties on her severed arms and legs. An elaborate headdress and huge, Toltec-style ear-spools top off the battlefield ensemble.

EXAMINING THE EVIDENCE

1. How does the Coyolxauhqui stone reflect women's roles in Aztec society?

2. What does the stone suggest about death in Aztec thought?

Empire was characterized by three core features: human sacrifice, warfare, and tribute. All were linked to Aztec and broader Mesoamerican notions of cosmic order, specifically the fundamental human duty to feed the gods.

Sacrifice　　Like most Mesoamerican peoples, the Aztecs traced not only their own but all human origins to sacrifices made by a wide range of deities. In most origin stories male and female gods threw themselves into fires, drew their own blood, and killed and dismembered one another, all for the good of humankind. These forms of sacrifice were considered essential to the process of releasing and renewing the generative powers that drove the cosmos (see Seeing the Past: The Coyolxauhqui Stone).

According to Aztec belief, humans were expected to show gratitude by following the example of their creators in an almost daily ritual cycle. Much of the sacred calendar had been inherited from older Mesoamerican cultures, but the Aztecs added many new holidays to celebrate their own special role in cosmic history. The Aztecs' focus on sacrifice also appears to have derived from their acute sense that secular and spiritual forces were

Aztec Human Sacrifice

This image dates from just after the Spanish Conquest of Mexico, but it was part of a codex about Aztec religious practices and symbols. Here a priest is removing the beating heart of a captive with a flint knife as an assistant holds his feet. The captive's bloody heart, in the form of a cactus fruit, ascends, presumably to the gods (see the same icon in Seeing the Past: An Aztec Map of Tenochtitlán, page 521). At the base of the sacrificial pyramid lies an earlier victim, apparently being taken away by noble Aztec men and women responsible for the handling of the corpse. (Scala/Art Resource, NY.)

inseparable and interdependent. Affairs of state were affairs of heaven, and vice versa. Tenochtitlán was thought to be the foundation of heaven, its enormous temple-pyramids the center of human-divine affairs. Aztec priests and astrologers believed that the universe, already in its fifth incarnation after only three thousand years, was inherently unstable, always on the verge of chaos and collapse. Only human intervention in the form of sustained sacrificial ritual could stave off apocalypse.

As an antidote, or at least a brake against impending doom, the gods had given humans the "gift" of warfare. Human captives, preferably able-bodied, energetic young men, were to be hunted and killed so that the release of their blood and spirits might satisfy the gods. Warrior sacrifice was so important to the Aztecs that they believed it kept the sun in motion. Thus the act of human sacrifice, which involved removing the hearts of live victims using a flint knife, was in part a reenactment of several creator gods' own acts of self-sacrifice.

Devout Aztec subjects, rather like the classic Maya before them, also took part in non-lethal cosmic regeneration rituals in the form of personal bloodletting, or **autosacrifice**. According to a number of eyewitness sources, extremities and genitals were bled using thorns and stone blades, with public exhibition of suffering as important as blood loss. Blood offerings were absorbed by thin sheets of reed paper, which were burnt before an

autosacrifice The Mesoamerican practice of personal bloodletting as a means of paying debts to the gods.

altar. These bloodlettings, like captive sacrifices, emphasized the frailty of the individual, the pain of life, and most of all indebtedness to the gods. Autosacrifice was, in short, a physical expression of the empathy and subordination humans were to feel before their creators. Human blood fueled not only the Aztec realm, but the cosmos.

Warfare Given these sacrificial obligations, Aztec warfare was aimed not at the annihilation, but rather at live capture of enemies. This is not to say that "stone age" weapons technology was an impediment to determined killers: two-handed broadswords with razor-sharp obsidian blades could slice feather-clad warriors to ribbons, and ceramic projectiles could be hurled from slings with deadly accuracy. Spears, lances, clubs, and other weapons were equally menacing. Still, according to most sources, Aztec combat was ideally a stylized and theatrical affair similar to royal jousts in contemporary Eurasia, with specific individuals paired for contest.

In the field, Aztec warriors were noted for their fury, a trait borrowed from their patron deity, Huitzilopochtli. Chronic enemies such as the Tlaxcalans of east-central Mexico, and the Tarascans to the west, apparently learned to match the ferocious Aztec style. Despite their proximity to Tenochtitlán, they remained unconquered when Europeans arrived. Some enemies, such as the nearby Otomí, were eventually overwhelmed, then incorporated into Aztec warrior ranks.

All Mesoamerican warriors considered death on the battlefield the highest honor. But live capture was the Aztecs' main goal, and most victims were marched naked and bound to the capital to be sacrificed. Although charged with religious meaning, Aztec warrior sacrifices were also intended to horrify enemies; visiting diplomats were made to watch them, according to sources. Aztec imperial expansion depended in part on religious terror, or the ability to appear chosen by the gods for victory.

Tribute In addition to sacrificial victims, the Aztecs demanded **tribute** of conquered peoples, a common imperial practice worldwide. In addition to periodic labor drafts for temple building and other public works, tribute lists included useful things such as food, textiles, and craft goods, crucial subsidies for the empire's large priestly and warrior classes. Redistribution of certain tribute items to favored subjects of lower status, a tactic also practiced by the Incas, further helped cement loyalties. Other tribute items were purely symbolic. Some new subjects were made to collect filth and inedible insects, for example, just to prove their unworthiness before the Aztec sovereign. As an empire that favored humiliation over co-optation and promotion of new subjects, the Aztecs faced an ever-deepening reservoir of resentment.

Daily Life Under the Aztecs

Class Hierarchy Aztec society was highly stratified, and class divisions firm. As in most imperial societies, Mexica nobles regarded commoners, particularly farming folk, as uncouth and generally beneath contempt. In between were imperial bureaucrats, priests, district chiefs, scribes, merchants, and artisans. Although elites at several levels showed off the fruits of their subordinates' labors in lavish displays, most Aztec art seems to have been destined not for wealthy people's homes but rather for temples, tombs, and religious shrines. Despite heavy emphasis on religious ceremonies, the Aztecs also maintained a multitiered civil justice system. In many instances, and quite unlike most of the world's imperial cultures, including the Incas, Aztec nobles received harsher punishments than commoners for similar misdeeds.

Class hierarchy was further reinforced by a host of detailed dress and speech codes, along with many other social rules and rituals. The tlatoani, for example, could not be touched or even looked in the face by any but his closest relatives, consorts, and servants. Even ranking nobles were supposed to lie face down on the ground and put dirt in their mouths before him. Nobles guarded their own rank with vigilance, going so far as to develop a restricted form of speech. Chances for social advancement were severely limited, but some men, all of whom were expected to serve in the military for a period, gained status on the battlefield.

At the base of the social pyramid were peasants and slaves. Some peasants were ethnic Aztecs, but the vast majority belonged to city-states and clans that had been conquered after 1430. In either case, peasants' lives mostly revolved around producing food for subsistence

tribute Taxes paid to a state or empire, usually in the form of farm produce or artisan manufactures but sometimes also human labor or even human bodies.

and providing overlords with tribute goods and occasional labor. Slavery usually took the form of crisis-driven self-indenture; it was not an inherited social status. Chattel slavery existed, in which slaves were treated as property and traded in the marketplace, but slavery remained unimportant to the overall Aztec economy.

Merchants, particularly the mobile pochteca, responsible for long-distance trade, occupied an unusual position. Although the pochteca sometimes accumulated great wealth, they remained resident aliens much like other ethnic merchant communities operating in the contemporary Mediterranean and Indian Ocean basins. They had no homeland, but made a good living supplying elites with exotic goods, including slaves. Yet even among merchants there seems to have been little interest in capital accumulation in the form of money, land, or saleable goods. There is no evidence of complex credit instruments, industrial-style production, or real estate exchange of the sort associated with early merchant capitalism in other parts of the world at this time. The Aztec state remained at root tributary, the movement of goods mostly a reflection of power relations underpinned by force. Merchants, far from influencing politics, remained ethnic outsiders. Thus, both the Aztec economy and social structure reinforced the insularity of Aztec elites. The inflexible Aztec society could not incorporate outsiders, and economic exchange, even long-distance trade, did little to add new ideas and beliefs to Aztec culture.

Women's Roles

The life of an Aztec woman was difficult even by early modern standards. Along with water transport and other heavy household chores, maize grinding and tortilla making became the core responsibilities of most women in the Valley of Mexico, and indeed throughout Mesoamerica. Without animal- or water-driven grain mills, food preparation was an arduous, time-consuming task, particularly for the poor. Only noblewomen enjoyed broad exemption from this and other forms of manual work.

Sources suggest that some women achieved shaman status, performing minor priestly roles and working as surgeons and herbalists. Midwifery was also a fairly high-status, female occupation (see Lives and Livelihoods: The Aztec Midwife). These were exceptions; women's lives were mostly hard under Aztec rule. Scholars disagree, however, as to whether male political and religious leaders viewed women's substantial duties and contributions as complementary or subordinate. Surviving texts do emphasize feminine mastery of the domestic sphere and its social value. However, this emphasis may simply reflect male desire to limit the sphere of women's actions, since female reproductive capacity was also highly valued as an aid to the empire's perpetual war effort.

Indeed, Aztec society was so militarized that giving birth was referred to as "taking a captive." This comparison reflects the generalized Aztec preoccupation with pleasing their gods: women were as much soldiers as men in the ongoing war to sustain human life. Women's roles in society were mostly domestic rather than public, but the home was a deeply sacred space. Caring for it was equivalent to caring for a temple. Sweeping was a genuine ritual, for example, albeit one with hygienic benefits. Hearth tending, maize grinding, spinning, and weaving were also highly ritualized tasks, each accompanied by chants and offerings. Insufficient attention to any of these daily rituals put families and entire lineages at risk.

Children's Lives

Aztec children, too, lived a scripted existence, their futures predicted at birth by astrologers. Names were derived from birthdates, and in a way amounted to a public badge of fate. According to a variety of testimonies taken just after the Spanish Conquest, Aztec society at all levels emphasized duty and good comportment rather than rights and individual freedom. Parents were admonished to police their children's behavior and to help mold all youths into useful citizens. Girls and boys at every social level were assigned tasks considered appropriate for their sex well before adolescence. By age fourteen, children of both sexes were fully engaged in adult work. One break from the constant chores was instruction between ages twelve and fifteen in singing and playing instruments, such as drums and flutes, for cyclical religious festivals. Girls married at about age fifteen, and boys nearer twenty, a pattern roughly in accordance with most parts of the world at the time. Elder Aztec women usually served as matchmakers, and wedding ceremonies tended to be elaborate, multiday affairs. Some noblemen expanded their prestige by retaining numerous wives and siring dozens of children.

The Aztec Midwife

Aztec Midwife

Women were expected to be tough in Aztec culture, which described giving birth as "taking a captive." But as in war, medical attention was often required, so a trained class of professional midwives stood by to administer aid. This image accompanies a description in Nahuatl, the Aztec language, of the midwife's duties written soon after the Spanish Conquest. (Firenze, Biblioteca Medicea Laurenziana, Ms. Med. Palat. 219, c. 132v.)

In Aztec culture, childbirth was a sacred and ritualized affair. Always life-threatening for mother and child, giving birth and being born were both explicitly compared to the battlefield experience. Aside from potential medical complications, the Aztecs considered the timing of a child's birth critical in determining his or her future. This tricky blend of physical and spiritual concerns gave rise to the respected and highly skilled livelihood of midwife. It is not entirely clear how midwives were chosen, but their work and sayings are well described in early postconquest records, particularly the illustrated books of Aztec lore and history collectively known as the *Florentine Codex*. The following passage, translated directly from sixteenth-century Nahuatl, is one such description. Note how the midwife blends physical tasks, such as supplying herbs and swaddling clothes, with shamanistic cries and speeches.

And the midwife inquired about the fate of the baby who was born.

When the pregnant one already became aware of [pains in] her womb, when it was said that her time of death had arrived, when she wanted to give birth

already, they quickly bathed her, washed her hair with soap, washed her, adorned her well. And then they arranged, they swept the house where the little woman was to suffer, where she was to perform her duty, to do her work, to give birth.

If she were a noblewoman or wealthy, she had two or three midwives. They remained by her side, awaiting her word. And when the woman became really disturbed internally, they quickly put her in a sweat bath [a kind of sauna]. And to hasten the birth of the baby, they gave the pregnant woman cooked *ciuapatli* [literally, "woman medicine"] herb to drink.

And if she suffered much, they gave her ground opossum tail to drink, and then the baby was quickly born. [The midwife] already had all that was needed for the baby, the little rags with which the baby was received.

And when the baby had arrived on earth, the midwife shouted; she gave war cries, which meant the woman had fought a good battle, had become a brave warrior, had taken a captive, had captured a baby.

Then the midwife spoke to it. If it was a boy, she said to it: "You have come out on earth, my youngest one, my boy, my young man." If it was a girl, she said to it: "My young woman, my youngest one, noblewoman, you have suffered, you are exhausted.". . . [and to either:] "You have come to arrive on earth, where your relatives, your kin suffer fatigue and exhaustion; where it is hot, where it is cold, and where the wind blows; where there is thirst, hunger, sadness, despair, exhaustion, fatigue, pain. . . ."

And then the midwife cut the umbilical cord. . . .

Source: Selection from the *Florentine Codex* in Matthew Restall, Lisa Sousa, and Kevin Terraciano, eds., *Mesoamerican Voices: Native-Language Writings from Colonial Mexico, Oaxaca, Yucatan, and Guatemala* (New York: Cambridge University Press, 2005), 216–217.

QUESTIONS TO CONSIDER

1. Why was midwifery so crucial to the Aztecs?
2. How were boys and girls addressed by the midwife, and why?

For Further Information:

Carrasco, Davíd, and Scott Sessions. *Daily Life of the Aztecs, People of the Sun and Earth*, 2d ed. Indianapolis, IN: Hackett Publishing, 2008.

Clendinnen, Inga. *Aztecs: An Interpretation*. New York: Cambridge University Press, 1994.

At around harvest time in September, Aztec subjects of all classes ate maize, beans, and squash lightly seasoned with salt and ground chili peppers. During other times of the year, and outside the chinampa zone, food could be scarce, forcing the poor to consume roasted insects, grubs, and lake scum. Certain items, such as frothed cocoa, were reserved for elites. Stored maize was used to make tortillas year-round, but two poor harvests in a row, a frequent occurrence in densely populated highland Mexico, could reduce rations considerably.

Food and Scarcity

In addition to periodic droughts, Aztec subjects coped with frosts, plagues of locusts, volcanic eruptions, earthquakes, and floods. Given such ecological uncertainty, warfare was reserved for the agricultural off-season, when hands were not needed for planting, weeding, or harvesting. In the absence of large domesticated animals and advanced metallurgy, agricultural tasks throughout Mesoamerica demanded virtual armies of field laborers equipped only with fire-hardened digging sticks and obsidian or flint knives.

Animal protein was scarce in highland Mexico, especially in urban areas where hunting opportunities were limited and few domestic animals were kept. Still, the people of Tenochtitlán raised significant numbers of turkeys and plump, hairless dogs (the prized Xolo breed of today). Even humble beans, when combined with maize, could constitute a complete protein, and indigenous grains such as amaranth were also highly nutritious. Famines still occurred, however, and one in the early 1450s led to mass migration out of the Valley of Mexico. Thousands sold themselves into slavery to avoid starvation.

The Limits of Holy Terror

As the Aztec Empire expanded in the later fifteenth century, sacrificial debts grew to be a consuming passion among pious elites. Calendars filled with sacrificial rites, and warfare was ever more geared toward satisfying what must have seemed a ballooning cosmic budget.

By 1500 the Aztec state had reached its height, and some scholars have argued that it had even begun to decline. Incessant captive wars and related tribute demands had reached their limits, and old enemies such as the Tlaxcalans and Tarascans remained belligerent. New conquests were blocked by difficult terrain, declining tributes, and resistant locals. With available technologies, there was no place else for this inherently expansive empire to grow, and even with complex water works in place, agricultural productivity barely kept the people fed. Under the harsh leadership of Moctezuma II ("Angry Lord the Younger") (r. 1502–1520), the future did not look promising. Although there is no evidence to suggest the Aztec Empire was on the verge of collapse when several hundred bearded, sunburnt strangers of Spanish descent appeared on Mexico's Gulf Coast shores in 1519, points of vulnerability abounded.

Underlying Weaknesses

Tributes of Sweat: The Inca Empire 1430–1532

At about the same time as the Aztec expansion in southernmost North America, another great empire emerged in the central Andean highlands of South America. There appears to have been no significant contact between them. Like the Aztecs, the Incas burst out of their highland homeland in the 1430s to conquer numerous neighboring cultures and huge swaths of territory. They demanded tribute in goods and labor, along with allegiance to an imperial religion. Also like the Aztecs, the Incas based their expansion on a centuries-long inheritance of technological, religious, and political traditions.

> **FOCUS**
> What core features characterized Inca life and rule?

Despite enormous geographical, technological, and cultural barriers, by 1500 the Incas ruled one of the world's most extensive, ecologically varied, and rugged land empires, stretching nearly three thousand miles along both sides of the towering Andean mountain range from just north of the equator to central Chile. Like most empires ancient and modern, extensive holdings proved to be a mixed blessing (see Map 16.3, page 531).

From Potato Farmers to Empire Builders

Inca Origins

Thanks to abundant archaeological evidence and early postconquest interviews and narratives, much is known about the rise and fall of the Inca state. Still, like the early Ottoman, Russian, and other contemporary empires, numerous mysteries remain. As in those cases, legends and sagas of the formative period in particular require careful and skeptical analysis. The Inca case is somewhat complicated by the fact that their complex knotted-string records, or *khipus* (also *quipus*, KEY-poohs), have yet to be deciphered.

Scholars agree that the Incas emerged from among a dozen or so regional ethnic groups or allied clans living in the highlands of south-central Peru between 1000 and 1400 C.E. Living as scattered and more-or-less egalitarian potato and maize farmers, the Incas started out as one of many similar groups of Andean mountaineers. Throughout the Andes, clan groupings settled in and around fertile valleys and alongside lakes between eighty-five hundred and thirteen thousand feet above sea level. Though often graced with clear mountain springs and fertile soils, these highland areas were subject to periodic frosts and droughts, despite their location within the tropics. Even more than in the Aztec realm, altitude (elevation above sea level), not latitude (distance north or south of the equator), was key.

Environment and Exchange

Anthropologist John Murra once described Inca land use as a "**vertical archipelago**," a stair-step system of interdependent environmental "islands." Kin groups occupying the altitudes best suited to potato and maize farming established outlying settlements in cold uplands, where thousands of llamas and alpacas—the Americas' only large domestic animals—were herded, and also in hot lowlands, where cotton, peanuts, chilis, and the stimulant coca were grown. People, animals, and goods traveled constantly between highland and lowland ecological zones using well-maintained and often stone-paved trails and hanging bridges, yet the incredibly rugged nature of the terrain (plus the stubborn nature of llamas) made use of wheeled vehicles impractical.

vertical archipelago Andean system of planting crops and grazing animals at different altitudes.

Clans with highland ties and even some states of considerable size inhabited Peru's long desert coast. Here, urban civilization was nearly as old as that of ancient Egypt. Andean coast dwellers engaged in large-scale irrigated agriculture, deep-sea fishing, and long-distance trade. Trading families outfitted large balsawood rafts with cotton sails and plied the Pacific as far as Guatemala. Inland trade links stretched over the Andes and deep into the Amazon rain forest. Stopping at pilgrimage sites along the way, coast-dwelling traders exchanged salt, seashells, beads, and copper hatchets for exotic feathers, gold dust, and pelts. The Incas would move rapidly to exploit all of these diverse Andean regions and their interconnections, replacing old exchange systems and religious shrines with their own. Around 1200 C.E. they established a base near Cuzco (KOOS-coh), deep in the highlands of Peru not far from the headwaters of the Amazon, and soon after 1400 they began their remarkable drive toward empire.

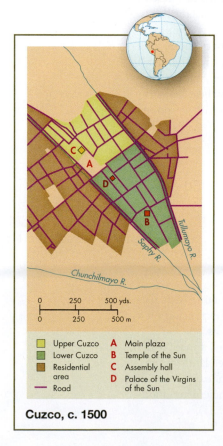

Cuzco, c. 1500

0   250   500 yds.

0   250   500 m

■ Upper Cuzco   **A** Main plaza
■ Lower Cuzco   **B** Temple of the Sun
■ Residential   **C** Assembly hall
   area   **D** Palace of the Virgins
— Road   of the Sun

The Great Apparatus: Inca Expansion and Religion

Cuzco, located in a narrow valley at a breathtaking altitude of over two miles above sea level, served as the Incas' political base and religious center. Like the Aztecs, the Incas saw their capital as the hub of the universe, calling it the "navel of the world." An array of dirt paths and stone-paved roads radiated out in all directions and tied hundreds of subsidiary shrines to the cosmically-ordained center. Much like the Aztecs' Tenochtitlán, Cuzco served as both the preeminent religious pilgrimage site and the empire's administrative capital. Compared with the Aztec capital, however, the city was modest in size, perhaps home to at most fifty thousand. Still, Cuzco had the advantage of being stoutly built of hewn stone. Whereas most of Tenochtitlán's temples and palaces were dismantled in the centuries following the Spanish Conquest, Cuzco's colossal stone foundations still stand.

For obscure reasons, the Incas in the early fifteenth century began conquering their neighbors. In time each emperor, or Sapa ("Unique") Inca, would seek to add more territory to the realm, called Tawantinsuyu (tuh-wahn-tin-SUE-you), or, "The Four Quarters Together." The Sapa Inca was thought to be descended from the sun and was thus regarded as the natural lord and sustainer of all humanity. To worship the sun was to worship the Inca, and vice versa. Devotion to lesser mountain and ancestor deities persisted, however, absorbed over time by the Incas in a way reminiscent of the Roman Empire's assimilation of regional deities and shrines. This religious inclusiveness helped the empire spread quickly even as the royal cult of the sun was inserted into everyday life. In a similar way, *runasimi*, later mislabeled "Quechua" (KETCH-wah) by the Spanish, became the Incas' official language even as local languages continued to be spoken.

Inca expansion was so rapid that the empire reached its greatest extent within a mere four generations of its founding. In semilegendary times, Wiracocha Inca (r. 1400–1438) was said to have led an army of followers to defeat an invading ethnic group called the Chankas near Cuzco. According to several royal sagas, this victory spurred Wiracocha to improve the defensive position of his people further by annexing the fertile territories of other neighbors. Defense turned to offense, and thus was primed the engine of Inca expansion.

Wiracocha's successor, Pachacuti Inca Yupanki (r. 1438–1471), was far more ambitious, so much so that he is widely regarded as the true founder of the Inca Empire. Substantial archaeological evidence backs this claim. Pachacuti (literally "Cataclysm") took over much of what is today Peru, including many coastal oases and the powerful Chimú kingdom. Along the way, Pachacuti perfected the core strategy of Inca warfare: amassing and mobilizing such overwhelming numbers of troops and backup forces that actual fighting was usually unnecessary.

Thousands of peasants were conscripted to bear arms, build roads, and carry grain. Others herded llamas, strung bridges, and cut building stone. With each new advance, huge masonry forts and temples were constructed in the imperial style, leaving an indelible Inca stamp on the landscape still visible today from Ecuador to Argentina. Even opponents such as the desert-dwelling Chimú, who had their aqueducts cut off to boot, simply capitulated in the face of the Inca juggernaut. Just after the Spanish Conquest, Pachacuti was remembered by female descendants:

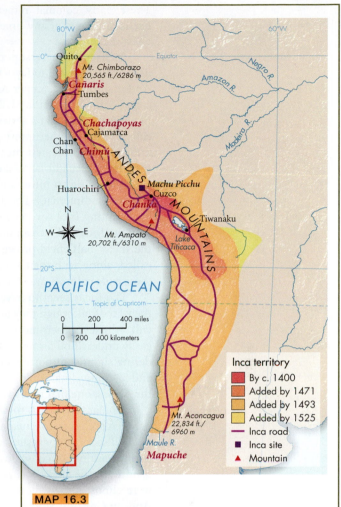

MAP 16.3

The Inca Empire, 1325–1521

Starting from their base in Cuzco, high in the Andes, the Incas built the most extensive empire in the Americas, and the second most populous after that of the Aztecs. They linked it by a road system that rivaled that of the ancient Romans. Inca expansion was extremely rapid as each ruler competed with his predecessor to extend tributary control. Some groups, such as the Cañaris and Chachapoyas, resisted Inca domination for many years, and the Mapuche of Chile were never conquered.

Imperial Expansion

As [Pachacuti] Inca Yupanki remained in his city and town of Cuzco, seeing that he was lord and that he had subjugated the towns and provinces, he was very pleased. He had subjugated more and obtained much more importance than any of his ancestors. He saw the great apparatus that he had so that whenever he wanted to he could subjugate and put under his control anything else he wanted.[3]

These early colonial remembrances underscore the Sapa Inca's tremendous power. Pachacuti could at any time deploy the "great apparatus" of empire as his personal conquest machine.

Pachacuti's successors continued in the same vein, extending conquests southward deep into what are today Chile and Argentina, and also eastward down the slope of the Andes and into the upper Amazon Basin. It is from this last region, the quarter the Incas called Antisuyu (auntie-SUE-you), that we derive the word *Andes*. On the northern frontier, the Incas fought a series of bitter wars with Ecuadorian ethnic groups to extend Inca rule into the southernmost part of present-day Colombia (see again Map 16.3). Here the imperial Inca conquest machine met its match: instead of capitulating, awestruck by the Inca, many Ecuadorian and Colombian highlanders fought to the death.

According to most sources, Inca advances into new territory were couched in the rhetoric of diplomacy. Local headmen were told they had two options: (1) to retain power by accepting Inca sovereignty and all the tributary obligations that went with it, or (2) to defy the Inca and face annihilation. Most headmen went along, particularly once word of the Incas' battlefield prowess spread. Those who did not were either killed in battle or exiled, along with their subject populations, to remote corners of the empire. Several of these exile colonies are still identifiable today in southern Ecuador and northern Bolivia.

The Incas seem to have been most interested in dominating productive peoples and their lands, although they also succeeded to some extent in spreading their imperial solar cult. Whatever their motives, like the Aztecs they defined political domination in simple, easily understood terms: tribute payment. Conquered subjects showed submission by rendering significant portions of their surplus production—and also labor—to the emperor and his subordinates. Tribute payment was a grudgingly accepted humiliation throughout the Andes, one that many hoped to shake off at the first opportunity.

Inca Religion

Scholars argue that to understand Inca religion one must set aside familiar distinctions between sacred and secular and between life and death. As the chapter-opening description of child sacrifice suggests, a continuum of life was assumed throughout the Andes, despite permanent loss of consciousness, and spirit and body were deemed inseparable. Likewise, features in the landscape, ranging from mountain springs and peaks to ordinary boulders, were almost always thought to house or emit spiritual energy (see Reading the Past: An Andean Creation Story). Even practical human-made landforms, such as irrigation canals, walls, and terraces, were commonly described as "alive." These sacred places, **wakas** (or *huacas*), received sacrifices of food, drink, and textiles from their human caretakers in exchange for good harvests, herd growth, and other bounties. In addition, most Andeans venerated images and amulets carved from wood, shell, stone, metal, and bone.

Andeans also venerated the human corpse. As long as something tangible remained of one's deceased relatives or ancestors, they were not regarded as entirely dead. It was generally thought wise to keep them around. Of course it helped that the central Andes' dry highland and coastal climates were ideal for mummification: preservation often required little more than removal of internal organs. In wetter areas, the dead were sometimes smoked over a slow fire, a process that led some outsiders to suspect cannibalism. In fact, it would have been fairly common in Inca times to encounter a neighbor's "freeze-dried" or smoked grandparents hanging from the rafters, still regarded as very much involved in household affairs. Andeans sometimes carried ancestor mummies to feasts and pilgrimages as well. Thus, Inca society included both past and present generations.

The Incas harnessed these and other core features of Andean society at its most ancient, yet like the Aztecs they put a unique stamp on the vast and diverse region they came to dominate. Though warlike, the Incas rarely sacrificed captive warriors, a ritual archaeologists now know was practiced among ancient coastal Peruvians. As for cannibalism, it was something the Incas associated with barbaric forest dwellers. Inca stone architecture, though clearly borrowing from older forms such as those of Tiwanaku, a temple complex in modern Bolivia, is still identifiable thanks to the frequent use of trapezoidal (flared) doors, windows, and niches (see the illustration of Machu Picchu in At a

waka A sacred place or thing in Andean culture.

An Andean Creation Story

The small Peruvian town of Huarochirí (wahr-oh-chee-REE), located in the high Andes east of Lima, was the target of a Spanish anti-idolatry campaign at the end of the sixteenth century. The Spanish conquest of the Incas, which began in 1532 (see Chapter 17), had little effect on the everyday life of Andean peasants, and many clung tenaciously to their religious beliefs. In Huarochirí, Spanish attempts to root out these beliefs and replace them with Western, Christian ones produced written testimonies from village elders in phonetically rendered Quechua, the most commonly spoken language in the Inca Empire. Like the Aztec codices, the resulting documents—aimed at eradicating the beliefs they describe—have unwittingly provided modern researchers with a rare window on a lost mental world. The passage here, translated directly from Quechua to English, relates an Andean myth that newly arrived or converted Christians considered a variation on the biblical story of Noah and the Great Flood. In the Christian story, God, angered by the wickedness of man, resolves to send a flood to destroy the earth. He spares only Noah, whom he instructs to build an ark in which Noah, his family, and a pair of every animal were saved from the Great Flood.

In ancient times, this world wanted to come to an end. A llama buck, aware that the ocean was about to overflow, was behaving like somebody who's deep in sadness. Even though its owner let it rest in a patch of excellent pasture, it cried and said, "In, in," and wouldn't eat. The llama's owner got really angry, and he threw a cob from some maize he had just eaten at the llama. "Eat, dog! This is some fine grass I'm letting you rest in!" he said. Then that llama began speaking like a human being. "You simpleton, whatever could you be thinking about? Soon, in five days, the ocean will overflow. It's a certainty. And the whole world will come to an end," it said. The man got good and scared. "What's going to happen to us? Where can we go to save ourselves?" he said. The llama replied, "Let's go to Villca Coto mountain. There we'll be saved. Take along five days' food for yourself." So the man went out from there in a great hurry, and himself carried both the llama buck and its load. When they arrived at Villca Coto mountain, all sorts of animals had already filled it up: pumas, foxes, guanacos [wild relatives of the llama], condors, all kinds of animals in great numbers. And as soon as that man had arrived there, the ocean overflowed. They stayed there huddling tightly together. The waters covered all those mountains and it was only Villca Coto mountain, or rather its very peak, that was not covered by the water. Water soaked the fox's tail. That's how it turned black. Five days later, the waters descended and began to dry up. The drying waters caused the ocean to retreat all the way down again and exterminate all the people. Afterward, that man began to multiply once more. That's the reason there are people until today.

[The scribe who recorded this tale, an Andean converted by Spanish missionaries, then adds this comment:] "Regarding this story, we Christians believe it refers to the time of the Flood. But they [i.e., non-Christian Andeans] believe it was Villca Coto mountain that saved them."

Source: Excerpt from *The Huarochirí Manuscript: A Testament of Ancient and Colonial Andean Religion*, trans. and ed. Frank Salomon and George L. Urioste (Austin: University of Texas Press, 1991), 51–52.

EXAMINING THE EVIDENCE

1. What do the similarities and differences between the Andean and Judeo-Christian flood stories suggest?

2. What do the differences between them reveal?

For Further Information:

Spalding, Karen. *Huarochirí: An Andean Society Under Inca and Spanish Rule*. Stanford: Stanford University Press, 1988.

Urton, Gary. *Inca Myths*. Austin: University of Texas Press, 1999.

Crossroads, page 512). It is worth noting, however, that the cult of the sun, which the Incas transformed and elevated to something new and imperial, proved far less durable than local religious traditions once the empire fell. Despite the Incas' rhetoric of diplomacy, most Andeans appear to have associated their rule with tyranny. Like the Aztecs, they failed to inspire loyalty in their subjects, who saw Inca government as a set of institutions designed to exploit, rather than protect, the peoples of the empire.

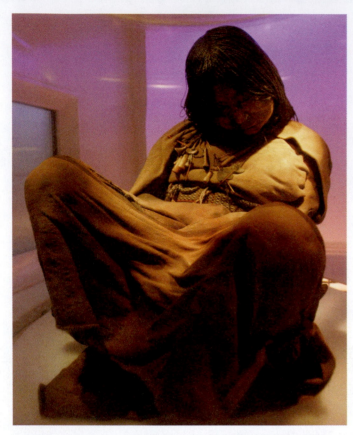

Inca Mummy

The Incas did not sacrifice humans as often as the Aztecs did, but headmen in newly conquered regions were sometimes required to give up young sons or daughters for live burial on high mountains. The victims, including this adolescent girl found in a shallow tomb atop 20,000-foot Mount Lullaillaco in the Argentine Andes, died of exposure after the long climb, but the Incas believed them to remain semiconscious and in communication with the spirit world. The girl seen here wears fine camelid-fiber garments bound by a *chumbi* (traditional Andean belt) and silver *topos* (shawl pins). She is also adorned with a shell necklace and other amulets, and her hair is pleated as described in early postconquest accounts. Such sacrifices were known as *capacocha*, or "debt payment." (AP Photo/Natacha Pisarenko.)

Daily Life Under the Incas

Inca society, like Aztec society, was highly stratified, with few means of upward mobility. Along with class gradations tied to occupation, the Incas maintained a variety of divisions and ranks according to sex, age, and ethnic or regional origin. Everyday life thus varied tremendously among the Inca's millions of subjects, although the vast peasant majority probably had much in common with farming folk the world over. Seasonal work stints for the empire were a burden for men, whereas women labored constantly to maintain households, raise children, and care for elderly kin. Unlike that of the Aztec, the Inca legal system, in common with most such systems in early modern times, appears to have been more harshly punitive against commoners than nobles. Exemplary elite behavior was expected, but not so rigidly enforced.

At the pinnacle of society was the Sapa Inca himself, the "son of the Sun." As in most imperial cultures, the emperor's alleged divinity extended to matters of war; he was believed to be the greatest warrior in the world. As a sign of unworthiness, everyone who came before him was obliged to bear a symbolic burden, such as a load of cloth or large water vessel. Only the Inca's female companions had intimate, daily contact with him. Although the ideal royal couple according to Inca mythology was a sibling pair, it was in fact dozens of wives and concubines who assured that there would be numerous potential heirs. Unlike monarchs in Europe and parts of Africa, the imperial household did not practice primogeniture, or the automatic inheritance of an estate or title by the eldest son. Neither did they leave succession to a group of elders, the method preferred by the Aztecs. Violent succession struggles predictably ensued. Though barred from the role of Inca themselves, ambitious noblewomen came to exercise considerable behind-the-scenes power over imperial succession.

Just beneath the Inca imperial line was an assortment of Cuzco-based nobles, readily identifiable by their huge ear-spools and finely woven tunics. Rather like their Aztec counterparts, they spoke a dialect of the royal language forbidden among commoners. Among this elite class were

Class Hierarchy decorated generals and hereditary lords of prominent and ancient clans. Often drawn from these and slightly lower noble ranks was a substantial class of priests and astrologers, charged with maintaining a vast array of temples and shrines.

Many noble women and girls deemed physically perfect, like the sacrificial victim described at the start of this chapter, were also selected for religious seclusion, somewhat like nuns in contemporary Western societies. Seclusion was not always permanent, because some of these women were groomed for marriage to the Inca. Still more noblewomen, mostly wives and widows, were charged with maintaining the urban households and country estates of the Incas, dead and alive.

Next came a class of bureaucrats, regional military leaders, and provincial headmen. Bureaucrats kept track of tribute obligations, communal work schedules, and land appropriations. Following conquest, up to two-thirds of productive land was set aside in the name of the ruling Inca and the cult of the sun. Bureaucrats negotiated with headmen as to which lands these would be, and how and when their subjects would be put to work on behalf of their new rulers. If negotiations failed, the military was called in for a show of force. Lower-ranking Inca military men, like bureaucrats, often faced service at the most hostile fringes of empire. They had little beyond the weak hold of local power to look forward to. As a result, in sharp distinction with the Aztecs, death in battle was not regarded as a glorious sacrifice among the Incas, but rather as yet another humiliation. Furthermore, many officers were themselves provincial in origin and thus had little hope of promotion to friendlier districts closer to the imperial core.

The Inca and his substantial retinue employed and received tribute from numerous artisans, mostly conquered provincials. Such specialists included architects, khipu-keepers, civil engineers, metalworkers, stonecutters, weavers, potters, wood-carvers, and many others. Unlike the Aztecs, the Incas did not tolerate free traders, instead choosing to manage the distribution of goods and services as a means of exercising state power. Partly as a result, chattel, or market-oriented, slavery appears not to have existed under the Incas, although some conquered young men and women spared from death or exile were absorbed into the labor force as personal servants. Most Inca subjects and tribute payers were peasants belonging to kin groups whose lives revolved around agriculture and rotational labor obligations. For them, the rigors of everyday life far outweighed the extra demands of Inca rule. Only in the case of recently conquered groups, or those caught in the midst of a regional rebellion or succession conflict, was this not true. Even then, subsistence remained the average Andean's most pressing concern; battlefields were abandoned at planting and harvest times.

Andean artisans living under Inca rule produced remarkable textiles, metalwork, and pottery, but the empire's most visible achievements were in the fields of architecture and civil engineering. The Incas' extensive road systems, irrigation works, and monumental temples were unmatched by any ancient American society. No one

Inca Road

Stretching nearly 10,000 miles across mountains, plains, deserts, and rain forests, the Inca Royal Road held one of the world's most rugged and extensive empires together. Using braided fiber bridges to span chasms and establishing inns and forts along the road, the Incas handily moved troops, supplies, and information—in the form of khipu records and messages—across vast distances. The Royal Road had the unintentional consequence of aiding penetration of the empire by Spanish conquistadors on horseback. (akg-images/Aurélia Frey.)

Material Achievements

else moved or carved such large stones or ruled such a vast stretch of terrain. Linking coast, highlands, and jungle, the Incas' roads covered nearly ten thousand miles. Draft workers and soldiers paved them with stones whenever possible, and many sections were hewn into near-vertical mountainsides by hand. Grass weavers spanned breathtaking gorges with hanging bridges strong enough to sustain trains of pack llamas for years at a time. These engineering marvels enabled the Incas to communicate and move troops and supplies across great distances with amazing speed, yet they also served the important religious function of facilitating pilgrimages and royal processions. Massive irrigation works and stone foundations, though highly practical, were similarly charged with religious power. Thus, the Inca infrastructure not only played an important practical role in imperial government, but it also expressed the Incas' belief in the connection between their own rule and the cosmic order.

The Incas appropriated and spread ancient Andean metalworking techniques, which were much older and thus far more developed than those of Mesoamerica. On the brink of a genuine Bronze Age by 1500, Inca metallurgy ranged from fine decorative work in specially prepared alloys to toolmaking for the masses. As in many parts of the early modern world, the forging of metals was as much a religious as an artistic exercise in the Andes, and metals themselves were regarded as semidivine. Gold was associated with the sun in Inca cosmology, and by extension with the Sapa Inca and his solar cult. Silver was associated with the moon and with several mother goddesses and Inca queens and princesses. Copper and bronze, considered less divine than gold and silver, were put to more practical uses.

Another ancient Andean tradition inherited by the Incas was weaving. Weaving in fact predates even ceramics in the Andes. Inca textiles, made mostly from native Peruvian cotton and alpaca fibers, were of extraordinary quality, and cloth became in essence the coin of the realm. Cooperative regional lords were rewarded by the Incas with substantial gifts of blankets and ponchos, which they could then redistribute among their subjects. Unlike some earlier coastal traditions, Inca design features favored geometric forms over representations of humans, animals, or deities. Fiber from the vicuña, a wild relative of the llama, was reserved for tunics and other garments worn only by the Sapa Inca. Softer than cashmere, it was the gold standard of Andean textile components. Some women became master weavers, but throughout most of the Inca Empire men wove fibers spun into thread by women, a gendered task division later reinforced by the Spanish.

With such an emphasis on textiles, it may come as no surprise that the Incas maintained a record-keeping system using knotted strings. Something like the Chinese abacus, or accounting device, in its most basic form, the **khipu** enabled bureaucrats and others to keep track of tributes, troop movements, ritual cycles, and other important matters. Like bronze metallurgy, the khipu predates the Inca Empire, but was most developed by Inca specialists. Although the extent of its capabilities as a means of data management remains a subject of intense debate, the khipu was sufficiently effective to remain in use for several centuries under Spanish rule, long after alphabetic writing was introduced.

Social Relations

Other ancient Andean traditions appropriated and spread by the Incas include reciprocity, the expectation of equal exchange and returned favors, complementary gender roles, and a tendency to view all social relations through the lens of kinship. Villagers, for example, depended on one another for aid in constructing homes, maintaining irrigation works, and tilling and harvesting fields. Whereas they chafed at service to the Inca ruler, they regarded rotational group work and communal care for disadvantaged neighbors not as burdens, but rather—after the work was done—as excuses for drinking parties and other festivities. Even in such a reciprocal environment, stresses and strains accumulated. In some villages, aggression was periodically vented during ritual fights between clan divisions.

Throughout the Andes, women occupied a distinct sphere from that of men, but not a subordinate one. For example, sources suggest that although the majority of Andeans living under Inca rule were patrilineal, or male-centered, in their succession preferences, power frequently landed in the hands of sisters and daughters of headmen. Literate Inca descendants described a world in which both sexes participated equally in complementary agricultural tasks, and also in contests against neighboring clans. Women exempted from rotational labor duties handled local exchanges of food and craft goods. Whether or not they were allowed to accumulate property as a result of these exchanges remains unknown.

Women's fertility was respected, but never equated with warfare, as in Aztec society. Interestingly, Andean childbirth was almost regarded as a nonevent, and rarely involved midwives. The Andean creator god, Wiracocha (weer-ah-COACH-ah), somewhat similar to the Aztecs' Tlaloc, had both male and female aspects. As in many traditional societies, Andean social hierarchy was described in terms of age and proximity of kin relation. "Mother" and "father," for example, were terms used to describe both gods and the most prominent earthly individuals (including one's parents). Next in line were numerous aunts, uncles, cousins, and so on down the family tree. Almost any respected elder was referred to as "uncle" or "aunt."

As in most early modern societies, parents treated Inca children much like miniature adults, and dressed them accordingly. Parents educated children by defining roles and duties early, using routine chores deemed appropriate to one's sex and status as the primary means of education. Girls and boys also participated in community and even state-level

khipu Knotted cotton or alpaca fiber strings used by the Incas and other Andeans to record tributes, troop numbers, and possibly narratives of events.

work projects. The expectation of all children was not to change society but to reproduce and maintain it through balanced relations with deities and neighbors. Contact with the Inca himself was an extremely remote possibility for most children living in the empire. A rare exception was capacocha sacrificial victims, such as the headman's daughter described at the opening of this chapter.

Just as maize was native to highland Mesoamerica and served as the base for urban development, the potato was the indigenous staple of the central Andes. A hearty, high-yield tuber with many varieties, the potato could be roasted, stewed, or naturally freeze-dried and stored for long periods. Control of preserved food surpluses was a hallmark of enduring imperial states, in large part because marching armies needed to eat. Maize could also be dried or toasted for storage and snacking, but among Andeans it was generally reserved for beer making. Along with maize, many lowland dwellers subsisted on manioc, peanuts, beans, and chili peppers.

Unique in the Americas, though common in much of Eurasia and Africa, Andean pastoralism played a critical role in Inca expansion. Andean domesticated animals included the llama, alpaca, and guinea pig. Llamas, in addition to carrying light loads, were sometimes eaten, and alpacas provided warm cloth fiber, much appreciated in the cold highlands. Slaughter of domestic animals, including fertilizer-producing guinea pigs, usually accompanied ritual occasions such as weddings or harvest festivals. Although like most early modern elites, the Inca and other nobles preferred to dine on freshly hunted deer, wild pig, and other meats. The average Andean diet was overwhelmingly vegetarian. Nevertheless, a common component of Inca trail food was *charqui* (hence "jerky"), bits of dried and salted llama flesh. Apparently for cultural rather than practical reasons, llamas and alpacas were never milked. Like many other peoples, Andeans restricted consumption of and even contact with certain animal fluids and body parts.

Khipu
The Incas did not invent the knotted-string record-keeping method known as khipu, but they used it extensively as they rapidly built their vast empire. Khipu masters braided and knotted cords of different colors and thicknesses in many combinations. Some khipus were kept as stored records and others sent as messages carried across the Andes by relay runners. (The Art Archive/Archaeological Museum Lima/Gianni Dagli Orti.)

Food and Subsistence

The high Inca heartland, though fertile, was prone to periodic droughts and frosts. The warmer coast was susceptible to catastrophic floods related to the so-called El Niño phenomenon, or periodic fluctuation in the eastern Pacific Ocean's surface temperature and resulting onshore moisture flow. Only by developing food storage techniques and exploiting numerous microenvironments were the Incas and their subjects able to weather such events. Added to these cyclical catastrophes were volcanic eruptions, earthquakes, mudslides, tsunamis, and plagues of locusts. Still, the overall record suggests that subsistence under the Incas, thanks to the "vertical archipelago," was much less precarious than under the Aztecs.

The Great Apparatus Breaks Down

In its simplest form Inca expansion derived from a blend of religious and secular impulses. As in Aztec Mexico, religious demands seem to have grown more and more urgent, possibly even destabilizing the empire by the time of the last Sapa Inca. As emperors died, their mummy cults required permanent and extravagant maintenance. In a context where the dead were not separate from the living, such obligations could not be shirked. The most eminent of mummies in effect tied up huge tracts of land. Logically, if vainly, successive emperors strove to make sure their mummy cults would be provided for in equal or better fashion. Each hoped his legacy might outshine that of his predecessor. Given the extraordinary precedent set by Pachacuti Inca, some scholars have argued that excessive mummy veneration effectively undermined the Inca Empire.

Despite this potentially unsustainable drive to conquer new territories, it was the Incas' notable organizational and diplomatic skills that held their enormous, geographically fractured empire together until the arrival of the Spanish in 1532. The Incas' ability to control the distribution of numerous commodities over great distances, to maintain communications and transport despite the absence of written texts and wheeled vehicles, to erect temples and centralize religious observation, and finally, to monopolize violence, all marked them as an imperial people.

As with the Aztecs, however, rapid growth by means of competitive violence sowed seeds of discontent. On the eve of the Spanish arrival both empires appear to have been on the verge of contraction rather than expansion, with rebellion at court and in the provinces the order of the day. The Incas had never done well against Amazonian and other lowland forest peoples, and some such enemies kept up chronic raiding activities. Highlanders such as the Cañaris of Ecuador and the Chachapoyas of northern Peru had cost the Incas dearly in their conquest, only just completed in 1525 after more than thirty years. Like the Tlaxcalans of Mexico, both of these recently conquered groups would ally with Spanish invaders in hopes of establishing their independence once and for all.

The Inca state was highly demanding of its subjects, and enemy frontiers abounded. Yet it seems the Incas' worst enemies were ultimately themselves. A nonviolent means of royal succession had never been established. This was good for the empire in that capable rather than simply hereditary rulers could emerge one after another, but bad in that the position of Sapa Inca was always up for grabs. In calmer times, defense against outside challengers would not have been much trouble, but the Spanish had the good fortune to arrive in the midst of a civil war between two rivals to the throne, Huascar and Atawallpa (also "Atahualpa"). By 1532 Atawallpa defeated his half-brother in a series of epic battles, only to fall prey to a small number of foreign interlopers.

COUNTERPOINT

The Peoples of North America's Eastern Woodlands 1450–1530

FOCUS

How did the Eastern Woodlanders' experience differ from life under the Aztecs and Incas?

By 1450 a great variety of native peoples, several million in all, inhabited North America's eastern woodlands. East of the Great Plains, dense forests provided raw materials for shelter, cooking, and transportation, as well as habitat for game. Trees also yielded nuts and other edible byproducts, and served as fertilizer for crops when burned. The great mound-building cultures of the Mississippi Basin had mostly faded by this time, their inhabitants having returned to less urban, more egalitarian ways of life. Villages headed by elected chiefs, not empires headed by divine kings, were the most common form of political organization (see Map 16.4).

Most of what we know about the diverse native inhabitants of eastern North America in early modern times derives from European documents from the contact period (1492–1750), plus archaeological studies. Although far less is known about them than about the Aztecs or Incas, the evidence suggests that Eastern Woodlands peoples faced significant changes in both their politics and everyday lives at the dawn of the early modern period, just before Europeans arrived to transform the region in other ways. Climate change may have been one important factor spurring conflict and consolidation.

Population Growth and Political Organization

Eastern Woodlands peoples were like the Aztecs in at least one sense. Most were maize farmers who engaged in seasonal warfare followed by captive sacrifice. According to archaeological evidence, both maize planting and warrior sacrifice spread into the region from Mesoamerica around the time of the Toltecs (800–1100 c.e.). The century prior to European contact appears to have been marked by rapid population growth, increased warfare, and political reorganization. Multisettlement ethnic alliances or leagues, such as the Iroquois Five Nations of upstate New York and the Powhatan Confederacy of Tidewater, Virginia, were relatively new to the landscape. Some confederacies were formed for

MAP 16.4

Native Peoples of North America, c. 1500

To the north of Mesoamerica, hundreds of native American groups, most of them organized as chiefdoms, flourished in a wide array of climate zones, from the coldest Arctic wilderness to the hottest subtropical deserts. Populations were highest where maize and other crops could be grown, as in the Mississippi Valley, Great Lakes, and eastern woodlands regions. Dense, sedentary populations also developed in the Pacific Northwest, where peoples such as the Kwakiutl lived almost entirely from gathering, hunting, and fishing. Nomadic hunters lived throughout the Great Plains, the Rocky Mountains, the Sierra Nevada, and the desert Southwest. Conflict between sedentary farmers and nomadic hunters was common, and some groups formed alliances to defend themselves against these and other attackers.

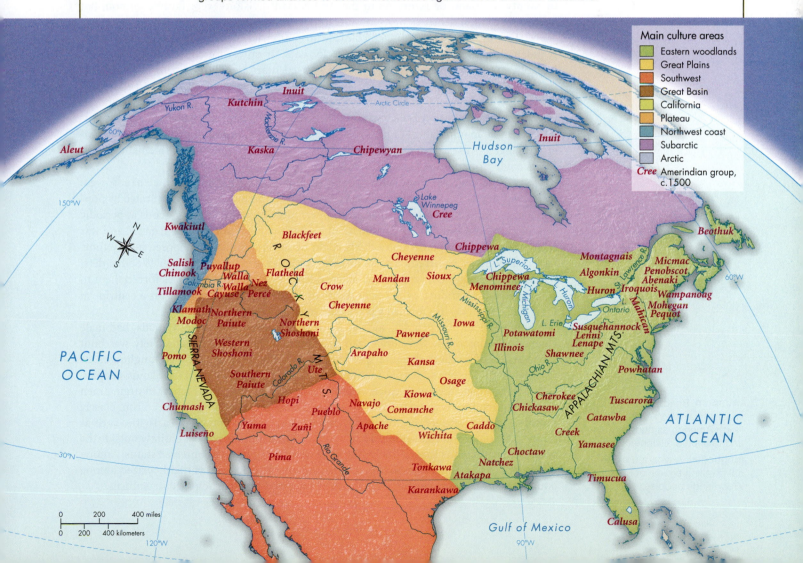

Huron Wampum Belt

For many Eastern Woodlands peoples such as the Huron, seashells like the New England quahog (a variety of clam) were sacred trade goods. Shell beads, generically called *wampum* after the arrival of Europeans, were woven into ceremonial belts whose geometrical designs and color schemes represented clans and sometimes treaties between larger groups. The linked-hands motif in this belt suggests a treaty or covenant. (National Museum of the American Indian, Smithsonian Institution. Catalog number: 1/2132. Photo by Katherine Fogden.)

Matrilineal Society

wampum Beads made of seashells; used in eastern North America as currency and to secure alliances.

longhouse A wooden communal dwelling typical of Eastern Woodlands peoples.

temporary defensive or offensive purposes, and others were primarily religious. Village populations sometimes exceeded two thousand inhabitants, and confederacies counted up to twenty thousand or more. As in the Andes, clan divisions were fairly common, but overall population densities were considerably lower.

Gathering-hunting groups, which made up a minority of the total Eastern Woodlands population, tended to occupy large but rocky, cold, or otherwise challenging landscapes. Notably, thanks to their varied diet, these nonsedentary peoples seem to have suffered fewer vitamin and mineral deficiencies than settled maize eaters. Even maize farmers, however, were generally taller than their European (or Mesoamerican) contemporaries. Throughout the eastern forests, including the vast Great Lakes region, metallurgy was limited to simple manipulation of native copper. Raw copper, found in abundance in northern Michigan, was regarded as a sacred substance and was associated with chiefly power. Beads made from polished seashells, or **wampum**, were similarly prized.

Nearly all Eastern Woodlands groups, including small gatherer-hunter bands, were headed by chiefs. These men were usually exceptional warriors or shamans elected by popular agreement. Chiefs retained power, however, only by redistributing goods at periodic ceremonies; generosity was the hallmark of leadership. Since surplus food, game, and war booty were far from predictable, chiefs could be unceremoniously deposed at any time. Few chiefdoms were hereditary. As in many societies, individual Eastern Woodlanders, particularly young men, yearned for independence even as circumstances forced them to cooperate and subordinate their wills to others. If the chief's generosity was a centripetal force, egalitarian desires formed a powerful centrifugal one.

Some agricultural peoples, such as the Huron of central Ontario, Canada, had male chiefs or headmen but were organized matrilineally. This meant that society was built around clans of mothers, daughters, and sisters. Matrilineal clans occupied **longhouses**, or wooden multifamily residential buildings, typical of most Eastern Woodlands peoples. Elder women consulted with chiefs regularly, and all women played a part in urging men to war. Agriculture was regarded as a strictly female preserve among the Huron, closely linked to human fertility. Huron men were relegated to risky, perennial activities such as hunting, warfare, and tree felling. Their sphere of influence lay almost entirely outside the village. Men's exploits abroad, including adolescent vision quests, conferred status. Among all Eastern Woodlanders, public speech making, or rhetoric, was as highly prized among adult men as martial expertise. Only the most esteemed men participated in councils.

Children's lives were generally unenviable among North America's Eastern Woodlanders (keeping in mind that this was true of childhood throughout the early modern world). Thanks to a multitude of vermin and pathogens, generally poor nutrition, smoky residences, and manifold hazards of war and accident, relatively few children survived to adulthood. Partly for these reasons, Eastern Woodlands cultures discouraged severe discipline for children, instead allowing them much freedom.

Children's Lives

Playtime ended early for surviving girls and boys, however, as each was schooled before puberty in the arts and responsibilities deemed appropriate for their sex. Girls learned to farm and cook, boys to hunt and make war. Soon after puberty young people began to "try out" mates until a suitable match was found. This preference for trial marriage over forced arrangements was found in the Andes and other parts of the Americas as well. Though this and the seemingly casual practice of divorce among Eastern Woodlanders were considered scandalous by early modern European standards, stable monogamy prevailed.

Warfare was endemic throughout the Eastern Woodlands in the summer season, when subsistence itself was less of a battle. In form, these wars resembled blood feuds, or vengeance cycles. According to European witnesses, wars among the Iroquois, Mahicans, and others were spawned by some long-forgotten crime, such as the rape or murder of a clan member. As such, they did not constitute struggles over land or other natural resources, which were relatively abundant, but rather male contests intended to prove courage and preserve honor.

Warfare

Warfare closely resembled hunting in that successful warriors gained status for their ability to ambush and capture their equivalents from the opposite camp. These unlucky individuals were then brought to the captor's longhouse for what can only be described as an excruciating ordeal, nearly always followed by slaughter and ritual consumption. (Female and child captives, by contrast, were "adopted" as replacements for lost kin.) The religious significance of captive sacrifice among Eastern Woodlands peoples has been less clearly explained than that of the Aztecs and other Mesoamericans, but it seems to have been tied to subsistence anxieties.

Religious thought among Eastern Woodlands peoples varied, but there were commonalities. Beyond the realm of everyday life was a complex spirit world. Matrilineal societies such as the Huron traced their origins to a somewhat malevolent female spirit whose grandsons were responsible for various technical innovations and practices considered essential to civilized human life. The sky itself was often more important than the sun or moon in Eastern Woodlands mythologies, and climatic events were associated with enormous bird spirits, such as the thunderbird.

Religion

Like Andean peoples, many Eastern Woodlanders believed that material things such as boulders, islands, and personal charms contained life essences, or "souls." Traders and warriors, in particular, took time to please spirits and "recharge" protective amulets with offerings and incantations. Periodic feasts were also imbued with spiritual energy, but were unlike those of the Aztecs or Incas in that none was held on a specified date. As in many nonurban societies, religious life was an everyday affair, not an institutionalized one. Instead of priesthoods, liturgies, and temples, most Eastern Woodlands peoples relied on elders and shamans to maintain traditions and remind juniors of core beliefs.

Dreams and visions were carefully analyzed for clues to personal and group destinies. Dreams were also analyzed for evidence of witchcraft, or malevolent spell casting, within the group. Stingy or secretive individuals were sometimes suspected of this practice, often associated with jealousy, greed, and other socially unacceptable impulses. As in many semisedentary cultures worldwide, malicious witchcraft was blamed for virtually all sickness and death.

Unlike many other native American groups, most Eastern Woodlanders did not regard death as a positive transition. They believed that souls lived on indefinitely and migrated to a new home, usually a recognizable ethnic village located in the western distance. Even dogs' souls migrated, as did those of wild animals. The problem with this later existence was that it was unsatisfying. Dead souls were said to haunt the living, complaining of hunger and other insatiable desires. The Huron sought to keep their dead ancestors together and send them off well through elaborate burial rituals, but it was understood that ultimately little could be done for them.

Conclusion

By the time Europeans entered the Caribbean Sea in 1492, the two continents and many islands that make up the Americas were home to over 60 million people. Throughout the Western Hemisphere, native American life was vibrant and complex, divided by language, customs, and sometimes geographical barriers, but also linked by religion, trade, and war. Cities, pilgrimage sites, mountain passes, and waterways served as crossroads for the exchange of goods and ideas, often between widely dispersed peoples. Another uniting factor was the underlying religious tradition of shamanism.

The many resources available in the highland tropics of Mesoamerica and the Andes Mountains promoted settled agriculture, urbanization, and eventually empire building. Drawing on the traditions of ancestors, imperial peoples such as the Aztecs and Incas built formidable capitals, road systems, and irrigation works. As the Inca capacocha and Aztec warrior sacrifices suggest, these empires were driven to expand at least as much by religious beliefs as by material desires. In part as a result of religious demands, both empires were in crisis by the first decades of the sixteenth century, when Europeans possessing steel-edged weapons, firearms, and other technological advantages first encountered them. Other native peoples, such as the Huron, Iroquois, and Powhatan of North America's eastern woodlands, built chiefdoms and confederacies rather than empires, and to some degree these looser structures would prove more resilient in the face of European invasion.

NOTES

1. For the archaeologist's own account of these discoveries, see Johan Reinhard, *The Ice Maiden: Inca Mummies, Mountain Gods, and Sacred Sites in the Andes* (Washington, DC: National Geographic, 2005).
2. Miguel León-Portilla, *Pre-Columbian Literatures of Mexico* (Norman: University of Oklahoma Press, 1969), 87.
3. Juan de Betanzos, *Narrative of the Incas*, c. 1557, trans. Roland Hamilton and Dana Buchanan (Austin: University of Texas Press, 1996), 92.

RESOURCES FOR RESEARCH

Many Native Americas

Native American history has long been interdisciplinary, combining archaeology, anthropology, history, linguistics, geography, and other disciplines. Here is a small sample of works on the last centuries before European arrival plus several venerable encyclopedias.

Conrad, Geoffrey, and Arthur Demarest. *Religion and Empire*. 1984.

Denevan, William, ed. *The Native Population of the Americas in 1492*, 2d ed. 1992.

National Museum of the American Indian, Washington, DC: http://www.nmai.si.edu/.

Steward, Julian, ed. *The Handbook of South American Indians*, 7 vols. 1946–1959.

Sturtevant, William E., ed. *The Handbook of North American Indians*, 20 vols. 1978–2008.

Trigger, Bruce, ed. *The Cambridge History of the Native Peoples of the Americas*, 3 vols. 1999.

Tributes of Blood: The Aztec Empire, 1325–1521

Scholarship on the Aztecs has exploded in recent years. The following small sample includes new works that synthesize the perspectives of history, anthropology, and comparative religions.

Carrasco, Davíd. *City of Sacrifice: The Aztec Empire and the Role of Violence in Civilization*. 1999.

Carrasco, Davíd, and Scott Sessions. *Daily Life of the Aztecs, People of the Sun and Earth*, 2d ed. 2008.

Clendinnen, Inga. *Aztecs, an Interpretation*. 1994.

For more on Mexico City's Templo Mayor, see: http://archaeology.asu.edu/tm/index2.htm.

Hassig, Ross. *Aztec Warfare: Imperial Expansion and Political Control*, 2d ed. 2006.

Townsend, Richard F. *The Aztecs*, rev. ed. 2000.

Tributes of Sweat: The Inca Empire, 1430–1532

As with the Aztecs, studies of the Incas have proliferated in recent years. Exciting work has taken place in many fields, including archaeology, linguistics, history, and anthropology.

D'Altroy, Terrence. *The Incas*. 2002.

McEwan, Gordon F. *The Incas: New Perspectives*. 2006.

On khipus, see also Prof. Urton's Web site: http://khipukamayuq .fas.harvard.edu.

Urton, Gary. *Signs of the Inka Khipu: Binary Coding in the Andean Knotted-String Records*. 2004.

Von Hagen, Adriana, and Craig Morris. *The Cities of the Ancient Andes*. 1998.

COUNTERPOINT: The Peoples of North America's Eastern Woodlands, 1450–1530

The history of North America's Eastern Woodlands peoples was pioneered by Canadian and U.S.-based anthropologists and historians. It has continued to grow and broaden in scope. Indigenous voices are best heard in James Axtell's documentary history.

The American Indian Studies Research Institute, University of Indiana, Bloomington. http://www.indiana.edu/%7Eaisri/ index.shtml.

Axtell, James. *Natives and Newcomers: The Cultural Origins of North America*. 2001.

Axtell, James, ed. *The Indian Peoples of Eastern North America: A Documentary History of the Sexes*. 1981.

Richter, Daniel. *The Ordeal of the Longhouse: The Peoples of the Iroquois League in the Era of European Colonization*. 1992.

Trigger, Bruce. *The Children of Aataentsic: A History of the Huron People to 1660*, 2d ed. 1987.

▶ **For additional primary sources from this period**, see *Sources of Crossroads and Cultures*.

▶ **For Web sites, images, and documents related to topics in this chapter**, see Make History at bedfordstmartins.com/smith.

REVIEW

The major global development in this chapter ▶ The diversity of societies
and states in the Americas prior to European invasion.

IMPORTANT EVENTS

c. 900–1600	Late Woodland period of dispersed farming and hunting
c. 1100	Aztecs leave Aztlán
c. 1200	Incas move into Cuzco region
c. 1270	Aztecs settle in Valley of Mexico
c. 1320	Aztecs ally with Colhua
c. 1325	Tenochtitlán founded at Lake Texcoco's edge
c. 1437	Incas defeat Chankas
c. 1440–1471	Sapa Inca Pachacuti expands empire into Ecuador and Bolivia
1450–1451	Great famine in Valley of Mexico
1471–1493	Incas conquer northern Chile and Argentina
1487–1502	Aztecs dedicate Coatepec (Templo Mayor) and expand sacrificial wars
1493–1525	Incas conquer northern Peru and highland Ecuador
1502–1519	Reign of Moctezuma II, conquered by Spanish
1525–1532	Inca succession war, followed by arrival of the Spanish
c. 1570	Formation of Huron Confederacy north of Lake Ontario and of Iroquois League south of Lake Ontario
c. 1580	Formation of Powhatan Confederacy in eastern Virginia

KEY TERMS

autosacrifice (p. 525)
chinampa (p. 523)
khipu (p. 536)
longhouse (p. 540)
shamanism (p. 518)

tribute (p. 526)
vertical archipelago (p. 530)
waka (p. 532)
wampum (p. 540)

CHAPTER OVERVIEW QUESTIONS

1. In what ways was cultural diversity in the Americas related to environmental diversity?

2. Why was it in Mesoamerica and the Andes that large empires emerged in around 1450?

3. What key ideas or practices extended beyond the limits of the great empires?

SECTION FOCUS QUESTIONS

1. What factors account for the diversity of native American cultures?

2. What core features characterized Aztec life and rule?

3. What core features characterized Inca life and rule?

4. How did the Eastern Woodlanders' experience differ from life under the Aztecs and Incas?

MAKING CONNECTIONS

1. Compare the Aztec and Inca empires with the Ming (see Chapter 15). What features did they share? What features set them apart?

2. How did Aztec and Inca sacrificial rituals differ, and why?

3. What were the main causes of warfare among native American peoples prior to the arrival of Europeans?

AT A CROSSROADS ▲

Painted on calfskins, portolan ("port finder") charts were used by mariners in the Mediterranean and North Atlantic beginning in the late fourteenth century. In addition to ports, the charts showed coasts and islands and corresponded, at least theoretically, to compass bearings. Like medieval manuscript illuminators, chart-makers occasionally filled blank or unknown spaces with renditions of ships, sea monsters, and freakish foreigners. After Christopher Columbus's momentous transatlantic voyage in 1492, portolan charts began to depict new European discoveries in the Americas with great accuracy. This 1500 map by Juan de la Cosa, who sailed with Columbus, is the earliest such chart. (Museo Naval, Madrid/Bridgeman Art Library.)

The Fall of Native American Empires and the Rise of an Atlantic World

1450–1600

The woman the Aztecs called Malintzin (mah-LEEN-tseen) was only a young girl when she was traded away by her parents around 1510. Malintzin was sent to serve a noble family living in what is today the state of Tabasco, on the Gulf coast of Mexico. She herself was of noble birth, a native speaker of the Aztec language, Nahuatl (NAH-watt). Malintzin's new masters were Chontal Maya speakers, and soon she learned this language, quite different from her own.

Throughout Malintzin's servitude in Tabasco, stories circulated there and in the neighboring Yucatan peninsula of bearded strangers. One day in the year 1519 eleven large vessels filled with these strangers arrived in Tabasco. The Tabascans assembled an attack when one party came ashore in a rowboat, but they were quickly defeated. In exchange for

BACKSTORY

By the mid-1400s, some 60 million people inhabited the Americas, about half of them subjects of the Aztec and Inca empires (see Chapter 16). These empires relied on far-flung tribute networks and drew from diverse cultural traditions even as they spread their own religious practices and imperial languages. Outside the Aztec and Inca realms, smaller states and chiefdoms occupied much of the hemisphere. Conflict between groups, whether in Peru, Brazil, Mexico, or eastern North America, was frequent.

The inhabitants of western Eurasia and North Africa were slowly recovering from the Black Death of 1347–1350 (see Chapter 15). Weakened nobilities and rebounding populations stimulated trade, political consolidation, and the adoption of new technologies for war and transport. The long-distance trade in luxury goods such as silk and spices also recovered, but by the early 1400s the rise of the Ottoman Empire in the eastern Mediterranean intensified competition and limited western European access to overland routes such as the Silk Road. The Asian luxury trade drained Europe of precious metals, prompting enterprising Italians and the seafaring Portuguese and Spanish of the Iberian peninsula to seek gold in Africa, to plant slave-staffed sugar colonies in the islands of the Mediterranean and eastern Atlantic, and to search for sea routes to Asia. In so doing they would link distant continents and initiate the development of a new Atlantic world.

Guns, Sails, and Compasses: Europeans Venture Abroad

FOCUS Why and how did Europeans begin to cross unknown seas in the fifteenth century?

New Crossroads, First Encounters: The European Voyages of Discovery, 1492–1521

FOCUS What were the main sources of conflict between Europeans and native Americans in the first decades after contact?

Spanish Conquests in the Americas, 1519–1600

FOCUS What factors enabled the Spanish to conquer the Aztec and Inca empires?

A New Empire in the Americas: New Spain and Peru, 1535–1600

FOCUS Why was the discovery of silver in Spanish America so important in the course of world history?

Brazil by Accident: The Portuguese in the Americas, 1500–1600

FOCUS How and why did early Portuguese Brazil develop differently from Spanish America?

COUNTERPOINT: The Mapuche of Chile: Native America's Indomitable State

FOCUS How did the Mapuche of Chile manage to resist European conquest?

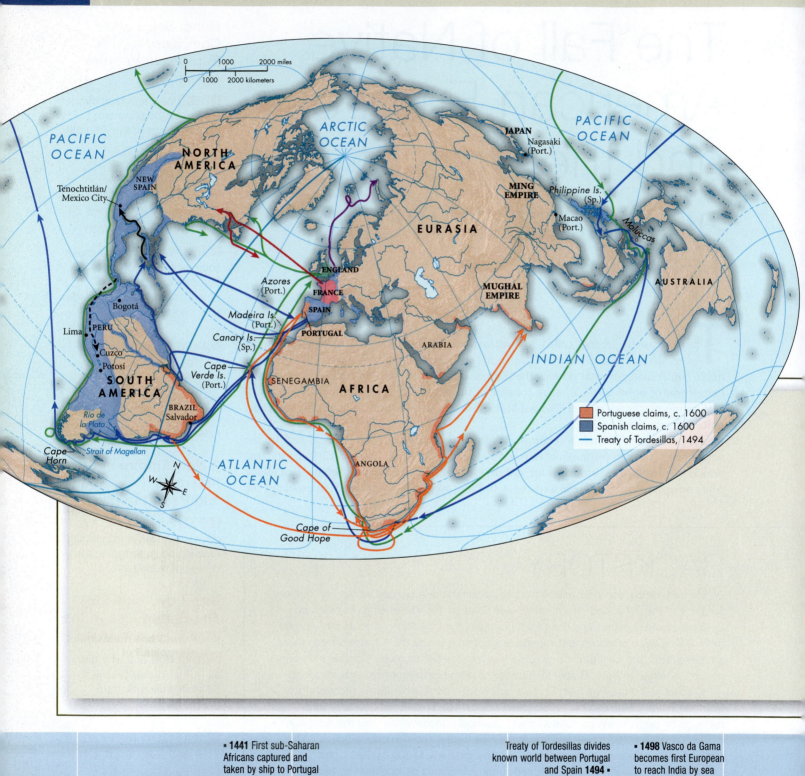

Portuguese claims, c. 1600
Spanish claims, c. 1600
Treaty of Tordesillas, 1494

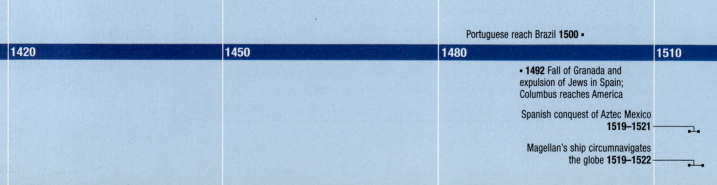

- **1441** First sub-Saharan Africans captured and taken by ship to Portugal

Treaty of Tordesillas divides known world between Portugal and Spain **1494** ▪

- **1498** Vasco da Gama becomes first European to reach India by sea

Portuguese reach Brazil **1500** ▪

| 1420 | 1450 | 1480 | 1510 |

- **1492** Fall of Granada and expulsion of Jews in Spain; Columbus reaches America

Spanish conquest of Aztec Mexico **1519–1521**

Magellan's ship circumnavigates the globe **1519–1522**

peace, they offered the strangers gold and feather work, and also several servant girls, among them Malintzin. When asked through an interpreter where the gold had come from, the Tabascans said "Mexico."

The strangers' interpreter was a bearded Spanish castaway called Jerónimo de Aguilar. He had lived several years in the Yucatan, but had now been ransomed by his countrymen. Aguilar soon discovered that Malintzin knew the language of Aztec Mexico. Their strangers' leader, Hernando Cortés, took a special interest in her for this reason, but as several of the strangers would later write, he also considered her the most beautiful and intelligent of the group of young female captives.

Twice given away now, and less certain than ever of her future, Malintzin joined the bearded foreigners in their cramped, floating homes. Heading west in the direction of the Aztec heartland, they reached a tiny island within sight of the mainland. Here Cortés ordered a party ashore to make contact with local villagers and, through them, to initiate a conversation with a group of traveling Aztec representatives. Only Nahuatl was spoken.

Suddenly the bilingual Malintzin was thrust into a mediating role of global significance. She passed along in Nahuatl the words the Spanish castaway gave her in Chontal Mayan. Then she did the reverse when the Aztec ambassadors replied. Aguilar made sense of the Mayan replies in the strangers' language for Cortés, who was already planning a risky march to take over the Aztec capital. Malintzin soon learned Castilian Spanish,

MAPPING THE WORLD

European Exploration and Conquest, c. 1450–1600

Combining a variety of shipbuilding and navigating technologies in innovative ways, and arming themselves with powerful new guns, western Europeans set out in search of spices, gold, and slaves. Some also sought Christian allies and converts. Merchants shared knowledge and pooled capital in Portugal's capital of Lisbon, the first seat of truly global maritime exploration. Soon after the Portuguese came the Spanish, among them settlers, traders, missionaries, and—most famously—conquistadors. These toppled the great American empires of the Aztecs and Incas within a generation of Columbus's landing in the Caribbean. The French, Dutch, and English followed the Iberian lead, but had little to show for their efforts before 1600.

ROUTES ▼

European exploration

→ Portuguese, 1487–1500
→ Spanish, 1492–1522
→ English, 1497–1580
→ French, 1534–1536
→ Dutch, 1596

Spanish conquistadors

→ Hernando Cortés, 1519–1521
--▸ Francisco Pizarro, 1531–1533

1532–1536 Spanish conquest of Inca Peru

▪ **1549** Portuguese establish royal capital of Salvador; first Jesuits arrive in Brazil

▪ **1572** Mita labor draft and mercury amalgamation formalized in Potosí

▪ **1555** French establish colony in Brazil's Guanabara Bay

1540	1570	1600

▪ **1545** Discovery of silver deposits at Potosí

1570–1571 Inquisition established in Lima and Mexico City

▪ **1592** Potosí reaches peak production

▪ **1564** Discovery of mercury mines in Huancavelica, Peru

▪ **1567** Portuguese drive French from Brazil

▪ **1599** Great Mapuche uprising in Chile

rendering Aguilar unnecessary. From here until the end of the conquest campaigns in 1521, Malintzin served as Cortés's key to Aztec Mexico.

In the midst of conquest Malintzin bore Cortés a son, but she ultimately married another Spaniard and lived with the respect given to European ladies in the first years of colonial rule. Malintzin joined a host of other former Aztec subjects who helped the foreigners build Mexico City from the rubble of the former Aztec capital of Tenochtitlán, and eventually a vast Christian kingdom called New Spain.

In modern Mexican mythology Malintzin, or Malinche (mah-LEEN-cheh), as she is commonly known, is regarded as a traitor, a collaborator, even a harlot. Recent scholars have shown these characterizations to be both anachronistic and unfair. Malintzin was not seen as a traitor in her own day, even by the Aztecs. In their paintings of the conquest, Nahuatl-speaking artists working shortly after the arrival of the Spanish often placed Malintzin at the center, poised and confident, speech scrolls emanating from her mouth. For a culture that called its kings *tlatoque*, or "speakers," this was significant.

But why was it mostly southern Europeans who were sailing across the Atlantic in Malintzin's and Cortés's time? In part it was because residents of the old European crossroads of Iberia (the peninsula occupied by Spain and Portugal), including colonies of Italian merchants, had begun charting the eastern Atlantic at least a century before. Also, in finishing what they called the *Reconquista* (Reconquest) of their homeland, Christian Iberians were driven to outflank the growing Ottoman Empire in North Africa and to revive the global crusade against Islam. Over time, a mix of commercial, political, and religious motives inspired the merchants and monarchs of Portugal and Spain, Europe's southwestern-most kingdoms, to develop the technologies needed to navigate open seas, exploring first the west coast of Africa and then crossing the vast Atlantic itself. Flush with capital, Italian bankers helped fund these enterprises (as we saw in Chapter 15).

The Iberian encounter with the Americas that resulted from all of these factors was an accident of monumental significance. In quest of legendary Asian riches, Columbus and his successors landed instead in the vast and populous but previously isolated regions they called the New World. It was new to them, of course, but hardly so to its roughly 60 million native American inhabitants. Cultural misunderstandings, political divisions among indigenous peoples, and European firearms aided conquest and settlement, but germs made the difference in a way not seen anywhere in Africa or Asia. Only certain Pacific Islanders proved as vulnerable.

Among the manifold effects of European expansion across the Atlantic was a biological exchange of profound importance for all humanity. Dubbed by historian Alfred Crosby "the Columbian Exchange," this was the first major biological relinking of the earth since the continents had drifted apart in prehuman times. Although the Columbian Exchange brought many deadly diseases to the Americas, it also brought new animals for transport, plowing, and consumption. Among the many effects of this global exchange was rapid population growth in parts of the world where American crops such as potatoes and maize took root. As a result of European expansion to the west, the Atlantic became a global crossroads, the center of a new pattern of exchange that would have consequences for the entire world.

Finally, we should not make the mistake of assuming that Europeans met little or no significant resistance in the Americas. As we shall see in the Counterpoint that concludes this chapter, one group of native Americans who successfully fought off European conquest, in part by adopting the horse and turning it against their oppressors, were the Mapuche of Chile.

OVERVIEW QUESTIONS

The major global development in this chapter: European expansion across the Atlantic and its profound consequences for societies and cultures worldwide.

As you read, consider:

1. What were the main biological and environmental consequences of European expansion into the Atlantic after 1492?

2. What roles did misunderstanding and chance play in the conquests of the Aztecs and Incas?

3. How did Eurasian demand for silver and sugar help bring about the creation of a linked Atlantic world?

Guns, Sails, and Compasses: Europeans Venture Abroad

Since late medieval times, Nordic and southern European mariners had been venturing farther and farther out to sea, testing seasonal winds and following currents as they founded new colonies and connected markets to regions of supply. Sailors and navigators shared information, but as in the Mediterranean, colonizing distant lands was a competitive, religiously charged, and violent process, one that also entailed fusing technologies from around the world. In the fifteenth century tiny Portugal emerged as the world's first truly global maritime empire. Neighboring Spain followed, spurred on by Christopher Columbus and a crusading spirit.

> **FOCUS**
> Why and how did Europeans begin to cross unknown seas in the fifteenth century?

Motives for Exploration

Early modern Europeans had many reasons for engaging in overseas ventures, but most shared a common interest in accumulating wealth, gaining power against their rivals, and spreading Christianity. Commerce was a core motive for expansion, as European merchants found themselves starved for gold and silver, which they needed to purchase Asian spices, silks, gems, and other luxuries. With the exception of Mediterranean coral and, increasingly, guns, Europe produced little to offer in exchange for eastern luxuries. In part because of Europe's relative poverty, ambitious monarchs and princes adopted violent means to extend their dominions overseas and to increase their tax and tribute incomes. Finally, Europe's many Christian missionaries hoped to spread their religion throughout the globe. These motives would shape the early encounters between Europeans and the peoples of the Americas, as well as the subsequent hybrid societies that would emerge in the conquered lands.

"Gold is most excellent," wrote Christopher Columbus in a letter to the king and queen of Spain. "Gold constitutes treasure, and anyone who has it can do whatever he likes in the world."[1] Columbus, a native of the Italian city-state of Genoa, knew what he was talking about. Genoese merchants had long traded for gold in North Africa, where Muslim traders who crossed the Sahara from West Africa brought it to exchange for a variety of goods. African gold lubricated Mediterranean and European trade, but population growth, commercial expansion, and intensifying competition among Christian and Islamic states

Gold and Spices

strained supplies. It was thus the well-placed Portuguese, who established a North African foothold in Morocco in 1415, who first sought direct access to African gold.

Italian merchants made some of their greatest profits on spices, which were used as both medicines and flavoring agents. Since most spices came from the farthest tropical margins of Asia, they rose considerably in value as they passed through the hands of mostly Islamic middlemen in the Indian Ocean and eastern Mediterranean. Indian pepper and Indonesian nutmeg were but a few of the many desired drugs and condiments that Portuguese and other European merchants hoped to purchase more cheaply by sailing directly to the source. This entailed either circumnavigating Africa or finding a western passage to the Pacific.

Slaves and Sugar

Throughout the Mediterranean basin, slaves were prized as field laborers and household servants, and demand for them grew with the expansion of commercial agriculture and the rise of wealthy merchant families. Prices also rose as source regions near the Black Sea were cut off after 1453 by the Ottomans. As the word *slave* suggests, most captives came initially from the Slavic regions of eastern Europe. Others were prisoners of war taken in battles and pirate raids. In part to meet growing Christian European demand, increasing numbers of sub-Saharan Africans were transported to North African ports by caravan. As with gold, southern European merchants engaged in this trade were quick to seek captives by sailing directly to West Africa.

Sugar, yet another exotic commodity in high and growing demand in Europe, required large investments in land, labor, and machinery. Produced mostly by enslaved workers on eastern Atlantic islands such as Portuguese Madeira by the mid-fifteenth century, cane sugar, in medieval times considered a spice or drug, increasingly became a common commodity in Europe as both a sweetener and preservative. As sugar took the place of honey in Old World cuisines, few consumers pondered its growing connection to overseas enslavement. In time, European demand for sugar would lead to the establishment of the Atlantic slave trade and the forced migration of millions of Africans to the Americas.

Technologies of Exploration

Firearms Manufacture

As they set sail for new horizons, Europeans employed innovations in three technological spheres: gun making, shipbuilding, and navigation. First was firearms manufacture. Gunpowder, a Chinese invention, had been known since at least the ninth century C.E. Chinese artisans experimented with rockets and bombs, but it was late medieval and early modern Europeans who developed gunpowder and gun making to their greatest destructive effect.

Europeans had also borrowed and improved on ancient Chinese papermaking and movable type technologies, and by 1500 they published treatises detailing the casting and operation of bronze and iron cannon. Soon, crude handguns and later muskets transformed field warfare, first in Europe, then worldwide. As gun and powder technologies improved and fighters acquired shooting and reloading skills, contingents of musketeers replaced archers, crossbowmen, and other foot soldiers.

Shipbuilding and Navigation

The second key technological leap was in ship construction. Although numerous small, swift-sailing vessels traversed the Mediterranean in late medieval times, long-distance carriers were cumbersome and even dangerous when overloaded. The Roman-style galley, used mostly in the Mediterranean, was a long and narrow fighting vessel propelled by captive oarsmen with occasional help from sails. Galleys functioned effectively where seas were calm, distances short, and prisoners plentiful. Galleys also worked well to defend against pirates and for massive showdowns, but they were almost useless for carrying cargo.

The galley proved unreliable for the rougher waters and longer voyages common in the North Atlantic. Here, in the old trading ports and fishing villages of Portugal, Spain, western France, the Netherlands, and England, shipwrights combined more rigid North Sea hull designs and square sail rigs with some of the defensive features of the galley, such as the high aft-castle, or fortified cabin built on the rear deck. They also borrowed and incorporated the galley's triangular or lateen sails, which in turn had been adapted from the Arabian *dhows* of the Indian Ocean.

The resulting hybrid vessel combinations, which included the caravel form used by ocean-crossing mariners such as Columbus, proved greater than the sum of their parts. Although slow and unwieldy by modern standards, these late-fifteenth-century European ships were the world's most durable, swift-sailing, and maneuverable means of heavy transport to date. Later modified into galleons, frigates, and clippers, they would serve as the basic models for virtually all European carriers and warships until the advent of steam technology in the early nineteenth century.

European innovations in navigational technology also propelled overseas expansion. Learned cosmographers believed the world to be more or less spherical by Columbus's time, but finding one's way from port to port beyond sight of land was still a source of worry. One aid in this dilemma was the magnetic compass, like gunpowder and printing a fairly ancient Chinese invention developed in a novel way by Europeans. We know from travelers' accounts that sailors in the Indian Ocean also used compasses in medieval and early modern times, but rarely in combination with sea charts, which contained detailed compass bearings and harbor descriptions. The combination of charts and compasses soon changed European navigators' perceptions of what had formerly been trackless seas.

Another borrowed instrument, apparently Arabic in origin, was the astrolabe. A calculator of latitude (one's location north or south of the equator), it proved even more critical for long-distance maritime travel than the compass. Precise knowledge of latitude was essential for early modern sailors in particular since longitude, a more complicated east-west calculation, was little known until the invention of seaworthy clocks in the mid-eighteenth century.

Thus armed with an impressive ensemble of borrowed and modified tools, weapons, and sailing vessels, Europeans were well poised to venture out into unknown or unfamiliar worlds. Add the recent development of the printing press, and they were also able to publicize their journeys in new if not altogether honest ways.

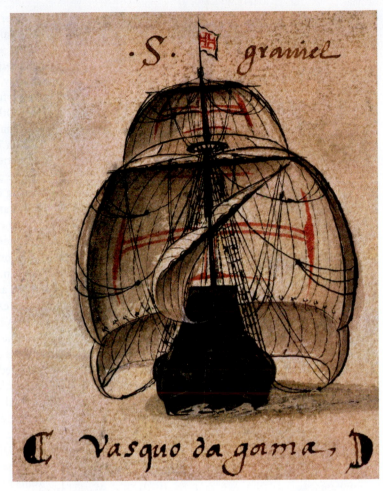

·S· graniel

Vasquo da gama,

Portuguese Ship

The Portuguese were the first Europeans to develop ocean-going ships for extended, return voyages. Initially they combined rigid hull designs from the Atlantic with maneuverable triangular sails of Arabic origin to build caravels, but these small vessels had limited cargo space and were vulnerable to attack. This evocative image from a contemporary manuscript shows Vasco da Gama's flagship, the *St. Gabriel*, on its way to India in 1497–1498 with every stitch of canvas out. For such long trips the Portuguese chose to sacrifice the maneuverability of the caravel in favor of maximizing sail surface and relying on trade winds. The resulting ships, which could carry up to 1200 tons of cargo and were built like floating fortresses, are known as "carracks." Portugal's national symbol until recent times, the red cross of the Order of Christ identified such ships as Portuguese. (The Art Archive/Science Academy Lisbon/Gianni Dagli Orti.)

Portugal Takes the Lead

Historians have long wondered why tiny Portugal, one of Europe's least populated and developed kingdoms, led the way in overseas expansion. A closer look at key factors helps solve this puzzle. First, the kingdom of Portugal was an ancient maritime crossroads straddling two vibrant commercial spheres, the Mediterranean and northeast Atlantic. Coastal shipping had grown efficient in late medieval times while overland transport between northern and southern Europe remained slow, costly, and prone to banditry. Well before 1400, long-distance merchants from as far away as Venice and Stockholm put in at Lisbon,

Overseas Incentives

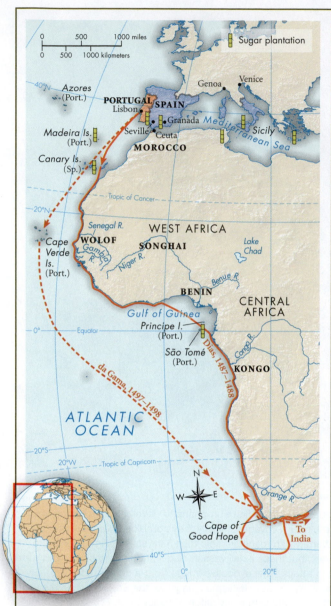

MAP 17.1

The East Atlantic, c. 1500

The Portuguese were the first Europeans to seek a sea route to Asia, and they did so by making their way south along the Atlantic coast of Africa. The diseases of tropical Africa limited Portuguese colonization to a few fortified enclaves, but they established lucrative settlement colonies in the eastern Atlantic island chains of the Azores, Madeiras, and Cape Verdes, along with the wet tropical island of São Tomé in the Gulf of Guinea. By 1500 the Portuguese had discovered that the fastest way to round the tip of Africa was to follow the prevailing winds and currents that swept to the west of the African coast before turning southeast.

the Portuguese capital, to break up their long journeys. Commercial competition was fostered by Portugal's kings, and along with money and exotic goods, important shipbuilding and sailing knowledge was exchanged. Capital, in the form of money, ships, and goods, also accumulated in the hands of powerful merchant clans, many of them foreign.

Other factors besides accumulating capital and foreign merchants pushed the Portuguese abroad. By the 1430s, fishermen regularly ventured far out into the Atlantic in pursuit of better catches. Moreover, arable land in Portugal grew scarce as populations grew and large estates expanded, rendering overseas colonization ever more attractive. Also, religious and strategic concerns drove Portuguese nobles to capture the Islamic port city of Ceuta (SYOO-tah), on Morocco's Mediterranean coast, in 1415. Crusade-like ventures such as this continued to overlap with commercial ones throughout early modern times. Thus, the push of limited resources at home and the pull of opportunities abroad stimulated Portuguese expansion.

With support from ambitious nobles such as Prince Henry "the Navigator" (1394–1460), Portuguese and foreign investors pooled capital accumulated in shipping and moneylending and invested it in a variety of new technologies to create a far-flung network of settlement colonies and *feitorias* (fay-toe-REE-ahs), or fortified trading posts. Some invested in overseas plantations in the eastern Atlantic and Mediterranean, others in the gold and slave trades of West Africa (see Map 17.1).

Gaining confidence with each new experience, Portuguese merchants and sailors learned to navigate the complex currents and prevailing winds of the West African coast. By 1430 they had come upon the Azores and Madeiras, uninhabited island chains in the eastern Atlantic. With incentives from the Crown and some Italian merchant investment, Portuguese settlers immediately colonized and farmed these islands. The Canaries, farther south, were somewhat different. Inhabited by dozens of bands and chiefdoms descended from pre-Islamic Moroccan immigrants, these rugged volcanic islands posed distinct political and moral challenges. "They go about naked without any clothes," wrote one Portuguese chronicler, "and have little shame at it; for they make a mockery of clothes, saying they are but sacks in which men put themselves."[2]

What was to be done? Should the inhabitants of the Canary Islands be conquered and their lands taken over by Europeans, and if so, by what right, and by whom? The presence of indigenous Canarians in fact spurred competition among a variety of European adventurers. Among them were Spanish missionaries and militant French and Portuguese nobles, but Spanish nobles under Isabella and Ferdinand, Columbus's future sponsors, ultimately won title to the islands. The Guanches (HWAN-chehs), as the Europeans called the largest group of native inhabitants, lost to the point of annihilation. A few survivors were enslaved and made to work on sugar plantations. In many ways, the Canarian experience foretold Iberian, and more generally European, actions in the Americas. When they stood in the way of European ambitions, the interests of indigenous peoples counted for little or nothing.

Always in search of gold, which the eastern Atlantic islands lacked, and spurred on by Prince Henry, the Portuguese in 1444 reached the mouth of the Senegal River. On the Senegal, the Portuguese traded Arabian warhorses for gold dust with representatives of the Muslim Wolof kingdoms. They also traded, and on a few occasions raided, for slaves. The victims of these 1440s raids and exchanges were the first Africans to be shipped en masse across Atlantic waters. Most ended up in the households and artisan workshops of Lisbon.

Origins of the Atlantic Slave Trade

Portuguese reconnaissance in the eastern Gulf of Guinea in the 1480s led to contacts with the kingdom of Benin and also to settlement of the offshore islands of Príncipe and São Tomé. Some captives from Benin were forced to plant and refine sugar on São Tomé. The slave-staffed tropical sugar plantation, which would define the economy and culture of colonial Brazil and much of the Caribbean basin from the fifteenth to nineteenth centuries, found a prototype here off the coast of central Africa in the years just before Columbus's famous voyages. Iberians developed similar plantations in the Canaries and Madeira.

By 1488, Bartolomeu Dias rounded Africa's Cape of Good Hope, and ten years later, Vasco da Gama became the first European to reach India by sea. Given the momentum, cumulative knowledge, and overall success of the Portuguese enterprise, it is understandable that when in the early 1480s Christopher Columbus proposed to open a westward route to "the Indies," the Portuguese king, on the advice of his cosmographers, declined. Columbus's calculations were in doubt, as was the need for an alternative of any kind. Once in the Indian Ocean, the Portuguese used their sturdy ships and superior firepower to terrifying effect, taking more than a dozen key ports from their mostly Muslim inhabitants by 1510. The emphasis on capturing ports reflected Portuguese ambitions. They sought to dominate the existing maritime Asian trade, not to establish a colonial land empire. Thus, as we shall see, Portuguese and Spanish expansion would take very different forms.

Push to Asia

New Crossroads, First Encounters: The European Voyages of Discovery 1492–1521

FOCUS
What were the main sources of conflict between Europeans and native Americans in the first decades after contact?

Portugal's Spanish neighbors had long been interested in overseas expansion as well, although by Columbus's time they lagged far behind. Spanish sailors and shipbuilders were as competent as those of Portugal, and some nobles and merchant families were tied to the early African trade. What would quickly distinguish Spain's overseas enterprises from Portugal's, however, was a stronger tendency to acquire large landmasses by force, colonize them with large numbers of settlers, and force Catholicism on all inhabitants. To some extent this pattern of expansion derived from the centuries-long Christian Reconquest of the Iberian peninsula that ended with the defeat of the Muslim caliphate of Granada in January 1492. As if fated, it was at Ferdinand and Isabella's royal military encampment, Santa Fe de Granada, that Columbus received his license to sail across the Ocean Sea, the name then given to the Atlantic.

Christopher Columbus in a New World

Christopher Columbus, born in the Italian city of Genoa in 1451, was just one of many ambitious merchants who came of age in the dynamic, profit-seeking East Atlantic world centered on Lisbon. Columbus married Felipa de Perestrelo, a Portuguese noblewoman, but did not settle down. Instead, he spent most of his time sailing on Portuguese merchant vessels bound for West Africa, England, and even Iceland. He soon became obsessed with a scheme to sail west to China and Japan, which he had read about in the already two-hundred-year-old account of the Venetian merchant Marco Polo. In around 1485 Columbus left for Spain,

feitoria A Portuguese overseas trading post, usually fortified.

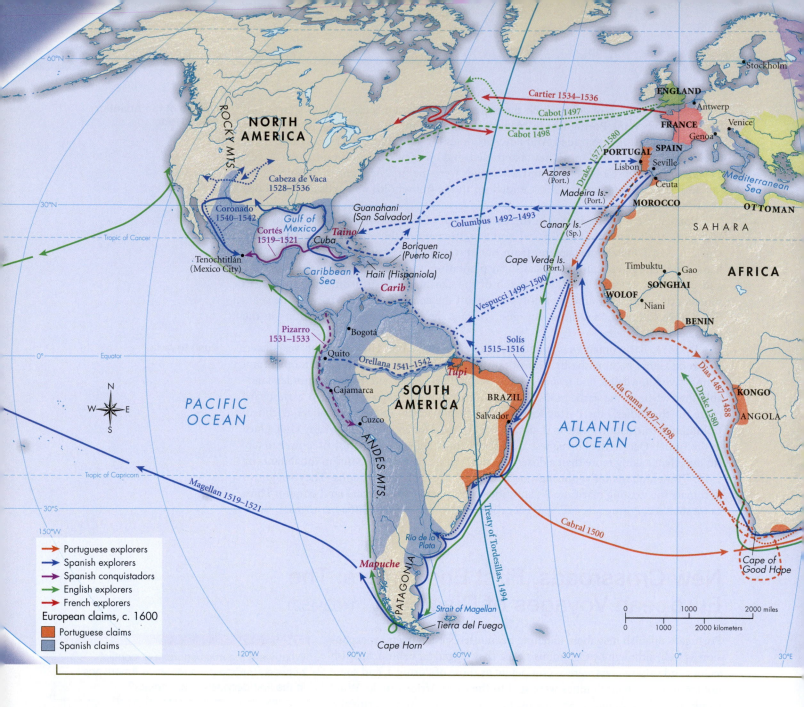

where he eventually won the sponsorship of Isabella and Ferdinand. By 1492 he was off to cross the Atlantic in search of the successors of Qubilai Khan, China's famed thirteenth-century Mongol ruler. "I set out for Your Highnesses' Canary Islands," he wrote to Ferdinand and Isabella in his ship's log, "in order to begin my journey from there and sail until I should arrive in the Indies, there to deliver Your Highnesses' embassy to those princes."[3]

On October 12, 1492, barely a month after leaving his last stopover point in the Canary Islands, Christopher Columbus and his mostly Spanish crew made contact with the native Taino (tah-EE-no) inhabitants of Guanahani, one of the smaller Bahama Islands. Unable to communicate with them, Columbus imagined himself somewhere near Japan, or at least "east of India." He christened the island San Salvador, or "Holy Savior," as a religious gesture of thanks, and called the native Bahamians and all other indigenous peoples he subsequently encountered "Indians" (see Map 17.2).

Remarking in his journal that the "Indians" he met in the Bahamas were tall, well built, scantily clad, and ignorant of iron weapons, Columbus proposed that they would make excellent slaves. The Indians reminded him of the native Canary Islanders whom the

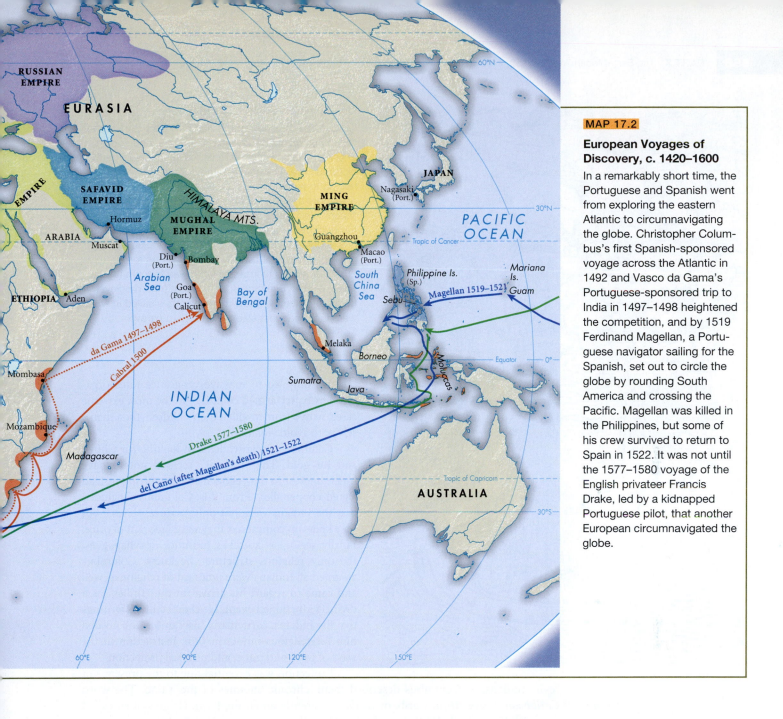

MAP 17.2

European Voyages of Discovery, c. 1420–1600

In a remarkably short time, the Portuguese and Spanish went from exploring the eastern Atlantic to circumnavigating the globe. Christopher Columbus's first Spanish-sponsored voyage across the Atlantic in 1492 and Vasco da Gama's Portuguese-sponsored trip to India in 1497–1498 heightened the competition, and by 1519 Ferdinand Magellan, a Portuguese navigator sailing for the Spanish, set out to circle the globe by rounding South America and crossing the Pacific. Magellan was killed in the Philippines, but some of his crew survived to return to Spain in 1522. It was not until the 1577–1580 voyage of the English privateer Francis Drake, led by a kidnapped Portuguese pilot, that another European circumnavigated the globe.

Spanish and Portuguese had conquered and enslaved. True to his word, Columbus eventually shipped some five hundred Caribbean natives to the markets of Seville.

After the first landfall in the Bahamas, Columbus sailed southwest to Cuba, then east to the large island known locally as Haiti. He renamed it "Española" ("Hispaniola," "Little Spain" in English) and began looking for a town site to settle in the name of his queen. In the course of this and three subsequent voyages, Christopher Columbus claimed and named everything and everyone that came into his view for his royal Spanish sponsors. In his logbook, Columbus constantly reiterated his hopes of finding gold, spices, and news of "the Great Khan." He died in 1506, still believing he was near China.

For the diverse American peoples who met Columbus and his crewmembers, the heavily clothed and armed foreigners provoked mixed feelings. They brought some useful goods, including hatchets and sewing needles, but when their incessant demands for food, gold, and sexual companionship were not met, they turned violent, torturing, raping, and murdering native islanders at will. No one, least of all Columbus, seemed willing to punish the newcomers or rein them in. Before long, some frustrated Taino hosts returned the violence in kind,

Exploring the Caribbean

Early Native American–Spanish Relations

557

Columbus Meets Native Americans

On October 12, 1492, the Italian navigator Christopher Columbus reached the Bahama Islands, and soon afterward Haiti, which he renamed "Española," partly pictured here. The native Taino welcomed Columbus, hoping to recruit him as an ally against fierce neighbors the admiral dubbed "Caribs," and later, "cannibals." News of these meetings soon spread throughout Europe, and very early images such as this one accompanying a portion of one of Columbus's published letters show how difficult it was for European artists to imagine what was to them a truly "New World." Even the ship is drawn from medieval tradition, since we know that Columbus sailed in what were then the most sleek and modern caravels. (Corbis.)

but this only led to massive vengeance raids organized by better-armed colonists. In the most extreme cases, native women killed their children, then themselves, to avoid violation.

Columbus, meanwhile, kept looking for China, and for gold. The "Indians" seemed not to have much interest in the yellow metal, preferring instead a gold-copper alloy. From this, Columbus concluded that the Indians were not only "natural slaves," but they knew no commerce; they were ignorant of price. Finally, seeing no churches, mosques, or synagogues, the only religious structures he knew, Columbus assumed all Indians were ignorant of religion as well and came to regard his arrival in the "Indies" as a divinely sanctioned event. He claimed in his writings that the Indians, particularly his Taino allies, needed him for religious indoctrination, instruction in the ways of work and trade, and physical protection.

Caribs Protection was essential due to the presence of "evil" Indians, as Columbus described them, chronic enemies of the Taino. The word *Caribbean* derives from Carib, or *caribe*, apparently an ethnic term. Groups of so-called Caribs did in fact inhabit the smaller islands to the east and south of Borinquen, the large island renamed Puerto Rico, or "Rich Port," by the Spanish. Although culturally similar to the Taino, these Caribs were said to have a particularly bad habit: they ate human flesh.

"Man-eating" natives were in some ways a predictable New World wonder, the sort of marvel medieval travelers had often described for sensation-hungry readers. Columbus happily played along. It appears he blended the Latin *canis* (dog) and local ethnic name *caribe* to produce a new word: *canibal*, or "cannibal." *Carib* and *cannibal* soon became interchangeable terms in the lexicon of Spanish conquest, and the image of the cannibal stuck fast in the European imagination. Indeed, almost as quickly as news of the Indies reached Europe, printers rushed to illustrate the alleged atrocities of the Caribbean "dog-people."

Given the circumstantial nature of the evidence, historians and anthropologists remain divided as to whether the so-called Caribs practiced cannibalism. What mattered for Columbus and his followers was that their allies, the "good Indians," said they did. With such a legal pretext (the eating of human flesh being regarded as a clear violation of natural law in the Western tradition), the newcomers could claim to be serving a necessary

Dog-Faced Cannibals
European readers of chivalry tales and travel accounts expected the American "New World" to yield fantastic and horrible creatures. Early news from the Caribbean and Brazil suggested the existence of humans with doglike, omnivorous appetites, seeming to confirm the alleged observations of Marco Polo and other medieval travelers. In this 1527 woodcut, a German artist fused Weimaraner-like dogs' heads with naked German butchers, one with a raised steel cleaver, to represent native Americans. Since this image predates the Spanish conquest of the Incas by five years, the horned llama-like animal at lower left is of special interest. (Courtesy of the John Carter Brown Library at Brown University.)

police role. By this argument, the Spanish alone could adequately "protect" and "punish"—that is, take over Western-style functions of government in the "New World." Thus, drawing on a variety of assumptions and preconceptions, Europeans imposed their own interpretations on the social and cultural patterns of New World peoples, interpretations that justified European domination.

Spanish sovereignty in the Americas was soon defined against the backdrop of Portugal's older overseas claims. With the pope's backing, in 1494 the Spanish and Portuguese split the world into two zones of influence. According to the terms of the Treaty of Tordesillas, the Spanish were to rule everyone living 370 leagues (roughly 1110 miles) or more west of the Canaries; all inhabitants beyond this line were now subjects of the crown of Spain according to European law. Africa, Asia, and eventually Brazil, which was not known to Europeans until 1500, fell to the Portuguese.

Why was the Roman Catholic pope involved in an agreement of this kind? First, fifteenth-century Europeans regarded his authority as above that of secular rulers. More important, however, was the matter of spreading the Christian gospel, a job Columbus himself embraced. Iberian monarchs, all pious Catholics at this time, promised to sponsor the conversion of everyone their subjects encountered abroad and also to continue the medieval fight against "infidels." Commerce may have supplied the initial and most powerful motive for overseas expansion, but a drive for religious and cultural hegemony soon came to play an important part in European colonization.

Treaty of Tordesillas

From Independence to Servitude: The Encomienda System

Although missionaries were present in the Caribbean from the 1490s, early Spanish colonization of this vast island region amounted mostly to a mad dash for gold and slaves. Early Spanish settlers had little interest in working the land themselves, preferring instead to live from the rents and labor provided by native American slaves and tribute payers. As news of massive abuse and alarming death rates among the Taino and captive Caribs reached Spain, Queen Isabella demanded an end to Amerindian slavery. After 1503 only violent rebels and alleged cannibals were to be enslaved.

Compromise on Native American Slavery

Would the Taino then be free in exchange for accepting Catholicism and Spanish protection against the Caribs? No, in large part because their labor was thought necessary to mine gold, which Spain's monarchs desperately wanted. Compromise came in the form of the *encomienda* system. Native villages headed by chieftains were entrusted to leading Spanish citizens in a manner resembling medieval European feudalism: village farming folk were to offer labor and surplus produce to their "lord" in exchange for military protection. Chiefs served as middlemen, exempted from tribute and manual work. The Spanish *encomenderos* who received these fiefdoms were self-styled men-at-arms, and from their ranks would come the conquerors of the mainland.

Indians deemed good and faithful subjects of Crown and Church paid tributes to their encomendero, or "trustee," as he was called, in farm products, textiles, and other local goods, twice a year. Adult men were also required to lend their labor to the encomendero from time to time, helping him clear farmland, round up livestock, and construct buildings. For his part, the encomendero was to protect his tributaries from outside attack and ensure their conversion to Christianity. However reciprocal in theory, the encomienda system was in fact used mostly to round up workers for the gold mines. It looked like slavery to the few Spanish critics who denounced it, and even more so to the many thousands of native peoples who suffered under it.

Bartolomé de Las Casas's Defense of Native American Rights

"And on the Day of Judgment it shall all be more clear," thundered Bartolomé de Las Casas in a sermon-like tract, "when God has His vengeance for such heinous and abominable insults as are done in the Indies by those who bear the name of Christians."[4] Las Casas was a Hispaniola encomendero's son turned Dominican priest who emerged as the leading defender of native American rights in early modern times. Some historians have argued that he represented another, more humanitarian side of the Spanish character in the otherwise violently acquisitive era of Columbus and his successors. Through constant pleading at court, and in widely publicized university debates and publications, Las Casas helped to suppress the indigenous slave trade and sharply restrict the encomienda system by the early 1540s. For the Tainos who first met Columbus, the reforms came too late. By 1510 there were only a few hundred encomienda subjects where a decade before there had been hundreds of thousands. By almost any measure, the Columbian era in the Caribbean was a disaster.

Columbus's Successors

Columbus's accomplishments as a navigator spawned dozens of like-minded expeditions (see again Map 17.2). These included the four voyages of Amerigo Vespucci (1497–1504), a Florentine merchant for whom the continents of the Western Hemisphere would later be named. Vespucci gained most fame as an early publicist of the new lands and peoples that southern Europeans were rapidly encountering throughout the American tropics. Vespucci came to realize that the Americas were not part of Asia. This did not, however, prevent him from embracing other European preconceptions. In relating his voyages to Brazil to Medici rulers in Florence, Vespucci calmly described the roasting and eating of human flesh among the local inhabitants. His reports only added to the European fixation on native American cannibalism.

Early Global Reconnaissance

Other voyages of reconnaissance included those of Juan de Solís and Ferdinand Magellan. Both were seasoned Portuguese explorers sailing in the service of Spain, and both, like Columbus, sought a westward route to Asia. Solís sailed up the Río de la Plata estuary near modern Buenos Aires in 1516, but was captured and killed in a skirmish with local inhabitants. Magellan learned details of the Argentine coast and its currents and winds from survivors of the Solís expedition, then organized a much more ambitious voyage to the Moluccas, or Maluku, in what is today Indonesia. The epic journey that followed, arguably one of the boldest ever undertaken, was recorded by yet another Italian, the Venetian Antonio de Pigafetta.

Of the five ships that left Spain in 1519, two were wrecked before Magellan reached the treacherous straits at the southern tip of South America that still bear his name. When food ran short, crewmembers shot, salted, and ate penguins and sea lions. Encounters with the native inhabitants of Tierra del Fuego and the neighboring mainland were mostly brief and hostile, reminiscent of Columbus's early encounters. Always the good publicist,

encomienda A feudal-style grant of a native American village to a conquistador or other Spaniard.

Columbian Exchange Historian Alfred Crosby's term for the movement of American plants, animals, and germs to the rest of the world and vice versa.

Pigafetta described exchanges and conflicts with primitive giants, giving rise to the legend of Patagonia, or "the land of Big Foot."

Once in the Pacific, Magellan set a northwesterly course that eventually led to Guam, in the Mariana Islands east of the Philippines. The four-month ocean crossing had left much of the crew suffering from malnutrition, and many others died from the effects of scurvy, a debilitating disease caused by lack of vitamin C. Magellan then sailed to the Philippine island of Sebu, where he became embroiled in a dispute between local chieftains. Alarmed to find Muslim merchants active in the region, Magellan sought to create an alliance with new converts to Christianity through a show of force. Instead, he and forty crewmembers were killed. Only one vessel managed to escape and return to Spain in 1522 by following the new Portuguese sailing route through the Indian and Atlantic oceans. For the first time in recorded history, the world had been circumnavigated (see again Map 17.2).

Meanwhile, in the Caribbean, Spanish colonists became rapidly disillusioned with the fabled "West Indies" of Columbus. Unhappiest of all were newly arrived immigrants from the Iberian peninsula, desperate young men with dreams of gold and a more promising future in a new world. Such men, and most immigrants were men in the early years, fanned out across the Caribbean in search of new sources of wealth, both human and metallic. Most failed, and many died, but some eventually found what they sought: fabled continental empires rich beyond belief.

The Columbian Exchange

In a landmark 1972 book, historian Alfred Crosby argued that the most significant consequences of 1492 were not political or even commercial, but biological.[5] What Crosby called the **Columbian Exchange** referred to the massive interoceanic transfer of animals (including humans), plants, and diseases that followed in Columbus's wake. Many of these transfers, such as the introduction of rats and smallpox to the Americas, were unintentional. Yet all had profound consequences.

Maize

Perhaps the most globally transformative native American crop (vying with the potato), maize was first domesticated in highland Mexico some 7000 years ago. This 1542 German depiction is the most accurate to survive from the first decades after maize was introduced to Europe. Similar varieties soon transformed global dietary patterns, particularly in sub-Saharan Africa. Some cultures adopted maize only as livestock feed. (*De Historia Stirpium*, 1542, Leonhard Fuchs, Typ 565.42.409(B), Houghton Library, Harvard University.)

Since European explorers circled the globe shortly after Columbus's time, this process of biological exchange was almost from the start a worldwide phenomenon. Indigenous cuisines, farming practices, and transportation modes were changed, sometimes for the better. Northern European populations, for example, grew rapidly following the introduction of Andean potatoes, which thrived in cool, wet climates. South and Southeast Asian cuisines were forever changed after the introduction of American capsicum peppers and peanuts, which flourished in the Old World tropics.

But European cattle, sheep, pigs, goats, horses, and other large domestic mammals also rapidly altered landscapes, sometimes with catastrophic consequences. In the worst case, the highlands of central Mexico were quickly denuded and reduced to deserts following the introduction of sheep in the sixteenth century. Lacking predators, and having access to vast new pastures, their populations exploded. Similar processes of environmental transformation were later repeated in Australia, New Zealand, Argentina, and the western United States.

Biological and Environmental Transformations

Epidemic Diseases and Population Loss

As in the case of ship borne rats, many unwanted exchanges took place in the first phases of global interaction. Worst among these were diseases, mostly caused by viruses, bacteria, and blood parasites, introduced to previously unexposed hosts. Since Africa and Eurasia had long been linked by waves of trade, warfare, migration, and pilgrimage, the repeated spread of diseases such as smallpox, measles, and mumps had allowed people over time to develop immunity against these and other pathogens. As seen in Chapter 15, pandemics of plague could be devastating in Africa and Eurasia, but never to the extent that they would be in long-isolated regions overseas. The peoples of the Americas, Australia, and Polynesia proved tragically vulnerable in this regard; they suffered what was probably the worst demographic collapse in history.

In the early modern Americas poor hygiene and medical care, chronic warfare, forced labor, and malnutrition all accompanied European conquest, rendering new disease agents more destructive. Documentary evidence suggests that throughout the Americas and Pacific Islands, indigenous populations declined by almost 90 percent within a century. Recovery and acquired immunity came slowly. With the introduction of malaria, yellow fever, and other mosquito-borne blood parasites—as deadly for Europeans as anyone else—America's lowland tropics did not recover their precontact populations until the introduction of insect-killing pesticides following World War II. On the plus side, world food exchanges spurred rapid population growth in Europe, Africa, and Asia, and contributed to the rebound of the Americas. Overall, the spread of American food crops boosted world population significantly before the end of early modern times. The peoples of the Americas, however, paid a steep price for these new and more productive connections between the world's societies.

Spanish Conquests in the Americas 1519–1600

FOCUS

What factors enabled the Spanish to conquer the Aztec and Inca empires?

Two men disappointed by their prospects in the Caribbean islands were Hernando Cortés and Francisco Pizarro. Cortés gained fame by the 1520s as conqueror of the Aztecs, and Pizarro after 1532 as conqueror of the Incas. Their extraordinary actions on the American mainland gave rise to the almost mythical Spanish-American livelihood of **conquistador**, or conqueror. Like Columbus, neither man acted alone, but both altered the course of global history. Also like Columbus, these two famous conquistadors, though made hugely rich by their exploits, both ended their lives unappreciated and disgraced. The sword of conquest was double-edged.

The Fall of Aztec Mexico

As we saw in Chapter 16, the people known as Aztecs called themselves Mexica (meh-SHEE-cah). By the time Spaniards arrived on Central America's Atlantic shores in the late 1510s, the Mexica ruled much of Mesoamerica, often by terror. The empire centered on the fertile highlands surrounding modern Mexico City, but extended south to the Pacific coast and east into Guatemala. Cortés would soon discover, however, that the Aztec Empire was vulnerable.

The Road to Tenochtitlán

A brash and ambitious leader, Hernando Cortés left his base in southern Cuba after a dispute with his sponsor, the governor. In Yucatan, as we have seen, he found an extraordinarily valuable translator in the person of Malintzin. By September of 1519 Cortés set out for the interior from the new town of Veracruz on Mexico's Gulf coast. With him were Malintzin and several hundred horses and well-armed men. The Spanish also brought with them fierce mastiffs, huge dogs bred for war. After a series of attacks on both Aztec allies and enemies, the Spanish and several thousand new allies entered Tenochtitlán in November 1519 as guests of the emperor, Moteuczoma, or "Moctezuma," II.

conquistador Spanish for "conqueror," a new livelihood in the Americas after Columbus.

Shortly after being welcomed and treated to a feast by the curious and gracious Moctezuma, Cortés and his followers managed to capture and imprison the unsuspecting emperor. Fearful for their ruler's life, the Aztec people, now leaderless, faced great uncertainty. Not afraid to use terror in his own way, Cortés ordered that anyone who opposed the Spanish and their allies would be publicly cut to pieces and fed to the dogs. Treachery, terror, and seizure of indigenous leaders were in fact stock tactics developed by Spanish conquistadors in the course of their decades of Caribbean slave raiding. These tactics proved even more effective against mainland imperial peoples who depended on divine kings. Attached to their subsistence plots, settled farmers had nowhere to run.

There followed almost eight months of looting and destruction, accompanied by a mix of open battles and informal skirmishes. Some former Aztec subjects supported the Spanish, most significantly the Tlaxcalans, but others resisted violently. Soon unfamiliar diseases such as smallpox and influenza swept through Tenochtitlán and the entire Valley of Mexico, decimating a vast and densely populated region already facing food shortages. Ironically, the people who would give the world maize, tomatoes, chocolate, vanilla, and a thousand other life-sustaining and pleasurable foods were now receiving only the most deadly ingredients of the Columbian Exchange: viruses and bacteria. Cortés ordered that images of the Virgin Mary be placed atop Aztec temples to assert the power of the invaders' Christian deities.

Cortés's Invasion of the Aztec Empire, 1519–1521

Spanish Setbacks

While Cortés went to negotiate with soldiers sent by Cuba's governor to arrest him in early 1520, the Spaniards left behind in Tenochtitlán provoked a siege by massacring Aztec nobles. Rushing to the city with Cuban recruits whom he had just won over, Cortés reached his comrades only to be trapped by the Aztec warriors. The desperate Spaniards brought out the captive emperor, Moctezuma, in hopes of calming tempers, but he was killed in a hail of stones. The besieged Spanish tried to flee Tenochtitlán, but there was no sneaking out of a city linked to the mainland by only three narrow causeways. Cortés and a handful of conquistadors escaped at the head of the pack, but many other Spaniards, about half the total number, fell into Aztec hands. One Spanish soldier recalled: "As we marched along we were followed by the Mexicans who hurled arrows and darts at us and stones from their slings, and the way in which they surrounded us and continually attacked us was terrifying."[6] According to Aztec accounts, when the city's male warriors fell dead or exhausted, women warriors took over, attacking the foreign enemy with equal vigor (see Reading the Past: Tlatelolcan Elders Recall the Conquest of Mexico). Despite the ravages of disease and the loss of their emperor, the Aztecs were still capable of dishing out terror in kind.

Final Victory

Cortés and his bedraggled Spanish forces eventually regrouped with aid from the Tlaxcalans, their staunchest allies, but it was over a year before Tenochtitlán and its twin city of Tlatelolco fell. Cut off from the mainland, the Aztecs faced starvation, then attack by land and water. Cortés ordered thirteen small, European-style sailing vessels built on the shores of Lake Texcoco, and armed with cannon these helped pound remaining Aztec warrior contingents in canoes. By August 1521 Cortés and his men and allies had forced the Aztecs to retreat to Tlatelolco. Soon, both cities were occupied and pillaged. Yet the Aztec capital proved hard to hold. Angry at the lack of valuable plunder, the Spanish responded to persistent urban rebels by razing virtually all residential buildings.

Soon after, a successor emperor to Moctezuma was captured and killed, after having been tortured for allegedly hiding booty. Dissatisfied conquistadors then fanned out across Mesoamerica in search of riches and empires. The self-promoting Cortés traveled to Spain in hopes of consolidating his gains, but found little support from the emperor Charles V. The material and political conquest of the Aztec center had not

Tlatelolcan Elders Recall the Conquest of Mexico

In what would become New Spain, or colonial Mexico, Spanish missionaries quickly introduced European-style writing systems. Indigenous scribes picked them up within a few decades of the conquest, rendering Nahuatl, Maya, and other local languages in a Latinate script with Spanish phonetics. Formal documents, including histories and sermons, were produced in this manner, but also interviews, myths, genealogies, criminal testimonies, and a host of everyday transactions. The following excerpt is a direct English translation of a Nahuatl document from about 1540 relating the conquest of both Tenochtitlán and its "twin city," Tlatelolco. The Tlatelolcan elders relating the story to junior scribes apparently witnessed and participated in the events in question.

And when they reached Yacocolco here, Spaniards were captured on the Tlilhuacan [tleel-WALK-on] road, as well as all the people from the various altepetl [allied city-states]. Two thousand died there, and the Tlatelolcans were exclusively responsible for it. At this time we Tlatelolcans set up skull racks; skull racks were in three places. One was in the temple courtyard at Tlillan, where the heads of our [present] lords [the Spaniards] were strung; the second was in Yacocolco,

where the heads of our lords [the Spaniards] were strung, along with the heads of two horses; the third place was in Çacatla, facing the Cihuateocalli (see-wah-tayoh-CAH-yee) [Woman-Temple]. It was the exclusive accomplishment of the Tlatelolcans. After this they drove us from there and reached the marketplace. That was when the great Tlatelolcan warriors were entirely vanquished. With that the fighting stopped once and for all. That was when the Tlatelolcan women all let loose, fighting, striking people, taking captives. They put on warriors' devices, all raising their skirts so that they could give pursuit.

Source: James Lockhart, ed. and trans. *We People Here: Nahuatl Accounts of the Conquest of Mexico* (Berkeley: University of California Press, 1993), 265–267.

EXAMINING THE EVIDENCE

1. What does this document tell us about Aztec political identity during the conquest?

2. What does it tell us about military culture and gender roles?

---

been easy, and at the fringes conquest was far from over. Far more difficult would be the winning of the hearts and minds of millions of former Aztec subjects now anxious to assert their own agendas. This would be the long story of colonial Mexico, a "New Spain" so unlike its Iberian namesake.

The Fall of Inca Peru

When Francisco Pizarro left the small Spanish settlement of Panama City in 1522 in search of "Pirú," a mythical chieftain, he had no idea that events high in the Andes Mountains to the south would conspire to favor his dream of repeating the success of Cortés. But as with Cortés and his many companions and aides, an empire—even with guns, germs, and steel on one's side—could not be toppled overnight.

In fact it took a decade of coastal reconnaissance and humiliating failure before Pizarro at last marched into what is today the Republic of Peru. In the meantime he had acquired Quechua translators immersed for several years in Castilian Spanish; a small army of men with horses, armor, and state-of-the-art weapons; and a license from Charles V. By late 1532, when Pizarro's forces began their inland march across a coastal desert reminiscent of southern Spain, Peru at last seemed ripe for the taking.

Tawantinsuyu (tuah-wahn-tin-SUE-you), as the Incas called their empire, was in deep crisis in 1532. A five-year battle over succession had recently ended with Atawallpa (also Atahualpa) emerging the winner. According to several eyewitness accounts, when

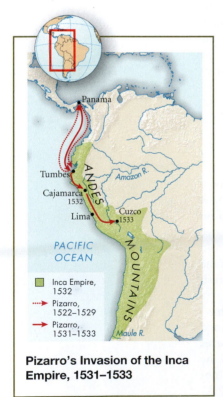

Pizarro's Invasion of the Inca Empire, 1531–1533

Pizarro Meets Atawallpa

Throughout colonial times native and European artists depicted the day in 1532 when Inca emperor Atawallpa met Francisco Pizarro. This is the first known image of the Peruvian encounter, a woodcut accompanying an eyewitness account published in Seville, Spain, in 1534. It depicts Atawallpa on a litter holding up what is probably the prayer book given him by the priest Vicente de Valverde, also pictured. Pizarro stands back with his fellow Spaniards, armed but not poised to attack. In the distance is a European-style castle presumably meant to stand for an Inca city. Notably absent is the native Andean interpreter whom we know only by his Christian name, "Little Philip." (Courtesy of the John Carter Brown Library at Brown University.)

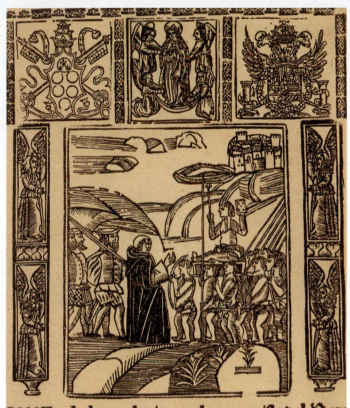

Pizarro and his 168 men climbed into the Andes to meet Atawallpa in the sacred city of Cajamarca, the new Sapa Inca was flush with victory. Atawallpa did not feel vulnerable, and in fact intended, rather like Moctezuma in Mexico, to draft the strangely bearded and well-armed foreigners into his service. Though their horses, firearms, and steel swords were cause for wonder, the Inca did not mistake the Spanish for gods.

According to survivor testimonies, in November 1532 Pizarro and his men captured Atawallpa in a surprise attack reminiscent of Cortés's seizure of Moctezuma. Humiliated, Atawallpa was held hostage for nearly a year as his subjects scrambled to gather up gold and silver to free him. The Incas possessed far more gold and silver than the Aztecs, and the hoard of metals offered to free their leader, whom most Andeans regarded as a divine being, was staggering. Suddenly Pizarro and his followers were rich beyond their wildest dreams.

Thus "Peru" became instantly synonymous with great wealth among Europeans, an association that would soon be reinforced by the discovery of immensely rich silver mines. Despite the ransom, however, Atawallpa was killed on Pizarro's orders in 1533. The treachery was complete, and by 1534 Tawantinsuyu was in Spanish hands.

The Conquest: Myths and Realities

How did a small number of Spanish men manage to topple two of the world's most populous and extensive empires in a relatively short time? Some biologists and anthropologists have claimed that these great, isolated indigenous empires faced inevitable defeat because they lacked iron, sufficient protein, draft animals, wheeled vehicles, writing, acquired immunity to numerous pathogens, and other advantages. Historians have long puzzled over this riddle, too, but more with an eye on human actors and the timing of events.

For their part, the conquistadors and their Spanish contemporaries regarded these victories as the will of their Christian God. Spain's enemies—and internal critics such as Las Casas—emphasized the conquistadors' "sins" of treachery, cruelty, lust, and greed. By the nineteenth century, historians less interested in judging the Spanish focused on the leadership abilities of individuals. They emphasized the intelligence and tenacity of Cortés and Pizarro, and the apparent weakness and indecisiveness of their adversaries, Moctezuma and Atawallpa. This emphasis on "great men" was aided by the conquistadors' own insistence that they were mistaken for gods everywhere they went.

Malintzin and the Meeting Between Moctezuma and Cortés

Malintzin Interprets for Cortés and Moctezuma
(The Granger Collection, New York.)

This image, taken from the early postconquest document known as the *Florentine Codex*, was drawn and colored by an indigenous Mexican artist who had been exposed to European prints and paintings while being schooled by Spanish friars. In it, Malintzin translates the words between Aztec emperor Moctezuma and Hernando Cortés at their momentous first meeting.

EXAMINING THE EVIDENCE

1. How does this drawing reflect the indigenous artist's instruction by Spanish friars?

2. To what extent is it a reflection of Malintzin's perceived importance in the conquest of Mexico?

Factors of Conquest

Recently, historians have focused on other causal factors. These include the importance of indigenous allies and interpreters; the conquistadors' accumulated experience as "Indian fighters" in the Caribbean; internal imperial politics and the timing of Spanish arrival; indigenous adaptation to Spanish fighting methods; contrasting goals of warfare; and of course, the introduction of novel weapons, animals, and diseases. Most historians agree that the conquests resulted from the convergence of these many variables—a number of them, such as the appearance of Malintzin the able translator, completely unpredictable (see Seeing the Past: Malintzin and the Meeting Between Moctezuma and Cortés).

A final point worth emphasizing is that indigenous peoples were not overawed by Spanish horses and technology, nor did they view the newcomers as gods. As this quote from a Spanish soldier who participated in the conquest of Mexico suggests, Aztec warriors adapted rapidly to the threat of cannon and armored opponents on horseback:

> One day an Indian I saw in combat with a mounted horseman struck the horse in the chest, cutting through to the inside and killing the horse on the spot. On the same day I saw another Indian give a horse a sword thrust in the neck that laid the horse dead at his feet. . . . Among them are extraordinary brave men who face death with absolute determination.[7]

The evidence from Inca Peru barely differs. After the capture of Atawallpa in 1532, Andean warriors quickly learned to avoid open field engagements where they might be run down by mounted Spaniards, preferring instead to ambush their enemies as they crossed rivers and traveled through narrow canyons. Simple stones and slingshots proved a surprising match for guns and steel-edged weapons in these conditions. Rebellions and raids continued for decades in the Mexican and Peruvian backcountry, but the rapid Spanish conquest of the Aztec and Inca imperial cores was sealed by those empires' own former subjects; although they did not know what was in store for them, most were anxious for something different.

A New Empire in the Americas: New Spain and Peru 1535–1600

Within a few generations of conquest, Spanish settlers penetrated deep into the Americas, transforming the world's largest overseas land empire into the world's greatest source of precious metals. Spain's monarchs in turn used this mineral bounty to pursue their religious and territorial ambitions in Europe and beyond. Merchants used it to link the world economy in unprecedented ways. But for the millions of native Americans subjected to Spanish rule, life would revolve around negotiating a measure of freedom within an imperial system at least as taxing as those of the Aztecs and Incas.

> **FOCUS**
>
> Why was the discovery of silver in Spanish America so important in the course of world history?

American Silver and the Global Economy

In 1545 an indigenous prospector came across silver outcrops on a high, red mountain in what is today south-central Bolivia. The Cerro Rico, or "Rich Hill," of Potosí (poh-toe-SEE), as it was soon known, turned out to be the most concentrated silver deposit ever discovered (see Map 17.3). Indeed, no other silver strike approached the extraordinary wealth of Potosí until modern times. This and related silver discoveries in early Spanish America radically transformed not only life in the colonies, but the global economy. As we will see in subsequent chapters, in regions as distant as China and South Asia, American silver affected people's livelihoods in profound and unexpected ways. Even before Potosí, silver mines had been discovered in highland Mexico in around 1530, and many new finds followed. Mexican districts such as Zacatecas (zah-cah-TAY-cus) and Guanajuato (hwan-uh-WAH-toe) were expanding rapidly by the 1550s and would continue to drive Mexico's economy well into the modern period.

Refining Innovations

Although the Spanish quickly adopted efficient Old World techniques of tunneling and refining, the silver boom also spurred important technical innovations. Chief among these was the use of mercury to separate silver from crushed ore. Amalgamation, as this process is known, was practiced in antiquity, but it was Bartolomé de Medina, a merchant working in the Mexican mines of Pachuca in the mid-1550s, who developed and patented a low-energy, large-scale refining process suitable for New World environments. Medina's invention revolutionized Spanish-American silver mining even as it spread one of the world's most persistent toxins, mercury.

Amalgamation was implemented in Potosí on a large scale after 1572 as part of a crown initiative to stimulate production. Although Spain itself produced substantial mercury, New World sources had been avidly sought since Potosí's discovery. Before long, the mine owners' dreams came true; in the Peruvian highlands southeast of Lima, the mercury mines of Huancavelica (wan-kah-bell-EE-cah) were discovered in 1564. Thus the Spanish paired Andean mercury with Andean silver, touching off an enormous boom in production. Potosí yielded tens of millions of ounces of silver annually by the 1580s. It was enough to pave the main streets of the town with silver bricks during religious processions.

Environmental Hazards

Even with abundant mercury, silver production remained costly. Unlike gold panning, underground mining required massive capital inputs, especially in labor and technology. Water-powered silver-processing mills, first developed in Germany, were among the most complex machines in use in early modern times. Mercury remained expensive despite a crown monopoly meant to assure availability. Less often calculated, although well known even in the sixteenth century, were the environmental and health costs of mercury pollution. Soils, rivers, and refinery workers' clothing were saturated with mercury, leading to a range of neurological disorders and birth defects. "Trembling like someone with mercury poisoning" became a common colonial metaphor for fright, akin to "shaking like a leaf."

More costly than mercury and machines combined was labor. Mining was hard and deadly work, attracting few volunteers. African and African-descended slaves supplemented

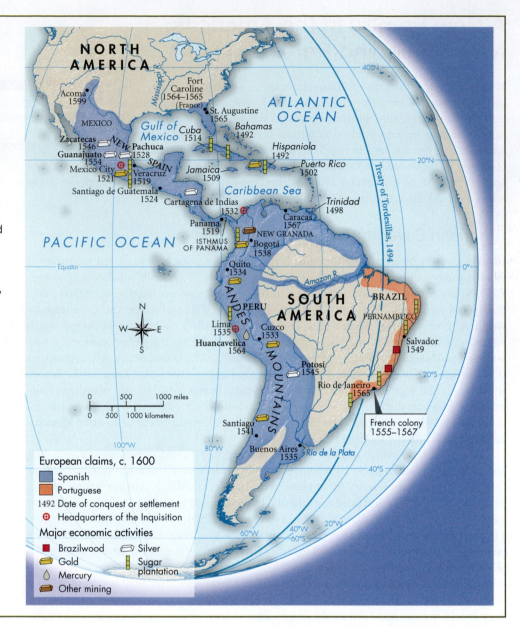

MAP 17.3

European Claims in the Americas, c. 1600

Beginning in the 1510s, the Spanish used bases in Cuba and on the Isthmus of Panama to launch the conquests of the Aztec and Inca empires. In search of similar empires, Spanish explorers drove deep into the interiors of North and South America; by the 1540s they had penetrated the U.S. Southwest and South America's Río de la Plata basin, and made their way down the Amazon. Other conquests in Central America, northwest Mexico, and New Granada led to the creation of a vast Spanish-American Empire, under the twin capitals of Mexico City and Lima. Portuguese Brazil, by contrast, consisted only of a few small settlements along the Atlantic coast, but by 1600 it was the world leader in sugar production, increasingly dependent on the labor of enslaved Africans.

The Mine Draft

the workforce from an early date in boomtowns such as Zacatecas and Potosí, but Spanish-American silver mines came to rely mostly on native American draft and wageworkers. The draft, or **mita** (MEE-tah) as it was called in the Andes, entailed a year of service in Potosí, Huancavelica, or some other mining center, followed by six years of work in one's own home region, usually in subsistence farming or herding. In Mexico the Spanish implemented a similar system called **repartimiento** (reh-par-tee-MYEN-toe).

Drafted indigenous laborers received a small wage and rations during their work stints, but given the danger of these jobs and the high cost of living in mining towns, the mita and repartimiento proved hugely disruptive of indigenous lifeways. Many considered draft work a death sentence. The miners of Huancavelica, in particular, faced lifelong degenerative illnesses caused by mercury poisoning. Others were killed by cave-ins and falls. Furthermore, indigenous women and children forced to occupy Spanish-American mining towns suffered from contaminated food, air, and water supplies. Exposure to heavy metals, a hazard usually associated with modern industrialization, was probably worst for native American draftees and African slaves engaged in refining tasks. Here in

mita A Spanish revival of the Inca draft labor system.

repartimiento An allotment of indigenous laborers in colonial Mexico, similar to the Andean mita.

The Rich Mountain of Potosí
This c. 1603 image of Potosí's famous Cerro Rico shows not only the legendary red mountain with its silver veins but also workers, most of them native Andeans, refining silver by mercury amalgamation, and antlike llamas carrying ore down the mountain. The ore-crushing mill in the foreground is powered by a stream of water supplied by canals coming down from artificial reservoirs built high in a neighboring mountain range. (The Hispanic Society of America Museum and Library, New York.)

the mills mercury was routinely vaporized, and large quantities of lead, arsenic, and other heavy metals were smelted along with silver. Such was the human cost of making money.

Potosí boomed in the first years of the mita, reaching peak production in 1592, but heightened demand for mine laborers in this remote and unhealthy site only worsened an already dramatic indigenous demographic collapse. Most eligible workers who remained in the region quickly learned to avoid the most dangerous tasks, and many sold whatever they could to pay a cash fee for exemption. Mine owners were increasingly forced to pay wages to stay in business.

American Silver and Everyday Life

The silver bonanza of the sixteenth century altered livelihoods worldwide. In the Spanish colonies, everything from ranch work to church building was connected in one way or another to the flow of silver. The armies of dependent miners living in towns such as Potosí and Zacatecas spurred merchants and landowners to expand their inventories, crops, and livestock herds. Mule-drivers, weavers, tanners, and countless other specialists came to rely on the continued productivity of the mines for their sustenance. In town centers, indigenous and mixed-heritage market women took advantage of crown-mandated tax exemptions to carve out a lucrative space as well. But along with this new orientation of the colonial economy toward silver production came an intensification of conversion efforts on the part of Spanish missionaries. Worldwide, Spanish-American silver funded a massive expansion of the Catholic Church.

Whereas most indigenous peoples adapted quickly to Spanish legal and civic traditions and even tolerated the oppressive obligations of mine work, most resisted total conversion to Catholicism. Confident in the universality of their religion, European missionaries expected indigenous populations to accept Christianity as the one true faith. When they did not, the process of cultural exchange shifted from conversion to coercion. After a brief period of optimism, in which a small number of newly arrived European priests met and mingled with tens of thousands of indigenous subjects, violence erupted. Within a few decades of military conquest, the Catholic Church was commonly using prosecution, public humiliation, and even torture and execution throughout Spanish America.

Challenges of Religious Conversion

Native Americans were not the only victims of religious intolerance. Offices of the **Inquisition**, a branch of the Catholic Church dedicated to enforcing orthodox beliefs and practices, were established in Mexico City and Lima in 1570 and Cartagena in 1610. Their purpose was to punish alleged deviants and heretics among the Spanish settlers, including a number of secretly practicing Jews and a few Muslims. In the indigenous majority (soon exempted from prosecution by the Inquisition due to their newness to the faith), complete conversion was limited by long-held, core religious beliefs. Most native American converts rejected monotheism, belief in a single, supreme god. Instead, they adopted the Christian God, his holy intermediaries, and saints on their own terms, as new additions to an already crowded pantheon. There were other misunderstandings. Thousands of native converts were baptized, only to return the next day to request that this new and pleasant ceremony be performed again. Catholic missionary priests became pessimistic and often angry with their seemingly stubborn parishioners. Conversion, unlike military conquest, was a slow process that depended on more than missionary zeal. It also required missionaries to achieve a better understanding of would-be converts.

It was only after some priests learned to speak indigenous languages fluently that Europeans began to fathom, and in some cases transform, native cosmologies. One way around the obstacle of conflicting core beliefs was to ignore elders and focus conversion efforts on native youths, particularly boys. Upon maturity, they would presumably serve as exemplary believers, leaders in the new faith. Many such boys were removed from their parents' custody, taught to read and write, and ordered to collect and collate essential myths and sagas. These stories were then rewritten by European priests to match Christian history and beliefs.

Yet even as the missionaries succeeded with some native men, they failed miserably with women. Indigenous women, despite repeated sexual assaults by conquistadors, merchants, overseers, and even priests, carried on with their lives, teaching their children the old ways and also pressing for social recognition and advancement within the new social order. Some, like Malintzin, refashioned themselves as something in between Spanish and indigenous, often bearing **mestizo** (meh-STEE-soh) or mixed-heritage children. But the extraordinary persistence of indigenous American languages, religious practices, food ways, and dress through modern times is due mostly to humble indigenous women, unsung keepers of the hearth. Despite the determination of Spanish priests and conquistadors to remake the Americas to serve European interests and ambitions, indigenous culture would continue to play a powerful role in colonial society.

Brazil by Accident: The Portuguese in the Americas 1500–1600

FOCUS

How and why did early Portuguese Brazil develop differently from Spanish America?

Despite some notable similarities with their Spanish neighbors north and south, the Portuguese followed a distinct path in colonizing Brazil. The general trend in the century after contact in 1500 was from benign neglect and small-scale trade with indigenous coast-dwellers toward a more formal royal presence and settled plantation agriculture, mostly concentrated along the northeast coast. By 1600, Brazil was the world's largest sugar producer. It also became the prime destination for sub-Saharan African slaves. A key stimulus for this tectonic shift in colonial policy and economy was French encroachment between 1503 and 1567. The arrival of French traders and religious refugees in Brazil forced the Portuguese to briefly take their eyes off India.

Native Encounters and Foreign Competitors

Inquisition A branch of the Catholic Church established to enforce orthodoxy.

mestizo A person of mixed European and native American ancestry.

It was on the way to India in early 1500 that the Portuguese captain Pedro Alvares Cabral and his large fleet were blown westward from Cape Verde, in West Africa. Toward the end of April the fleet unexpectedly sighted land, which the captain dubbed the "Island of the True Cross." The landmass was later found not to be an island, but rather a mountainous stretch of the continent of South America. Columbus and the Spanish were at this time only

First Encounter in Brazil: Cabral's Report to King Manoel of Portugal

On May 1, 1500, Pedro Alvares Cabral's scribe, Pero Vaz de Caminha, recorded the first known meeting between Europeans and Tupi-speaking tribespeople in a letter to the king. Unlike the Tainos who met Columbus, the indigenous peoples who met Cabral and his crew had no gold—perhaps luckily. Unimpressed, the foreigners dispatched a small vessel home to Lisbon to report on their "discovery," and the great fleet sailed on to India.

> In appearance they are dark, somewhat reddish, with good faces and good noses, well shaped. They go naked, without any covering; neither do they pay more attention to concealing or exposing their shame than they do to showing their faces, and in this respect they are very innocent. Both [captives taken from a canoe to see Cabral] had their lower lips bored and in them were placed pieces of white bone, the length of a handbreadth, and the thickness of a cotton spindle and as sharp as an awl [pointed tool] at the end. . . . Their hair is smooth, and they were shorn, with the hair cut higher than above a comb of good size, and shaved to above the ears. And one of them was wearing below the opening, from temple to temple towards the back, a sort of wig of yellow birds' feathers . . . very thick and very tight, and it covered the back of the head and the ears. This was glued to his hair, feather by feather, with a material as soft as wax, but it was not wax. Thus the headdress was very round and very close and very equal, so that it was not necessary to remove it when they washed. . . .
>
> One of them saw . . . some white rosary beads; he made a motion that they should give them to him, and he played much with them, and put them around his neck;

and then he took them off and wrapped them around his arm. He made a sign towards the land and then to the beads and to the collar of the captain, as if to say that they would give gold for that. We interpreted this so, because we wished to, but if he meant that he would take the beads and also the collar, we did not wish to understand because we did not intend to give it to him. And afterwards he returned the beads to the one who gave them to him. . . .

> There were also among them four or five young women just as naked, who were not displeasing to the eye, among whom was one with her thigh from the knee to the hip and buttock all painted with black paint and all the rest in her own color; another had both knees and calves and ankles so painted, and her privy parts so nude and exposed with such innocence that there was not there any shame.

Source: William Brooks Greenlee, trans., *The Voyage of Pedro Alvares Cabral to Brazil and India* (Nendeln/Lichtenstein: Kraus Reprint Limited, 1967, reproduced by permission of the Hakluyt Society, 1938), 10–21.

EXAMINING THE EVIDENCE

1. Why might Cabral's scribe have been so keen to describe the physical features, piercings, and personal adornments of Tupi men and women in such detail in a letter to the king of Portugal?

2. What does the passage concerning the captain's collar reveal about European and indigenous attitudes and communication?

---

beginning to touch upon its northern shores, and had no sense of its size. The huge portion of the continent claimed by Portugal would later be called Brazil (see again Map 17.3).

Brazil was of little interest to Portugal for some time despite the fact that it fell within the domain delineated by the 1494 Treaty of Tordesillas, signed with Spain and sanctioned by the pope (see Reading the Past: First Encounter in Brazil: Cabral's Report to King Manoel of Portugal). Without gold or some other lucrative export, there seemed to be little point in colonizing this distant land. Brazil's one obvious resource, and what earned it its name, was brazilwood, a tree with a deep-red, pithy heart. Portuguese traders, soon followed by French competitors, set up posts all along Brazil's vast coast to barter with indigenous Tupi speakers for precut, red-hearted logs.

Cut and carried to shore by indigenous men, brazilwood was then shipped to Europe, where dye was extracted and sold at profit. Native Brazilians willingly participated in this trade because it brought them tangible benefits: metal hatchets, knives, sewing needles, and other utilitarian items, along with beads, mirrors, bells, and other personal and ritual adornments. For some, it also brought military alliances against traditional enemies. In several places Portuguese *degredados*, or criminal castaways, survived their tropical exile and married into eminent indigenous families, becoming translators and commercial middlemen.

Early Dyewood Trade

This use of criminal exiles to spearhead colonization was quite different from Spanish practices in the Americas.

Portuguese Response to French Competition

French competition for control of Brazil and its dyewood pressed the Portuguese to assert their claims more forcefully. A fleet of warships was sent from Lisbon in 1532 to protect Portuguese traders and to punish French interlopers. Land claims were to be organized differently, too. After 1534 Brazil was carved into fifteen proprietary colonies, granted by King Manoel to courtiers ranging from noble warriors to scholars. Brazil's proprietary governors were told to encourage permanent settlement by farmers and artisans from their home districts. This was similar to Spanish plans in the early Caribbean, but the models the king had in mind were Madeira and the Azores, Portugal's earlier experiments with overseas settlement colonies. Brazil's new proprietors were also expected to organize the defense of their holdings against French and indigenous enemies. The closest the Spanish ever came to such private colonization schemes was Charles V's grant of parts of Venezuela to German banking families in the 1530s and 1540s, all of which failed.

With few exceptions, the Brazilian proprietary colonies also failed; the French were still a menace, and native Brazilians, not Portuguese colonists, had the run of the land. In 1549 the Crown tried another strategy: Salvador, a defensible hamlet located at the tip of the wide Bay of All Saints in northeastern Brazil, was made the royal capital and seat of a governor general. Jesuit missionaries, only a half dozen of them at first, also arrived. They soon fanned out across Brazil to convert tens of thousands of native, Tupi-speaking allies to Roman Catholicism. From here forward, enemies of the Crown or faith, indigenous and otherwise, would be given no quarter.

French Retreat from Brazil

The French did not easily give up on their Brazilian enterprise, and in fact redoubled their efforts at midcentury. In 1555 they established a new colony in Guanabara Bay, near modern Rio de Janeiro (see again Map 17.3). The colony's leader proved incapable of sorting out disputes between Catholics like himself and numerous Protestant refugees, or Huguenots. Divided by religion, like France itself at the time (as we will see in Chapter 20), the French colony was doomed. The Portuguese drove out Catholics and Protestants alike by 1567. As for indigenous enemies, including the allies of the French, Portuguese wars and slaving expeditions would continue throughout colonial times.

Bitter Sugar: Slavery and the Plantation Complex in the Early Atlantic World 1530–1600

A search for precious metals and gems came up short soon after the royal capital of Salvador was established in 1549, but the Portuguese found other ways beyond brazilwood to profit from a tropical colony. On Brazil's northeast coast, sugar cane was planted along the banks of several rivers as early as the 1530s. By 1570, Brazil was the world's number-one sugar producer, a position it still holds. Cane sugar was Brazil's answer to Spanish-American silver. It was an exotic cash crop with a growing market abroad. Europeans, in particular, could not get enough of it. First indigenous, then African, slaves were made to do the bulk of the burdensome work required to produce sugar (see Lives and Livelihoods: Atlantic Sugar Producers).

Dependence on Enslaved Africans

Sugar growers in the region surrounding Salvador competed vigorously with their counterparts in Pernambuco, one of the few surviving proprietary colonies to the north. Each region vied for the greater share of total output, with Pernambuco usually ahead. Native Brazilian slaves were exploited in large numbers in both regions, but well before 1600 Portuguese planters turned to Africa for still more enslaved laborers. Indigenous workers died in large numbers from disease and abuse, as happened in the early Spanish Caribbean, and were also prone to run away to the interior. As will be seen in greater detail in the next chapter, the Portuguese had the advantage of established market ties with dozens of western African chiefdoms and states from Senegambia to Angola. More even than the Spanish, they sought to replace indigenous cane cutters with enslaved Africans.

Though more resistant to Old World diseases than their native American co-workers, Africans died in alarming numbers in the early cane fields of Brazil. Many were literally worked to death. Instead of moderating workloads, improving nutrition and medical care, and encouraging family formation, Portuguese masters opted to exhaust the labor power of their slaves, the vast majority of them young men. The reason was as logical as it was cold-hearted: having direct access to more and more captives at relatively low cost in western Africa, sugar planters "used up" laborers much like mine owners did mita workers in Peru. Even when female slaves were introduced and families formed, high child mortality rates discouraged reproduction. Brazil would subsequently become so dependent on Africa for labor that by the time the slave trade ended in the nineteenth century over 40 percent of all slaves transported across the Atlantic had landed in this single destination.

COUNTERPOINT
The Mapuche of Chile: Native America's Indomitable State

The climate of southern Chile, a land of rugged coasts and dense forests, is wet and cool. Gently rolling hills are interspersed with picturesque lakes, rivers, and volcanoes. Near the coast is a temperate rain forest comparable to parts of the Pacific Northwest of the United States and Canada. Fish and wildlife are abundant and varied. Towering araucaria pines yield nuts rich in fat and protein, and vitamin-packed wild berries abound in the thickets. This is the homeland of the Mapuche (mah-POOH-cheh), or Araucanians (a term derived from the Bay of Arauca), one of the Americas' most resilient native cultures. Across nearly five centuries, they successfully resisted attempted conquests by the Incas, the Spanish, and the Chilean nation-state.

FOCUS

How did the Mapuche of Chile manage to resist European conquest?

Today, more than five hundred years after Columbus, the Mapuche, half a million strong, are still proclaiming their independence. It was only in the 1880s that Chilean armed forces managed to partially subdue the Mapuche using modern weapons and threats of annihilation, a process similar to that used against native peoples of western North America and the Argentine *pampas*, or plains, in the same era. But what of colonial times, the era of the conquistadors? There was substantial gold in the Mapuche heartland, yet the Spanish failed to conquer them despite knowing this since the time of Pizarro. Why?

A Culture of Warfare

The historical record suggests that successful Mapuche resistance owed much to entrenched cultural patterns. As poets, ex-captives, and Mapuche commentators themselves have noted since the sixteenth century, this was a fiercely independent people raised to fight. The Mapuche reared boys for a life of warfare, apparently before as well as after Spanish arrival in the region. Girls were raised to produce and store the food surpluses needed for the war effort. Despite their access to horses, iron and steel-edged weapons, and firearms, the Spanish fared little better than the Incas against the native Chileans.

There were early successes, however. The first conquistadors in Chile, headed by Pedro de Valdivia, in fact managed to reduce a large number of Mapuche to encomienda servitude by 1550. Rich gold deposits were subsequently discovered, and Mapuche men were forced to

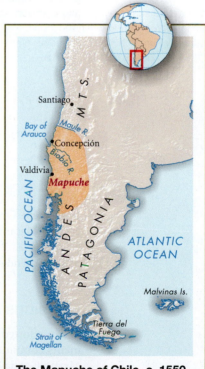

The Mapuche of Chile, c. 1550

Atlantic Sugar Producers

Found in countless foods and beverages, and now a major global source of biofuels, cane sugar was once a rare commodity. Introduced to the Mediterranean by Muslim traders and colonists in the eighth or ninth century C.E., sugar was at first a medicine and high-status condiment. Its source, sugar cane, a tall, thick grass, was eventually planted in Egypt, Sicily, Cyprus, and southern Iberia, and by at least the fourteenth century was processed not only by Muslims but also by Christian landowners in southern Spain and Portugal. Though later associated exclusively with slavery, sugar making in this era was done by a mixed free and enslaved labor force. Before long, women joined men in both cane fields and processing plants.

Sugar cane is so tough that considerable energy is required to extract maximum juice. Efficient presses were thus a technical hurdle for commercial producers. Like silver refining, sugar making required technical expertise and a complex sequence of chemical processes that allowed for few errors. In the Mediterranean basin, cane millers borrowed from long-established techniques of wine grape and olive pressing. Specialists were required to design and build ever larger and more powerful machines, which were among the most complex mechanical apparatus known at the time.

Animals such as oxen were often used for power, but waterwheels were preferred for their greater efficiency. In the

Sugar Plantations

Enslaved sugar-makers worked not only in fields but also in powerful mills and refining furnaces. Men, women, and children were all involved. This Dutch 1662 image of Pernambuco, Brazil, depicts enslaved sugar refinery and transport workers during the intense harvest period when the mills ran all night. The Dutch controlled Pernambuco and its sugar plantations from 1630 to 1654. (Courtesy of the John Carter Brown Library at Brown University.)

work them. Once it became clear that the Spanish were only after gold and captive laborers, the Mapuche resisted violently. To drive their point home, they captured, killed, and ate portions of Valdivia's corpse in a great public ceremony. Mapuche cannibalism was plainly intended to terrorize the enemy.

Uprisings Against the Spanish

What followed was a general uprising lasting from 1553 to 1557. Raids on Spanish settlements continued until 1598, when the Mapuche captured and ate yet another governor, Martín García de Loyola, a close relative of the founder of the Catholic Jesuit order, Ignatius Loyola (see Chapter 20). This incident was followed by a mass uprising in 1599, in

generally dry and sometimes frost-prone Mediterranean basin, access to warm, well-watered plains and consistently flowing millstreams was severely limited. Bounded by ecological and capital constraints, mill ownership remained a dream of most sugar producers. This soon proved equally true in the Atlantic islands and Brazil. For their part, mill workers, particularly the women and sometimes children who fed canes through the rollers, faced loss of limbs and sometimes death. "And in these Mills (during the season of making Sugar) they work both day and night," wrote English visitor Richard Flecknoe in 1654, "the work of immediately applying the canes to the Mill being so perilous [that] if through drowsiness or heedlessness a finger's end be but engaged between the posts, their whole body inevitably follows."[1] Rendering the precious juice into white crystal sugar was also difficult and labor intensive. Workers had to boil the juice in huge copper vats, then reduce it in a series of smaller vats into a concentrated syrup they poured into molds to crystallize. Women were usually in charge of whitening the resulting brown sugar loaves with wet clay and removing them from the molds and packing them for shipment. European consumers considered white sugar purer than brown, "purged" of imperfections. Each phase of the process required skill and close monitoring, and fires had to be stoked throughout the night. Sugar making thus produced a number of task-specific livelihoods, such as purger (purifier), mold-maker, and crating supervisor. Given its complexity, high capital investment, and careful attention to timing, sugar making has been described as an early modern precursor of industrial, or factory, production. However labeled, sugar work was monotonous and occasionally deadly.

On the consumer end of sugar making, first Muslim and then Jewish and Christian chefs made the most of the new sweetener, inventing a wide variety of candies, pastries, and preserves. Thus was born the livelihood of confectioner, or candy-maker. When American cacao took Europe by storm in the 1600s, the specialty of chocolatier emerged.

Europeans' taste for sugar grew slowly at first, but by 1600, sugar was an ordinary ingredient in many foods. Sugar's association with slavery also gradually increased. Numerous slaves labored in the early cane fields and mills of the eastern Atlantic islands of Madeira and the Canaries, but the pattern replicated in the Americas—predominantly African slaves manning large plantations—appeared first on the Portuguese island of São Tomé, off equatorial West Africa. By 1550, the so-called plantation complex was established in the Spanish Caribbean and Brazil. In the Americas, as in the Canaries, with the decimation of local cultures indigenous slavery gave way to African slavery.

---

1. E. Bradford Burns, ed., *A Documentary History of Brazil* (New York: Alfred A. Knopf, 1966), 82.

QUESTIONS TO CONSIDER

1. How did the rise of Atlantic sugar affect the global economy?
2. How did it transform livelihoods?

For Further Information:

Mintz, Sidney W. *Sweetness and Power*. New York: Viking, 1985.
Schwartz, Stuart B., ed. *Tropical Babylons: Sugar and the Making of the Atlantic World, 1450–1680*. Chapel Hill: University of North Carolina Press, 2004.

which established rebels united with Mapuches who had been subjected to Spanish rule. It was a resounding success. No Spanish town remained south of the Biobío River after 1600, and Spanish attempts to reconquer the Mapuche and occupy their lands failed throughout the colonial period.

What factors besides a culture of warfare allowed the Mapuche to succeed when so many other native American cultures fell to European invaders? As in North America's Great Plains, the inadvertent introduction of horses by the Spanish greatly enhanced Mapuche warrior mobility. Steel and iron guns, knives, and swords were also captured and quickly adopted. Further, the Mapuche "Columbian Exchange" included Old World foods and animals such as wheat, apples, chickens, and pigs, markedly increasing their subsistence base.

Mapuche Man and Woman

The Mapuche peoples of Chile proved as resistant to the Spanish as they had been to the Incas. Hostilities began in 1549, and by 1599 Mapuche warriors had destroyed all inland Spanish settlements south of the Biobío River. This image, painted by a Spanish priest who fled the Mapuche in 1600, depicts a Mapuche woman with her spinning equipment and trademark horned hairstyle. To the left is the great Mapuche leader Lautaro, who led the first uprisings. As is evident, the Mapuche adopted Spanish-style helmets and body armor, which they fashioned from the raw hides of introduced cattle. Like the Plains peoples of North America, the Mapuche also adopted the horse to great effect. (Courtesy of the University of Oviedo Library, Spain.)

Despite their new mounts and access to new weapons, Chile's native warriors did not alter their overall style of warfare. Rather than face the better-armed Spanish on the open field, as these European-trained fighters would have liked, the Mapuche preferred night attacks, long-distance raiding, captive-taking, and other tactics later termed *guerrilla*, or "little war," by the Spanish. Very long native-style bamboo lances remained the weapon of choice, not to be replaced by cumbersome and inaccurate handguns or dueling rapiers, and Mapuche men continued to fight barefoot. Alliances were another key to success. The great uprising of 1599 linked culturally related neighbors in a confederacy that the Spanish termed "the Indomitable State."

As a result of sustained Mapuche resistance, southern Chile became a permanent frontier of Spanish South America, a region of defensive rather than offensive operations. The Mapuche, though still frequently at war with their European neighbors, had proved the fact of their independence. Throughout the Spanish world, they became legendary. Only in the late nineteenth century was a tenuous peace established with the Chilean government and reservations created. Like many treaties between nation-states and indigenous peoples, this peace brought not integration but marginalization and poverty. As a result, the Mapuche are still fighting.

Conclusion

The first wave of European overseas expansion in the Atlantic was transformative in many ways, and would not be repeated in Africa, Asia, or Oceania for several centuries. Hundreds of isolated cultures were brought into contact with one another, often for the first time. Agents of the Columbian Exchange, European farmers and ranchers migrated to new landscapes, which they and their plants, livestock, and germs quickly transformed. Millions of sub-Saharan Africans, most of them captive laborers, joined a fast-emerging Atlantic, and soon globally integrated, world.

Spearheading this transformation were the uniquely positioned and highly motivated Portuguese, armed and outfitted to undertake risky voyages of reconnaissance and chart new routes to commercial gain abroad. By the 1440s they were trading for gold and slaves in sub-Saharan Africa, and by the 1540s they had reached Japan. Although most interested in commerce, the Portuguese also carried with them a militant Christianity that they promoted with some success alongside their expanding global network of trading posts. In Brazil they took another tack, establishing hundreds of slave-staffed sugar plantations.

Early modern Spaniards sought the same gold, spices, sugar, and slaves that motivated their Portuguese neighbors, but after encountering the Americas, they turned away from trading posts in favor of territorial conquest. Those they defeated were forced to extract wealth and accept conversion to the Catholic faith. Ironic as it may seem, it was imperial peoples such as the Aztecs and Incas who proved most vulnerable to the Spanish onslaught, and more especially to foreign disease. Mobile, scattered cultures such as the Mapuche of Chile proved far more resistant. Even at the margins, however, violent conquest and the beginnings of the Atlantic slave trade transformed livelihoods for millions. Some individuals swept up in the early phases of colonial encounter and the Columbian Exchange, such as young Malintzin, found advantages and even a means to social gain. Countless others found themselves reduced to servitude in an emerging social order defined by race as much as by wealth or ancestry. This new order forged in the Americas would soon affect much of western Africa.

NOTES

1. Christopher Columbus, *The Four Voyages*, trans. J. M. Cohen (New York: Penguin, 1969), 300.
2. Gomes Eannes de Azurara, quoted in John H. Parry and Robert G. Keith, *New Iberian World: A Documentary History of the Discovery of Latin America to the Seventeenth Century* (New York: Times Books, 1984), 1:256.
3. Geoffrey Symcox and Blair Sullivan, *Christopher Columbus and the Enterprise of the Indies: A Brief History with Documents* (Boston: Bedford/St. Martin's, 2004).
4. Bartolomé de las Casas, *An Account, Much Abbreviated, of the Destruction of the Indies*, ed. Franklin Knight, trans. Andrew Hurley (Indianapolis: Hackett, 2003), 61.
5. Alfred Crosby, *The Columbian Exchange: Biological and Cultural Consequences of 1492*, 2d ed. (Westport, CT: Praeger, 2003).
6. Bernal Díaz del Castillo, *The History of the Conquest of New Spain*, ed. David Carrasco, trans. A. P. Maudslay (Albuquerque: University of New Mexico Press, 2008), 230.
7. Quoted in Ross Hassig, *Aztec Warfare: Imperial Expansion and Political Control* (Norman: University of Oklahoma Press, 1992), 124.

RESOURCES FOR RESEARCH

General Works

There are several fine general surveys of early Latin America, but the following are exceptional for their helpful models and explanations of key colonial institutions such as the encomienda and early plantation complex, plus the tricky business of analyzing writings and images from the early postconquest era.

Brown University, John Carter Brown Library Archive of Early American Images. http://www.brown.edu/Facilities/ John_Carter_Brown_Library/pages/ea_hmpg.html.

Library of Congress, Exploring the Early Americas. http://www .loc.gov/exhibits/earlyamericas/.

Lockhart, James, and Stuart B. Schwartz. *Early Latin America*. 1983.

Schwartz, Stuart B., ed. *Implicit Understandings: Observing, Reporting, and Reflecting on the Encounters Between Europeans and Other Peoples in the Early Modern Era*. 1994.

University of Texas, Latin American Network Information Center. http://www.info.lanic.utexas.edu/la/region/history.

Guns, Sails, and Compasses: Europeans Venture Abroad

The topic of early Iberian overseas expansion has drawn scholarly attention for many years, and several of the following works, though relatively old, are still considered classics.

Fernández Armesto, Felipe. *Before Columbus: Exploration and Colonization from the Mediterranean to the Atlantic, 1229–1492*. 1987.

Newitt, Malyn. *A History of Portuguese Overseas Expansion, 1400–1668*. 2005.

Parry, J. H. *The Age of Reconnaissance*. 1963.

Phillips, William D., and Carla Rahn Phillips. *The Worlds of Christopher Columbus*. 1992.

Symcox, Geoffrey, and Blair Sullivan. *Christopher Columbus and the Enterprise of the Indies: A Brief History with Documents*. 2004.

New Crossroads, First Encounters: The European Voyages of Discovery, 1492–1521

The literature on the Columbian Exchange and environmental transformations has grown in recent years, with special emphasis on the role of disease as a major factor distinguishing European success in the Americas from their less penetrating early experiences in Africa and Asia.

Alchon, Suzanne Austin. *A Pest in the Land: New World Epidemics in a Global Perspective*. 2003.

Cook, Noble David. *Born to Die: Disease and New World Conquest, 1492–1650*. 1998.

Crosby, Alfred. *The Columbian Exchange: Biological and Cultural Consequences of 1492*, 2d ed. 2003.

Emmer, Pieter C., ed. *General History of the Caribbean*. Vol. 2. *New Societies: The Caribbean in the Long Sixteenth Century*. 1997.

Melville, Elinor. *A Plague of Sheep: Environmental Consequences of the Conquest of Mexico*. 1994.

Spanish Conquests in the Americas, 1519–1600

Recent scholarship on the Spanish conquests has evolved to emphasize the many factors, such as the help of thousands of indigenous allies, that enabled relatively small numbers of Europeans to bring down two of the world's most populous empires.

Powers, Karen V. *Women in the Crucible of Conquest: The Gendered Genesis of Spanish American Society, 1500–1600*. 2005.

Restall, Matthew. *Seven Myths of the Spanish Conquest*. 2003.

Schwartz, Stuart B., ed. *Victors and Vanquished: Spanish and Nahua Views of the Conquest of Mexico*. 2000.

Townsend, Camilla. *Malintzin's Choice: An Indian Woman in the Conquest of Mexico*. 2006.

Wood, Stephanie. *Transcending Conquest: Nahua Views of Spanish Colonial Mexico*. 2003.

A New Empire in the Americas: New Spain and Peru, 1535–1600

Good regional and topical studies of colonial Spanish America abound. The following have been selected to highlight the themes of this chapter. Bakewell's treatment of early mining, trade, and administration is superlative.

Bakewell, Peter. *A History of Latin America to 1825*, 3d ed. 2009.

Clendinnen, Inga. *Ambivalent Conquests: Maya and Spaniard in Yucatan, 1517–1570*, 2d ed. 2003.

Gibson, Charles. *The Aztecs Under Spanish Rule*. 1964.

Mangan, Jane E. *Trading Roles: Gender, Ethnicity, and the Urban Economy in Colonial Potosí*. 2005.

Brazil by Accident: The Portuguese in the Americas, 1500–1600

The early history of Brazil is becoming a more popular topic, mostly focusing on European-indigenous relations.

Bethell, Leslie, ed. *Colonial Brazil*. 1986.

Hemming, John. *Red Gold: The Conquest of the Brazilian Indians, 1500–1760*. 1978.

Léry, Jean de. *History of a Voyage to the Land of Brazil*. Translated by Janet Whatley. 1990.

Metcalf, Alida. *Go-Betweens in the History of Brazil, 1500–1600*. 2005.

Schwartz, Stuart B. *Sugar Plantations and the Formation of Brazilian Society*. 1985.

COUNTERPOINT: The Mapuche of Chile: Native America's Indomitable State

Few studies of the colonial Mapuche have been published in English. The following are three important exceptions.

Dillehay, Tom. *Monuments, Empires, and Resistance: The Araucanian Polity and Ritual Narratives*. 2007.

Jones, Kristine. "Warfare, Reorganization and Redaptation at the Margins of Spanish Rule: The Southern Margin (1573–1882)." In *The Cambridge History of the Native Peoples of the Americas*, vol. 3, pt. 2, 138–187. Edited by Stuart B. Schwartz and Frank Salomon. 1999.

Padden, Robert C. "Cultural Adaptation and Militant Autonomy Among the Araucanians of Chile." In *The Indian in Latin American History: Resistance, Resilience, and Acculturation*, rev. ed. 71–91. Edited by John Kicza. 2000.

▶ **For additional primary sources from this period**, see *Sources of Crossroads and Cultures.*

▶ **For Web sites, images, and documents related to topics in this chapter**, see Make History at bedfordstmartins.com/smith.

REVIEW

The major global development in this chapter ▶ European expansion across the Atlantic and its profound consequences for societies and cultures worldwide.

IMPORTANT EVENTS

1441	First sub-Saharan Africans captured and taken by ship to Portugal
1492	Fall of Granada and expulsion of Jews in Spain; Columbus reaches America
1494	Treaty of Tordesillas divides known world between Portugal and Spain
1498	Vasco da Gama becomes first European to reach India by sea
1500	Portuguese reach Brazil
1519–1521	Spanish conquest of Aztec Mexico
1519–1522	Magellan's ship circumnavigates the globe
1532–1536	Spanish conquest of Inca Peru
1545	Discovery of silver deposits at Potosí
1549	Portuguese establish royal capital of Salvador; first Jesuits arrive in Brazil
1555	French establish colony in Brazil's Guanabara Bay
1564	Discovery of mercury mines in Huancavelica, Peru
1567	Portuguese drive French from Brazil
1570–1571	Inquisition established in Lima and Mexico City
1572	Mita labor draft and mercury amalgamation formalized in Potosí
1592	Potosí reaches peak production
1599	Great Mapuche uprising in Chile

KEY TERMS

Columbian Exchange (p. 560)
conquistador (p. 562)
encomienda (p. 560)
feitoria (p. 555)

Inquisition (p. 570)
mestizo (p. 570)
mita (p. 568)
repartimiento (p. 568)

CHAPTER OVERVIEW QUESTIONS

1. What were the main biological and environmental consequences of European expansion into the Atlantic after 1492?

2. What roles did misunderstanding and chance play in the conquests of the Aztecs and Incas?

3. How did Eurasian demand for silver and sugar help bring about the creation of a linked Atlantic world?

SECTION FOCUS QUESTIONS

1. Why and how did Europeans begin to cross unknown seas in the fifteenth century?

2. What were the main sources of conflict between Europeans and native Americans in the first decades after contact?

3. What factors enabled the Spanish to conquer the Aztec and Inca empires?

4. Why was the discovery of silver in Spanish America so important in the course of world history?

5. How and why did early Portuguese Brazil develop differently from Spanish America?

6. How did the Mapuche of Chile manage to resist European conquest?

MAKING CONNECTIONS

1. How did Spanish and Portuguese imperial aims differ from those of the Incas and Aztecs (see Chapter 16)?

2. How would you compare the Spanish conquest of Mexico with the Ottoman conquest of Constantinople discussed in Chapter 15?

3. What role did European consumers play in the rise of the American plantation complex?

4. How did global demand for silver affect the lives of ordinary people in the Spanish colonies?

18

AT A CROSSROADS ▶

This dramatic brass plaque depicts the oba, or king, of Benin in a royal procession, probably in the sixteenth century. He is seated sidesaddle on a seemingly overburdened horse, probably imported and sold to him by Portuguese traders. The larger attendants to each side shade the monarch while the smaller ones hold his staff and other regal paraphernalia. Above, as if walking behind, are two armed guards. (Image copyright © The Metropolitan Museum of Art/Art Resource, NY.)

Western Africa in the Era of the Atlantic Slave Trade

1450–1800

In 1594 a youth of about seventeen was captured in a village raid in the interior of western Africa. The Portuguese, who controlled the Atlantic port of Luanda, where the young captive was taken, called this vast region Angola, a corruption of the Kimbundu term for "blacksmith." The young man was now a nameless body to be branded, examined like a beast, and sold; he was also, in the words of his captors, "a black." In Luanda, the captive was housed in a stifling barracks with many others, perhaps including some who spoke his language and probably even a few who came from his village. Most, however, were strangers whose words, looks, hairstyles, and "country marks," or ritual scars, were unfamiliar.

Eventually, men dressed in black robes appeared among the captives. These odd-looking men were Roman Catholic priests, members of the Jesuit order. They had only recently established a missionary base in Luanda. In grave tones and mostly unintelligible

BACKSTORY

Prior to 1450, the lives of most western Africans focused on hoe agriculture, supplementary herding and hunting, and in some places mining and metallurgy. Chiefdoms were the dominant political form throughout the region, from the southern fringes of Morocco to the interior of Angola, although several expansive kingdoms rose and fell along the Niger and Volta rivers, notably Old Ghana, which thrived from about 300 to 1000, and most recently, as the early modern period dawned, Mali, which flourished from about 1200 to 1400.

Trade in many commodities extended over vast distances, often monopolized by extended families or ethnic groups. Muslim traders were dominant along the southern margins of the Sahara Desert after about 1000 C.E. Some western African merchants traded slaves across the Sahara to the Mediterranean basin, and others raided vulnerable villages for captives, some of whom were sent as far away as the Red Sea and Indian Ocean. Islam predominated by 1450 along many trade routes into the savanna, or grasslands, but most western Africans retained local religious beliefs, usually combining ancestor veneration with healing and divination practices similar to native American shamanism (see Chapter 16).

Many Western Africas

FOCUS What range of livelihoods, cultural practices, and political arrangements typified western Africa in early modern times?

Landlords and Strangers: Peoples and States in West Africa

FOCUS What economic, social, and political patterns characterized early modern West Africa?

Land of the Blacksmith Kings: West Central Africa

FOCUS What economic, social, and political patterns characterized early modern West Central Africa?

Strangers in Ships: Gold, Slavery, and the Portuguese

FOCUS How did the early Portuguese slave trade in western Africa function?

Northern Europeans and the Expansion of the Atlantic Slave Trade, 1600–1800

FOCUS What were the major changes in the Atlantic slave trade after 1600?

COUNTERPOINT: The Pygmies of Central Africa

FOCUS How did the Pygmies' rain forest world differ from the better-known environment of savannas and farms?

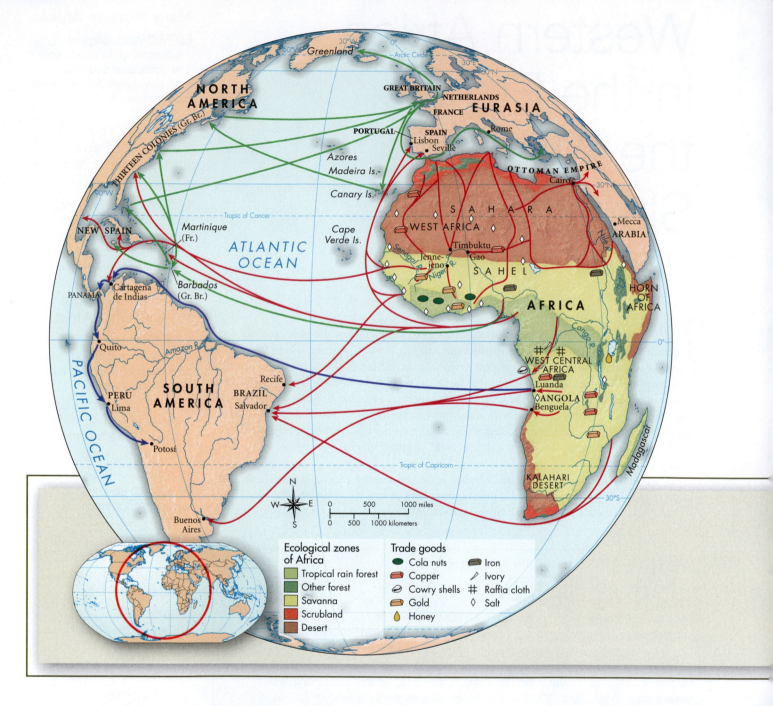

Ecological zones
of Africa

Tropical rain forest
Other forest
Savanna
Scrubland
Desert

Trade goods

Cola nuts
Copper
Cowry shells
Gold
Honey

Iron
Ivory
Raffia cloth
Salt

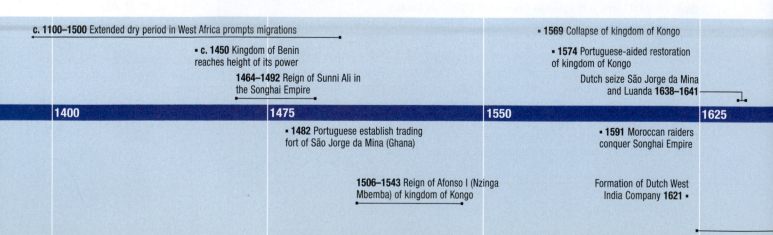

c. 1100–1500 Extended dry period in West Africa prompts migrations

• c. 1450 Kingdom of Benin
reaches height of its power

1464–1492 Reign of Sunni Ali in
the Songhai Empire

• 1569 Collapse of kingdom of Kongo

• 1574 Portuguese-aided restoration
of kingdom of Kongo

Dutch seize São Jorge da Mina
and Luanda 1638–1641

1400	1475	1550	1625

• 1482 Portuguese establish trading
fort of São Jorge da Mina (Ghana)

• 1591 Moroccan raiders
conquer Songhai Empire

1506–1543 Reign of Afonso I (Nzinga
Mbemba) of kingdom of Kongo

Formation of Dutch West
India Company 1621 •

words, they spoke to the captives. The young man must have listened with puzzlement. At last, after several weeks, each captive was sprinkled with water and made to accept a lump of salt on the tongue. After this conversion ritual, names were assigned. The young man was now called "Domingo," "Sunday" in Portuguese. Once in the Americas, Spanish scribes recorded his name as "Domingo Angola, black slave." His sale records are the only evidence we have of his existence.

Domingo was one of the lucky ones. He survived barracks life in Luanda and then the grueling two-month voyage, or "middle passage," from Luanda to Cartagena de Indias, a bustling port on the Caribbean coast of present-day Colombia. More than one in five died during these ordeals. After stumbling out of the sickening hold of the slave ship and into the bright Caribbean sun, Domingo Angola would have been washed, oiled, examined for signs of contagious illness, and fed a simple meal of maize gruel and tough, salted beef. Both foods were new to him, and they would form the core of his diet for the rest of his enslaved life in Spanish South America.

After being transported by ship to Panama, Domingo was sold to a merchant on his way to Quito, the former northern Inca capital high in the Andes Mountains of Ecuador. There, according to notary records for the year 1595, he was sold yet again, this time to two merchants planning a multiyear sales trip to the distant silver-mining town of Potosí, several thousand miles to the south. In all, Domingo spent almost another year of hard and dangerous tropical travel. Documents listing travel costs say he fell ill while waiting for a ship on the Pacific coast and had to be treated. In Potosí, Domingo was sold yet again, and probably not for the last time. He had not yet turned nineteen.[1]

Meanwhile, back in Angola, a terrifying story arose about men and women such as Domingo who had been captured and taken away across the sea. People began to imagine that they were being captured to feed a distant race of cannibals. These "people eaters," red in color, lived somewhere beyond the sunset, it was said, on the far side of an

MAPPING THE WORLD
Africa and the Atlantic, c. 1450–1800

The vast and ecologically diverse continent of Africa had long been linked together by trade in salt, copper, iron, cola nuts, and other commodities. It had also been connected since ancient times to the Mediterranean and the Indian Ocean maritime worlds. Goods traded beyond Africa consisted mostly of gold and ivory, but there was also substantial traffic in human captives. After 1450 the Portuguese extended this pattern into the growing Atlantic world, establishing fortified trading posts all along Africa's west coast.

ROUTES ▼

→ Slave and trade route, c. 1450–1800

→ Voyage of Domingo Angola, c. 1594–1597

→ Voyages of Olaudah Equiano, c. 1755–1797

▪ **1672** Formation of English Royal African Company

1750–1800 Atlantic slave trade reaches highest volume

1700

1775

1850

▪ **1807** British declare Atlantic slave trade illegal

1624–1663 Reign of Queen Nzinga in the Ndongo kingdom of Angola

enormous lake, and there they butchered ordinary Angolans. Human blood was their wine, brains their cheese, and roasted and ground long-bones their gunpowder. The red people—the sunburnt Portuguese—were slavish devotees of Mwene Puto, God of the Dead. How else to explain the massive, ceaseless traffic in souls, what Angolans called the "way of death"?[2]

Domingo's long journey from western Africa to highland South America was not unusual, and in fact he would have met many other Angolans arriving in Potosí via Brazil and Buenos Aires. Victims of the Atlantic slave trade in this period were constantly on the move, some sailing from Africa as far as India, the Molucca Islands in the East Indies, and even Japan. This trend of slave mobility diminished somewhat with the rise of plantation agriculture in the seventeenth and eighteenth centuries, but Africans continued to work on sailing ships and in port cities all over the world. On land or at sea, massive disruption and shuffling of ethnic groups was typical of the Atlantic slave trade and what historians call the **African diaspora**, or "great scattering" of sub-Saharan African peoples. As we will see in the next chapter, millions of slaves were sent across the Indian Ocean from East Africa as well, a phenomenon predating the Atlantic trade but in the end not as voluminous. This chapter focuses on western or "Atlantic" Africa, a vast portion of the continent that geographers normally split into two parts: West and West Central Africa (see Mapping the World, page 583).

Although slavery and slave trading were established practices in western Africa prior to the arrival of Europeans, both institutions and their effects changed dramatically as a result of the surge in European demand for African slaves that coincided with European colonization of the Americas. Beginning in the late sixteenth century, new patterns of behavior emerged. African warriors and mercenaries focused more and more on attacking and kidnapping their neighbors in order to trade them to foreign slavers for weapons, stimulants, and luxury goods; coastal farmers abandoned arable lands vulnerable to raiders; formerly protective traditions and customs were called into question; and Islam and Christianity made new inroads. We now know that even cultures inhabiting zones far inland from the Atlantic coast, such as the Batwa, or Pygmies, of the Congo rain forest, were affected by reverberations of the slave trade. They were driven deeper into the forest as other internal migrants, forced to move under pressure from slavers, expanded their farms and pasturelands. There, as we will see in the Counterpoint to this chapter, the Pygmies forged a lifestyle far different from that of their settled neighbors.

African diaspora The global dispersal, mostly through the Atlantic slave trade, of African peoples.

OVERVIEW
QUESTIONS

The major global development in this chapter: The rise of the Atlantic slave trade and its impact on early modern African peoples and cultures.

As you read, consider:

1. How did ecological diversity in western Africa relate to cultural developments?

2. What tied western Africa to other parts of the world prior to the arrival of Europeans along Atlantic shores?

3. How did the Atlantic slave trade arise, and how was it sustained?

Many Western Africas

It has been estimated that the African continent, comprising a little over 20 percent of the earth's landmass, was home to 100 million people at the time of Columbus's famous 1492 transatlantic voyage. About 50 million people inhabited West and West Central Africa, what we refer to here as "western Africa." Western Africa thus had a population comparable to that of all the Americas at that time. It contained several dozen aspiring tributary states in various stages of expansion and contraction, along with a vast number of permanent agricultural and mobile, warrior-headed chiefdoms. There were also wide-ranging pastoral or herding groups, trading peoples, fishing folk, and scattered bands of desert and rain forest gatherer-hunters. The array of livelihoods was wide, yet the vast majority of western Africans lived as hoe agriculturalists, primarily cultivators of rice, sorghum, millet, and cotton (see Map 18.1).

FOCUS

What range of livelihoods, cultural practices, and political arrangements typified western Africa in early modern times?

Cultural Diversity

Religious ideas and practices varied as much as livelihoods, but most Africans south of the Sahara, like many peoples the world over, placed great emphasis on fertility. Fertility rituals were an integral aspect of everyday life; some entailed animal sacrifice, and others, rarely, human sacrifice. Also as in many other early modern societies, discord, illness, and material hardship were often thought to be the products of witchcraft. The capacity to identify and punish witches helped define power in many societies.

Islam, introduced by long-distance traders and warriors after the seventh century C.E., became dominant in the dry *sahel* (from the Arabic for "shore") and savanna, or grassland, regions just south of the Sahara, and along the rim of the Indian Ocean. Christian and Jewish communities were limited to tiny pockets in the northeastern Horn and along the Maghreb, or Mediterranean coast. Over two thousand languages were spoken on the continent, most of them derived from four major roots. All told, Africa's cultural and linguistic diversity easily exceeded that of Europe in the era of Columbus.

Even where Islam predominated, local notions of the spirit world survived. Most western Africans believed in a distant creator deity, sometimes equated with Allah, and everyday ritual tended to emphasize communication with ancestor spirits, who helped placate a host of other, potentially malevolent forces. As in many ancient cosmologies, animal and plant spirits were considered especially potent.

Places were also sacred. Rather like Andean *wakas*, western African **génies** (JEHN-ees) could be features in the landscape: boulders, springs, rivers, lakes, and groves. Trees were especially revered among peoples living along the southern margins of the savanna, and villagers built alongside patches of old-growth forest. Through periodic animal sacrifice, western Africans sought the patronage of local tree spirits, since they were literally most rooted in the land.

Environmental Challenges

Western Africa fell entirely within the lowland tropics and was thus subject to a number of endemic diseases and pests. The deadly falciparum variety of malaria and other serious mosquito-borne fevers attacked humans in the hot lowlands, and the wide range of the tsetse fly, carrier of the fatal trypanosomiasis virus, limited livestock grazing and horse breeding. As in modern times, droughts could be severe and prolonged in some densely populated regions, spurring mass migration and warfare. Western Africans nevertheless adapted to these and other environmental challenges, in the case of malaria developing at least some immunity against the disease.

Animal Husbandry and Metalsmithing

In the arid north where Islam predominated, beasts of burden included camels, donkeys, and horses. Cattle were also kept in the interior highlands and far south, where they were safe from tsetse flies. Arabian warhorses were greatly prized, and were widely traded among kingdoms and chiefdoms along the southern margins of the Sahara. They were most valued where fly-borne disease made breeding impossible. Other domestic animals included goats, swine, guinea fowl, sheep, and dogs. In general, animal **husbandry**, as in greater Eurasia, was far more developed in western Africa than in the Americas. There were also more large wild mammals in sub-Saharan Africa than in any other part of the world, and these featured prominently in regional cosmologies.

génie A sacred site or feature in the West African landscape.

husbandry Human intervention in the breeding of animals.

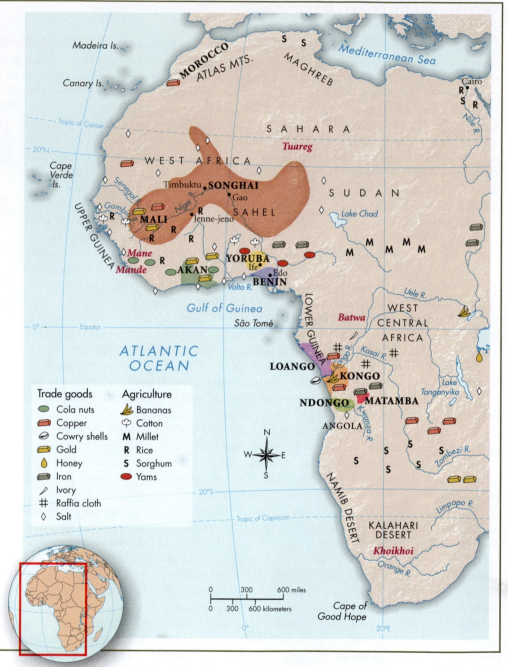

MAP 18.1

Western Africa, c. 1500

The huge regions of West and West Central Africa were of key importance to early modern global history as sources of both luxury commodities and enslaved immigrants. But western Africa was also marked by substantial internal dynamism. The Songhai Empire on the middle Niger rose to prominence about the time of Columbus. Large kingdoms and city-states also flourished on the Volta and lower Niger rivers and near the mouth of the Congo (Zaire). Rain forests and deserts were home to gatherer-hunters such as the Batwa (Pygmies) and Khoikhoi. Since tropical diseases severely limited the raising of large livestock, most western Africans used iron hand tools to plant and harvest millet, sorghum, rice, bananas, and, after trade with the Americas, maize and manioc.

Trade goods

- 🟢 Cola nuts
- 🟥 Copper
- 🥚 Cowry shells
- 🟨 Gold
- 🟡 Honey
- ⬛ Iron
- ⟋ Ivory
- # Raffia cloth
- ◇ Salt

Agriculture

- 🍌 Bananas
- ♇ Cotton
- M Millet
- R Rice
- S Sorghum
- 🔴 Yams

paramount chief A chief who presided over several headmen and controlled a large area.

Mining and metalsmithing technologies were also highly developed and widely dispersed. Throughout West and West Central Africa, copper and copper-alloy metallurgical techniques had grown complex by 1500. Goldsmithing was also advanced, though less widespread. This was in part because African gold was being increasingly drawn away into commercial trade networks extending to the Mediterranean Sea and Indian Ocean. To a large extent, western Eurasia's "bullion famine" spurred early European expansion into Africa.

Since ancient times, Africans had been great producers and consumers of iron. Whether in Mali or Angola, African ironmongers were not simply artisans but also shamanlike figures and even **paramount chiefs**—heads of numerous village clans. In fact, throughout sub-Saharan Africa, metalwork was a closely guarded and mystical process similar to alchemy (the transmutation of base metals into gold) in contemporary Europe, the Middle East, and China. African metalsmiths produced great quantities of tools, ornaments, and lasting works of art. They made the iron hoes most people tended crops with, and sometimes they traded in bulk over vast distances.

Africa's internal trade was linked to craft specialization, but mostly it served to redistribute basic commodities. Those who mined or collected salt, for example, usually bartered it for other necessities such as cloth. Highly prized in the vast West African interior, where springs and deposits were extremely scarce, Saharan salt was an essential dietary supplement. Similarly, manufactured goods such as agricultural tools were widely traded for food, textiles, and livestock, but bits of gold, copper, and iron also served as currency. Among the most important trade goods were cola nuts, the sharing of which cemented social relations in much of West Africa, particularly among elites.

Copper and bronze bracelets were prized by some of western Africa's coastal peoples, and eventually they were standardized into currency that the Portuguese called *manillas* (mah-KNEE-lahs). In some areas seashells such as the cowry, brought all the way from the Maldive Islands off the west coast of India, functioned in the same way. The desire for brightly colored cotton textiles from India fueled Africa's west coast demand for shell and copperbronze currency, which in time would also contribute to the expansion of the Atlantic slave trade. Africa's east coast, meanwhile, remained integrated into the vast and mostly separate Indian Ocean trade circuit through the monsoon-seasonal export of ivory, gold, and to a lesser extent, human captives, as we will see in Chapter 19.

African societies linked by trade were sometimes also bound by political ties. A shared desire to both expand household units and improve security led many Africans to form short- and long-term confederations and conglomerates. Like the Iroquois and Powhatan confederacies of eastern North America (discussed in Chapter 16), some of these alliances had a religious core, but just as often such collaborative actions were spurred by ecological stresses such as droughts. In this politically fluid context, ethnic and other forms of identity often blended and blurred as groups merged and partially or wholly adopted each other's languages, cosmologies, farming techniques, and modes of dress and adornment.

Nevertheless, as in the Americas, intergroup conflict was hardly unusual in western Africa prior to the arrival of Europeans. Expansionist, tributary empires such as Mali and Songhai grew independently of outside forces, and both managed to make lifelong regional and internal enemies. The motives of African warfare varied, but they frequently had to do with the control of resources, and especially people, sometimes as slaves put to work on agricultural estates. As in other parts of the early modern world, European trading and political meddling on Africa's Atlantic coast would spawn or exacerbate major new conflicts that would reverberate deep within the continent. Full-blown imperialism would come much later, with the development of new technologies and antimalarial drugs, but it would benefit in part from this earlier political disruption.

A Young Woman from West Africa

Since at least medieval times, West African women surprised outside visitors with their independence, visibility, and political influence, in both Islamic and non-Islamic societies. This drawing by an English artist during a slave-trading voyage to West Africa in around 1775 depicts a young woman with elaborately braided hair, pearl earrings, and a choker strung with coral or large stones. It is possible that she is a member of an elite family given these proudly displayed ornaments, but we do not know. The portrait reveals neither her identity nor her destiny, though it is clear that she made a strong impression on the foreign artist. (National Maritime Museum, London/The Image Works.)

Trade, Politics, and Warfare

West Africa's Gold Miners

Implements of the Gold Trade

West Africa was long legendary for its gold, which was first traded across the Sahara and later to Europeans arriving along the Atlantic coast. In the Akan region of present-day Ghana, gold dust circulated as currency, with portions measured by merchants in a hanging balance against tiny, fancifully designed brass weights. Gold dust was stored in brass boxes and dished out with decorated brass spoons. Smaller exchanges employed cowry shells, brought to Atlantic Africa from the Maldive Islands in the Indian Ocean. (Aldo Tutino/Art Resource, NY.)

Until 1650, gold was a more valuable West African export than slaves, and it remained highly significant for many years afterward. The mines and their workers, some of whom were enslaved, were controlled by local kings, whose agents traded the gold to long-distance merchants with ties to Europeans on the coast. Gold diggings were concentrated along the upper reaches of the Senegal, Niger, and Volta rivers, mostly in and around streams flowing down from eroded mountain ranges. Sources describing West African gold mining in early modern times are rare, but anecdotal descriptions combined with somewhat later eyewitness accounts suggest that women did many

of the most strenuous tasks. The Scottish traveler Mungo Park described nonenslaved West African women miners among the Mande of the upper Niger in the 1790s as follows:

> About the beginning of December, when the harvest is over, and the streams and torrents have greatly subsided, the Mansa, or chief of the town, appoints a day to begin *sanoo koo*, "gold washing"; and the women are sure to have themselves in readiness by the time appointed. . . . On the morning of their departure, a bullock is killed for the first day's

Landlords and Strangers: Peoples and States in West Africa

FOCUS

What economic, social, and political patterns characterized early modern West Africa?

According to mostly archaeological and some textual references, West Africans in the period following 700 C.E. faced several radical new developments. Two major catalysts for change were the introduction and spread of Islam after the eighth century and a long dry period lasting from roughly 1100 to 1500 C.E. At least one historian has characterized human relations in this era in terms of "landlords" and "strangers," a reference to the tendency toward small and scattered agricultural communities offering safe passage and hospitality to a variety of travelers and craft specialists.[3] In return, these "strangers"—traders, blacksmiths, tanners, bards, and clerics—offered goods and services. The model "landlord" was an esteemed personage or even group of elders capable of ensuring the security and prosperity of a wide range of dependents and affiliates, usually conceived of as members of an extended family.

entertainment, and a number of prayers and charms are used to ensure success; for a failure on that day is thought a bad omen. . . . The washing of the sands of the streams is by far the easiest way of obtaining the gold dust, but in most places the sands have been so narrowly searched before that unless the stream takes some new course, the gold is found but in small quantities. While some of the party are busied in washing the sands, others employ themselves farther up the torrent, where the rapidity of the stream has carried away all the clay, sand, etc., and left nothing but small pebbles. The search among these is a very troublesome task. I have seen women who have had the skin worn off the tops of their fingers in this employment. Sometimes, however, they are rewarded by finding pieces [nuggets] of gold, which they call *sanoo birro*, "gold stones," that amply repay them for their trouble. A woman and her daughter, inhabitants of Kamalia, found in one day two pieces of this kind.

Mande men, according to Park, participated in excavating deep pits in gold-bearing hills "in the height of the dry season," producing clay and other sediments "for the women to wash; for though the pit is dug by the men, the gold is always washed by the women, who are accustomed from their infancy to a similar

operation, in separating the husks of corn from the meal." To be efficient, panning required intense concentration and careful eye-hand coordination, and use of several pans to collect concentrates. This skill was appreciated, as Park explains: "Some women, by long practice, become so well acquainted with the nature of the sand, and the mode of washing it, that they will collect gold where others cannot find a single particle." Gold dust was then stored in quills (the hollow shafts of bird feathers) plugged with cotton, says Park, "and the washers are fond of displaying a number of these quills in their hair."

Source: Mungo Park, *Travels in the Interior Districts of Africa*, ed. and introduced by Kate Ferguson Masters (Durham, NC: Duke University Press, 2000), 264–267.

QUESTIONS TO CONSIDER

1. Why was West African gold mining seasonal?

2. How were tasks divided between men and women, and why?

3. Was gold washing demeaning labor, or could it be a source of pride?

For Further Information:
Philip D. Curtin. *Economic Change in Precolonial Africa: Senegambia in the Era of the Slave Trade*. Madison: University of Wisconsin Press, 1975.

Empire Builders and Traders

The late medieval dry period also witnessed the rise of mounted warriors: the stranger as conqueror and captive-taker. On the banks of the middle and upper Niger River rose the expansionist kingdoms of Mali and Songhai, both linked to the Mediterranean world via the caravan terminus of Timbuktu (see again Map 18.1). Both empires were headed by devout, locally born Muslim rulers. One, Mansa Musa (*mansa* meaning "conqueror") of Mali, made the pilgrimage to Mecca in 1325. Musa spent so much gold during a stop in Cairo that his visit became legend.

It was gold, concentrated near the headwaters of the Senegal, Niger, and Volta rivers, that put sub-Saharan Africa on the minds—and maps—of European and Middle Eastern traders and monarchs. Most West African mines were worked by farming peoples forced to pay tribute in gold dust unearthed in the fallow (inactive) season (see Lives and Livelihoods: West Africa's Gold Miners). As in North America, India, and many other parts of the world at this time, warfare was also limited by the seasonal demands of subsistence agriculture. Yet land was a less-prized commodity than labor in West Africa. Prestige derived not from own-

Politics of the Gold Trade

ership of farmland or mines but from control over productive people, some of whom—and in places like Songhai, many of whom—were enslaved. Captive-taking was thus integral to warfare at all political levels, from the smallest chiefdom to the largest empire. Like the seasonal production of gold, the seasonal production of slaves, who for centuries had been sent north across the Sahara to Mediterranean markets and east to those of the Red Sea and Indian Ocean, would vastly expand once Europeans arrived on Atlantic shores.

With the exception, as we will see, of the Songhai Empire, West African politics in this period was mostly confederated. Dozens of paramount chiefs or regional kings relied on a host of more-or-less-loyal tributaries and enslaved laborers for their power, wealth, and sustenance. In general, as in much of Southeast Asia (see Chapter 19), early modern West Africa witnessed the periodic rise of charismatic and aggressive rulers, with few bureaucrats and judges. Rulers typically extended their authority by offering to protect vulnerable agricultural groups from raiders. Some coastal rice growers in Upper Guinea drifted in and out of these kinds of regional alliances, depending on political and environmental conditions. Alliances did not always spare them from disaster. Still, as actors in the Columbian Exchange, enslaved rice farmers from this region transferred techniques and perhaps grains to the plantations of North and South America.

From Western Sudan to Lower Guinea, town-sized units predominated, many of them walled or otherwise fortified. Archaeologists are still discovering traces of these extensive enclosures, some of which housed thousands of inhabitants. As in medieval Europe, even when they shared a language, walled cities in neighboring territories could be fiercely competitive. These were not tribal units but rather highly stratified and populous urban enclaves.

Songhai Empire

Dating to the first centuries C.E., West Africa was also home to sizable kingdoms. Old Ghana flourished from about 300 to 1000 C.E., followed by Mali, which thrived from about 1200 to 1400. From about the time of Columbus, the Songhai Empire, centered at Gao, rose to prominence under Sunni Ali (r. 1464–1492). Similar to the mansas of Mali, Sunni Ali was a conqueror, employing mounted lancers and huge squads of boatmen to great and terrifying effect. Sunni Ali's successor, Muhammad Touré, extended Songhai's rule even farther. At his zenith Touré, who took the title *askiya* (AH-skee-yah), or hereditary lord, and later *caliph*, or supreme lord, controlled a huge portion of West Africa (see again Map 18.1). Ultimately, like many Eurasian contemporaries, he was limited more by sheer logistics and distance than armed resistance.

The wealth and power of Songhai derived from the merchant crossroads cities of the middle Niger: Jenne, Gao, and Timbuktu (see Reading the Past: Al-Sa'di on Jenne and Its History). Here gold from the western mines of the upper Niger and Senegal, salt from the Sahara, and forest products from the south such as cola nuts and raffia palm fiber were exchanged, along with a host of other commodities. Slaves, many of them taken in Songhai's wars of expansion, were also traded to distant buyers in North and East Africa. Stately Timbuktu, meanwhile, retained its reputation as a major market for books and a center of Islamic teachings.

Touré's successors were less aggressive than he, and as Songhai's power waned in the later sixteenth century, the empire fell victim to mounted raiders from distant Morocco. With alarming audacity, and greatly aided by their state-of-the-art firearms and swift mounts, the Moroccans (among them hundreds of exiled Spanish Muslims, or Moriscos) captured the cities of Gao and Timbuktu in 1591. As their victory texts attest, these foreign conquistadors took home stunning quantities of gold and a number of slaves. Yet unlike their Spanish and Portuguese contemporaries in the Americas, they failed to hold on to their new conquest. The mighty Sahara proved a more formidable barrier to colonial governance than the Atlantic Ocean. After the fall of Songhai there emerged a fractured dynasty of Moroccan princes, the Sa'dis, who were in turn crushed by new, local waves of warfare in the late seventeenth and early eighteenth centuries. Most fell victim to the Sahara's best-known nomads, the Tuareg (TWAH-regh).

Sculptors and Priest-Kings

Farther south, near the mouth of the Niger River, was the rain forest kingdom of Benin, with its capital at Edo. Under King Ewuare (EH-woo-AH-reh) (r. c. 1450–1480), Benin

Al-Sa'di on Jenne and Its History

The historian known as Al-Sa'di (1594–c. 1656) was an imam, or religious scholar, descended from the Moroccan Sa'dis who invaded and toppled the Songhai Empire on the middle Niger River in 1591. He lived in the cities of Timbuktu and Jenne, and he appears to have learned most of what he knew about the region's past from a mix of written Arabic sources and local oral historians who spoke the Songhai language. The following passage, from about 1655, is translated from Al-Sa'di's Arabic history of the middle Niger region from medieval times to his own.

Jenne is a large, well-favored and blessed city, characterized by prosperity, good fortune, and compassion. God bestowed these things upon that land as innate characteristics. It is the nature of Jenne's inhabitants to be kind, charitable, and solicitous for one another. However, when it comes to matters of daily life, competitiveness is very much a part of their character, to such an extent that if anyone attains a higher status, the rest uniformly hate him, though without making this apparent or letting it show. Only if there occurs some change of fortune—from which God protect us—will each of them display his hatred in word and deed.

Jenne is one of the great markets of the Muslims. Those who deal in salt from the mine of Taghaza meet there with those who deal in gold from the mine of Bitu. These two blessed mines have no equal in the entire world. People discovered their great blessing through going to them for business, amassing such wealth as only God—Sublime is He—could assess. This blessed city of Jenne is why caravans come to Timbuktu from all quarters—north, south, east, and west. Jenne is situated to the south and west of Timbuktu beyond the two rivers [the Niger and Bani]. When the [Bani] river is in flood, Jenne becomes an island, but when the flood abates, the water is far from it. It begins to be surrounded by water in August, and in February the water recedes again. . . .

With the exception of Sunni Ali [of Songhai], no ruler had ever defeated the people of Jenne since the town was founded. According to what its people tell, Sunni Ali besieged them for seven years, seven months, and seven days, finally subduing them and ruling over them. His army was encamped at Joboro [original site of Jenne, south of the city] and they would attack the people of Jenne daily until the flood encircled the city. Then he would retire with his army to a place called Nibkat Sunni ("the hillock of Sunni"), so named because he stayed there. His army would remain there and keep watch until the waters receded and then would return to Joboro to fight. I was told by Sultan Abd Allah son of Sultan Abu Bakr that this went on for seven years. Then famine struck and the people of Jenne grew weak. Despite that, they contrived to appear still strong, so that Sunni Ali had no idea what condition they were really in. Weary of the siege at last, he decided to return to Songhai. Then one of the Sultan of Jenne's senior army commanders, said to be the grandfather of Unsa Mani Surya Muhammad, sent word to Sunni Ali and revealed the secret, and told him not to return home until he saw how things would turn out. So Sunni Ali exercised patience and became even more eager [to take Jenne].

Then the sultan took counsel with his commanders and the senior men of his army. He proposed that they should surrender to Sunni Ali, and they agreed. . . . So the Sultan of Jenne and his senior army commanders rode forth to meet Sunni Ali, and when he got close to him he dismounted and walked towards him on foot. Sunni Ali welcomed him and received him with honor. When he saw that the sultan was only a young man, he took hold of him and seated him beside him on his rug and said, "Have we been fighting with a boy all this time?" Then his courtiers told him that the young man's father had died during the siege, and that he had succeeded him as sultan. This is what lies behind the custom of the Sultan of Songhai sitting together with the Sultan of Jenne on a single rug until this day.

Source: John O. Hunwick, ed. and trans., *Timbuktu and the Songhay Empire: Al-Sadi's Tarikh al-sudan Down to 1613 and Other Contemporary Documents* (Leiden, the Netherlands: Brill, 1999), 13–21.

EXAMINING THE EVIDENCE

1. How does Al-Sa'di characterize the city and people of Jenne?

2. Why is the city's location on the Niger River important?

3. How does Al-Sa'di characterize the Songhai Empire founder Sunni Ali's conquest of Jenne?

Art of the Slave Trade: A Benin Bronze Plaque

Copper and bronze metallurgy were advanced arts in western Africa long before the arrival of Europeans. Metal sculpture, in the form of lifelike busts, historical plaques, and complex representations of deities, was most developed in western Nigeria and the kingdom of Benin. Realistic representations of elite men and women appear to have served a commemorative function, as did relief-sculpted plaques depicting kings, chiefs, and warlords in full regalia. Beginning in the 1500s, sculptors in Benin and neighboring lands began to depict Portuguese slave traders and missionaries, bearded men with helmets, heavy robes, and trade goods, including primitive muskets. This plaque depicts Portuguese slavers with a cargo of manillas, the bronze bracelets that served as currency in the slave trade until the mid-nineteenth century.

EXAMINING THE
EVIDENCE

1. How were Portuguese newcomers incorporated into this traditional Benin art form?

2. How might this bronze representation of foreigners and their trade goods have been a commentary on the slave trade?

Plaque of Portuguese Traders with Manillas
(Gift of Mr. and Mrs. Klaus G. Perls, 1991 (1991.17.13). The Metropolitan Museum of Art, New York, NY/Art Resource, NY.)

reached the height of its power in the mid-fifteenth century, subjecting dozens of neighboring towns and chiefdoms to tributary status. Benin grew wealthy in part by exporting cloth made by women working on domestic looms in tributary villages. This trade expanded substantially with the arrival of Portuguese coastal traders around 1500, revitalizing Benin's power. Some of the most accomplished sculptors in African history worked under King Ewuare and his successors, producing a stunning array of cast brass portraits of Benin royalty, prominent warriors, and even newly arrived Europeans. This was but one of the many specialized livelihoods afforded by urban living (see Seeing the Past: Art of the Slave Trade: A Benin Bronze Plaque).

Yoruba City-States

Just west of Benin were a number of city-states ruled by ethnic Yoruba clans. At their core was the city of Ife (EE-feh), founded in around 1000 C.E. Ife metalsmiths and sculptors were as accomplished as those of Benin, and their large cast works, especially in copper, have been hailed as inimitable. As in the precontact Americas, Yoruba political leaders, called *obas*, performed a mix of political and religious duties. Most of these priest-kings were men, but a significant number were women. One of the obas' main functions was to negotiate with an array of ancestor deities thought to govern key aspects of everyday life. Some slaves later taken from this region to the Americas appear to have adapted these ideas to Christian monotheism, masking multiple ancestor worship behind the Roman Catholic cult of saints.

Akan City-States

oba A priest-king or queen of the Yoruba culture (modern southern Nigeria).

Urban life also matured along the banks of the lower Volta River, in what is today Ghana, at the beginning of early modern times. Here Akan peoples had formed city-states, mostly by controlling regional gold mines and trading networks. The Akan initially focused on transporting gold and cola nuts to the drier north, where these commodities found a ready market among the imperial societies of the middle Niger. With the arrival of Europeans on the Atlantic coast in the late fifteenth century, however, many Akan traders turned their attention toward the south. Throughout early modern times, women held great power in Akan polities, and matrilineal inheritance was the recognized standard. Matrilineal societies were relatively rare in West Africa, but other exceptions included the nomadic Tuareg. Even in patrilineal empires such as Mali and Songhai, women could wield considerable power, especially in matters of succession.

Land of the Blacksmith Kings: West Central Africa

Human interaction in West Central Africa, called by some historians "land of the blacksmith kings," was in part defined by long-term control of copper and iron deposits. As in West Africa, however, the vast majority of people were engaged in subsistence agriculture, limited to hoe tilling because the tsetse fly eliminated livestock capable of pulling plows. For this reason, few people other than gatherer-hunters such as the Pygmies inhabited the most prominent geographical feature of the region, Africa's great equatorial forest (see again Mapping the World, page 583). Most preferred to farm the surrounding savanna and fish along the Atlantic coast and major riverbanks.

> **FOCUS**
>
> What economic, social, and political patterns characterized early modern West Central Africa?

The Congo (Zaire) River basin and estuary, second only to the Amazon in terms of forest cover and volume of freshwater catchment, were of central importance to human history in West Central Africa. Although patterns of belief and material culture varied, most people spoke derivations of Western Bantu, an ancestral root language. Islam was known in some areas but remained marginal in influence. Most inhabitants of West Central Africa lived in matrilineal or patrilineal kin-based villages, a small minority of them subordinate to paramount chiefs or small kings. In all, the region was marked by a cultural coherence similar to that of Mesoamerica (discussed in Chapter 16).

Farmers and Traders

Farmers

The hoe-agriculturalists who formed the vast majority of West Central Africans grew mostly millet and sorghum, complemented by yams and bananas in certain areas. Bananas, a crop introduced to the region some time before 1000 C.E., enabled farmers to exploit the forest's edge more effectively and devote more energy to textile making and other activities. Some forested areas were too wet for staple crops but still offered game, medicinal plants, and other products. Pygmy forest dwellers, for example, traded honey, ivory, and wild animal skins to their farming neighbors for iron points and food items. Tsetse flies and other pests limited the development of animal husbandry in West Central Africa, except in the drier south. In the vast plains of southern Angola, livestock survived, but rains were highly uncertain.

Wherever they lived, West Central Africans, like Europeans and Asians, embraced a host of native American crops in the centuries following Columbus's voyages. Maize became a staple throughout Central Africa, along with cassava (manioc), peanuts, chili peppers, beans, squash, and tobacco. Peanuts, probably introduced by the Portuguese from Brazil soon after 1500, were locally called *nguba* (NGOO-bah), from which the American term "goober peas" derives.

Traders

As the introduction of American crops demonstrates, West Central Africa may have had less direct ties to global trade than coastal West Africa, but it was still part of the system. Likewise, the internal African trade networks were of great importance to West Central African life. As in West Africa, salt was traded over great distances, along with food products, textiles, metal goods, and other items. Raffia palm fiber was used to manufacture a supple and durable cloth, and coastal lagoons were exploited for cowry shells for trade.

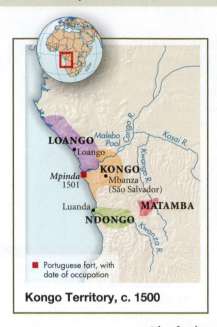

Kongo Territory, c. 1500

■ Portuguese fort, with date of occupation

Throughout the region political power came to be associated with control of these sorts of trade goods and also of routes of access to the interior. For example, in around 1300 two kingdoms arose above and below the Malebo Pool alongside the Congo River. This was the first major cataract, and hence portage site, for all traders moving between the coast and interior. The kings of Loango, living above the falls but also controlling access to the Atlantic coast, taxed trade and also drew legitimacy from their role as caretakers of an ancient religious shrine. Below the falls and to the south, in Kongo—a kingdom misnamed by the Portuguese after the title of its warlords, the ***manikongos*** (mah-nee-CONE-goes)—leaders came to power in part by monopolizing copper deposits. The kings of Kongo also controlled access to cowry shells, the region's main currency.

Smiths and Kings

As in West Africa, power also derived from the mystique surrounding metallurgy. The introduction of ironworking to the region sometime early in the Common Era had made the majority of farmers dependent on smiths for hoes, blades, and other implements. Making the most of this reliance, some blacksmiths became kings. By 1500, Kongo commanded an area stretching inland from the right bank of the Congo River south and east some 185 miles, absorbing numerous villages, slaves, and tributaries along the way. A few small kingdoms existed to the north and east, often with copper deposits serving as their lifeblood. These kingdoms eventually challenged Kongo directly, in part because they were subjected to Kongo slave-raiding. In what is today Angola, just north of the Kwanza River, there emerged in the sixteenth century the Ndongo (NDOAN-go) kingdom. Just northeast of Ndongo lay the Matamba kingdom. Initially tributaries of Kongo, the people of Matamba shifted their relations in favor of Ndongo as Portuguese influence there grew in the sixteenth century. By 1600, the Portuguese held forts deep in Ndongo country, using them to procure slaves from farther inland.

Less is known about the peoples of the more isolated and forested middle Congo basin, but archaeologists have recently shown that large chiefdoms were being consolidated there as early as the thirteenth century, and they lasted into early modern times. Here, innovations in sword manufacture seem to have enabled some paramount chiefs to monopolize trade along Congo River tributaries. Like elites everywhere, these chiefs considered themselves the spiritual kin of various predatory lords of the animal kingdom, in this case the leopard and eagle.

We know less about women's livelihoods than men's, but it appears that in early modern West Central Africa, as in many preindustrial societies, women tended to work mostly at domestic tasks such as child rearing, food preparation, and other aspects of household management. Men were frequently engaged in hunting, herding, trade, and warfare, so women's responsibilities often extended to agriculture. In many places, women planted yams in hard soils by slicing through the crust with machetes made by village men. Almost everywhere, women tended the food crops and men cleared forest.

Women formed the foundation of West Central African society in terms of both subsistence and reproduction. Yet

Mbundu Blacksmiths

This late-seventeenth-century watercolor depicts a Mbundu blacksmith and assistant at work. As the assistant operates the typical African bellows with rods attached to airbags, the master smith hammers a crescent-shaped iron blade on an anvil. Other blades, including what may be a sickle or hoe, lie on the ground to the left of the anvil. In the background a curious audience looks on. (Illumination by Padre Giovanni Antonio Cavazzi da Montecuccolo (died 1692) from the Manoscritti Araldi; reproduction courtesy of Michele Araldi.)

women did still more. Evidence for the early modern period is slim, but it appears that while men controlled metal smelting and smithing, women both managed and worked in mining crews. Some were probably enslaved, but others were likely associated with ethnic groups famed for their expertise in these tasks. Even children were employed in mines, particularly salt and copper mines. Experienced West and West Central African miners, including women and children, were probably among the first slaves sent by the Portuguese to work the gold mines of the Spanish Caribbean. Many later found their skills in demand in Colombia, Mexico, Peru, and Brazil.

Strangers in Ships: Gold, Slavery, and the Portuguese

As we saw in Chapter 17, the Portuguese arrived in western Africa soon after 1400 in search of gold and a sea route to India. For well over a century they were the only significant European presence in the region. During that time, a number of Portuguese explorers, merchants, missionaries, and even criminal castaways established a string of *feitorias*, or fortified trading posts, and offshore island settlements. There were no great marches to the interior, no conquests of existing empires. Instead, the Portuguese focused their efforts on extracting Africa's famed wealth in gold, ivory, and slaves through intermediaries. In a pattern that would be continued in Asia, the Portuguese sought to dominate maritime trade.

> **FOCUS**
>
> How did the early Portuguese slave trade in western Africa function?

From Voyages of Reconnaissance to Trading Forts 1415–1650

On the wide Gambia River the Portuguese sailed far inland, seeking the famed gold of Mali, at this time an empire in decline but still powerful in the interior (see again Map 18.1). The warring states of the region were happy to trade gold for horses, which were far more valuable than the crude European guns available at this time. Chronic conflicts yielded a surplus of captives. With explicit backing from the pope, Portuguese merchants did not hesitate to accept African slaves as payment. Once in Portuguese hands, each healthy young male was reduced to an accounting unit, or *peça* (PEH-sah) literally "piece." Women, children, the disabled, and the elderly were discounted in terms of fractions of a peça.

African enslavement of fellow Africans was widespread long before the arrival of Europeans, and the daily experience of slavery in most African households, farms, or mines was no doubt unpleasant. What differed with the arrival of the Portuguese in the fifteenth century was a new insistence on innate African inferiority—in a word, racism—and with it a closing of traditional avenues of reentry into free society, if not for oneself, then for one's children, such as faithful service, or in Islamic societies, religious conversion. The Portuguese followed the pope's decree that enslaved sub-Saharan Africans be converted to Catholicism, but they also adopted an unstated policy that regarded black Africans as "slaves by nature." To sidestep the paradox of African spiritual equality and alleged "beastly" inferiority, the Portuguese claimed that they sold only captives taken in "just war." Many such slaves were sold, like young Domingo Angola, to the Spanish, who took the Portuguese sellers at their word (see Reading the Past: Alonso de Sandoval, "General Points Relating to Slavery").

Iberian demand for African slaves remained limited prior to American colonization. Word of goldfields in the African interior encouraged the Portuguese to continue their dogged search for the yellow metal. By 1471 caravels reached West Africa's so-called Gold Coast, and in 1482 the Portuguese established a feitoria in present-day Ghana. Built by

Racism as Justification for Slavery

manikongo A "blacksmith" king of Kongo.

peça Portuguese for "piece," used to describe enslaved Africans as units of labor.

Alonso de Sandoval, "General Points Relating to Slavery"

Alonso de Sandoval (1577–c. 1650) was a Jesuit priest born in Seville, Spain, and raised in Lima, Peru. He spent most of his adult life administering sacraments to enslaved Africans arriving at the Caribbean port city of Cartagena de Indias, in present-day Colombia. In 1627 he published a book entitled *On Restoring Ethiopian Salvation*. In it, he focused on cultural aspects of sub-Saharan African societies as he understood them, with the aim of preaching to Africans more effectively, but he also discussed the Atlantic slave trade and its justifications.

> The debate among scholars on how to justify the arduous and difficult business of slavery has perplexed me for a long time. I could have given up on explaining it and just ignored it in this book. However, I am determined to discuss it, although I will leave the final justification of slavery to legal and ecclesiastical authorities. . . . I will only mention here what I have learned after many years of working in this ministry. The readers can formulate their own ideas on the justice of this issue. . . .
>
> A short story helps me explain how to morally justify black slavery. I was once consulted by a captain who owned slave ships that had made many voyages to these places. He had enriched himself through the slave trade, and his conscience was burdened with concern over how these slaves had fallen into his hands. His concern is not surprising, because he also told me that one of their kings imprisoned anyone who angered him in order to sell them as slaves to the Spaniards. So in this region, people are enslaved if they anger the king. . . .
>
> There is a more standard way in which slaves are traded and later shipped in fleets of ships to the Indies. Near Luanda are some black merchants called pombeiros worth a thousand pesos. They travel inland eighty leagues [c. 250 miles], bringing porters with them to carry trade goods. They meet in great markets where merchants gather together to sell slaves. These merchants travel 200 or 300 leagues [c. 650–1000 miles] to sell blacks from many different kingdoms to various merchants or pombeiros. The pombeiros buy the slaves and transport them to the coast. They must report to their masters how many died on the road. They do this by bringing back the hands of the dead, a stinking, horrific sight. . . .
>
> I have spent a great deal of time discussing this subject because slaves are captured in many different ways, and this disturbs the slave traders' consciences. One slave trader freely told me that he felt guilty about how the slaves he had bought in Guinea had come to be enslaved. Another slave trader, who had bought 300 slaves on foot, expressed the same concerns, adding that half the wars fought between blacks would not take place if the Spanish [or more likely, Portuguese] did not go there to buy slaves. . . . The evidence, along with the moral justifications argued by scholars, is the best we can do to carefully address this irredeemable situation and the very difficult business of the slave trade.

Source: Alonso de Sandoval, *Treatise on Slavery*, ed. and trans. Nicole Von Germeten (Indianapolis, IN: Hackett Publishers, 2008), 50–55.

EXAMINING THE EVIDENCE

1. Who was Alonso de Sandoval, and why did he write this passage?
2. How does Sandoval try to justify African enslavement?
3. Are Africans themselves involved in this discussion?

Early Portuguese Slave Trade enslaved Africans, São Jorge da Mina, or "St. George of the mine," served for over a century as Portugal's major West African gold and slaving fort.

After 1500, as slave markets in Spanish America and Brazil emerged, new trading posts were established in choice spots all along the West African coast. It so happened that invasions of Mande and Mane (MAH-nay) peoples into modern Guinea, Liberia, Sierra Leone, and Ivory Coast in the fifteenth and sixteenth centuries produced yet more streams of captives through the seventeenth century (see Map 18.2). As in the first years after their arrival, the Portuguese continued to trade copper, iron, textiles, horses, and guns (now much more advanced) for gold, ivory, and a local spice called malaguetta pepper, but by the early 1500s the shift toward slave trading was evident. The coexistence of rising

MAP 18.2

The Early Atlantic Slave Trade, c. 1450–1650

The first enslaved Africans transported by ship in Atlantic waters arrived in Portugal in 1441. The Portuguese won a monopoly on African coastal trade from the pope, and until 1500, they shipped most enslaved African captives to the eastern Atlantic islands, where plantations were booming by the 1450s. Soon after 1500, Portuguese slave traders took captives first to the Spanish Caribbean (West Indies), then to the mainland colonies of New Spain and Peru. Claimed by the Portuguese in 1500, Brazil was initially a minor destination for enslaved Africans, but this changed by about 1570, when the colony's sugar production ballooned. Another early Atlantic route took slaves south to Buenos Aires, where they were marched overland to the rich city of Potosí. Death rates on the ships and on overland marches were always high in this traffic in human lives.

demand for slaves in the Americas and increased supply in Africa as the result of warfare made the dramatic growth of the Atlantic slave trade all but inevitable.

Throughout western Africa the Portuguese both extracted and transported wealth. They frequently ferried luxury goods such as cola nuts and textiles, as well as slaves, between existing African trade zones. As we will see, a similar pattern would emerge when the Portuguese reached India, and later China, Japan, and the Spice Islands. Virtually everywhere the Portuguese docked their lumbering but well-armed ships, Africans found that they benefited as much from access to the foreigners' shipping, which was relatively secure and efficient, as from their goods. As a result, many competing coastal lords made the most of these new trade ties, often to the detriment of more isolated and vulnerable neighbors.

At times commerce with the Portuguese, which increasingly turned to the import of bronze and copper bracelets, or manillas, as currency, would upend a region's balance of power, touching off a series of interior conflicts. Some such conflicts were ignited by Portuguese convicts, who survived abandonment along the coast to establish marriage alliances with local chiefdoms. As seen in Chapter 17 in the case of Brazil, this was in fact the Portuguese plan, to drop expendable subjects like seeds along the world's coasts. Some took root, learned local languages, and built trading posts. In several West African coastal enclaves, mulatto or "Eurafrican" communities developed. These mixed communities were nominally Catholic, but much cultural blending occurred. Some scholars now refer to these new intermediaries of global exchange as "Atlantic creoles."

**New Markets in the
Niger Delta**

After 1510, the Portuguese moved eastward. Here among the Niger delta's vast tidal flats and mangroves, Ijaw (EE-jaw) boatmen were initially willing to trade an adult male captive for fewer than a dozen copper manillas. Rates of exchange moderated with competition and a steadier flow of goods, but overall, Portuguese demand for slaves remained relatively low and was met by other captive-producing zones. What historians call the "Nigerian diaspora" mostly developed later in this densely populated region, in the seventeenth and eighteenth centuries. By then rival Dutch and English slavers had begun operating posts to the west and east of the Niger delta (see Map 18.4, page 602). After 1650 this region was known simply as the Slave Coast.

Portuguese Strategy in the Kingdom of Kongo

Portuguese interest in Atlantic Africa shifted southeastward after 1500, based in part on alliances with the kingdom of Kongo. Within West Central Africa generally, ongoing cycles of trade, war, and drought profoundly influenced relationships with outsiders. Once again, local nobles forced the Portuguese to operate according to local systems of influence and local rules. Still, whereas Portuguese slavers were to be largely displaced by the French, English, and Dutch in West and even northern West Central Africa by 1650, in the southern portion of the continent they held on for much longer. As a result, the fortunes of Kongo and Angola became ever more intimately entwined with those of Brazil, Portugal's vast colony on the other side of the Atlantic. Historians now speak of a functionally separate South Atlantic slave trade circuit.

Missionary Efforts

Portuguese religious initiatives in Africa had long been split between armed conflict with Muslim kingdoms in the far north, epitomized by the 1415 conquest of Ceuta in Morocco (see Chapter 17), and more peaceful, although scattered and inconsistent, missionary efforts in the south. Portuguese missionaries, like merchants, tended not to survive long in the tropical interior, where malaria and other diseases took a heavy toll. Thus scores of Franciscans, Jesuits, and others died denouncing the persistent **fetishism** (roughly, "idolatry") of their local hosts.

Quite unlike their Spanish contemporaries in the Americas, the Portuguese made barely a dent in African religious traditions, despite centuries of contact. This was not for lack of trying—the Portuguese worked much harder at conversion than did later-arriving northern Europeans—but rather due to a mix of hardening Portuguese racism and sub-Saharan Africa's punishing disease regime. Falciparum malaria, in particular, severely restricted the movements of European missionaries, who also faced language barriers and other cultural obstacles. The obvious solution was to train African priests, and for a time this option was pursued and even sponsored by the Portuguese royal family.

In the early sixteenth century, African priests were trained in Lisbon, in the university city of Coimbra, and even in Rome. African seminaries also were established, notably in the Cape Verde Islands and the island of São Tomé, located off the western coast in the Gulf of Guinea. Despite promising beginnings, however, these endeavors met with sharp opposition from an increasingly racist and self-righteous Portuguese clergy. A similar process had taken place in Spanish America, where ambitious plans for training and ordaining a native American clergy were scrapped within a few generations of contact. Emerging colonial racial hierarchies, indelibly linked to status, trumped the universal ideal of spiritual equality. An African clergy could also prove subversive of the slave trade and other such commercial projects. Already in decline before 1600, most of the local African seminaries languished in the seventeenth and early eighteenth centuries. Only with the Enlightenment-inspired reforms of the later eighteenth century (discussed in Chapter 23) were African novices again encouraged to become priests beyond the secular, or parish, level, and only after the abolition of slavery did their numbers become significant. Thus, although the Atlantic slave trade would result in the forced migration of millions of Africans and the creation of new hybrid cultural communities in the Americas, in Africa itself the racial basis of the trade inhibited cultural merger and exchange.

Portuguese Soldier
Here a Benin artist depicts a Portuguese soldier in what appears to be light armor and a crested metal helmet typical of the later sixteenth century. Portuguese soldiers like this one aided several African allies, including the Christian kings of Kongo, as they fought for regional supremacy and engaged in the growing slave trade. (Snark/Art Resource, NY.)

This did not mean that Christianity had no impact on early modern Atlantic Africa. Rather, it meant that its presence was less deeply felt than might otherwise have been the case. Aside from the offshore islands, only in Kongo and Angola did Christianity play a critical historical role. Beginning in the 1480s, the Portuguese applied their usual blend of trade, military alliances, and religious proselytizing to carve out a niche in West Central Africa. By 1491 they had managed to convert much of the Kongo aristocracy to Roman Catholicism. Key among the converts was the paramount chief's son, Nzinga Mbemba, who later ruled as Afonso I (r. 1506–1543).

Afonso's conversion was apparently genuine. He learned to read, studied theology tirelessly, and renamed Mbanza, the capital city, São Salvador ("Holy Savior"). One of his sons became a priest in Lisbon and returned to Kongo following consecration in Rome. He was one of the earliest exemplars of western African indigenous clergy.

Ultimately, however, Christianity, like copper, tended to be monopolized by Kongo's elites; the peasant and craft worker majority was virtually ignored. Most Kongolese commoners recognized deities called **kitomi** (key-TOE-mee), each looked after by a local (non-Catholic) priest. Meanwhile, Portuguese military aid buttressed Kongo politically while fueling the slave trade.

Here, as elsewhere in Africa, the slave trade, though it offered considerable gains, also exacerbated existing dangers and conflicts and almost always created new ones. King Afonso wrote to the king of Portugal in 1526, complaining that "every day the merchants carry away our people, sons of our soil and sons of our nobles and vassals, and our relatives, whom thieves and people of bad conscience kidnap and sell to obtain the coveted things and trade goods of that [Portuguese] Kingdom."[4] Even in its earliest days, the slave trade in West Central Africa was taking on a life of its own.

As a result of Kongo's slaving-based alliance with the Portuguese, King Afonso's successors faced growing opposition from every direction. The kingdom of Kongo finally collapsed in 1569. São Salvador was sacked, and its Christian nobles were humiliated and sold into slavery in the interior. Lisbon responded to the fall of its staunchest African ally with troops, in this case six hundred Portuguese harquebusiers (the precursor of musketeers). With this violent intervention, the monarchy was effectively restored in 1574. In exchange, Kongo traders called *pombeiros* (pohm-BEH-rohs) supplied their Portuguese saviors with a steady stream of slaves. The process of propping up regimes in exchange for captives was to continue throughout the long history of the slave trade.

Kongo-Portuguese Slaving Alliance

Portuguese Strategy in Angola

A second pillar of Portuguese strategy in West Central Africa entailed establishing a permanent military colony in Angola, home of the young man named Domingo whose story began this chapter. Beginning with the port city of Luanda, this new colony was to become one of the largest and longest-lived clearinghouses for the Atlantic slave trade (see Map 18.3). It was perhaps here more than anywhere else in Africa that the Portuguese, aided again by droughts and other factors, managed to radically alter local livelihoods.

According to Portuguese documents and climatological evidence, the major stimulus to the early Angolan slave trade was a severe and prolonged drought affecting the interior in the 1590s. The drought uprooted numerous groups of villagers already weakened by slave-raiding, and these luckless refugees in turn were preyed upon by still more parasitic and aggressive warrior-bandits calling themselves Imbangala. The Imbangala, organized around secret military societies, soon became slaving allies of the Portuguese. These were probably Domingo Angola's captors.

Employing terrifying tactics, including human sacrifice and—allegedly—cannibalism, Imbangala raiders eventually threatened to snuff out the Ndongo kingdom. That Ndongo survived at all, in fact, depended on the creativity and wile of a powerful woman, Queen Nzinga (r. 1624–1663). Following the maxim "if you can't beat 'em, join 'em," Queen Nzinga sought to thwart the Imbangala by allying with their sometime business partners, the Portuguese. In Luanda she was baptized "Dona Ana," or "Queen Ann."

fetishism The derogatory term used by Europeans to describe western African use of religious objects.

kitomi Deities attended by Kongo priests prior to the arrival of Christian Europeans.

pombeiro A slave-trade middleman in the West Central African interior.

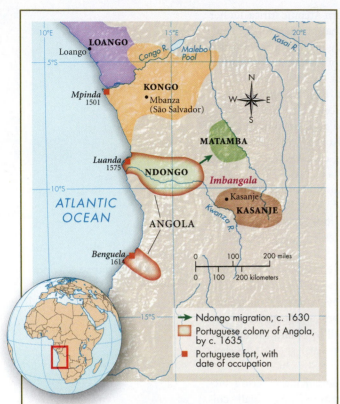

MAP 18.3   **West Central Africa, c. 1500–1635**

No African region was more affected by European interlopers in early modern times than West Central Africa, the Atlantic world's main source of enslaved captives, nearly all of them shipped abroad by the Portuguese. At first, Portuguese missionaries and diplomats vied for the favor of the kings of Kongo. Before long, however, the Portuguese shifted their interest south to Luanda, a base built almost exclusively for slave trading. Peoples of the interior suffered periodic slave raids as the Portuguese extended their networks south to Benguela. Some refugees migrated eastward, only to encounter new enemies— most of them allies of the Portuguese.

Adopting the example of the kings of Kongo, Queen Nzinga promised to supply slaves to her new friends. She soon discovered that the Portuguese had little authority over the Imbangala, however. Their warriors continued to attack the Ndongo, who were forced to move to a new homeland, in deserted Matamba. From this newer, more secure base Queen Nzinga built her own aggressive slaving and trading state. When the Dutch occupied Luanda in the 1640s, the queen adapted, trading slaves to them in exchange for political immunity for her followers. Before her death at the age of eighty-one, Queen Nzinga reestablished ties with the Portuguese, who again controlled the coast in the 1650s.

To the south and west, meanwhile, Imbangala warriors began to intermingle with various peoples, eventually establishing the kingdom of Kasanje (see again Map 18.3). After 1630, Kasanje merchant-warriors operated alternately as slavers and middlemen, taking or trading for captives from the east. Farther south, other warriors began to interact with Portuguese settlers around the Atlantic port of Benguela. By the later seventeenth century Benguela rivaled Luanda as the key conduit for the South Atlantic slave trade.

By this time, Portuguese trade in Africa focused almost entirely on slaves. Overall, West Central Africa, mostly Kongo and Angola, supplied over 5 million, or nearly half of the about 12 million recorded slaves sent to the Americas between 1519 and 1867. The victims were overwhelmingly peasants, poor millet and sorghum farmers struggling to eke out a living in a largely drought-prone and war-torn region. Very occasionally, as in the case of Kongo, the enslaved included nobles and prominent warriors. At least two-thirds of all African captives sent across the Atlantic were men, a significant number of them boys. Some historians have argued that growing demand for young men abroad and the African desire to be rid of these potentially vengeful captives proved mutually reinforcing. Into the vortex were thrust young men such as Domingo Angola, who was sent all the way to the Andean boomtown of Potosí.

Due to Portuguese entrenchment on the West Central African coast and a fairly formalized system of enslavement, a majority of Angolan and Kongolese slaves reached the Americas as baptized Catholics more or less fluent in Kimbundu or Kikongo, the common languages of the coast, and sometimes even Portuguese. Ethnic differences existed, but on the whole slaves given the monikers "Kongo" and "Angola," like Domingo, had more in common than any comparable group of Africans taken to the Americas.

Northern Europeans and the Expansion of the Atlantic Slave Trade 1600–1800

FOCUS

What were the major changes in the Atlantic slave trade after 1600?

Other Europeans had vied for a share of the Portuguese Atlantic slave trade since the mid-sixteenth century, among them famous figures such as the English corsair Francis Drake, but it was only after 1600 that competition grew significantly. First the French, then the English, Dutch, Danish,

Queen Nzinga's Baptism
Here the same late-seventeenth-century artist who painted the Mbundu blacksmiths (see page 594) portrays the baptism of the central African Queen Nzinga. Queen Nzinga's Catholic baptism did not prevent her from making alliances with non-Catholics, both African and European, in long and violent struggles with neighbors and the Portuguese in her district of Matamba, Angola. Some witnesses say she was attended by dozens of male servants dressed as concubines. (Illumination by Padre Giovanni Antonio Cavazzi da Montecuccolo (died 1692) from the Manoscritti Araldi; reproduction courtesy of Michele Araldi.)

and other northern Europeans forcibly displaced Portuguese traders all along the western shores of Africa. Others set up competing posts nearby. By 1650, the Portuguese were struggling to maintain a significant presence even in West Central Africa. They began to supplement western African slaves with captives transshipped from their outposts in the Indian Ocean, primarily Mozambique and Madagascar. As a result, slaves arriving in Brazil in the seventeenth century were of increasingly diverse ethnic origins (see Map 18.4).

Since it was both profitable and logistically complex, the slave trade was among the most thoroughly documented commercial activities of early modern times. Beginning after 1650, we can cross-check multiple documents for numbers of slaves boarded, origin place-names, and age or sex groupings. These sources, a bland accounting of mass death and suffering, suggest that the volume of the trade grew slowly, expanding gradually after 1650 and very rapidly only after 1750. The British, despite profiting greatly from the slave trade in western Africa through the 1790s, when volume peaked, suddenly reversed policy under pressure from abolitionists in 1807. After 1808, the British Navy actively suppressed the Atlantic slave trade until it was formally abolished by international treaty in 1850. Despite these measures, contraband slaving continued, mostly between Angola and Brazil. In terms of numbers of lives, families, and communities destroyed, the Atlantic slave trade was primarily a modern phenomenon with deep early modern roots.

The Rise and Fall of Monopoly Trading Companies

Following the example of the Spanish and Portuguese, northern European participation in the Atlantic slave trade grew in tandem with colonization efforts in the Americas. Tobacco-producing Caribbean islands such as Barbados and Martinique and mainland North American regions such as Virginia and the Carolinas were initially staffed with indentured, or contracted, European servants and only a small number of African slaves. As sugar cultivation increased in the Caribbean after 1650 and tobacco took off in Virginia,

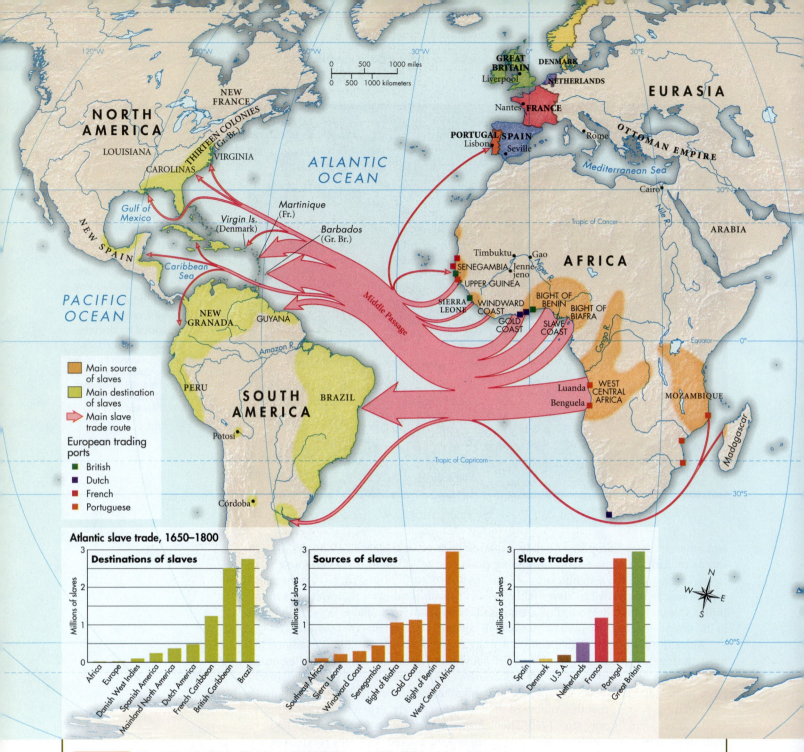

Atlantic slave trade, 1650–1800

Destinations of slaves
(y-axis: Millions of slaves, 0 to 3)
Categories: Africa, Europe, Danish West Indies, Spanish America, Mainland North America, Dutch America, French Caribbean, British Caribbean, Brazil

Sources of slaves
(y-axis: Millions of slaves, 0 to 3)
Categories: Southeast Africa, Sierra Leone, Windward Coast, Senegambia, Bight of Biafra, Gold Coast, Bight of Benin, West Central Africa

Slave traders
(y-axis: Millions of slaves, 0 to 3)
Categories: Spain, Denmark, U.S.A., Netherlands, France, Portugal, Great Britain

MAP 18.4 The Atlantic Slave Trade at Its Height, c. 1650–1800

Though always terrible and deadly, the Atlantic slave trade grew dramatically after 1650. The Portuguese were no longer the only slave traders, and demand was no longer limited to Spanish America and Brazil. New slaving nations included the Netherlands, England, France, and Denmark, all of which had colonies in the Caribbean and on the North American mainland that relied on plantation agriculture. The regions from which enslaved Africans came also shifted during this long period. West Central Africa remained a major source region, but the Upper Guinea Coast was increasingly overshadowed by the so-called Slave Coast located between the Bight of Benin and the Bight of Biafra.

however, planters shifted overwhelmingly to African slavery. This had been their wish, as their documents attest, and a declining supply of poor European contract laborers, particularly after 1700, accelerated the trend.

Origins of American Racism

For historians of the North Atlantic, this transition from indentured servitude to African slavery has raised a host of questions about the origins of American racism. In sum, can modern notions of racial difference be traced to early modern American slavery and the Atlantic slave trade? Some prominent scholars of English and French colonialism have argued that racist ideologies grew mostly *after* this shift from European to African labor. Before that, they argue, "white" and "black" workers were treated by masters and overseers with equal cruelty. In Virginia and Barbados during the early to mid-1600s, for instance, black and white indentured servants labored alongside each other, experiencing equal exploitation and limited legal protection in the brief years before racial slavery was codified by law. Scholars working in a broader historical context, however—one that takes into account Spanish, Portuguese, Dutch, and Italian experiences in the Atlantic, Mediterranean, and beyond—have been less convinced by this assertion. They argue that while racist notions hardened with the expansion of slavery in the Caribbean and North America after 1650—and grew harder still following the Scientific Revolution with its emphasis on biological classification—European views of sub-Saharan Africans had virtually never been positive. Put another way, racism was more a cause of slavery than a result.

Although numerous challengers were gathering force by 1600, Portuguese slavers remained the most significant suppliers to early English and French planters in the Americas. As we have seen, the Portuguese had a distinct advantage in that over several centuries they had established the financial instruments and supply networks necessary to run such a complex and risky business. To compete, northern Europeans were forced to establish state-subsidized monopoly trading companies. The highly belligerent Dutch West India Company was founded in 1621 to attack Spanish and Portuguese colonial outposts and take over Iberian commercial interests in the Atlantic. Several slaving forts in western Africa were eventually seized. São Jorge da Mina fell in 1638, and Luanda, Angola, in 1641. Although these colonial outposts were returned in subsequent decades, the era of Portuguese dominance was over.

The French, whose early overseas activities had been stunted by the religious wars described in Chapter 20, finally organized a monopoly trading company in 1664 to supply their growing Caribbean market. The English, fresh from their own civil conflicts, followed suit by forming the Royal African Company in 1672. By 1700, the French and English were fighting bitterly to supply not only their own colonial holdings but also the highly lucrative Spanish-American market. Dutch slavers also competed, supplying nearly one hundred thousand slaves to the Spanish up to the 1730s. After 1650, Spanish-Americans were not

Formation of Northern European Trading Companies

Filling the Slave Ships
The upper half of this 1732 engraving by Dutch artist Johannes Kip shows West African fishermen in canoes off the coast of present-day Ghana, with the old Portuguese fortress of São Jorge da Mina in the distance. The lower half shows slaves being ferried to a Dutch ship in a somewhat longer canoe, with a string of other European slave-trading forts in the distance. Slave ships often cruised African coasts for several months, acquiring a diverse range of captives before crossing the Atlantic. (Beinecke Rare Book and Manuscript Library, Yale University.)

buying as many slaves as in the first century after conquest, but unlike other colonists they paid for them with gold and silver. Danish slavers also entered the competition by the 1670s, when they established several Caribbean sugar plantations in the Virgin Islands.

The company model did not last. By 1725, if not before, most of the northern European monopoly companies had been dismantled. Stuck with costly forts, salaried officers, and state-mandated contract obligations, they proved to be too inflexible and inefficient to survive in a world of limited information and shifting supply and demand. Thus the French, English, and Dutch resorted to a system more like that long practiced by the Portuguese, in which small numbers of private merchants, often related to one another by marriage if not blood, pooled capital to finance individual voyages. Like their Mediterranean predecessors in Venice, Genoa, and elsewhere, the trade in slaves was but one of many overlapping ventures for most of these investors. Their profits, usually averaging 10 percent or so, were reinvested in land, light industry, and numerous other endeavors. In time, investors inhabiting bustling slave ports such as Liverpool, England, and Nantes, France, had little to do with the actual organization of slaving voyages. Nonetheless, the profits slavery produced would flow through these ports into Europe, fueling the continent's economic growth and development.

How the Mature Slave Trade Functioned

The slave trade proved most lucrative when European investors cut every possible corner. Profit margins consistently trumped humanitarian concerns. By the late seventeenth century, ships were packed tightly, food and water rationed sparingly, and crews kept as small as possible. Unlike other shipping ventures at this time, the value of the captives held as cargo far exceeded the costs of ship and crew on typical slaving voyages. In part this was a reflection of the considerable risks involved.

European Risk and Profit   Risks and uncertainties abounded in the slave trade. Despite a growing number of more or less friendly European forts scattered along Africa's vast Atlantic coast, slavers were mostly on their own when it came to collecting captives. In short, the system was much more open and African-dominated than has generally been acknowledged. Ships spent an average of three months cruising coastal towns and estuaries in search of African middlemen willing to trade captives for commodities. By the late seventeenth century, competition was on the rise, affecting supply and thus price. Violence, mostly in the form of slave uprisings and hostile attacks by fellow Europeans, was a constant concern.

European ship captains in charge of this dangerous and drawn-out leg of the trip hoped to receive at the other end a bounty of 2 to 5 percent on all surviving slaves. Somewhat like modern human traffickers, they were in fact betting their lives on a relatively small fortune. As we saw with regard to Portuguese missionaries, western Africa was notoriously unhealthy for "unseasoned" Europeans, due mostly to endemic falciparum malaria, and according to the documentary record, as many as one in ten ship captains died before leaving the African coast for the Americas. Few who survived repeated the trip. Ships' doctors had scant remedies on hand even for common ailments such as dysentery, which also afflicted slaves and crewmembers to a great extent. When not ill themselves, doctors inspected slaves before embarkation, hoping to head off premature death or the spread of disease aboard ship and thereby to protect the investment.

African Gains and Losses   On the African consumer side, few northern European products were attractive enough to stimulate trade. More than anything, Africans wanted colorful cotton fabrics from India to supplement their own usually indigo-dyed or plain products. Thus the Dutch, French, English, and others followed the Portuguese example yet again by importing huge quantities of cotton cloth from South Asia, cowry shells from the Indian Ocean, and iron, brass, and copper from parts of Europe, particularly Spain and Sweden. European traders struggled to meet the particular and often shifting demands of each slaving region's inhabitants. Cloth was the most sought-after trade item throughout the period of the slave trade, constituting at least two-thirds of imports carried by British slavers between the 1690s and 1808. Other tastes were introduced by Europeans. By 1700, American plantation commodities such as rum and tobacco were being exchanged for slaves in significant quantities. Thus, the Atlantic slave trade was a global concern, drawing in people and goods from around the world.

It is clear from many contemporary sources that chiefs and kings throughout western Africa greatly augmented their prestige by accumulating and redistributing the commodities they procured through the slave trade. The captives they sent abroad were not their kin, and western Africans appear to have had no sense of the overall magnitude of this commerce in human bodies. There were few internal brakes on captive-taking besides the diminishing pool of victims and shifting political ambitions; the African desire to hold dependents to boost prestige and provide domestic labor meshed with European demands. Along these lines, whereas female war captives might be absorbed into elite households, men and boys were generally considered dangerous elements and happily gotten rid of. It so happened that European planters and mine owners in the colonies valued men over women by a significant margin. Thus, however immoral and disruptive of African life it appears in retrospect, the slave trade probably seemed at the time to be mutually beneficial for European buyers and African sellers. Only the slaves themselves felt otherwise.

The Middle Passage

It is difficult to imagine the suffering endured by the more than 12 million African captives forced to cross the Atlantic Ocean in early modern times. The ordeal itself has come to be known as the **Middle Passage** (see again Map 18.4). As noted at the opening of this chapter, some West Central Africans imagined the slavers' ships to be floating slaughterhouses crossing a great lake or river to satisfy white cannibals inhabiting a distant, sterile land. Portuguese sailors unambiguously dubbed them "death ships" or "floating tombs." Perhaps troubled by this sense of damnation, Portuguese priests in Luanda, Benguela, and elsewhere baptized as many slaves as they could before departure. Portuguese ships were virtually all named for Catholic saints.

Slave Conditions and Mortality

Northern Europeans, increasingly in charge of the slave trade after 1650, took a more dispassionate approach. Slaves, as far as they were concerned, were a sort of highly valued livestock requiring efficient but impersonal handling. Put another way, the care and feeding of slaves were treated as pragmatic matters of health, not faith. Rations were the subsistence minimum of maize, rice, or millet gruel, with a bit of fish or dried meat added from time to time. Men, women, and children were assigned separate quarters. Women were given a cotton cloth for a wrap, whereas men were often kept naked, both to save money and to discourage rebellion by adding to their already abject humiliation. Exercise was required on deck in the form of dancing to drums during daylight hours. Like cattle, slaves were showered with seawater before the nighttime lockdown. The hold, ventilated on most ships after initial experiences with mass suffocation and heatstroke, was periodically splashed with vinegar.

Despite these measures, slave mortality on the one- to three-month voyage across the Atlantic was high. On average, between 10 and 20 percent of slaves did not survive the cramped conditions, physical abuse, and generally unsanitary environment aboard ship. This high mortality rate is all the more alarming in that these slaves had been selected for their relative good health in the first place, leaving countless other captives behind to perish in makeshift barracks, dungeons, and coastal agricultural plots. Many more died soon after landing in the Americas, often from dysentery and other intestinal ailments. Some who were emotionally overwhelmed committed suicide along the way by hurling themselves into the ocean or strangling themselves in their chains. A few enraged men managed to kill a crewmember or even a captain before being summarily executed. Slaves from different regions had trouble communicating. Thus successful slave mutinies, in which women as well as men participated, were rare but not unknown.

The general conditions of the Middle Passage worsened over time. In the name of increased efficiency, the situation belowdecks went from crowded to crammed between the seventeenth and eighteenth centuries. On average, crews of 30 to 40 common

Middle Passage The Atlantic crossing made by slaves taken from Africa to the Americas.

Olaudah Equiano

Olaudah Equiano, whose slave name was Gustavus Vassa, became a celebrity critic of the Atlantic slave trade in the late eighteenth century after writing a memoir of his experiences as a slave and free man of color in Africa, North America, the Caribbean, and Europe. The book, published in 1789, offered a rare victim's perspective on the Atlantic slave trade and the daily humiliations and punishments suffered by slaves in the Americas. (British Library, London/© British Library Board. All Rights Reserved/Bridgeman Art Library.)

sailors oversaw 200 to 300 slaves in around 1700, whereas the same number oversaw 300 to 400 slaves after 1750. These are only averages; even in the 1620s, some ships carried 600 or more slaves.

Although some Iberian clergymen protested the horrors of this crossing as early as the sixteenth century, it took the extraordinary eighteenth-century deterioration of conditions aboard slave ships to awaken the conscience of participating nations. In England, most importantly, African survivors of the Middle Passage such as Olaudah Equiano (c. 1745–1797) were called to testify before Parliament by the late eighteenth century. "Permit me, with the greatest deference and respect," Equiano began his 1789 autobiography, "to lay at your feet the following genuine Narrative, the chief design of which is to excite in your august assemblies a sense of compassion for the miseries which the Slave-Trade has entailed on my unfortunate countrymen."[5] Such testimonies, backed by the impassioned pleas of prominent Quakers and other religious figures, were finally heard. Abolition of the Atlantic slave trade, first enforced by the British in 1808, would come much more easily than abolition of slavery itself.

Volume of the Slave Trade

It is important to note that the trans-Saharan and East African slave trades preceded the Atlantic one discussed here, and that these trades continued apace throughout early modern times. In fact, the volume of the Atlantic trade appears only to have eclipsed these other avenues to foreign captivity after 1600. That said, the Atlantic slave trade ultimately constituted the greatest forced migration in early modern world history. Compared with the roughly 2 million mostly free European migrants who made their way to all parts of the Americas between the voyage of Columbus in 1492 and the British abolition of the slave trade in 1808, the number of enslaved Africans to cross the Atlantic and survive is astounding—between 10 and 12 million.

Also astounding is the fact that the vast majority of these Africans arrived in the last half century of the slave trade, that is, after 1750. Up until 1650 a total of approximately 710,000 slaves had been taken to American markets, most of them to Spanish America (262,700). Brazil was the next largest destination, absorbing about a quarter of a million slaves to that date. São Tomé, the sugar island in the Gulf of Guinea, and Europe (mostly Iberia) absorbed about 95,000 and 112,000 slaves, respectively. Madeira and the Canaries imported about 25,000 African slaves, and the English and French West Indies, 21,000 and 2500, respectively. The average annual volume for the period up to 1650 was approximately 7500 slaves per year.

Eighteenth-Century Explosion

The second (1650–1750) and third (1750–1850) stages of the Atlantic slave trade witnessed enormous, historically transformative growth. By 1675, nearly 15,000 slaves were being carried to the colonies annually, and by 1700 nearly 30,000. The total volume of the trade between 1700 and 1750 was double that of the previous fifty years, bringing some 2.5 million slaves to the Americas. The trade nearly doubled yet again between 1750 and 1800, when some 4 million Africans were transported. By this time the effect of the Atlantic slave trade on western African societies was considerable. The trade was increasingly restricted by British naval interdiction after 1808, but slavers still managed to move some 3 million slaves, mostly to Brazil, and to a lesser extent Cuba and the United States, by 1850. Northern U.S. shipbuilders were key suppliers to Brazilian slavers to the very end.

It appears that in the first three centuries of the Atlantic slave trade most African captives came from the coastal hinterland. This changed only after about 1750, when colonial demand began to outstrip local sources of supply. Thereafter, slaves were brought to the coast from increasingly distant interior regions. In West Africa this amounted to something of an inversion of the caravan trading routes fanning out from the Niger River basin, but in West Central Africa entirely new trails and trade circuits were formed. Also, whereas war captives and drought refugees had been the main victims in the past, now random kidnapping and slave-raiding became widespread.

COUNTERPOINT
The Pygmies of Central Africa

As in the Americas, certain forest, desert, and other margin-dwelling peoples of Africa appear to have remained largely immune to the effects of European conquest, colonization, and trade throughout early modern times. But such seeming immunity is difficult to gauge, especially since we now know some margin-dwelling groups once thought to be naturally isolated were in fact refugees from conquest and slaving wars. Many were driven from the more accessible regions where they had once hunted or otherwise exploited nature to survive. Distinct cultures such as the Batwa (BAH-twah), a major Pygmy group of the great Congo rain forest, and the Khoikhoi (COY-coy) and other tribespeople of southern Africa's Kalahari Desert, were until only recently thought to have been unaffected by outsiders before the nineteenth century. Recent scholarship, and most surviving gatherer-hunters themselves, suggest otherwise.

FOCUS

How did the Pygmies' rain forest world differ from the better-known environment of savannas and farms?

Life in the Congo Rain Forest

Still, for the Pygmies, as for many of the world's tropical forest peoples, life has long been distinct from that of settled agriculturalists. Even now, Pygmies live by exploiting the natural forest around them, unaided by manufactured goods. These forests, marked by rugged terrain and washed by superabundant rains, make agriculture and herding impossible. Short of cutting down huge swaths of trees, which in this region often leads to massive soil erosion, neither can be practiced. This is not to say space is limited. Indeed, the Congo River basin is home to the world's second-largest rain forest, after that of the Amazon in South America; it is vast. As in the Amazon, most forest animals are modest in size, with the important exception of the African elephant, which early modern Pygmies occasionally hunted for food and tusks.

Until recent times, most Pygmies were gatherer-hunters. Their superior tracking abilities, limited material possessions, and knowledge of useful forest products such as leaves for dwellings and natural toxins for bow hunting allowed them to retreat in times of external threats such as war. Herding and farming Bantu-speaking and Sudanic neighbors were at a disadvantage in Pygmy country, which

Pygmies of the Congo Rain Forest

Modern-day Pygmies
Here Baka Pygmies of Cameroon and the Central African Republic hunt in the Congo rain forest using nets, sticks, and vines. The woman also carries a machete for butchering the catch and a basket for the meat. Pygmy hunters arrange nets fashioned from vines in forest enclosures to catch small antelope and other game lured or scared into the trap by chants and songs. (Martin Harvey/Peter Arnold/Photolibrary.)

seems to have prevented Pygmy militarization or formation of defensive confederacies. The Congo rain forest is also attractive in that it is much less affected by malarial mosquitoes than the surrounding farmland. In recent times only a few Pygmy groups, such as the much-studied Mbuti (M-BOOH-tee), have remained separate enough from neighboring farmers and herders to retain their famously short stature and other distinct characteristics. The Pygmies' highly distinctive singing style and instrumentation, most of it Mbuti, has become renowned with the rise of world music recording and distribution.

Everyday Pygmy life has been examined in most detail by anthropologists, many of whom have emphasized differences between Pygmy and neighboring Bantu rituals. Whereas Bantu speakers have venerated dead ancestors in a way that has deeply affected their long-term settlement patterns, warfare, and kin groupings, the Pygmies have long preferred to "let go" of their dead—to move on, as it were. Similarly, whereas Bantu coming-of-age rituals such as circumcision have tended to be elaborate and essential to social reproduction, Pygmies have traditionally marked few distinct phases in life. Most important, the Pygmies have venerated the forest itself as a life-giving spirit, whereas outsiders have treated it as a threatening space and potential source of evil. Has it always been so?

Legendary since ancient Egyptian times for their small, reedlike bodies, simple lifestyles, good-natured humor, and melodious music, the Pygmies have long been held up as the perfect counterpoint to urban civilization and its discontents. It is only recently that the Pygmies and other nonsedentary peoples like them have been treated historically, as makers rather than "nonactors" or victims of history. The absence of written records produced by the Pygmies themselves has made this task difficult, but anthropologists, historians, linguists, and archaeologists working together have made considerable headway.

Pygmy-Bantu Relations

It seems that some time after 1500, the introduction of iron tools and banana cultivation to the central African interior began to alter settlement patterns and overall demography. This change placed Pygmies and Bantu neighbors in closer proximity, as more and more forest was cut for planting and Bantu moved into Pygmy territory. Bantu speakers, some of them refugees from areas attacked by slavers or afflicted by drought, appear to have displaced some Pygmy groups and to have intermarried with others. They seem to have adopted a variety of Pygmy religious beliefs, although Bantu languages mostly displaced original Pygmy ones. Also after 1500, American crops such as peanuts and manioc began to alter sedentary life at the forest's edge, leading to still more interaction, not all of it peaceful, between the Pygmies and their neighbors. Pygmies adopted American capsicum peppers as an everyday spice.

Were the Pygmies driven from the rain forest's edge into its heart as a result of the slave trade? Perhaps in some places, yes, but the evidence is clearer for increased interaction with Bantu migrants. Early effects of globalization on Pygmy life are more easily tracked in terms of foods adopted as a result of the Columbian Exchange. Despite these exchanges and conflicts, the Pygmies have managed to retain a distinct identity that is as intertwined with the rhythms of the forest as it is with the rhythms of settled agriculture.

Although the story of the Pygmies' survival is not as dramatic as that of the Mapuche of Chile (see Chapter 17), their culture's richness and resilience serve as testaments to their peoples' imagination, will, and ingenuity. Their extraordinary adaptation to the rain forest—probably in part a result of early modern historical stresses, which pushed them farther into the forest—reminds us of a shared human tendency to make the most of a given ecological setting, but also that the distinction between civilized and "primitive" lifestyles is a false one, or at least socially constructed.

Conclusion

Western African societies grew and changed according to the rhythms of planting, harvest, trade, and war, and these rhythms continued to define everyday life in early modern times. Droughts, diseases, and pests made subsistence more challenging in sub-Saharan Africa than in most parts of the world, yet people adapted and formed chiefdoms, kingdoms, and empires, often underpinned, at least symbolically, by the control of iron and other metals. Iron tools helped farmers clear forest and till hard soils.

Islam influenced African society and politics across a broad belt south of the Sahara and along the shores of the Indian Ocean, but even this powerful religious tradition was to a degree absorbed by local cultures. Most African states and chiefdoms were not influenced by outside religious influences—or by the conquistadors who wished to impose them—until the late nineteenth century. It was malaria, a disease against which many sub-Saharan Africans had at least some acquired immunity, that proved to be the continent's best defense.

But Africa possessed commodities demanded by outsiders, and despite their failure to penetrate the interior in early modern times, it was these outsiders, first among them the seaborne Portuguese, who set the early modern phase of African history in motion. The Portuguese came looking for gold in the mid-fifteenth century, and once they discovered the dangers of malaria, they stuck to the coast and offshore islands to trade through intermediaries, including coastal chiefs and kings. First they traded for gold, but very soon for war captives. In return, the Portuguese brought horses, cloth, wine, metal goods, and guns. Local chiefs became powerful by allying with the newcomers, and they expanded their trading and raiding ventures deep into the continental interior. Thus began a symbiotic relationship, copied and expanded by the English, Dutch, French, and other northern Europeans, that swelled over four centuries to supply the Americas with some 12 million enslaved African laborers, the largest forced migration in world history. Among these millions of captives, most of whose names we shall never know, was young Domingo Angola, a West Central African teenager caught up in a widening global web of trade, conquest, and religious conversion.

NOTES

1. The story of Domingo Angola is reconstructed from notary documents found in the Ecuadorian National Archive in Quito (Archivo Nacional del Ecuador, Protocolos notariales 1:19 FGD, 1-x-1601, ff. 647–746, and 1:6 DLM, 5-x-1595, f. 287v.) and various studies of the early slave trade, especially Linda Heywood and John Thornton, *Central Africans, Atlantic Creoles, and the Foundation of the Americas, 1585–1660* (New York: Cambridge University Press, 2007). On the Jesuits in Luanda and their involvement in the slave trade at this time, see Dauril Alden, *The Making of an Enterprise: The Society of Jesus in Portugal, Its Empire, and Beyond, 1540–1750* (Stanford, CA: Stanford University Press, 1996), 544–546.
2. Joseph Miller, *Way of Death: Merchant Capitalism and the Angolan Slave Trade, 1730–1830* (Madison: University of Wisconsin Press, 1988), 4–5.
3. George E. Brooks, *Landlords and Strangers: Ecology, Society, and Trade in Western Africa, 1000–1630* (Boulder, CO: Westview Press, 1994).
4. This and other letters are published in António Brásio, ed., *Monumenta Missionaria Africana*, vol. 1, *África Ocidental (1471–1531)* (Lisbon: Agência Geral do Ultramar, 1952), 470–471. (Special thanks to José Curto of York University, Canada, for pointing out this reference.)
5. Olaudah Equiano, *The Interesting Narrative of the Life of Olaudah Equiano, Written by Himself*, 2d ed., introduction by Robert J. Allison (Boston: Bedford/St. Martin's, 2007), 7.

RESOURCES FOR RESEARCH

Many Western Africas

General surveys of precolonial Africa have proliferated in recent years, many incorporating a new range of findings from archaeology, climate studies, and linguistics. The Collins and Burns text is exceptional.

Bisson, Michael, S. Terry Childs, Philip de Barros, and Augustin Holl. *Ancient African Metallurgy: The Socio-cultural Context*. 2000.

Collins, Robert O., and James M. Burns. *A History of Sub-Saharan Africa*. 2007.

Connah, Graham. *African Civilizations: An Archeological Perspective*, 2d ed. 2001.

Ehret, Christopher. *The Civilizations of Africa: A History to 1800*. 2002.

McCann, James C. *Maize and Grace: Africa's Encounter with a New World Crop, 1500–2000*. 2005.

Northrup, David. *Africa's Discovery of Europe, 1450–1850*. 2002.

Webb, James L. A., Jr. *Humanity's Burden: A Global History of Malaria*. 2009.

Landlords and Strangers: Peoples and States in West Africa

Works on West Africa in the early modern period have begun to link internal developments to external factors such as the slave trade and the rise of global markets in a variety of innovative ways, including a focus on metals such as gold, copper, and bronze and crops such as rice, peanuts, and oil palm.

Brooks, George E. *Eurafricans in Western Africa: Commerce, Social Status, Gender, and Religious Observance from the Sixteenth to the Eighteenth Century*. 2003.

Brooks, George E. *Landlords and Strangers: Ecology, Society, and Trade in Western Africa, 1000–1630*. 1994.

Charney, Judith A. *Black Rice: The African Origins of Rice Cultivation in the Americas*. 2001.

Herbert, Eugenia. *Iron, Gender, and Power: Rituals of Transformation in African Societies*. 1993.

Herbert, Eugenia. *Red Gold of Africa: Copper in Precolonial History and Culture*. 1984.

Wright, Donald R. *The World and a Very Small Place in Africa: A History of Globalization in Niumi, The Gambia*, 2d ed. 2004.

Land of the Blacksmith Kings: West Central Africa

Works on early modern West Central Africa have become more detailed and transatlantic in nature in recent years, thanks in part to a host of newly discovered (or newly appreciated) sources in Portuguese, Spanish, and Italian.

Heywood, Linda M., and John Thornton. *Central Africans, Atlantic Creoles, and the Foundation of the Americas, 1585–1660*. 2007.

Hilton, Anne. *The Kingdom of Kongo*. 1985.

Sweet, James H. *Recreating Africa: Culture, Kinship, and Religion in the African-Portuguese World, 1441–1770*. 2003.

Vansina, Jan. *Paths in the Rainforest*. 1990.

Strangers in Ships: Gold, Slavery, and the Portuguese

Literature about the Atlantic slave trade is vast and fast growing. The following is only a small selection of helpful introductory works on the Portuguese era of the slave trade.

Barry, Boubacar. *Senegambia and the Atlantic Slave Trade*. 1998.

Blackburn, Robin. *The Making of New World Slavery from the Baroque to the Modern, 1492–1800*. 1997.

Hawthorne, Walter. *From Africa to Brazil: Culture, Identity, and an Atlantic Slave Trade, 1600–1830*. 2010.

Miller, Joseph. *Way of Death: Merchant Capitalism and the Atlantic Slave Trade, 1780–1830*. 1988.

Thomas, Hugh. *The Slave Trade: The Story of the Atlantic Slave Trade, 1440–1870*. 1997.

Northern Europeans and the Expansion of the Atlantic Slave Trade, 1600–1800

Among the burgeoning literature on the later stages of the Atlantic slave trade are these helpful works. Eltis and Klein offer clear overviews that draw in part from recently constructed databases.

Eltis, David. *The Rise of African Slavery in the Americas*. 2001.

Equiano, Olaudah. *The Interesting Narrative of the Life of Olaudah Equiano, Written by Himself*, 2d ed. Introduction by Robert J. Allison. 2007.

Handler, Jerome S., and Michael L. Tuite Jr. *The Atlantic Slave Trade and Slave Life in the Americas: A Visual Record* (University of Virginia/Virginia Foundation for the Humanities). http://hitchcock.itc.virginia.edu/Slavery/index.php.

Klein, Herbert. *The Atlantic Slave Trade*. 1999.

Law, Robin C. *The Slave Coast of West Africa, 1550–1750: The Impact of the Atlantic Slave Trade on an African Society*. 1990.

COUNTERPOINT: The Pygmies of Central Africa

The Mbuti Pygmy culture has been described in most detail by the anthropologist Colin Turnbull, and his works remain essential. Klieman offers a more historical look at Pygmy relations with Bantu neighbors over the long term.

Klieman, Kairn. *"The Pygmies Were Our Compass": Bantu and Batwa in the History of West Central Africa, Early Times to c. 1900 C.E.* 2003.

Turnbull, Colin. *The Forest People*. 1968.

Turnbull, Colin. *The Mbuti Pygmies: Change and Adaptation*. 1983.

Turnbull, Colin, Francis Chapman, and Michelle Kisliuk. *Mbuti Pygmies of the Ituri Rainforest*. Sound recording. 1992.

▶ **For additional primary sources from this period**, see *Sources of Crossroads and Cultures*.

▶ **For Web sites, images, and documents related to topics in this chapter**, see Make History at bedfordstmartins.com/smith.

The major global development in this chapter ► The rise of the Atlantic slave trade and its impact on early modern African peoples and cultures.

IMPORTANT EVENTS

c. 1100–1500	Extended dry period in West Africa prompts migrations
c. 1450	Kingdom of Benin reaches height of its power
1464–1492	Reign of Sunni Ali in the Songhai Empire
1482	Portuguese establish trading fort of São Jorge da Mina (Ghana)
1506–1543	Reign of Afonso I (Nzinga Mbemba) of kingdom of Kongo
1569	Collapse of kingdom of Kongo
1574	Portuguese-aided restoration of kingdom of Kongo
1591	Moroccan raiders conquer Songhai Empire
1621	Formation of Dutch West India Company
1624–1663	Reign of Queen Nzinga in the Ndongo kingdom of Angola
1638–1641	Dutch seize São Jorge da Mina and Luanda
1672	Formation of English Royal African Company
1750–1800	Atlantic slave trade reaches highest volume
1807	British declare Atlantic slave trade illegal

KEY TERMS

African diaspora (p. 584)
fetishism (p. 599)
génie (p. 585)
husbandry (p. 585)
kitomi (p. 599)
manikongo (p. 595)

Middle Passage (p. 605)
oba (p. 592)
paramount chief (p. 586)
peça (p. 595)
pombeiro (p. 599)

CHAPTER OVERVIEW QUESTIONS

1. How did ecological diversity in western Africa relate to cultural developments?

2. What tied western Africa to other parts of the world prior to the arrival of Europeans along Atlantic shores?

3. How did the Atlantic slave trade arise, and how was it sustained?

SECTION FOCUS QUESTIONS

1. What range of livelihoods, cultural practices, and political arrangements typified western Africa in early modern times?

2. What economic, social, and political patterns characterized early modern West Africa?

3. What economic, social, and political patterns characterized early modern West Central Africa?

4. How did the early Portuguese slave trade in western Africa function?

5. What were the major changes in the Atlantic slave trade after 1600?

6. How did the Pygmies' rain forest world differ from the better-known environment of savannas and farms?

MAKING CONNECTIONS

1. How does the Moroccan conquest of Songhai compare with the Spanish conquest of the Aztecs (see Chapter 17)?

2. How did gender roles differ between the kingdoms of West Africa and those of North America's Eastern Woodlands (see Chapter 16)?

3. How did the Portuguese experience in Africa differ from events in Brazil (see Chapter 17)?

4. How did growing European competition for enslaved Africans alter the nature of enslavement and trade in Africa itself?

19

AT A CROSSROADS ▶

In this exquisite miniature painting from the 1590s, the Mughal emperor Akbar receives the Persian ambassador Sayyid Beg in 1562. The painting is an illustration commissioned for Akbar's official court history, the *Akbarnama*, and thus would have been seen and approved by the emperor himself. The meeting is emblematic of the generally amiable relationship between the Mughals and their Safavid neighbors in Iran. (Victoria & Albert Museum, London/Art Resource, NY.)

Trade and Empire in the Indian Ocean and South Asia

1450–1750

Born to Persian immigrants in the Afghan city of Kandahar, Princess Mihr un-nisa (meer oon-NEE-sah), known to history as Nur Jahan, or "Light of the World," married the Mughal emperor Jahangir (jah-hahn-GEER) in 1611, at the age of thirty-four. As the emperor increasingly turned his attention to science and the arts, as well as to his addictions to wine and opium, Nur Jahan increasingly assumed the ruler's duties throughout the last decade of her husband's life, which ended in 1627. She had coins struck in her name, and most importantly, she made certain that a daughter from an earlier marriage and her brother's daughter both wed likely heirs to the Mughal throne.

As her husband withdrew from worldly affairs, Nur Jahan actively engaged them. After a visit from the English ambassador in 1613, she developed a keen interest in European manufactures, especially quality textiles. She established domestic industries in cloth manufacture and jewelry making and developed an export trade in indigo dye. Indigo from her farms was shipped to Portuguese and English trading forts along India's west coast, then sent to Lisbon, London, Antwerp, and beyond.

In 1614, Nur Jahan arranged for her niece, Arjumand Banu Begum (AHR-joo-mond bah-noo BEH-goom), to marry Jahangir's favorite son, Prince Khurram, known after he became emperor as Shah Jahan. Arjumand Banu Begum, who took the title Mumtaz Mahal,

BACKSTORY

For centuries before the rise of the Atlantic system (see Chapter 17), the vast Indian Ocean basin thrived as a religious and commercial crossroads. Powered by the annual monsoon wind cycle, traders, mainly Muslim, developed a flourishing commerce over thousands of miles in such luxury goods as spices, gems, and precious metals. The network included the trading enclaves of East Africa and Arabia and the many ports of South and Southeast Asia. Ideas, religious traditions—notably Islam—and pilgrimages moved along the same routes. Throughout the Indian Ocean basin, there was also a trade in enslaved laborers, mostly war captives, including many non-Africans, but this trade grew mostly after the rise of plantation agriculture in the later eighteenth century. The vast majority of the region's many millions of inhabitants were peasant farmers, many of them dependent on wet-rice agriculture.

At the dawn of the early modern period, Hindu kingdoms still flourished in southern India and parts of island Southeast Asia, but these were on the wane. By contrast, some Muslim kingdoms began an expansive phase. After 1500, a key factor in changes throughout the Indian Ocean basin was the introduction of gunpowder weapons from Europe.

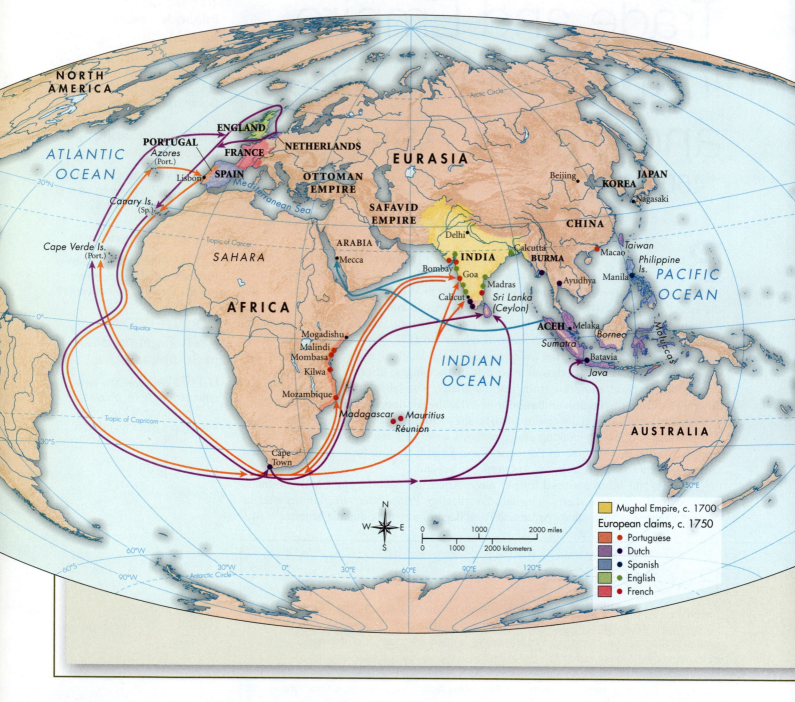

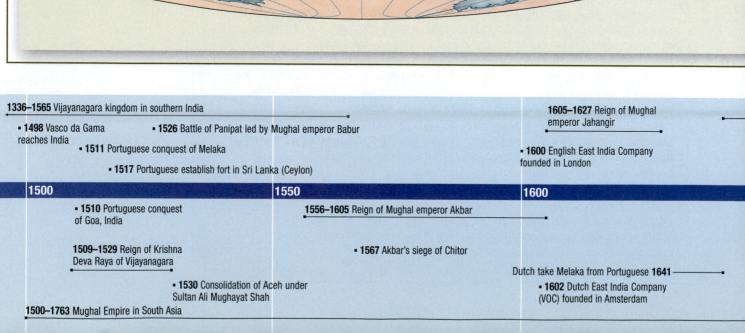

died in 1631 while bearing her fourteenth child for her emperor husband. Heartbroken, Shah Jahan went into mourning for two full years. He commissioned the construction of an extraordinary mausoleum for his beloved Mumtaz in the sacred city of Agra. This graceful structure of white marble, among the architectural wonders of the world, is known as the Taj Mahal.

Nur Jahan attended court with her head and breasts covered only by wisps of gauze. She rode horses proudly in public without her husband. Such conduct was not considered inappropriate for a woman of her status in her time. Like other South Asian noblewomen, Nur Jahan expressed her rank through public piety, commissioning a number of religious buildings, including her father's and her husband's mausoleums, as well as many elaborate gardens, several of which survive. She continued to play an active and sometimes controversial role in politics until her death in 1644, occasionally supporting rivals of Shah Jahan.

For most of the early modern period the lands surrounding the Indian Ocean remained in the hands of powerful local rulers, as exemplified by Nur Jahan. As in western Africa, but in stark contrast to much of the Americas, it took European interlopers several centuries to gain the lasting footholds that enabled the widespread imperial takeover after 1800 (discussed in Chapter 26). Again like western Africans and unlike the native peoples of the Americas, the inhabitants of the greater Indian Ocean basin had acquired over time at least some immunity to European microbes, so their resistance was not hobbled by waves of deadly disease.

Trade on the Indian Ocean during the age of sail followed the **monsoons**, semiannual alternating dry and humid winds generated by the seasonal heating and cooling of air masses above the vast Asian continent. To exploit these reliable winds, Arab sailors developed swift, triangular-rigged vessels. Southeast Asians introduced much larger square-riggers influenced by Chinese shipbuilding techniques, and by 1500 the Portuguese arrived from the North Atlantic in well-armed, sturdy vessels rigged with both square and triangular sails and capable of years-long voyages through heavy seas. It was the wide array of luxury trade goods, along with religious pilgrimage sites such as Mecca and Benares, that made this area a vibrant saltwater crossroads.

monsoon A wind system that influences large climatic regions such as the Indian Ocean basin and reverses direction seasonally.

MAPPING THE WORLD
The Indian Ocean and South Asia, 1450–1750

Harnessing the power of monsoon winds, Arab and Asian sailors traversed the Indian Ocean and Arabian Sea for centuries before the Portuguese arrived in the 1490s, in search of pepper and other commodities. In subsequent years, competing Eurasian interlopers, including the Ottomans, conquered key ports from East Africa to Southeast Asia in an attempt to control both exports to Europe and interregional trade. The Ottomans retreated after the mid-sixteenth century, but many Muslims continued to sail to the Arabian peninsula to make the pilgrimage to Mecca and to engage in trade.

ROUTES ▼

→ Portuguese *Carreira da India* (Voyage to India)
→ Dutch trade route
→ Major pilgrimage route

1641–1699 Sultanate of Women in Aceh

1764 British East India Company controls Bengal

1700   1750   1800

1658 Dutch drive Portuguese from Ceylon

1701 William Kidd hanged in London for piracy

1739 Persian raiders under Nadir Shah sack Delhi

The Indian Ocean basin, which some historians and linguists have termed the Afrasian Sea, was defined by interlinked maritime and overland networks. Despite repeated attempts, no state ever totally controlled the great basin's exchange of goods, people, and ideas. Religious diversity and relative political independence were the rule. Even Islam, the most widespread religion, was not practiced in exactly the same way in any two places. Muslims from East Africa, Arabia, Persia, and South, Southeast, and East Asia all maintained distinct identities despite a shared religion, distant mercantile connections, and even long-term residence and intermarriage in foreign ports.

India, with its huge, mostly Hindu population, lay at the center of the Afrasian Sea trading system. The black pepper of Malabar, on the southwest coast, was world-famous, as were the diamonds of Golconda, in the southern interior. But it was India's cotton fabrics, linking countless farmers, artisans, and brokers, that brought in most foreign exchange. As in the Mediterranean and Atlantic trading systems, gold from sub-Saharan Africa and later silver from the Americas were the essential lubricants of trade. Nur Jahan minted rupees in American silver and African gold.

The Portuguese reached India in 1498. They had three key goals: to monopolize the spice trade to Europe, to tax or take over key shipping lanes, and to fight the expansion of Islam and spread Christianity instead. With the brief exception of the Ottomans in the first half of the sixteenth century, no land-based empire in the region attempted to stop them. Persia's Safavids and South Asia's Mughals might have done so, but they preferred to play off the later-arriving English, French, and Dutch against the Portuguese—and against one another. Given these empires' overwhelming strength on land, this strategy made sense, but as in Africa, leaving sea power to the Europeans proved a fateful decision.

The arrival of the Portuguese coincided with the rise of the Islamic Mughal Empire in India beginning about 1500. Though a land empire much like China under the Ming (see Chapter 15), the Mughal state was thoroughly connected to the outside world. Wealthy and well armed, the Mughals seemed invincible to many neighbors and outsiders. Certainly European conquest was unthinkable in the seventeenth century, the era of Nur Jahan. Her life exemplifies both the colorful court life typical of Eurasia's so-called gunpowder empires, as well as the outward gaze and self-consciousness these states' rulers exhibited.

The term "gunpowder empire" was coined by historian Marshall Hodgson to help explain the rise of the Mughal, Safavid, Ottoman, and other states whose rapid expansion after 1500 was enabled by Western-style cannons, muskets, and other firearms.[1] Historians also apply the term to the Safavid and Ottoman states and the Spanish, Portuguese, and other European kingdoms that took their new and powerful weaponry abroad in the name of commerce and Christianity. Unlike their ocean-going European adversaries, however, the great land empires of Central and South Asia were motivated by neither trade nor religion; their goal in expanding was to extract tributes from neighboring populations.

Despite the rise and fall of gunpowder empires on land and at sea, historical records suggest that most inhabitants of the greater Indian Ocean carried on much as they had before. There were certain changes, however. Especially in cash-crop-producing regions, such as Ceylon (Sri Lanka) off India's south coast and Aceh in Indonesia, demands on ordinary laborers and on productive lands sharply increased. Religious change took place, too. Although Islamic land empires such as that of the Mughals advanced, Islam grew most notably in politically fractured Southeast Asia. As in western Africa and unlike in the Americas, very few people in this vast region adopted Christianity.

For a time, South Asia held competing Europeans at bay in spite of their advanced gun-making and shipbuilding technologies. Starting in the seventeenth century, however, the European powers began to exploit the region's open seas and political divisions to advance land-based conquest and colonization. As they had done in the Americas, Europeans divided the Indian Ocean's shores, waterways, and islands into rigidly controlled colonial plantations and monopoly trading zones. Local lords were co-opted or, if resistant, deposed. In the end, the relative peace, prosperity, and cultural diversity that had once blocked foreign control helped facilitate it.

Trading Cities and Inland Networks: East Africa

The history of early modern East Africa is best understood in terms of linkages among the numerous Indian Ocean traders from as far away as China and the cities and peoples of the African interior. Brokering Africa's ties to Asia were merchant families and local princes clustered along a string of port towns and cities stretching from Ethiopia in the northeast to Mozambique in the southeast.

FOCUS

How did Swahili Coast traders link the East African interior to the Indian Ocean basin?

By 1500, it was mainly Muslims who lived in these thriving East African trading ports. Some were descendants of early Persian, Arabian, and South Asian overseas traders and missionaries, but the vast majority were native Africans, mostly Bantu speakers. Swahili, still commonly spoken in much of this region, is a Bantu language laced with Arabic terms. In early modern times, scribes recorded transactions in Swahili using Arabic script. Thus, the society and culture of East African trading ports blended African and Asian elements, reflecting the economic connections between the two regions.

Portuguese and Ottoman traders arrived in these ports around 1500, but neither managed to control more than a few of them at a time. Dutch, French, and English merchants arrived in the seventeenth century, but they, too, failed to monopolize East African trade. Offshore, the French established a minor presence on the huge island of Madagascar and then on much smaller Réunion, a future plantation colony, but neither island had been vital to the ancient monsoon trading circuit. As free from each other as they were from outsiders, the hundred-odd ports of East Africa's Swahili Coast remained largely independent until the imperial scramble of the late nineteenth century (discussed in Chapter 26).

Port Towns and Beginnings

By the early modern period, the East African coast had served as a regional crossroads for more than a thousand years. Archaeologists have recently determined that Muslim trader-missionaries had reached

East African Port Cities

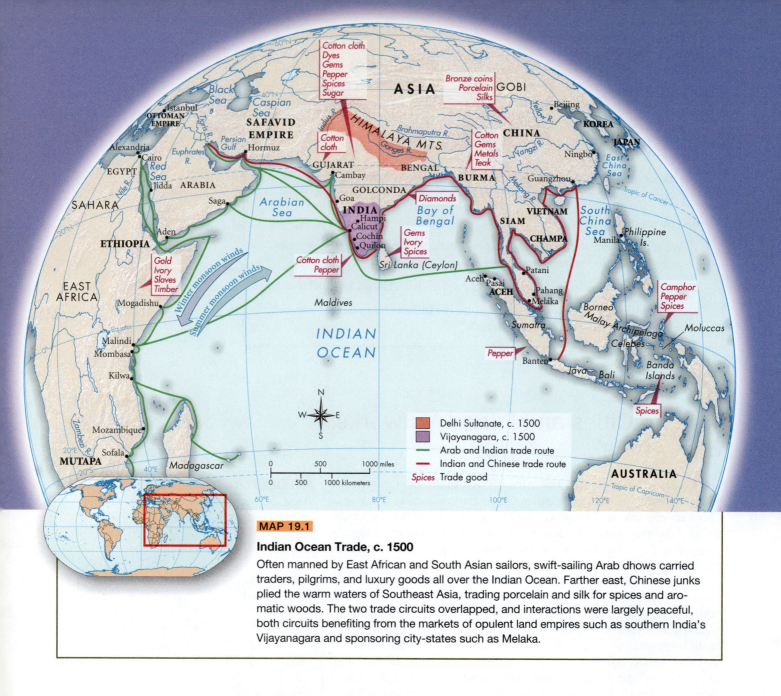

MAP 19.1

Indian Ocean Trade, c. 1500

Often manned by East African and South Asian sailors, swift-sailing Arab dhows carried traders, pilgrims, and luxury goods all over the Indian Ocean. Farther east, Chinese junks plied the warm waters of Southeast Asia, trading porcelain and silk for spices and aromatic woods. The two trade circuits overlapped, and interactions were largely peaceful, both circuits benefiting from the markets of opulent land empires such as southern India's Vijayanagara and sponsoring city-states such as Melaka.

many East African port towns by the eighth century C.E., soon after the founding of Islam. Seaborne trade in ivory, gold, ceramics, and other items was even older, however, dating back to classical antiquity. Early modern East African traders continued this commerce, bringing luxury goods from Central, South, and even East Asia to the coast in exchange for Africa's treasured raw materials. Traders also exchanged slaves for luxuries on occasion, but the scale of the Indian Ocean slave trade seems to have remained relatively small until the rise of plantations in the nineteenth century.

By modern urban standards, most East African trading ports were small towns. The largest, such as Kilwa, Sofala, Malindi, and Mombasa, had no more than 10,000 inhabitants at their height. Most towns were much smaller, home to only several hundred permanent residents. Quelimane (keh-lee-MAH-neh) and Mogadishu fell somewhere in between, with a few thousand inhabitants. Nearly all of the region's cities and many of the towns were walled, but only the most opulent had mosques of stone or coral block rather than adobe. Merchants, resident and foreign, occupied house blocks clustered within each city's walls. In exchange for tributes, local princes protected merchant families, negotiating with sometimes hostile inland chiefdoms for trade goods and subsistence items.

Indian Ocean Connections

East African traders exported elephant tusks and gold in exchange for South Asian cloth, much of it from Cambay in the Gujarat region of northwest India (see Map 19.1). They also imported Persian and even Chinese ceramics, along with spices, tobacco (after 1500), and a host of other items. African ivory was especially prized throughout Asia for its soft texture, and African gold, mostly from the southern interior, was always in high demand as currency. In much of India, women brought dowries of gold when they married, displaying it in the form of fine jewelry. As we have seen in previous chapters, African gold was an essential world currency prior to European expansion into the Americas.

Most goods were carried in **dhows** (dowz), swift, single-decked ships with triangular sails and about two hundred tons' capacity. Traders used smaller vessels and dugout canoes to navigate rivers such as the great Zambezi and to ferry goods through the treacherous coral reefs that lay between East Africa's towns.

Despite the extraordinary value of most Indian Ocean trade goods, shippers traveled only lightly armed. Although piracy had long been known, and was even expected in waters such as India's Malabar Coast, violent theft at sea seems to have become a serious threat to Indian Ocean commerce only after the arrival of the Portuguese, who sought to establish and defend their trading monopolies through brute force. Their actions in turn encouraged contraband trade and the fencing of stolen goods.

Chinese maritime visits to East Africa, though memorable, were few and far between. As we saw in Chapter 15, the famous Ming admiral Zheng He arrived first in Malindi in the late 1410s, and then at Mogadishu in the early 1430s. Zheng He's vessels were enormous, more than double the size of the largest Portuguese ships to arrive about a century later. In addition to the standard gold and ivory, the Ming admiral filled his ample holds with local items, including a veritable zoo for the Chinese emperor. There is no evidence of attempts to conquer or to establish trading posts or colonies, and afterward Chinese goods came to East Africa

Swahili Coast Traders

China's Retreat from the Indian Ocean

dhow A small sailing vessel with triangular rigs used in monsoon trade to East Africa.

Exchanger of Cambay

In this early-sixteenth-century watercolor, apparently by a self-taught Portuguese artist, a merchant in Cambay, on India's northwest coast, collects and changes gold, silver, and other coins of many mint marks and denominations. A tiny balance hangs behind him on one side, and a strongbox seems to float in midair on the other. To the right, people of many faiths, clothing styles, and colors come to seek his services. At least two are women bearing gold coins. (Ms 1889 at the Biblioteca Casanatense, Rome.)

again only through Southeast Asian intermediaries, often Muslim Malays. The Chinese retreat from the Indian Ocean left a void that early modern European interlopers were happy to fill.

Links to the Interior

Less often described than East Africa's ties to overseas merchants were its links to the African interior. The extent of each port's productive hinterlands or subsistence grounds was generally small, but coastal towns and cities did not simply face outward, as once believed. Almost all Swahili town-dwellers relied on nearby agricultural plots for their day-to-day survival, and many engaged in regular exchanges with independent cattle herders. Many Swahili elites owned slaves purchased from the interior, who produced food for both their masters and themselves. The African products in greatest demand overseas, however, came from the more densely populated southern interior.

Products from the Interior

This was most true of gold dust, traded northward from the mouth of the Zambezi River (see again Map 19.1). Its main sources were the many goldfields of the Mutapa kingdom (formerly Great Zimbabwe), located on the Zimbabwe Plateau. Here, as in parts of contemporary West Africa, men and women panned for gold in the agricultural off-season. A few mines went underground. The historical record is spotty, but it appears that an annual average of at least a ton of gold entered the Indian Ocean trade circuit during the sixteenth century.

Ivory was a different sort of product; collecting it required the hunting and slaughter of wild animals. Although modern demand for ivory has led to the extinction of elephants in parts of Africa, it appears that most of the tusks fed into the early modern Indian Ocean circuit were a byproduct of subsistence hunting. Hunters only went out seasonally, and without firearms. Bringing down an adult elephant with spears and longbows was an extremely dangerous business, and the compensation was not attractive enough to make it a livelihood. Aside from the dangers of ivory procurement, interior peoples such as the Shona speakers of the Mutapa kingdom were not easily pressured into market exchanges of any kind. With no particular need for Asian products, they carried ivory and gold to the seaports at their leisure.

An important export from the north Swahili Coast was lumber, specifically mangrove hardwoods for residential construction in desert regions of Arabia and the Red Sea. The exact ecological consequences of this enterprise have yet to be determined, but like the trade in tusks and gold, it appears not to have exhausted the resource. Extractive industries in the early modern period usually damaged the environment only in relation to their scale.

Arrival of the Portuguese

By 1500 trade was thriving throughout East Africa and its partners in the Indian Ocean basin. The arrival of the Portuguese at about that time would disrupt that valuable balance. With nothing to offer the well-off merchants of East Africa, India, and the Arabian Sea region, the Portuguese turned to force. Using their guns, stout vessels, and Mediterranean fort-building techniques, they sought to profit from the Indian Ocean trade by impeding it—that is, by enforcing monopolies on certain items and taking over vital ports. Ultimately this worked better in India than elsewhere, but the Portuguese tried desperately to gain control of East African trade, and even to penetrate the continent's southeast interior in search of Mutapa's fabled gold. Although they failed to conquer the Mutapa state, the Portuguese traded with its rulers and gained control of gold exports. As they had done in western Africa, in East Africa the Portuguese concentrated most of their energies on capturing and fortifying posts, or *feitorias*, which they established at Mozambique, Sofala, and Mombasa. The Dutch and English would soon follow.

Trade and Empire in South Asia

FOCUS

What factors account for the fall of Vijayanagara and the rise of the Mughals?

As in East Africa, despite competition and occasional violence, dozens of independent trading enclaves in South Asia prospered in early modern times. Many coastal cities and their surrounding hinterlands were subject to Muslim sultans or Hindu princes, most of whom drew their sustenance from the merchants they protected. Trading populations were larger than those of East

Africa and more diverse. Religious minorities included Jains, Jews, Parsis (Zoroastrians), and Christians. Among the region's most densely packed commercial crossroads, India's port cities maintained close ties to the subcontinent's rich and well-interconnected interior, at this time home to two major empires. One was in ascendance, the Muslim Mughal Empire in the north, and the other in decline, the Hindu kingdom of Vijayanagara (vizh-ah-ya-na-GAR-ah) in the south (see again Map 19.1).

Vijayanagara's Rise and Fall 1336–1565

Vijayanagara grew into an empire around 1500, only to disintegrate due to internal factionalism and external, mostly northern Muslim (although not Mughal) attacks. Because of its swift demise and the near-total loss of its written records, Vijayanagara remains one of the most enigmatic empires of the early modern period. With Muslim kingdoms dominating much of the subcontinent by the time the Portuguese arrived offshore around 1500, Hindu Vijayanagara appears to have been something of an anachronism. Like the contemporary Aztec and Inca empires of the Americas, Vijayanagara was neither a gunpowder empire nor an early modern, bureaucratic state. Its material record constitutes a major but still limited source for historians. Massive stone temple structures and lively artistic works hint at great opulence and power, but the nature of daily life for commoners remains obscure, although it has been reconstructed in part by archaeological work and from the observations of early European visitors.

Literally, "city of triumph," the kingdom of Vijayanagara was said to have been founded by two brothers in 1336. They chose the town site of Hampi, deep in the southern interior, to revive a purist version of the Hindu state. According to legend, the brothers had been captured in northern frontier wars and forced to convert to Islam in Delhi, but once back in their homeland they renounced that faith and sought the advice of Hindu Brahmans.

Hampi

This is an aerial view of part of Hampi, ancient capital of the Hindu kingdom of Vijayanagara in south-central India. The main temple rises in the smoky distance, marking the end of a long ceremonial promenade fronted by stone structures. The Tungabhadra River winds alongside, and all around are hills strewn with granite boulders, giving the city a primeval, almost timeless feel. Hampi fell to northern invaders in 1565. (Colin McPherson/Corbis.)

Hundreds of temples were quickly built along the Tungabadhra River gorge to venerate the state's patron deity, Virupaksha (vee-rooh-PAHK-shah), among others. Thus, the kingdom's identity was explicitly Hindu. By 1370, the empire covered most of southern India, with the exception of Malabar in the far southwest.

Divine Kingship

Whereas Muslim and Christian rulers were generally regarded as pragmatic "warriors of the faith," Hindu rulers were often seen as divine kings. Their most important duties involved performing the sacred rituals believed to sustain their kingdoms. Whether in Vijayanagara or in distant Bali in Southeast Asia, Hindu kingship relied on theatricality and symbolism quite removed from the everyday concerns of imperial administration. Early modern Hindu kings did participate in warfare and other serious matters, but their lives were mostly scripted by traditional sacred texts. Their societies believed that they would ensure prosperity in peacetime and victory in war by properly enacting their roles, which bordered on the priestly.

Life in Vijayanagara cycled between a peaceful period, when the king resided in the capital and carried out rituals, and a campaign season, when the king and his retinue traveled the empire battling with neighboring states and principalities. Like so much under Hindu rule, even victory on the field was scripted, and the warring season itself served as a reenactment of legendary battles. Each campaign started with a great festival reaffirming the king's divinity. Although he was renowned for his piety, it was his martial prowess that most set him apart from mere mortals. He was the exemplar of the **Kshatriya** (K-SHAH-tree-yah) or warrior **caste**, not the technically higher-ranking **Brahman** or priestly caste.

Krishna Deva Raya

Celebratory temple inscriptions record the names and deeds of many monarchs, but thanks to the records of foreign visitors the Vijayanagara king we know most about was Krishna Deva Raya (r. 1509–1529). Portuguese merchants and ambassadors traveled to his capital and court on several occasions, and all were stunned by the monarch's wealth and pomp. At his height, Krishna Deva Raya controlled most of India south of the Krishna River. Most of India's famed diamonds were mined nearby, providing a significant source of state revenue. But it was the constant flow of tribute from the *rajas*, the subject princes, that built his "city of triumph." Imperial demand drove the rajas to trade their products for Indian Ocean luxuries such as African gold and ivory. The king sat upon a diamond-studded throne, and two hundred subject princes attended him constantly at court. Each wore a gold ankle bracelet to indicate his willingness to die on the king's behalf.

Krishna Deva Raya welcomed the Portuguese following their 1510 conquest of Muslim-held Goa (GO-ah), a port on India's west coast that would become the keystone of Portugal's overseas empire. His armies required warhorses in the tens of thousands, and an arrangement with the Portuguese would give him easier access to horses from Arabia and Iraq. As they had done in western Africa, the Portuguese happily served as horse-traders to conquering non-Christian kings in exchange for access to key trade goods. Krishna Deva Raya used the imported mounts to extend Vijayanagara's borders north and south, and the Portuguese sent home some of the largest diamonds yet seen in Europe.

Imperial Organization

Vijayanagara shared some features with the roughly contemporaneous Aztec and Inca states—it was a tributary empire built on a combination of military force and religious charisma. Subject princes were required to maintain substantial armies and give surpluses to their king at periodic festivals; material display reaffirmed the king's divinity. Proper subordination of the rajas was equally important. Krishna Deva Raya was said to require so much gold from certain rajas that they were forced to sponsor pirates to generate revenue. Most tribute, however, came from the sale of farm products, cloth, and diamonds.

Above the rajas, Krishna Deva Raya appointed district administrators called *nayaks*. These were usually trusted relatives, and each oversaw a number of lesser kingdoms. The whole system was intended to both replicate and feed the center, with each raja and nayak sponsoring temple construction and revenue-generating projects of various sorts. Large-scale irrigation works improved agricultural yields, and at bridge crossings and city gates, officials taxed goods transported by ox-cart, donkey, and other means. The demands of the city and empire inevitably placed great pressure on southern India's forests and wetlands, and increased diamond mining sped deforestation and erosion of riverbanks. As in most

Kshatriya A member of the warrior caste in Hindu societies.

caste A hereditary social class separated from others in Hindu societies.

Brahman A member of the priestly caste in Hindu societies.

instances of imperial expansion, environmental consequences quickly became evident but were not, as far as we know, a major cause of decline.

Dependent as it was on trade, the expansion of Vijayanagara required a policy of religious tolerance similar to that later practiced by the Mughals. Jain merchants and minor princes were particularly important subjects since they helped link Vijayanagara to the world beyond India. Brahmanic or priestly law largely restricted Hindu trade to the land, whereas Jains could freely go abroad. Muslim coastal merchants were also allowed into the imperial fold, especially because they had far greater access than the Jains to luxury imports and warhorses. They had their own residential quarter in the city of Hampi. The early Portuguese policy in India was to exploit niches in this pre-existing trade system—not to conquer Vijayanagara, but simply to drive out competing Muslim merchants.

Though connected to the outside world mainly through the luxury goods trade, the empire's economy was based on large-scale rice cultivation. While kings and Brahmans reenacted the lives of the gods, the vast majority of Vijayanagara's subjects toiled their lives away as rice farmers. Around 1522 the Portuguese visitor Domingos Paes (see Reading the Past: Portuguese Report of a Vijayanagara Festival) described work on a huge, stone-reinforced reservoir: "In the tank I saw so many people at work that there must have been fifteen or twenty thousand men, looking like ants, so that you could not see the ground on which they walked."[2]

Rice Cultivation and Export

Vijayanagara's irrigated rice fed its people, but it was also a key export product. Special varieties were shipped as far abroad as Hormuz, on the Persian Gulf, and Aden, at the mouth of the Red Sea. More common rice varieties, along with sugar and some spices, provisioned the merchants of many Indian Ocean ports, including those of East Africa and Gujarat. It was through the sale of rice abroad that many subject princes obtained African gold for their king, with annual payments said to be in the thousands of pounds each by the time of Krishna Deva Raya. Hence, like luxury goods, rice was not only a key component in the trade relationships connecting the kingdom to the outside world; it also connected Vijayanagara's elites to each other, helping to define their political and social relationships.

Following Krishna Deva Raya's death in 1529, Vijayanagara fell victim first to internal succession rivalries, and then to Muslim aggressors. In 1565, under King Ramaraja, a coalition of formerly subject sultans defeated the royal army. Hampi, the capital city, was sacked, plundered, and abandoned; it was an overgrown ruin by 1568. Remnant Hindu principalities survived for a time in the southeast but eventually fell to the expansionist Mughals. By the seventeenth century only a few Hindu states remained around the fringes of South Asia, including remote Nepal. The Hindu principalities of Malabar, meanwhile, fell increasingly into the hands of Europeans and Muslim Gujarati merchants. Still, the memory of Vijayanagara's greatness and wealth lived on, to be revived much later by Hindu nationalists.

The Power of the Mughals

Another empire was expanding rapidly in India's north as Vijayanagara crumbled in the south. Beginning around 1500, under a Timurid (from Timur, the famed fourteenth-century Central Asian ruler discussed in Chapter 15) Muslim warlord named Babur (the "Tiger," r. 1500–1530), the Mughal Empire emerged as the most powerful, wealthy, and populous state yet seen in South Asia. By the time of Nur Jahan in the early 1600s, the Mughals (literally "Mongols," the great fourteenth-century emperors from whom the Mughals descended) had over 120 million subjects, a population comparable only to that of Ming China. Accumulating wealth from plunder and tribute and employing newly introduced gunpowder weapons and swift warhorses to terrifying effect, the Mughals subdued dozens of Hindu and Muslim principalities as they pushed relentlessly southward (see Map 19.2). Like many early modern empire builders, the Mughals were outsiders who adapted to local cultural traditions to establish and maintain legitimacy. In terms of Indian Ocean commerce, their rapid rise drove up demand for luxury imports, and, as in the case

Portuguese Report of a Vijayanagara Festival

The Portuguese merchant Domingos Paes (PAH-ish) visited Vijayanagara in 1520 with a larger diplomatic and commercial mission sent from Goa, the Portuguese trading post on India's southwest coast. Paes's report of the capital of Hampi and King Krishna Deva Raya's court, apparently written for the Portuguese court's official chronicler back in Lisbon, is among the richest to survive. Below, Paes describes part of a multiday festival that served to glorify the king and reaffirm the hierarchy of the state, and also to reenact cosmic battles.

At three o'clock in the afternoon everyone comes to the palace. They do not admit everyone at once . . . but there go inside only the wrestlers and dancing-women, and the elephants, which go with their trappings and decorations, those that sit on them being armed with shields and javelins, and wearing quilted tunics. As soon as these are inside they range themselves around the arena, each one in his or her place. . . . Many other people are then at the entrance gate opposite to the building, namely Brahmins, and the sons of the king's favorites, and their relations; all these noble youths who serve before the king. The officers of the household go about keeping order amongst all the people, and keep each one in his or her own place. . . .

The king sits dressed in white clothes all covered with [embroidery of] golden roses and wearing his jewels—he wears a quantity of these white garments, and I always saw him so dressed—and around him stand his pages with his betel [to chew], and his sword, and the other things which are his insignia of state. . . . As soon as the king is seated, the captains who waited outside make their entrance, each one by himself,

attended by his chief people. . . . As soon as the nobles have finished entering, the captains of the troops approach with shields and spears, and afterwards the captains of archers. . . . As soon as these soldiers have all taken their places the women begin to dance. . . . Who can fitly describe to you the great riches these women carry on their persons?—collars of gold with so many diamonds and rubies and pearls, bracelets also on their arms and upper arms, girdles below, and of necessity anklets on their feet. . . .

Then the wrestlers begin their play. Their wrestling does not seem like ours, but there are blows [given], so severe as to break teeth, and put out eyes, and disfigure faces, so much so that here and there men are carried off speechless by their friends; they give one another fine falls, too. They have their captains and judges who are there to put each one on equal footing in the field, and also to award the honors to him who wins.

Source: Robert Sewell, *A Forgotten Empire (Vijayanagara): A Contribution to the History of India* (London: Sonnenschein, 1900), 268–271.

EXAMINING THE EVIDENCE

1. What does the selection suggest regarding social hierarchy and prescribed gender roles in Vijayanagara?

2. How does the divine kingship described here compare with that of the Incas (see Chapter 16)?

---

of Nur Jahan, some high-ranking Mughal nobles invested directly in exports of items such as indigo and gems.

Religious Toleration Despite rule by Muslim overlords, most South Asians remained Hindus in early modern times, but those who converted to Islam enjoyed some benefits. Initially, conversion to Islam brought exemption from certain taxes, but these exemptions were suspended in the late sixteenth century under Emperor Akbar. As we will see, during and after his reign, lasting fusions between Hinduism and Islam emerged in various parts of the subcontinent.

Expanded Trade Like its religion, South Asia's dynamic and highly productive economy was little changed after conquest. Under Mughal rule, South Asia's legendary textiles, grains, spices, gems, and many other products continued to find buyers worldwide. Truly new markets for Indian goods emerged in the Americas and parts of sub-Saharan Africa, supplied by Portuguese and other European shippers. Lacking commodities Indians wanted, European traders paid for South Asia's goods in hard cash. As a result India, like China, enjoyed a consistently favorable balance of trade throughout early modern times. Along with funding armies, this wealth from abroad fueled construction, especially of religious buildings. With royal sponsorship like that of Nur Jahan, many of India's most famous architectural gems, such as the Taj Mahal and Red Fort, were built along the Ganges River plain.

True to the Timurid heritage it shared with its Safavid Persian and Ottoman Turkish neighbors (discussed in the next chapter), Mughal rule in India was marked by both extraordinary court opulence and near-constant power struggles and rebellions. As in many other empires not constrained by rules of primogeniture, factionalism and succession crises eventually led to Mughal decline. Soon after 1700, this decline in central authority left Mughal India vulnerable to European as well as Persian imperial designs. Persian raiders sacked the capital of Delhi in 1739, and by 1763 the English East India Company won rights to tax former Mughal subjects in the vast province of Bengal, effectively exercising sovereignty in the Indian interior. Despite these top-level reversals of fortune, life for the bulk of South Asia's millions of poor farmers and artisans scarcely changed.

Gunpowder Weapons and Imperial Consolidation 1500–1763

The emperor, or "Mughal," Babur spent most of his life defeating Afghan warlords. Horses and archers were still critical in these early victories, as was Babur's charismatic leadership, but by the 1510s some of the emperor's most important forces were using matchlock guns in battle. By the 1526 Battle of Panipat, outside Delhi, Babur's armies had perfected the use of cannons (see again Map 19.2). As Babur recalled nonchalantly in his memoir, the *Baburnama*: "Mustafa the artilleryman fired some good shots from the mortars mounted on carts to the left of the center [flank]." Some 16,000 men were said to have died in this battle, and Babur celebrated by plundering the great city of Agra. In 1527, although hugely outnumbered by a Hindu Rajput alliance of some 80,000 cavalry and 500 armored war elephants, Babur and his army won handily. "From the center [flank of troops commanded by] our dear eldest son, Muhammad Humayun, Mustafa Rumi brought forward the caissons, and with matchlocks and mortars broke not only the ranks of the infidel but their hearts as well."[3] Gunpowder weapons continued to prove decisive as Babur and his successors drove south.

Humayun, as Babur's son was known, took over the emerging Mughal Empire at his father's death in 1530, but he suffered setbacks. In 1535, he employed Ottoman military engineers and Portuguese gunners to attack the kingdom of Gujarat, a major textile exporter facing the Arabian Sea, but sources say his crippling addiction to opium cost valuable time and led to a forced withdrawal of troops. In the course of this ill-fated adventure, an Afghan warlord rose from the ashes to reconquer almost everything Babur had won in the north. Humayun went into exile in Safavid

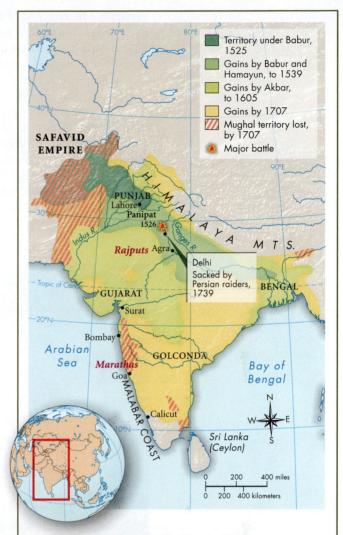

MAP 19.2 **The Mughal Empire, c. 1700**

Descendants of mounted Central Asian raiders, the Mughals expanded their control over the Indian subcontinent from the northwest after 1500. They did so with devastating, gunpowder-backed force followed by ethnic and religious accommodation. The majority of Mughal subjects did not practice the conquerors' Islamic faith, and some historians have even argued that India conquered the Mughals rather than the other way around. By 1700, the empire was approaching its greatest extent, after which rebellions and invasions began to force it to contract.

Persia, but he returned to India aided by gun-toting Safavid forces. By 1555, Humayun had used this expanded firepower to regain his father's conquests, only to die in 1556 after hitting his head on the stairs of his library. Councilors decided the next Mughal would be Humayun's twelve-year-old son, Akbar.

Akbar the Great

India's historic role as an interfaith and intercultural crossroads was only heightened during the long reign of Akbar (literally "the Great," r. 1556–1605). Though founded by Timurid horsemen who regarded themselves as warriors of the Islamic faith in the Sunni tradition, by the time of Akbar a quick succession of marriages had linked Shi'ite Safavid and Hindu royalty to the central Mughal line. For over a century Persian remained the language of the court, and relations with the Safavids were friendly. Most notable, however, was the steady "Indianization" of the Mughal emperors themselves. The wealth and diversity of the subcontinent, not to mention the beauty and charm of Hindu Rajput princesses, absorbed them. Akbar was no exception; his son Jahangir, the next emperor, was born to a Hindu princess.

Taj Mahal

The Mughal emperor Shah Jahan (r. 1627–1658) commissioned this spectacular mausoleum, the Taj Mahal, in memory of his wife, Mumtaz Mahal. The structure includes Persian elements, in part because many Persian artisans worked in the Mughal court. But its quality of near-ethereal lightness, rising from the delicately carved white marble and long reflecting pool, marks it as Indian and Mughal. (Marco Pavan/Grand Tour/Corbis.)

This process of absorption was greatly accelerated by Akbar's eclectic personality. Fascinated with everything from yogic asceticism to the fire worship of India's Parsi, or Zoroastrian, minority, by the 1570s Akbar began formulating his own hybrid religion. It was a variety of emperor worship forced mostly upon high-ranking subjects. Somewhat like the early modern Inca and Japanese royal cults that tied the ruling house to the sun, Akbar's cult emphasized his own divine solar radiance. Staunch Muslim advisers rebelled against this seeming heresy in 1579, but Akbar successfully repressed them. In the end, Akbar's faith won few lasting converts—and left visiting Jesuit missionaries scratching their heads—yet its mere existence demonstrated an enduring Mughal tendency toward accommodation of religious difference.

Despite his eclecticism and toleration, Akbar clung to core Timurid cultural traditions, such as moving his court and all its attendant wealth and servants from one grand campsite to another. He was said to travel with no fewer than 100,000 attendants. He also never gave up his attachment to gunpowder warfare. Recalcitrant regional lords such as the Rajput Hindu prince Udai Singh defied Akbar's authority in the 1560s, only to suffer the young emperor's wrath. A protracted 1567 siege of the fortified city of Chitor ended with the deaths of some 25,000 defenders and their families. Akbar himself shot the commander of the city's defenses dead with a musket, and his massive siege cannons, plus the planting of explosive mines, brought down its formidable stone walls. A similar siege in 1569 employed even larger guns, hauled into position by elephants and teams of oxen. Few princes challenged Akbar's authority after these devastating demonstrations of Mughal firepower.

Akbar's Successors

By the end of Akbar's reign, the Mughal Empire stretched from Afghanistan in the northwest to Bengal in the east, and south to about the latitude of Bombay (today Mumbai; see again Map 19.2). Emperor Jahangir (r. 1605–1627) was far less ambitious than his father Akbar, and as we saw in the opening paragraphs to this chapter, his addictions and interests led him to hand power to his favored wife, Nur Jahan, an effective administrator and business woman but not a conqueror. Jahangir's reign was nevertheless culturally significant. A devoted patron of the arts and an amateur poet, Jahangir took Mughal court splendor to new heights (see Seeing the Past: Reflections of the Divine in a Mughal Emerald). His illustrated memoir, the *Jahangirnama*, is a remarkably candid description of life at the top of one of the early modern world's most populous and wealthy empires.

New conquests under Shah Jahan (r. 1628–1658) and Aurangzeb (aw-WRONG-zeb) (r. 1658–1707) carried the empire south almost to the tip of the subcontinent. These rulers had made few innovations in gunpowder warfare; as in the days of Babur, religion was as important a factor in imperial expansion as technology. Shah Jahan was an observant but tolerant Muslim, whereas Aurangzeb was a true holy warrior who called for a return to orthodoxy and elimination of unauthorized practices. Aurangzeb's religious fervor was a major force in the last phase of Mughal expansion.

The emperor's main foe was Prince Shivaji (c. 1640–1680), leader of the Hindu Marathas of India's far southwest. Aurangzeb employed European gunners, whose state-of-the-art weapons and high-quality gunpowder helped him capture several of Shivaji's forts, but he mostly relied on muskets, cannons, and other weapons designed and cast in India. Many large swivel guns were mounted on camels, a useful adaptation. For his part, Shivaji was never able to field more than a few hundred musketeers, relying instead on swift mounts and guerrilla raids. Despite a major offensive sent by Aurangzeb after Shivaji's death, the Marathas bounced back within a few decades and won recognition of their homeland.

Only with the accession of Aurangzeb's successor, Muhammad (r. 1720–1739), did Mughal stagnation and contraction set in. Rebellions by overtaxed peasants and nobles alike sapped the empire's overstretched bureaucratic and defensive resources, and Muhammad's guns proved increasingly outmoded. Europeans were by this time shifting to lighter and more mobile artillery, but the Mughals were casting larger and ever-more-unwieldy cannons. A cannon said to be capable of shooting 100-pound balls, dubbed "Fort Opener," was so heavy it had to be pulled by four elephants and thousands of oxen. Most of the time, it remained stuck in the mud between siege targets. Muhammad Shah

Jahangir Being Helped to Bed

This Mughal miniature from about 1635 shows the emperor Jahangir being put to bed by the ladies of his court after celebrating a Hindu new year's eve festival called Holi. As one of the illustrations in Jahangir's own memoir, the *Jahangirnama*, this image matches well with the emperor's self-description as a regular user of alcohol and other intoxicating substances. Though his interests were not as eclectic as those of his father, Akbar, Jahangir was tolerant of religious diversity.

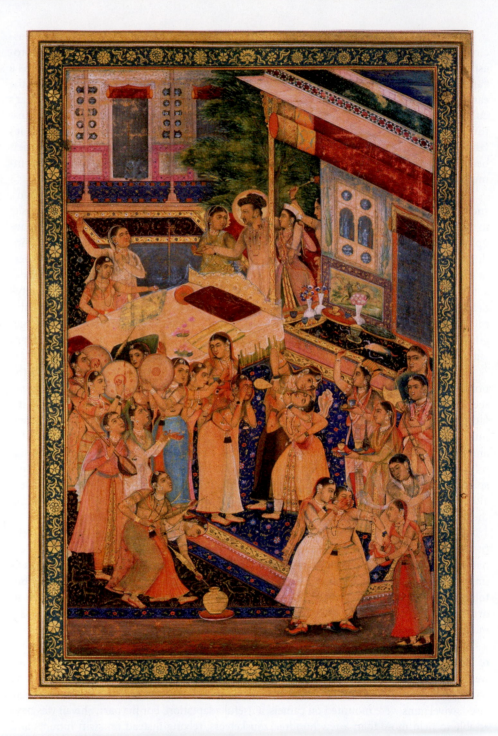

finally lost Delhi and the great Mughal treasury to Iran's Nadir Shah, successor to the Safavids, in 1739. The empire fell into disarray until the reign of Shah Alam II, who took the throne in 1759, only to fall under British influence in 1763. He ruled as a puppet of English East India Company until 1806.

Typical of early modern empire builders, the Mughals shifted between peaceful pragmatism and deadly force. They made a variety of alliances with subject peoples, offering them a share of power and the right to carry on established livelihoods. When not engaged in wars of expansion, emperors such as Akbar and Shah Jahan spent considerable time

Reflections of the Divine in a Mughal Emerald

Mughal Emerald (Van Pelt Photography.)

In the seventeenth century, foreign visitors repeatedly claimed that the Mughal court was the richest in the world. The Mughal emperor and his family wore delicately tailored silk garments and other luxurious clothes, dripping with jewels. Many great stones, such as the one pictured here, have survived in museums or private collections. Fabulous gemstones weighing hundreds of carats were routinely exchanged and given as gifts to important visitors, loyal subjects, and favored heirs.

India's early modern rulers had direct access to precious metals, diamonds, rubies, and pearls, but emeralds—especially prized because green was the color of Islam—were hard to come by. Old mines in Egypt had long since played out, and sources in Afghanistan and Pakistan remained unknown, or at least untapped.

Emeralds were found, however, in faraway New Granada, the Spanish-American colony now roughly comprised by the Republic of Colombia. Beginning in the late sixteenth century, Spanish mine owners traded emeralds dug from the high Andes to Spanish and Portuguese merchants with ties to Goa, Portugal's most important trading post in India. From there, merchants traded the stones inland to intermediaries and even to the Mughal emperor himself. Once in the hands of the renowned artisans of the world's most opulent court, raw Colombian emeralds were faceted, tumbled, and carved for incorporation into a wide variety of royal jewels. Some were carefully inscribed with Arabic verses from the Qur'an or special prayers. The one pictured here contains a Shi'a prayer praising the Twelve Imams. It was meant to be sewn into a ritual garment, prayer-side in, as a protective amulet.

EXAMINING THE EVIDENCE

1. How does this precious object reflect patterns of early modern globalization?

2. Why would the royal owner commission a religious object of such magnificence?

---

mediating disputes, expanding palace structures, and organizing tribute collection. Elite tax-collectors and administrators called *zamindars* (SAW-mean-dars) lived off their shares of peasant and artisan tribute, ruling like chiefs over zones called *parganas*, similar to the Ottoman *timars* (discussed in the next chapter). Somewhat medieval in structure, this sort of decentralized rule bred corruption, which in turn led to waves of modernizing reform.

As in the similarly populous and cash-hungry empire of Ming China, Mughal tax reform moved in the direction of a centralized money economy (India's rulers had long enjoyed the privilege of minting gold, silver, and copper coins), stimulating both rural and urban markets. By Akbar's time, most taxes were paid in cash. Meanwhile, European merchants, ever anxious for Indian commodities such as pepper, diamonds, and cotton textiles, reluctantly supplied their South Asian counterparts with precious metals. As in China, this boost to the Mughal money supply was critical, since India had few precious metals mines of its own. The influx of cash, mostly Spanish-American silver pesos, continued even after the 1739 Persian sack of Delhi, but it was arguably a mixed blessing. As in contemporary China, and indeed in Spain itself, the heightened commercial activity and massive influx of bullion did not beget modern industrialization in India. Instead, it bred increased state belligerence and court grandeur. In a sense, the old "Mongolian" notions of governance were simply magnified, financed in a new, more efficient way. Even gunpowder weapons became little more than objects of show.

Tax Reform and Its Effects

Everyday Life in the Mughal Empire

Continuance of the Caste System

Despite its Islamic core and general policy of religious toleration, Mughal India remained sharply divided by status, or caste, as well as other types of social distinctions. India's caste divisions, like the so-called estates of Europe (nobility, clergy, and commoners), were thought to be derived from a divine order, or hierarchy, and could scarcely be challenged. Women's lives were circumscribed, if not oppressed, in virtually all but regal and wealthy merchant circles. The Hindu practice of **sati**, in which widows committed suicide by throwing themselves onto their husbands' funeral pyres, continued under Islamic rule,

sati The ancient Indian practice of ritual suicide by widows.

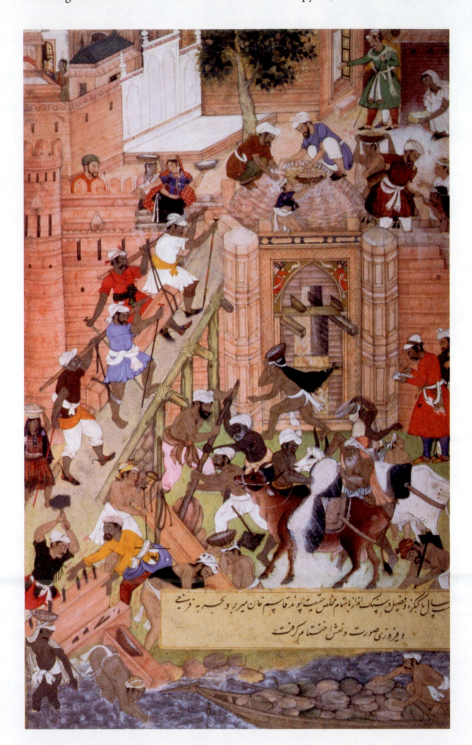

Building a Palace

This Mughal miniature from the 1590s is quite unusual in depicting ordinary working folk, along with a pair of animal helpers. Men of several colors, ages, and states of dress engage in heavy labor, transporting and lifting stones, beams, and mortar; splitting planks; setting stones; and plastering domes. Several women are sifting sand or preparing mortar, and at center-right are two well-dressed men who appear to be architects or inspectors. Two similar inspectors appear in the upper right, and only in the upper left corner do we glimpse the elite palace inhabitants, seemingly oblivious to the goings-on below. (Victoria & Albert Museum, London/Art Resource, NY.)

although there is much debate about its frequency. Akbar opposed the practice, but he did not ban it. Polygamy, sanctioned by Islam and embraced by Akbar and other rulers, was practiced by any man who could afford to support what amounted to multiple households.

Lower-caste folk, meanwhile, suffered regardless of gender. Men, women, and children were equally banished to a humiliated, slavelike existence in many areas, urban and rural. Worst off were the so-called Untouchables, who were relegated to disposing of human waste, animal carcasses, and other jobs requiring the handling of filth. Like those in many other parts of the early modern world, Mughal elites defined their own dignity most clearly by denying it to those around them—all the while displaying their innate goodness and superiority through ritualized, ostentatious acts of charity. After Akbar, the Mughal emperors had themselves publicly and lavishly weighed on their solar and lunar birthdays against piles of gold and silver coins, which they then distributed to the poor. Similar charitable practices were copied down to the lowest levels of society.

Farmers

As in much of the early modern world, the vast majority of Mughal subjects were subsistence farmers, many of them tied to large landlords through tributary and other customary obligations. The Mughal state thrived mostly by inserting itself into existing tributary structures, not by reordering local economies. Problems arose when Mughal rulers raised tax quotas sharply, or when droughts, floods, and other natural disasters upset the cycle of agricultural production. Unlike the Ming and Qing Chinese, or even the Spanish in Mexico, the Mughals devoted very little of their tremendous wealth to dams, aqueducts, and other massive public works projects. What was new, or modern, was that paper-pushing bureaucrats recorded farmers' tax assessments.

Even in good times, most South Asians lived on only a small daily ration of rice or millet, seasoned with ginger or cumin and—lightly—salt, an expensive state-monopoly item. Some fruits, such as mangoes, were seasonally available, but protein sources were limited. Even in times of bounty, religious dietary restrictions kept most people thin. After centuries of deforestation, people used animal dung as cooking fuel. Intensive agriculture using animal-drawn plows and irrigation works was widespread, but mass famines occurred with notable frequency. The Columbian Exchange was marginally helpful. After about 1600, American maize and tobacco were commonly planted, along with the capsicum peppers that came to spice up many South Asian dishes. Maize spurred population growth in some parts of India, whereas tobacco probably shortened some people's lives. Most tobacco was produced as a cash crop for elite consumption.

Urban Artisans

India's cities grew rapidly in Mughal times, in part due to stress-induced migration. Nine urban centers—among them Agra, Delhi, and Lahore—exceeded 200,000 inhabitants before 1700. After Akbar's rule, the shift to tax collection in cash was a major stimulus to urban growth and dynamism. Even smaller towns bustled with commercial activity as the economy became more thoroughly monetized, and all urban centers formed nuclei of artisan production.

A number of South Asian coastal and riverside cities and nearby hinterlands produced cotton and silk textiles in massive quantities. They usually followed the putting-out, or piecework, system, in which merchants "put out" raw materials to artisans working from home. As in China and northern Europe, women formed the backbone of this industry, not so much in weaving but rather in the physically harder tasks of fiber cleaning and spinning. Other, mostly male artisans specialized in woodworking, leather making, blacksmithing, and gem cutting. Perhaps the most visible artisanal legacy from Mughal times was in architecture. Highly skilled stonemasons produced Akbar's majestic Red Fort and Shah Jahan's inimitable Taj Mahal, both in the early Mughal capital of Agra.

Some men found employment in the shipyards of Surat, Calicut, and the Bay of Bengal, and others set sail with their seasonal cargoes of export goods and pilgrims. Gujarati Muslim merchants were dominant in the Arabian Sea even after the arrival of Europeans, but Hindus, Jains, and members of other faiths also participated. Unlike the Ottomans, the Mughals never developed a navy, despite their control of maritime

Gujarat since Akbar's conquest of the region in 1572 (see again Map 19.2). On land, by contrast, the empire's vast military apparatus absorbed many thousands of men. Frontier wars with fellow Muslims and southern Hindus were nearly constant. Christian Europeans were mostly seen as tangential commercial allies, technical advisers, and arms suppliers.

The Sikh Challenge

In the northwestern Punjab region an internal challenge of lasting significance emerged, this time mounted by leaders of a relatively new religious sect, Sikhism. Sikhism was something of a hybrid between Islam and Hinduism, but it tended more toward the latter and thus found deeper support among Hindu princes than among Islamic ones. Merchants and artisans were particularly attracted to the faith's recognition of hard work and abstinence (as we saw in Chapter 15). Peasant and artisan followers of Guru Gobind Singh (1666–1708) rebelled in 1710, and their plundering raids reached Delhi. The rebellion was violently quashed by Shah Farrukhsiyar (far-ROOK-see-yar) (r. 1713–1720) in 1715, but sporadic raids and uprisings continued until the end of the eighteenth century, when the Sikhs at last established a separate state.

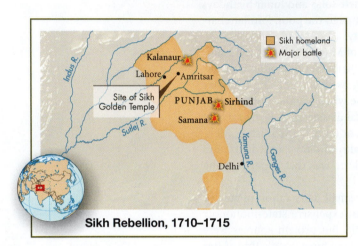

Sikh Rebellion, 1710–1715

In sum, the mighty Mughals ruled over the richest and most populous of Eurasia's early modern Islamic empires, and theirs remained by far the most culturally diverse. Mounted warriors used guns to crush or intimidate neighbors in new and terrifying ways, quickly absorbing huge swaths of terrain and millions of subject peoples. Yet generally, the resulting rule was neither intolerant nor authoritarian. As long as they paid cash tributes, regions could preserve their religious diversity and a degree of local autonomy. Problems arose with imperial overstretch, succession crises, and excessive taxation. Rebels, particularly non-Muslim ones, increasingly shook imperial foundations. More subtle but ultimately more serious were the inroads made by European commercial agents, in particular those of Britain's East India Company. These men, from Connecticut-born clerk Elihu Yale to Governor-general Robert Clive, formed the spearhead of a new imperialism.

European Interlopers

FOCUS

What factors enabled Europeans to take over key Indian Ocean trade networks?

Direct trade for Indian luxuries had been a dream of Europeans since the days of Marco Polo. Unfortunately, as the Portuguese explorer Vasco da Gama and his followers quickly discovered, Europeans had little that appealed to South Asians. With the exception of certain types of guns and clocks, the Portuguese had no products that could not be had in some form already, often more cheaply, and guns would soon be copied. Like Portugal, India was an ancient crossroads, but it was far larger and richer, and vastly more productive. Complex trade circuits had long linked India's rich interior and bustling ports to the wider world. In such a crowded marketplace, only silver and gold found universal acceptance because they functioned as money. Frustrated, the Portuguese turned to piracy, financing their first voyages by plunder rather than trade.

Portuguese Conquistadors 1500–1600

As would prove true in China, only precious metals opened India's doors of trade to new-comers. Even with powerful guns and swift ships on their side, the vastly outnumbered Portuguese had no choice but to part with their hard-won African gold and Spanish-American silver. Taking a somewhat different track than in western Africa, the Portuguese inserted themselves into Indian Ocean trade circuits with an uncompromising mix of belligerence and silver money. They were fortunate in that silver soon arrived in quantity through Portugal's growing Atlantic trade with the Spanish, particularly after 1550. Profits made in the slave trade were routinely reinvested in spices and other goods from India. Meanwhile, the security of all exchanges was guaranteed with brute force, and in some places, such as Goa in India and Melaka in Malaysia, outright conquest.

Portuguese Advances

Genuine Portuguese conquests in Asia were few but significant. Crown-sponsored conquistadors focused on strategic sites for their fortified trading posts, mostly traditional mercantile crossroads and shipping straits not effectively monopolized or defended by local princes. These *feitorías* resembled those already established along the western coast of Africa, but most proved far more expensive and difficult to maintain. The Indian Ocean's sea traffic was already huge, by comparison, and competition was fierce.

The Portuguese grand plan, one that was never realized, was to monopolize all trade in the Indian Ocean by extracting tolls and tariffs from local traders of various ethnicities and political allegiances. For a time they sold shipping licenses to Gujarati Muslim and other long-distance shippers. If traders failed to produce such licenses when passing through Portuguese-controlled ports, their goods were confiscated. On top of this, they had to pay duties.

Within a half-century of da Gama's 1498 voyage to India the Portuguese controlled access to the Persian Gulf, Red Sea, South China Sea, and Atlantic Ocean, along with many major coastal trading enclaves, from Mombasa on the coast of Kenya to Macao on China's Pearl River delta (see Map 19.3). Being so few in a region of millions, the Portuguese strategy was pragmatic. By tapping existing trade networks and setting up feitorías, they could efficiently collect spices and textiles, along with what were essentially extortion payments. Friends would be given silver, enemies lead. The method worked as long as the Portuguese faced no competition from other belligerent sea powers and remained unified and consistent in their use of violence.

Despite some early Ottoman attacks, seaborne trade competitors would not arrive until about 1600, but given the distance to Lisbon, it immediately proved impossible to enforce Portuguese unity and consistency in dealing with Indian Ocean merchants and princes. Ironically, it was "friendly" local merchants, rajas, and sultans—Arab, Hindu, and otherwise—who benefited most from Portuguese sponsorship and protection. As in western Africa, for several centuries the Portuguese unwittingly did as much to facilitate local aspirations as to realize their own. What they grandly called the "State of India," *Estado da Índia*, gradually proved more "Indian" than Portuguese, though for a short time it was highly profitable to the Crown.

Failed Efforts at Religious Conversion

Portugal's grand religious project was similarly absorbed. In 1498 Vasco da Gama expressed confidence in the spread of Roman Catholicism to East Africa: "On Easter day the Moors [Muslims] we had taken captive told us that in the town of Malindi [a Swahili port on the coast of Kenya] there were four vessels belonging to Christians from India, and if we should like to convey them there they would give us Christian pilots, and everything else we might need, including meats, water, wood, and other things."[4] Da Gama wrongly took this to mean that there was a pre-existing Christian base or network in the region upon which the Catholic Portuguese could build. Ultimately, Portuguese efforts to convert the many peoples of the Indian Ocean basin failed even more miserably than in Atlantic Africa, though not for lack of trying. Francis Xavier, an early Jesuit missionary (see Chapter 20), worked tirelessly and died an optimist. Whereas he focused on converting the region's countless slaves and lower-caste people, others sought to bend the will of monarchs such as Akbar, hoping they would set an example. Small Christian communities formed at Goa and other strongholds, but everywhere they went, Portuguese missionaries faced literally millions of hostile Muslims and perhaps equal or greater numbers of uninterested Hindus, Buddhists, Confucianists, Jains, Parsis, Sikhs, Jews, and others. In short, Christianity, at least in the form presented by the Portuguese, did not appeal to the vast majority of people inhabiting the Indian Ocean basin. As we will see in Chapter 21, only in

MAP 19.3

Portugal's Seaborne Empire, c. 1600

With their castle-like sailing vessels and potent gunpowder weapons, the Portuguese inserted themselves violently into the greater Indian Ocean basin beginning in 1498. From their stronghold in Goa, they monopolized regional and export trade in luxury goods, either by shipping these items themselves or by forcing others to purchase licenses. After 1580, the Portuguese were under Spanish rule, which linked the lucrative East and South Asia trade routes to New World silver arriving in the Philippines.

Japan, the Philippines, East Timor, and other select areas, mostly in the western Pacific, did early modern Catholic missionaries appear to strike a chord.

The "India Voyage"

Despite the failure of Christian missionary efforts, trade was brisk, at least for a time. The so-called *carreira da India* (cah-HEY-rah dah EENDJ-yah), or India voyage, became legendary in Portuguese culture, and for good reason. Even on successful trips, death rates on this annual sail between Lisbon and Goa were high due to poor onboard sanitation, prolonged vitamin C deprivation, questionable medical therapies such as bloodletting, and other health challenges typical of the era. Also, although early modern navigators were arguably more adept than medieval ones, shipwrecks were not uncommon on the India voyage. Unlike local dhows, sixteenth- and seventeenth-century Portuguese vessels were huge, round-hulled, and built for cargo rather than speed or maneuverability, and foundered due to overloading. The coral reefs of southeast Africa became a notorious graveyard of the carreira.

By the later sixteenth century, Portuguese monopolies on East Indian spices and sea-lanes had weakened considerably. With so much wealth at stake and so few enforcers on hand, corruption and contraband flourished. Spices were, after all, the drugs of their day, more valuable by weight than gold. Shipwrecks and piracy became more frequent throughout Portugal's ocean empire, as did competition from new, better-armed Europeans—Protestants, to boot. As Luiz Vaz de Camões (cah-MOYSH), veteran of many adventures in the East Indies, composed the triumphant poem that would become Portugal's national epic, *The Lusíads*, Portugal was actually on the eve of losing not only its heirless king but also its hard-won trading monopolies in the Indian Ocean. It was the Spanish under Philip II who would offer the first humiliation. Shortly after, Spain's sworn enemies, the Dutch, would deal the Portuguese a series of crushing blows.

Weakening of Portuguese Power

The Dutch and English East India Companies 1600–1750

As Portuguese fortunes declined and Mughal expansion continued toward the turn of the seventeenth century, South Asia's overseas trade underwent notable reorganization. This shift involved many players, including the familiar Gujarati merchants, the increasingly powerful Ottomans, Persia's expanding Safavids, and others. But ultimately it was Dutch and English newcomers, and to a lesser extent the French, who would have the greatest long-term impact. All formed powerful **trading companies** in the seventeenth and eighteenth centuries, each backed by state-of-the-art cannons and first-rate sailing ships.

Despite these important changes, it would be highly misleading to project the later imperial holdings of these foreigners back onto the seventeenth and early eighteenth centuries. Only the Dutch came close to establishing a genuine "Indian Ocean Empire" during early modern times. Meanwhile, East Africans, South and Southeast Asians, and other native peoples of the Indian Ocean continued to act independently, in their own interests. It was the sudden, unexpected collapse of the Mughals and other gunpowder-fueled Asian states in the later eighteenth century that allowed Europeans to conquer large landmasses and to plant colonies of the sort long since established in the Americas.

The Dutch East India Company, known by its Dutch acronym VOC, was founded in 1602. The company's aim was to use ships, arms, and Spanish-American silver to displace the Portuguese as Europe's principal suppliers of spices and other exotic Asian goods. Though not officially a state enterprise, the Dutch East India Company counted many ranking statesmen among its principal investors, and its actions abroad were as belligerent as those of any imperial army or navy. In the course of almost two centuries, the VOC extended Dutch influence from South Africa to Japan. Its most lasting achievement was the conquest of Java, base for the vast and diverse Dutch colony of Indonesia.

Dutch VOC

Although they never drove the Portuguese from their overseas capital at Goa, the mostly Protestant Dutch displaced their Catholic rivals nearly everywhere else. Their greatest early successes were in southern India and Java, followed by Sri Lanka (Ceylon), Bengal, Melaka, and Japan (see Map 19.4). In Southeast Asia their standard procedure was to follow conquest with enslavement and eventually plantation agriculture of the sort established by the Spanish and Portuguese in the Americas. They also imposed this sequence on Ceylon (see Lives and Livelihoods: Cinnamon Harvesters in Ceylon).

The monopolistic mentality of contemporary Europe is what drove Dutch aggression: profits were ensured not by open competition but by absolute control over the flow of commodities and the money to pay for them. Faced with competition from both regional authorities such as the Mughals and fellow foreign interlopers such as the English and Portuguese, the VOC concentrated on monopolizing spices. After seizing the pepper-growing region of southern Sumatra, the VOC turned to the riskier business of establishing plantations to grow coffee and other tropical cash crops. Like the Portuguese before them, the Dutch devoted at least as much cargo space to interregional trade as to exports. Thus clever local traders and many thousands of Chinese merchants benefited from the Dutch determination to monopolize trade.

trading companies Private corporations licensed by early modern European states to monopolize Asian and other overseas trades.

Cinnamon Harvesters in Ceylon

Harvesting Cinnamon

This engraving, based on a simpler one from 1672, depicts cinnamon harvesters in Ceylon (Sri Lanka). The Portuguese were the first Europeans to attempt to monopolize the global export of this spice, but local kings were difficult to conquer and control. Only in the later seventeenth century did the Dutch manage to establish plantation-type production, with the final product, the now familiar cinnamon sticks, monopolized by the Dutch East India Company. (The Granger Collection, New York.)

Long before the arrival of Europeans in 1506, the island of Sri Lanka, or Ceylon (its colonial name), was world-renowned for its cinnamon exports. As far away as Persia this wet tropical island off India's southeast tip, largely under control of competing Buddhist kings, was famous for its sapphires, rubies, pearls, and domesticated elephants (see again Map 19.3). Like India's pepper and Southeast Asia's cloves, mace, and nutmeg, Ceylonese cinnamon fetched extraordinary prices throughout Eurasia

and parts of Africa, where it was used as a condiment, preservative, and even medicine. As late as 1685 a Portuguese observer noted: "Every year a great number of vessels arrive from Persia, Arabia, the Red Sea, the Malabar Coast [of India], China, Bengal, and Europe to fetch cinnamon." Attempts to transplant the spice elsewhere, including Brazil, consistently failed, and early conquistador claims of finding cinnamon in Ecuador's eastern jungles proved false. As part of the Columbian Exchange,

Ceylonese cinnamon became a necessary ingredient in hot chocolate, a beverage developed in colonial Mexico that soon took Europe by storm.

The spice grew wild in forests belonging to the kingdom of Kandy, in Ceylon's southwest highlands. In 1517, the Portuguese struck a deal with the king of Kandy that allowed them to use and fortify the port of Colombo to monopolize cinnamon exports in exchange for cloth, metalware, and military assistance against rivals. The Portuguese did not engage directly in cinnamon production, but rather traded for it with the king and certain nobles. The king and his nobles in turn collected cinnamon as a tribute item produced on feudal-type estates called *para-wenia*. A special caste of male workers known as *chalias* was specifically responsible for planting, harvesting, slicing, drying, and packaging Ceylon's most prized crop. The chalias were not enslaved, but rather served as dependents of the king and various noblemen and military officers in exchange for the right to use land for subsistence farming in the off-season, plus rations of rice and occasionally a cash wage.

Cinnamon is derived from the shaved and dried inner bark of the small *Cinamomum verum* tree, a variety of laurel. Although the spice can be harvested wild, Ceylon's chalias pruned, transplanted, and even grew the trees from seed to maximize output and improve quality. With southwest Ceylon's white sand soils and reliable monsoon rains, the crop flourished year after year. Cinnamon is best when taken from young saplings three to five years old, no more than ten feet high, and about the thickness of a walking stick. Due to Ceylon's latitude, two harvests were possible, one concentrated in May-June and another in November-December. At harvest time the chalias cut ripe cinnamon trees with hatchets and then removed the bark. Daily collection quotas were set by the king and other holders of parawenia estates.

Next came peeling, the key process and the one for which the chalias were best known. As a seventeenth-century Portuguese writer described them: "These cinnamon peelers carry in their girdle a small hooked knife as a mark of their occupation." Working in pairs, one chalia made two lengthwise incisions on the ripe sticks using his hooked knife and carefully removed the resulting half-cylindrical strips of bark. His companion then used other tools to separate a gray outer bark from the thin, cream-colored inner bark. Leaving even a tiny amount of the outer bark on the inner bark made the cinnamon inedibly bitter. The inner bark was then left to dry, curling, thickening, and turning brown as it oxidized. The chalias then packaged the resulting "cinnamon sticks" in cloth-covered bundles weighing about 100 lbs. These were given to overlords; the king of Kandy alone was said to demand over 500 tons each year. Cinnamon was often bundled with black pepper for long sea voyages to help draw out moisture.

We have no documents written by the chalias to give us a sense of their views, but we do know that a leader of a 1609 rebellion against the Portuguese was a member of this caste and the son of a cinnamon cutter. Tapping into local discontent, the Dutch East India Company (VOC) displaced the Portuguese in 1658 after making an alliance with the king of Kandy. Once established on the island, the Dutch shifted to direct planting and harvesting, using enslaved laborers and totally monopolizing trade in cinnamon to maximize profits. The king was reduced to the status of client. Work on cinnamon plantations was not as difficult a livelihood as gem mining or pearl diving, but Dutch work demands were rigorous and punishments harsh for even light offenses. Dissatisfaction with the VOC administrators ran deep. The British took over Ceylon in 1796 following the collapse of the VOC, but their management of the cinnamon economy was not as careful or exacting, and both price and quality fell. Ceylon's export sector would be revived after 1800 with the introduction of American tropical crops adapted by British botanists: cinchona (quinine), cacao, and rubber.

QUESTIONS TO CONSIDER

1. How was cinnamon grown, harvested, and prepared for export?

2. How did cinnamon harvesting fit into traditional, pre-colonial landholding and labor systems?

3. How did Dutch rule change the lives and livelihoods of cinnamon harvesters? Of Sri Lanka (Ceylon) in general?

For Further Information:

Valentijn, François. *Description of Ceylon,* ed. Sinnappah Arasaratnam. London: Hakluyt Society, 1978 [orig. publ. 1720].

Winius, George D. *The Fatal History of Portuguese Ceylon: Transition to Dutch Rule.* New York: Cambridge University Press, 1971.

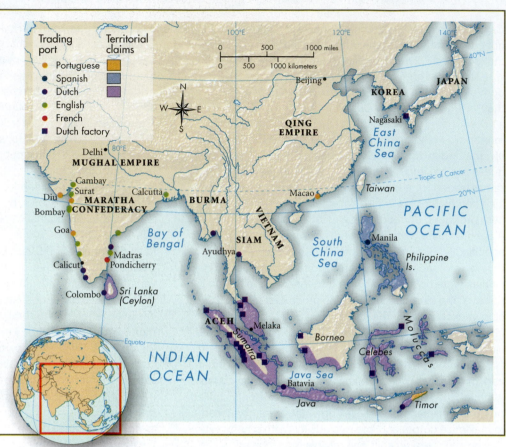

MAP 19.4

Dutch and English Colonies in South and Southeast Asia, to 1750

Although the Portuguese remained active in the Indian Ocean basin and South China Sea until the twentieth century, after 1600 the Dutch and English had largely displaced them. The East India Companies of these two countries sought to conquer and defend key trading enclaves, both against each other and against the later-arriving French. Outside the Spanish Philippines, only the Dutch managed to establish a significant land empire before 1750. In the hands of the company, or VOC, Dutch holdings grew to encompass most of Indonesia. The English and French would follow suit in South and Southeast Asia in subsequent decades.

The VOC, like other Indian Ocean traders, relied on a steady supply of Spanish-American silver to lubricate commerce. Between 1600 and 1648, when these rival empires were at war, some silver was plundered from the Spanish in the Caribbean by Dutch pirates, but most was extracted through trade, both official and contraband. Recent research has revealed the importance of illegal Dutch slave traders in Buenos Aires after a major peace agreement was signed with Spain in 1648. The silver of Potosí in this case bypassed Europe entirely to go to Dutch trading posts in India, Southeast Asia, and China. Mexican silver, meanwhile, flowed out of Dutch Caribbean ports such as Curaçao, through Amsterdam, and into the holds of outbound company ships. Trade in Manila extracted still more Spanish silver. Though ever more divided in its political loyalties, the world was becoming ever more unified in its monetary system.

English East India Company

Compared with the VOC, the English East India Company (EIC), founded two years earlier in 1600, had more modest aims and much less capital. Nevertheless, it used brute force and a royal charter to displace the Portuguese in several strategic ports, especially around the Arabian peninsula and on the coasts of India. Given England's civil wars and other internal problems in the seventeenth century (discussed in the next chapter), progress was slow and uneven. Only in the late seventeenth century did English traders in India begin to amass considerable fortunes, mostly by exporting spices, gems, and cloth from their modest fortresses at Surat, Bombay, Madras, and Calcutta (see again Map 19.4). Like the VOC, however, the EIC grew increasingly powerful over time, eventually taking on a blatantly imperial role.

Two very different individuals from the turn of the eighteenth century illustrate the slow but steady ascent of the English East India Company. Elihu Yale, a native New Englander whose book collection was used to establish a college in Connecticut in his name, rose from the position of Company clerk to serve for over a dozen years as the

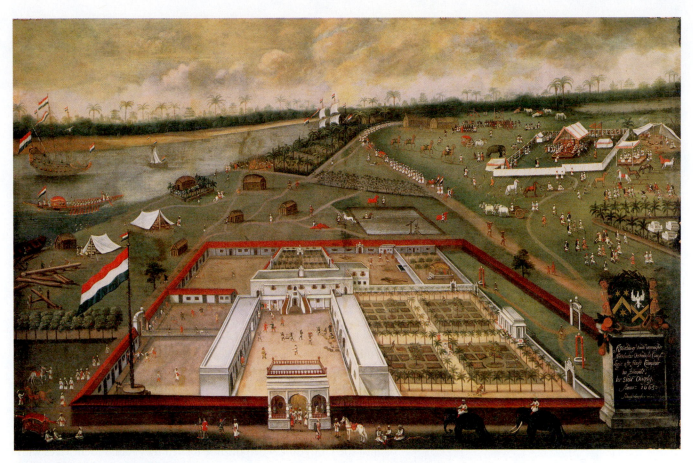

Dutch Headquarters in Bengal

This painting from 1665 depicts the Dutch East India Company (VOC) trading fort at Hugly, on the banks of the Ganges River branch of the same name in the Indian province of Bengal. As they did elsewhere along the rim of the rich and populous Indian Ocean basin, the Dutch sought to establish exclusive control over specific commodities, usually after driving out the Portuguese. In Bengal, the main export items were fine cotton print fabrics, which, along with a variety of products already circulating in the region, they traded mostly for Spanish-American silver. The VOC would eventually be displaced by the English East India Company. (Courtesy of Rijksmuseum, Amsterdam, The Netherlands.)

governor of the East India Company's fort at Madras. He quickly learned to exploit his post to export cloth, pepper, saltpeter, opium, and diamonds. Upon his return to England in 1699, Yale was the contemporary equivalent of a multimillionaire. Although he never visited New Haven, his philanthropic capital, skimmed from East India Company profits, was piously invested in colonial higher education.

At about the same time, England's Admiralty, under pressure from EIC investors, commissioned a Scottish-born but New York City–based privateer named William Kidd to search for English pirates interfering with Company-protected trade in the Indian Ocean, especially in the Red Sea. Instead, Kidd foolishly attacked and plundered a Mughal-sponsored merchantman off the southwest coast of India. Now a pirate himself, Kidd fled to Madagascar in the stolen vessel, then across the Atlantic to the Caribbean. Eventually, Kidd tried to contact his wife in New York, but he was captured and sent in chains to Boston, then London. At the urging of East India Company officials, whose friendship with Emperor Aurangzeb had been severely strained by the renegade pirate hunter's actions, Kidd was hanged in 1701. The company's interests in distant seas were, it seems, increasingly the government's.

COUNTERPOINT
Aceh: Fighting Back in Southeast Asia

FOCUS

Why was the tiny sultanate of Aceh able to hold out against European interlopers in early modern times?

The province and city of Aceh (AH-cheh), at the northwest tip of the island of Sumatra in Indonesia, was transformed but not conquered in early modern times. Like many trading enclaves linked by the Indian Ocean's predictable monsoon winds, Aceh was a Muslim sultanate that lived by exchanging the produce of its interior, in this case black pepper, for the many commodities supplied by other, distant kingdoms. Aceh's rulers participated directly in trade, dictating its terms and enjoying many of its benefits. Yet unlike most such enclaves, which fell like dominoes to European interlopers, Aceh held out. For a variety of reasons, but perhaps most importantly a newfound religious fervor, the Acehnese defeated a long string of would-be conquistadors.

The Differing Fortunes of Aceh and Melaka

Aceh's rulers were probably related to those of the less fortunate Malay trading city of Melaka. Melaka was a former fishing village with a fine natural harbor and highly strategic location on the east end of the narrow Melaka Strait. It was said to have been founded by a Hindu prince who converted to Islam in around 1420. Melaka's rulers forged deft, profitable alliances to regions as far away as China, but ties to the interior were weak, drawing predators. Melaka was attacked repeatedly by Javanese sultans, and in the end it fell to Portuguese cannons in 1511. Although Melakan forces had guns of their own and fought valiantly against the Europeans, when the tide turned they found themselves without a backcountry into which guerrilla warriors might flee and reorganize. The Dutch followed in 1641, displacing the Portuguese.

Unlike Melaka, Aceh's influence reached deep into the interior and across hundreds of miles of coast. After defeating Portuguese invaders in 1518, Aceh emerged as one of the most assertive seaborne Islamic states in the entire Indian Ocean, tapping military aid from the distant Ottomans and shipping considerable quantities of pepper to the Mediterranean via the Red Sea. But Aceh's repeated efforts to conquer Portuguese-controlled Melaka failed, and by the late seventeenth century the kingdom declined as both a political and commercial force. Still, it was not until the late nineteenth century that the Dutch reduced Aceh to colonial status.

Aceh, "the Veranda of Mecca"

Aceh

Islamic Identity

Aceh's early modern history has been gleaned from a variety of outside sources, and also local, sometimes official, chronicles, including epic poems written in Malay and Acehnese in the sixteenth and seventeenth centuries to celebrate the deeds of its sultans. Although poets tended to exaggerate the greatness of their patrons and to conflate or compress events, the epics express Acehnese Islamic pride, mostly as the region's bulwark against the militant Christian Portuguese. Ottoman, Portuguese, Dutch, and English sources note that Aceh was a great meeting place for Southeast Asian pilgrims on their way to Mecca, and it came to be known as *Serambi Mekkah*, the Veranda of Mecca.

Despite its intensely Islamic identity, Acehnese culture respected female independence. Women controlled and inherited nearly all property, from houses to rice fields, and at marriage men moved to their wives' households. Men in fact spent much of their time

Dutch Merchants Learn How to Act in Aceh

In this passage, originally composed in the Malay language just after 1600, a Dutch merchant in Aceh created a dialogue between an imaginary European visitor, "Daud," and a local informant, "Ibrahim." The sample exchange was meant to instruct future Dutch visitors. Should they come to Aceh for business, they would know something of the cultural intricacies of local exchange, and also how to ask about them. This passage describes the formal reception of a Gujarati merchant from western India by the local raja. Every detail of court etiquette was critical. To make mistakes in the course of observing and participating in these rituals, particularly when one had little knowledge of local languages, was to risk permanent expulsion, and in some cases death.

Daud: Who is it coming on this great elephant, who has such a crowd of people behind him?

Ibrahim: It is the Shahbandar with the Penghulu kerkun [secretary].

Daud: I also see some foreign traders sitting up there. Who are they?

Ibrahim: That is a Gujarati *nakhoda* [merchant], who has just come with his ship, and whom they are going to take to salute the raja.

Daud: What does it mean, that elephant caparisoned in red cloth, with those people in front of it playing on tambourines, trumpets, and flutes?

Ibrahim: The elephant you see and the man sitting in a palanquin [curtained couch] upon it, means that a letter is being brought from their raja to our lord. . . .

Daud: Who is seated up there?

Ibrahim: It is one of the sultan's *orangkaya* [courtier], that he has chosen for that.

Daud: And what is all that for?

Ibrahim: To honor the raja whose letter it is.

Daud: And what is that I see, so many men and slaves, each bringing a painted cloth in his hands?

Ibrahim: These are the presents which the nakhoda will offer to the king.

Daud: Is that the tariff he must pay for his goods, or must he pay another tariff?

Ibrahim: No, the tariff is extra, seven percent.

Daud: What honor will the raja give them in return?

Ibrahim: Indeed, when they enter the raja's palace, they will be given great honor.

Daud: What happens there?

Ibrahim: There they eat and drink, all sorts of food and fruits are brought, they play, dance, with all sorts of entertainments, they play on the trumpet, flute, clarinet, and *rebab,* and then the king asks for a garment of our local style to be brought, which he gives to the nakhoda.

Source: Frederick de Houtman, 1603, quoted in of Anthony Reid, *Southeast Asia in the Age of Commerce* (New Haven: Yale University Press, 1993), 2: 237–238. Credit: Anthony Reid. *Southeast Asia in the Age of Commerce*, Volume 2. Yale University Press, 1993. Copyright © Yale University Press, 1993. Used by permission of the publisher.

EXAMINING THE EVIDENCE

1. What does this dialogue suggest about the balance of power in Aceh?

2. What does it reveal about the interplay of rulership and trade?

---

away on business or engaged in religious study, leaving women in charge of most aspects of everyday life. Pre-Islamic kin structures governed daily affairs, while *ulama*, or religious scholars, oversaw matters of business and state. Criminal cases reveal that local custom could override Islamic prescriptions, especially when it came to capital punishment. The result was a somewhat mild, woman-friendly Southeast Asian blend of secular and religious life reminiscent of West Africa.

Aceh was immediately recognized as a powerful state by northern European visitors in the early seventeenth century. The first Dutch envoys were jailed from 1599 to 1601 for

Trade and Diplomacy

mishandling court etiquette (see Reading the Past: Dutch Merchants Learn How to Act in Aceh), but soon after, English visitors representing Queen Elizabeth I and the newly chartered East India Company made a better impression. Of particular interest to the Acehnese shah was Dutch and English hostility to Portugal, which also sent ambassadors. Playing competing Europeans off one another soon became an absorbing and sometimes profitable game. And the Europeans were by no means alone—sizable trading and diplomatic missions arrived in Aceh from eastern and western India, Burma, and Siam. Sultan Iskandar Muda used English and Dutch traders to drive the Gujaratis out of the pepper trade in the 1610s, only to force the Europeans out of it in the 1620s. He continued to ship pepper to Red Sea intermediaries, but steadily lost market share to both English and Dutch merchants, who turned to other Southeast Asian sources.

Sultanate of Women

Aceh's decline has been traditionally associated with the rise of female sultans in the seventeenth century, much as occurred in the Ottoman Empire at about the same time (as we will see in Chapter 20). Sultana Taj al-Alam Safiyat al-Din Shah ruled from 1641 to 1675. She was the daughter of the renowned conqueror and deft handler of foreign envoys, Iskandar Muda Shah (r. 1607–1636), but her politics focused mostly on domestic affairs, in part because Aceh was in a period of restructuring after her father's failed 1629 attack on Portuguese Melaka. Like her counterparts in Istanbul and Agra, Safiyat al-Din was a great patron of artists and scholars. Under her sponsorship, Acehnese displaced Malay as the language of state and the arts.

Safiyat al-Din was succeeded by three more sultanas, the last of whom, Kamalat Shah, was deposed following a 1699 decree, or **fatwa**, from Mecca declaring women unfit to serve as sultans. Careful reading of sources suggests that female sultans were not the cause of Aceh's declining power in the region, but rather a symptom of a general shift toward the Malay style of divine kingship. Even in decline, Aceh held out throughout early modern times and beyond against European attempts to subject it to colonial rule.

Conclusion

Thanks to reliable monsoon winds, the vast Indian Ocean basin had long been interconnected by ties of trade and religion, and this general pattern continued throughout early modern times. The region's countless farmers depended as they had for millennia on the monsoon rains.

Change came, however, with the rise of gunpowder-fueled empires both on land and at sea. Beginning about 1500, seaborne Europeans forcibly took over key ports and began taxing the trade of others, while Islamic warriors on horseback blasted resistant sultans and rajas into tribute-paying submission in South and Southwest Asia. Smaller sultanates and kingdoms also adopted gunpowder weapons after 1500, both to defend themselves against invaders and to attack weaker neighbors. Although such armed conflict could be deadly or at least disrupt everyday life, for most ordinary people in the long run it meant a rise in tribute demands, and in some places a turn to forced cultivation of export products such as cinnamon or pepper.

Despite the advances of increasingly belligerent Islamic and Christian empires throughout the Indian Ocean, most inhabitants, including India's 100 million-plus Mughal subjects, did not convert. Religious tolerance had long been the rule in this culturally complex region, and although the Portuguese were driven by an almost crusading fervor to spread Catholicism, in the end they were forced to deal with Hindus, Buddhists, Jews, and Muslims to make a profit. Later Europeans, most of them Protestants, scarcely bothered to proselytize prior to modern times, choosing instead to offer themselves as religiously neutral intermediaries, unlike the intolerant Portuguese.

fatwa A decree issued by Islamic religious officials.

The Mughals, like the kings of Vijayanagara before them, followed a tradition of divinely aloof religious tolerance, although conversion to the state faith had its benefits, particularly in trade. Emperor Akbar went so far as to create his own hybrid cult, although it never took root, and in the provinces Sikhism emerged as an alternative to Hinduism or Islam. As with Christianity, Islamic practices varied greatly throughout this vast region, and these differences were visible in customs of female mobility, dress, and access to positions of power. Nur Jahan represented a temporary period of Mughal openness to feminine power and public expression, and Aceh's Sultanate of the Women represented another in Southeast Asia.

Europeans sought to adapt to local cultures of trade when using force was impractical. For most of the early modern period, they had no choice, at least outside their tiny, fortressed towns. Only with the decline of great land empires such as that of the Mughals in the eighteenth century did this begin to change. Though it happened much more slowly than in contemporary Latin America or western Africa, by the end of the early modern period European imperial designs had begun to alter established lifeways throughout the Indian Ocean region. Expansion into the interior, first by overseas trading companies such as the English East India Company and the Dutch VOC, would grow in the nineteenth century into full-blown imperialism. Only a few outliers, such as the Muslim revivalist sultanate of Aceh, managed to hold out, and even their time would come.

NOTES

1. Marshall Hodgson, *The Venture of Islam,* 2 vols. (Chicago: University of Chicago Press, 1974), 2: 34.
2. Robert Sewell, *A Forgotten Empire (Vijayanagar): A Contribution to the History of India* (London: Sonnenschein, 1900), 245.
3. Thackston Wheeler, ed. and trans., *The Baburnama: Memoirs of Babur, Prince and Emperor* (Washington, D.C.: Smithsonian Institution, 1996), 326, 384.
4. Vasco da Gama, *The Diary of His Travels Through African Waters, 1497–1499,* ed. and trans. Eric Axelson (Somerset, U.K.: Stephan Phillips, 1998), 45.

RESOURCES FOR RESEARCH

General Works

The Indian Ocean has recently become a unit of study on par with the Atlantic and Mediterranean, but synthetic interpretations are still few. For the early modern period, Barendse's synthesis is essential.

Barendse, R. J. *The Arabian Seas: The Indian Ocean World of the Seventeenth Century.* 2002.

Risso, Patricia. *Merchants and Faith: Muslim Commerce and Culture in the Indian Ocean.* 1995.

The Sultan Qaboos Cultural Center at Washington D.C.'s Middle East Cultural Center maintains a superb site on the Indian Ocean in world history at http://www.indianoceanhistory .org/.

The University of Wisconsin's Center for South Asia maintains a Web site with links to texts, timelines, maps, and other materials relevant to the study of South Asia and the Indian Ocean. http://www.southasia.wisc.edu/resources.html.

Trading Cities and Inland Networks: East Africa

The following authors are among the leading specialists writing on early modern East Africa, including in their work both African and Portuguese perspectives.

Newitt, Malyn. *A History of Portuguese Overseas Expansion, 1400–1668.* 2005.

Pearson, Michael N. *Port Cities and Intruders: The Swahili Coast, India, and Portugal in the Early Modern Era.* 1998.

Trade and Empire in South Asia

The literature on maritime India is vast and growing, but the following works offer a good sense of both the questions being pursued and the types of sources available. Whereas works on Vijayanagara are few, and based mostly on art and archaeology, document-based studies on Mughal India have multiplied more rapidly than for any of the other gunpowder empires.

Dale, Stephen. *Indian Merchants and Eurasian Trade, 1600–1750.* 1994.

Mukhia, Harbans. *The Mughals of India.* 2004.

Pearson, Michael N. *The Portuguese in India* (The New Cambridge History of India, Part 1, vol. 1). 1987.

Schimmel, Annemarie. *The Empire of the Mughals: History, Art, and Culture.* Translated by Corinne Attwood. 2004.

Stein, Burton. *Vijayanagara.* 2005.

European Interlopers

The literature on Europe's "East India Companies" and related enterprises is voluminous, but recent work has attempted to go beyond a focus on business and bureaucracy to fathom cross-cultural meanings.

Boyajian, James C. *Portuguese Trade in Asia Under the Habsburgs, 1580–1640.* 1993.

Chaudhury, Sushil, and Michel Morineau, eds. *Merchants, Companies, and Trade: Europe and Asia in the Early Modern Era.* 1999.

Gaastra, Femme S. *The Dutch East India Company: Expansion and Decline.* 2003.

Keay, John. *The Honourable Company: A History of the East India Company.* 1993.

Ritchie, Robert C. *Captain Kidd and the War Against the Pirates.* 1986.

COUNTERPOINT: Aceh: Fighting Back in Southeast Asia

Work on the early modern history of island Southeast Asia has ballooned in recent years. The following authors treat Aceh in this wider context.

Lockard, Craig. *Southeast Asia in World History.* 2009.

Reid, Anthony. *Southeast Asia in the Age of Commerce.* 2 vols. 1988.

Reid, Anthony, ed. *Southeast Asia in the Early Modern Era: Trade, Power, and Belief.* 1993.

Reid, Anthony, ed. *Verandah of Violence: The Background to the Aceh Problem.* 2006.

▶ **For additional primary sources from this period**, see *Sources of Crossroads and Cultures*.

▶ **For Web sites, images, and documents related to topics in this chapter**, see Make History at bedfordstmartins.com/smith.

The major global development in this chapter ▶ The Indian Ocean trading network and the impact of European intrusion on maritime and mainland South Asia.

IMPORTANT EVENTS

1336–1565	Vijayanagara kingdom in southern India
1498	Vasco da Gama reaches India
1500–1763	Mughal Empire in South Asia
1509–1529	Reign of Krishna Deva Raya of Vijayanagara
1510	Portuguese conquest of Goa, India
1511	Portuguese conquest of Melaka
1517	Portuguese establish fort in Sri Lanka (Ceylon)
1526	Battle of Panipat led by Mughal emperor Babur
1530	Consolidation of Aceh under Sultan Ali Mughayat Shah
1556–1605	Reign of Mughal emperor Akbar
1567	Akbar's siege of Chitor
1600	English East India Company founded in London
1602	Dutch East India Company (VOC) founded in Amsterdam
1605–1627	Reign of Mughal emperor Jahangir
1641	Dutch take Melaka from Portuguese
1641–1699	Sultanate of Women in Aceh
1658	Dutch drive Portuguese from Ceylon
1701	William Kidd hanged in London for piracy
1739	Persian raiders under Nadir Shah sack Delhi
1764	English East India Company controls Bengal

KEY TERMS

Brahman (p. 622)
caste (p. 622)
dhow (p. 619)
fatwa (p. 642)
Kshatriya (p. 622)

monsoon (p. 615)
sati (p. 630)
trading companies (p. 635)

CHAPTER OVERVIEW QUESTIONS

1. What environmental, religious, and political factors enabled trading enclaves to flourish in the Indian Ocean basin?

2. How did the rise and fall of India's land empires reflect larger regional trends?

3. How did Europeans insert themselves into the Indian Ocean trading network, and what changes did they bring about?

SECTION FOCUS QUESTIONS

1. How did Swahili Coast traders link the East African interior to the Indian Ocean basin?

2. What factors account for the fall of Vijayanagara and the rise of the Mughals?

3. What factors enabled Europeans to take over key Indian Ocean trade networks?

4. Why was the tiny sultanate of Aceh able to hold out against European interlopers in early modern times?

MAKING CONNECTIONS

1. In what ways did Indian Ocean trade differ from the contemporary Atlantic slave trade (see Chapter 18)? What role did Africa play in each?

2. How did traditional kingdoms such as Vijayanagara differ from those of the Americas prior to the Spanish conquest (see Chapter 16)?

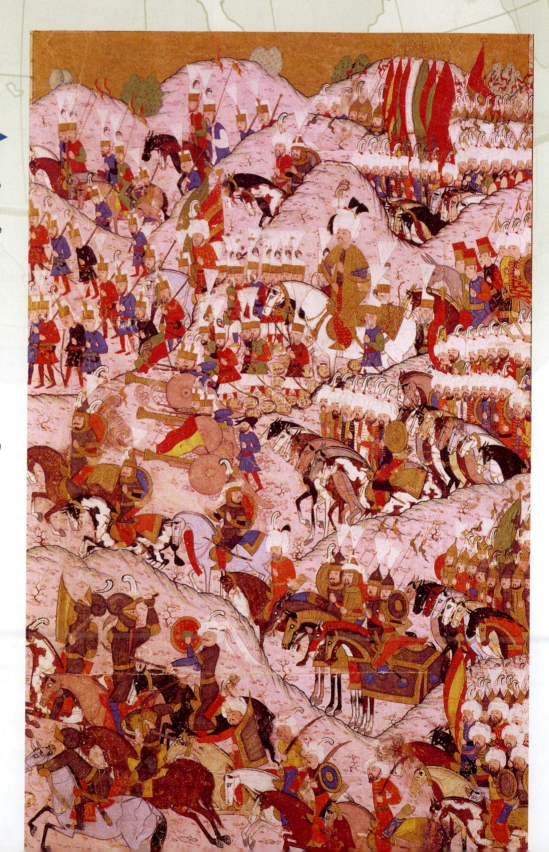

20

AT A CROSSROADS ▶

Court artists painted this 1588 Ottoman miniature to illustrate Suleiman the Magnificent's 1526 victory over Christian forces at the Battle of Mohacs, which left Hungary without a monarch and divided between the Habsburg and Ottoman empires. Traditional cavalry forces face off in the left foreground, but most prominent is the sultan himself in the upper right, on a white horse just behind a line of large Ottoman cannon. (Topkapi Palace Museum, Istanbul/ Giraudon/Bridgeman Art Library.)

Consolidation and Conflict in Europe and the Greater Mediterranean

1450–1750

In 1590, forty-three-year-old Miguel de Cervantes Saavedra, an office clerk working in the Spanish city of Seville, applied for a colonial service job in South America. Such assignments usually went to applicants with nobler connections than Cervantes enjoyed, but perhaps he hoped his military service would count in his favor. Cervantes had been wounded in a major naval conflict, the Battle of Lepanto, in 1571, fighting against the mighty Ottomans. He also suffered five years of captivity in Algiers as the prisoner of North Africa's Barbary pirates. Despite all of this, he was turned down.

Before taking up his desk job in Seville, Cervantes had tried his hand at writing, publishing a modestly successful novel in 1585. Spain at this time was a literary leader in Europe. The novels, plays, and poems of Spain's "Golden Century" drew on medieval models, but they were both enriched and transformed by the changes resulting from overseas colonization and religious upheavals. Playwrights and poets rewrote the conquests of the Aztecs and Incas as tragedies, and one writer, "El Inca" Garcilaso de la Vega, son of a Spanish conquistador and an Inca princess, thrilled his Spanish readers with tales of a

BACKSTORY

Europe and the greater Mediterranean basin gradually recovered from the devastating Black Death of 1347–1350 (see Chapter 15), but the inhabitants of this geographically divided region faced many challenges at the start of the early modern period. Christian Europeans grew increasingly intolerant of religious diversity. In the most extreme case, Iberian Muslims and Jews were forced to convert to Catholicism or leave the peninsula after 1492, prompting a great diaspora, or scattering, largely into Morocco and Ottoman lands, but also into Italy, France, and northern Europe. Resource-poor and avid for Asian trade goods and precious metals, western Europeans raced to develop new technologies of war and long-distance transport to compete with one another as well as with non-Europeans abroad. In contrast, the Muslim Ottomans of the eastern Mediterranean had been expanding their tributary land empire since the fourteenth century. By the later fifteenth century they would take to the sea to extend their conquests into the Mediterranean and the Indian Ocean.

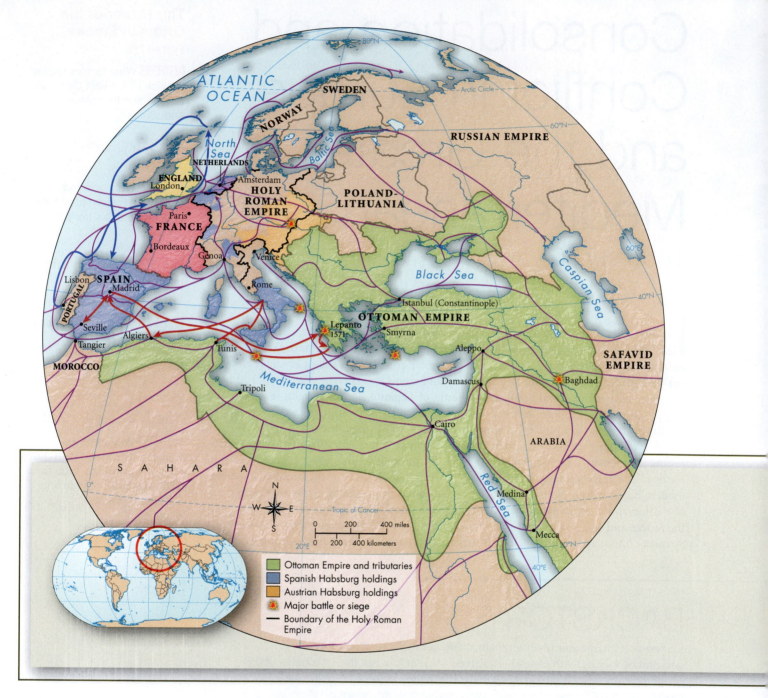

Ottoman Empire and tributaries
Spanish Habsburg holdings
Austrian Habsburg holdings
Major battle or siege
Boundary of the Holy Roman Empire

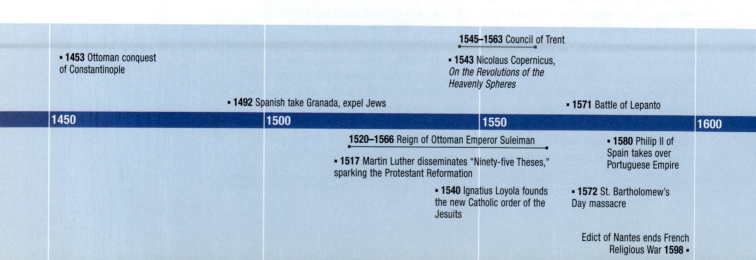

1545–1563 Council of Trent

1453 Ottoman conquest of Constantinople

1543 Nicolaus Copernicus, *On the Revolutions of the Heavenly Spheres*

1492 Spanish take Granada, expel Jews

1571 Battle of Lepanto

1450	1500	1550	1600

1520–1566 Reign of Ottoman Emperor Suleiman

1580 Philip II of Spain takes over Portuguese Empire

1517 Martin Luther disseminates "Ninety-five Theses," sparking the Protestant Reformation

1540 Ignatius Loyola founds the new Catholic order of the Jesuits

1572 St. Bartholomew's Day massacre

Edict of Nantes ends French Religious War **1598**

vanished Inca paradise. He based his best-selling *Royal Commentaries of the Incas*, composed in the Spanish countryside, on stories told by his mother in Cuzco.

Cervantes never crossed the Atlantic, but he found plenty to inspire him in the vibrant crossroads city of Seville, Spain's largest city with over one hundred thousand inhabitants. Yet as Cervantes' 1605 masterpiece, *Don Quixote*, revealed, it was the author's experiences as a prisoner in Algiers that most prepared him to bridge cultures and upend literary conventions. Although regarded as the quintessential Spanish novel—set in the Spanish countryside, with poor Catholic villagers as its central characters—*Don Quixote* includes long passages describing the many peoples, especially forced converts to Christianity from Islam and renegade Christians living in North Africa, who routinely crossed borders and seas, risking their lives to find love or maintain family fortunes. Cervantes died in 1616, in the midst of a brief truce between Spain and its greatest rival of the day, the emerging Dutch Republic. "El Inca" Garcilaso died the same year.

Europe and the greater Mediterranean in the age of Cervantes was, like the Indian Ocean basin, home to diverse peoples who had long been linked by deep and multifaceted connections. Yet it was increasingly divided by political, religious, and ethnic conflict. Christians fought Jews and Muslims, and, in the movements known as the Protestant and Catholic reformations, one another. Emerging national identities based on language and shared religion began to harden, even as local and regional trade increased. Christian Europe viewed Ottoman expansion with alarm, and fear of growing Muslim power contributed to rising tension and conflict between Christians and Muslims. Piracy flourished from the Atlantic to the Indian Ocean, and war raged from the Low Countries to the Balkans, eventually engulfing nearly all of Europe by 1618. In the course of the Thirty Years' War that followed, Catholics and Protestants, led by ambitious princes, slaughtered each other by the tens of thousands. Economic woes compounded the chaos, exacerbated by a sudden drop in silver revenues from

MAPPING THE WORLD
Europe and the Greater Mediterranean, c. 1600

The Mediterranean was an ancient global crossroads, and its role in connecting Africa, Asia, and Europe only intensified during early modern times. After 1450, African gold and Spanish-American silver lubricated trade, but they also financed warfare, notably an increasingly bitter rivalry between the Ottoman and Habsburg empires. The period also witnessed the rise of the so-called Barbary pirates, based mostly in Algiers, Tunis, and Tripoli, who offered only a tenuous allegiance to the Ottomans against their Christian foes. Mediterranean trade, sea routes to the Indian Ocean, and overland routes to East Asia were all increasingly tied to Europe's North Atlantic trade. As trade grew, conflict became ever more intense.

ROUTES ▼

— Major trade route

→ Voyages of Miguel de Cervantes Saavedra, c. 1571–1609

→ Route of the Spanish Armada, 1588

1618–1648 Thirty Years' War

1642–1646 English Civil War

1687 Isaac Newton, *Principia Mathematica*

1688 Glorious Revolution in England

1650   1700   1750

1643–1715 Reign of Louis XIV of France

1640 Portugal wins independence from Spain

1683 Ottomans defeated in Vienna by Polish-Austrian alliance

1701–1714 War of the Spanish Succession

the mines of Spanish America. Prolonged cold weather led to a cycle of failed harvests. Amid growing anxiety, large-scale rebellions broke out from Scotland to the Persian frontier.

Out of this prolonged period of religious, political, and economic instability, which some historians have labeled the "seventeenth-century crisis," came profound and eventually world-changing innovations in science, government, and the economy. The combination of growing religious skepticism, deep interest in the physical world sparked by overseas discoveries, and new optical technologies led a small cluster of European intellectuals to turn to scientific inquiry, initiating what later would be hailed as a "scientific revolution." Political innovations included absolutism and constitutionalism, two novel approaches to monarchy. Whatever their political form, nearly all of Europe's competing states engaged in overseas expansion, using the Atlantic as a gateway to the wider world. With the support of their governments, merchants and investors in western Europe launched new efforts to challenge the long-established global claims of the Spanish and Portuguese.

Christian Europe's overseas expansion was driven in part by the rise of its powerful Sunni Muslim neighbor, the Ottoman Empire. The Ottoman state, which by 1550 straddled Europe, the Middle East, North Africa, Arabia, and parts of Central Asia, was strategically located between three vast and ancient maritime trade zones. To the west lay the Mediterranean, Atlantic, and all of Europe; to the east and north, the Silk Road and Black Sea region; and to the south, East Africa, Arabia, and the vast Indian Ocean basin. Along with such major commercial crossroads as Istanbul (formerly Constantinople), Aleppo, and Cairo, the Ottomans controlled key religious pilgrimage sites, including Mecca and Jerusalem. No early modern European state approached the Ottomans' size, military might, or cultural and religious diversity, and no contemporary Islamic empire, not even the mighty Mughals, did as much to offset rising Christian European sea power. The Ottomans were arguably the most versatile of the early modern "gunpowder empires."

OVERVIEW
QUESTIONS

The major global development in this chapter: Early modern Europe's increasing competition and division in the face of Ottoman expansion.

As you read, consider:

1. To what degree was religious diversity embraced or rejected in early modern Europe and the greater Mediterranean, and why?

2. How did Christian Europe's gunpowder-fueled empires compare with that of the Ottomans?

3. What accounts for the rise of science and capitalism in early modern western Europe?

The Power of the Ottoman Empire 1453–1750

FOCUS

What factors explain the rise of the vast Ottoman Empire and its centuries-long endurance?

Founded by mounted Turkic warriors in the early fourteenth century, the Ottoman Empire grew rapidly after its stunning 1453 capture of the Byzantine capital, Constantinople (see Chapter 15). As in Mughal India, gunpowder weapons introduced by Christian Europeans sped the Ottomans' rise and helped them spread their dominions deep into Europe as well as the Middle East and North Africa. The Ottomans also took to the sea, challenging the Venetians, Habsburgs, and other contenders in the Mediterranean, as well as the Portuguese in the Indian Ocean. But it was arguably clever governance, minimal trade restrictions, and religious tolerance, not gunpowder weapons or naval proficiency, that permitted this most durable of Islamic empires to survive until the early twentieth century.

Tools of Empire

As we saw in Chapter 15, Mehmed II's conquest in 1453 of Constantinople not only shocked the Christian world but also marked a dramatic shift in the Ottoman enterprise. The sultans no longer viewed themselves as the roving holy warriors of Osman's day. Instead, they took on the identity of Islamic rulers with supreme authority over a multinational empire at the crossroads of Europe and Asia.

Devshirme System

Like other expansive realms, the Ottoman state faced the challenge of governing its frontier regions. To maintain control over the provinces, the Ottomans drew on the janissary corps, elite infantry and bureaucrats who owed direct allegiance to the sultan. Within a century of the capture of Constantinople, the janissaries were recruited nearly exclusively through the *devshirme* (dev-SHEER-may), the conscription of Christian youths from eastern Europe. Chosen for their good looks and fine physiques, these boys were converted to Islam and sent to farms to learn Turkish and to build up their bodies. The most promising were sent to Istanbul to learn Ottoman military, religious, and administrative techniques. Trained in Ottoman ways, educated in the use of advanced weaponry, and shorn of all family connections, the young men recruited through the devshirme were thus prepared to serve as janissaries wholly beholden to the sultan and dedicated to his service. In later years the janissaries would directly challenge the sultan's power, but for much of the early modern era, these crack soldiers and able administrators extended and supported Ottoman rule. A few rose to the rank of Grand Vizier (roughly, "Prime Minister").

Timar System

The *timar* system of land grants given in compensation for military service was another key means through which the Ottomans managed the provinces while ensuring that armed forces remained powerful. It was similar to Mughal India's *parganas* and Spanish America's *encomiendas* in that all three imperial systems were put in place to reward frontier warriors while preventing them from becoming independent aristocrats. Sultans snatched timars and gave them to others when their holders failed to serve in ongoing wars, an incentive to keep fighting. Even in times of stability, the timars were referred to as "the fruits of war." Timar-holders slowly turned new territories into provinces. Able administrators were rewarded with governorships. Although the timar and devshirme systems changed over time, it was these early innovations in frontier governance and military recruitment that stabilized and buttressed Ottoman rule in the face of succession crises, regional rebellions, natural disasters, and other shocks.

Expansion and Consolidation

Mehmed II's 1453 capture of Constantinople earned him the nickname "Conqueror." By 1464, Mehmed had added Athens, Serbia, and Bosnia to the Ottoman domain, and by 1475, the Golden Horde khanate of the Crimean peninsula was paying tribute to the Ottomans (see Map 20.1). In the Mediterranean, powerful Venice was put on notice that its days of dominance were coming to an end, and the Genoese were driven from their trading posts in the Black Sea. In 1480 the Ottomans attacked Otranto, in southern Italy, and in 1488 they struck Malta, a key Mediterranean island between Sicily and North Africa. At the imperial center, Constantinople, now named Istanbul, became a reflection of Mehmed's power, and also his piety. The city's horizon was soon dotted with hundreds of domes and minarets. With over one hundred thousand

devshirme The Ottomans' conscription of Christian male youths from eastern Europe to serve in the military or administration.

timar A land grant given in compensation for military service by the Ottoman sultan to a soldier.

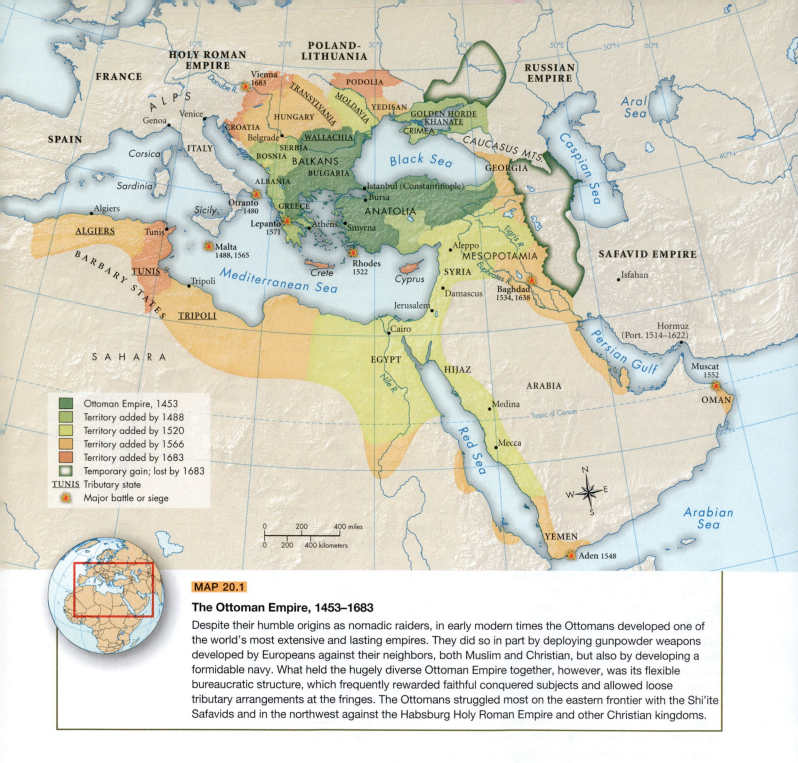

MAP 20.1

The Ottoman Empire, 1453–1683

Despite their humble origins as nomadic raiders, in early modern times the Ottomans developed one of the world's most extensive and lasting empires. They did so in part by deploying gunpowder weapons developed by Europeans against their neighbors, both Muslim and Christian, but also by developing a formidable navy. What held the hugely diverse Ottoman Empire together, however, was its flexible bureaucratic structure, which frequently rewarded faithful conquered subjects and allowed loose tributary arrangements at the fringes. The Ottomans struggled most on the eastern frontier with the Shi'ite Safavids and in the northwest against the Habsburg Holy Roman Empire and other Christian kingdoms.

inhabitants by the time of the sultan's death in 1481, Istanbul was one of the largest capitals in Eurasia.

The Ottomans turned newly obtained European artillery and highly trained janissary fighters on Islamic neighbors such as the Safavids and Mamluks in Syria and Egypt. Under Selim I (r. 1512–1520), called "the Grim," both were overwhelmed, although the Safavids would continue to challenge Ottoman power. Ottoman influence now touched the shores of the Indian Ocean, where Selim and the Ottomans challenged Portuguese expansion. The Muslim holy cities of Medina and Mecca became Ottoman protectorates, a boon for the state's religious reputation. Ottoman control of the Arabian peninsula would not be challenged until the end of the eighteenth century by the Wahhabi Saudis (discussed in Chapter 23).

Reign of Suleiman the Magnificent

Christian Europe again felt the sting of Ottoman artillery under Selim's successor, Suleiman (soo-lay-MAHN) (r. 1520–1566), called "the Magnificent." Suleiman ended

Istanbul's Skyline

When the former Constantinople became the capital of the Ottoman Empire, its rulers and court patrons soon transformed its architecture and overall skyline. The domes in the foreground make up part of the formerly Christian basilica Hagia Sophia, which was transformed into a mosque after 1453. In the distance rises Istanbul's imposing Blue Mosque, built between 1609 and 1616 for Sultan Ahmed I. (Photo by Ketan Gajria.)

the first year of his reign with the capture of two more symbolic prizes, Belgrade and Rhodes. The former feat gave Suleiman near-total control of eastern Europe, and the latter gave him effective rule over the eastern Mediterranean. In the western Mediterranean, the sultan supported Muslim pirates such as the Barbarossa brothers of Algiers, who targeted Europeans and held thousands of Christian captives for ransom (see Counterpoint: The Barbary Pirates). In 1565 the Ottomans laid siege to Malta. Though ultimately unsuccessful, this huge expedition provided yet another display of "the Great Turk's" naval capacity.

As the siege of Malta and other gunpowder-fueled seaborne offensives attested, Suleiman was determined to challenge the Habsburg Holy Roman Empire, as was his successor, Selim II (r. 1566–1574). But the Ottomans were dealt a terrible blow in 1571 when Habsburg forces sponsored by Spain's Catholic king Philip II (r. 1556–1598) overpowered Selim's navy at the Battle of Lepanto off the Greek coast (see again Map 20.1). Some six thousand janissaries armed with matchlock handguns faced off against over twenty thousand similarly armed European recruits and missionaries, among them the future author of *Don Quixote*. The Christians prevailed and commemorated their victory against the "infidels" in artwork ranging from painting to tapestry.

Although the Battle of Lepanto marked the beginning of a general decline in Ottoman sea supremacy, Selim II's will was far from broken. His forces managed to capture Tunis and Cyprus, and the navy was quickly rebuilt. A poet praised the sultan's vision:

> If it were not for the body of Sultan Selim,
> This generous king, this source of happiness
> The enemy would have occupied
> The country from one end to the other
> God would not have helped us.
> Neither would he have granted us conquest.[1]

Conflict with the Catholic Habsburgs

Battle with the Habsburgs reached a crescendo with the 1683 siege of Vienna. Ottoman gun technology had kept pace with that of western Europe, and some observers claimed that Ottoman muskets in fact had better range and accuracy than those used by Vienna's defenders. Heavy siege artillery was not employed here on the scale regularly practiced in Persia and Mesopotamia, however, and this may have proved a fatal mistake. Ottoman attempts to mine and blow up Vienna's walls failed just as tens of thousands of allies led by the Polish king arrived to save the day for the Habsburgs. At least fifteen thousand Ottoman troops were killed. Never again would the Ottomans pose a serious threat to Christian Europe.

Conflict with the Shi'ite Safavids

To the east, war with Persia occupied the sultans' attention throughout the sixteenth century. Since 1500, Safavid shahs had incited rebellions against Ottoman rule in outlying provinces, denouncing its Sunni leadership as corrupt and illegitimate. The Ottomans responded by violently persecuting both rebels and many innocents caught in between. Under Suleiman, campaigns against the Safavids in the 1530s and 1540s were mostly successful thanks to new guns, but territorial advances proved difficult to sustain. As one Ottoman eyewitness put it in the 1550s, "The territories called Persia are much less fertile than our country; and further, it is the custom of the inhabitants, when their land is invaded, to lay waste and burn everything, and so force the enemy to retire through lack of food."[2] The Safavids were just far enough away to prove unconquerable, leaving intermediate cities such as Baghdad as the key battlegrounds (see Reading the Past: Weapons of Mass Destruction: Ottomans vs. Persians in Baghdad).

Beginning in the late 1570s, Murad III took advantage of Safavid political instability to expand Ottoman influence beyond the frontier established by Suleiman. By the time a peace was arranged in 1590, the Ottomans controlled Mesopotamia and had established a firm presence in the Caucasus region. Still, the empire was rocked in the decades around 1600 by price inflation caused by a massive influx of Spanish-American silver, which flowed into the empire from Europe in exchange for Ottoman silks and spices. Ottoman attempts to fix prices of basic commodities and reduce the silver content of their coins only worsened the problem, and troops facing food shortages and poor pay rioted.

Some historians have argued that the Ottoman Empire was in decline following the reign of Suleiman the Magnificent, even though expansion continued into the seventeenth century, beginning with a long struggle for Hungary (1593–1606). Like Habsburg Spain, also said to be in decline in this era despite its vast size and wealth, Ottoman efforts to conquer new lands increasingly ended in stalemate, with military expenses far exceeding the value of the territory gained. The crushing weight of rising costs forced sultans and viziers to make humiliating concessions. Among the worst of these were losses to the Safavids that amounted to a total reversal of Murad III's gains. Frontier setbacks were not always evident from the center. Istanbul, with some four hundred thousand inhabitants by this time, was by far Eurasia's largest and most opulent city.

Sultanate of the Women

Murad IV (r. 1623–1640) managed to recapture Baghdad and several other eastern losses, but a crippling succession crisis ensued. Only after 1648 was the matter settled, with seven-year-old Mehmed IV (r. 1648–1687) on the throne. A child emperor required interim rule by regency, and in this case Mehmed's mother, Turhan, took control after fighting off challenges from other powerful women at court whose sons claimed a right to the throne. As a result of this direct feminine management of the Ottoman Empire, analogous to that of much tinier Aceh in these years (see Chapter 19), the period of Turhan's regency has been called "the Sultanate of the Women."

Indeed, as the Ottoman realm consolidated, court women became a powerful political force, despite their strict seclusion from society. First, the politics of succession dictated close control over the sultan's sexual life. Women came to dominate this key arena as early as the mid-sixteenth century. It was not seductive young wives and concubines who counted most, but rather elder women, particularly the Queen Mother. Second, much like

Weapons of Mass Destruction: Ottomans vs. Persians in Baghdad

In 1722 an Afghan army invaded the Safavid Empire from the east, seized the capital of Isfahan, and repulsed an Ottoman invasion from the west. The ambitious Afghan warlord Nadir Shah took over. Until his murder in 1747 Nadir attacked virtually all of Persia's neighbors, including the Mughals, but spent most of his energies fighting the Ottomans. Below is an excerpt from a chronicle of Nadir's campaigns written in around 1733 by an Armenian participant, Abraham of Erevan.

> After laying siege to the city [Baghdad] for forty-eight days, Nadir received the twenty-five cannons that he had left behind in Zohab. They began to place the cannons and to fire on the city. Both sides exchanged cannon fire. Since the Ottoman cannons were larger than Nadir's, they were capable of hurtling larger cannon balls. One particular cannon, the largest, could hurl a cannon ball filled with approximately forty *okhas* [about one hundred pounds] of gunpowder. Although Nadir's forces were not concentrated in one area, such a cannon ball was fired from the fort. It exploded in the middle of the camp and killed one hundred troops. Seeing such casualties, Nadir moved the front further back. After that, the Ottoman cannon balls could not harm his troops, but neither could his cannon balls reach Baghdad. Thus they faced each other for fifty-five days without firing their artillery. The Ottomans then fired the large cannon once again, but the explosion damaged a wall of the fortifications and destroyed many houses, after which the Turks did not use it again. After fifty-five days of siege, the Ottomans, fully armed, made a sudden sortie with the intention of attacking the Persians. . . . The Pasha, however, remained in the city and did not permit the citizens to leave either, for half of them were Persians and he suspected that they would join the troops of Nadir.

> The minute Nadir saw that the Ottomans had attacked him, he moved his troops forward without his cannons. The Ottomans, who had brought ten loaded cannons with them, began to fire on the Persian forces. Nadir then divided his troops into four groups so that he would not subject his entire army to the cannon fire. Having used their guns, the Ottomans could not reload their cannons fast enough, and while they were busy reloading, the Persians fell upon them from four sides and stopped the enemy from using its firepower. The two armies clashed and began to slaughter each other with swords and muskets for some seven hours. Eight thousand Ottomans and six thousand Persians perished. The Ottoman army suffered a defeat and fled back into the fortress and did not venture out again.

Source: Abraham of Erevan, *History of the Wars (1721–1738)*, ed. and trans. George A. Bournoutian (Costa Mesa, CA: Mazda Publishers, 1999), 77–78.

EXAMINING THE EVIDENCE

1. What role did cities such as Baghdad play in the battles between the Ottomans and Persians?

2. How do battles such as this one reveal the advantages and drawbacks of heavy guns?

Nur Jahan in Mughal India, powerful Ottoman women were important patrons of the arts and of pious works, and they figured prominently in royal rituals and mosque and hospital construction. The sultan was the ultimate patriarch, but it was his larger family that constituted the model of Ottoman society. Documents reveal that the royal harem, source of much lurid speculation by Europeans, was in fact a kind of sacred, familial space, more haven than prison.

Daily Life in the Ottoman Empire

Social Structure

As in most early modern states, the vast majority of Ottoman subjects lived in the countryside and were peasants and herders. Urban society, by contrast, was hierarchical, divided by occupation. Beneath the Osman royal family was the *askeri* (AS-keh-ree),

Istanbul Street Scene
This rare sixteenth-century Ottoman street scene depicts men and women exchanging a variety of goods near the famous bazaar of Istanbul, formerly Constantinople. A proud merchant holds up a bouquet of flowers, and another weighs what may be almonds. Two women with different head coverings bring what appear to be ducks and bread for sale, while a woman in the left foreground seems to be making a cash purchase from a merchant balancing a basket of fruit or flowers on his head. The exchanges take place right next to the Column of Constantine, a relic of Roman rule under the city's namesake emperor. (The Art Archive/Museo Correr Venice/Alfredo Dagli Orti.)

or "military" class, which was exempt from taxes and dependent on the sultan for their well-being. In addition to military leaders, the askeri included bureaucrats and *ulama*, religious scholars versed in Arabic and canon law. Whereas the Safavids considered religious authorities superior to the shahs, the Ottoman sultans only took the advice of their chief ulama—a distinction that persists today in Shi'ite and Sunni states. Beneath the askeri was a much broader class of taxpayers called *reaya* (RAH-ya), or "the flock." The reaya included everyone from common laborers and artisans to traders and merchants. Thanks to a long-established Ottoman tradition of meritocracy and inclusion, provincial members of the lower classes could make considerable gains in status through education or military service.

In the countryside, peasant farmers' and pastoralists' lives revolved around cycles of planting and harvest, seasonal movement of animal herds, and the rhythms of commerce and religious observance. Some men were drafted into military service, leaving women to manage households, herds, and farms. Women in both rural and urban contexts also engaged in export crafts such as silk weaving, carpet making, and ceramic manufacture. Thus, although few country folk of either gender experienced urban life for more than a few days in a lifetime, rural life in the Ottoman Empire was shaped by the larger forces of international trade and the demands of the Ottoman military.

More mobile by far were merchants, whose livelihood was considered highly respectable. The merchants of trading crossroads such as Aleppo, Damascus, Smyrna, and Cairo profited handsomely from their access to Asian and African luxuries. Ottoman taxes on trade were relatively low, and the empire rarely resorted to the burdensome wartime demands made by European states on their often less-well-regarded merchant communities. On the flip side, the Ottoman state invested little in trading infrastructure beyond maintenance of **caravanserais**, or travelers' lodges located along otherwise desolate trade routes. Like the Inca roadside inns taken over by the Spanish after conquest in 1532, these structures also served a military purpose.

Women's Experience

Recent research has revealed that ordinary women under Ottoman rule, much like court women, enjoyed more power than previously thought. Women had rights to their own property and investments, fully protected by shari'a, or Islamic law, before, during, and after marriage. This was, however, a rigidly patriarchal society. Women were expected to marry, and when they did they had few legal rights in relation to their husbands, who were permitted multiple wives and could divorce them at any time. Although women were treated as inferiors under Ottoman rule, it is worth noting that they had greater access to divorce than women in most early modern European societies.

caravanserai A roadside inn for merchants on the Silk Road and other overland trade routes.

The religious diversity of their subjects led the Ottomans to compromise in matters of gender. Islamic judges, or *qadis*, occasionally intervened in Christian married life, for example. Some Christian women won divorce by converting to Islam, as happened in the following case from Cyprus, decided in 1609: "Husna, daughter of Murad, Armenian wife, says before her husband Mergeri, son of Kuluk, Armenian: 'He always treats me cruelly. I do not want him.' He denies that. But now Husna becomes honored with Islam. After she takes the name Ayisha, her husband is invited to Islam, but he does not accept, so Ayisha's separation is ordered."[3] Although such conversions could be insincere, it is certain that religious diversity and legal oversight under Ottoman rule increased the range of options for female victims of domestic oppression.

Although devoutly Muslim at its core, the Ottoman state, with some 40 million subjects by the mid-seventeenth century, was at least as tolerant of religious diversity as the Islamic Mughal Empire, with policies similarly dictated by a practical desire to gain the cooperation of its diverse subjects. Religious tolerance and coexistence were most tested in frontier districts such as Cyprus and the Balkans. A description of Belgrade from 1660 illustrates just how diverse a frontier city could be: "On the banks of the river Sava there are three Gypsy neighborhoods, and on the banks of the Danube there are three neighborhoods of Greek unbelievers [i.e., Christians], as well as Serbs and Bulgarians also living in three neighborhoods. Right by the fortress is a neighborhood of Jews, those belonging to the seven communities known as the Karaim Jews. There is also a neighborhood of Armenian unbelievers. . . . All the rest are Muslim neighborhoods, so that families of the followers of Muhammad possess all the best, the most spacious and the airiest parts, located on the high or middle ground of the city."[4] Converts to Islam gained tax benefits (plus residential preferences, apparently), but punitive measures to force subjects to convert to the state religion were never used.

Religious Tolerance

Many Jews in the Ottoman Empire maintained their religious independence permanently. Some Jewish communities were centuries old and had local roots, but many more came as *Sephardim*, refugees from Iberian expulsions in the late fifteenth and early sixteenth centuries. Sephardic physicians, merchants, and tax collectors were a common sight in the capital city of Istanbul, and by the later sixteenth century many Ottoman towns had full-fledged Jewish communities. Members of the prominent Jewish Mendes family served as merchants, bankers, and advisers to the sultan in the sixteenth and seventeenth centuries.

In large part because of its incorporative nature and flexible structures, the Ottoman state proved one of the most durable in world history. Gunpowder weapons, though always important, were most critical in the early phases of expansion. Individual rulers varied widely in terms of aptitude and ambition, but the state itself remained quite stable. Fierce allegiance to Sunni Islam and control of its key shrines lent the Ottomans religious clout, yet their system of governance did not persecute Jews, Christians, or others who followed the state's rules regarding non-Muslims. Shi'ite Muslims faced more difficulties, by contrast, and this religious schism fueled a lasting rivalry with neighboring Persia.

Ottoman Rule: A Summing Up

Finally, in the realm of commerce, powerful merchants and trade guilds could be found in several Ottoman cities, notably Aleppo, but overseas ventures and entrepreneurial activities remained limited, at most sizable family businesses (see Lives and Livelihoods: Ottoman Coffeehouse Owners and Patrons). The state placed minimal restrictions on trade and provided some infrastructure in the form of caravanserais, but there was no policy equivalent to Iberian support of overseas commerce in the form of trading forts and convoys. In this regard the Ottoman Empire was profoundly different from the rising "merchant empires" of western Europe, where an increasingly global and highly competitive mercantile capitalism hitched state interests directly to those of bankers and merchants.

Ottoman Coffeehouse Owners and Patrons

Ottoman Coffeehouse

This late-sixteenth-century miniature depicts a packed Ottoman coffeehouse. The patrons and serving staff all appear to be male, but they represent many classes and age groups, and possibly several religious traditions. In the upper middle, elite men with large turbans are conversing; a worker prepares a tray of cups in a small room to their right. In the lower middle, one man appears to be speaking as others turn their attention to a backgammon game under way near his feet. When rebellions or other political troubles brewed, coffeehouses were a source of concern for Ottoman authorities. (The Trustees of the Chester Beatty Library, Dublin.)

An institution of modern life in much of the world today, the coffeehouse, or café, originated on the southern fringes of the Ottoman Empire in around 1450. The coffee bean, harvested from a small tree that scientists would later call *Coffea arabica*, had long been roasted, ground, and brewed in the Ethiopian and Somalian highlands of East Africa. At some point, coffee was transplanted to the highlands of Yemen, at the southern tip of the Arabian peninsula (see again Map 20.1). Here members of Sufi Muslim brotherhoods adopted coffee drinking to aid them in their all-night meditations and chants. Merchants sailing north on the Red Sea carried the new habit-forming beverage to Cairo and Constantinople. From there it spread quickly throughout the entire Mediterranean commercial world. By the late seventeenth century, there were coffeehouses in all the major cities of western Europe. By the early eighteenth century, coffee itself was planted in the tropical Americas.

Despite coffee's sobering effects, many *imams*, or religious scholars, were initially skeptical of its propriety. The

Europe Divided 1500–1650

FOCUS

What sparked division in Europe after 1500, and why did this trend persist?

Europe in the age of Ottoman ascendancy was diverse, fractured, and dynamic. By 1500, commerce and literacy were on the rise, populations were growing, and armies of craftsmen were perfecting technologies of warfare, manufacture, and navigation. Savvy publishers capitalized on demand for fiction long before Cervantes, but they also made available new thoughts on religion and science as well as new translations of classical works. Thus, the growth of literacy helped unsettle old notions of time, space, and human potential. A less visible transformation was taking place in the countryside, where traditional, reciprocal relationships tying peasants to feudal lords were increasingly replaced with commercial ones. Most notable in western Europe, especially in England, this shift entailed a rise in renting, sharecropping, and wage work, a proliferation of market-oriented farms owned by urban elites, and the privatization of lands formerly enjoyed as common community resources. Peasants displaced by this early capitalist restructuring of the countryside increasingly filled Europe's cities. Some went overseas to try their luck in the colonies.

word coffee apparently derives from *qahwa*, one of several Arabic terms for wine. Imams used this word since the beverage altered consciousness in a noticeable, if not necessarily debilitating, way. Eventually, coffee was decreed an acceptable drink in accordance with scripture, and was widely consumed during fasts such as Ramadan. Both men and women were allowed to drink coffee, but several *fatwas*, or religious prohibitions, were issued against female coffee vendors in the early sixteenth century. As a result, both the public sale and public consumption of coffee became male preserves in the Ottoman Empire.

Coffee's troubles were far from over. If coffee itself was declared wholesome, the places where it was commonly consumed were not. Coffeehouses, sometimes run by non-Muslims, proliferated in major market cities such as Cairo by the early 1500s, drawing hoards of lower-class traders, artisans, and even slaves. Unable to suppress the café even at the core of their empire, Ottoman religious leaders simply denounced them as places of iniquity, dens of sinners. Female musicians played and danced scandalously in some, conservative clerics argued, while other cafés promoted homosexual prostitution. Some coffeehouses served as well-known hangouts for opium and hashish addicts, further tainting their reputation. Then came the vice of tobacco smoking, introduced from the Americas by European merchants in the early seventeenth century.

As later proved true in Europe, there were other reasons to fear the coffeehouse. Ottoman officials suspected the cafés as hotbeds of insurrection and treason. Still, they proved impossible to suppress, and coffee vendors quickly sprang back into action when the authorities closed them down. The Ottomans finally relented, deciding that the coffeehouse was an ideal place to gauge popular reactions to state policy and planting spies. In an era before restaurants, and in a religious climate hostile to alcohol and hence taverns, the coffeehouse met a variety of social needs. It was first a place where traveling merchants far from the comforts of home could exchange information, buy their associates a few rounds of satisfying coffee, and perhaps relax with a game of backgammon and a water-cooled smoke. For men of the working class, the coffeehouse became a place of rest and collegiality, and occasionally of political ferment.

QUESTIONS TO CONSIDER

1. How did Islamic clerics' attitude toward coffee change? What factors might account for this shift?

2. How and why did the Ottoman state come to accept the coffeehouse as a social institution?

For Further Information:

Hattox, Ralph. *Coffee and Coffee Houses: The Origins of a Social Beverage in the Medieval Near East*. Seattle: University of Washington Press, 1985.

Schivelbusch, Wolfgang. *Tastes of Paradise: A Social History of Spices, Stimulants, and Intoxicants*. Translated by David Jacobson. New York: Vintage, 1993.

Everyday Life in Early Modern Europe

Historians estimate that Europe in 1492 had a population of about 70 million, or slightly more than the population of the Americas just prior to Columbus's arrival. By 1550, Europe counted some 85 million inhabitants, and it was still growing rapidly. This population increase was mostly due to reduced mortality rather than increased births. Unlike larger Ming China and Mughal India, Europe's high growth rate was not sustained. A series of epidemics and climatic events beginning in around 1600, coupled with the effects of the Thirty Years' War (1618–1648) and numerous other conflicts, led to population stagnancy and even decline. Europe's population in 1630 was below 80 million, and would not reach 100 million until just before 1700.

The Columbian Exchange was largely responsible for the sixteenth-century population increase. In both city and countryside, American crops radically altered European diets after 1500. Maize, potatoes, tomatoes, capsicum peppers, and many other foods reordered both peasant and elite tastes and needs. In some cases this sped population growth, and in others it simply spiced up an otherwise bland diet. Potatoes came to be associated with Ireland and

Changing Patterns of Consumption

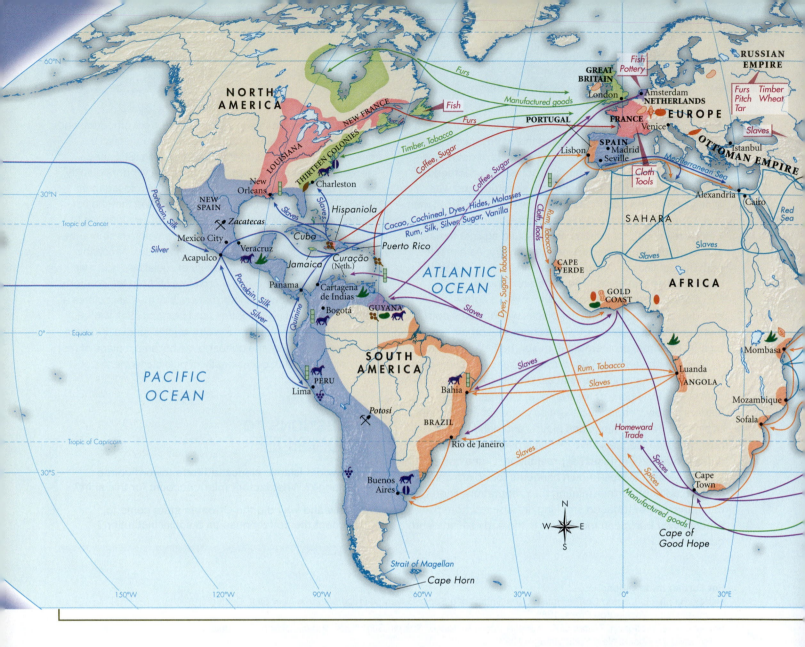

paprika with Hungary and Spain, but these and other American foods were widely embraced and helped spur an increasingly sophisticated consumer culture. American-grown sugar, tobacco, and later chocolate, vanilla, and coffee also figured prominently in Europe's taste revolution, as did Asian-grown tea and a host of exotic spices. European consumers also demanded new drugs such as opium and quinine bark, and merchants who trafficked in these and other tropical goods often made enormous profits. Thus, Europe's new connection with the Americas had a profound impact on its population, culture, and economy (see Map 20.2).

Environmental Transformations

The rise of commercial farming and peasant displacement, as well as overseas expansion, transformed ecosystems. Throughout Europe, more and more forest was cleared. Some princes passed decrees to limit deforestation, usually to preserve hunting grounds rather than for the good of the forest itself, but peasants still entered reserves in search of fuel and timber. Laws against such common use did little to relieve the stress, turning environmental problems into social ones. Shipbuilders, metalsmiths, and construction workers consumed forest as well, and wars and fires destroyed still more. By 1500, many Mediterranean cities, and even some northern European ones, relied on imported wood, sometimes looking as far afield as the Americas for new supplies. Not all environmental transformations were negative, however. The Dutch improved transportation by building canals and reclaimed land for agriculture from the sea by erecting dikes and filling wetlands.

Life Expectancy and Marriage Patterns

More people than ever crowded into European cities. Naples, London, and Paris were each home to more than two hundred thousand inhabitants by 1600. Nearly a dozen other

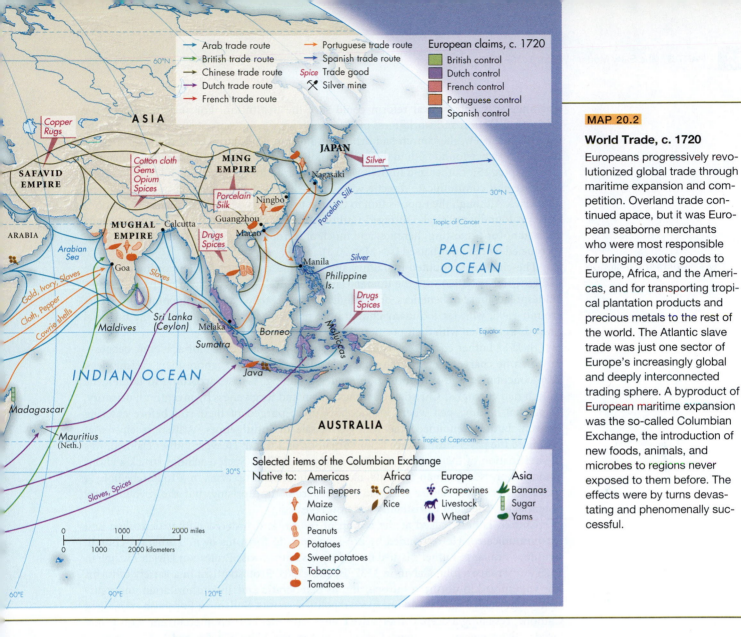

Arab trade route
British trade route
Chinese trade route
Dutch trade route
French trade route
Portuguese trade route
Spanish trade route
Spice **Trade good**
Silver mine

European claims, c. 1720
British control
Dutch control
French control
Portuguese control
Spanish control

Selected items of the Columbian Exchange

Native to:

Americas
- Chili peppers
- Maize
- Manioc
- Peanuts
- Potatoes
- Sweet potatoes
- Tobacco
- Tomatoes

Africa
- Coffee
- Rice

Europe
- Grapevines
- Livestock
- Wheat

Asia
- Bananas
- Sugar
- Yams

MAP 20.2

World Trade, c. 1720

Europeans progressively revolutionized global trade through maritime expansion and competition. Overland trade continued apace, but it was European seaborne merchants who were most responsible for bringing exotic goods to Europe, Africa, and the Americas, and for transporting tropical plantation products and precious metals to the rest of the world. The Atlantic slave trade was just one sector of Europe's increasingly global and deeply interconnected trading sphere. A byproduct of European maritime expansion was the so-called Columbian Exchange, the introduction of new foods, animals, and microbes to regions never exposed to them before. The effects were by turns devastating and phenomenally successful.

cities in Iberia, the Netherlands, and Italy were close behind, with populations over one hundred thousand. Still, the vast majority of Europeans remained in the countryside. Life for most, including the nobility, was short. A lucky few survived into their eighties and even nineties in both urban and rural settings, but high infant mortality yielded overall life expectancies of only eighteen to thirty-six years.

Most early modern Europeans did not rush to marry, nor were they compelled to enter arranged marriages, as in some Asian societies. Women were between twenty and twenty-five, on average, when they married. Men married slightly later, between twenty-three and twenty-seven, in part due to itinerant work and military obligations. Relatively few children were born out of wedlock, at least according to surviving church records, but many were conceived before marriage. Most partners could expect to be widowed within twenty years, in which time half a couple's offspring would probably also have died. Moreover, one in ten women died in childbirth. In Europe, as in much of the world at this time, the prospect of death was never far away.

Protestant and Catholic Reformations

Like Islam, Christianity had long been subject to disagreements and schisms. Yet the critiques of Roman Catholicism presented by several sixteenth-century northern European theologians marked the deepest split thus far. Catholic reformers beginning with the German monk Martin Luther argued that the church had so deviated from early Christian teachings that only radical reform could save the institution. For such reformers, the evident corruption and worldliness of the church were symptoms of a much deeper problem. In their view, the church had drifted into profound doctrinal and theological error. Inspired by a newfound faith in the individual that had its roots in Renaissance humanism (see Chapter 15), Luther and his followers emphasized the individual's ability to interpret scripture and communicate directly with God, without the intercession of priestly intermediaries. Although their opposition to Church teachings was theological, its implications were profoundly political. Outraged Catholic officials branded Luther and his followers Protestant (or protesting) heretics, and much of Europe fell into a century of bloody conflict fueled by religious hatred (see Map 20.3).

The Protestant Challenge

The challenge mounted by Luther amplified old complaints. Many ordinary people had grown dissatisfied with the Roman Catholic Church, particularly in northern Europe. Widespread abuse of benefices, or parish territories, reached a breaking point in the years around 1500, with far too many church officeholders concerned only with the financial rewards associated with their positions.

In 1517 Luther circulated "Ninety-five Theses"—propositions for academic debate—in which he charged that church policy encouraged priests to ignore their parishioners, keep concubines, and concentrate on money-grubbing. Worse, according to Luther, the church had corrupted Christian teachings on sin and forgiveness by inventing Purgatory, a spiritual holding pen where the deceased were purged of their sins before entering Heaven. Luther denounced the widespread sale of **indulgences**, written receipts that promised the payer early release from Purgatory, as a fraud. Heaven, Luther claimed, was the destination of the faithful, not the wealthy or gullible. Such teachings struck a chord among oppressed German peasants, many of whom took up arms in a 1525 rebellion. A social conservative, Luther withheld support from the uprising, but the revolutionary potential of Protestant Christianity was now revealed.

Church fathers balked at the notion of reform and ordered Luther defrocked and excommunicated. He responded by breaking away to form his own "Lutheran" church. Critiques similar to Luther's issued from the pens of the Swiss Protestant Ulrich Zwingli in 1523 and France's John Calvin in 1537. By the 1550s, Protestantism in a variety of forms was widespread in northern Europe, and its democratic and antiauthoritarian undercurrents soon yielded radical and unexpected political results. Still, most Europeans remained Catholic, revealing a deep, conservative countercurrent. That countercurrent soon resurfaced with a vengeance, although Catholicism, too, would be transformed.

Anglican Protestant Church

Another major schism occurred in 1534 when England's King Henry VIII declared his nation Protestant. Although Henry broke with the church for personal and political reasons rather than theological ones (the king wanted a divorce that the pope refused to grant), Anglican Protestantism was quickly embraced as the new state religion. Critics were silenced by Henry's execution of England's most prominent Catholic intellectual, Sir Thomas More, author of *Utopia* (1517). As in central and northern Europe, however, this early, mostly peaceful break hardly marked the end of Catholicism in England.

Founding of the Jesuit Order

The Catholic Church's leaders responded to Protestantism first with stunned disbelief, then vengeful anger. Some among the outraged Catholic majority launched strong but peaceful assaults. In Spain, for example, a Basque soldier calling himself Ignatius of Loyola became a priest and in 1534 founded a new religious order. Approved by the pope in 1540, the Society of Jesus, or Jesuits, soon became the Catholic Church's greatest educators and wealthiest property managers. More importantly for global history, they set out as missionaries to head off Protestant initiatives overseas. Within a few decades of Loyola's founding of the order there were Jesuit preachers in places as far-flung as Brazil, West Africa, Ceylon, and Japan (see Seeing the Past: Gift Clocks for the Emperors of China). Others stuck closer to home and won back converts in central Europe on the eve of the Thirty Years' War.

In the face of the Protestant challenge, some high officials within the church called for self-examination, and even the pope ultimately agreed that it was time for the church to

indulgence In early modern Europe, a note sold by the Catholic Church to speed a soul's exit from Purgatory.

MAP 20.3   Protestant and Catholic Reformations in Europe

In the midst of early overseas expansion, a great schism among Christians emerged in Europe. What Protestants called the Reformation was a fundamental questioning of Roman Catholic doctrine and practice. The dispute quickly produced violence and led some kingdoms, such as England, to break entirely from papal authority. France dissolved into civil war pitting Catholics against Protestants, and Spain and Portugal used their Inquisitions to persecute Protestants as heretics. A Catholic Reformation sought to reform and strengthen the church, but conflict continued to bubble up, leading soon after 1600 to the disastrous Thirty Years' War, the most deadly for civilians yet experienced in world history.

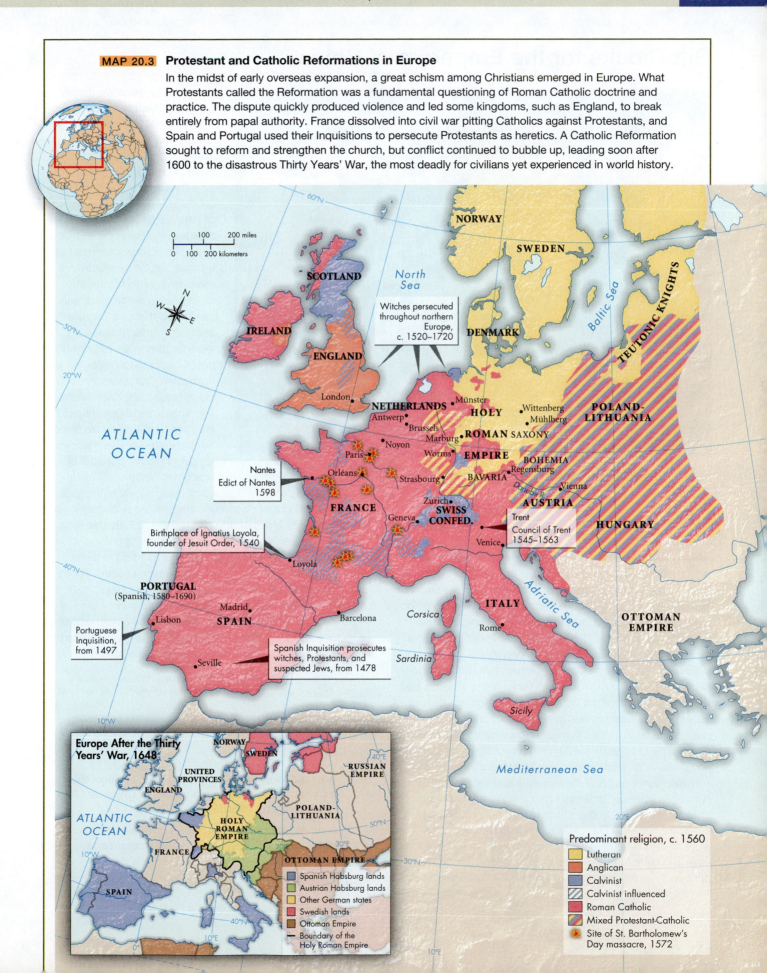

Witches persecuted throughout northern Europe, c. 1520–1720

Nantes
Edict of Nantes 1598

Birthplace of Ignatius Loyola, founder of Jesuit Order, 1540

Trent
Council of Trent 1545–1563

PORTUGAL
(Spanish, 1580–1690)

Portuguese Inquisition, from 1497

Spanish Inquisition prosecutes witches, Protestants, and suspected Jews, from 1478

Europe After the Thirty Years' War, 1648

- Spanish Habsburg lands
- Austrian Habsburg lands
- Other German states
- Swedish lands
- Ottoman Empire
- — Boundary of the Holy Roman Empire

Predominant religion, c. 1560

- Lutheran
- Anglican
- Calvinist
- Calvinist influenced
- Roman Catholic
- Mixed Protestant-Catholic
- ✳ Site of St. Bartholomew's Day massacre, 1572

Gift Clocks for the Emperors of China

Courting the Qing: European Gift Clocks in the Forbidden City (The Palace Museum, Beijing/ChinaStock.)

With the exception of raw silver, China had little need of products introduced by Europeans hoping to trade for silk, porcelain, and eventually, tea. This presented a great problem for merchants short of silver, but it also challenged early modern European missionaries. The first Jesuits arrived in China in the 1550s, barely a decade after the pope's formal recognition of their order. They spent their first years trying to win poor converts inhabiting the cities along the South China Sea, but by the 1580s some Jesuit priests, such as the Italian Matteo Ricci, began working their way toward Beijing. Given China's huge population, it made sense to try to convert those at the top of the social order in hopes that they would mandate the conversion of their many millions of subjects. Chinese officials, courtiers, and princes were not easily swayed even by the most sophisticated philosophical arguments, but they were almost universally fascinated by advances in Western science and technology.

Aware of this, Ricci developed a special program of "Christian science," attempting to link Western cartography, optics, metallurgy, and clockmaking to notions of divine order. He carried a European clock to Beijing in hopes of wowing the emperor in 1601, and it proved a big hit. A Chinese chronicle from 1603 records the event as follows: "In the twenty-eighth year of the reign of Wanli of the Ming

dynasty, the great Westerner Li Madou [Matteo Ricci] presented a self-sounding bell, a mysterious and unknown art. The great bell sounds the hours, at midday, one sound."

The Chinese were relatively uninterested in Western notions of timekeeping in itself because they had their own means and units of measurement. Instead, the Chinese admired the clocks for their intricate mechanical construction and welcomed them as "high-tech" status symbols. The Jesuits were for many years allowed special access to Beijing's Forbidden City primarily as clock repairmen. Their efforts to link clockwork to godliness in a Western Christian sense failed, but they did eventually spawn royal workshops capable of producing elaborate if not particularly accurate timepieces by the early eighteenth century. Under Qing rule, the Royal Office of Clock Manufacture opened in 1723. By this time, advances in English clock- and watchmaking coincided with increased British interest in China, leading to a new wave of gift timepieces meant to win favor at court. Those shown here are on display today in the Forbidden City, the Ming and Qing imperial palace in Beijing that now houses the Palace Museum. Gifts from a range of Western ambassadors, they reveal European states' centuries-long effort to curry favor with the powerful Chinese Empire.

Source: Catherine Pagani, *Eastern Magnificence and Western Ingenuity: Clocks of Late Imperial China* (Ann Arbor: University of Michigan Press, 2001).

EXAMINING THE EVIDENCE

1. Why did Western missionaries such as Ricci think that introducing European clocks to China would aid conversion efforts?

2. How did Chinese appreciation of these clocks reflect cultural differences between them and Europeans?

clarify its mission. The Council of Trent (1545–1563) yielded a new charter for the Roman Catholic Church. Far from offering compromises, however, Trent reaffirmed the Catholic Church's conservatism. Purgatory and indulgences were not eliminated, nor was priestly celibacy. Sacraments such as marriage were reinforced and sexual behavior more circumscribed than ever before. The church also policed ideas and banned books. Cervantes was fortunate to have only one sentence of *Don Quixote* removed. In some places, such as the staunchly Catholic Iberian world, the Holy Office of the Inquisition acted as enforcer of the new precepts, rooting out and punishing alleged deviance. Historians have shown that ordinary Catholics could be skeptical of the church's dogmatic claims, but much of what we know about these freethinkers comes from their Inquisition trial records.

Council of Trent

In the wake of Trent, France's Catholics began persecuting Huguenots, as Calvinist Protestants were known in France, in earnest. This culminated in the Saint Bartholomew's Day massacre of 1572, in which tens of thousands of Huguenots were slaughtered and their bodies mutilated (see again Map 20.3). Just back from America, horrified Huguenot Jean de Léry wrote how "civilized" French Christians had proved themselves far more barbaric than Brazil's Tupinamba cannibals, who at least killed one another according to rigid honor codes. Hostilities ended only in 1598 when the French king Henry IV signed the Edict of Nantes granting Protestants freedom to practice their religion. It helped that Henry IV was a former Protestant, but the Huguenots' troubles were not over.

French Wars of Religion

Imperial Spain and Its Challenges

With religiously and politically fractured kingdoms and duchies the rule in early modern Europe, unified Spain proved to be the exception. Largely financed by the wealth of their numerous overseas colonies, Spain's Catholic Habsburg monarchs sought to consolidate their gains in Europe, and more importantly, to challenge the much larger and more powerful Ottoman Empire to the east. As we have seen, the fight against the "Great Turk," to use the language of the day, forever altered the lives of veterans such as Miguel de Cervantes.

Philip II came to the throne of Spain in 1556, when his father, Holy Roman Emperor Charles V (r. 1516–1556), abdicated. The title of "Emperor" passed to Ferdinand, Charles's brother, but Philip inherited extensive holdings of his own. Taken together, his kingdoms were much larger and richer than his uncle's. Indeed, by 1598, the year of his death, Philip II ruled the world's first empire "upon which the sun never set." The distant Philippines were claimed and named for him in 1565. Still, governing a far-flung and culturally diverse empire brought more burden than pleasure. A forceful but pious monarch, Spain's so-called Prudent King would die doubting his own salvation.

Reign of Philip II

One of Philip's first concerns, inherited from his father, was centralization in the core kingdoms. Castile and Aragon had been nominally united with the marriage of Isabella and Ferdinand in 1469, but local nobles and semiautonomous cities such as Barcelona continued to challenge royal authority. Charles's attempts to assert his will had sparked rebellions in the 1520s, and regional resentments in Iberia itself continued to fester throughout the period of overseas expansion. Philip responded in part by turning Madrid, formerly a dusty medieval crossroads in central Castile, into a world-class capital and Spain's unequivocal center. The capital's building boom was funded in large part by American treasure. Palaces, churches, monasteries, and residential structures proliferated, often blending traditional Castilian and northern European architectural styles. Envious neighbors joked that the Spanish had discovered a magic formula for turning silver into stone.

Thanks to New World treasure, Spain had become Europe's most formidable state by the second half of the sixteenth century. Among other successes, Philip's forces had beaten, as we have seen, the Ottoman navy at Lepanto in 1571. Philip's biggest setback was the revolt of the Netherlands, a politically and religiously divided region inherited from his father. The so-called Dutch Revolt, which began in 1566, taxed Iberian resources severely before its end in 1648. This was a war the Spanish lost, despite enormous effort.

Annexation of Portugal

Two other key events in Philip II's reign were the assumption of the Portuguese throne in 1580 and the 1588 attempt to invade England by sea. Both events had global significance. Portugal's King Sebastian died without an heir in 1578, and the subsequent succession crisis ended only when Philip, whose mother was Isabella of Portugal, stepped in to take the crown. Legitimate or not, Philip's move required an armed invasion, and the Portuguese always regarded Spanish rule, which lasted from 1580 until 1640, as unlawful and oppressive. In global terms, Spanish-Portuguese union meant that one monarch now ruled a substantial portion of Europe, much of the Americas, and dozens of far-flung Asian and African ports, islands, and sea routes. No European challenger was even close.

Philip knew this, and he assumed his good fortune was a reflection of divine will. Like many powerful individuals at their peak, Philip overstretched his mandate. Irritated by English harassment of the Spanish in the Americas and by English aid to the Dutch rebels, and motivated first and foremost by a determination to bring England back into the Catholic fold, Philip decided to launch a full-scale invasion of the British Isles. Such an undertaking would require the concentration of an enormous amount of military resources, and as at Lepanto, the stakes were correspondingly huge.

The Spanish Armada

The Spanish **Armada** of 1588, the largest and most expensive naval force assembled up to that time, appears in retrospect to have been an ill-considered enterprise. Means of communication were few and slow, and most Spanish sailors were poorly equipped for foul weather. Neither side regarded the invasion as foolish at the time, however, and ultimately it was defeated due to a host of factors, only some of them within Spanish control. The Spanish stockpiled supplies for years, and even Cervantes took part, as a clerk charged with cataloguing stores of olive oil and other foods. When it came time to fight, English defenders such as the famous pirate Francis Drake, aided by numerous Dutch allies, were critical; they knew the English Channel and understood Spanish tactics and technology. English guns were also powerful, carefully placed, and well manned. Aiding this defense were harsh weather, contrary winds, poorly mounted cannon, and numerous other complications. Spanish luck went from bad to worse.

Route of the Spanish Armada, 1588

Ships not sunk by English and Dutch artillery were battered by waves and drawn off course by fierce gusts. The great Spanish fleet scattered, and the remaining vessels were forced to sail north around Scotland to avoid capture. Here in the cold North Atlantic, Spanish sailors died by the hundreds of hunger and exposure. Some survivors were captured off the coast of Ireland. The English, hardly the sea power they would later become, were jubilant. Subjects of the fiercely Protestant Elizabeth I had proved that mighty Philip and his great armada were not invincible after all.

Spain's misfortunes only compounded in the wake of the armada disaster, and although the world's most extensive empire was hardly crumbling, Philip II's successors faced a potent new competitor in the form of the breakaway Dutch Republic. The Dutch projected their power overseas beginning in the 1590s, and by 1640 the Dutch East and West India companies took over many of the key trading posts held by the joint Spanish-Portuguese Empire from the Caribbean islands to Japan. Beginning in 1630, the West India Company occupied northeastern Brazil, calling this vast territory New Holland. What the Dutch did not know was that at precisely this time the main sources of Spanish wealth, the great silver mines of Potosí in present-day Bolivia, were petering out.

armada A fleet of warships; usually used in reference to the Spanish naval fleet defeated by England in 1588.

Much of the world was deeply affected. Declining silver revenues combined with other chance factors sparked what has become known as "the seventeenth-century crisis" (see Figure 20.1).

Defeat of the Spanish Armada

Gunpowder weapons are very much on display in this dramatic 1601 painting by Dutch marine artist Hendrik Cornelisz Vroom of the 1588 Anglo-Dutch defeat of the Spanish Armada in the English Channel. High winds, shown by the stretched sail canvas, helped English and Dutch forces to outmaneuver and trap Spanish ships, which they blasted with their superior cannon. Several large vessels went down, and all on board drowned. Surviving Spanish ships sailed north around Scotland, where many crewmembers died of exposure. Others were captured in Ireland. It was one of the greatest naval defeats of early modern times. (Scala/White Images/Art Resource, NY.)

The Seventeenth-Century Crisis

Few topics have generated as much debate among historians as the seventeenth-century crisis, a complex series of events and trends that affected much of Europe and the Mediterranean basin from about 1600 to 1660. Some scholars have even claimed that no general crisis occurred, only a cluster of unrelated catastrophes. In any case, Europe's post-1660 rebound and push toward global maritime dominance seems remarkable. How did one of the world's most politically divided, religiously intolerant, and economically fractured regions give rise, in a relatively short time, to secular models of government, rational scientific inquiry, and financial capitalism, all hallmarks of modernity?

Historians focus on different causes, depending on their interpretive bent. Political and military historians focus on the "modern" horrors and early nationalism of the Thirty Years' War and related conflicts. Here, unlike in Asia and North Africa, gunpowder led to the dissolution rather than consolidation of empires. Economic historians focus on the shifting influx of American silver and its effects on food and other commodity prices. Some argue that inflated prices and economic depression had both negative and positive effects, sparking riots while prompting technical and financial innovations. Still other historians, informed by modern scientific techniques, focus on climate, analyzing ice cores and tree rings, along with traditional historical sources, to document the extent of the so-called Little Ice Age, which, as we will see, enveloped Europe from about 1550 to 1700. In the end it is hard to say which of these factors was most responsible for either the widespread turmoil or the swift turnaround that followed, but most historians agree that something transformative had occurred.

In the midst of a twelve-year truce between the Spanish and Dutch, the Thirty Years' War (1618–1648) broke out in

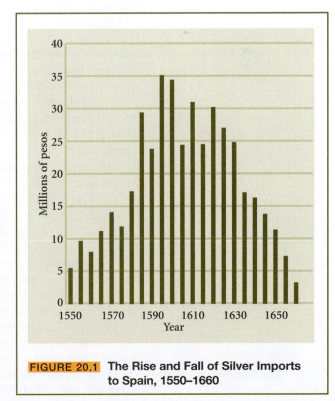

FIGURE 20.1   **The Rise and Fall of Silver Imports to Spain, 1550–1660**

The Thirty Years' War

Dutch artist Jan Maertszen de Jonghe graphically depicts the horrors of the battlefield in this 1634 rendering of the 1627 Battle of Dirschau, near Gdansk, Poland. The battle pitted Swedish king Gustav II, whose slain body appears in the foreground, against Polish-Lithuanian forces led by General Stanislaw Koniecpolski, shown here astride a chestnut horse. Soldiers and horses lie dead or wounded in this picture, but later in the Thirty Years' War, it was civilian casualties that reached levels not seen before in Europe. The Battle of Dirschau was one of several bloody encounters leading to stalemate in 1629, and this painting emphasizes the war's chaos and destruction more than its heroism. (akg-images.)

The Thirty Years' War

central Europe. This complex conflict pitted Christian factions against one another in a civil and international war that radically reshaped Europe's borders. The Thirty Years' War was devastating for civilians. Caught in the crossfire, they were forced to support occupying troops, only to be massacred for doing so when the tide turned and the other side's troops moved in.

In essence, the Thirty Years' War was over the internal politics of the Holy Roman Empire in central Europe (see again Map 20.3). This was really only a loose confederacy—since the days of Emperor Charles V, substantial autonomy had been ceded to an increasing number of Lutheran and Calvinist principalities and duchies. Inhabitants of these Protestant enclaves rightly feared a more assertive Catholic emperor. Emperor Ferdinand II was such a person, an ambitious, Jesuit-educated militant. When it became clear that Ferdinand might re-Catholicize central Europe, the various enemies of the Habsburgs sent aid, then joined the fray.

Before the war ground to a close, a variety of German and Bohemian princes, the kings of Denmark, Poland, and Sweden, plus the English, French, Dutch, and finally the Spanish had all been drawn into the conflict. Contemporary engravings and paintings from its last phase depict the full range of human cruelty, a blatant reminder, like the Saint Bartholomew's Day massacre, that Europeans were as capable of savagery as America's famous warrior cultures. At war's end at least a third of the population of Germany had died, and the region's infrastructure lay in ruins. From population decline to decreased agricultural production, the war was a manifestation of the seventeenth-century crisis.

Silver and Depression

It was also enormously costly in terms of money, the supply of which was shifting. Economic historians have found that throughout Europe prices rose even as demand fell. In one interpretation, an overabundance of silver in the late sixteenth century drove prices up, after which a sequence of plagues, droughts, wars, and other disasters killed off both consumers and suppliers of basic goods throughout Europe, leading to depression. A sustained drop in silver income beginning in around 1600 made hard money scarce when it was already overvalued, forcing many people to resort to barter. Thus, the fabulous wealth of the Americas proved both a blessing and a curse, shifting the global balance of power in Europe's favor at the same time that it led to dangerous and destructive economic volatility.

The Dutch Exception

Hard times for the masses could be good for some, and it appears that the Dutch fared rather well, particularly in comparison with the Spanish and Portuguese. The Netherlands' unique mix of financial capitalism, religious toleration, and overseas conquest seemed to

READING THE PAST

An Exiled European Muslim Visits the Netherlands

After an Ottoman-supported rebellion in Andalusia from 1569 to 1571, Spain's remaining forced converts to Christianity from Islam, or Moriscos, faced increasing persecution. Many fled to Morocco, Algeria, and other Muslim havens in North Africa, especially during a last wave of expulsions ordered by Philip III from 1609 to 1614. Among the refugees was Ahmad Ibn Qasim al-Hajari, born with the Spanish surname Bejarano in around 1569 in a village in Extremadura, not far from the birthplaces of Francisco Pizarro and Hernando Cortés. Al-Hajari went on to become a major spokesman for the Morisco community in exile, and he wrote and traveled widely. His best-known work, composed and circulated in both Arabic and Spanish, is called *The Supporter of Religion Against the Infidel* (c. 1637). In this passage, al-Hajari describes his visit to the Netherlands.

About the Netherlands: You should know that I set out for that country deliberately, although it lies farther from our own country than France. But a man should seek protection from others or from himself, and after I had experienced the way French sailors were treating Muslims, I said: I will not return to my country in one of those ships, but I will go to the country of the Netherlanders, because they do not harm Muslims but treat them well. . . .

After I reached the City of Amsterdam, I marveled at the beauty of its architecture and the style of its buildings, its cleanness and the great number of its inhabitants. Its population was almost like that of the City of Paris in France. There is no city in the world with so many ships as it has! One says that the total number of its ships, including the smaller and the bigger ones, is six thousand. As for the houses, each of these is painted and decorated with marvelous colors from top to bottom. Not one resembles another in the art of its painting. All the streets are made of paved stones. . . .

One should know that the Netherlands consists of seventeen islands, all of which used to belong to the Sultan of al-Andalus [the king of Spain]. At a certain time, a man appeared in those lands who was held as a great scholar by them, called Luther, as well as another scholar called Calvin. Each of them wrote his view of the corruption and deviation from the religion of our lord Jesus and the Gospel that had come about in the religion of the Christians. They said the popes in Rome misled the people by worshiping idols and by the additions they introduced into the faith by forbidding priests and monks to marry, and many other things. All the people of the Netherlands . . . embraced this doctrine and they rose up against their sultan until today. The people of the Sultanate of the English also follow this doctrine. There are also many of them in France. Their scholars warn them against the popes and the worshiping of idols. They tell them they should not hate Muslims because they are the Sword of God on His earth against the worshipers of idols.

Source: Ahmad Ibn Qasim al-Hajari, *The Supporter of Religion Against the Infidel*, ed. and trans. P. S. Van Koningsveld, Q. al-Samarrai, and G. A. Wiegers (Madrid: Consejo Superior de Investigaciones Científicas, 1997), 194–195.

EXAMINING THE EVIDENCE

1. What aspects of the Netherlands most impress al-Hajari?

2. How clear is al-Hajari's understanding of the Protestant Reformation?

---

offset many of the difficulties faced by other states (see Reading the Past: An Exiled European Muslim Visits the Netherlands). The Dutch East India Company's spice-island takeovers in Southeast Asia were critical, as seen in Chapter 19, but Dutch pirates, many sponsored by the West India Company, were also busy capturing Spanish silver fleets in the Caribbean.

Historians have long suggested that the climatic change known as the Little Ice Age may have spurred rebellion and even war during the seventeenth century, but only recently have enough data been assembled to generate a fairly clear picture of the century's weather cycles. It now appears that four of the five coldest summers ever recorded in the Northern Hemisphere occurred in the seventeenth century, and that global volcanic activity was probably a major contributing factor to the cooldown. Global cooling shortened growing seasons just as Europeans were pushing into more marginal and thus vulnerable agricultural lands. In alpine valleys, for example, peasants and herders were driven from their highland homes by advancing glaciers. Unprecedented droughts ravaged traditionally wet regions such as Scotland in the 1630s and 1640s, sparking violent uprisings in the midst of an already unstable political climate.

Little Ice Age

The Little Ice Age affected regions far beyond European borders. The worst drought in five hundred years was recorded on the Yangzi River between 1641 and 1644, probably contributing to the 1644 fall of the Ming dynasty in China (discussed in Chapter 21). Ottoman territories were also hit: Egypt's Nile River fell to its lowest recorded levels between 1640 and 1643. Troops on the Persian frontier rebelled when their pay in silver coin proved insufficient to buy food.

Increased Persecutions

Within Europe, the seventeenth-century crisis took on more sinister social dimensions with the rise of witchcraft trials and Inquisition prosecutions. In Protestant Europe, thousands of women were executed for alleged acts of sorcery, and in Catholic Spain and its colonies an unprecedented number of Jews were killed by order of the Inquisition between 1637 and 1649. It is difficult to know why these repressive outbursts occurred in the midst of war, famine, and other problems, but the tendency to scapegoat vulnerable persons in uncertain times has been documented elsewhere. More positive outcomes of the seventeenth-century crisis included scientific discoveries and novel political ideas that eventually took on global importance.

European Innovations in Science and Government 1550–1750

FOCUS

What factors enabled European scientific and political innovations in the early modern period?

In the aftermath of the religious wars of the sixteenth and early seventeenth centuries, a new wave of political consolidation took place in northern and central Europe in the form of absolutist and constitutionalist monarchies. Many of these states, like their Spanish, Portuguese, and Dutch predecessors, took their expansionist energies overseas. Global expansion, as these earlier players had learned, entailed great risks and huge defense costs. In addition to building professional navies, states created licensing agencies and sponsored monopoly trading companies. Financial innovations included stock markets and double-entry accounting, essential ingredients of modern capitalism. Also emerging from the divided world of Europe was a new development aided by the printing press and other technologies: the "scientific revolution." Although restricted for many years to a small number of theorists and experimenters who shared their work in Latin treatises, Europe's embrace of science was to prove globally significant.

The Scientific Revolution

The rise of modern Western science is often described, rather like the Protestant Reformation, as a heroic struggle against a hidebound Catholic tradition. Certainly church patriarchs clung to traditional ideas when challenged by the new science. Still, it was very often Catholic-educated priests and seminarians, along with the odd basement alchemist, who broke the mold in early modern times. Even the Protestants' access to scientific books owed everything to the labors of countless Catholic monks who over centuries had transcribed, translated, and sometimes composed key treatises. They were in turn indebted to numerous medieval Islamic scholars based in cities such as Baghdad and Córdoba. Finally, in early modern times, the printing press and a general interest in technical improvements helped give thousands access to knowledge.

As with the "seventeenth-century crisis," historians have long debated whether or not Europe experienced a genuine "scientific revolution" in the early modern era. Skeptics argue that the key innovations of the period were too restricted to educated elites and court patrons to justify the term *revolution*. In contrast, proponents describe an unprecedented shift in worldview that resonated beyond the small circle of known "scientific rebels."

Call it what we may, European intellectuals after about 1550 increasingly expressed skepticism about received wisdom and began to employ mathematical formulas and empirical (observable) data in an effort to discover the rules by which nature operated. Inductive and deductive reasoning were guiding principles in their efforts. Inductive reasoning—deriving general principles from particular facts and empirical evidence—was most clearly articulated by the English statesman and writer Sir Francis Bacon. Its complement, deductive reasoning—the process of reasoning from a self-evident general principle to a specific fact—was the contri-

geocentrism The ancient belief that the earth is the center of the universe.

The Copernican Universe

The earth still appears quite large in relation to other planets in this 1660 rendering of a heliocentric, or sun-centered, cosmos, but the breakthrough initiated by Nicolaus Copernicus in 1543 is fully evident. Copernicus did not know that planets such as earth traced elliptical rather than perfectly circular orbits, but this was a minor error compared to the older view of a geocentric universe claimed since the days of the great ancient Greek philosopher Aristotle. (akg-images/historic-maps.)

bution of French thinker and mathematician René Descartes. One result of this new search for universal rules was a developing understanding of the way things worked, including the cosmos. Since this was akin to describing "Heaven" in a secular way, many churchmen bristled.

The first breakthroughs were made by a Polish monk, Nicolaus Copernicus. Copernicus was the first to systematically question the ancient Ptolemaic model of the cosmos, which was geocentric, or earth-centered. Copernicus's collected observations of solar, lunar, and planetary movements did not support **geocentrism**, suggesting instead that the stars and planets, including the earth, revolved around a fixed sun. Fearing ridicule, Copernicus did not publish his *On the Revolutions of the Heavenly Spheres* until 1543, the year of his death. Following Copernicus, the Danish astronomer Tycho Brahe compiled a wealth of "eyeball" data relating to planetary and stellar movements. This data was precise enough to help the German Johannes Kepler work out an elegant if not yet persuasive heliocentric, or sun-centered, model in which the planets circled the sun in elliptical orbits.

Many of Europe's most probing minds were open to the truth of **heliocentrism**, and some went on to risk not only reputations but lives to advance the project of wedding mathematics to observed phenomena. In works such as *The Advancement of Learning* (1605), Sir Francis Bacon attacked reliance on ancient writers and ardently supported the scientific method based on inductive reasoning and empirical experimentation. Bacon had his critics, but he was shielded from persecution by the Protestant English state, which he served as lord chancellor. By contrast, the Italian scientist Galileo Galilei is best remembered for his insistence, against an unforgiving Catholic Church, that nature was governed by mathematical laws. Although the Inquisition placed Galileo under house arrest, his use of new, high-grade telescopes to observe the moons of Jupiter furthered the cause of heliocentrism and challenged reliance on received wisdom.

Ultimately, minor deviations between Kepler's model and careful empirical observation were worked out in large part by the English scientist Isaac Newton. The elliptical planetary orbits discovered by Kepler, Newton argued through word and formula in *Principia Mathematica* (*Mathematical Principles*, 1687), resulted from the laws of motion, including the principle of gravity, which explained the forces that controlled the movement not only of

Early Breakthroughs

Newton's Synthesis

heliocentrism The early modern discovery that the sun is the center of our solar system.

planets but of objects on earth. The whole universe was brought together in one majestic system. Whereas Copernicus had feared publishing his findings in his lifetime, Newton faced a much more receptive audience. His synthesis would prevail until the twentieth century.

Advance of the New Science Beyond Europe

Other educated Europeans were testing boundaries in distant corners of the world. In the last years of the sixteenth century the Italian Jesuit Matteo Ricci stunned the Ming court with his vast knowledge of mechanics and mathematics. The Spanish-American metallurgist and parish priest Alvaro Alonso Barba went further, challenging received wisdom through experimentation in his 1627 treatise, *The Art of Metals*. Here in the remote silver mines of Potosí, high in the mountains of what is today Bolivia, Barba was sufficiently informed to comment on Galileo's observations of the moons of Jupiter as outlined in his 1610 publication, *Sidereus Nuncius* (*The Starry Messenger*).

The Emergence of Capitalism

Another great puzzle of early modern Europe regards the emergence of **capitalism**—an economic system in which private individuals or groups make their goods and services available on a free market and seek to take advantage of market conditions to profit from their activities. In developing a capitalist economic system, Europe diverged from the rest of the world, especially after 1650. To be sure, the desire to accumulate wealth and realize profits was by no means new. Ever since the introduction of agriculture and the production of surplus crops, some individuals and groups had accumulated great wealth. As we saw in Chapter 15, merchants in the fifteenth-century "global bazaar" avidly pursued profits from overseas trade. During early modern times, however, European merchants and entrepreneurs transformed their society in a way that none of their predecessors had.

Role of Trading Companies

Historians and economists remain divided as to how capitalism came about, as well as where it started. Most agree, however, that there were two overlapping stages: first commercial, and later industrial. Large trading companies such as the English East India Company and its Dutch competitor, the VOC, were especially important institutions in the commercial stage of capitalism. They spread the risks attached to expensive business enterprises and also took advantage of extensive communications and transportation networks. The trading companies organized commercial ventures on a larger scale than ever before in world history. They were supported by an array of businesses and services. Banks, for example, appeared in all the major commercial cities of Europe to safeguard funds and to grant loans to launch new ventures. Insurance companies mitigated financial losses from risky undertakings. Stock exchanges provided markets where investors could buy and sell shares in the trading companies, and they dealt in other commodities as well. Thus, innovative financial institutions and services created new connections among Europeans that facilitated expansion into global markets.

Rise of Wageworkers and the Bourgeoisie

In the countryside, meanwhile, innovations in mechanization and transport led to gains in productivity that exceeded population growth, especially in northwestern Europe. The arrival of potatoes and other New World crops boosted yields and filled peasant bellies. American sugar was increasingly used to preserve fruits through the long winter. Better food security enabled some peasants to sell their surplus labor for cash wages. Wages made peasants small-scale consumers, a new kind of market participant.

More dependable food supplies came with a social cost, however, most immediately felt by English peasants. Only landowners with secure titles to their property could take advantage of the new crops to practice commercial farming. Rich landowners therefore "enclosed" the land—that is, consolidated their holdings—and got Parliament to give them title to the common lands that in the past had been open to all. Land enclosure turned tenant farmers and sharecroppers into landless farm laborers. Many moved to the cities to seek work.

Cities became increasingly home to merchants, or burghers, as well as to wageworkers. The burghers, or **bourgeoisie**, grew to compete with the old nobility, particularly in England, the Netherlands, and parts of France, Germany, and Italy, as consumers of luxury goods. Especially after 1660 their economic power was boosting their political power.

capitalism In early modern Europe, a new way of conducting business by pooling money, goods, and labor to make a profit.

bourgeoisie In early modern Europe, a new class of burghers, or urban-dwelling merchants.

Role of Textile Manufacture

Europe's manufacturing sector was also deeply transformed. Beginning in the late Middle Ages, rising demand for textiles led to expanded production of woolen and linen fabrics. The major growth of the cloth industries took place in northern Europe beginning in the sixteenth century, when Spanish-American silver flowed through Spain to France, England, and Holland, despite ongoing conflicts. Asians did not much care for Europe's products, but colonists did. Millions of bolts of Dutch and French linens, as well as English woolens, were sent across the Atlantic, and even the Pacific, to Spanish and Portuguese colonies. Global interdependence grew ever tighter through the circulation of fabrics and silver. Europe's textile manufacturers begged Amsterdam and London merchants for Spanish-American dyes, along with Brazilian and Central American dyewood. Profits from growing international trade in textiles were then reinvested in more land for flax growing, larger weaving shops, and wages for increasing numbers of specialized workers. With the application of scientific principles and ever more innovative mechanical apparatus by the early eighteenth century, the stage was set for the emergence of industrial capitalism in England (discussed in Chapter 24).

Capitalism and Politics

England's commercial leadership in the eighteenth century had its origins in the mercantilism of the seventeenth century. European **mercantilism** was a system of economic regulations aimed at increasing the power of the state. It rested on the general premise that a nation's power and wealth were determined by its supply of precious metals, which were to be acquired by increasing exports (paid for with gold) and reducing imports to achieve domestic self-sufficiency. What distinguished English mercantilism was the notion that government economic regulations could and should serve the private interests of individuals and groups as well as the public needs of the state. For example, the Navigation Acts of the seventeenth century required that English goods be transported in English ships and restricted colonial exports to raw materials, enriching English merchants and manufacturers as well as the Crown.

Cornering the Atlantic slave trade and Indian Ocean cloth trade were England's two key overseas commercial objectives in the eighteenth century, and profits from both fueled industrial growth at home. As we will see in Chapter 22, English settlers amassed huge plantations in the Caribbean and North American mainland, based primarily on the labor of enslaved Africans, the profits from which they mostly sent home. English inroads in the Indian Ocean trade circuit, meanwhile, grew to eclipse all other European competitors. Capital that had been accumulated in the slave trade, Atlantic plantation complex, and East India monopolies was soon invested in industrial production in several English cities. Goods thus manufactured were subsequently forced on buyers in captive overseas markets, such as the North American colonies, enabling still greater capital accumulation in the imperial center. State power was exercised at every step, from the seizure of native American lands to the sale of African bodies, harsh reminders that the rise of industrial capitalism in England was not a magical or even a natural process, but rather the result of concerted applications of force in many parts of the world.

New Political Models: Absolutism and Constitutionalism

Europe in the wake of the Thirty Years' War witnessed the rise of two new state forms: absolutism and constitutionalism. Worn out by the costs of conflict, the Habsburg Empire fell into decline. A number of challengers sought to fill the void, including the commercially savvy Dutch, but it was the French under the Bourbon king Louis XIV who emerged pre-eminent. Not far behind, however, were the English, who despite a midcentury civil war moved to consolidate control over the British Isles and many overseas possessions by the early eighteenth century. As the great imperial rivals of the time, Britain and France developed distinct systems of governance later copied and modified by others. The monarchs of England found themselves sharply restricted by elected parliaments, whereas those of France sought absolute authority and claimed quasi-divinity. Despite their differing models of rule, the British and French managed to create the largest, most heavily armed, and widest-ranging navies yet seen in world history.

Although Spain's Philip II and other Habsburgs had acted in autocratic and grandiose ways since the mid-sixteenth century, no European monarch matched the heady blend of

mercantilism A system of economic regulations aimed at increasing the power of the state.

Absolutism in France

state drama and personal charisma of France's Louis XIV (r. 1643–1715). The "Sun-King," as he came to be known, personified the absolutist ruler who shared power with no one. Louis XIV spent much of his long reign centralizing state authority in order to make France a global contender. Though successful in the short run, Louis's form of **absolutism**—propped up in large part by rising taxes and a general contempt for the common masses—sowed the seeds of its own destruction.

Louis XIV came to the throne as a five-year-old, and his mother, Anne of Austria, and her Italian-born adviser and rumored lover, Cardinal Mazarin, ruled in his name. Under the regency, resistance quickly emerged in the form of the *Fronde*, a five-year period of instability from 1648 to 1653 that grew from a regional tax revolt into a potential civil war. Critics coined the term *Fronde*, French for a child's slingshot, to signify that the revolts were mere child's play. In fact, they posed an unprecedented threat to the Crown. Historians of the seventeenth-century crisis have often linked the uprisings to climate change, agricultural stresses, and price fluctuations. Whatever the Fronde's causes, nobles and district courts, or *parlements* (PARLE-mohn), asserted their power against the regency. In the end, the revolt was put down, and when Mazarin died in 1661, Louis XIV assumed total control. He would not forget the Fronde, drawing from it the lesson that the independent power of the French aristocracy must be eliminated and that all power and authority in France must derive from the king.

Like many other monarchs faced with entrenched power structures, Louis XIV spent the next several decades co-opting nobles and potential religious opponents through a mix of patronage and punishment. His rule was authoritarian, and like that of his Spanish Habsburg precursor, Philip II, intolerant of religious difference. After persecuting nonconformist Catholics in the 1660s, Louis exiled the country's remaining Huguenots, French Protestants whose protection had been guaranteed by Henry IV in the Edict of Nantes of 1598. Absolutism was extended to the press as well, with pro-state propaganda and harsh censorship of criticism the order of the day.

The French absolutist state also relied on loyal crown officers, called *intendants* (ON-tohn-don), whose authority superseded that of local parlements and nobles. These officials governed districts, or departments, in the king's name, administering justice, collecting taxes, and organizing defense. Loyal bureaucrats also included high-ranking commoners such as Jean-Baptiste Colbert, Louis's minister of finance. As a trusted favorite, Colbert also oversaw naval and overseas trade affairs, taking a close interest in French expansion in the Caribbean and North America. As the Ottomans had already shown, rewarding merit-worthy commoners with high office was as much a part of early modern government as containing the aspirations of high nobles. Building an overseas empire greatly expanded the scope of patronage politics.

Court Culture and State Power

More than any other early European monarch, Louis XIV arranged court life to serve as a sort of state theater. As in Inca Peru or Ming China, the ruler was allegedly divine, and physical proximity to him was regarded as both desirable and dangerous. A constant stream of propaganda in the form of poems, processions, statues, and medals celebrated the greatness of the monarch. "The state?" Louis asked rhetorically. "It is I."

To house his bulging court, which included growing numbers of fawning and reluctantly drafted nobles, Louis XIV ordered thousands of artisans and laborers to construct a palace befitting his magnificence. Built between 1662 and 1685, Versailles, just outside Paris, was to exceed the ambitious dimensions of Philip II's Escorial. Though hardly the pleasure dome outsiders and common folk imagined it to be, and far less opulent than the palace of Louis's near contemporary, Mughal emperor Shah Jahan, Versailles set a new model for European court grandeur. It was also a physical embodiment of Louis's political ideology. Versailles was a central point from which, at least in theory, all political power and authority flowed.

absolutism A political theory holding that all power should be vested in one ruler; also such a system of government.

constitutionalism An early modern system of government based on a written charter defining a power-sharing arrangement between a monarch and representative bodies, or parliaments.

Tax increases helped to cover the costs of building and maintaining Versailles. The point of raising taxes during Louis XIV's rule was not simply to underwrite court opulence, however. More costly by far were the armed forces. Naval construction grew tremendously under Colbert's direction, but the professionalization and reorganization of land forces was even more extensive. By 1700 France, a country of some 20 million people, could field three hundred thousand soldiers. This was more than ten times the number of soldiers in England, a country with about half of France's total population.

Palace of Versailles
In this 1668 aerial view of Versailles, painter Pierre Patel seeks to encompass the full grandeur and orderliness of French king Louis XIV's famous palace and retreat. Begun in 1661, Versailles instantly became a symbol of absolutist power, a virtual city unto itself. Many early modern rulers ordered the construction or expansion of similarly opulent structures, such as the Ottomans' Topkapi Palace in Istanbul and the Mughals' Red Fort complex in Delhi. (akg-images.)

Louis used his army and navy primarily to confront his powerful Habsburg neighbors to the east and south, although his aggression upset many others, including the English, Swedes, and Dutch. First were incursions into the Spanish Netherlands in the 1660s and 1670s, then into Germany in the 1680s and 1690s. Both conflicts ended with only minor gains for France, but Louis was feared enough to be dubbed the "Christian Turk." Meanwhile, the Crown sponsored French trading companies that vied with their Dutch and English counterparts to penetrate the markets of Africa, the Middle East, India, and Southeast Asia.

Wars of Expansion

Most important in global terms was the War of the Spanish Succession (1701–1714). This long, bloody, and complex conflict proved disastrous for the French because most of Europe allied against them, fearing the consequences of French control over Spanish territories. It ended with England the ultimate victor and France forced to cede exclusive trading privileges with Spanish America (see Map 20.4). Military service, meanwhile, became a standard feature of life for French commoners, along with high taxes and periodic food shortages. Absolutism was good for centralizing authority, but not, as it would turn out, for keeping the peace.

The turmoil of seventeenth-century Europe resulted in both absolute monarchy and a lasting alternative form of government. **Constitutionalism** requires rulers to share power with representative bodies, or parliaments. In England, birthplace of constitutionalism, taxation was always at issue, but so were other matters such as religious freedom and class representation.

Constitutionalism in England

Constitutions were charters guaranteeing subjects certain rights, but which subjects and what rights? For a time, it was mostly elites whose economic and religious interests won out. Indeed, far from being democratically elected representatives of the popular classes, members of the constitutionalist parliament—whether in England, Holland, or Poland—were generally landlords and merchants. Some were prominent clergymen. None were artisans or peasants.

English constitutionalism did not emerge peacefully. Instead, when in 1641 King Charles I (r. 1625–1649) attempted to play absolutist monarch before England's centuries-old Parliament of wealthy property owners, he met a resistance so violent it cost him his life. Charles's timing, as historians of the seventeenth-century crisis have pointed out, could not have been worse: thousands were starving after a sequence of failed harvests. In what was surely among the most startling if not revolutionary acts of the early modern period, subjects decided that if the king was judged to be acting out-of-bounds, he should go.

England's showdown with the king had a long backstory. Charles had distrusted Parliament from the start of his rule and refused to call it into session throughout the 1630s.

English Civil War

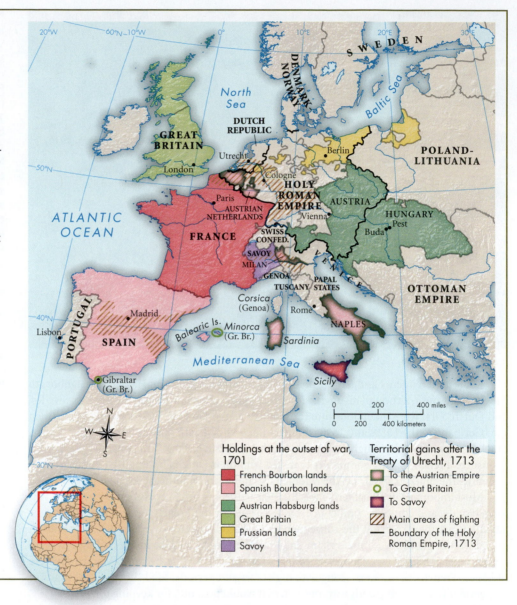

MAP 20.4

War of the Spanish Succession, 1701–1714

Unlike the Thirty Years' War of the previous century, the War of the Spanish Succession was openly understood to be a global power contest rather than a conflict over religious faith. With the Ottomans, Iberians, and even the Dutch in decline, the main contestants were Great Britain and France. Great Britain and its allies won the war, but in the Treaty of Utrecht they allowed the French prince to take the throne as Philip V in exchange for a monopoly on the slave trade to Spanish America and other concessions, such as the strategic Mediterranean post of Gibraltar and the island of Minorca.

Holdings at the outset of war, 1701

- French Bourbon lands
- Spanish Bourbon lands
- Austrian Habsburg lands
- Great Britain
- Prussian lands
- Savoy

Territorial gains after the Treaty of Utrecht, 1713

- To the Austrian Empire
- To Great Britain
- To Savoy
- Main areas of fighting
- Boundary of the Holy Roman Empire, 1713

Unconventional taxes and religious edicts eroded the king's support in England and provoked a rebellion in Scotland. Parliament was called in 1640 to meet this last crisis, but representatives surprised the monarch by demanding sweeping reforms. Many Protestants felt that the king supported Catholicism, the religion of his French wife, and the most radical among them, the Puritans, pushed hardest for checks on royal power. Charles reacted with force, touching off the English Civil War of 1642 to 1646.

After intense fighting, the Puritan faction under Oliver Cromwell emerged victorious. Cromwell and his Puritan supporters took over Parliament and brought Charles to trial. The king was convicted of tyranny and executed by beheading in 1649.

The Cromwell Dictatorship and Restoration

Cromwell, who styled himself "Lord Protector," proved instead to be a military dictator. Dissenters were killed or oppressed, and Cromwellian forces subjugated Scotland and Ireland with terror and mass displacement. Overseas conflicts with the Dutch and French resulted in few victories and expanded taxes. When Cromwell died in 1658, few English subjects mourned his passing. Instead, the reaction was a sweeping revival of Anglicanism and restoration of the monarchy in 1660.

The Glorious Revolution

King and Parliament, however, soon resumed their conflicts. After coming to power in 1685, James II ran afoul of Parliament with his absolutist tendencies and apparent desire to impose his and his wife's Catholicism on English subjects. In 1688 Parliament deposed James, an act that proved far less bloody than the removal of Charles I, and invited James's Protestant daughter Mary (r. 1689–1694) and her Dutch husband, William of Orange (r. 1689–1702), to assume the throne. The event was called the Glorious Revolution since it entailed the monarchs' signing an agreement to share power with Parliament. A genuine constitutional system, much copied worldwide in later years, was now in place.

COUNTERPOINT
The Barbary Pirates

To the vast land empire of the Ottomans and the fractured states of Europe, Africa's north coast, or Maghreb, offers a dual counterpoint. The early modern Maghreb consisted of sea-hugging city-states and tribal enclaves stretching from Morocco to present-day Libya. Although fiercely Islamic and sympathetic to the Ottoman cause against the Habsburgs and their allies, no Maghribi city ever fell completely under the sway of the Ottoman Empire. Instead, the greatest threats to this centerless region's autonomy came from Christian Europe, whose merchants had long traveled to Africa in pursuit of slaves and gold. Energized by its gunpowder-fueled 1492 conquest of Granada, Spain invaded North Africa with fury, but struggled mightily and at great cost to hold onto a few rocky outposts. Subsequent European interlopers fared little better.

> **FOCUS**
>
> Why were the Barbary pirates of North Africa able to thrive from 1500 to 1800 despite Ottoman and European overseas expansion?

Reign of the Sea Bandits

After 1500, sea banditry flourished along what Europeans called the Berber, or Barbary, Coast. Early pirate leaders of great renown included Oruç and Hayreddin Barbarossa, Greek brothers from the island of Lesbos who settled in Algiers and ruled it from 1516 to 1546. The Barbarossa (Italian for "red beard") brothers were already famous for their bold raids on the coast of Italy. They briefly combined forces with neighboring Tunis to launch large-scale attacks and share out booty, but regional jealousies prevailed and the cities again competed. The raiders focused on capturing merchant vessels at sea, but what made the Barbarossas household names were their increasingly audacious land attacks and kidnappings. Hayreddin later strengthened ties to the Ottomans, but he remained independent of the sultan's orders.

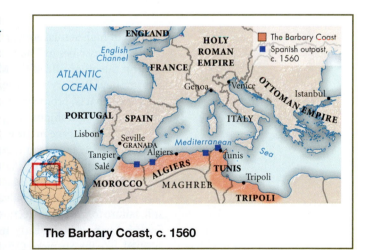

The Barbary Coast, c. 1560

As Ottoman sea power declined after 1580 and Atlantic shipping ballooned, other pirate bases sprang up along the west coast of Morocco. Key after 1600 was the tiny city of Salé (sah-LAY), whose pirate attacks on Spanish and Portuguese shipping were financed and sometimes manned by exiled Iberian Jews and Muslims. Some such foreign-born pirates were deeply involved in European court intrigues, acting as double agents and seeking support for pretenders to the Spanish-held Portuguese throne. Others were simply outlaws hoping to get rich at the expense of their former tormentors. Aside from these vengeful European "renegades," as they were called, a number of Morocco's own seafaring Berber tribes engaged in piracy and extortion as an extension of their culture. Countless young men came of age beneath the pirate flag.

By the time Miguel de Cervantes was held captive in Algiers in the late 1570s, Maghribi hostage trafficking and extortion rackets formed the core of a sophisticated business. The pirates used swift sailing vessels and state-of-the-art European guns to steal money and merchandise, but mostly they kidnapped Christian Europeans, preferably men and

Ransoming Christians

Piracy in the early modern Mediterranean entailed many daring captures at sea, along with several audacious ones on land. Unlike in the Americas, where piracy also thrived at this time, the Barbary pirates of Africa's north coast specialized in kidnapping and extortion. The ransom of Christian captives held in cities such as Algiers and Tunis was organized by Catholic religious orders, who collected sums from as far away as Spanish America to free men and women whose relatives in Spain, Italy, France, and elsewhere could produce no ransom. This seventeenth-century European engraving depicts Catholic priests heroically carrying ransom money, while Christian prisoners appear as cruelly mistreated victims cowering behind their Muslim captors. (The Art Archive.)

women of high status. Some hostages were mistreated and forced to do hard labor, but as Cervantes describes in *Don Quixote*, most were allowed to send letters to friends and relatives on the other side of the Mediterranean in hopes that they would raise sufficient ransom money. Barbary Coast extortion also consisted of selling safe passage to European shippers—that is, promising *not* to kidnap them or steal their merchandise in exchange for money, arms, and shipbuilding materials.

Unable to engage in the expensive conquest enterprises tried by the Spanish and Portuguese, northern European merchants, who were more answerable to shareholders than to kings after about 1600, struck deals with various sultans and tribal leaders in the Maghreb in exchange for safe passage. Maghribi leaders mostly welcomed these Protestant newcomers, because they had access to advanced weapons and shared their hatred of Catholic Iberians. Still, failure to pay for protection led to harsh reprisals. Some pirates raided as far away as the English Channel in the early 1600s, and before long thousands of northern Europeans languished, like the Spaniard Cervantes before them, in the jails of Algiers, Tunis, and Tripoli. In time, England, France, and the Netherlands funded permanent embassies in these and other competing city-states, but their primary purpose was to gather information and keep allied Muslim princes happy, not to seek the release of unlucky Christian subjects. After 1660, the English became a permanent presence in the Moroccan city of Tangier, a strategic base won from the Portuguese through royal marriage.

The Barbary Wars

Although internal divisions and poor leadership among Maghribi sovereigns became more evident over time, it was sustained rivalry among the Europeans that prevented any coordinated attack on the Barbary pirates until the early nineteenth century. Only then, when merchants from the fledgling United States reacted angrily to demands for protection money, did the Barbary pirates see a reversal in fortune. Outraged by what the merchants considered hypocrisy in an era of loudly proclaimed free trade, they proposed a new approach to the Mediterranean's piracy problem. In a pet project of President Thomas Jefferson, the United States won the support of traditional European powers, most significantly the French, to bomb the Barbary pirates into submission. The so-called Barbary Wars' unexpected result was near-total French takeover of North Africa, which ended only in the 1960s.

Conclusion

Fueled by gunpowder, silver, and religious fervor, Europe and the Mediterranean basin exploded after 1500 as the world's most belligerent region, but it was also the most commercially dynamic. Relative resource poverty had long compelled Europeans to trade with one another, but regional identities, exacerbated by religious differences, had led them to fight as often as they cooperated. This trend only continued in the late sixteenth century, when nationalist loyalties were hardened by the Protestant Reformation and its aftermath.

By contrast, in these years the Sunni Muslim Ottomans built a vast land empire encompassing eastern Europe, Southwest Asia, Egypt, and much of Arabia. They did so with force, but also by cleverly integrating new subjects into the ranks of government and the armed forces. Ottoman pragmatism also included a policy of religious tolerance. The Ottoman world became a haven for many of Europe's persecuted Jews, and conquered Christians were not forced to convert to Islam. Chronic wars with the Habsburgs and Safavids provided many opportunities for social advancement, but they also absorbed a huge portion of state resources, eventually bogging the empire down.

A battered Europe emerged from its seventeenth-century crisis to begin a new phase of national division. The century between 1650 and 1750 was no less bloody than the one before, but it marked the beginnings of three globally significant trends: a new science based on direct observation and experimentation, an increasingly capitalist economy, and increasingly centralized, national government. All of this sounds quite modern, but western Europe's competing kingdoms still saw the quest for wealth and power as a zero-sum game, in which gain by one side meant loss by the others, driving them to seek monopolies over resources and lay claim to ever more distant lands and peoples. To a degree, Europeans saw the world through the same mercantilist lens as the Portuguese of previous centuries, but the languages of science and rational economics, rather than religion, were increasingly used to justify conquest of traditional societies. Soon after, in the first years of the nineteenth century, it was a new language, that of free trade, rather than religious animosity that drove the fledgling United States and its European allies to attack the Barbary Coast pirates. Former Barbary captive Miguel de Cervantes of Spain could hardly have known what lay ahead for Europe and the greater Mediterranean, but his vision of a newly interconnected world continued to inspire his imagination. In the opening to the second part of *Don Quixote*, published in 1615, Cervantes jokingly claimed that he had received a letter from the Chinese emperor inviting him to establish a Spanish school at court for which his "world-famous" novel would be the main text. Cervantes claimed that he had declined the offer only because he was ill and could not afford the trip.

NOTES

1. Celalzade, Mustafa, *Selim-name* [In praise of Selim] (eds. Ahmet Uğur, Mustafa Huhadar), Ankara 1990; as it appears in Halil Berktay and Bogdan Murgescu, *The Ottoman Empire* (Thessaloniki: CDRSEE, 2005), 53.
2. Habsburg ambassador Ghiselin de Busbecq, quoted in Gérard Chaliand, ed., *The Art of War in World History from Antiquity to the Nuclear Age* (Berkeley: University of California Press, 1994), 457.
3. Jennings, Ronald C., *Christians and Muslims in Ottoman Cyprus and the Mediterranean World, 1571-1640,* New York – London 1993; as it appears in Halil Berktay and Bogdan Murgescu, *The Ottoman Empire* (Thessaloniki: CDRSEE, 2005), 116.
4. Evlija Celebi, Putopis. *Odlomci o jugoslovenskim zemljama* [Travel-records. Fragments about Yugoslav Countries], Sarajevo 1996; as it appears in Halil Berktay and Bogdan Murgescu, *The Ottoman Empire* (Thessaloniki: CDRSEE, 2005), 82.

RESOURCES FOR RESEARCH

General Works

Few historians have attempted to treat early modern Europe and the wider Mediterranean in a global context, but the following books are some of the best general syntheses in the field. Braudel remains the grand inspiration. Crosby challenges us to see what was special about growing European interest in numbers and calculation, which owed much to Islamic precedent.

Braudel, Fernand. *The Mediterranean and the Mediterranean World in the Age of Philip II*. 2 vols. Translated by Sian Reynolds. 1996.

Crosby, Alfred W. *The Measure of Reality: Quantification and Western Society, 1250–1600*. 1997.

Elliott, John H. *Spain, Europe, and the Wider World, 1500–1800*. 2009.

Elliott, John H. *Europe Divided, 1556–1598*, 2d ed. 2000.

Kamen, Henry. *Early Modern European Society*. 2000.

The Power of the Ottoman Empire, 1453–1750

Ottoman history is a vibrant field, and new work continues to link the empire to both West and East. A recent wave of regional studies of Ottoman Egypt and Syria joins better-known work on Ottoman eastern Europe and Anatolia. Giancarlo Casale's book takes the Ottomans overseas.

Casale, Giancarlo. *The Ottoman Age of Exploration*. 2010.

Goffman, Daniel. *The Ottomans and Early Modern Europe*. 2002.

Kafadar, Cemal. *Between Two Worlds: The Construction of the Ottoman State*. 1995.

Mansel, Philip. *Constantinople: City of the World's Desire, 1453–1924*. 1996.

Pierce, Leslie. *The Imperial Harem: Women and Sovereignty in the Ottoman Empire*. 1993.

Europe Divided, 1500–1650

Histories of the "seventeenth-century crisis" have come back into vogue in recent years, and now stress global linkages in trade, climate, and other spheres. Other authors, such as Davis and Schwartz, have expanded the study of women's self-fashioning and the popular religious toleration that existed despite harsh decrees from above.

Cunningham, Andrew, and Ole Peter Grell. *The Four Horsemen of the Apocalypse: Religion, War, Famine and Death in Reformation Europe*. 2000.

Davis, Natalie Zemon. *Women on the Margins: Three Seventeenth-Century Lives*. 1995.

"Introduction." AHR Forum: The General Crisis of the Seventeenth Century Revisited. *The American Historical Review* 113, no. 4 (October 2008): 1029–1030. http://www.jstor.org/stable/10.1086/ahr.113.4.1029.

Parker, Geoffrey. *Europe in Crisis, 1598–1648*, 2d ed. 2001.

Schwartz, Stuart B. *All Can Be Saved: Religious Tolerance and Salvation in the Iberian Atlantic World*. 2008.

Sturdy, David J. *Fractured Europe, 1600–1721*. 2002.

European Innovations in Science and Government, 1550–1750

Historians of science continue to debate the meaning and timing of the so-called Scientific Revolution, but when seen in a global context, the changes initiated in sixteenth-century Europe appear starkly important. Economic historians are even less in agreement with regard to the origins of modern capitalism, but the topic remains huge, and as treated by Chaudury, Pomeranz, and others, it has become more globally integrated.

Beik, William. *Louis XIV and Absolutism: A Brief Study with Documents*. 2000.

Chaudury, Sushil, and Michel Morineau, eds. *Merchants, Companies, and Trade: Europe and Asia in the Early Modern Era*. 1999.

Edwards, Philip. *The Making of the Modern English State, 1460–1660*. 2001.

Henry, John. *The Scientific Revolution and the Origins of Modern Science*, 2d ed. New York: Palgrave, 2002.

Pomeranz, Kenneth. *The Great Divergence: China, Europe, and the Making of the Modern World Economy*. 2000.

Smith, Pamela H., and Paula Findlen, eds. *Merchants and Marvels: Commerce, Science, and Art in Early Modern Europe*. 2002.

Smyth, Jim. *The Making of the United Kingdom, 1660–1800*. 2001.

COUNTERPOINT: The Barbary Pirates

The Barbary pirates have been a source of many legends, but serious historical research has also been undertaken. Braudel's classic study of the Mediterranean, cited above under General Works, includes considerable information on the sixteenth-century pirates, whereas Heers and Wolf provide more scope and detail.

Heers, Jacques. *The Barbary Corsairs*. 2003.

Pennell, C. R. *Bandits at Sea: A Pirates Reader*. 2001.

Vitkus, Daniel J., and Nabil Matar, eds. *Piracy, Slavery, and Redemption: Barbary Captivity Narratives from Early Modern England*. 2001.

Wolf, John B. *The Barbary Coast: Algeria Under the Turks*. 1979.

▶ **For additional primary sources from this period**, see *Sources of Crossroads and Cultures*.

▶ **For Web sites, images, and documents related to topics in this chapter**, see Make History at bedfordstmartins.com/smith.

REVIEW

The major global development in this chapter ▶ Early modern Europe's increasing competition and division in the face of Ottoman expansion.

IMPORTANT EVENTS

1453	Ottoman conquest of Constantinople
1492	Spanish take Granada, expel Jews
1517	Martin Luther disseminates "Ninety-five Theses," sparking the Protestant Reformation
1520–1566	Reign of Ottoman emperor Suleiman
1540	Ignatius Loyola founds the new Catholic order of the Jesuits
1543	Nicolaus Copernicus, *On the Revolutions of the Heavenly Spheres*
1545–1563	Council of Trent
1571	Battle of Lepanto
1572	St. Bartholomew's Day massacre
1580	Philip II of Spain takes over Portuguese Empire
1598	Edict of Nantes ends French Religious War
1618–1648	Thirty Years' War
1640	Portugal wins independence from Spain
1642–1646	English Civil War
1643–1715	Reign of Louis XIV of France
1683	Ottomans defeated in Vienna by Polish-Austrian alliance
1687	Isaac Newton, *Principia Mathematica*
1688	Glorious Revolution in England
1701–1714	War of the Spanish Succession

CHAPTER OVERVIEW QUESTIONS

1. To what degree was religious diversity embraced or rejected in early modern Europe and the greater Mediterranean, and why?

2. How did Christian Europe's gunpowder-fueled empires compare with that of the Ottomans?

3. What accounts for the rise of science and capitalism in early modern western Europe?

SECTION FOCUS QUESTIONS

1. What factors explain the rise of the vast Ottoman Empire and its centuries-long endurance?

2. What sparked division in Europe after 1500, and why did this trend persist?

3. What factors enabled European scientific and political innovations in the early modern period?

4. Why were the Barbary pirates of North Africa able to thrive from 1500 to 1800 despite Ottoman and European overseas expansion?

MAKING CONNECTIONS

1. How did battles for control of the Mediterranean compare with those for control of Indian Ocean trade (see Chapter 19)?

2. How globally important was the Protestant Reformation?

3. In what ways were the Barbary pirates similar to the Atlantic slave traders (see Chapter 18)? How were they different?

KEY TERMS

absolutism (p. 674)
armada (p. 666)
bourgeoisie (p. 672)
capitalism (p. 672)
caravanserai (p. 656)
constitutionalism (p. 674)

devshirme (p. 651)
geocentrism (p. 670)
heliocentrism (p. 671)
indulgence (p. 662)
mercantilism (p. 673)
timar (p. 651)

21

AT A CROSSROADS ▶

This life-size portrait from Beijing's Palace Museum depicts China's Emperor Qianlong (1711–1799) at a grand old age. The use of perspective—the illusion of three-dimensional space—reflects the influence of European Jesuit artists who resided at court after the early seventeenth century, but the emperor's pose reflects a Chinese taste for a more statuelike representation of imperial power. His elaborate silk garments and pearl-encrusted headgear and necklace suggest the wealth of the Qing treasury, which despite massive expenditures and waste, boasted a huge surplus in silver for much of the emperor's reign. (The Palace Museum, Beijing/©Hu Weibiao/ChinaStock.)

Expansion and Isolation in Asia

1450–1750

W ang Yangming (1472–1529) had trouble on his hands. As governor of the south western Chinese province of Jiangxi, he was expected to collect taxes and keep the peace for his Ming overlords. Wang had risen through the ranks of the civil service through a mix of intelligence, connections, and raw ambition. Now he was faced with a rebellious prince, Zhu Chen-hao, and his loyal followers. Acting as general, Wang successfully attacked the rebels with every weapon at hand, including novel bronze cannon probably copied from the Portuguese. More important than the suppression of the rebellion was the aftermath. Wang chose not to terrorize the populace and destroy the land as his predecessors might have, but instead moved quickly to rebuild, pardoning many rebels and winning their loyalty to the Ming emperor.

Wang Yangming's effective governorship won praise, but he was far better known as a philosopher. Wang was among the most renowned **Neo-Confucianists** of early modern China. As described in Chapter 15, the broad philosophical movement known as Neo-Confucianism was a revival of an ancient tradition. The fifth-century B.C.E. Chinese philosopher Kongzi (Latinized as "Confucius") envisioned the ideal earthly society as a mirror of divine harmony. Although he prescribed ritual ancestor worship, Confucius

BACKSTORY

By the fifteenth century, Russia, a largely agrarian society straddling Eurasia, had shaken off Mongol rule and was beginning to expand from its base in Moscow. Russian expansion would eventually lead to conflict with China, which by the fifteenth century was by far the world's most populous state. Self-sufficient, widely literate, and technically sophisticated, China vied with Europe for supremacy in both practical and theoretical sciences. As we saw in Chapter 15, the Ming dynasty had also become a global power capable of mounting long-distance sea voyages, yet by the 1430s its rulers had chosen to withdraw and focus on consolidating internal affairs. By contrast, Japan was deeply fractured in the fifteenth century, its many districts and several islands subject to feuding warlords. Korea, though less densely populated than either of its neighbors east or west, was relatively unified under the Yi dynasty, which came to power in the late fourteenth century. In mainland Southeast Asia, several Buddhist kingdoms were by this time undergoing a major reconfiguration. Neo-Confucianism was on the rise in Vietnam. The Philippine Islands, meanwhile, remained politically and ethnically diverse, in part due to their complex geography.

Straddling Eurasia: Rise of the Russian Empire, 1462–1725

FOCUS What prompted Russian territorial expansion?

China from Ming to Qing Rule, 1500–1800

FOCUS How did the shift to a silver cash economy transform Chinese government and society?

Japan in Transition, 1540–1750

FOCUS How did self-isolation affect Japan?

Korea, a Land in Between, 1392–1750

FOCUS How did life for common folk in early modern Korea differ from life in China or Japan?

Consolidation in Mainland Southeast Asia, 1500–1750

FOCUS What trends did mainland Southeast Asia share with China, Korea, Japan, and Russia?

COUNTERPOINT: "Spiritual Conquest" in the Philippines

FOCUS In contrast to the general trend of political consolidation in early modern Asia, why did the Philippines fall to a European colonizing power?

Neo-Confucianism The revival of Confucius's ancient philosophy stressing agrarian life, harmony between ruler and ruled, and respect for elders and ancestors.

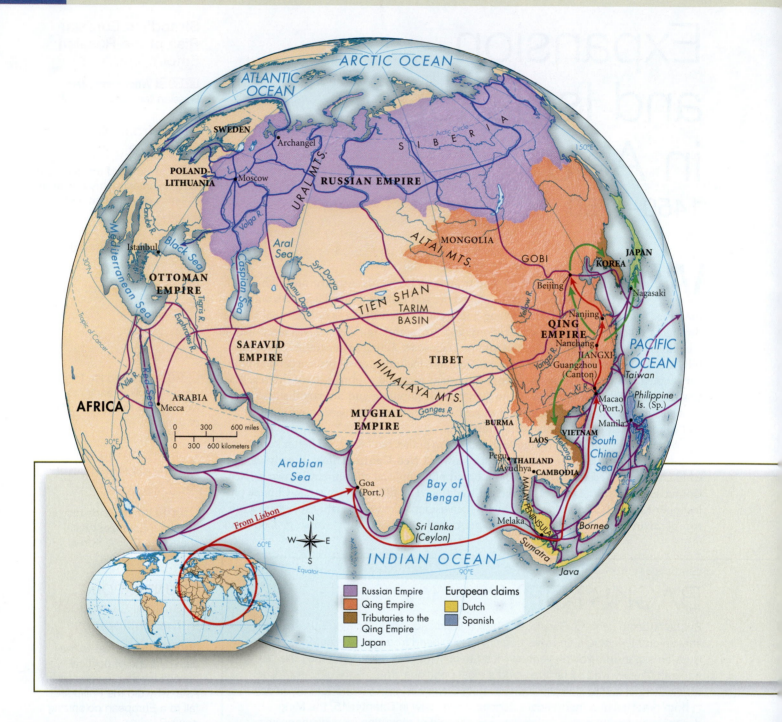

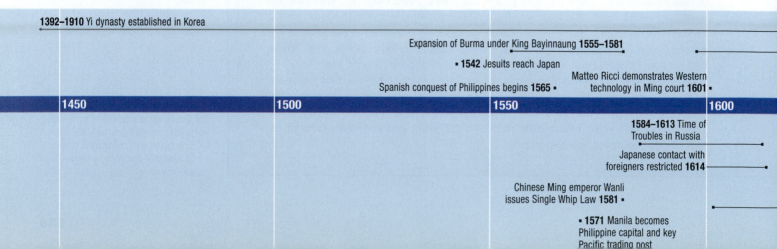

Expansion of Burma under King Bayinnaung **1555–1581**

• **1542** Jesuits reach Japan

Spanish conquest of Philippines begins **1565** •

Matteo Ricci demonstrates Western technology in Ming court **1601** •

| 1450 | 1500 | 1550 | 1600 |

1584–1613 Time of Troubles in Russia

Japanese contact with foreigners restricted **1614**

Chinese Ming emperor Wanli issues Single Whip Law **1581** •

• **1571** Manila becomes Philippine capital and key Pacific trading post

developed a system of ethics rather than a formal religion. Education and scientific experimentation were highly valued, but so was submission to elders and other social superiors. Ideal Chinese citizens had duties rather than rights. Some of Confucius's core ideas were further developed by his fourth-century B.C.E. successor, Mengzi, or Mencius, whose commentaries inspired Wang Yangming.

As his response to the rebels in Jiangxi suggested, Wang was as much a man of action as he was a scholar. In fact, Wang saw no clear distinction between his military and intellectual lives, arguing that only by doing could one learn, and that action was in fact inseparable from learning. In addition to challenging older notions that privileged scholarly reflection in matters of policy, Wang argued that individuals possessed an innate sense of right and wrong, something akin to the Western notion of conscience. Some scholars have argued that at least one result of the wide diffusion of Wang's teachings was a heightened sense among Chinese elites of the worthiness of the individual as a historical actor.

Neo-Confucianists sought to restore order to societies they felt had descended into chaos and decadence. For Wang, putting Ming society back on track required forceful action. Other Neo-Confucianists argued in favor of more passive reflection, but Wang's ideas seemed to strike the right chord in early sixteenth-century China, and were widely promoted by educators, first in China and later in Korea and Vietnam. Japan borrowed more selectively from Neo-Confucianism. When blended with the underlying Buddhist beliefs already deeply rooted in all these regions, Neo-Confucianism emerged as a largely uncontroversial religion of state. A foundation for many legal as well as moral principles, it helped hold together millions of ethnically diverse and socially divided people. In other parts of Asia, however, religion fueled division and conflict. The Philippines were a battleground between recent converts to Islam and Roman Catholicism. Russia, meanwhile, was defining itself as a revived Byzantium, expanding frontiers across Asia in the name of Orthodox Christianity. Muslims and other non-Christians were treated as enemies of faith and state.

MAPPING THE WORLD

Eurasian Trade and Empires, c. 1700

With the decline of the Mongols, Central Asia returned to its former role as a trading crossroads, mostly for silk, gems, furs, and other high-value commodities, yet it also became a meeting ground for two new, expansive empires: Russia under the Romanovs and China under the Qing, or Manchu, dynasty. Despite their focus on land expansion, both empires sought trade ties with the outside world by sea, mostly to win foreign exchange in the form of silver. More isolated areas in the region included Korea and Japan, both of which experienced political consolidation influenced by the spread of Chinese Neo-Confucianist principles. Similar processes appeared in Vietnam, whereas most of mainland Southeast Asia remained under expansionist Buddhist kings.

ROUTES ▼

— Fur trade route
— Other trade route
→ Spread of Neo-Confucianism
→ Travels of Matteo Ricci, 1582–1598

1597–1630s Persecution of Japanese Christians

1644 Manchu invasion of Beijing; Ming dynasty replaced by Qing

| 1650 | 1700 | 1750 |

1627, 1636 Manchu invasions of Korea

1661–1722 Qing expansion under Emperor Kangxi

1751 Qing annexation of Tibet

1602–1867 Tokugawa Shogunate in Japan

1689–1725 Russian imperial expansion under Tsar Peter the Great

Over the course of early modern times, Asian monarchs varied between absolutist-style rulers, as in Ming and Qing China and in Russia, and more symbolic figureheads, as in Tokugawa Japan. Korea's Yi (yee) dynasty kings fell somewhere in between, as did some of the kings of mainland Southeast Asia. Ordinary people, as in most of the Middle East and Europe, had little chance to contact or communicate with their rulers, dealing only with royal intermediaries or provincial authorities. The vast majority of Asians worked at subsistence farming and paid tribute in cash or foodstuffs to landlords or royal adminis-trators. Men were usually more mobile than women in that they were more likely to be caught up in public works or military drafts. Childhood—everywhere difficult to survive—was mostly an apprenticeship to adult labor.

Despite this continuity in everyday life, the early modern period was a time of sweep-ing change across Asia, sometimes sparked by the provocations of foreigners, but mostly resulting from long-range, internal developments. The overall trend was toward political consolidation under powerful dynasties. These centralizing governments sought to sup-press internal dissent, encourage religious unity, and expand territorial holdings at the expense of weaker neighbors, often using new military technologies to achieve this end. Dependence on outsiders was for the most part limited to strategic items such as guns and hard currency. Whole new classes of bureaucrats and merchants flourished, and with them came wider literacy in vernacular languages, support of the arts, and conspicuous consumption. Despite some punishing episodes of war, rebellion, and natural disaster, the early modern period in East Asia was arguably more peaceful than in most of Europe, the Middle East, or Africa. It was an era of steady population growth, commercial expansion, political consolidation, and cultural florescence.

OVERVIEW
QUESTIONS

The major global development in this chapter: The general trend toward political and cultural consolidation in early modern Asia.

As you read, consider:

1. What factors led to imperial consolidation in Russia and China? Who were the new rulers, and what were the sources of their legitimacy?

2. Why was isolation more common in these empires than overseas engage-ment, and what were some of the benefits and drawbacks of isolation?

3. In what ways did early modern Asians transform their environments, and why?

Straddling Eurasia: Rise of the Russian Empire 1462–1725

FOCUS

What prompted Russian territorial expansion?

Whereas the emerging nation-states of western Europe expanded largely through overseas conquests, early modern Russia followed a land-based path of expansion and consolidation more like that of the Ottomans and other so-called gunpowder empires to the south and east. Beginning in 1462, Moscow-based princes combined new weapons technology with bureaucratic innovations to expand their holdings. By the time Tsar Peter the Great died in 1725, the Russian Empire encompassed a huge swath of northern Asia, stretching from the Baltic to the Pacific (see Map 21.1).

Russian imperialism was basically conservative, with Russian Orthodoxy, the state religion, serving as a kind of nationalist "glue" throughout early modern times. Religious and cultural unity, plus a tendency toward isolation, inhibited efforts at social and agricultural reform. Although Peter the Great would end his reign by copying elements of western European governance and science, Russia remained an essentially tributary, agricultural regime until the nineteenth century. Military reforms such as those embraced by the Ottomans were Peter's most modern legacy. Although a modest merchant class had long existed in cities such as Moscow and Novgorod, the majority of Russians remained **serfs**, bound peasants with little more freedom than slaves.

Consolidation in Muscovite Russia

After the fall of Constantinople in 1453, some Russian Christians prophesied that the principality of Muscovy was to be the new Byzantium, and Moscow the "third Rome." The

serf A dependent agricultural laborer attached to a property and treated much like a slave.

MAP 21.1   **Rise of Russia, 1462–1725**

Beginning with the consolidation of Muscovy in the mid-fifteenth century, Russia grew steadily to become one of the world's largest—albeit least densely populated—land empires. By the time of Peter the Great's death in 1725, the Russian Empire encompassed much of northern Eurasia and included key ports in the Atlantic, Arctic, and Pacific oceans, with links to the Mediterranean via the Black Sea and to Persia via the Caspian Sea. Alongside military and commercial endeavors, the Russians spread their Orthodox Christian faith as far as northwest North America.

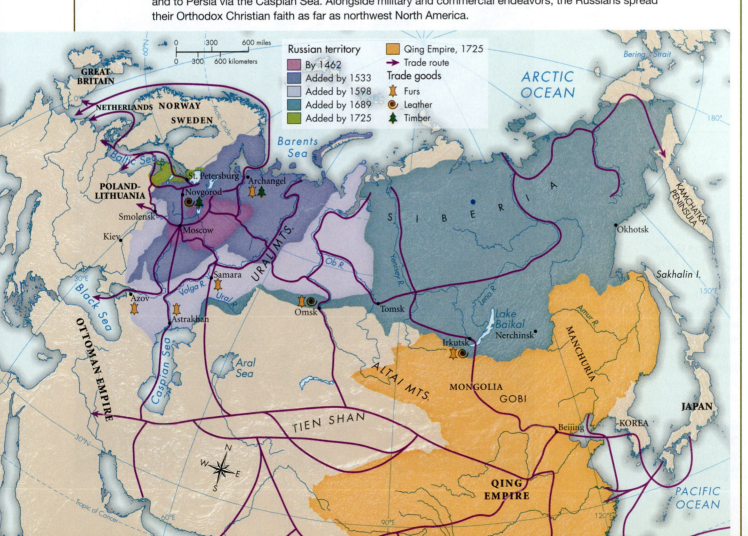

Rise and Expansion of Muscovy

Russian Orthodox Church was fiercely anti-Catholic and frequently energized by apocalyptic visionaries. These visionaries inspired a succession of grand princes who ruled Moscow following the Black Death, and each seemed more determined than the last to expand both Muscovy and the Orthodox Church's domain. As the early modern period progressed, the Ottomans and their allies came to pose the greatest threat to Russia in the south, and the Poles, Lithuanians, and Swedes periodically threatened in the west. The eastern Tatars, though in decline after Timur (see Chapter 15), were also a chronic menace.

Russia took shape under Moscow's grand prince, Ivan III (r. 1462–1505), nicknamed "the Great." Under Ivan the Great, the Muscovites expanded northward, tying landlocked Muscovy to the commercially vibrant Baltic Sea region. By the later sixteenth century, Russian monarchs began to allow English, Dutch, and other non-Catholic northwest European merchants to settle and trade in the capital. Like other Europeans, these merchants sought to circumvent the Ottomans and Middle Eastern intermediaries in the quest for East and South Asian fabrics and spices. As a result of alliances with foreign merchants, Muscovite rulers gained access to artillery, muskets, and other Western gunpowder technologies in exchange for furs and Asian textiles. These new weapons in turn fueled Russian imperial expansion, mostly across the steppes to the east and south (see again Map 21.1).

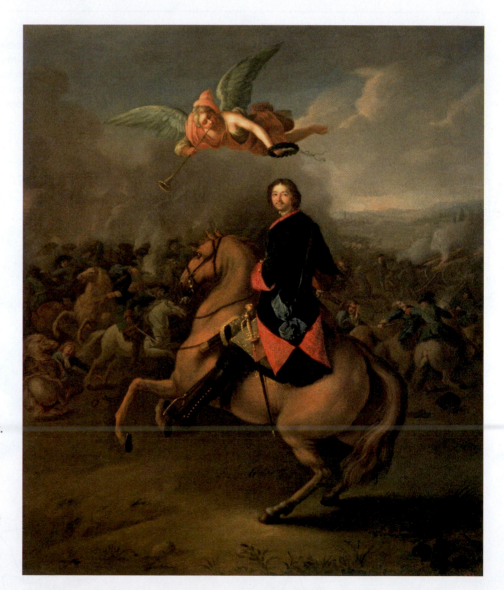

Peter the Great

Truly a giant of Russian history, the Romanov tsar Peter the Great spent much of his adult life trying to modernize and expand his vast realm, which spanned the Eurasian continent. He is shown here, tall in the saddle and supremely confident, at the 1709 Battle of Poltava (in present-day Ukraine), where he and his modernized army defeated Sweden's King Charles XII. The artist depicts Peter as blessed by an angel, whereas King Charles was forced to seek refuge with the Ottomans. (Tretyakov Gallery, Moscow/Bridgeman Art Library.)

Russia's next great ruler, and first tsar (literally, "Caesar"), was Ivan IV (r. 1533–1584), "the Terrible." Although remembered mostly for bizarre and violent behavior in his later years, Ivan IV was for the most part an effective monarch. In addition to conquering cities in the distant territories of the Golden Horde in the 1550s and acquiring lucrative fur-producing territories in Siberia, Ivan IV also reformed the Muscovite bureaucracy, judiciary, and treasury in a manner befitting a growing empire. The church, always at the heart of Russian politics, was also reorganized and partly subordinated to the state.

Ivan earned his nickname beginning in the 1560s when he established a personal fiefdom called the *oprichnina* (oh-preech-NEE-nah), which, like the Ottoman *timar* and *devshirme* systems, was in part intended to break the power of nobles and replace them with dependent state servants. This abrupt political shuffling crippled vital commercial cities such as Novgorod, however, and generally threw the empire into disarray. Meanwhile, wars begun in 1558 with Poland and Sweden went badly for Ivan's outgunned and undertrained forces. Things went no better on the southern front, and in 1571 Moscow fell to the eastern Tatars. Increasingly psychologically unstable during the last decade of his life, Ivan died of a stroke in 1584. Thanks in part to Ivan's personal disintegration, which included his killing of the heir apparent, Russia descended into chaos after Ivan's death. Historians have designated the subsequent three decades Russia's "Time of Troubles."

The Time of Troubles (1584–1613) was punctuated by succession crises, but it was also an era of famine, disease, military defeat, and social unrest, akin to Europe's "seventeenth-century crisis." Taking advantage of the dynastic chaos, the king of Poland and Lithuania tried to place his son on the Russian throne. The prospect of a Catholic ruler sparked Russia's first massive peasant rebellion, which ended with the humiliating occupation of Moscow by Polish forces. In 1613 an army of nobles, townspeople, and peasants drove out the intruders and put on the throne a nobleman, Michael Romanov (r. 1613–1645), founder of Russia's last royal line.

Time of Troubles

The Romanovs' New Frontiers

Under Romanov leadership, the seventeenth century saw the rebuilding and expansion of Muscovy and the slow but steady return to empire. Starting at 7 million in 1600, Russia's population roughly doubled by 1700. Impressive as this growth was, all of Russia's inhabitants could have fit into a small corner of China. Further, they looked more to leadership from the church, which had regained the authority it lost under Ivan the Terrible, than from the crown.

By the time of Peter the Great (r. 1689–1725), the Russian tsar faced a powerful and insubordinate church. Peter responded by prosecuting wandering preachers as enemies of the state. But what made Peter "great" was not his harsh dealings with the church but his relentless push to make Russia a competitor on par with France and other emerging western European nation-states. To this end, he kept stoking the fires of expansion-driven war, importing arms and military experts, building a navy, and professionalizing the armed forces. The Imperial Russian Army soon became not only a major force against the strongest of European and Central Asian challengers, but also a gargantuan consumer of state revenue.

Peter, a man of formidable size and boundless energy, is often remembered for his attempts to Westernize Russia, to purge it of what he regarded as backward, mostly Asian characteristics. Boyars, or nobles, were ordered to shave their beards and change their dress, and all courtiers were required to learn French. A new capital, St. Petersburg, was built on the Baltic shore in the French style, complete with a summer palace inspired by Louis XIV's Versailles. Not

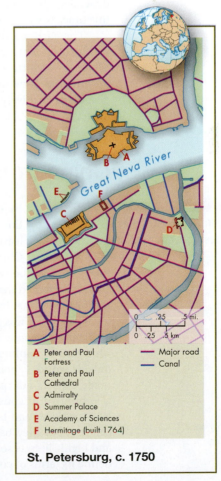

A	Peter and Paul Fortress
B	Peter and Paul Cathedral
C	Admiralty
D	Summer Palace
E	Academy of Sciences
F	Hermitage (built 1764)

— Major road
— Canal

St. Petersburg, c. 1750

everything Asian was bad, however. On southern expansion, Peter had this to say: "Approach as close to Constantinople and India as possible. He who rules there will be the real ruler of the world."[1]

Russian expansion across Asia was not only a military process. The growth of the fur trade reverberated ever more deeply through the many complex ecosystems of Siberia, and settling the great steppes of the south and east entailed wrenching social change and a wholesale transformation of the landscape. As frontier forts and agricultural colonization advanced, indigenous nomads were massacred, driven out, incorporated into trade or tributary networks, or forced to convert to Christianity. Well-watered riverbanks were tilled and planted in traditional fashion, and prairie grasslands became pasturage for large herds of domestic livestock. The steppe frontier was to some extent a haven for fugitives, too, including a number of runaway serfs, and it also proved to be a source of rebel leaders. The government was always playing catch-up, trying to bring order to the unruly fringe.

Foreign merchants, meanwhile, came to Russia not only from the west, but from the south and east. In addition to small colonies of northern Europeans, Moscow was home to thriving communities of Middle Eastern, Central Asian, South Asian, and Armenian merchants by the seventeenth century. As in most other mercantilist systems, however, the government granted foreign merchants only limited access to Russian urban markets and even less to interior supply regions. Thus Russian merchants continued to dominate both internal and long-distance trade, despite limited access to credit and precious metals. Mostly based in Moscow, they used distant ports such as Archangel, on the White Sea, to trade leather and other goods with the English and Dutch (see again Mapping the World, page 685). Furs were traded westward to eastern and central Europe, and also southward to the Ottoman and Persian empires. By the time of Peter the Great, England had become dependent on Russian timber, which it paid for with gold (coming mostly from Brazil by this time, as we will see in the next chapter).

The early modern Russian Empire, in sum, drew from a blend of religious self-confidence, demographic growth, commercial links, and the personal ambitions of its Moscow-based tsars. More gunpowder empire than modern state in many regards, Russia nevertheless grew to encompass more terrain than any other Eurasian state in its time, despite its relatively sparse population. The continued subjugation of the serf majority, however, would spark a new wave of rebellions before the end of the eighteenth century.

China from Ming to Qing Rule 1500–1800

FOCUS

How did the shift to a silver cash economy transform Chinese government and society?

By 1500, thanks to several millennia of intensive agriculture and a tradition of vast and innovative public works projects, China was home to at least 110 million people, almost twice as many as Europe. Moreover, China under the Ming dynasty (1368–1644) was virtually self-sufficient. Rice and other foodstuffs, along with livestock and manufactured goods, were transported and redistributed throughout the empire by way of a complex system of canals, roads, and fortified posts that had been constructed by drafted peasant laborers over the centuries.

Only silver was in short supply as Ming rulers shifted China's economy from copper or bronze currency and simple barter to silver money exchanges, especially after 1550. This shift to commercialization and a "hard money" economy necessitated links to the outside world. China's surplus of silk, a versatile fiber in demand abroad since antiquity, made exports not only possible, but highly profitable. Fine porcelain and lacquer wares also brought in considerable foreign exchange, and tea would later be added to the list. Western ideas and technologies arrived with Christian missionaries in the mid-sixteenth century, but they barely influenced Chinese culture. China, a technologically advanced and highly literate society, wanted only silver from the West, and, for a time, it managed to define its terms of connection and exchange with the outside world.

The final century of Ming rule, from about 1540 to 1644, witnessed a commercial revival and overall improvement in standards of living. It also saw the return of mounted enemies in the north, the Manchu. And, despite the general prosperity, there were no perfect guarantees against the famine and disease that plagued previous centuries due to the density of China's population and the primitive state of its medical care. Bureaucratic structures, though efficient by contemporary world standards, were inadequate to the task of mass relief. Peasant families could at best hope for community cooperation in hard times.

Late Ming Imperial Demands and Private Trade

The most important emperor of late Ming times was Wanli (r. 1573–1620). Wanli was a creature of the imperial palace and notoriously out of touch with his subjects, yet one of his policies had global implications. Previous emperors had enacted similar decrees on a small scale, but it was Wanli who ordered many of China's taxes collected in silver rather than in the form of labor service, rice, or other trade goods. The shift to hard currency eased price standardization across the empire. This was the "Single Whip Law" of 1581, so named since it bundled various taxes into one stinging payment.

Single Whip Law and the Shift to Hard Currency

Given China's immense population, approaching 200 million by this time, demand for silver soared. Portuguese merchants moved quickly to import Japanese silver acquired in exchange for guns, silk, and other items, but soon Chinese merchants all but eclipsed them. These merchants moored their ships in Nagasaki Bay alongside the Portuguese and later Dutch, but many more set up shop in Manila, the Philippine capital, where they exchanged silk, porcelain, and other goods for Spanish-American silver that had arrived from Mexico (see Map 21.3, page 709). Thanks to Wanli, a vibrant Chinese commercial colony emerged in Manila virtually overnight. Large numbers of Chinese merchants also settled in Thailand, Malaysia, and Java, where they offset the growing commercial power of Europeans.

Demand for Silver and the Manila Trade

Despite the great distances and risks involved, the Manila trade was particularly profitable for both Spanish and Chinese merchants. The annual transpacific voyages of the *naos de la China*, or "Manila galleons," that left Acapulco, Mexico, each year loaded with the silver of Potosí (Bolivia), Zacatecas (Mexico), and other American mining centers, continued unabated through the early nineteenth century. Like the arrival of the Atlantic silver fleet in Spain each fall, the safe arrival of the galleons in Manila was a longed-for and celebrated event in all quarters. Still more Spanish-American silver reached China from the West, traveling through Europe, the Middle East, and the Indian Ocean basin to ports such as Macao and Guangzhou (Canton). Since China, compared with contemporary Europe or India, valued silver at a relatively higher rate than gold, substantial profit could be made in almost any exchange. Put another way, the historically close relationship between favorable exchange rates and export profitability was quickly exploited by merchants on both sides of the exchange divide.

How China's economy managed to absorb millions of ounces of silver annually over the course of decades without dramatic price inflation or some other notable effect remains a matter of much scholarly debate. One outlet was government spending, for by the early seventeenth century Ming rulers became more like their western European contemporaries in outfitting costly armies. Defense against Manchu and other northern raiders as well as disgruntled peasants grew increasingly expensive, but in the end proved ineffectual. Were fluctuations in silver income to blame for Ming decline?

Echoing historians of the seventeenth-century crisis in Europe, scholars long claimed that a dip in silver revenues after about 1630 rendered the state unable to defend itself. More recent research, however, suggests no such dip occurred; silver kept pouring in through the 1640s. Other factors must have trumped the Ming state's budget issues. Meanwhile, private merchants who supplied the military with food, weapons, and other necessities clearly benefited from China's new, silver-based economy, as did those who exported silk to Manila and other overseas bazaars. Only in the nineteenth century would China's vast silver holdings begin to flow outward in exchange for opium and other imports brought by European traders.

Demand for Chinese Exports

China's new commercial links to the outside world stimulated the economy in several ways, especially in the coastal regions around Nanjing and Canton. Men continued to work in intensive rice agriculture since taxes in the form of raw commodities were still required despite rapid monetization of the overall economy. Women, however, were increasingly drawn into the production of silk thread and finished textiles for export. After silk, China's most admired product was its porcelain, known as "chinaware" in the West (see Seeing the Past: Blue-on-White: Ming Export Porcelain).

As in parts of northwest Europe described in the last chapter, Chinese textile making grew more efficient in response to export demands, but without the mechanization, standardization, and wage labor usually associated with modern industry. By the early sixteenth century not only finished fabrics were traded widely in China, but also their components, raw fiber and thread. Even mulberry leaves, which were fed to silkworms to produce thread, were traded on the open market. Only labor was not yet commodified in

SEEING THE PAST

Blue-on-White: Ming Export Porcelain

Ming Blue-on-White Export Porcelain (Paul Freeman/Bridgeman Art Library.)

Before industrialization, China's artisans produced a vast range of consumer goods, from ordinary metal nails to fine silk textiles. After silk, China was most renowned for its porcelain, a special variety of clay pottery fired to the point that it was transformed into glass. The center of this artisanal industry was (and remains) Jingdezhen (JING-deh-juhn) in southern China. The combination of properly mixed clay and high heat made it possible for artisans, mostly men, to fashion durable vessels, plates, and other items

of extraordinary thinness. Over many centuries, Chinese painters and calligraphers developed a range of styles and techniques for decorating porcelain, including the application of cobalt blue pigments that emerged from the kiln in stark contrast to the white base. The Ming developed this "blue-on-white" porcelain specifically for export, first, as we saw in Chapter 15, to the Muslim world and later to regions throughout the globe. The example shown here from about 1600 features Li Tieguai, a legendary Chinese religious figure, but many blue-on-white porcelain products were decorated with Western and other foreign images, including monograms and pictures of the Virgin Mary.

Porcelain making continued throughout the Qing period, as well, but with a shift toward individual artistic virtuosity rather than mass, anonymous production.

EXAMINING THE EVIDENCE

1. How did Ming craftsmen adapt their blue-on-white porcelain to match the tastes of foreign buyers?

2. Compare this Ming plate of around 1600 with the example on page 796 of "Wedgwood blue" china created in industrializing Britain around two centuries later. What aesthetic and physical qualities were the British manufacturers seeking to duplicate, and why?

the modern "hourly" or salaried sense. Unlike in neighboring Korea, chattel slavery, or full ownership of workers' bodies, was extremely rare in China, although penal labor—forced work by prisoners—was exploited in many public projects.

The explosive demand for export textiles that resulted from overseas expansion and American conquest had profound consequences for Chinese women. Women did most spinning and weaving in their own households in the form of piecework. This yielded essential income for the household but also added significantly to an already burdensome workload. Although being paid by the piece or task kept female workers at the mercy of male merchants, this new demand brought Chinese women, much like their Dutch and Irish contemporaries in the linen industry, fully into the global commercial economy. The products of their labors were consumed at the far edges of the world (see Lives and Livelihoods: Silk Weavers in China, page 696).

Manchu Expansion and the Rise of the Qing Empire

Some of the same environmental shocks that exacerbated the seventeenth-century crisis in Europe struck China in the last years of Ming rule. Droughts were particularly severe in the north from 1641 to 1644, but other factors also contributed to Ming decline. Court intrigues, often prompted by increasingly powerful eunuchs (castrated court officials), weakened Ming rulership just as China's economy grew in size and complexity. Manchu raids, meanwhile, became a severe threat and, consequently, a drain on resources as early as the 1620s. The Manchu were also on the march in Korea, which they reduced to tributary status in 1637. By 1642 the raiders reached Shandong province, but it was a local rebel, Li Zicheng, who ushered in the Manchu capture of Beijing in 1644. As the capital fell to Li, both the Ming emperor and his wife committed suicide rather than face the humiliation of captivity. To rid the capital of the rebels, a Ming official sought Manchu aid. The Manchus took advantage of the moment and occupied the capital. Calling themselves the Qing, or "Pure," dynasty, the Manchus quickly adapted to the role of ruling minority (see Map 21.2).

The transition to Qing rule after 1644 proved surprisingly smooth, and most Chinese subjects' lives were barely changed. Although the new Qing emperors maintained a distinct ethnic identity and often dealt harshly with dissenters, they tended to improve on rather than revolutionize established patterns of Chinese governance. As a result, the empire rebounded with remarkable speed. Under Qing rule, Western gunpowder technology was so fully embraced that it enabled the rapid conquest of much of Mongolia, Tibet, and the Amur River basin (claimed by Russia) by the 1750s. Tributaries from these distant provinces trekked to Beijing to pay homage to the "pure" emperor.

Qing Governance

The ascendancy of the Qing dynasty (1644–1911) was cemented with the accession of Emperor Kangxi (kang-shee) in 1661. By the end of his rule in 1722, China was for the first time in centuries an expansionist empire, with westward expansion by land China's principal aim. Mongolia, annexed in 1697, was a critical base for this project, and a buffer against Peter the Great's Russia. Even the traditionally defiant south began to give in, and by 1700 much of mainland Southeast Asia, including Burma, Thailand, Cambodia, and Vietnam, paid tribute to the Qing emperor in exchange for political autonomy. Kangxi's successors sought to follow his example. By 1751 Tibet and Nepal fell to the Qing. Chinese colonists, some of them hungry and homeless after floods and other disasters, were encouraged to move west with tax breaks, homesteads, and other incentives.

Qing Expansion

Most outlying regions were ruled indirectly, and some, like Korea, remained virtually autonomous, but by the 1750s, under the long-lived emperor Qianlong (chee-YEN-loong), China seemed to be reaching the limits of its bureaucratic and military capabilities. Victory in massive wars against southern Siberian peoples demonstrated Qing military might, but trouble was brewing, and not just at the fringes. Rebellions were now common throughout the realm. Subjects in the core districts grew increasingly restless, and guerrilla warfare and massacres of ethnic Chinese colonists became constant features of frontier life. Qianlong clung to power until 1796, and despite ballooning war costs, the emperor's reign

MAP 21.2

The Qing Dynasty, 1644–1799

MAP 21.2

The Qing Dynasty, 1644–1799

The Qing were mounted outsiders who developed a vast Asian empire, first by toppling the Ming dynasty to their south in 1644, then by annexing interior regions one by one through the eighteenth century. Taiwan was the only significant offshore conquest, but overseas trade with Japan and Southeast Asia, particularly the Spanish Philippine port of Manila, was critical to China's economy. Although conquered interior regions such as Tibet and Mongolia were extensive, most Qing subjects lived in the former Ming core, home to the world's largest concentration of people.

had boasted some of the biggest treasury surpluses in early modern history. The silver of the Americas had funded Qing expansion.

Environmental Transformations

Historians have only recently begun to examine how China's environment was changed by the general expansion of trade and population in the Ming and Qing eras. The disasters most remarked upon by contemporaries were floods, but their relationship to human rather than divine action was rarely explored except by a few alert public works officials. Deforestation, though not in itself a cause of floods, often exacerbated them. As peasants cleared more and more land for planting and cut forests for firewood and building materials, effective rainfall catchment areas were greatly diminished. Monsoon rains thus swept away more and more exposed soil, creating massive erosion upstream and devastating river sedimentation downstream. The problem became so widespread that Chinese territorial expansion and colonization in Qing times were in part aimed at resettling peasants displaced by environmental catastrophes in the heartland. In early modern times China was arguably the most human-molded landscape in the world in proportion to its population, and subsistence requirements absorbed an extraordinary amount of energy even before the rise of the Ming.

Everyday Life in Ming and Qing China

Ming intellectuals made note of China's broad shift to commercialism as early as the sixteenth century, and most found it annoying. As in many traditional societies (except Islamic ones), merchants and traders were something of a suspect class, esteemed only slightly above actors and musicians. Chinese society as defined by Confucius emphasized production over exchange, the countryside over the city, and continuity over change or mobility. The ideal was a linked grouping of agriculturally self-sufficient provincial units overseen by patriarchal figures. These units were to be connected not by trade, but by a merit-based governing hierarchy headed by a divine monarch.

Within this model, even peasant households were supposed to achieve self-sufficiency, relying on the market only in times of duress. Men were supposed to farm and women were supposed to spin and weave, both remaining in their home villages and producing only for their own consumption. Surpluses, a divine gift to the pious and industrious, were not to be sold but rather yielded up to the emperor at periodic intervals to express fealty and submission. Bureaucrats and scholars, who lived from these surpluses, kept track of them on paper.

Struggles of the Common Folk

Such was the ideal Neo-Confucian society. As we have seen, however, times of duress proved frequent in early modern China: droughts, floods, plagues, and even pirates took their toll. Peasants, as usual, suffered most, especially those driven to frontier lands by continued population growth. These stresses, along with increasing state demands for cash payment of taxes, compelled many individuals and families to migrate and sell their labor to whoever

Chinese Beggars
Although most early modern Chinese artists depicted idealized things of beauty, such as rugged landscapes and fanciful creatures in flight, some turned their attention to ordinary people. This c. 1500 Ming image depicts two wandering beggars, one apparently talking to himself as he walks and the other brandishing a serpent, presumably his helper at winning alms from curious or terrified passersby. The image offers a rare glimpse at an impoverished yet colorful Chinese subculture not often mentioned in historical documents. (The Granger Collection, New York.)

Silk Weavers in China

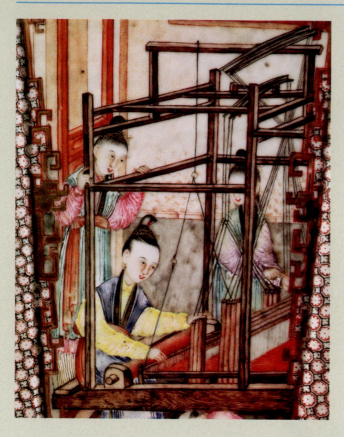

Chinese Silk Weaving

This rare detail from a Ming ceramic vase shows a group of Chinese women weaving silk on a complex loom. Chinese silk manufacture employed many thousands of women as well as men, doing everything from tending the mulberry bushes that produced the silkworms' food to finishing elaborate brocades and tapestries for export to the wider world, often in exchange for Spanish-American silver. Both highly technical and vast in scale, Chinese silk production was unmatched in early modern times. (Giraudon/ Bridgeman Art Library.)

Silk production, or sericulture, dates back several thousand years in China, but export volume grew most dramatically in early modern times, beginning with the late Ming. It was stimulated in particular by the massive influx of Spanish-American silver after China shifted to a silver-based economy in 1581. Most Chinese silk producers were concentrated in the southeast, especially along the lower Yangzi River (see again Map 21.2). Imperial factories were established under the Ming in Nanjing and Beijing, but most work was spread among peasants who worked at home at specific tasks assigned by private merchants. The merchants paid peasants for their mulberry leaves, cocoons, spun fiber, and finished fabrics.

Silk fiber is spun from the cocoons of the silkworm, produced by the worms' digestion of large quantities of

could pay. There is strong evidence that couples of even middling status practiced various forms of birth control to avoid the financial pressure of additional children.

The Newly Wealthy   Meanwhile, landlords and merchants accumulated increasing amounts of cash through market exchange. They were buying low and selling high, moving goods and getting rich. The social inequity resulting from this process was in part what bothered Chinese traditionalist intellectuals. What struck them as worse, however, since it had profound ethical and hence philosophical implications, was the market economy's tendency to reward nonproductive and even outright dishonest behavior. It was the appearance of the uppity rich, not the miserably poor, that most bothered the educated old guard.

The Flourishing of Art and Culture

As in Golden Age Spain, the arts and literature thrived in China during an era of political decline. This seeming paradox was due in part to the patronage of merchants who had made fortunes in the economic upswing, but it was also a function of the surplus of unemployed, literate civil servants. More and more smart people, in short, were angling for work and recognition. The end of the Ming was an era of increased literacy and mass distribution of books as well, and ideas and scientific knowledge were disseminated more widely than ever before. Novels and plays were also hugely popular. The play *The Lute*, published in 1610, included woodblock prints of scenes, for readers not able to see a live performance. Some writers devoted themselves to adventure travel in the interior, describing rugged landscapes and wild rivers for curious urban readers.

mulberry leaves. The worms are fragile creatures susceptible to diseases and in need of constant supervision and feeding. Since they were tended in environments susceptible to drastic temperature changes, the worms' welfare was a constant source of worry. This codependent relationship between humans and insects was perhaps matched only by that of beekeeping for honey collection or cochineal dye production in Mexico (cochineal bugs thrive on prickly pear cacti).

Rather like the linen industry in early modern Holland and Ireland, silk production in Ming and Qing China was extremely labor-intensive and largely dependent on women. Care of silkworms added to a host of domestic and agricultural tasks, and spinning, which had to be finished rapidly before the cocoons rotted, often lasted late into the night. Many households stopped interacting with neighbors entirely until silk season had passed, so intense and delicate was the work. Silk for export had to be reeled twice to guarantee consistent fineness. Still, silk making was attractive to peasants since it allowed them to enter the market economy at greater advantage than with food products, which were heavy and susceptible to spoilage or consumption by rodents and other vermin. Because the industry itself was not taxed, many peasants planted mulberry bushes and tended cocoons to meet the emperor's silver cash tax demands.

Commercial producers eventually developed large reeling machines operated by men, but in early modern times most reeling was done by women on small hand-turned devices. Some peasants also wove textiles, but often not those who produced the raw fiber. With time, like European linen manufacture, Chinese silk production became a highly capitalized industry.

QUESTIONS TO CONSIDER

1. From its origins as an ancient Chinese art, how did silk manufacture change in early modern times?

2. Consider the Lives and Livelihoods essays in Chapters 17 and 18. How did silk weaving differ from sugar making in the Americas and gold mining in Africa?

For Further Information:
Shih, Min-hsiung. *The Silk Industry in Ch'ing China*. Translated by E-tu Zen Sun. 1976.
Vainker, S. J. *Chinese Silk: A Cultural History*. 2004.

In the years around 1600, foreign visitors, notably the Italian Jesuit Matteo Ricci in 1601, impressed the Chinese court with their knowledge of mathematics, alchemy, optics, and mechanics, though not with their religion. When he was not fixing European clocks brought as gifts for the emperor (see page 664), Ricci devoted his time to translating Confucius for a Western audience and composing religious tracts in court Chinese. As in Mughal India, Jesuit visitors at court had some influence on painting styles, particularly royal portraiture. Some artists also adopted European techniques of representing depth and perspective. The Jesuit presence at court and in the trading port of Macao remained important through the Qing era, even though the number of Chinese converts to Christianity remained very small in relation to China's population. They were never expelled from China, as happened in Japan.

Japan in Transition 1540–1750

Located in the temperate latitudes of the North Pacific Ocean, Japan was shut off from the rest of the world for most of the early modern period. A brief opening in the feuding sixteenth century allowed foreign ideas and technologies to flow in and permitted a large but ineffectual invasion of Korea. Soon after 1600, however, Japan's leaders enforced seclusion from the outside world and, like their neighbors in China, concentrated their efforts on consolidating power. Japan would not be reopened for over two centuries.

FOCUS

How did self-isolation affect Japan?

Most inhabitants of the three major islands, Honshu, Kyushu, and Shikoku, were peasants, nearly all of them subjects of regional lords, called **daimyo**. Above Japan's rice-farming peasant majority was a class of warriors called **samurai**, some of them mercenaries and others permanent employees of powerful daimyo. Above the daimyo a small group of generals, including the top-ranking **shogun**, jockeyed to become Japan's supreme ruler. By 1600 the royal family had been reduced to ceremonial figureheads. In the peace that came with closure, Japan's population expanded steadily and the arts flourished.

Rise of the Tokugawa Shogunate and the Unification of Japan

As we saw in Chapter 15, following what is often described in Japanese history as a golden age of imperial unity and courtly life in the eleventh and twelfth centuries there ensued a breakdown of central authority and a rise in competing military factions. This politically chaotic period, heyday of the samurai warriors, lasted several centuries. The daimyo sometimes succeeded in bringing a measure of order to their domains, but no one daimyo family could establish predominance over others.

At the end of the sixteenth century several generals sought to quell civil war and to unify Japan. One such general, Toyotomi Hideyoshi (1535–1598), not only conquered his rivals but, with the Kyoto emperor's permission, assumed the role of top shogun. After Hideyoshi died, Tokugawa Ieyasu (1542–1616), a powerful military leader, seized control. Assuming the title of shogun in 1603, he declared that thereafter rulership was hereditary. The Tokugawa (TOH-koo-GAH-wah) Shogunate would endure until 1867.

Tokugawa Japan

With the uncompromising Tokugawa shoguns in charge of Japan's core districts, regional lords and military men found themselves forced to accept allegiance to the emerging unified state or face its growing might. The vast majority chose submission, and a long period of peace ensued. Peasant rebellions occurred from time to time, sometimes led by disgruntled samurai, but the state's adoption of Neo-Confucian ideals similar to those embraced in contemporary China and Korea stressed duty and hierarchy over rights and individual freedom. No elaborate, Neo-Confucianist civil service exam system was developed to match those of the mainland, but most Japanese accepted the benefits of peace and worked within their assigned roles.

Hideyoshi's rule had been notable for tolerating Iberian Christian missionaries and launching two massive invasions of Korea in 1593 and 1597, part of a more ambitious project aimed at conquering China. Ieyasu reversed course, banning missionaries and making peace with Korea. Contact with foreigners, particularly Europeans—called *nanban*, or "southern barbarians," a reference to their arrival from southern seas—was restricted after 1614 to the tiny offshore island of Deshima near the city of Nagasaki, in westernmost Kyushu. Foreign families were not permitted to reside on Japanese soil, and by the 1630s all remaining Catholic priests and bachelor merchants had been expelled with the exception of one Dutch merchant. A representative of the Dutch East India Company, or VOC, he was strictly forbidden to discuss religion. The Dutch thus gained access, albeit limited, to the Japanese market, and the Tokugawa shoguns gained access to select information from the West, especially that regarding advances in science and technology. The much more numerous Chinese residents in Nagasaki, most of them silver-hungry merchants, were treated with similar suspicion. Scholars dispute the importance of Christianity in driving the early Tokugawa shoguns toward a policy of seclusion, but it clearly played a role. It was not the foreignness of the nanbans' religion that worried the shoguns, but rather its believers' insistence that it was the one true religion. Japan had long been a land of religious diversity, with a variety of foreign and local sects coexisting more or less peacefully. One

Containment of Foreigners

daimyo A regional lord in feudal and early modern Japan.

samurai The hereditary warriors who dominated Japanese society and culture from the twelfth to the nineteenth centuries.

shogun The supreme military commander in Japan, who also took political control.

nanban A Japanese term for "southern barbarians," or Europeans; also applies to hybrid European-Japanese artistic style.

could follow imported Confucian ethical principles, for example, as promoted by the Tokugawa state, yet also be a devout Buddhist. Taoist ideas and rituals were also embraced to a greater or lesser degree by most Japanese. Beyond this, one was expected to venerate nature spirits according to ancient Shinto traditions.

What was most unattractive about Christianity from the Tokugawa shogun's point of view was its intolerance of these or any other belief systems. Strictly monotheistic, focused on eternal salvation rather than everyday behavior, and fully understood only by foreign specialists, Christianity was branded subversive. Thus Roman Catholicism was harshly persecuted. The first executions of priests and followers began in 1597 and continued, with some breaks, to the end of the 1630s, when a major Christian-led rebellion was suppressed. Then, the shoguns ordered unrepentant priests and converts publicly beheaded, boiled, or crucified. The only remnants of Catholicism to survive this violent purge were scattered names of priests and saints, most of them venerated in older Japanese fashion by isolated peasants and fishing folk (see Reading the Past: Selections from the Hidden Christians' Sacred Book).

Harsh as it was, the shoguns considered their repression of Christianity a political rather than religious action. Stories of Spain's lightning-fast conquests in the distant Americas and nearby Philippines had long circulated in Japan, and Dutch and English contacts were quick to inform the Japanese of alleged Spanish cruelties. Portugal's similarly violent actions in India, Africa, and Southeast Asia were also well known, suggesting to Japan's new rulers that Catholic missionaries, particularly Iberians, were probably a spearhead for imperial designs. Several indiscreet Spanish visitors suggested as much in the 1590s, confirming Japanese fears.

There was an economic basis for seclusion as well. Japanese exports of silver surged in about 1600 in response to China's shift to a silver cash economy, then declined precipitously. A mining crisis in southwest Honshu in the 1630s forced the shoguns to keep as much silver as possible within the country to avert a currency shortage. This further isolated Japan from outside contact. With silver in short supply, the Dutch exported Japan's other metals, gold and copper, but connections to China and other outsiders gradually diminished. Japan, in short, had little need for the outside world. Even matchlock handguns, which had been successfully copied from early European imports, were abandoned soon after 1600 in favor of more traditional swords. Gunpowder was relegated to fireworks.

Following Christian suppression in the 1630s, the shoguns established firm control of the interior by forcing subordinate lords to maintain households in the new capital of Edo (modern Tokyo). Wives and children lived in the city and its growing suburbs as virtual hostages, and the daimyo themselves had to rotate in and out of the capital at least every other year. A new version of court life was one result of this shifting center, and with it grew both a vibrant capital city and a complex road and inn system lacing the rugged topography of Japan together. With Edo's primacy firmly established, Osaka became a major marketplace, producing its own class of newly rich merchants, and Kyoto thrived as a major cultural center.

Some Tokugawa subjects carried on trade with the Ryukyu Islands to the southwest, but only in the north was there anything like imperial expansion after the failed invasions of Korea in the 1590s. Japanese merchants had long traded rice for gold dust and rare seafoods with the Ainu of Hokkaido. The Ainu (EYE-new), who sported tattoos and whose men wore long beards, descended from Siberians from the north and probably also Austronesian islanders from the south. The Japanese considered them barbarians, and the Ainu considered the Japanese treacherous. By 1650 Japanese trading families had colonized portions of southernmost Hokkaido, but increasing pressures on the Ainu sparked rebellion. The Tokugawa state was reluctant to spend the necessary money to invade and fortify Hokkaido, but it did claim the island as Japanese territory. Only when the Russians threatened in the late eighteenth century to annex Ainu-inhabited islands farther north did the Japanese cement their claims and back them with force. Ainu culture was violently suppressed, but survives to the present day.

Suppression of Christianity

Withdrawal from Global Connections

Edo, the New Tokugawa Capital

Conquest of the Ainu

READING THE PAST

Selections from the Hidden Christians' Sacred Book

As seen in the last chapter with regard to Judaism and Islam in early modern Iberia, oppressed religions have survived in secret for centuries. Sometimes theologies endured with little change thanks to a preserved text or a sequence of tradition-keepers with good memories; in other cases only traces of old ritual behaviors persisted. In regions where a complex religious tradition had only recently been introduced before being harshly persecuted, considerable blending of local and imported ideas and forms was usually still in process. This yielded yet a third result, a kind of stunted blend. Thus Christianity's brief appearance in Japan produced an unusual underground religious tradition that was in general more Japanese than Christian. Compare the version of Genesis below to the standard Western text.

In the beginning Deusu [Dios] was worshiped as Lord of Heaven and Earth, and Parent of humankind and all creation. Deusu has two hundred ranks and forty-two forms, and divided the light that was originally one, and made the Sun Heaven, and twelve other heavens. The names of these heavens are Benbo or Hell, Manbo, Oribeten, Shidai, Godai, Pappa, Oroha, Konsutanchi, Hora, Koroteru, and a hundred thousand Paraiso [Paradise] and Gokuraku.

Deusu then created the sun, the moon, and the stars, and called into being tens of thousands of anjo [angels] just by thinking of them. One of them, Jusuheru [Lucifer], the head of seven anjo, has a hundred ranks and thirty-two forms. Deusu is the one who made all things: earth, water, fire, wind, salt, oil, and put in his own flesh and bones. Without pause Deusu worked on the Shikuda, Terusha, Kuwaruta, Kinta, Sesuta, and Sabata [all days of the week, mostly from Portuguese]. Then on the seventh day Deusu blew breath into this being and named him Domeigosu-no-Adan [Adam], who possessed thirty-three forms. So this is the usual number of forms for a human being.

For this reason the seventh day of one cycle is observed as a feast day.

Deusu then made a woman and called her Domeigosu-no-Ewa [Eve], had the man and woman marry, and gave them the realm called Koroteru. There they bore a son and a daughter, Chikoro and Tanho, and went every day to Paraiso to worship Deusu.

Source: Christal Whelan, ed. and trans., *The Beginning of Heaven and Earth: The Sacred Book of Japan's Hidden Christians* (Honolulu: University of Hawai'i Press, 1996) (portions of an early nineteenth-century Tokugawa-era Kakure Kirishitan, or "Hidden Christian," manuscript).

EXAMINING THE EVIDENCE

1. What elements of Christian teachings survive in this origin tale of the world?
2. What elements of the story are distinctly Japanese?

Everyday Life and Culture in Tokugawa Japan

Agricultural Expansion

Japan's population grew from about 10 million in 1600 to nearly 30 million in 1700, when it stabilized. This rapid growth was made possible in part by relative peace, but expansion and integration of the rice economy contributed as well. Rice's high yields encouraged creation of even the smallest irrigated fields, and some daimyo proved to be skillful marketers of their tributaries' main product. Most rice was sold in cities and to elites, while peasants ate a healthier diet of mixed grains, vegetables, and soy products. Urban-rural reciprocity was key, and processed human excrement collected in cities and villages was the main fertilizer. As surprising as it may seem, Japan's complex system of waste collection and recycling was easily the most hygienic and efficient in the world. Whole guilds were dedicated to the collection and marketing of what in the West was regarded as dangerous filth. The water supply of Edo, with over half a million people by the eighteenth century, was cleaner and more reliable than that of London. Thus, this system improved the health of the Japanese population as it created connections between urban and rural Japanese.

New strains of rice introduced from Southeast Asia also allowed farmers to extend cultivation into previously unproductive areas. By contrast, American crops such as maize and peanuts were not embraced in Japan as they were in China. Only sweet potatoes were appreciated, and they saved millions of lives during times of famine. As in China, however, Japanese agricultural expansion and diversification had profound ecological consequences. Leaders immediately recognized that deforestation intensified floods, and they responded to this problem with striking efficiency, organizing armies of workers to replant many depleted woodlands by the eighteenth century.

Improvements in Infrastructure

Transportation infrastructure was everywhere improved, from roads and bridges to ports and canals. Shoguns kept daimyos in check after 1615 by permitting only one castle in each domain, and sharply limiting improvement or expansion, but peace encouraged other forms of private construction. Like agriculture, the construction boom soon took a toll on Japan's forests, as did increased shipbuilding and other transport-related industries. Vulnerability to earthquakes gave rise to building codes and design innovations. A German-born employee of the Dutch VOC, Engelbert Kaempfer, described this Edo scene in 1691: "Today, one hour before noon, in bright and calm weather, a terrible earthquake shook the house with a loud sound. . . . This earthquake taught me that the country's laws limiting the height of buildings are based on necessity. It is also necessary that buildings be constructed of light wood, partitions, boards, and wood chips and then, below the timbers, be topped with a heavy pole, which with its weight pushes together the whole construction so that it does not collapse during an earthquake."[2] Hence, in agriculture, infrastructure, and construction, the leaders of Tokugawa Japan demonstrated the power of centralized government, controlling Japan's growth and development and shaping the connections between their subjects.

Rise of a Leisure Class and Expansion of the Artisan Sector

Although the majority of Tokugawa subjects remained peasants, a genuine leisure class also emerged, mostly concentrated in Kyoto. Merchants imported raw silk from China, which Japanese artisans processed and wove. Other imports included sandalwood, sugar, and spices from Southeast Asia. Consumption of fine fabrics and other products by the wealthy greatly expanded the artisan sector, but did not spark industrialization. There was simply not a large enough wage-earning consumer class in Japan to sustain industrial production. Instead, the trend was toward increasingly high-quality "boutique" goods such as samurai swords and ceremonial kimonos, rather than mass-produced consumer goods.

Growth of Cotton Textile Production

The period did, however, see the emergence of a precursor to modern Japanese industrialization. Like elites, peasants had to be clothed, if less opulently. What they wore most were locally produced cotton garments. Both the demand and supply of these textiles were new developments historically. Most traditional peasant clothing prior to the sixteenth century had been made from hemp fiber, and only through trade with Korea and China had cotton come to figure in Japan's economy. Initially, cotton was in demand among sixteenth-century samurai warriors, who used it for clothing, lining for armor, and fuses for matchlock handguns. Fishing folk also consumed cotton sailcloth. Trade restrictions in the Tokugawa era stimulated internal production of cotton textiles to such a degree that it reached near-industrial levels by the eighteenth century.

Commoners' Diet

Japanese commoners got by on a diet of just under two thousand calories a day according to population historians, mostly consisting of grain porridges. They consumed very little meat and no milk or cheese, and away from coastal areas where seafood and fish could be harvested, most protein came from beans and soy products such as tofu. A huge variety of fruits, vegetables, herbs, grasses, fungi, insects, and larvae were roasted or pickled for consumption in winter or in lean times. Tobacco, an American crop, grew increasingly popular under Tokugawa rule. It was smoked by men and women of all social classes in tiny clay pipes, serving a social function much like the sharing of tea. When tea was too expensive, as it often was, common folk drank boiled water, which was at least safe. In all, the peasant diet in Tokugawa Japan, though short of protein, was at least as nourishing as that of western Europe at the same time.

The Japanese Calendar

Both elite and ordinary Japanese folk lived according to a blend of agricultural and ritual calendars. In the simplest sense, time was measured according to lunar months and solar years, but there were numerous overlapping astrological and imperial cycles measured by Buddhist monks, who tolled bells to remind villagers and urbanites alike of ritual obligations. Western-style clocks, though known, were not adopted.

Kyoto Festival

This c. 1750 painting of a festival in Kyoto, Japan, depicts not only the daimyo, or local lord, and his ox-drawn cart and procession of armed samurai, but also daily goings-on about town. Many people seem to be engaged in conversation indoors, although they are quite visible thanks to open screens, allowing them to view the procession. Near the top of the panel, women and children walk leisurely toward what appears to be a recitation, possibly given by a samurai, and accompanied by a drummer. The use of patterned gold clouds to fill in empty spaces was a standard convention of early modern Japanese art, and here it adds a foglike layer to the painting's depth. (The Granger Collection, New York.)

Women's Lives   Women of every class faced obstacles to freedom in Japan's male-dominated and often misogynist society. Most were expected to marry at an early age and spend the majority of their lives serving their husbands, children, and in-laws. Still, as in other traditional societies, there were significant openings for female self-expression and even access to power in Tokugawa Japan. At court, noblewomen exercised considerable influence over succession and the everyday maintenance of proper decorum, and in the peasant sphere women managed household affairs, particularly when men were away on military duty or business. Widows could become quite powerful, especially those managing the affairs of dead merchant husbands.

Emergence of a National Culture

With the growth of cities and rise of a leisure class, Japanese literature and painting flourished, along with flower arranging, stylized and puppet theater, board games, and music. The writer Ihara Saikaku (EH-hah-rah sigh-kah-KOO) grew immensely popular at the end of the seventeenth century with his tales contrasting elite and working-class life. Saikaku idealized homosexual relations between senior and junior samurai, and also those among actors and their patrons, mostly wealthy townsmen. In "The Great Mirror of Male Love," Saikaku described most of these relationships as temporary, consensual, and often purchased. More than a hint of misogyny pervades the writings of Saikaku, but that sentiment is less evident in his "Life of an Amorous Woman" and other stories relating the adventures of courtesans and female prostitutes. In short, homosexuality, bisexuality, and prostitution were not only accepted but institutionalized in Tokugawa society.

In Edo, Kyoto, and especially the rice-trading city of Osaka, entertainments were many and varied. Daimyo and samurai landlords came to Osaka to exchange their rice tributes for money, which they then spent locally or in Edo, where they had to pay obeisance to the emperor. The frequent visits by regional elites to these two cities helped make them economic and cultural crossroads for Japan as a whole. Many samurai moved to these cities permanently as their rural estates diminished in size across generations. Social tension arose as the old warrior class tried to adapt to the cooperative requirements of urban life, but fortunately, there was much to distract them. Some worked for little compensation as teachers or policemen, but the wealthier samurai found time for the theater, musical concerts, and poetry readings. **Sumo** wrestling matches were popular even among non-samurai urbanites, as were board games, the tea ceremony, calligraphy, bonsai cultivation, and garden landscaping. More costly pursuits such as gambling, drinking, and sexual diversions were restricted to the so-called Licensed Quarters of the major cities. In general these activities were not considered "vices" as long as they did not prevent individuals from performing their civil duties.

Early modern European visitors, especially Catholic priests, found the general Japanese tolerance of prostitution, female impersonation, and homosexuality shocking, but they made little effort to understand Japanese cultural attitudes about sex and shame. Prostitution often was degrading to women and in some places approached the level of sex slavery. Still, there were groups of female escorts such as the geisha whom outsiders mistook for prostitutes. The **geisha** were indentured servants who made their living as private entertainers to the wealthiest merchants and landowners visiting or inhabiting cities. Geisha dress, makeup, and general comportment were all highly ritualized and distinctive. Although the geisha had control over their adult sexual lives, their first coital experience, or "deflowering," was sold to the highest bidder. Many young male prostitutes also acted as female impersonators in kabuki theater.

Kabuki was a popular form of theater that first appeared in Kyoto in 1603 as a way to advertise a number of female prostitutes. Subsequent shows caused such violence among potential customers that the Tokugawa government allowed only men to perform. As these female impersonators became associated with male prostitution, the state established official theaters that punished actors and patrons who engaged in sexual relations. By the eighteenth century, kabuki performances had become so "sanitized" that they included moralizing Neo-Confucian speeches. Even so, playwrights such as Chikamatsu Monzaemon (1653–1724) managed to retain ribald humor amid lessons in correct behavior. At the other end of the spectrum was the somber and ancient tradition of Noh theater, associated with Buddhist tales and Shinto shrines.

Poetry flourished as never before during the era of seclusion, and poets such as the itinerant and prolific Matsuo Bashō (1644–1684) were widely read. Here is a sample of his work:

> On my way through Nagoya, where crazy Chikusai is said to have practiced quackery and poetry, I wrote:
>
> With a bit of madness in me,
> Which is poetry,
> I plod along like Chikusai
> Among the wails of the wind.

Urban Sophistication

sumo A Japanese professional wrestler known for his heft.

geisha A professional female entertainer in Tokugawa Japan.

kabuki A popular Japanese theater known for bawdy humor and female impersonation.

Kabuki Theater

Something of a counterpoint to Neo-Confucian ideals of self-control and social order was Tokugawa Japan's ribald kabuki theater tradition, which became wildly popular in major cities after 1600. Kabuki actors were initially prostitutes, first young women and then young men, but objections from the samurai led by 1670 to the creation of a class of older men licensed to act in drag. In this c. 1680 screen painting by Hishikawa Moronobu, actors, costume designers, makeup artists, washerwomen, and stagehands all appear to be absorbed in their own little worlds. The painting seems to confirm early modern Japan's inward gaze and seemingly total cultural and material self-sufficiency. (The Granger Collection, New York.)

> Sleeping on a grass pillow
> I hear now and then
> The nocturnal bark of a dog
> In the passing rain.[3]

Despite isolation, Japan was among the most literate societies in the world in early modern times. By 1700 there were some fifteen hundred publishers active between Edo, Kyoto, and Osaka, publishing at least 7300 titles. Books on everything from tobacco farming to how young brides could find marital bliss were sold or rented in both city and countryside. Early forms of comic books were circulating by the eighteenth century, with the greatest sellers resembling what today would be classed as pulp fiction. Most books continued to be published on woodblock presses despite the fact that movable type was known from both mainland Asian and European sources—another example of the fact that early modern Japan, like China, had little need of the West.

Korea, a Land in Between 1392–1750

The Korean peninsula falls between China and Japan, with the Yellow Sea to the west and the Sea of Japan to the east. In 1392 Korea came to be ruled by the Yi (or Choson) dynasty, which remained in power until 1910. Though unified since the late seventh century, the Korean peninsula developed its distinctive culture primarily during Yi times, partly in response to Chinese and Japanese invasions. Korea had long been influenced by China, and had likewise served as a conduit linking the Asian mainland to Japan. The guiding principles of the early Choson state were drawn from the work of Confucius, as in contemporary China and Japan, and grafted onto a society that mostly practiced Buddhism, yet another imported tradition. Still, Koreans regarded themselves as a distinct and autonomous people, unified by a language and culture.

FOCUS

How did life for common folk in early modern Korea differ from life in China or Japan?

Capital and Countryside

It was under the first Yi ruler that Seoul, then known as Hanyang, became Korea's undisputed capital. Following Chinese principles of geomancy, or auspicious site selection, the Choson capital, backed by mountains and spread along the Han River plains, was considered blessed. Successive rulers drafted nearby peasants to expand the city and add to its grandeur. By 1450 Hanyang was home not only to substantial royal palaces but also bureaucratic buildings, markets, and schools.

The Choson state was not secular, but its leaders did move quickly to reduce the political and economic power of Buddhist temples and monasteries. Temple lands were widely confiscated and distributed to loyal officials. A kind of Neo-Confucian constitution was drafted in the first years of Yi rule advocating more radical state takeover and redistribution of land to peasants, but nobles balked and for the most part tenant farming persisted. Early modern Korea's government mirrored neighboring China's in some ways, but a significant difference was the prominence of a noble class, the **yangban**. Ancient ruling clans dominated the highest ranks of the bureaucracy, which consisted of a broad range of councils and regional governorships. A uniquely Korean institution known as the Samsa, a kind of academic oversight committee, had power even over the king himself, acting as a type of moral police force. Official historians, also drawn from the educated noble class, were allowed to write what they observed, keeping their work secret from the king. The Korean state did follow the Chinese model of civil service examinations, however, and through the hardest of these a few rare individuals of medium rank gained access to positions of power. The pressure was so great that some enterprising students hid tightly rolled crib-notes in their nostrils. Military service proved unpopular, partly because it was associated with slavery, and enrollment in school won exemption.

Korea still needed a defense apparatus, though, and the early Yi rulers responded directly. The nobles' private forces were consolidated into a national, standing army by the mid-fifteenth century, and a complex system of ranks and divisions was instituted. Professional military men took exams, and peasants soon faced periodic draft service in frontier outposts. The Jurchen and other horse warriors threatened Korea's northern provinces from time to time, but many chieftains were successfully co-opted by the Choson state in the fifteenth century. Another defense strategy was to settle the northern frontier with land-hungry peasants from the south.

Japanese invasions, 1592, 1597
Manchu invasions, 1627, 1637

Choson Korea

Foreign Challenges

yangban The noble class in early modern Korea.

Social Order in Early Modern Korea

Korean life under the Yi dynasty was marked by sharp class divisions, with a large portion of the poorer country folk living as slaves. This eighteenth-century painting on silk shows a notable individual on promenade, elaborately dressed, shaded, and otherwise attended, as more humble figures kneel in submission in the foreground. The broad-brimmed black hats and flowing garments were typical of high-ranking Koreans. Although Korean artists also depicted humble workers with some dignity, the Neo-Confucian ideal of a rigid social order comes through most strongly here. (The Art Archive/Musée Guimet Paris/Gianni Dagli Orti.)

After these early initiatives, defense became less of a concern, and the general devaluing of military service, which some Neo-Confucian reformers tried to address through incentives and fund-raising schemes, left Korea vulnerable by the time the Japanese invaded the peninsula in 1593 and 1597. Despite their massive forces and lightning speed, the Japanese under Shogun Hideyoshi were soon driven out with aid from Ming China. The Manchus were not so easily subdued, however. They invaded Korea in 1627 and 1636, reducing it to tributary status by 1637. Still, Korea managed to retain considerable autonomy.

Korea exported ginseng, furs, and a few other items to China in exchange for silk and porcelain, but its overseas trade was generally small, and only a few Korean merchants ventured beyond Japan or the nearby Ryukyu Islands, especially Okinawa. Aside from a general lack of high-value exports, which also dampened European interest, Korean merchants in the south faced constant threats from mostly Japanese pirates, the same ones who menaced China and its merchants from the thirteenth to seventeenth centuries. The Choson government attempted to suppress the pirates through both force and diplomacy, but Japan's fractured political system and occasional sponsorship of the pirates had the same hindering effect on Korean overseas trade felt in coastal China.

Everyday Life in Choson Korea

Despite rugged terrain, most Koreans under Yi rule were rice farmers. Wet-field rice cultivation expanded dramatically in the south beginning in the fifteenth century thanks to government initiatives and adaptation of Chinese techniques. Southern populations grew accordingly. Population estimates are debated, but it appears that Korea grew from about 5 million inhabitants in 1450 to some 10 million by 1600. In colder and drier parts of the peninsula, especially in the far north, peasants relied on millet and barley. As in Japan, these healthy grains were widely disdained as hardship rations in early modern times. Soybeans were later planted, adding a new source of protein. Koreans also exploited seacoasts and rivers for mollusks and fish, and some raised pigs and other livestock. Vegetables such as cabbage were pickled for winter consumption, spiced by the eighteenth century with capsicum peppers introduced from the Americas.

Gender Roles and Religious Beliefs

Ordinary folk probably did not obsess over genealogies and proper marriage matches to the extent that the noble class, or yangban, did, but their mating customs could still be rigid. Some marriages were arranged, occasionally between young children. Women appear to have lost a great deal of their former autonomy thanks to the rise of Neo-Confucianism, and widows were even presented with a knife with which to kill themselves should they be sexually violated or otherwise dishonored. According to some sources,

Korean women more often used their suicide knives to kill attackers. Female entertainers, or **kisaeng**—like their Japanese counterparts, the geisha—were sometimes able to accumulate capital and achieve literary fame.

Teachers in Choson Korea took on the moral advisory role played by priests or imams in early modern Christian or Islamic societies, and in the seventeenth century Neo-Confucian scholars, following the lead of China's Wang Yangming, attempted to reform Korean society and government wholesale. Education in general was highly valued, and literacy widespread (see Reading the Past: Scenes from the Daily Life of a Korean Queen). It was in the Choson era that Korean students became outspoken critics of the state, launching a number of mass protests in the late seventeenth and early eighteenth centuries. Despite the ruling class's attachment to Neo-Confucian philosophy and suppression of Buddhist monasteries, popular religious ideas persisted, especially in the countryside. Alongside some rooted Buddhist beliefs, mountain deities and sacred stones or trees continued to be venerated on a regular basis, much as in western Africa and the Andes Mountains of South America, and shamanism was widely practiced for divination and healing. Many of the best-known healing shamans were women.

kisaeng A geisha-like female entertainer in early modern Korea.

READING THE PAST

Scenes from the Daily Life of a Korean Queen

The following selection is taken from the diary of Lady Hong (1735–1815), a queen during Korea's Yi dynasty. Unlike most male authors of the time, who wrote in Chinese (in part to show off their education, much as many European men at this time wrote in Latin rather than their own vernaculars), Lady Hong wrote in the Korean script. She also devoted great attention to the details of everyday life, including close observations of individual emotions. After stating that she began to write her memoirs at the urging of a nephew, Lady Hong describes her birth and early upbringing:

I was born during the reign of King Yongjo, at noon on 6 August 1735, at my mother's family's home in Kop'yong-dong, Pangsongbang. One night, before I was born, my father had dreamed of a black dragon coiled around the rafters of my mother's room, but the birth of a daughter did not seem to fit the portent of his dream. . . .

My paternal grandfather, Lord Chong-hon, came to look at me, and took an immediate fancy to me, declaring, "Although it is a girl, this is no ordinary child!" As I grew up, he became so fond of me that he was reluctant to let me leave his lap. He would say jokingly, "This girl is quite a little lady already, so she is sure to grow up quickly!". . .

The womenfolk of our family were all connected with the most respected clans of the day. My mother came from the Yi family—an upright clan. My father's eldest sister was married to a famous magistrate; while his second sister was a daughter-in-law of Prince Ch'ong-nung; and his youngest sister was a daughter-in-law of the minister of the board of civil office. Despite these connections, they were not haughty or extravagant, as is so often the case. When the family gathered together on festival days, my mother always treated the elder members with respect, and greeted the younger ones with a kind smile and an affectionate word. Father's second brother's wife was likewise virtuous, and her esteem for my mother was exceeded only by that for her mother-in-law. She was an outstanding woman—noble-minded and well educated. She was very fond of me; taught me my Korean alphabet and instructed me in a wide range of subjects. I loved her like a mother and indeed my mother used to say I had grown too close to her.

Source: Lady Hong, *Memoirs of a Korean Queen*, ed. and trans. Choe-Wall Yangh-hi (London: KPI, 1985), 1–4, 49.

EXAMINING THE EVIDENCE

1. In what ways do these passages reveal Neo-Confucian values?

2. What do these passages tell us about gender roles in a Neo-Confucian court society?

Slavery

Choson Korea appears unique among early modern states in that it was both ethnically homogeneous and heavily reliant on slave labor. Korea's enslaved population, perhaps as much as 30 percent of the total by 1550, appears to have emerged as a result of several factors: debt peonage (self-sale due to famine or debt) and penal servitude (punishment for crimes, including rebellion). Debt peonage and penal servitude were not unusual in the early modern world, and both could be found in neighboring China. What made slavery different in Korea was that the legal status of the enslaved, once proclaimed, was likely to be inherited for many generations. Self-purchase was extremely difficult, and slave owners clung to their chattels tenaciously. Korea's rigid social structure, far more hierarchical than neighboring China's or Japan's, only reinforced the notion of perpetual bondage. Moralists criticized slavery as early as the seventeenth century, but it was not until forced contact with outsiders after 1876 that the institution died out. Korea's last slaves were freed only in 1894.

Consolidation in Mainland Southeast Asia 1500–1750

FOCUS

What trends did mainland Southeast Asia share with China, Korea, Japan, and Russia?

Mainland Southeast Asia, encompassing the modern nations of Burma (Myanmar), Thailand, Cambodia, Laos, and Vietnam, followed a path more like that of China than of the Southeast Asian islands discussed in Chapter 19. Overall trends on the mainland included political consolidation, mostly by Buddhist kings; growth of large, tribute-paying populations due to intensive wet rice cultivation; and a shift toward planting of cash crops such as sugar for export. Unlike the more politically fractured islands of Indonesia and the Philippines, which fell increasingly into the hands of European interlopers (see Counterpoint: "Spiritual Conquest" in the Philippines), mainland Southeast Asia in early modern times experienced gunpowder-fueled, dynastic state-building.

Political Consolidation

The mainland Southeast Asian kingdoms in place by 1700 formed the basis for the nation-states of today. As happened in Muscovite Russia, access to European guns enabled some emerging dynasties, such as those of southern Burma, to expand and even briefly conquer their neighbors in the sixteenth and seventeenth centuries. Another catalyst for change was the rapid growth of global maritime trade, evident since the early fifteenth century (see Map 21.3). Overseas commerce transformed not only traditional maritime hubs such as Melaka and Aceh, as seen in Chapter 19, but also Pegu in Burma, Ayudhya (or Ayutthaya) in Thailand, and Lovek (near modern Phnom Penh) in Cambodia. The Buddhist kings who dominated these cities used trade revenues to expand and enhance their realms by attracting scholars, building libraries and monasteries, and constructing temples and images of the Buddha. The most confident saw themselves as incarnations of the Buddhist ideal of the universal king. Funded in part by growing trade, a massive bronze Buddha and supporting temple complex were built in the city of Luang Prabang, in Laos, beginning in 1512. A solid gold Buddha was also commissioned. Religious monuments on this scale, as seen in Europe, the Middle East, and even Spanish America, are a lasting reminder of early modern devotion and wealth.

The Example of Burma

A notable example of mainland Southeast Asian state-building driven by commercial wealth and access to European gunpowder weapons arose in southern Burma beginning in the 1530s. Portuguese mercenaries aided a regional king's takeover of the commercial city of Pegu, and a new, Pegu-based Buddhist dynasty with imperial ambitions soon emerged. Under King Bayinnaung (r. 1551–1581) the Burmese expanded into neighboring Thailand and Laos, conquering the prosperous capital of Ayudhya in 1569 and Vientiane, on the

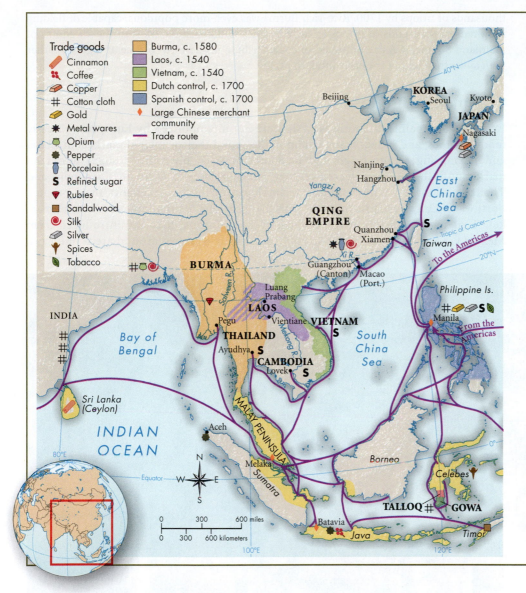

MAP 21.3

Southeast Asian Trade, c. 1500–1700

Maritime trade between the Indian Ocean and the western Pacific went back thousands of years, but it grew exponentially in volume and value after 1500, when Europeans arrived with gunpowder weapons and Spanish-American silver, eager to carve out trading enclaves and establish monopolies on key commodities such as pepper and opium. Non-European commercial networks expanded in turn, and many Chinese merchants set up shop in European outposts such as Nagasaki, Manila, and Batavia. Several mainland kingdoms, notably Burma and Thailand, became suddenly powerful by adopting imported weapons technology and monopolizing exports or restricting access to waterways and ports. Island kingdoms such as Aceh did likewise, taking advantage of their access to pepper and other goods. By 1700, Europeans had deeply affected this ancient crossroads, yet fell far short of controlling it.

upper Mekong River, in 1574. After building numerous pagodas, or ceremonial towers, in his new conquests, admirers referred to Bayinnaung as the "Victor of Ten Directions." He preferred the title "King of Kings."

Vietnam's Different Path

Vietnam followed a different path, largely as a result of Chinese influence. Even before Ming expansion southward in the fourteenth and early fifteenth centuries, Neo-Confucian principles of law and governance had been adopted by Vietnamese royalty under the Le dynasty (1428–1788). Yet like Korea, whose nobility had also embraced the kinds of reformist ideas promoted by Wang Yangming, the Chinese veneer in Vietnam barely masked a vibrant regional culture whose sense of distinct identity was never in question. China brokered power-sharing arrangements between the northern and southern halves of Vietnam in the 1520s, but new, competitive dynasties, led by the Trinh and Nguyen clans, were already in the making. Their battles for control lasted until the late seventeenth century and hindered Vietnamese consolidation despite the region's shared language and culture.

Mainland Southeast Asia resembled China more than neighboring islands in another sense: high overall population. This was largely the result of wet-rice agriculture and acquired immunity to a range of lowland tropical maladies. Massive water-control projects reminiscent of those in China and Japan allowed Vietnam's feuding clans to field tens of thousands of troops by 1700. Rice-rich Burma was even more populous, capable of fielding hundreds of thousands of troops as early as 1650. Unlike China, most of the kingdoms of mainland Southeast Asia continued to collect tribute in the form of rice and goods rather than silver throughout the early modern period.

Commercial Trends

Exports   Exports from mainland Southeast Asia were not monopolized by Europeans in early modern times, and in fact many commodities found their principal markets in China and Japan. Sugar cane originated in Southeast Asia, but refined sugar found no market until the late seventeenth century, when growers in Vietnam, Cambodia, and Thailand adopted Chinese milling technology and began to export their product northward. Only Taiwan competed with these regions for the Japanese "sweet" market. That most addictive of Columbian exchange crops, tobacco, introduced from Mexico via Manila, joined betel leaves (traditionally wrapped around areca nuts) as a

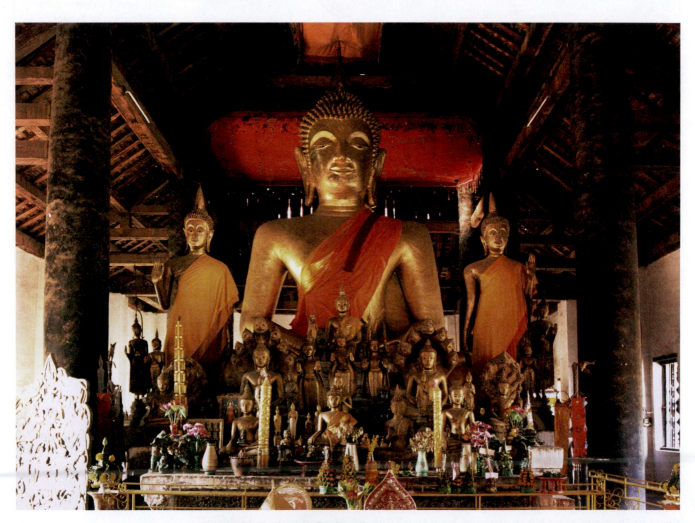

Buddha from Luang Prabang

This enormous gilt bronze Buddha was cast in the early sixteenth century in the former royal capital of Laos, Luang Prabang, where it is still at the center of an active temple. For several centuries the temple also housed a solid gold Buddha, which is now in the nearby palace museum. The remarkably well-preserved city and temples of Luang Prabang evoke the heyday of the Buddhist kings of mainland Southeast Asia, when new gunpowder weapons and access to more distant foreign markets stoked expansionist urges. (Yoshio Tomii Photo Studio/Aflo FotoAgency/Photolibrary.)

popular stimulant throughout the region by the seventeenth century. Other drugs had more profound consequences. The Dutch were the first to push the sale of opium from India in the 1680s (initially as a tobacco additive), and it soon created a class of addicts among Southeast Asia's many Chinese merchants and others willing to pay any amount of silver cash for it.

Imports to mainland Southeast Asia consisted primarily of cloth from India, an old "monsoon circuit" trade good that fostered resident communities of merchants, most of them Muslims, from as far away as Gujarat, in the Arabian Sea. Chinese merchants brought cloth from home, too, along with metal wares, porcelain, and a wide range of goods acquired through interregional trade. On the whole, the Chinese were by far more competitive and successful middlemen in mainland Southeast Asia than Europeans in early modern times, a fact that led to much resentment.

Imports

Interregional and interethnic commerce and urbanization enabled many Southeast Asian women to engage in trade as well, and whether they were Islamic, Buddhist, or otherwise observant, this pattern fit well with the general regional tendency toward female independence noted in Chapter 19. The wives and concubines of prominent long-distance merchants not only carried on important business transactions on land, they traveled with their husbands and lovers at sea. Some Southeast Asian women served as fully autonomous intermediaries for European merchants, most famously Soet Pegu, a Burmese woman who lived in the Thai capital of Ayudhya. She was the principal broker for the Dutch in Thailand (then known as Siam) for many years beginning in the 1640s.

Women's Commercial Pursuits

The global financial crisis of the seventeenth century, coupled with a number of regional wars, epidemics, and droughts, left mainland Southeast Asia in a weakened state. Burma contracted considerably, as did neighboring Siam. Laos survived as a separate kingdom only due to its isolation from these two neighbors, and it became even more inward-looking. Cambodia was similarly introverted under Khmer rule, and Vietnam suffered an even more severe decline. Mainland Southeast Asia submitted to paying tribute to China's Qing emperors in the course of the eighteenth century. In spite of the trend toward contraction, however, the region remained nearly impervious to European designs.

Economic Contraction

COUNTERPOINT
"Spiritual Conquest" in the Philippines

The Philippine Islands are a large volcanic chain in the warm tropical waters of the western Pacific (see Map 21.4). Like most Southeast Asian islands, the Philippines were settled by Austronesian mariners who left southern China and Taiwan some three thousand years ago. With the exception of a few small Islamic sultanates in the southern islands, the Philippines at the dawn of early modern times had no dynastic rulers or overarching religious or ethical traditions to unify its population. Over one hundred languages were spoken throughout the archipelago, and material culture differed radically from one river valley or island to the next.

> **FOCUS**
>
> In contrast to the general trend of political consolidation in early modern Asia, why did the Philippines fall to a European colonizing power?

Kin-based political units rarely exceeded two thousand members, and most were mutually hostile, sometimes murderously so. The islands' total population was relatively high, probably between 1 and 2 million in 1500, and acquired immunity to Old World diseases appears to have been relatively robust, certainly superior to that of Europeans who came later. As in most of Southeast Asia, women in the Philippines were relatively powerful and autonomous in politics, business, and domestic affairs. Both slavery and long-distance trade were established, though not deeply entrenched institutions, and a writing system using bamboo slats, now lost, was more or less common.

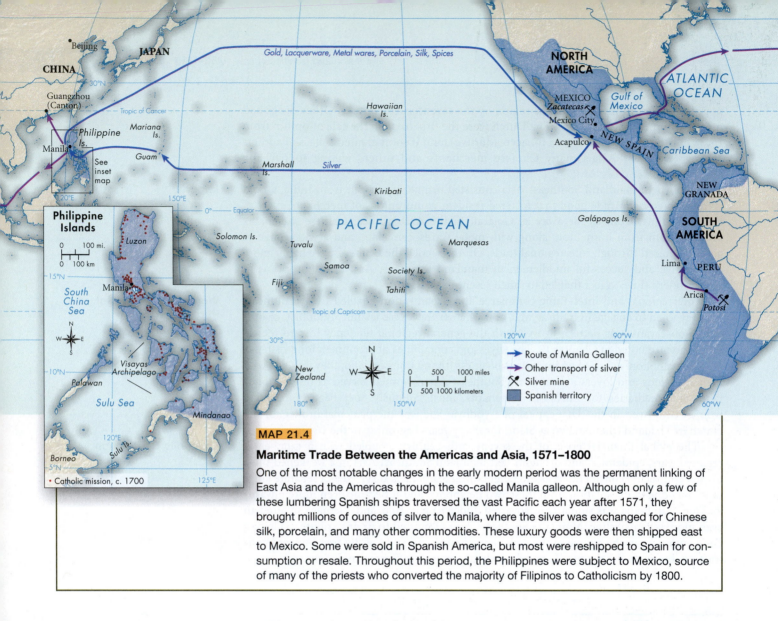

MAP 21.4

Maritime Trade Between the Americas and Asia, 1571–1800
One of the most notable changes in the early modern period was the permanent linking of East Asia and the Americas through the so-called Manila galleon. Although only a few of these lumbering Spanish ships traversed the vast Pacific each year after 1571, they brought millions of ounces of silver to Manila, where the silver was exchanged for Chinese silk, porcelain, and many other commodities. These luxury goods were then shipped east to Mexico. Some were sold in Spanish America, but most were reshipped to Spain for consumption or resale. Throughout this period, the Philippines were subject to Mexico, source of many of the priests who converted the majority of Filipinos to Catholicism by 1800.

Filipino traders sailing large outrigger vessels maintained contact with the East and Southeast Asian mainland, as well as with southern Japan, and Chinese merchants had long operated small trading posts in the Philippines, including one at Manila on the northern island of Luzon. Filipino exports included future plantation crops such as sugar and cotton, along with a bit of gold panned from mountain streams. Imports included metal goods, porcelain, spices, and a wide range of textiles. Most Filipinos mixed farming with fishing and the raising of small livestock, mostly pigs and chickens.

Arrival of the Spanish

Conquistadors Filipino life was suddenly and forever altered when Spanish conquistadors arrived in 1565, following up on the claims of Ferdinand Magellan, who was killed on the islands in 1521. By 1571 the Spanish had made Manila their capital city: a base for trade with China and a springboard for regional conquest. Shipyards were established at nearby Cavite to outfit the great galleons sent annually to Mexico (see again Map 21.4). Conquest was not easy in such a divided region, but these same divisions prevented a unified effort to repulse the Spanish. European invaders managed to gradually dominate many regions of the Philippines by making alliances with local chieftains in exchange for gifts and favors. Where local headmen resisted, obedient substitutes were found and placed in power.

Early Spanish colonists feverishly searched for gold, pearls, and other exportable local commodities, but their hopes fizzled before the end of the sixteenth century. There was ultimately little to collect in the way of marketable tribute, and the small enclave around

An Elite Filipino Couple

When the Spanish established their Philippine capital at Manila in 1571, they began to deal regularly with local nobles as well as visiting Chinese merchants. This rare image from about 1600 shows a Filipino husband and wife with the local label of Tagalog. Although Filipinos spoke many languages and practiced many distinct religions, the Tagalog language was the one chosen by Spanish priests for evangelization. Alongside Spanish, it became the islands' official language. The couple shown here displays dress and grooming similar to those of Malay elites living throughout Southeast Asia. The man holds the hilt of a kris dagger, a key symbol of high status, while his demure wife stands draped in the finest Chinese silk. (Courtesy, The Lilly Library, Indiana University, Bloomington, Indiana.)

Manila became, rather like a contemporary Portuguese outpost, the exclusive preserve of Spanish merchants, soldiers, and missionaries. A few bureaucrats eventually followed, linking Manila to its official capital in faraway Mexico City.

Outside Manila's Spanish core there grew a substantial Chinese merchant community, and many of its residents eventually converted to Catholicism and intermarried with local Filipino elites. In the end it was Catholic priests arriving on the annual ships from Mexico who proved responsible for what has come to be known as the "spiritual conquest" of the Philippines. As a result of lax crown oversight, the absence of precious minerals or other high-value exports, and general Filipino receptiveness to Roman Catholicism, before the end of early modern times a fairly small number of highly energetic priests managed to transform much of the archipelago into a veritable theocracy (a state ruled by religious authority), amassing huge amounts of territory and much political power in the process.

Missionaries

Missionaries from several Catholic orders learned to preach in Tagalog, the language of the greater Manila area, as well as a few other regional languages. Lack of standardized languages and writing systems complicated missionary efforts in some places, as did the racist refusal to train an indigenous clergy, yet the absence of a regionwide state religion or code of ethics similar to Buddhism or Confucianism probably eased acceptance of Catholicism's universalist claims. Indigenous deities and interpretations of Catholicism nevertheless persisted, usually manifested through the cult of the saints and in hybrid practices described by priests as witchcraft. In time, scores of Spanish and Mexican missionaries established hundreds of rural churches and frontier missions, most of them concentrated in the northern islands but some stretching south through the Visayas archipelago and into northern Mindanao.

The Limits of "Spiritual Conquest"

The Muslim South   Southern Mindanao and the Sulu Islands remained staunchly Muslim, however, and hence enemy territory in the Spanish view. Periodic battles pitted self-styled crusading Spaniards against the so-called Moors of this region, and some missionaries related harrowing stories of martyrdom and captivity among "pirate infidels" reminiscent of accounts from North Africa's Barbary Coast (discussed in Chapter 20). Indeed, hundreds of letters to Spain's kings and to the pope describe these mostly fruitless struggles.

Other threats to Christian hegemony came from bands of headhunters inhabiting the mountainous interior of Luzon and smaller islands. According to surviving documents, the ritual practice of headhunting, known in many parts of island Southeast Asia, was fairly widespread when the Spanish arrived, and it was periodically revived in some areas into modern times. Despite all these challenges to Spain's unarmed "Christian soldiers," the Philippines emerged from early modern times deeply transformed, in some ways more like Latin America than any other part of Asia. It would ironically be Filipino youths such as José Rizal, trained by the Jesuit and Franciscan successors of these early missionaries, who would lead the struggle to end Spanish colonialism at the last years of the nineteenth century.

Conclusion

China, Japan, Korea, and mainland Southeast Asia were home to a large portion of the world's peoples in early modern times. Russia was, by contrast, vast but thinly populated. In all cases, however, the most notable trend in northern and eastern Asia was toward internal political consolidation. The Philippines, though relatively populous, proved to be an exception, falling with relative ease into the hands of Spanish invaders. Outside Orthodox Russia and the Buddhist regions of Southeast Asia, Neo-Confucian principles of agrarian order and paternalistic harmony guided imperial consolidation. Despite some shocks in the seventeenth century, steady population growth and relative peace in China, Japan, and Korea only seemed to reinforce Confucius's ideal notions of educated self-sufficiency and limited need for foreign trade. Dynasty building and territorial expansion took on more charismatic and even prophetic religious tones in Orthodox Russia and Buddhist Southeast Asia.

Internal changes, however, particularly in China, did have profound effects on the rest of the world, and some regional political trends were accelerated by foreign imports such as gunpowder weapons. Wang Yangming, whose story began this chapter, was just one of many new imperial officials to use these deadly tools of power. Western weapons also aided Burmese and later Qing overland expansion in a way reminiscent of the Islamic "gunpowder empires" discussed in Chapters 19 and 20. Global trade also proved highly susceptible to East Asia's centralizing early modern policies. China's shift to a silver-based currency in the sixteenth century radically reordered world trade patterns. Suddenly, the Americas, Europe, and many Asian neighbors found themselves revolving in an increasingly tight, China-centered orbit. Virtually overnight, the village of Manila was transformed into one of the world's most vibrant trading crossroads. Manila was also an outlying colony, as will be seen in the next chapter, of an increasingly autonomous Spanish America. It was only in the nineteenth century that many parts of East and Southeast Asia began to experience the types of outside domination long experienced by these early established colonies.

NOTES

1. Peter the Great, quoted in Gérard Chaliand, ed., *The Art of War in World History from Antiquity to the Nuclear Age* (Berkeley: University of California Press, 1995), 578.
2. Engelbert Kaempfer, *Kaempfer's Japan: Tokugawa Culture Observed*, ed. and trans. Beatrice M. Bodart-Bailey (Honolulu: University of Hawai'i Press, 1999), 356.
3. Bashō, "The Records of a Weather-exposed Skeleton" (c. 1685), ed. and trans. Nobuyuki Yuasa, *The Narrow Road to the Deep North and Other Sketches* (London: Penguin, 1966).

RESOURCES FOR RESEARCH

General Works

Few works survey the many cultures treated as a cluster in this chapter, but some recent comparative studies have challenged established national categories of analysis. Liebermann and other contributors to the following volume try to relink Europe and Asia in early modern times.

Liebermann, Victor, ed. *Beyond Binary Histories: Re-imagining Eurasia to c. 1830.* 1999.

Straddling Eurasia: Rise of the Russian Empire, 1462–1725

The emphasis in early modern Russian history has largely moved away from court intrigues and suffering serfs toward broader processes of expansion into frontiers, environmental impacts, and cultural interaction. Other current scholarship focuses on the importance of the Orthodox Church. In economic history, classic works on the fur trade are still frequently cited.

For a broad-ranging Web site introduced by veteran Russian historian James H. Billington (author of *The Icon and the Axe: An Interpretive History of Russian Culture*, 1966), see http://www.pbs.org/weta/faceofrussia/intro.html.
Engel, Barbara A. *Women in Russia, 1700–2000.* 2004.
Kivelson, Valerie, and Robert H. Greene, eds. *Orthodox Russia: Belief and Practice Under the Tsars.* 2003.
LeDonne, John P. *The Grand Strategy of the Russian Empire, 1650–1831.* 2004.
Poe, Marshall T. *The Russian Moment in World History.* 2003.
Sunderland, Willard. *Taming the Wild Field: Colonization and Empire on the Russian Steppe.* 2004.

China from Ming to Qing Rule, 1500–1800

The literature on Ming and Qing China is vast. The following selections highlight both key internal developments and global interactions. Environmental history has experienced a recent boom.

Brook, Timothy. *The Confusions of Pleasure: Commerce and Culture in Ming China.* 1998.
Clunas, Craig. *Empire of Great Brightness: Visual and Material Cultures of Ming China, 1368–1644.* 2007.
Princeton University professor Benjamin Elman maintains a comprehensive Web site for Chinese history and culture: http://www.princeton.edu/~classbib.
Elvin, Mark. *The Retreat of the Elephants: An Environmental History of China.* 2004.
Mungello, D. E. *The Great Encounter of China and the West, 1500–1800*, 2d ed. 2005.
Struve, Lynn A., ed. *The Qing Formation in World-Historical Time.* 2004.
Von Glahn, Richard. *Fountain of Fortune: Money and Monetary Policy in China, 1000–1700.* 1996.

Japan in Transition, 1540–1750

The literature on Tokugawa Japan is extensive, and increasingly diverse. Some of the most exciting recent work treats cultural trends and environmental impacts.

Elison, George, and Bardwell L. Smith, eds. *Warlords, Artists, and Commoners: Japan in the Sixteenth Century.* 1981.
Fitzhugh, William W., and Chisato O. Dubreuil, eds. *Ainu: Spirit of a Northern People.* 1999.
Nakane, Chie, and Shinzaburō Ōishi, eds. *Tokugawa Japan: The Social and Economic Antecedents of Modern Japan.* Translated by Conrad Totman. 1990.
Perez, Louis G. *Daily Life in Early Modern Japan.* 2002.
The Public Broadcasting Service maintains a Web site with many Edo period images and links at http://www.pbs.org/empires/japan/.
Totman, Conrad. *The Lumber Industry in Early Modern Japan.* 1995.

Korea, a Land in Between, 1392–1750

Very few English-language histories of Korea give much attention to the early modern period. Seth is an exception.

Seth, Michael J. *A Concise History of Korea: From the Neolithic Period Through the Nineteenth Century*. 2006.

Consolidation in Mainland Southeast Asia, 1500–1750

Histories of mainland Southeast Asia are only beginning to break the old nationalist paradigm and take into account broad regional trends. Liebermann, a specialist on Burma, nicely complements Reid, whose work has mostly been on the islands.

Liebermann, Victor. *Strange Parallels: Southeast Asia in Global Context, c. 800–1830*. 2 vols. 2003–2004.

Northern Illinois University maintains a Southeast Asian digital library at http://sea.lib.niu.edu.

Reid, Anthony, ed. *Sojourners and Settlers: Histories of Southeast Asia and the Chinese*. 2001.

Tarling, Nicolas, ed. *The Cambridge History of Southeast Asia*. Vol. 1., *From Early Times to c. 1800*. 1992.

COUNTERPOINT: "Spiritual Conquest" in the Philippines

The colonial history of the Philippines still requires more scholarly examination, though many primary sources, such as that of Antonio de Morga, have been published in English translation. Phelan's account of early missionary endeavors remains a useful introduction.

Brewer, Carolyn. *Shamanism, Catholicism, and Gender Relations in the Colonial Philippines, 1521–1685*. 2004.

*de Morga, Antonio. *Sucesos de las Islas Filipinas*. Translated and edited by J. S. Cummins. 1971.

Majul, Cesar A. *Muslims in the Philippines*. 1973.

Phelan, John L. *The Hispanization of the Philippines: Spanish Aims and Filipino Responses, 1565–1700*. 1959.

Rafael, Vicente. *Contracting Colonialism: Translation and Christian Conversion in Tagalog Society Under Early Spanish Rule*, 2d ed. 1993.

*Primary source.

▶ **For additional primary sources from this period**, see *Sources of Crossroads and Cultures*.

▶ **For Web sites, images, and documents related to topics in this chapter**, see Make History at bedfordstmartins.com/smith.

REVIEW

The major global development in this chapter ▶ The general trend toward
political and cultural consolidation in early modern Asia.

IMPORTANT EVENTS

1392–1910	Yi dynasty established in Korea
1542	Jesuits reach Japan
1555–1581	Expansion of Burma under King Bayinnaung
1565	Spanish conquest of Philippines begins
1571	Manila becomes Philippine capital and key Pacific trading post
1581	Chinese Ming emperor Wanli issues Single Whip Law
1584–1613	Time of Troubles in Russia
1597–1630s	Persecution of Japanese Christians
1601	Matteo Ricci demonstrates Western technology in Ming court
1602–1867	Tokugawa Shogunate in Japan
1614	Japanese contact with foreigners restricted
1627, 1636	Manchu invasions of Korea
1644	Manchu invasion of Beijing; Ming dynasty replaced by Qing
1661–1722	Qing expansion under Emperor Kangxi
1689–1725	Russian imperial expansion under Tsar Peter the Great
1751	Qing annexation of Tibet

KEY TERMS

daimyo (p. 698)   **samurai** (p. 698)
geisha (p. 703)   **serf** (p. 687)
kabuki (p. 703)   **shogun** (p. 698)
kisaeng (p. 707)   **sumo** (p. 703)
nanban (p. 698)   **yangban** (p. 705)
Neo-Confucianism
    (p. 683)

CHAPTER OVERVIEW QUESTIONS

1. What factors led to imperial consolidation in Russia and China? Who were the new rulers, and what were the sources of their legitimacy?

2. Why was isolation more common in these empires than overseas engagement, and what were some of the benefits and drawbacks of isolation?

3. In what ways did early modern Asians transform their environments, and why?

SECTION FOCUS QUESTIONS

1. What prompted Russian territorial expansion?

2. How did the shift to a silver cash economy transform Chinese government and society?

3. How did self-isolation affect Japan?

4. How did life for common folk in early modern Korea differ from life in China or Japan?

5. What trends did mainland Southeast Asia share with China, Korea, Japan, and Russia?

6. In contrast to the general trend of political consolidation in early modern Asia, why did the Philippines fall to a European colonizing power?

MAKING CONNECTIONS

1. How did imperial Russia's rise compare with that of the Ottomans or Habsburgs (see Chapter 20)?

2. How did China under the Ming and Qing compare with the other most populous early modern empire, Mughal India (see Chapter 19)?

3. How did Iberian missionaries' efforts in the Philippines compare with those in western Africa (see Chapter 18)?

AT A CROSSROADS ▲

Scenes of everyday life in eighteenth-century Brazil are extremely rare, but fortunately an Italian military engineer known in Portuguese as Carlos Julião chose to depict enslaved and free people of color in Salvador da Bahia, Rio de Janeiro, and the diamond diggings of northern Minas Gerais during several tours of duty. This image of a free woman of color in the diamond town of Tejuco, home of Chica da Silva (whose story opens this chapter), suggests that she is attracting the romantic attention of a bespectacled Portuguese immigrant. Both are clothed with a mix of fine Asian and European fabrics, testament to the wealth of the diamond diggings. Opulence, violence, and the constant mixing of peoples were core features of life on Brazil's colonial mining frontier. (Acervo da Fundação Biblioteca Nacional, Rio de Janeiro, Brazil.)

Transforming New Worlds: The American Colonies Mature

1600–1750

Born of an enslaved African mother and a Portuguese father in a small diamond-mining camp deep in the highlands of Brazil, the legendary Chica da Silva, "the slave who became queen," has long fired the imagination. In 1753, when Chica was about twenty, she was purchased by João Fernandes de Oliveira, who had come from Portugal to oversee diamond mines granted by the Crown to his father. Before long, Chica became the overseer's mistress and the talk of Tejuco, capital of the diamond district. Freed on Christmas Day, 1753, less than a year after being purchased, Chica established a household of her own, in the most opulent style. In time, she would bear Fernandes de Oliveira thirteen children. Her lover lavished upon Chica and her children gifts, fine clothing, a large town-house, and country estates. Together, the couple owned hundreds of slaves. When Chica went down the street with her bright silk gowns and retinue of servants, people made way.

BACKSTORY

As we saw in Chapter 17, the Americas were transformed in early modern times, emerging as a global crossroads whose products, including silver, sugar, and tobacco, would change the world. The wealth of the Americas would be extracted at incalculable cost. By the early seventeenth century millions of native Americans had died from the effects of conquest, overwork, and epidemic disease. As a result, the Spanish and Portuguese enslaved West and West Central Africans and brought them to work the plantations and mines. Livestock imported from Europe roamed far and wide in the Americas, transforming the landscape and displacing native species.

Despite increasing challenges from northern Europeans, the Spanish remained dominant in the Americas through the early 1600s, and they retained control of all known sources of mineral wealth. Their colonies became increasingly mixed racially, and the people were ranked along a steep social hierarchy, but everyone was officially Catholic. In the early seventeenth century, Portuguese Brazil was a coast-hugging sugar colony dependent on the labor of enslaved Amerindians and Africans. Its European settler population was still a tiny minority, for whom most of Brazil was an unknown, untamed frontier. Although the great empires of the Aztecs and Incas had long since fallen, much of North and South America remained native territory.

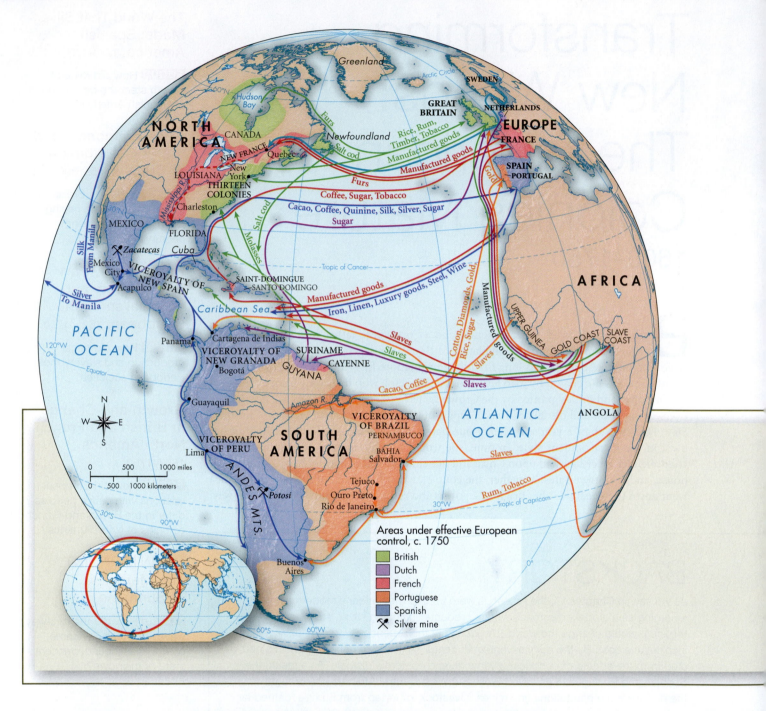

Areas under effective European control, c. 1750

- British
- Dutch
- French
- Portuguese
- Spanish
- ✗ Silver mine

1570 Spanish galleons begin annual service linking Acapulco to Manila

1630 Dutch capture northeast Brazil

1654 Portuguese drive Dutch from Brazil; some colonists move to Suriname

1618 Dutch establish colony of New Netherland on upper Hudson River

1655 English seize Jamaica from the Spanish

| 1600 | 1625 | 1650 | 1675 |

1607 English establish colony at Jamestown, Virginia

1625 Dutch settle New Amsterdam on Manhattan Island; English establish colony on Barbados

Bacon's Rebellion in Virginia **1676**

Henry Morgan's buccaneers sack Panama City **1671**

1608 French establish colony at Quebec City

1664 English take New Amsterdam from Dutch, rename it New York

Visitors from Portugal were scandalized that an illegitimate "half-breed" woman could flaunt such extravagance. Indeed, numerous laws forbade such public display by persons of "free-colored" status. In Brazil's diamond and gold districts, however, such laws seemed made to be broken. After her death, storytellers surmised that Chica da Silva used cruelty and promiscuity to advance her wealth and status. According to the legends they constructed, Chica da Silva was a kind of Brazilian archetype: the sexually insatiable and power-hungry *mulata* (mulatto). In the popular imagination, the exceptional woman of color could make good only by seducing and manipulating her white oppressor.

However, the Brazilian historian Júnia Furtado has challenged this view of Chica. First, Furtado asks, how could a woman who bore thirteen children in fifteen years have been a seductress? Second, Chica was hardly unique: of 510 family residences in Tejuco, 197 were headed by free women of color, several of them recent slaves like Chica. More-over, records show that Chica da Silva did attend to some matters of propriety: she did her best to educate her children and used much of her fortune to build churches, fund religious brotherhoods, organize church processions, and pay for baptisms, burials, and weddings, including those of her slaves. She was in these ways a typical elite "Portu-guese" woman who happened to live in an atypical, racially mixed, mining frontier world.

The story of Chica da Silva highlights several features of colonial life in the Americas. First, these colonies were often born of the exploitation of slaves in the production of raw wealth for export. Second, the proximity of peoples of different colors, or "races," in these colonies led to racial mingling, a subject still marked by considerable taboo. For some, the

MAPPING THE WORLD

New World Colonies, c. 1750

Arguably the most profoundly transformed world region in the early modern period, the Americas soon came to be linked not only to western Europe, but also to Atlantic Africa and East Asia. Native American populations declined drastically due to disease and conquest. Their numbers began to rebound after 1650, however, and in Spanish America they served as the major producers of silver, dyes, hides, and other commodities exported to the rest of the world. Africa's role was also critical. The number of enslaved Africans forcibly brought to the Americas by 1750 far exceeded the number of Europeans who migrated voluntarily, and it was they and their descendants who produced the bulk of the world's sugar, cacao, tobacco, and eventually coffee. Colonial American life entailed more than forced labor and primary resource extraction, but both, like the Christianity introduced by missionaries and colonists, remained core features of the region long after colonialism ended.

ROUTES ▼

→ British trade route
→ Dutch trade route
→ French trade route
→ Portuguese trade route
→ Spanish trade route
⇢ Travels of Robert de la Salle, 1679–1682
→ Travels of Pehr Kalm, 1749

1695–1800 Discovery in Brazilian interior of gold and diamonds inaugurates Brazil's "gold rush"

▪ **1720** Brazil elevated to status of viceroyalty

1700	1725	1750

▪ **1694** Great Brazilian maroon community of Palmares destroyed

Rio de Janeiro elevated to status of capital of Brazil **1763** ▪

1701–1714 War of the Spanish Succession

emergence of new populations of mixed heritage upset notions of racial purity, ethnicity, hierarchy, and propriety. For others, breeding across color lines was a natural but not uncomplicated consequence of proximity. Although the abuses of colonialism can hardly be overstated, the life of Chica da Silva embodies the complexities and contradictions of colonial life in the Americas.

Beginning with the arrival of Columbus in the Caribbean in 1492 and Pedro Álvares Cabral on the coast of Brazil in 1500, waves of European conquerors, missionaries, and colonists, along with a host of alien plants, animals, and pathogens, swept across the Western Hemisphere. By 1750 few indigenous Americans remained unaffected. Even in the vast unconquered areas of the Amazon Basin and the Great Plains of North America, where native American refugee populations had been pushed by European encroachment, European-introduced diseases, animals, and trade goods steadily transformed everyday life. In some places native peoples were joined by runaway African slaves.

Despite its slower start, Portuguese Brazil came to resemble Spanish Mexico and Peru. Busy with their far-flung African and Asian colonies and trading posts, at first the Portuguese maintained only coastal plantations in Brazil. This situation began to change after 1695 when gold and diamonds were discovered in the interior. Along the northeast coast, the Portuguese created the first of several "neo-Africas" in the Americas, uprooting and enslaving hundreds of thousands of West and West Central Africans to plant, harvest, and refine sugar and other cash crops. The Atlantic slave trade and the plantation economy, both defining features of the Caribbean and of British North America after 1700, started in earnest in the Brazilian districts of Pernambuco and Bahia, where the Americas are nearest to Africa.

Desire for empire attracted the French, Dutch, and English to first prey on Spanish and Portuguese ships and ports, and then to establish American colonies of their own. They also searched desperately for a passage to China in hopes of outflanking the Spanish and Portuguese. Piracy and privateering, or state-sponsored piracy, proved to be serious problems for Iberian colonists and merchants until the end of early modern times, and both practices helped generate the initial capital and official interest needed to establish rival colonies. Despite some poor planning and occasional violent ejections, entrepreneurs and planters from northern European countries eventually developed thriving settlements. In time, Caribbean island and mainland colonies such as Barbados and Virginia came to compete with Spanish and Portuguese colonies in the export of sugar and tobacco.

Like the Spanish and the Portuguese, Dutch, French, and English planters in the Caribbean and eastern seaboard colonies of North America employed African slaves from an early date. Amerindian slavery was also practiced, despite proud claims by colonists that they treated native Americans more fairly than the Spanish and Portuguese had. Unlike their Iberian-American counterparts, however, northern European masters relied more heavily on indentured servants, poor women and men from their own countries who contracted terms of servitude in exchange for passage to the Americas, plus room and board. However, most terms of **indenture** were short, usually three years, and before long their masters reinvested the capital accumulated from their labors in African slavery.

In the far north, yet another model emerged. Here the French, Dutch, and English competed with a variety of indigenous groups for access to furs, timber, agricultural land, fish, and other natural resources. These European colonists, like their counterparts in the tropics, kept Amerindian and a few African slaves, but they did not rely wholly on them for subsistence or export products. Swedes, Germans, and Danes also entered into the competition for colonies in some regions, though less forcefully. To the chagrin of all northern Europeans, gold and silver were nowhere to be found in the regions not occupied by the Spanish and Portuguese. A water passage to China's fabled silk and porcelain was similarly elusive. The colonists would have to make do with less glamorous exports, such as salted cod and timber.

indenture A labor system in which Europeans contracted for several years of unpaid labor in exchange for free passage across the Atlantic and housing.

OVERVIEW
QUESTIONS

The major global development in this chapter: The profound social, cultural, and environmental changes in the Americas under colonial rule.

As you read, consider:

1. How did the production of silver, gold, and other commodities shape colonial American societies?

2. How and where did northern Europeans insert themselves into territories claimed by Spain and Portugal?

3. How did racial divisions and mixtures compare across the Americas by the mid-eighteenth century?

The World That Silver Made: Spanish America 1570–1750

As we saw in Chapter 17, following the discovery of precious metals in the early sixteenth century, the Spanish moved quickly to reconnoiter their claims while also building cities, widening roads, and fortifying ports. Their two great bases were Lima and Mexico City, each home to tens of thousands of Spaniards, Indians, Africans, mixed people of color, and even some Asians, mostly Filipinos, by the end of the sixteenth century. Although much territory remained in indigenous hands, the Spanish established themselves as far afield as northern New Mexico and southern Chile. A complex imperial bureaucracy functioned all over the colonies by 1570, and various arms of the Catholic Church were firmly in place, occupying stone buildings as imposing as many in Europe. Armed fleets hauled tons of gold and silver to Europe and Asia each year, returning with a wide array of luxury consumer goods, including Chinese silk and Dutch linen. The plundering of pirates could make only a small dent in this rich commerce in both Atlantic and Pacific waters (see Map 22.1).

> **FOCUS**
> How did mineral wealth steer the development of Spanish America?

Gold and silver also financed the purchase of slaves, and soon men, women, and children of African descent were found throughout Spanish America. Young Domingo Angola, whose story opened Chapter 18, was one of many such uprooted Africans. Captive Africans served on galleons in the Pacific, and some visited China, Japan, the Spice Islands, and the Philippines. Major port cities such as Lima and Cartagena de Indias counted black majorities soon after 1600, and highland mining boomtowns such as Zacatecas and Potosí had large African and African-descended populations throughout early modern times.

Perhaps the most significant trend in this long period, however, was the decline of the indigenous population. Ranking among the worst population collapses in world history, this decline was largely a result of sudden exposure to new diseases from Europe and Africa, against which native Americans had built up no natural immunities during thousands of years of isolation. From a total of some 40 million in 1500, the number of native Americans living within the sphere of Spanish dominance fell to less than 5 million by 1600. Labor conditions, displacement, and physical abuse greatly accelerated indigenous population decline in the early years. Although some recovery was evident by the mid-eighteenth century, native populations in the former Inca and Aztec realms never returned to precontact levels.

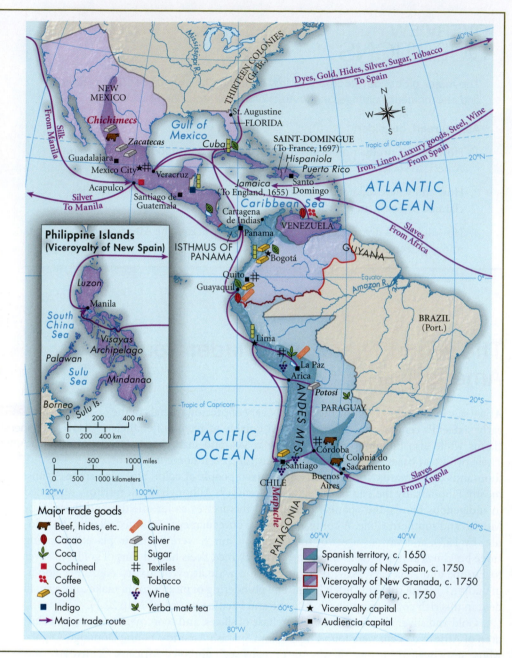

MAP 22.1

Spanish America, 1580–1750

In early modern times Spain was the most significant power in the Americas. Although Dutch, English, and French competitors gained ground in North America and the Caribbean after 1600, and the Portuguese finally moved to expand Brazil after 1700, during this period Spanish America, divided into three viceroyalties by 1750, remained the richest and most densely populated region in the Western Hemisphere by far. The mines of Potosí and Zacatecas alone supplied the bulk of the world's silver, and internal demand for cacao, sugar, and hides, among many other commodities, kept the colonies humming and interconnected. Meanwhile, the distant Philippines, governed from Mexico City, served as both a trade node with East Asia and a base for missionary expansion.

Philippine Islands (Viceroyalty of New Spain)

Major trade goods
- Beef, hides, etc.
- Cacao
- Coca
- Cochineal
- Coffee
- Gold
- Indigo
- Quinine
- Silver
- Sugar
- Textiles
- Tobacco
- Wine
- Yerba maté tea
- Major trade route

Spanish territory, c. 1650
Viceroyalty of New Spain, c. 1750
Viceroyalty of New Granada, c. 1750
Viceroyalty of Peru, c. 1750
★ Viceroyalty capital
■ Audiencia capital

Governing and Profiting from the Colonies

Control Through Bureaucracy

To maintain control and authority over its ambitious settlers, the Spanish crown quickly spun a complex web of overlapping institutions for colonial governance. Some institutions, such as the high appeals court, or *audiencia*, were based on Spanish models; others were American innovations or hybrids. The process of bureaucratization was surprisingly rapid, in part thanks to Spain's growing ranks of university-trained lawyers. These lawyers often clashed with the conquistadors and their offspring, but by 1570 most government institutions were in place.

Spanish culture had long centered on towns and cities, and hundreds of new ones were founded throughout the Americas, some displacing pre-Columbian settlements. Santo Domingo, Mexico City, Lima, Bogotá, and Buenos Aires became capitals of vast districts,

audiencia The high appeals court in Spanish America.

Mexico City's Plaza Mayor

Mexico City's *plaza mayor*, or great square, painted here in 1695, served as the city's main marketplace, exposition grounds, and social crucible. In addition to ceremonial processions and religious devotions, the square was the site of public executions and *autos-da fé*, punishments of those convicted by the Inquisition. It was a place to see and be seen. In this anonymous painting one gets a sense of the size and grandeur of New Spain's capital at its height, although nature's wrath is on the horizon in the form of Popocatépetl, a huge, active volcano, spewing ash ominously into the darkened sky. (Corsham Court, Wiltshire/Bridgeman Art Library.)

but even small provincial towns exerted power over the surrounding countryside. As in Spain, town councils were the basic unit of governance throughout Spanish America.

Legally, the colonies were divided between a "republic of Indians," complete with separate legal codes, and a "republic of Spaniards." This divided system was created not out of fears of racial mixing, which occurred constantly regardless of the Crown's desires, but rather to shelter and thus more efficiently exploit Spanish America's indigenous population. In short, it was in the government's best interest to keep the number of officially registered "Indians" high, since only they were subject to tribute payment and labor drafts. Much like Russian peasants in the same period, native Americans under Spanish rule were legally bound to assigned villages. Officially recognized indigenous headmen were required to collect tributes from their subjects twice a year and to organize labor pools.

Spanish colonies were divided into provinces headed by crown-appointed governors or magistrates. Clusters of these provinces made up audiencia jurisdictions, or regions subject to the authority of a royal court of appeals. Audiencia judges were nearly all Spanish-born lawyers hoping to climb the ranks of colonial bureaucracy and one day return to Spain. Few subjects' legal appeals went beyond these courts, and indigenous groups quickly learned to use the audiencias to their advantage in disputes with Spanish landlords and mine owners.

Above the audiencias were two viceroyalties: New Spain and Peru. New Spain, with its capital at Mexico City, covered Spanish North America, Central America, the Caribbean islands, Venezuela, and the Philippine Islands across the Pacific. The Viceroyalty of Peru, which was subdivided in the eighteenth century, covered all of Spanish South America with the exception of Venezuela, but included the Isthmus of Panama (see again Map 22.1). Spain's king thus appointed only two viceroys for all of his overseas holdings. Both reported to the king and to a court council in Spain, the Council of the Indies. Consequently, at least in theory, all colonial officials were part of a political hierarchy headed by the Crown, the ultimate source of power and decision making.

Spain's transatlantic mail service was slow, and the transpacific one even slower, but both were surprisingly reliable once the annual fleet system was in place after the mid-sixteenth century. Word of trouble in the colonies—or new mineral finds—always reached the king, and his decrees and tax demands always made the return trip. Thanks to this complex bureaucracy and regular transportation system, Spain's many distant colonies felt connected to the motherland.

The first Spanish settlers in the Americas were few in number compared to the vast native populations. Still, these early settlers were an ambitious lot, and they quickly fanned out over an enormous area in search of gold, silver, and other commodities. Conquistadors gained land and encomiendas, or grants of the compelled labor and tribute of native Americans. Foreshadowing African slavery, the encomienda system allowed Spaniards to accumulate capital and gain access to credit without having to pay wages. The system persisted in frontier areas until the mid-eighteenth century, subsidizing development of cattle ranches, wheat farms, fruit orchards, and vineyards. The Spanish crown, meanwhile, also claimed its share of New World income.

Even without the encomienda, all men identified in census records as "Indian," with the exception of chiefs and nobles, were required to pay tribute to the Crown biannually as a reminder of their conquered status. By 1600, tribute had to be paid in cash, a requirement that forced native peoples to produce marketable goods or sell their labor. Tributes and taxes in raw commodities such as grains or textiles were no longer accepted; everyone had to participate in the market economy. Indigenous women and children were increasingly drawn into the workforce to help produce cash. In many cities, including Potosí, single indigenous women, exempt from tribute obligations and also exempt from the Spanish sales tax, became relatively

Spanish "Piece of Eight"

Most Spanish-American silver flowed out into the wider world in the form of large, brick-sized bars, but the Spanish also minted millions of coins throughout early modern times, both in the colonies and in Spain. This crudely struck *peso de a ocho,* or "piece of eight," was minted in the famous silver mining city of Potosí in 1688, during the reign of the last Habsburg king, Charles II. In addition to the coin maker's initials, "VR," the piece of eight bears symbols of Spain's overseas empire, including the Pillars of Hercules (the Strait of Gibraltar) and the great waves of the "Ocean Sea," or Atlantic. "Plus Ultra," or "Further Beyond," the motto of Spain's first Habsburg king and Holy Roman Emperor Charles V, became the motto of empire as well. The Spanish piece of eight served for several centuries as the standard world currency. (Hoberman Collection/Corbis.)

READING THE PAST

An Iraqi Traveler's Impressions of Potosí

The following selection was originally written in Arabic by an Iraqi Christian, Elias al-Musili, who traveled throughout Spanish America between 1675 and 1680 hoping to raise money for his church, which was located in Ottoman territory but sponsored by Rome. Al-Musili was among the very few foreigners permitted to visit Spain's colonies in the early modern era due to persistent crown fears of subversion and spying, and he was the only Middle Eastern Arabic speaker of whom we have record. He was given alms throughout the Andes, particularly by native Americans, for preaching in the ancient Aramaic language. He left Potosí with several mule-loads of silver.

A Visit to the Mint and Silver Mine

One day I went to the place where they minted dinars, piastres ["pieces of eight"], halves, and quarters. In this mint house there are forty black slaves and twelve Spaniards working. We saw the piles of coins, like hillocks on one side, the halves on another, and half-quarters still on another, heaped on the floor and being trampled underfoot like dirt that has no value.

On one side of this town is the mountain containing the mine[s]. It is known throughout the world on account of its excessive wealth; countless treasures have been extracted from all four sides of it for 140 years. They had fenced it off, dug it up, and reached the very bottom of it to extract the silver. They had prepared wooden props for it, to make sure the mountain did not cave in. From the outside it looks whole, but on the inside it is empty. Up to 700 Indians work inside to cut out stone for men who had already bought the rights from the king. Every miner has assigned a certain number of Indians to work his share of the mine. There is a royal decree ordering every village to offer a number of Indian men to mine. According to the law one out of five men is to be assigned to such a task.

Describing the Extraction of Silver

There are 37 mills used for grinding silver-bearing stones day and night, except for Sundays and holidays. After grinding it finely, they take it in quantities of fifty qintârs [about 5000 lbs.] and form separate piles with it. They add water to each . . . then add mercury to it according to need. They then stir it with shovels several times; and should it require more mercury, they add it up until perfected. If it is cold by nature, they add copper until it warms up. If it is warm by nature, they add lead until it cools. How can they tell whether it is warm or cool? They scoop up samples in a clay utensil and wash it with water until the dirt disappears and the mixture of silver and mercury remains. The sample is then smeared by finger on a piece of the aforementioned clay pot. If it crumbles, it is considered hot; if it sticks, it is considered cold. When perfect, or well tempered, it adheres to the clay and shines. Next they put it in a large basin with water flowing over it and stir it all the while with finesse. Silver and mercury settle on the bottom and dirt is carried off by the water. After thus completing the "washing" of this mixture, the overflow of water is cut off and the basin cleaned. The mixture of silver and mercury is taken out and put in gunnysacks hung from trees, under which are placed containers lined with cattle skin. Mercury flows out of the sacks into these containers underneath and only silver remains in them, like loaves of sugar.

Source: Cesar E. Farah, ed. and trans., *An Arab's Journey to Colonial Spanish America: The Travels of Elias al-Mûsili in the Seventeenth Century* (Syracuse, NY: Syracuse University Press, 2003).

EXAMINING THE EVIDENCE

1. What aspects of silver production seem to have most amazed al-Musili?

2. How does he portray workers in Potosí's mint, mines, and refineries?

wealthy, and soon ran afoul of town authorities for wearing silk garments and other adornments deemed inappropriate for their class.

Along with indigenous tributes, sales taxes, and customs duties, the Spanish crown and its many bureaucrats relied on mining taxes in the form of silver, the so-called *quinto real*, or "royal fifth," of the silver mined. The Crown also rented out the mercury monopoly, which was crucial in processing silver. However, by 1600 corruption was common, and crown control of mining and silver exports became weak. Mine owners and merchants found increasingly clever ways to avoid tax collectors. By the 1640s a vibrant contraband trade was flourishing, especially around Buenos Aires and along Caribbean shores, where newly arrived slaves and luxury merchandise were traded for silver ingots and "pieces of eight," all tax-free.

Despite a growing culture of corruption and tax evasion, some mine owners managed to follow the rules and still do very well for themselves. One who stood out was Antonio López de Quiroga, who used his profits from selling silver to the mint in Potosí to buy up abandoned mines, hire the most skilled workers available, and employ innovations such as black-powder blasting (see Reading the Past: An Iraqi Traveler's Impressions of Potosí). By the 1670s, López de Quiroga was the local equivalent of a billionaire, a major benefactor of churches, and even a sponsor of lowland conquest expeditions in the upper Amazon. Similar stories were repeated in the mining frontiers of northern Mexico.

Commodities Beyond Silver

Although the mining economy was most critical in stimulating the expansion of frontiers, much else was happening in Spanish America. Venezuela, for example, developed a vibrant economy based on the production of raw chocolate beans, or cacao. These were first destined for Mexico, a huge Spanish-American market, and subsequently for Europe, once the taste for chocolate developed there in the later seventeenth century. Partly due to Venezuela's location along the slave route to New Granada (present-day Colombia) and Mexico, in the cacao groves surrounding the regional capital of Caracas, African laborers soon displaced native Americans held in encomienda. Coffee was introduced from Arabia in the early eighteenth century and soon became another major export.

There were other ways to make money in Spanish America without entering the global export market. In Paraguay a tea called *yerba maté* was collected in the forest by native Guaraní speakers, many of whom lived on and around Jesuit missions. The tea was then carried by mule throughout the Andes, where it was consumed by all classes. This habit, unlike chocolate drinking, was not picked up in Europe. Huge cattle ranches developed in the hinterland of Buenos Aires and in north-central Mexico. Beef, tallow, and hides were consumed in great quantities in mining towns such as Potosí and Zacatecas. In seventeenth-century Mexico what historians call a "mining-ranching complex" developed, tying distant regions together across expanses of desert. Elites invested profits from mining in trade, and vice versa. By 1600, cheap cotton and woolen textiles were produced in quantity in both Mexico and the northern Andes, enough to nearly satisfy the substantial working-class market.

Spanish America's Unique Economy

Spanish America was unusual among early modern overseas colonies in that its economy was both export-oriented and self-sufficient from an early stage. Only luxury goods such as fine textiles and iron and steel items were not produced locally. Why a local iron industry did not develop might seem strange since iron deposits were available, but the short answer is silver. Spanish-American merchants simply had so much silver to export that they struggled to find enough imports to balance the trade. Spanish authorities later outlawed local iron production to protect merchant interests.

After textiles, which included vast quantities of Chinese silks and South Asian chintzes and calicoes along with a wide range of European cloths, common iron goods such as horseshoes were among the main items consumed. The Basques of northern Spain had long produced iron and steel products, and some artisan clans in cities such as Bilbao became wealthy by sending their wares to the colonies. Wine was another favorite import from Spain, mostly produced in the hinterland of Seville, but even this was being produced in large quantities on the coasts of Peru and Chile by the 1580s.

The net effect of silver exports on such a grand scale from both Mexico and the Andes was a colonial economy that was both internally interdependent in terms of food, common cloth, hides, and other basic items and dependent on the outside world for luxury products. As with iron, the Crown actively discouraged industrialization of the textile sector, but scientific innovations in mining and metallurgy—anything to increase the flow of silver—were rewarded with patents. Thus, the colonial system increased the density of economic connections within the Americas at the same time as it forged new connections between the Americas and the larger world.

Spanish Mercantile Policy

As we saw in Chapter 20, Spain's Habsburg monarchs and ministers envisioned the colonial economy as a closed mercantile system, intended to benefit the mother country through taxation while enabling subjects of varying status to seek and consolidate wealth (although not to gain crown-challenging titles of nobility). No foreigners were supposed to trade with the American colonies except through approved monopoly holders based in Seville. These monopolists also controlled (theoretically) all trade through Acapulco to Manila and back. Although this closed-system ideal was realized to a surprising degree given the great distances, cultural divides, and other obstacles involved, it soon fell prey to individual wiles and corrupt cartels as Spain itself fell into decline under a succession of weak kings after Philip II (r. 1556–1598). Only after 1700, with the rise of the Bourbon dynasty, did the Crown manage to reassert itself forcefully in colonial economic affairs. As we will see in the next chapter, widespread rebellion would follow.

Everyday Life in Spanish America

As the colonies matured, Spain's increasingly diverse American subjects found new possibilities for social and material improvement, but they also faced many bureaucratic and natural constraints. Life spans in colonial Spanish America were similar to those of contemporary Europe for elites, but as we have seen, they were considerably shorter for people of indigenous and African descent. Epidemics, particularly of smallpox, hit everyone from time to time. Slaves, draft workers, and mixed-race criminals sent to fight the Mapuche in Chile or the Chichimecs of northern Mexico were often described in identification documents as having smallpox scars on their faces. Infant mortality was very high at all levels of society.

Many of the regions settled by the Spanish were prone to earthquakes and volcanic eruptions, which led many to regard natural disasters as judgments of God. When in 1661 a volcano dumped several feet of ash on Quito, now the capital of Ecuador, Catholic priests ordered that an image of the Virgin Mary be paraded through the streets until the eruption ceased. Such religiosity was manifest in many aspects of colonial Spanish-American society, including art and literature, and it helped shape local norms of gender and race relations. In fact, Catholicism came to serve as a common cultural touchstone, connecting the members of an ethnically and culturally diverse society.

Unlike parts of English, French, and Dutch America, as we will see, Spanish America was never intended as a refuge for religious dissenters. From the beginning the region was a Roman Catholic domain. Even recent converts to Christianity were not allowed to emigrate for fear of allowing Judaism or Islam into the colonies. Spain's Romas, or gypsies, were likewise banned due to their alleged fondness for fortunetelling and witchcraft. Still, some recent converts and Romas, along with miscellaneous "unorthodox" foreigners from Portugal, France, Italy, Germany, the Low Countries, and even Greece, managed to sneak aboard Indies-bound ships leaving Seville. In the colonies, the beginning of the Inquisition after 1570, plus waves of anti-idolatry campaigns after 1560, soon led to widespread persecution of nonconformists.

Religious Conformity and Resistance

How did the mass of subject peoples, most of them indigenous peasants and enslaved Africans, respond to these demands for spiritual conformity? Faced with constant threats and punishments from priests and officials, along with the sometimes persuasive efforts of missionaries, the vast majority of native and African-descended subjects at least nominally accepted Catholicism. What soon emerged, however, was a complex fusion of Catholic practices with a more secretive, underground world of non-Christian cults, shamanistic healing practices, and witchcraft. Scholars have learned much about these alternative religious spheres in recent years from Inquisition and anti-idolatry records, and some have sought to trace their roots to parts of Africa and elsewhere.

According to Christian scripture, all human beings were redeemable in the creator's eyes, regardless of sex, age, status, color, or birthplace. Thus, many church leaders believed that non-Western habits such as nudity and even cannibalism could be reformed

Gentlemen of Esmeraldas

Andrés Sánchez Gallque, *Gentlemen of Esmeraldas* (The Art Archive/American Museum Madrid.)

In 1599 Andrés Sánchez Gallque, an indigenous artist from Quito, the former Inca capital located high in the Andes, painted a group portrait of three men who had climbed up from the Pacific coast province of Esmeraldas to sign a treaty with the colonial government. The three men, Don Francisco de Arobe and his two sons, Pedro and Domingo, were maroons, descendants of escaped slaves who swam ashore following a shipwreck in the 1540s. They were in Quito to sign a treaty agreeing not to ally with pirates. The Spanish honorific title "Don" was used for all three men since they were recognized as indigenous chiefs. As it happened, Don Francisco de Arobe was the son of an African man and a native woman from Nicaragua. Other Esmeraldas maroons had intermarried with local indigenous inhabitants.

In exchange for agreeing to defend the coast against intruders, the Arobes were sent to a professional tailor in Quito and given a wide variety of luxury textiles, including ponchos and capes made from Chinese silk brought to Acapulco by the Manila galleon, then south to Quito via Panama. The maroon leaders also received linen ruff collars from Holland and iron spearheads, probably from the Basque region of northern Spain. Their own adornments included shell necklaces and gold facial jewelry typical of South America's northwest Pacific coast. The painting was sent to Philip III in Madrid as a memento of peace. It is now housed in Spain's Museo de América.

Source: Kris Lane, Quito 1599: City and Colony in Transition (Albuquerque: University of New Mexico Press, 2002.)

EXAMINING THE
EVIDENCE

1. What might these men's wide array of adornments symbolize?

2. What image does Sánchez Gallque seem to wish to convey to the king of Spain?

and did not justify permanent discrimination. It was on such grounds that Spanish priests such as Bartolomé de las Casas had argued so successfully against Amerindian slavery (see Chapter 17).

Condoning Slavery

By contrast, African slavery was hardly debated by Spanish priests and theologians. Some church leaders even sought to justify it. Settlers, particularly those in need of workers, were inclined to view both native Americans and Africans as inferior and uneducable; such racist views suited their interests. For its part, the Spanish crown sought protection of subject Amerindians not so much for reasons of faith, but because natives were a source of state revenue and paid their tributes in silver. Slaves, being outside the tributary economy, were left mostly to their own devices, although Spanish law contained some protections, certainly more than those developed by later colonists such as the Dutch, French, and English. It was assumed, often wrongly, that rational masters would be loath to harm their chattels.

By the seventeenth century, Spanish America was molded by a variety of religious, economic, and political forces. But it was only biology—some would say the law of human attraction—that could subvert the system. To start, a surplus of male European settlers, including farmers, artisans, and merchants, in the early years quickly led to *mestizaje* (mess-tee-ZAH-hey), Spanish for "mixture," and a significant mixed-heritage population. In some places it was indigenous women, ranging in status from servants such as Malintzin to Aztec and Inca princesses, who gave birth to a new generation of *mestizos*, as mixed-blood offspring were called. In other cases it was enslaved or free women of African descent who bore **mulatto** children to Spanish colonizers. There were many examples resembling Brazil's Chica da Silva throughout Spanish America, though none so rich or famous. Indigenous women also had children by African men, free and enslaved, and countless other "mixtures" occurred in the course of three centuries of colonial rule. The Mexican nation-state would later celebrate mestizaje as something dynamic and new, a "cosmic race."

To attribute all this to the power of physical attraction would be an oversimplification. Some relationships across color lines were forced and criminal, others merely fleeting, and still others were permanent and even church-sanctioned. Though some bureaucrats and bishops might have wished it so, neither state nor church outlawed interracial marriage in colonial Spanish America. Only marriage across huge status gaps, as, say, between a nobleman and a slave, was forbidden. By 1750 Spanish-American society was so "mixed" at virtually all social levels that the term *casta*, or "caste," formerly applied by the Portuguese in India, was adopted to categorize the bewildering range of socioracial types. Hundreds of paintings depict the various unions and offspring comprising Spanish America's so-called *sistema de castas*, or "system of castes" (see Seeing the Past: *Gentlemen of Esmeraldas*).

The experiences of women in colonial Spanish America varied more by social class than color. In time, immigrants born in Spain looked down upon even the whitest **creole**, or locally born Spaniard. Under the influence of age-old superstitions about sub-Saharan Africa, Europeans believed that life in the tropics was inherently debilitating, even for aristocratic Christians from northern Spain. Still, most creole women in Spanish America brushed off such suggestions of inferiority and made the most of their situations.

Peruvian Blacksmiths

Although all iron and steel were imported by privileged wholesalers to the Spanish-American colonies, it was local blacksmiths who fashioned these raw materials into horseshoes, hinges, nails, tools, and many other items. In this mid-eighteenth-century watercolor from the Pacific-coast city of Trujillo, Peru, a man and woman work together to forge tools. By this time, nearly all artisans were of indigenous, African, or mixed background, since hand labor was generally disdained by those claiming to be of pure European stock. This pair appears to be of mestizo, or mixed Spanish and indigenous, heritage. (Iberfoto/The Image Works.)

Racial Mixing

mestizaje Spanish for "mixture," referring to racial blending of any type.

mestizo Spanish for "mixed," or offspring of Europeans and native Americans.

mulatto Offspring of Europeans and Africans.

creole A European born in the Americas and his or her descendants.

Late marriage by men left many Spanish-American women widowed at a relatively young age. This gave some women a boost in terms of economic security and independence. Despite a generally stifling patriarchal culture, Spanish inheritance law, similar to Islamic law from which it borrowed, was relatively generous to women. The wives of merchants, in particular, frequently found themselves in charge of substantial enterprises and estates, with much freedom to administer them. More significantly, widows wielded extraordinary influence over their children's marriage choices. When children married well, estates could be combined and expanded over time, cementing a family's fortunes in the face of uncertainties and disruption. Such was the story of the family of Simón Bolívar, whose story opens the next chapter. Among his ancestors, it was women who made many of the most important choices.

Although elite women were concerned with maintaining wealth and improving the status of their offspring, poor women had other worries. Virtually all poor women were engaged in market-oriented activity at some level, even if they lived in the countryside. Weaving, spinning, and pottery-making were often female tasks. Urban women of poor to middling status were usually either servants or vendors, with some working alongside artisan husbands as cobblers, tanners, tailors, cigar-rollers, and even blacksmiths. Along with their burdensome duties as wet nurses, cooks, and cleaners, female domestic servants and slaves were also hired out, handing over the wages to their masters. Despite harsh conditions, access to markets meant access to cash, and even some socially marginalized urban women accumulated small fortunes or purchased freedom for their children.

In a different category altogether were Catholic nuns. Most were of elite parentage, but some were of humble background, including women born out of wedlock. Every Spanish-American city of note had at least one convent, and often half a dozen or more. Inside lived not only the nuns themselves, but their female servants and slaves. Lima, for example, in 1630 counted over 1366 nuns served by 899 female African slaves out of a total city population of about forty thousand. Convents also served as shelters for widows and women facing hardships, and as reformatories for those accused of prostitution and minor crime. Though confining, Spanish-American nunneries occasionally nurtured female intellectuals and mystics of great renown, such as St. Rose of Lima (1586–1617) and Juana Inés de la Cruz (1651–1595). Famous for her biting wit, de la Cruz even took on the misogynist ways of Mexican society in verse:

> Who would have the greatest blame
> In an errant love affair,
> She who falls to him who begs
> Or he who plays the beggar?
>
> Or who should be more guilty
> Though each is evil-doing,
> She who sins for pay,
> Or he who pays for sinning?[1]

Gold, Diamonds, and the Transformation of Brazil 1695–1800

FOCUS

How was Brazil transformed by the mining boom of the eighteenth century?

Beginning in around 1695, the coastal, sugar-based export economy of Portuguese Brazil began to change, sparked by the discovery of gold and diamonds in Brazil's south-central highlands. What followed was the greatest bonanza in world history prior to California's gold rush. The consequences were profound and lasting. First, over half a million Portuguese immigrants flowed into Brazil between 1700 and 1800. Second, the African slave trade was expanded,

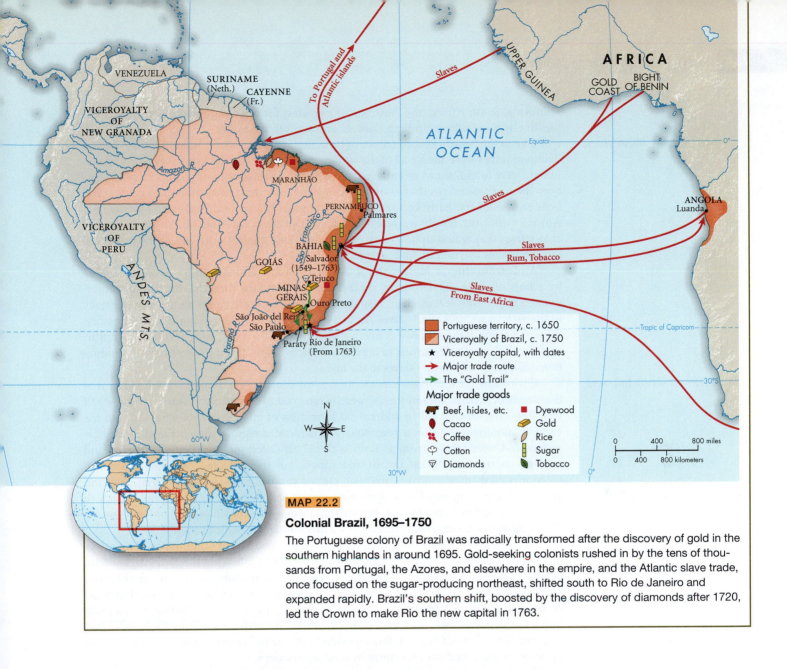

MAP 22.2

Colonial Brazil, 1695–1750

The Portuguese colony of Brazil was radically transformed after the discovery of gold in the southern highlands in around 1695. Gold-seeking colonists rushed in by the tens of thousands from Portugal, the Azores, and elsewhere in the empire, and the Atlantic slave trade, once focused on the sugar-producing northeast, shifted south to Rio de Janeiro and expanded rapidly. Brazil's southern shift, boosted by the discovery of diamonds after 1720, led the Crown to make Rio the new capital in 1763.

particularly in the hinterland of Angola. Third, the Portuguese crown elevated Brazil to the status of viceroyalty in 1720. Finally, Brazil's center of political and economic gravity shifted southward, away from the sugar zone of the northeast. Rio de Janeiro became Brazil's new capital in 1763 (see Map 22.2). On a global scale, Brazilian gold's importance briefly rivaled that of Spanish-American silver, flowing through Lisbon and into allied England, helping to finance the early stages of the Industrial Revolution.

Boom Times for Colonial Brazil

In the mid-1690s, while searching for indigenous slaves, a mulatto aide traveling with Brazilian backwoodsmen and slave hunters discovered gold in the rugged highlands northeast of São Paulo. By 1800 Brazil had exported between 2.5 and 4.5 million pounds of gold, and several million carats of raw diamonds. Up to this time diamonds had come almost entirely from India, and gold from West Africa and Spanish America. Soon after 1700, a district capital was set up in the town of Ouro Preto (OR-ooh PREH-too), or "Black Gold," and the region was dubbed Minas Gerais (MEAN-us jheh-HICE), or "General Mines." Prospectors and slaves flowed into Minas Gerais in droves, among them Chica da Silva's African mother and Portuguese father. Hordes of itinerant and wholesale merchants came close on their heels. As would happen in the later gold rush frontiers of

California, South Africa, and Australia, the greatest fortunes were made not by prospectors but by those selling clothing, shovels, and maps to the mines.

Mine Work

Due to the heavily eroded nature of its mountain ranges, Brazil's substantial gold and diamond mines were almost all of the surface, or "placer," variety. Wherever gold and diamonds were found, teams of enslaved workers, the vast majority of them young African-born men, excavated riverbanks while others panned or redirected streams to get at gravel beds and sandbars. Early commentators such as an Italian Jesuit using the pseudonym Antonil (since the Jesuits were officially forbidden from entering Minas Gerais, due to crown fears they would siphon away profits) described mining work as hellishly hard, and food shortages as common and severe.

Aside from chronic hunger and abuse, slaves in the mining country were endangered by a host of diseases, venomous snakes, and the constant threat of drowning in rain-swollen rivers. Murderous claim disputes and uprisings were common as well, especially in the early years, and many slaves ran away simply to avoid being caught in the crossfire. Slave mortality in the mines was much higher than in the sugar cane fields of the northeast. Some slave owners turned to the less risky activities of farming and livestock production, selling off only unruly slaves to the mines.

Environmental Impacts

Environmental historians estimate that in the course of the Brazilian gold rush tens of thousands of square miles of topsoil were overturned to a depth of at least one and a half feet. Resulting erosion led to widespread formation of gullies, deep ditches cut into the earth by running water after a downpour, and deforested regions were invaded by inedible grasses and weeds. Laws from as early as the 1720s called for preservation of forest and bush to control rainfall catchment and runoff, but these decrees were not observed. Uncontrolled digging and river diversion created vast badlands, areas of barren, arid land visible to the present day. Deforestation to support farming and the raising of livestock to feed the miners went even further, forever transforming the Brazilian highlands and greatly diminishing the Atlantic coast forest, only a tiny remnant of which remains.

Expansion of Portuguese Emigration and Atlantic Slave Trade

As happened in Spain soon after the discovery of Potosí and other major silver mines in Spanish America, a wave of emigration swept Portugal following the Brazilian bonanza of 1695. Never a very populous country, Portugal could ill afford the loss of tens of thousands of residents, especially when most of those leaving were young, able-bodied men. So many Portuguese men came to Minas Gerais in the first years after 1700 that a minor war broke out between them and the creole "Paulistas," or residents of São Paulo, who had discovered the mines. Crown authorities sided with the newcomers, and eventually sought to establish order in the backcountry by sending in troops.

The Atlantic slave trade expanded dramatically in response to the discovery of gold and diamonds in the Brazilian interior. Brazil's proximity to Africa and Portugal's long involvement in the slave trade led to a development quite distinct from the silver mines of Spanish America. In Mexico and Peru, most mine work was carried out by indigenous draft and later mestizo or mulatto wageworkers. By contrast, in the goldfields of Brazil, whose indigenous populations had been decimated by disease and slave raiding by 1700, African slavery quickly became the only form of labor employed. By 1800, there were nearly a million slaves in Minas Gerais. The few women to enter Minas Gerais in the early years of the rush were also primarily enslaved Africans, and they were in such high demand that most became the prized concubines of Portuguese men. Some were rented out as prostitutes in exchange for gold dust and diamonds. One such woman gave birth to Chica da Silva. Thus, the discovery of gold and diamonds in Brazil drew millions of migrants, some voluntary but many more forced, to the Americas. The cultural heritages these migrants brought with them have shaped Brazilian society to this day.

Royal Control and Its Limits

The Portuguese crown took an immediate interest in the Brazilian gold rush, establishing a taxation and monopoly trade system similar to that developed by the Spanish in Mexico and Peru. Gold taxes, the same "royal fifth" demanded by the Spanish crown, were collected at official sites in Ouro Preto and other towns, and all trade was directed along royal, stone-paved roads complete with official stations where mule-loads were inspected and taxed. The "gold trail" initially terminated in the tiny coastal town of Paraty, on Brazil's lush South Atlantic coast just beyond the Tropic of Capricorn, but soon it led to Rio de Janeiro, (see again Map 22.2). Rio became Brazil's largest city, and was elevated to the status of capital of the viceroyalty in 1763.

As in Spanish America, royal control over mining districts was more easily imagined than realized, and smuggling, particularly of diamonds, soon became a huge problem. Official control centered on the town of Tejuco (today's Diamantina) and was headed by royal contractors from Portugal, such as Chica da Silva's common-law husband, João Fernandes de Oliveira. Although the diamond mines were closely monitored and slaves were subjected to physical inspections, there were always ways of hiding and secretly trading stones. As an incentive to be honest and work hard, slaves were promised instant freedom if they found diamonds above a very large size, but few were so lucky.

Much more often, enslaved diamond miners set aside a few stones from time to time to trade to corrupt bureaucrats and merchants for cash. Slaves in the gold mines did the same. Wealth thus accumulated was then used to purchase the workers' freedom or the freedom of their children. One of the ironies of the Brazilian gold and diamond mines was that although the work itself was more dangerous than that of the cane fields and sugar mills of the northeast, the odds of obtaining freedom were considerably higher. Knowing that enslaved Africans outnumbered them by a huge margin here in the mountainous backlands, Portuguese masters and crown officials accepted a measure of secret trade and self-purchase.

Everyday Life in Golden-Age Brazil

With slavery such a central feature of Brazil's colonial economy, it is no surprise that this core institution deeply influenced society. Its influence would only increase over time. At first indigenous and then African cultural elements fused with Portuguese imports to create a new, hybrid culture. Only certain elites proved resistant to this hybridization, doing their best to mimic metropolitan styles and ideas. Some members of this elite class, such as the Portuguese diamond contractor João Fernandes de Oliveira, embraced "Afro-Brazil" in a more literal sense, by forming families of mixed ancestry. Other Brazilians practiced Catholicism while seeking the aid of numerous folk healers, clairvoyants, and other officially illegal religious figures, many of them of African ancestry.

As in Spanish America, a pressing matter for Portuguese authorities was the presence of Judaism and people of Jewish ancestry. In Brazil's early years some New Christians, or forced converts, had been allowed to immigrate. By the 1590s, some of these settlers were discovered to be secretly practicing Judaic rituals. Infrequent visits by the Inquisition, which never set up a permanent tribunal in Brazil, uncovered evidence of "heresy," or at least

Brazilian Diamond Diggers

Images of colonial mineworkers in the Americas are rare. Fortunately, the Italian military engineer Carlos Julião sought to depict the labors of Brazil's enslaved and mostly African-born diamond workers in Minas Gerais in the eighteenth century, precisely when Chica da Silva was the richest woman in the district and her common-law husband was possibly the wealthiest man in Portugal. The workers here are searching through diamond-bearing gravel under close surveillance (although the first overseer appears to be napping). When slaves found a diamond, they were to stand up and hold the stone above their heads before handing it to the overseer for safekeeping. Despite these and other controls, many slaves managed to hide diamonds in their mouths, ears, hair, and elsewhere, trading them later for food, clothing, alcohol, or cash. (The Art Archive/Biblioteca National do Rio de Janiero Brazil/Dagli Orti.)

unorthodox religious practices (such as kosher food preparation), but few were prosecuted. Brazil's Jewish community became more evident when several New Christians joined the Dutch during their occupation from 1630 to 1654 of Pernambuco in northeast Brazil. Under the Dutch, Brazil's Jews were allowed to build a synagogue and practice their religion openly. When the Portuguese regained control of the northeast in 1654, several New Christian planter families relocated to Dutch Suriname, where they set up slave-staffed plantations (see Counterpoint: The Maroons of Suriname). The Inquisition also persecuted secret Jews in Minas Gerais in the early eighteenth century, in part to confiscate their valuable estates and stocks of merchandise.

Afro-Brazilian Religion

The Portuguese Inquisition in Brazil also prosecuted Afro-Brazilian religious practitioners. None were burned, but many were publicly shamed, exiled, or sentenced to galley service. Usually denounced as "fetishists," devil-worshipers, and witches, these people maintained a wide variety of West and West Central African religious traditions, usually blended with some degree of Catholicism and native American shamanism. Often, Catholic saints were used to mask male and female West African deities, as later happened in Cuba and Saint-Domingue (Haiti). In other cases, religious brotherhoods combined West Central African spirit possession with Catholic Christianity. These brotherhoods, often devoted to black saints such as St. Benedict the Moor and St. Efigenia, were common throughout Brazil, but were especially powerful in Minas Gerais, where the missionary orders were banned for fiscal reasons. Orthodox black Catholics also enlivened their ceremonies, especially funerals and patron saints' days, with rhythmic music and dance.

Maroon Communities

Even before the discovery of gold, Brazil hosted the largest communities of **maroons** in the Western Hemisphere. By 1650 the maroon (from the Spanish term *cimarrón*, meaning "runaway") community of Palmares, really a confederation of a dozen fugitive villages, was home to some ten thousand or more ex-slaves and their descendants. Despite numerous military campaigns organized by planters in coordination with slave hunters, Palmares was only broken up in the 1690s and finally destroyed in 1694. With the development of Minas Gerais, dozens of new maroon villages popped up in the gold-rich backcountry. Several of their descendant communities have been formally recognized by the Brazilian government in recent years.

Artistic Legacies

As in Spanish America, it was in the cities most affected by the great mining boom—and later by sugar wealth—that Brazilian material culture grew most opulent. Churches modeled after European ones, such as those in Salvador in the northeast and Rio de Janeiro in the south, testify to the piety of both elites and poor religious brotherhoods. Even more stunning and original are the many churches and chapels of Minas Gerais, stretching from lonely Tejuco to São João del Rei (see again Map 22.2). A significant number of these extraordinary structures were designed, built, and decorated by slaves and their descendants. In Tejuco, several were commissioned by Chica da Silva, whose house still stands.

As the case of Chica da Silva illustrates, people of mixed heritage rose to prominent positions in Brazil, particularly in frontier districts. Arguably the colony's greatest artistic genius was the sculptor and architect Francisco Lisboa, like Chica the child of an enslaved African mother and free Portuguese father. Popularly known as Aleijadinho, or "Little Cripple" (due to leprosy), Lisboa was among the most original architects and sculptors of his era, carving fantastic soapstone façades with chisels strapped to the stumps of his hands.

Brazil's gold rush sputtered out around 1800, but by this time the northeastern sugar industry was undergoing a revival, along with tobacco, rice, cotton, and other cash crops. For the first time, Portuguese officials encouraged diversification and experimentation. The vast Amazon Basin was now being explored as a potential source of minerals, cacao, medicinal barks, and other export commodities. Coffee, which would later become Brazil's prime export, was also experimentally planted in various tropical climate zones, starting in the north. In export agriculture, Brazil's greatest competitors were in the Caribbean.

maroon In the seventeenth and eighteenth centuries, a runaway slave and his or her descendants.

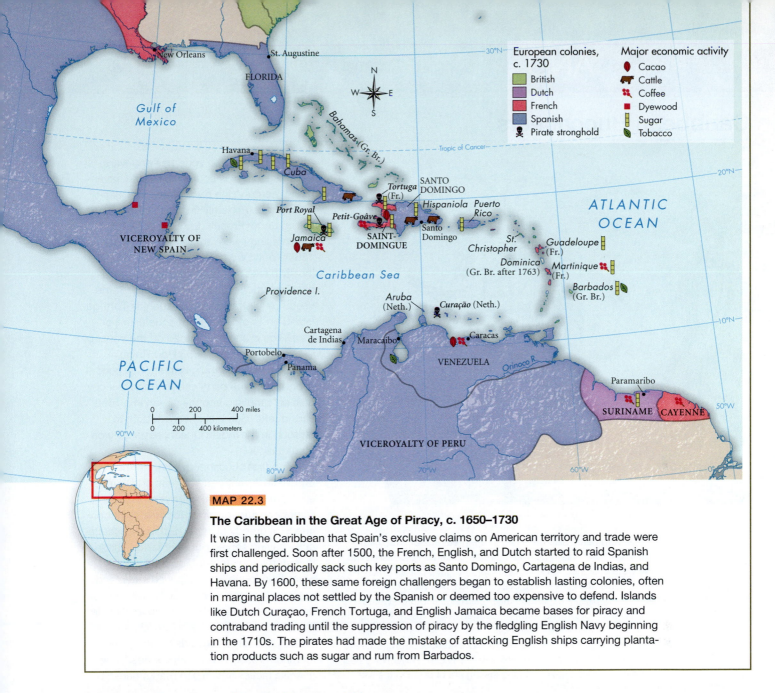

MAP 22.3

The Caribbean in the Great Age of Piracy, c. 1650–1730

It was in the Caribbean that Spain's exclusive claims on American territory and trade were first challenged. Soon after 1500, the French, English, and Dutch started to raid Spanish ships and periodically sack such key ports as Santo Domingo, Cartagena de Indias, and Havana. By 1600, these same foreign challengers began to establish lasting colonies, often in marginal places not settled by the Spanish or deemed too expensive to defend. Islands like Dutch Curaçao, French Tortuga, and English Jamaica became bases for piracy and contraband trading until the suppression of piracy by the fledgling English Navy beginning in the 1710s. The pirates had made the mistake of attacking English ships carrying plantation products such as sugar and rum from Barbados.

Bitter Sugar, Part Two: Slavery and Colonialism in the Caribbean 1625–1750

When the Dutch captured Pernambuco in 1630, they were most interested in sugar. How had the Portuguese managed to produce so much of it so cheaply? What the Dutch discovered was northeast Brazil's peculiar blend of loamy tropical soils, high-technology mills, and slave labor. By the time the Dutch abandoned Brazil in 1654, they had learned all they needed to know about the sugar business.

English and French visitors had also taken careful notes as they displaced the Spanish in various parts of the Caribbean, such as Jamaica and western Hispaniola (later known as Saint-Domingue, then Haiti). These techniques of sugar manufacture were closely copied, and from the mid-seventeenth century onward the story of the Caribbean was but the story of sugar and slavery, continued. After Brazil, this diverse island region was the largest destination for enslaved Africans brought across the Atlantic—over one-third of the total (see Map 22.3).

FOCUS

How did sugar production and slavery mold Caribbean societies?

Caribbean Buccaneers

"Black Bart"

The great age of maritime commerce also gave rise to the great age of piracy, an activity that peaked between 1660 and 1730. Most pirates preyed on Spanish ships and towns, since these were imagined to be rich in silver and gold, but as Spain's competitors gained footholds in the Caribbean, coastal Africa, and parts of the American mainland after 1600, pirates expanded their reach and captured whatever they could, including slave ships belonging to their outraged countrymen. Among the most successful pirates was Bartholomew "Black Bart" Roberts, shown here near the African port of Whydah, where he captured and ransomed a number of English slave ships. Roberts was killed in 1722 in an engagement with the English Royal Navy near present-day Gabon. There followed a new and long-lasting era of policing the sea. (National Maritime Museum, London/The Image Works.)

Atlantic colonization schemes and wars gave rise to a new social type in the seventeenth century: the **buccaneer**, or Caribbean pirate. Privately financed sea raiders sailing under French, English, or Dutch commissions were active from the early 1500s, but it was only in the mid-1600s that locally based sea bandits acting on their own became an endemic problem. Some used French trading posts such as Tortuga Island north of Saint-Domingue (Haiti) or the Dutch island of Curaçao off the coast of Venezuela, but after 1655 Port Royal, Jamaica, became the greatest of all buccaneer bases. The party ended when this city built on sand slid into the ocean in a 1692 earthquake. Some survivors sought to regroup in the Indian Ocean, especially on Madagascar.

The first buccaneers were northern European indentured servants and war veterans, many of whom were sent to the Caribbean sugar islands to meet the labor needs of greedy planters. Either by escape or by having served out their terms, these indentures took to living off the land in Saint-Domingue, shooting wild cattle and roasting their meat on crude barbecues, or *boucans*. Known by 1650 as *boucaniers* in French, and buccaneers in English, the hunters began to organize raids on straggling merchant vessels in dugout canoes. Their guerrilla tactics and expert marksmanship

Pirates and Planters

Development in the Caribbean was slow and not very methodical. Throughout the sixteenth century, French, English, and Dutch traders and raiders challenged Spanish monopolies, particularly on the mainland. Pirates and privateers preyed on slow-moving ships and lightly defended port towns. One of the most famous privateers was Sir Francis Drake, who in the late 1570s plundered one Spanish port after another. He also dabbled in the contraband slave trade, but the grateful English crown looked the other way to award him a knighthood. Only in around 1600 did these interlopers begin to establish permanent colonies. The Dutch focused on Guyana (later Suriname) and several small islands, such as Curaçao and St. Christopher. The English followed on Providence Island off the coast of modern Nicaragua. The French focused on western Hispaniola and Tortuga, a small island just offshore to the north. All these efforts combined experimental plantations, usually to grow tobacco or sugar, with contraband trade and piracy (see Lives and Livelihoods: Caribbean Buccaneers).

buccaneer A Caribbean-based pirate of the seventeenth century.

made them difficult to counter. Some, such as the Welshman Henry Morgan, made deals to share booty with colonial governors in exchange for legal protection, and later joined the colonial service. Others, such as François L'Ollonais, were unattached terrors of the Spanish Main. L'Ollonais was said to have carved the heart from a living victim and taken a bite. Piracy was about booty, not terror, however, and Spanish ships and towns, since they often contained silver and other portable treasures, were the main objects of buccaneer desire.

Once a raid was carried off, the pirates rendezvoused in the bars and brothels of Port Royal, whose markets thrived from the influx of stolen goods and money. When the buccaneers began to attack English, French, and Dutch ships with the same ferocity formerly reserved for Spanish ones in the late 1660s, the hunters became the hunted. Antipiracy laws from as early as the 1670s led to arrests and hangings, and by 1680 many buccaneers had fled to the Pacific and Indian oceans. A group of pirates who set out from the Virginia coast in the early 1680s returned to the Chesapeake with treasure stolen along the coast of Peru, only to land in jail and have their booty confiscated by royal officials. A portion of their loot was used to found the College of William and Mary in 1693.

At about the same time, a new pirate base was created on the island of Madagascar, which no Europeans had successfully colonized. From here buccaneers sailed north to stalk Muslim vessels traveling from India to the Arabian peninsula. The capture of several rich prizes by Henry Avery and other famous pirates in the 1690s led the English to send pirate hunters, among them the former buccaneer William Kidd. Kidd reverted to piratical activity off the coast of India; he was eventually arrested and jailed in New England before being sent to London for execution in 1701. After a break during the War of the Spanish Succession (1701–1714), which absorbed many buccaneers as privateers and even navy men, the war on Caribbean piracy returned in force, prosecuted mostly by the English Admiralty.

In the midst of England's war on piracy emerged some of the greatest figures of the era, among them Bartholomew Roberts. "Black Bart," as he was sometimes known, was one of the first pirates to prey on Portuguese ships carrying gold and diamonds to Europe from Brazil. When killed by English pirate hunters off the coast of Gabon in 1722, he was wearing a diamond-studded gold cross taken near Rio. By about 1725 the last wave of Anglo-American pirates, including the only known female pirate duo of Ann Bonny and Mary Read, was squelched.

QUESTIONS TO CONSIDER

1. What factors made buccaneer society possible in the seventeenth-century Caribbean?

2. What trends led to the sudden demise of the buccaneers' livelihood?

For Further Information:
Earle, Peter. *The Pirate Wars*. Boston: St. Martin's Griffin, 2006.

Spanish retaliation was fierce at first, but declined along with the empire's fortunes after 1648. The deepening seventeenth-century crisis rendered defense expenditures prohibitive. A massive English attack on Santo Domingo was successfully repulsed in 1655, but Jamaica was seized. Lacking minerals or a substantial native population, the Spanish had barely settled the island. Within a decade Port Royal, opposite Kingston Harbor on Jamaica's south coast, was a major base for contraband traders and buccaneers, among them Henry Morgan. Morgan and his followers sacked Panama City in 1671. The French followed a similar path on Martinique, Guadeloupe, and Saint-Domingue. Pirates of various nationalities meanwhile plagued the Spanish just as planters built a slave-staffed sugar economy farther inland. Some pirates, such as Henry Morgan, invested their plunder in their own Jamaican plantations, eventually gaining noble titles and general respectability.

Seizing Spanish Bases

The English colony of Barbados was a surprising success. A small and virtually uninhabited island at the easternmost edge of the Caribbean, Barbados had been of no interest

Developing Colonies

to the Spanish and Portuguese. The first English settlers came to plant tobacco in around 1625, and for a time the island's fortunes rested on production and export of this addictive drug. In time, capital accumulated from tobacco, along with advice and capital lent by Dutch refugees from Brazil, led the colony's planters to shift to sugar. Indentured servitude rapidly gave way to African slavery, and with slavery came rebellions. Even so, by the 1680s Barbados was a major world exporter of high-quality sugar, a position it held through the eighteenth century. Barbados showed that the Brazilian plantation model could transform even the smallest tropical island into a veritable gold mine.

With the expansion of slavery and sugar-growing on other Caribbean islands and parts of the mainland (especially Dutch Suriname), non-Iberian colonists began to surpass their predecessors in overall exports. In the course of the eighteenth century, the English, Dutch, and French embraced slavery on a scale and with an intensity not seen in Spanish America or Brazil. Slave codes grew increasingly harsh, and punishments cruel. There was virtually no interest expressed in protecting slaves' families or dignity, much less their souls. By 1750 the planters of Jamaica routinely tortured, raped, and otherwise terrorized enslaved Africans. They themselves admitted it, and wrote that such harsh measures were necessary to quell rebellion while maximizing production. Visitors to eighteenth-century Suriname described public executions as run-of-the-mill events, and those who visited Saint-Domingue wrote of sugar production on a vast, industrial scale. Slaves were consumed like so much timber.

The Rise of Caribbean Slave Societies

Whereas Brazilian planters used cheaper, enslaved native American workers as a bridge to mass African slavery, French, Dutch, and English planters in the Caribbean used indentured European servants. Throughout the seventeenth century thousands of poor servants and convicts staffed tobacco and sugar plantations alongside growing numbers of Africans and their descendants. If they survived the harsh conditions of the tropics, these servants could expect freedom within three to seven years. Many did not live to see that day, but the profits accumulated during these few years enabled plantation owners to purchase a permanently enslaved workforce. Scholars remain divided as to whether indentured Europeans were treated as badly as enslaved Africans.

Island Culture By the early eighteenth century, Caribbean plantation society had begun to achieve the opulent material culture and African-influenced diversity found in Brazil's mining districts. Great houses in the European style dotted many islands, and slave communities grew into neo-African villages. Churches in these often Protestant lands were far more modest than in Catholic Brazil, however, and of several denominations. African religious traditions flourished, often with little influence from the colonizers' faiths. In Jamaica and Saint-Domingue, the constant influx of African-born slaves, coupled with general disdain for slaves' spiritual lives among planters, priests, and missionaries, led to the formation of new, hybrid religious traditions, called Obeah and Vodoun (or Voodoo), respectively.

A great difference that did exist between Brazil and the Caribbean sugar colonies lay in the realms of racial mixture and shared religious traditions. European men routinely kept African and mulatto mistresses, as in Minas Gerais and other parts of Brazil, but they were usually loath to recognize their children, much less educate them in Europe and incorporate them into high society. Treated as a dirty secret and even a petty crime, racial mixture soon gave rise to sharply graded color categories quite distinct from Spanish America's fluid *sistema de castas*. As for religion, Europeans showed nothing but contempt for "Obeah men" and "Voodoo priestesses," treating them as frauds and quacks. Partly as a result, some of these new religious leaders, male and female, played key roles in slave uprisings.

Maroons and Slaves As in Brazil, *marronage* or slave flight was common throughout the Caribbean. Refuges for long-term runaways proved scarce on smaller, low-lying islands such as Barbados and Curaçao, but larger and more rugged islands such as Jamaica, Dominica, and Saint Domingue abounded with possibilities for safe haven. Here in rugged highlands such as Jamaica's Blue

Mountains, maroons were so successful they were able to negotiate treaties with planters and colonial officials by the early eighteenth century. Jamaican maroon leaders such as Nanny and Cudjoe were folk heroes to the enslaved and a constant thorn in the side of the British.

Sugar production as practiced by northern Europeans in the eighteenth century provided significant capital gains and, like Brazilian gold, probably helped to spark England's industrialization. Yet slavery of such horrific cruelty and scale also sowed the seeds of its own destruction. Slave traders responded to ratcheting Caribbean demand by packing their ships ever more tightly, turning slaving itself into an increasingly predatory exercise in more and more regions of West and West Central Africa. Some slaves were brought from as far away as the Indian Ocean island of Madagascar. By the late eighteenth century, white abolitionists at last began to join the long-ignored chorus of African and African-American voices against this enormous crime against humanity in the name of profit. For the first time, English tea drinkers thought twice before sweetening their brew.

Growth and Change in British and French North America 1607–1750

European colonization of the eastern seaboard of North America followed a different path than that of Spanish America or Brazil. There were, however, similarities: plantations developed, missionaries preached, people bred or married across color lines, and in places slave labor came to dominate. But overall, nontropical, Atlantic North America was characterized by a slow advance of European settler families practicing subsistence agriculture, livestock-raising, fishing, and commerce according to Old World norms. Eastern North America, both French and English, was to become, in the words of historian Alfred Crosby, a "neo-Europe" (see Map 22.4). Indigenous peoples, unlike in Spanish and Portuguese America where they had been absorbed and forcibly converted, were mostly driven from their lands or annihilated.

FOCUS

How did European relations with native peoples differ in the British and French colonies of North America?

Experiments in Commercial Colonialism

French, Dutch, and English colonization of eastern North America took root in the first decades of the seventeenth century. English Jamestown was founded on Virginia's Powhatan River (renamed "James" after the king) in 1607 and French Quebec, on Canada's St. Lawrence, in 1608. Henry Hudson, for a time an employee of the Dutch East India Company, began reconnoitering the river that took his name in 1609. Once it was clear that the Hudson River did not lead to the Pacific Ocean, a Dutch fur-trading post was established in 1618. As early as 1605 French Huguenots (or Protestant refugees) had also begun farming the coast of Maine and Nova Scotia, which they called Acadia.

Mariners such as Hudson continued searching in vain for a **northwest passage** to China. Others probed the soils of Newfoundland for signs of gold or silver. The survival of the earliest colonies in the tiny, fortified enclaves of "New France," "New Netherland," and "Virginia" depended on alliances with indigenous inhabitants. At the same time, all three European competitors were preoccupied with each other's designs on the region, a source of lasting conflict. Moreover, everyone worried about the Spanish, who had violently driven the French from Florida and the Dutch from Venezuela.

New France, first governed by Samuel de Champlain, marked France's renewed effort to colonize the Americas. Jacques Cartier and other mariners had explored the St. Lawrence Basin shortly after Columbus's time, and French colonists had planted forts in Florida and Brazil before being expelled by the Spanish and Portuguese in the 1560s. Only after France itself returned to calm, after the religious wars of 1562 to 1598 (discussed in Chapter 20), was a permanent colony deemed feasible. In North America, serious conflicts with the English

New France

northwest passage Searched-for sea route to Asia via North America.

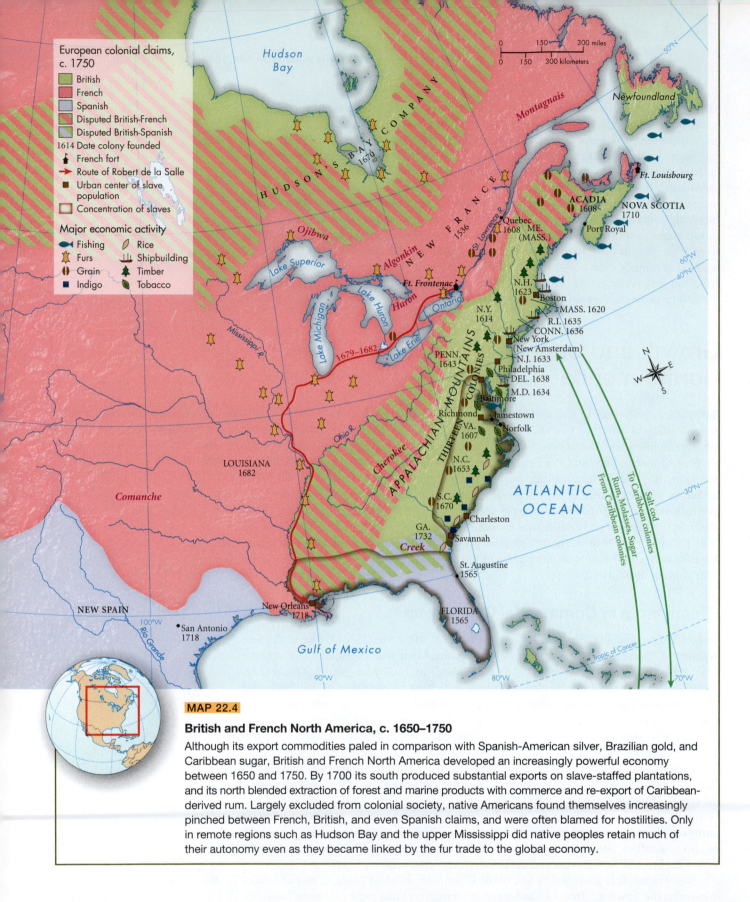

European colonial claims, c. 1750

- British
- French
- Spanish
- Disputed British-French
- Disputed British-Spanish
- 1614 Date colony founded
- French fort
- → Route of Robert de la Salle
- Urban center of slave population
- Concentration of slaves

Major economic activity

- Fishing
- Furs
- Grain
- Indigo
- Rice
- Shipbuilding
- Timber
- Tobacco

MAP 22.4

British and French North America, c. 1650–1750

Although its export commodities paled in comparison with Spanish-American silver, Brazilian gold, and Caribbean sugar, British and French North America developed an increasingly powerful economy between 1650 and 1750. By 1700 its south produced substantial exports on slave-staffed plantations, and its north blended extraction of forest and marine products with commerce and re-export of Caribbean-derived rum. Largely excluded from colonial society, native Americans found themselves increasingly pinched between French, British, and even Spanish claims, and were often blamed for hostilities. Only in remote regions such as Hudson Bay and the upper Mississippi did native peoples retain much of their autonomy even as they became linked by the fur trade to the global economy.

broke out by the 1610s and 1620s; they were resolved by treaty in 1632. Quebec would subsequently survive for over a century as a fortified trading post funded by absentee investors. Military alliances with indigenous groups such as the Montagnais and Huron proved critical throughout New France's history.

Unlike the Spanish and Portuguese, French, English, and Dutch colonizers created **joint-stock companies** that attracted numerous investors in the mother country and took on a financial and even political life of their own. Amsterdam's stock market was by far Europe's most vibrant, and the Dutch VOC was considered the shining model of such enterprises, because it successfully combined commercial, military, and diplomatic functions to turn a private profit from colonialism.

New France managed to survive through many a long winter only by tapping into the long chain of indigenous and *métis*, or mixed-heritage, fur traders and trappers extending deep into the Great Lakes and beyond. The beaver pelts they brought from the interior were processed for the European hat market. Only these men in canoes, the famed *coureurs de bois* ("runners of the woods," as the independent fur traders were known), and a few Jesuits went much beyond the fort. Settlers concentrated mostly in the St. Lawrence Valley, eking out a living in subsistence agriculture supplemented by fishing and hunting.

The early government of Jamestown, Virginia, funded like New France by a group of absentee investors, blended business and military models. This proved to be a bad idea. Despite investment and high hopes, the Virginia Company experiment failed disastrously, and it was nearly abandoned after only a few years. Men such as John Smith, though in some ways capable leaders, could not keep restless fellow settlers from antagonizing local indigenous groups, many of which belonged to a confederacy headed by the chieftain Powhatan. The settler-soldiers refused to farm, and theft of indigenous food stores led to reprisals, spawning decades-long cycles of vengeance. Tsenacommocah (sen-uh-COMB-uh-cuh), as Powhatan's subjects called the Chesapeake Bay region, was not easily conquered, and indigenous attacks in the 1620s nearly wiped out the first English settlers' plantations.

Chesapeake Bay, c. 1650–1700

Eventually, English settlers got the upper hand and began to make money from tobacco exports. Although enslaved Africans arrived as early as 1619, initially indentured English servants were the primary source of labor. Soil exhaustion was rapid, causing the tobacco frontier to sweep inland toward the Appalachian Mountains and southward into North Carolina. Soaring demand for land to cultivate tobacco prompted Indian attacks and culminated in a settler rebellion led by Nathaniel Bacon in 1676. Bacon and some five hundred followers ran Virginia's governor out of Jamestown for allegedly dealing too kindly with the Powhatan and other native groups. Although colonial authorities rejected Bacon's calls to uproot the Indians, English policy turned sharply toward "removal." As Indians were forced westward, indentured servitude and small plots gave way to African slavery and large plantations.

The stony region dubbed New England, initially settled by religious dissenters called "Puritans," followed a distinct trajectory. Soon after arriving more or less by accident in Plymouth, Massachusetts, in 1620 the first "pilgrims," as they called themselves, faced the problem of establishing a working relationship with indigenous peoples in a land of limited agricultural and commercial potential. The colony, farther north than initially planned, was sponsored by the Virginia Company, but in 1629 a new corporation, the Massachusetts Bay Company, was chartered by prominent Puritans in England. Elder churchmen latched onto the ample rights of self-governance entailed by this charter, and Boston emerged as capital of the deeply religious Massachusetts Bay colony. As in cold New France, survival was a challenge. Servants suffered most in the first hard years; indigenous peoples were largely ignored.

Religious and labor discipline led to some success for early New Englanders, but both also bred division. Dissenters fled southward to found Rhode Island and Connecticut; others were punished internally. Expansion of subsistence farms throughout the region yielded surplus wheat and other grains in time, and cod fishing in the Newfoundland Banks

Jamestown

New England

joint-stock company A colonial commercial venture with a royal charter and private shareholders.

métis French for "mixed," or offspring of Europeans and native Americans.

Champlain Fires on the Iroquois

Violent European encounters with native Americans continued long after the arrival of Christopher Columbus in the Caribbean in 1492. Soon after Columbus, French navigators explored Canada's St. Lawrence estuary, partly in hopes of finding a northwest passage to the Pacific Ocean and to Asia. Yet it was only in the early seventeenth century that the French established a lasting colony based in Quebec City. This image shows French commander Samuel Champlain firing on Iroquois warriors in 1613 near what is today Fort Ticonderoga, New York. The engraving puts European technology in stark relief as Champlain (aided by two armed men in the trees above) confronts a mass of naked warriors flowing out of their stockade. Champlain's armor renders him immune to enemy arrows, which mostly sail overhead. According to an accompanying report of the engagement, a single shot by Champlain felled two of the most feared Iroquois warriors. (Bettmann/Corbis.)

grew ever more important, as did whaling. Colonial authorities signed treaties with compliant indigenous neighbors; those who resisted faced enslavement or death. The Puritans were not pacifists, and like Samuel de Champlain and John Smith, they knew how to use firearms to terrorizing effect. They also had no qualms about enslaving war captives. As in Virginia, missionary efforts were few, perhaps in part because of emerging English notions of individual religious freedom, but also because of racism. The general pattern of European-indigenous relations in New England, as it would eventually be throughout British North America, was total displacement.

New Commercial Ventures   Newfoundland and Nova Scotia were chartered for commercial reasons in the 1620s, the latter disputed with the French for over a century. Proprietary colonies soon followed to the south of New England. Court favorites were given vast tracts of American lands in exchange for promises to defend and develop them as havens for settlers and for the export of raw materials to benefit the mother country. These proprietary colonies later yielded states such as Pennsylvania, Delaware, and Maryland. In 1664, the English captured Dutch

Pilgrims Set Sail on the *Mayflower* In this iconic seventeenth-century woodcut, a trio of English separatists leaves the temporary refuge of Leiden, a major Dutch university town, to sail to North America on the *Mayflower*. The Pilgrims, as they came to be known, hoped to found a colony in Virginia territory, but after landing by accident on the coast of Massachusetts in 1620, they chose to stay. (Private Collection/Bridgeman Art Library.)

New Amsterdam, a fur-trading post established in 1625 and increasingly a site of contraband trade; they renamed it New York. By 1700, England dominated eastern North America from Newfoundland to the Carolinas. Religiously diverse, British North America lacked an overarching structure of governance. In this the English differed from the bureaucratic and centralizing Spanish.

Southeastern Plantations

By the early eighteenth century, Virginia, Maryland, the Carolinas, and England's other mid-Atlantic and southern colonies were home to huge, export-oriented plantations. Planters focused first on tobacco, then rice, indigo, and other cash crops. More like the Caribbean and parts of Iberian America than New France or New England, the mid-Atlantic and southeast colonies grew quickly into slave-based societies. The region's trade was dominated by port towns such as Norfolk, Baltimore, and Charleston, their vast hinterlands dotted with great plantation houses and substantial, almost townlike slave quarters. Pockets of indigenous resistance could still be found in the eighteenth century, but native groups wishing to remain independent were increasingly forced westward beyond the Appalachian Mountains.

Northeastern Commerce

The northeast seaboard colonies, including the thriving port of New York, followed a different, less export-oriented path, although mercantile connections to the Caribbean and other primary goods-producing regions were strong. Rum distilling and re-export became a major New England industry, alongside shipbuilding and fishing. All of these businesses connected northeastern British America to the Atlantic slave trade, and bulk items such as salt cod soon became central to the diet of enslaved Africans in Jamaica. Perhaps most significant compared with Spanish and Portuguese America was the great freedom to trade with foreigners that English colonists generally enjoyed. This was not legal, but as Chapter 23 will show, England failed to enforce its colonial trading policies until after 1750. When it finally did so, it provoked violent rebellion.

Everyday Life in the Northern Colonies

Given the long winters and relative isolation of the St. Lawrence River Basin, life for early French Canadians was both difficult and lonely. Food stores were a major concern, and settlers long relied on a blend of native generosity and annual supply ships from France. Thousands of colonists were sent to develop the land, along with soldiers to guard against English or Indian attacks. The result was the militarization of the backcountry, displacing and massacring native groups in a way reminiscent of England's uncompromising "removal" policy.

Jesuit Missionaries

Jesuit missionaries, meanwhile, set out to convert these embattled, indigenous inhabitants to Roman Catholicism. The priests, relatively few in number, concentrated on large semisedentary groups such as the Huron, Algonkin, and Ojibwa, among others. Sometimes the missionaries learned local languages, made friends with prominent chieftains or their sons, and found success. At other times, their failures ended in their deaths, memorialized by their brethren as religious martyrdom. French Jesuits did not give up on North American Indians, in any case, and eventually worked their way from the Great Lakes down the Mississippi Basin. Military explorers followed, including the nobleman Robert de la Salle, who in 1682 claimed the lower Mississippi, which he called Louisiana, for King Louis XIV (see again Map 22.4).

Frontier Society

Life in the American backcountry claimed by France was in many ways dominated by native peoples, a frontier arrangement historian Richard White has labeled "the middle ground." Here at the edge of imperial control indigenous Americans, métis fur traders, and European missionaries, soldiers, and homesteaders all found themselves interdependent, none claiming a monopoly. Not everyone found this arrangement to their liking, least of all crown representatives, but on the frontier the social divisions of race, religion, gender, and culture were blurred or overlooked (see Reading the Past: A Swedish Traveler's Description of Quebec). Put another way, "the middle ground" was the most egalitarian space in the early modern Americas. Like Chica da Silva's fluid world in backcountry Brazil, the possibilities could be astonishing, at least in the eyes of outsiders.

Limited Racial Relations

Unlike in Spanish or Portuguese America, sexual relations across color lines were relatively rare in British North America, except in frontier outposts. In part, this was a result of demography: European men and women migrated to the eastern seaboard in close to equal numbers over time, and indigenous peoples were relatively few and were rarely incorporated into settler society. When racial mixture occurred, it was most commonly the result of illicit relations between white men and enslaved women of African descent. Such relations, which according to surviving documents were more often forced than consensual or long-term, were most common in the plantation districts of the Chesapeake and Carolina Low Country. Still, some mixed-race children were born in northern cities such as New York and Boston, where considerable numbers of slaves and free people of color could be found in close proximity to whites. Throughout the British colonies, blatantly racist "antimiscegenation" laws dating to the seventeenth century also discouraged black-white unions, because these were thought to undermine the social hierarchy. Racial codes and covenants were most rigidly enforced in regions highly dependent on African slavery, namely the mid-Atlantic and southeast. Still, as Virginia planter and future U.S. president Thomas Jefferson's long-term, child-producing relationship with his slave, Sally Hemings, demonstrates, human urges and affinities could override even the strictest social taboos and legal codes.

Slave Culture and Resistance

Slavery existed in New France, but on a small scale. A few Africans could be found in growing towns such as Montreal, but most slaves were indigenous war captives used for household labor. In early New England, enslaved Africans and a few indigenous slaves served in similar roles, and also in artisan workshops and on board ships. Thousands of enslaved Africans lived and worked in the bustling shops and port facilities of New York City by the early eighteenth century, and many more lived and worked on farms in rural Pennsylvania. Slave rebellions were relatively rare in these regions, although the slaves of New York were highly outspoken and sometimes alarmed city authorities. Slave resistance mostly consisted of work stoppages, tool breaking, truancy, and other "passive" means. Faced with racist exclusion, small black religious communities, mostly of the Anglican, Methodist, and Baptist denominations, eventually formed.

Even more distinct slave cultures emerged in regions where Africans predominated, from Maryland to Georgia. Here plantation life took on some of the features of the English Caribbean, with large numbers of enslaved Africans and their descendants concentrated in prisonlike barracks within view of great plantation houses. As archaeologists

A Swedish Traveler's Description of Quebec

Pehr ("Peter") Kalm was a Swedish naturalist who visited Canada in around 1749. In the following passages, translated from the Swedish in the 1770s, Kalm describes the inhabitants of the Christian Huron village of Lorette, just outside the capital of French Canada, Quebec City.

August the 12. This afternoon I and my servant went out of town, to stay in the country for a couple of days that I might have more leisure to examine the plants that grow in the woods here, and the state of the country. In order to proceed the better, the governor-general had sent for an Indian from Lorette to show us the way, and teach us what use they make of the spontaneous plants hereabouts. This Indian was an Englishman by birth, taken by the Indians thirty years ago, when he was a boy, and adopted by them, according to their custom, instead of a relation of theirs killed by the enemy. Since that time he constantly stayed with them, became a Roman Catholic and married an Indian woman: he dresses like an Indian, speaks English and French, and many of the Indian languages. In the wars between the French and English, in this country [a reference to chronic conflicts preceding the Seven Years' War], the French Indians have made many prisoners of both sexes in the English plantations [i.e., farms], adopted them afterwards, and they married with people of the Indian nations. From hence the Indian blood in Canada is much mixed with European blood, and a great part of the Indians now living owe their origin to

Europe. It is likewise remarkable that a great part of the people they had taken during the war and incorporated with their nations, especially the young people, did not choose to return to their native country, though their parents and nearest relations came to them and endeavored to persuade them to it, and though it was in their power to do it. The licentious life led by the Indians pleased them better than that of their European relations; they dressed like the Indians and regulated all their affairs in their way. It is therefore difficult to distinguish them except by their color, which is somewhat whiter than that of the Indians. There are likewise examples of some Frenchmen going amongst the Indians and following their way of life. There is on the contrary scarce one instance of an Indian's adopting the European customs.

Source: Peter Kalm, *Travels into North America*, trans. John Reinold Forster (Barre, MA: Imprint Society, 1972) 3:184.

EXAMINING THE EVIDENCE

1. How does Kalm assess the "cultural divide" and racial mixture in French Canada?

2. What made Indian customs preferable to European ones in this region, according to Kalm?

and historians are increasingly discovering, enslaved Africans had a thriving religious and material world of their own, one that contrasted sharply to the tidy, well-heeled world of the English planter families who claimed lordship over them. African religious practices, while muted by comparison with those of the Caribbean or Brazil, were widely known and respected among the enslaved population. Secret shamanistic and medicinal practices were also common. Whites appear to have known virtually nothing about the slaves' hidden culture.

Violent rebellions and mass marronage along the Atlantic seaboard were rare in comparison with the Caribbean or even Brazil. There were simply far more whites who could be mustered to put down an uprising in Virginia or North Carolina than in Jamaica or Barbados, where slaves outnumbered white settlers by huge margins. Geography limited marronage as well. The mountains were distant and inhabited by Indians. During winter, maroons could be more easily tracked by hunters due to diminished forest cover, and they were hard-pressed to find food in the wild. Some slaves ran away to cities, and even to Spanish Florida, but it was nearly impossible to form lasting maroon communities. Unlike Spanish and Portuguese America, slaves' legal access to freedom through self-purchase or emancipation was severely limited, as was access to the religion of the planters. Only in places such as South Carolina were concentrations of recently arrived Africans great enough to create the kinds of "neo-Africas" found in much of Brazil and the Caribbean. Thus, while societies throughout the Americas included a mixture of Europeans, Africans, and indigenous Americans, the relationships among these groups and the hybrid cultures that emerged varied from region to region, depending on local conditions and the goals and beliefs of the colonizers in question.

COUNTERPOINT
The Maroons of Suriname

FOCUS

How did the runaway slaves of Dutch Suriname create a lasting independent state of their own?

In defiance of slavery on plantations and in mines, fugitive Africans and their descendants established free, or "maroon," communities throughout the Americas. Slaves ran away as soon as they could from brutal conditions in Hispaniola, Puerto Rico, Cuba, and Panama. Others fled into the hills east and southwest of Mexico City. Still others found refuge in backcountry Venezuela, Colombia, Ecuador, Peru, and Bolivia. Slaves in Portuguese Brazil did likewise, forming in the hills of Alagoas, a small province of northeastern Brazil, the largest maroon confederacy in history: the Quilombo (key-LOAM-boh) of Palmares. Similar maroon settlements emerged in English Jamaica, as well as French Saint-Domingue, Guadeloupe, and Martinique. But it was in the small colony of Dutch Suriname on South America's northern coast that African and African-American fugitives established the Americas' most resilient and distinctive maroon culture.

From Persecution to Freedom

Dutch and Portuguese Jewish planters ejected from Brazil after 1654 brought enslaved Africans to Suriname to grow and process sugar cane. By the 1660s, dozens of plantations dotted the banks of the Saramaka, Suriname, and Marowijne rivers. Faced not only with intensive, uncompensated labor in the hot sun but also with physical and psychological torture, many of the enslaved escaped upriver into dense forests once inhabited by Carib and Arawakan-speaking indigenous peoples. Sheltered by cataracts, rapids, and winding tributaries, dozens and then hundreds of runaways settled beyond the reach of planters and colonial authorities. If captured, the maroons, male and female, faced dismemberment and public execution, tactics of terror meant to dissuade those on the plantations from fleeing.

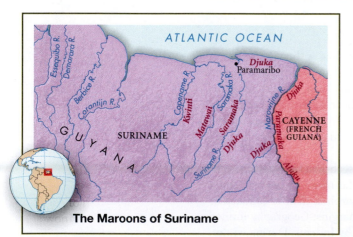

The Maroons of Suriname

By 1700 Suriname's maroons had formed several independent chiefdoms, each augmenting its numbers through periodic raids on the plantations downriver. Women were especially prized. Within a few decades the maroons numbered in the thousands. Taking advantage of the rugged geography of the Suriname interior and adapting to its challenging environment, the maroons carved out a "neo-Africa" in the backlands. After numerous failed expeditions to capture and re-enslave the maroons, plantation owners sought peace in the 1740s, only to return with even larger and better-armed expeditions after 1750. The maroons remained resolute and eventually won freedom from the Dutch government, which sent them arms and other trade goods to keep peace. As early as the late eighteenth century a few maroon groups allowed small numbers of Christian missionaries to visit them, but the missionaries won few converts and most of them soon died of malaria and other tropical diseases.

Suriname's Distinctive Maroon Culture

Six major maroon groups, the Saramaka, Djuka, Aluku, Paramaka, Matawai, and Kwinti, continue to live in Suriname and neighboring French Guiana, and many retain, thanks to vibrant oral traditions, substantial memories of the period of slavery and the punishing wars the planters prosecuted against them. Some maroon descendants began writing histories of these events as early as the 1880s. Others have moved in the decades following Suriname's independence from the Dutch in 1975 to the coastal capital of Paramaribo or even to Dutch cities such as Amsterdam and Leiden. Maroon culture nevertheless remains very much alive.

Maroon culture in Suriname, built around matrilineal villages, was so striking to early outside visitors that they assumed its rituals and complex artistic traditions to be direct transfers from some part of western Africa. The distinctive architecture, decorative patterns, textile traditions, and musical styles all hark back to Africa. Anthropologists looked for specific links in African art, language, and religion, but found no single traceable root—only broad associations and isolated words. Anthropologists Richard and Sally Price have argued that Suriname's distinctive maroon culture was something new, a product of resistance to colonialism. By combining archival and anthropological research they have shown how strands of western African thought and practice converged with the contingencies of fugitive life at the margins of a European-dominated plantation society. To survive, runaway Africans and their descendants learned to select the best local forest products such as wood for canoes and thatch for roofs, then planted known, imported crops such as bananas and plantains, as well as local ones like maize. Through raids and treaties they obtained cooking pots, textiles, and other manufactured goods, all of which they combined, then decorated, to create a new and distinctive material culture.

Descendants of the original maroon elders have preserved and passed along memories of the long-past horrors and escape from slavery, as in the following passage, recited by the Saramakan leader Lántifáya and recorded by Richard Price in 1978:

Maroon of Suriname

As slavery expanded throughout the Caribbean and many parts of the mainland Americas after 1650, so too did slave flight and the formation of "maroon," or runaway, communities. Although scattered throughout the tropics as well as the swamplands of the U.S. southeast, the largest and best-armed maroon communities in the Americas emerged in the backlands of Dutch Suriname, on the north coast of South America. Here escaped slaves armed themselves by raiding coastal plantations. Their raids sparked reprisals, which included full-blown wars by the later eighteenth century. A soldier in these wars, John Gabriel Stedman, wrote a sympathetic account of the struggles of slaves and maroons in Suriname that became evidence used by the emerging abolitionist cause in England. Engraver Francesco Bartolozzi followed Stedman's descriptions to depict this maroon warrior on the march, stolen gun in hand and death—or slain enemies—literally at his feet. (British Library/The Image Works.)

In slavery, there was hardly anything to eat. It was at the place called Providence Plantation. They whipped you till your ass was burning. Then they would give you a bit of plain rice in a calabash [bowl made from the fruit of a tropical American tree]. (That's what we've heard.) And the gods told them that this is no way for human beings to live. They would help them. Let each person go where he could. So they ran.[2]

Conclusion

The colonial Americas underwent the deepest alterations of the world's regions in early modern times, environmentally and socially. Mining of precious metals for export to Europe and Asia drove the Spanish and Portuguese deep into the interior, transforming vast landscapes and giving rise to a wide range of new social and economic relations. Autonomous indigenous groups, followed later by enslaved Africans, were driven farther inland as they searched for refuge. Punishing forms of labor persisted at the old Aztec and Inca core through the eighteenth century, but indigenous populations began to recover from postconquest disease shocks. In the lawless mining frontier of Brazil, as in backcountry New France, racial mixing proved a pragmatic response to demographic realities, challenging notions of propriety and permissiveness.

More rigidly racist social orders developed in the French, Dutch, and English Caribbean and along the eastern seaboard of North America. That a successful and publicly recognized woman of color such as Chica da Silva could have emerged in such a place as Jamaica or Virginia is almost impossible to imagine. The intense religiosity of the seventeenth and early eighteenth centuries, manifested in both Spanish-American Catholicism and English Puritanism, faded only slowly and left a long-lasting legacy. American dependence on slavery and other forms of forced labor would also die a lingering death. In these and other key ways, the Americas and their European motherlands grew steadily and irreconcilably apart.

NOTES

1. Sor Juana Inés de la Cruz, quoted in Irving Leonard, *Baroque Times in Old Mexico: Seventeenth-century Persons, Places, and Practices* (Ann Arbor: University of Michigan Press, 1959), 189.
2. Saramakan elder Lántifáya, quoted in Richard Price, *First-Time: The Historical Vision of an Afro-American People* (Baltimore, MD: Johns Hopkins University Press, 1983), 71.

RESOURCES FOR RESEARCH

General Works

General surveys of the early modern Americas remain to be written, but the following are examples of border-crossing works. Benjamin and Egerton et al. are pioneering textbooks in Atlantic history, incorporating Africa and western Europe as well as the Americas.

Alchon, Suzanne Austin. *A Pest in the Land: New World Epidemics in a Global Perspective.* 2003.

Benjamin, Thomas. *The Atlantic World: Europeans, Africans, Indians, and Their Shared History, 1400–1900.* 2009.

Egerton, Douglas R., Alison Games, Jane Landers, Kris Lane, and Donald Wright. *The Atlantic World.* 2007.

Library of Congress: Hispanic Reading Room. This Web site features a wealth of materials on early Spanish and Portuguese America: http://www.loc.gov/rr/hispanic/onlinecol.html.

Socolow, Susan. *The Women of Colonial Latin America.* 2000.

University of Pennsylvania Library: Cultural Readings: Colonization and Print in the Americas. A useful mix of printed and pictorial sources on the early Americas: http://www.library.upenn.edu/exhibits/rbm/kislak/index/cultural.html.

The World That Silver Made: Spanish America, 1580–1750

Thanks to many researchers, Spanish America is at last beginning to come into focus as a global region. The following is a sampling of key studies and solid overviews. Bakewell is especially good on the mining economy, as are Guy and Sheridan on frontiers.

Andrien, Kenneth. *Andean Worlds: Indigenous History, Culture, and Consciousness Under Spanish Rule, 1532–1825.* 2001.

Bakewell, Peter. *A History of Latin America to 1825,* 3d ed. 2010.

Guy, Donna, and Thomas Sheridan, eds. *Contested Ground: Comparative Frontiers on the Northern and Southern Edges of the Spanish Empire.* 1998.

Hoberman, Louisa Schell, and Susan Socolow, eds. *Cities and Society in Colonial Latin America.* 1986.

Hoberman, Louisa Schell, and Susan Socolow, eds. *The Countryside in Colonial Latin America.* 1996.

Gold, Diamonds, and the Transformation of Brazil, 1695–1800

The story of Golden-Age Brazil is still being researched, but several classic and new works in English, including Charles Boxer's fine overview and Júnia Furtado's new biography of Chica da Silva, offer a solid start. Dean's is an excellent environmental study.

Boxer, Charles R. *The Golden Age of Brazil: Growing Pains of a Colonial Society.* 1964.

Dean, Warren. *With Broadax and Firebrand: The Destruction of Brazilian Atlantic Forest.* 1995.

Furtado, Júnia F. *Chica da Silva.* 2008.

Higgins, Kathleen. *"Licentious Liberty" in a Colonial Gold Mining Region: Sabará, Minas Gerais, in the Eighteenth Century.* 1999.

Schwartz, Stuart B. *Slaves, Peasants, and Rebels: Reconsidering Brazilian Slavery.* 1992.

Bitter Sugar, Part Two: Slavery and Colonialism in the Caribbean, 1625–1750

Caribbean history is a fast-growing field. This area is only starting to be treated as a region rather than as clusters of islands with a shared language, or "proto-nations." Dunn's work on the English Caribbean is classic, the Schwartz collection offers a sweeping update, and Moya Pons is a superb overview.

Burnard, Trevor. *Mastery, Tyranny, and Desire: Thomas Thistlewood and His Slaves in the Anglo-Jamaican World.* 2004.

Common-Place. A Web journal with research links sponsored by the American Antiquarian Society: http://www.common-place.org/.

Dunn, Richard S. *Sugar and Slaves: The Rise of the Planter Class in the English West Indies, 1624–1713,* 2d ed. 2000.

Moya Pons, Frank. *The Caribbean: A History.* 2007.

Schwartz, Stuart B., ed. *Tropical Babylons: Sugar and the Making of the Atlantic World, 1450–1680.* 2005.

Growth and Change in British and French North America, 1607–1750

The literature on British and French North America is vast. What follows is only a small sample of classic and recent contributions.

Gleach, Frederic W. *Powhatan's World and Colonial Virginia: A Conflict of Cultures.* 1997.

Hall, David D. *Worlds of Wonder, Days of Judgment: Popular Religious Belief in Early New England.* 1990.

Karlsen, Carol F. *The Devil in the Shape of a Woman: Witchcraft in Colonial New England.* 1987.

Morgan, Philip D. *Slave Counterpoint: Black Culture in the Eighteenth-Century Chesapeake and Lowcountry.* 1998.

Society of Early Americanists. Web site with links to teaching resources and documents: http://www.societyofearlyamericanists.org/.

White, Richard. *The Middle Ground: Indians, Empires, and Republics in the Great Lakes Region, 1650–1815.* 1991.

COUNTERPOINT: The Maroons of Suriname

Scholarship on maroon societies is growing, but few have written more on the maroons of Suriname than anthropologists Richard and Sally Price.

Price, Richard. *Alabi's World.* 1990.

———. *First-Time: The Historical Vision of an Afro-American People.* 1983.

———, ed. *Maroon Societies: Rebel Slave Communities in the Americas,* 3d ed. 1996.

Price, Richard, and Sally Price. *Maroon Arts.* 2000.

▶ **For additional primary sources from this period**, see *Sources of Crossroads and Cultures*.

▶ **For Web sites, images, and documents related to topics in this chapter**, see Make History at bedfordstmartins.com/smith.

The major global development in this chapter ▶ The profound social, cultural, and environmental changes in the Americas under colonial rule.

IMPORTANT EVENTS

1570	Spanish galleons begin annual service linking Acapulco to Manila
1607	English establish colony at Jamestown, Virginia
1608	French establish colony at Quebec City
1618	Dutch establish colony of New Netherland on upper Hudson River
1625	Dutch settle New Amsterdam on Manhattan Island; English establish colony on Barbados
1630	Dutch capture northeast Brazil
1654	Portuguese drive Dutch from Brazil; some colonists move to Suriname
1655	English seize Jamaica from the Spanish
1664	English take New Amsterdam from Dutch, rename it New York
1671	Henry Morgan's buccaneers sack Panama City
1676	Bacon's Rebellion in Virginia
1694	Great Brazilian maroon community of Palmares destroyed
1695–1800	Discovery in Brazilian interior of gold and diamonds inaugurates Brazil's "gold rush"
1701–1714	War of the Spanish Succession
1720	Brazil elevated to status of viceroyalty
1763	Rio de Janeiro elevated to status of capital of Brazil

KEY TERMS

audiencia (p. 724)
buccaneer (p. 738)
creole (p. 731)
indenture (p. 722)
joint-stock company (p. 743)
maroon (p. 736)

mestizaje (p. 731)
mestizo (p. 731)
métis (p. 743)
mulatto (p. 731)
northwest passage (p. 741)

CHAPTER OVERVIEW QUESTIONS

1. How did the production of silver, gold, and other commodities shape colonial American societies?

2. How and where did northern Europeans insert themselves into territories claimed by Spain and Portugal?

3. How did racial divisions and mixtures compare across the Americas by the mid-eighteenth century?

SECTION FOCUS QUESTIONS

1. How did mineral wealth steer the development of Spanish America?

2. How was Brazil transformed by the mining boom of the eighteenth century?

3. How did sugar production and slavery mold Caribbean societies?

4. How did European relations with native peoples differ in the British and French colonies of North America?

5. How did the runaway slaves of Dutch Suriname create a lasting independent state of their own?

MAKING CONNECTIONS

1. How did Spanish America's imperial bureaucracy compare with those of the Ottomans and other "gunpowder empires" discussed in Chapters 19 to 21?

2. How did the labor systems of the American colonies compare with those of western Eurasia (see Chapter 20)? With those of Russian and East Asia (see Chapter 21)?

3. What role did religious diversity play in colonial American life compared with contemporary South and Southeast Asia (see Chapter 19)?

4. In what ways did economic developments in colonial Brazil differ from developments in Spanish America?

ADDITIONAL CREDITS

Text Credits

Chapter 9

N. J. Dawood. Passages from the Qur'an from *The Koran: With Parallel Arabic Text*, translated with notes by N. J. Dawood (Penguin Books, 1990). Copyright © N. J. Dawood 1956, 1959, 1966, 1968, 1990. Reproduced by permission of Penguin Books Ltd.

A. S. Tritton. *The Caliphs and Their Non-Muslim Subjects*, by A. S. Tritton (1930): "The Pact of Umar." By permission of Oxford University Press.

Chapter 11

Allen J. Christenson. Popul Vuh, *The Sacred Book of the Maya*, translated by Allen Christenson. Copyright © 2003 by O Books. University of Oklahoma Press, 2007. Used by permission of the publisher.

Chapter 12

Patricia Buckley Ebrey. *Family and Property in Sung China*, by Patricia Buckley Ebrey. © 1984 Princeton University Press. Reprinted by permission of Princeton University Press.

Chapter 13

Ichisada Miyazaki. From *China's Examination Hell*, by Ichisada Miyazaki, translated by Conrad Schirokauer, 1st edition, 1976. Protected by copyright under terms of the International Copyright Union. Reprinted by arrangement with Shambhala Publications, Inc., Boston, Mass., www.shambhala.com.

Franz Rosenthal. Ibn Khaldun, *The Muqaddimah*, translated by Franz Rosenthal. © 2005 by Princeton University Press. Reprinted by permission of Princeton University Press.

Richard Bowring. From *The Diary of Lady Murasaki* by Lady Murasaki, translated by Richard Bowring (Penguin Books, 1996). Translation copyright © Richard Bowring, 1996. Used by permission of Penguin Group, UK.

Spot Map: Mesoamerican Scripts. Based on Andrew Robinson, *Lost Languages: The Enigma of the World's Undeciphered Scripts*. Copyright © 2002 McGraw-Hill Companies, Inc. Used by permission of the publisher.

Chapter 14

Francesco Gabrieli. *Arab Historians of the Crusades*, edited by Francesco Gabrieli. Copyright © 1957 by Giulio Einaudi Editore S.p.A., Turin. Translation © Routledge & Kegan Paul Limited, 1969. Reproduced by permission of Taylor & Francis Books UK.

Bruno Scott James. *Bernard of Clairvaux, Letters*, translated by Bruno Scott James, Burns, Oates, 1953. Reproduced by kind permission of Continuum International Publishing Group.

Robert Bartlett. *The Making of Europe*, © 1993 Robert Bartlett. First published in Great Britain by Penguin Books Ltd. 1994 Princeton University Press paperback edition. Reprinted by permission of Princeton University Press.

Chapter 15

Richard A. Newhall. *The Chronicle of Jean de Venette*, edited by Richard A. Newhall, Columbia University Press, 1953. Used by permission of Columbia University Press.

Chapter 16

Miguel Leon-Portilla. *Pre-Columbian Literatures of Mexico*, by Miguel Leon-Portilla, translated from the Spanish by Grace Lobanov. Copyright © 1969 by The University of Oklahoma Press. Used by permission of the publisher.

Matthew Restall, Lisa Sousa, and Kevin Terraciano, editors. *Mesoamerican Voices: Native-Language Writings from Colonial Mexico, Oaxaca, Yucatan, and Guatemala*. Copyright © 2005 Matthew Restall, Lisa Sousa, and Kevin Terraciano. Reprinted with the permission of Cambridge University Press.

Frank Salomon and George L. Urioste. From *The Huarochirí Manuscript: A Testament of Ancient and Colonial Andean Religion*, translated and edited by Frank Salomon and George L. Urioste, Copyright © 1991. By permission of the University of Texas Press.

Chapter 17

William Brooks Greenlee. *The Voyage of Pedro Alvares Cabral to Brazil and India*, translated by William Brooks Greenlee, Hakluyt Society, 1938; as it appears in Kraus Reprint Limited, Nendeln/Liechtenstein, 1967. Used by permission of the Hakluyt Society.

Chapter 18

Kate Ferguson Masters. "Travels in the Interior of Africa," in *Travels in the Interior Districts of Africa* by Mungo Park, edited by Kate Ferguson Masters, pp. 264–267. Copyright 2000, Duke University Press. All rights reserved. Reprinted by permission of the publisher.

John O. Hunwick. *Timbukto and the Songhay Empire: Al-Sadi's Tarikj al-sudan down to 1613 and Other Contemporary Documents*, edited and translated by John O. Hunwick, Brill 1999. Used by permission of Koninklijke BRILL NV.

Nicole Von Germeten. *Treatise on Slavery*, by Alonso de Sandoval, edited and translated by Nicole Von Germeten. Hackett Publishers, 2008. Used by permission of the publisher.

Chapter 19

Anthony Reid. *Southeast Asia in the Age of Commerce*, Volume 2. Yale University Press, 1993. Copyright © Yale University Press, 1993. Used by permission of the publisher.

Chapter 20

Abraham of Erevan, *History of the Wars* (1721–1738), edited and translated by George A. Bournoutian (Costa Mesa, CA: Mazda Publishers, 1999), 77–78. Used by permission of Mazda Publishers.

Chapter 21

C. Whelan. From "An early 19th-century Tokugawa-era Kakure Kirishitan, or 'Hidden Christian,'" manuscript, edited and translated by C. Whelan. © 1966 University of Hawaii Press. Reprinted with permission.

Nobuyuki Yuasa. "The Records of a Weather-exposed Skeleton," by Matsuo Basho, c. 1685, in *The Narrow Road to the Deep North and Other Sketches*, edited and translated by Nobuyuki Yuasa, Penguin, 1966. Reproduced by permission of Penguin Books Ltd.

Map 21.4: Maritime Trade Between the Americas and Asia, 1571–1800. From John Leddy Phelan, *The Hispanization of the Philippines: Spanish Aims and Filipino Responses, 1565–1700*. © 1959 by the Board of Regents of the University of Wisconsin System. Reprinted by permission of The University of Wisconsin Press.

Choe-Wall Yangh-hi. Lady Hong, *Memoirs of a Korean Queen*, edited and translated by Choe-Wall Yangh-hi (London: KPI, 1985), pp. 1–4, 49. Used by permission of Taylor & Francis Books.

Chapter 22

Cesar E. Farah. *An Arab's Journey to Colonial Spanish America: The Travels of Elias al-Musili in the Seventeenth Century*, edited and translated by Cesar E. Farah, Syracuse University Press, 2003. Used by permission of Syracuse University Press.

Richard Price. *First-Time: The Historical Vision of an Afro-American People* (Baltimore: Johns Hopkins University Press, 1983), p. 71. Used by permission of the author.

Art Credits

Opener to Part 2

Chapter 9: Erich Lessing/Art Resource, NY; Chapter 10: Arthur M. Sackler Museum, Harvard University Art Museums/Bequest of Grenville L. Winthrop/Bridgeman Art Library; Chapter 11: Giraudon/Bridgeman Art Library; Chapter 12: Bibliothèque Nationale, Paris, France/ Bildarchiv Preussischer Kulturbesitz/Art Resource, NY; Chapter 13: ISESCO; Chapter 14: The Art Archive; Chapter 15: Candace Feit

Opener to Part 3

Chapter 16: The Art Archive/Museo del Templo Mayor Mexico/Gianni Dagli Orti; Chapter 17: The Art Archive/Science Academy Lisbon/Gianni Dagli Orti; Chapter 18: Image copyright © The Metropolitan Museum of Art/Art Resource, NY; Chapter 19: Marco Pavan/Grand Tour/Corbis; Chapter 20: Photo by Ketan Gajria; Chapter 21: Yoshio Tomii Photo Studio/Aflo FotoAgency/Photolibrary; Chapter 22: Acervo da Fundação Biblioteca Nacional, Rio de Janeiro, Brasil

INDEX

A note about the index:

Letters in parentheses following pages refer to:
  (*b*) boxed features
  (*i*) illustrations, including photographs and artifacts
  (*m*) maps

About the authors

BONNIE G. SMITH (Ph.D., University of Rochester) is Board of Governors Professor of History at Rutgers University. She has written numerous works in European and global history, including *Ladies of the Leisure Class*; *Changing Lives: Women in European History since 1700*; and *Imperialism*. She is editor of *Global Feminisms since 1945* and *Women's History in Global Perspective*; coeditor of the New Oxford World History series; and general editor of *The Oxford Encyclopedia of Women in World History*. Currently she is studying the globalization of European culture and society since the seventeenth century. **Bonnie treats the period 1750 to the present (Part 4) in *Crossroads and Cultures*.**

MARC VAN DE MIEROOP (Ph.D., Yale University) is Professor of History at Columbia University. His research focuses on the ancient history of the Near East from a long-term perspective and extends across traditionally established disciplinary boundaries. Among his many works are *The Ancient Mesopotamian City*; *Cuneiform Texts and the Writing of History*; *A History of the Ancient Near East*; *The Eastern Mediterranean in the Age of Ramesses II*; and *A History of Ancient Egypt*. **Marc covers the period from human origins to 500 C.E. (Part 1) in *Crossroads and Cultures*.**

RICHARD VON GLAHN (Ph.D., Yale University) is Professor of History at the University of California, Los Angeles. A specialist in Chinese economic history, Richard is the author of *The Country of Streams and Grottoes: Expansion, Settlement, and the Civilizing of the Sichuan Frontier in Song Times*; *Fountain of Fortune: Money and Monetary Policy in China, 1000–1700*; and *The Sinister Way: The Divine and the Demonic in Chinese Religious Culture*. He is also coeditor of *The Song-Yuan-Ming Transition in Chinese History* and *Global Connections and Monetary History, 1470–1800*. His current research focuses on monetary history on a global scale, from ancient times to the recent past. **Richard treats the period 500 to 1450 (Part 2) in *Crossroads and Cultures*.**

KRIS LANE (Ph.D., University of Minnesota) is the France V. Scholes Chair in Colonial Latin American History at Tulane University. Kris specializes in colonial Latin American history and the Atlantic world, and his great hope is to globalize the teaching and study of the early Americas. His publications include *Pillaging the Empire: Piracy in the Americas, 1500–1750*; *Quito 1599: City and Colony in Transition*; and *Colour of Paradise: The Emerald in the Age of Gunpowder Empires*. He also edited Bernardo de Vargas Machuca's *The Indian Militia and Description of the Indies* and *Defense and Discourse of the Western Conquest*. **Kris treats the period 1450 to 1750 (Part 3) in *Crossroads and Cultures*.**

About the cover image

Venice, Italy

A romantic tourist destination today, the northern Italian city of Venice was once an independent world power. Thanks to its location on the sheltered Adriatic Sea, with access both to the rich trading ports of the eastern Mediterranean and to the interior of Europe, Venice grew in the late Middle Ages to become one of the wealthiest and largest cities in Eurasia. After the 1453 Ottoman seizure of Constantinople, the Venetians lost their dominance of the Mediterranean trade, although the city remained a vibrant cultural and commercial crossroads into modern times.